STUDY GUIDE TO ACCOMPANY
SAMUELSON: ECONOMICS

STUDY GUIDE TO ACCOMPANY
SAMUELSON: ECONOMICS
Tenth Edition

ROMNEY ROBINSON

McGraw-Hill Book Company

New York   St. Louis   San Francisco   Auckland   Düsseldorf   Johannesburg   Kuala Lumpur   London
Mexico   Montreal   New Delhi   Panama   Paris   São Paulo   Singapore   Sydney   Tokyo   Toronto

STUDY GUIDE TO ACCOMPANY
SAMUELSON: ECONOMICS

ISBN 0-07-053267-2

  34567890 BABA 783210987

This book was set in Caledonia by University Graphics, Inc.
The editors were J. S. Dietrich, Marjorie Singer, and Edwin Hanson;
the designer was J. E. O'Connor;
the production supervisor was Joe Campanella.
George Banta Company, Inc., was printer and binder.

CONTENTS

TO THE STUDENT

This Study Guide has a single objective: to help you learn the basic principles and ideas of economics.

Specifically, this Guide is prepared to accompany the tenth edition of the textbook *Economics* by Professor Paul A. Samuelson. The Guide is *not* a substitute for careful study of the text or for regular classroom attendance. But experience has shown that a guide such as this can be of great help in getting you *involved* in the material you learn in text and classroom. It involves you by asking questions and providing correct answers. It is planned to help you in grasping the ideas set out in the text, and to enable you to test for yourself your mastery of these ideas.

Before tackling any Study Guide chapter, you should read the corresponding textbook chapter—twice. Your first reading should be a rapid one. Don't stop for details; just try for some perspective on what the chapter is about. Your second reading should be a little more careful. But again: don't try to master every detail.

Then turn to the review questions in the Study Guide. These questions have been carefully written to bring out the most essential and important ideas within the text chapter. Most of them are of the multiple-choice variety, in which you are asked to pick one (or more) correct alternatives, or to circle whichever one of several phrases in italic type you think is correct. A few questions are of the fill-in-the-blank variety.

The answer to each review question follows immediately after that question, in lighter type. As you tackle the question, cover the answer with a piece of paper, to prevent an overhasty look. But never work up too much frustration on any question. If you can't answer it, look at the answer; if necessary, go back to the text to find out why this *is* the correct answer.

Study Guide chapters vary considerably in length. A few occupy only three or four pages, and you can polish them off quickly. At the other extreme, you will find several chapters with ten or twelve pages. They were prepared with the utmost care to carry you through difficult or important material as smoothly as possible. But you must expect to spend time on these chapters. Where experience has shown that the topic can be a difficult one, there is often some introductory discussion material preceding the actual questions.

No attempt has been made to cover *everything* discussed in the text, since that would call for a work thicker than the textbook itself. The Study Guide has by intent been confined to those topics which—in one instructor's lengthy teaching experience—are most likely to bring students to grief.

The review questions are followed by quiz material. All chapters have multiple-choice questions, and some few have "other" questions. Answers for the first few of these questions (usually the first five multiple choice and the

viii | To the Student

first one or two "other") will be found at the back of the Study Guide. Answers for the remaining quiz questions are not provided. These questions are intended for classroom assignment and discussion. In some earlier Study Guide editions, answers for *all* these questions were furnished, in a deliberate effort to find how the maximum of effectiveness as a learning aid might be accomplished. Experience showed that there was more motivation to tackle these questions if answers were withheld.

To answer the multiple-choice questions, select *one* of the five alternatives—the one you think makes the sentence correct, or most nearly correct. You may feel reasonably confident of your knowledge of the chapter if you can correctly answer about seven of every ten questions. If your instructor is exacting in examinations, you may find you must increase this level to eight or nine.

No matter how difficult the multiple-choice question, all are expected to conform to one test of fairness: The answer is supposed to be within the text, directly or indirectly. One choice among the five available is intended to be correct, and the other four are all intended to be explicitly wrong, or demonstrably inferior to the correct one. The arbiter in all cases is what Samuelson has to say in the text.

If you find any question which you think fails to meet such a test, or which you feel adds more confusion than illumination, a note to the author (in care of the McGraw-Hill Book Company) will be appreciated. It may help other students who later use the Study Guide.

Thirty years ago, economics was often considered one of the dullest subjects in the college or university curriculum. Today, it is considered one of the most interesting—but also one of the more challenging—courses. It is my hope that this Study Guide will help not only your mastery of the subject but your interest in it as well.

Sincere thanks are due to numerous instructors who have commented on parts of this Study Guide and made suggestions for its improvement. In particular, I owe thanks to Professor Paul J. Hanley of Rice University, Professor Carl Kreider of Goshen College, Professor Lynne Pierson of Chapman College, and Professor John L. Wortham of Texas Christian University.

And I am most grateful to Marjorie Singer for efficient and considerate supervision in the preparation of this edition of the Study Guide.

Romney Robinson

ORIENTATION: HOW TO READ AND UNDERSTAND GRAPHS

ECONOMICS makes extensive use of graphs or charts, and they appear in almost every chapter of this text. If you are not familiar with graphs, you must invest a little of your time in learning how to read and use them.

Fortunately, this is not a difficult job. Graphs are intended to make life easier for you, not to complicate your study of economics. A good graph reveals things which might otherwise be very difficult to grasp.

Remember this:

▶ A graph is always an illustration picturing how two sets of figures are related to one another.

First Example: Study Hours and Leisure Hours.

Suppose you decide to plan your working day. A considerable part of each 24 hours must be given over to sleep, meals, and class attendance. Suppose these matters take up 14 hours per day. This leaves the remaining 10 hours to divide between study on the one hand, leisure and recreation on the other.

That 10 hours could be divided in an infinite number of ways. At one extreme would be 10 hours for leisure and zero hours for study. This particular time allocation must be considered unsatisfactory in the sense that its pursuit tends to lead to unpleasant interviews with the dean of students or similar people of limited imagination.

At the other extreme would be 10 hours for study and zero for leisure and recreation, or the week-before-examinations allocation. Among the possible choices are these:

	A	B	C	D	E	F	G
Leisure hours	10	8	7	6	4½	2½	0
Study hours	0	2	3	4	5½	7½	10

What we have is two sets, or lists, of figures. One set gives possible study hours; the other set gives possible leisure hours. More important, *these figures are tied to one another. Each study-hour figure is paired off with a leisure-hour figure.* If we start with the assumption of only 10 available hours, then the figure of 6 leisure hours *must* be linked with 4 study hours, and with no other figure; 5½ study hours is linked with 4½ leisure hours, and so on. Here, the linking rule is simple: The two members of each pair must together add up to 10.

Review. The illustration above is a simple one, but confirm your grasp of it by completing the following blanks before you go on.

1. The example involves leisure time and _____ time. Total daily time to be allocated between these two is _____ hours, so that 4 hours of leisure time must be linked with _____ hours of _____ time.

2. If hours are divided into half hours, quarters, and so on, we can have as many pairs of numbers as we please, but each pair must satisfy the rule that _____ _____ .

---

1. study; 10; 6; study.
2. the two members must add up to 10.

Graphical Illustration. This example reveals precisely the kind of situation a graph always illustrates: *a series of pairs of numbers, all linked together by some rule.*

Figure 1 is a graph illustrating the study-leisure situation. Go over it carefully—but before starting, remember that all unfamiliar things appear complicated. You cannot tell whether they are really complicated or not until you have spent at least a little time in growing familiar with them. It may help your familiarizing process if you know that the whole system of graphical illustration began with a bored man lying in bed, gazing at a crack in the ceiling.

The man was René Descartes, the French philosopher and mathematician. Descartes had been abed with illness; as he lay on his back, going through the tedium of recovery, this thought struck him: To locate the position of any point or small spot on the ceiling, you need two measurements—a pair. You must have two—one is insufficient—but two is all you need. Thus a particular point might be exactly 8 feet from that edge of the ceiling toward your feet, and 2 feet from the left-hand ceiling edge.

It is all quite simple. You start by agreeing to take these two edges of the ceiling as base lines or zero lines. Every point on the ceiling has associated with it two figures (each of the figures being a measurement from one of the two edges or base lines). From a point, you can obtain a pair of figures which locate that point.

But Descartes was more interested in the fact that you can turn things around: start with the pair of figures rather than the point. Given any pair of figures, you can illustrate them as a particular and unique point on a two-dimensional surface, whether that surface happens to be a ceiling or a sheet of paper. Even more interesting, if you have a *series* of pairs somehow linked together, as in the study-leisure example, you can illustrate them as a *line*. (A line, for our purpose here, is just a particular accumulation of points.) And the way that line runs—whether up or down, whether curved or straight, and so on—is an illustration of the kind of linking rule which those pairs of points must satisfy.

Economics is filled with topics in which this linking together of two sets of numbers is important, and graphs are useful just because they illustrate so readily the nature of the relationship involved. They are useful, that is, once you have spent sufficient time to grasp the mechanics of their construction.

In Fig. 1, the vertical line at left and the horizontal line at bottom correspond to the two edges of Descartes' ceiling. Each is divided off with a number scale, and the meaning of these numbers is indicated by the labels: "Hours of study time" (horizontally) and "Hours of leisure time" (vertically).

The slanting line carrying points labeled *A* through *G* is the actual graph illustrating the study-leisure relation. But you should concentrate first on the horizontal and vertical measuring lines.

The horizontal line is the *horizontal axis* (or sometimes

the *X axis*). This horizontal axis is just a convenient line for measuring distances in the horizontal or west-and-east dimension. In the study-leisure example, one member in each number pair must stand for a certain number of study hours. In Fig. 1, study time has been given the west-and-east dimension, and the space in this dimension has been divided into numbers from 0 to 10, with 0 at extreme left, 10 at right.

This horizontal or *X* axis goes at the bottom of the diagram as a matter of convenience and custom, not because it *must* sit there. Think of this horizontal axis as a kind of sliding line which could be moved up or down the diagram as you would move a ruler—always keeping it exactly horizontal. For example, look at the 2 mark on the *X* axis. Above it is a broken line extending up to point *B*. Any point on this broken line stands for 2 study hours, because it is 2 measuring units away from the left-hand edge. If the horizontal axis were slid upward, the 2 mark thereon would touch all points on this broken line up to *B* (and beyond), and only points on this line.

Similarly, the vertical line at left is the *vertical axis* or *Y axis*. It should be regarded as a measuring line which could be swept from left to right across the diagram in order to measure off amounts of leisure time. Thus any point on the broken horizontal line running through *B* stands for 8 hours of leisure time.

It is convenient to give the two axis lines their positions at bottom and at left because each of them can then perform a service for the other. In Fig. 1, the vertical axis is primarily the measuring lines for leisure time. But because of its position, it is also the zero line for study time. Any point on this vertical axis stands for 0 study hours. Similarly, any point on the horizontal study-time axis records 0 leisure hours.

The lower left-hand corner at which the two axis lines meet is the *origin*. It signifies 0 study hours and 0 leisure hours. (In the text, you will occasionally find a graph which does not have this double-zero origin. Most of these are "time series" in which one member of each number pair is an actual year, so that the horizontal axis of the graph is taken over by a sequence of years, say, from 1900 to 1975. Text Figs. 14-1 and 14-2 illustrate this type of graph. Such graphs are easily understood and do not require attention now.)

Review. Add the proper word in each blank below, or circle the correct alternative among those given.

3. A graph has _____ dimensions, horizontal or west and east, and _____ or south and north. Hence any pair of numbers, such as a combination of study and leisure hours, can appear on the graph as a single

_____.

4. In the horizontal or west-east dimension, a figure of 0 would be recorded on the line at(*extreme left* / *extreme right* / *very bottom* / *very top* / *exact center*). In the vertical dimension, 0 would be recorded on the line at(*extreme left* / *extreme right* / *very bottom* / *very top* / *exact center*).

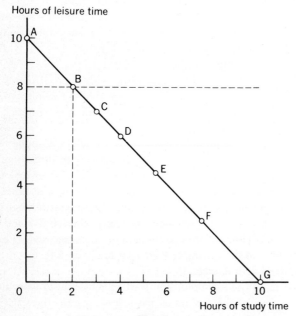

Hours of leisure time

Hours of study time

Fig. 1

5. The measuring line used to place numbers shown in the west-east dimension is called the _____ _____or the _____. The south-north measuring line is the _____ _____or the _____.

6. In Fig. 1, point *B* stands for the combination of 2 *(study/ leisure)* hours and 8 *(study / leisure)* hours. In Fig. 1, leisure hours are measured *(vertically / horizontally)* and study hours *(vertically / horizontally)*. Point *D* stands for _____ leisure hours and _____ study hours; 9 study hours and 1 leisure hour would be a pair indicated by a point between points *(A and B / D and E / F and G)*.

---

3. two; vertical; point.
4. extreme left; very bottom.
5. horizontal axis or *X* axis; vertical axis or *Y* axis.
6. study; leisure; vertically; horizontally; 6; 4; *F* and *G*.

Drawing a Graph. If you have to learn about graphs, then draw graphs. Figure 2 is blank except for a series of vertical and horizontal "grid lines," used to help locate the point that matches up with any given pair of measurements. The grid lines correspond to some of the positions the vertical axis would occupy if slid to the right, or the horizontal axis if slid upward.

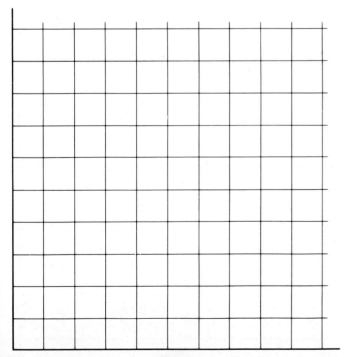

Fig. 2

On Fig. 2, redraw Fig. 1 yourself. First label your **axis** lines. What are you measuring in the vertical, **south-north** direction? Write this at top of the vertical axis. Often in **the** text this label is written along the side of the vertical axis line. This saves space, although it sometimes necessitates twisting the book around to read the label. Pick a scale for each of **the** axes—that is, choose how much distance you are going to use to represent 1 hour. Then record as many pairs of numbers as you please—10 leisure hours and 0 study hours, 9 and 1, 5 and 5, 6½ and 3½, and so on. They should all lie along a line comparable to *AG*. After you have satisfied yourself about **this** fact, you may draw the entire line. It sums up all the possible points you could mark if you had sufficient time and patience.

This last idea bears repeating. You cannot possibly find **any** add-up-to-10 combination that does not appear somewhere **on** *AG*. *AG* includes every possible pair that satisfies this **linking** rule. Moreover, *AG* can be trusted in another respect. It **has** no point that does *not* meet the linking rule. In other **words,** *AG* is an exact graphical representation of the add-up-to-**10** rule in the sense that (1) it includes *all* points that satisfy **this** rule, and (2) it includes *only* points that satisfy this rule.

Review. In each question below, circle the correct alternative among the four offered.

7. Take *any* point *inside* the triangle formed by the **three** lines of Fig. 1 (the *AG* line and the two axis lines). The **pair** of measurements for any such point:
a. must together total more than 10.
b. must together total less than 10.
c. must together total 10.
d. may total more than 10 or less than 10.

8. Which alternative in question 7 correctly describes the pair of measurements belonging to any point outside *AG* (above and to the right)? .... *(a / b / c / d)*

9. If we redid this example by assuming that there **was** a total of 11 hours rather than 10 to allocate, what would happen to *AG* (as the line indicating all possible combinations)?
a. It would move outward—i.e., upward and to the right— remaining parallel to the present line.
b. It would move inward—i.e., downward and to the left— remaining parallel to the present line.
c. Its position would not change.
d. It would pivot or rotate outward on point *A*.

---

7. *b.* (For example, take any point—other than *B*—on **the** vertical broken line running between *B* and the 2 **mark on** the horizontal axis. This is a typical point inside the **triangle.** That point must stand for 2 study hours and—because it is *below B*—less than 8 hours of leisure time, or a total of **less** than 10.)
8. *a.* 9. *a.*

Second Example: The Guns-or-Butter Diagram. One of the first graphical diagrams you will encounter in the text is the guns-or-butter chart of Chapter 2. As the following table (reproduced from the text) shows, it involves pairs of figures once again.

	A	B	C	D	E	F
Butter (millions of pounds)	0	1	2	3	4	5
Guns (thousands)	15	14	12	9	5	0

The background of the guns-or-butter case is this: The economy has only a limited and fixed stock of machinery, labor, and all the other things needed to produce such items as guns or butter. To some degree, these resources can be used in either occupation; a man can help to make guns by working in a steel mill or by being a machinist, or he can help make butter by milking cows or working in a dairy. Insofar as these versatile either-occupation resources exist, the production of either commodity can be increased if such resources can be taken from their employment in the other commodity. The cost of an increase in butter production is of course a decrease in gun production, and vice versa.

As a further exercise in graph drawing, do the guns-or-butter diagram for yourself in Fig. 3. Use the figures in the preceding table. As before, first label your two axes. Measure quantity of guns in the vertical dimension (as the text does) and quantity of butter horizontally. Ordinarily, you want to make use of all the space available on a graph. In Fig. 3, the maximum butter quantity to be recorded is 5 (million pounds); so put 5 at the bottom right-hand corner. There are 15 little squares sitting on the horizontal axis line; if 5 goes below the end of the fifteenth square, then 1 must go below the end of the third one, 2 below the end of the sixth, and so on. As to guns, your maximum is 15 (thousand); so put 15 at top left, with the smaller numbers correspondingly below. Notice that (in the matter of graph distances) your two number scales can be different. Here, the same distance in inches which measures 5 million pounds of butter (horizontally) records 15 thousand guns (vertically).

Having put labels and numbers on your axes, indicate on the graph the six points in the table. (This is known as *plotting* the points.) Join them with a smooth curve.

The Utility of Graphical Illustrations. If a text uses graphs as illustrations, the assumption is that you, as student, will be helped by this means of presentation. If unfamiliar with graphs, you are not yet sufficiently advanced to be able to decide for yourself whether or not this illustrative device is worth the trouble of learning about it. But even now, it is worth considering what—if anything—is accomplished by taking the simple guns-or-butter case and presenting it in graphical form.

At this stage the text seeks to make the point that all economies, regardless of their form of political organization, regardless of whether they are rich or poor, face certain identical problems. These problems arise out of the basic scarcity of productive agents—machines, men, and materials. These productive agents are the source of finished consumer goods and services, and they are scarce in the sense that they cannot produce a sufficient quantity of such goods and services to satisfy fully everybody's wants for everything. One of the economy's problems is accordingly that it must decide WHAT to produce; and the guns-or-butter example is intended to reveal the nature of this problem and of the decision it demands. Matters are simplified to the point of assuming that there are only two final consumer goods wanted and producible. (It may help if you think of "guns" strictly as a consumer good. People use them for hunting, or they find guns useful on social occasions, or they use them for whatever other purpose your imagination can supply.)

Each pair of figures in the gun-butter table is assumed to represent a combination which the resources in the economy *could* produce per period of time (a) when fully employed and (b) when employed to the best possible advantage—i.e., when the best possible use is made of the gun-producing and butter-producing technologies known in the economy.

The use of a graphical illustration is intended to bring out more clearly at least four points:

1. The area of the graph above and to the right of the *ABCDEF* line represents more desirable but unattainable

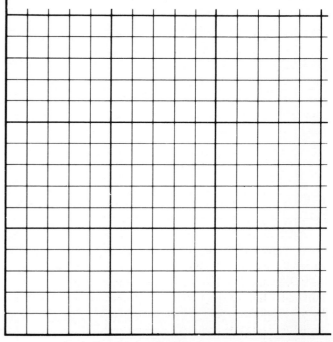

Fig. 3

territory. Points therein represent larger gun-butter combinations than those represented by *ABCDEF*. But they are unattainable—unless or until the economy acquires more productive agents or develops better techniques for using what it has. The process of economic growth can be represented as a gradual pushing outward of the *ABCDEF* line.

2. The graph area below and to the left of *ABCDEF* is fully attainable. But if the economy's actual gun-butter production were to be represented by a point in this area, it would signify (a) that the economy was not fully using all its available resources, or else (b) that although it was employing them, it was somehow failing to use them to the best advantage. We assume that the economy *can* reach any point on the *ABCDEF* line without disrupting its social order and without undue strain on its productive agents; and its people will want production to reach this line, since both of the two commodities are scarce relative to the desire for them. If actual production lands at some point in the area below *ABCDEF*, it means there has been some failure in the area of economic or social organization. In this sense, the area below *ABCDEF* is undesirable.

3. If both unattainable and undesirable areas are taken away, only the line *ABCDEF* itself remains. The decision which the people in this economy (or their leaders) must somehow make with respect to WHAT goods to produce can be represented as the problem of choosing a point somewhere on *ABCDEF*. To describe this as a "guns *or* butter" decision can be a bit misleading, for it suggests that the only choice is between A (all guns, no butter) and F (all butter, no guns). If both butter and guns are desirable goods, it is likely that points A and F would both be rejected as much less desirable than an intermediate point such as C or D.

4. In actual life, decisions on WHAT to produce have somehow been made for a long time; and they are still being made. A decision of this nature is not something that need be made only once and can then be forgotten, for tastes change and so do productive conditions. It is a little more realistic, then, to think of an economy which is currently operating at some point such as D, and which is disposed, say, toward having a little more butter. That would mean a shift from D toward E. Now think of this as a two-part shift:

a. First, there is a movement away from D horizontally and to the right, of a distance equal to the contemplated increase in butter production—say ¼ million pounds.
b. The movement in *a* takes the economy into unattainable territory. So it must be followed by another movement, vertically downward, of sufficient length to get back to the *ABCDEF* line. (On Fig. 3, starting at the D point, draw a short horizontal line to the right. This is the desired increase in butter production, and the move into unattainable territory. From the end of this line, draw another, this time vertical and downward, to reach the *ABCDEF* line. This is the reduction

in gun production needed in order to get back to "attainable output.")

The point about making a simple movement along the line into a two-part, right-angled shift is that the lengths of the sides on the little right angle spell out the crucial swapping terms involved. The horizontal side measures the contemplated increase in butter—and the vertical side measures the required decrease in gun output. Whether or not an extra ¼ million pounds of butter is really worth having depends on whether it is considered worth the sacrifice of (about) 1,000 guns. As to a contemplated move of this kind (what the text would later call a *marginal* shift), it is correct to speak of "guns *or* butter." The real cost of extra butter is not a cost in money, or even (except indirectly) in resources taken up to produce that butter; the real cost is in guns sacrificed.

Review. Circle the correct alternative, or write the appropriate answer in the space provided.

10. The figures in the guns-and-butter table represent (*maximum/minimum*) combinations of these two commodities which some imaginary community could produce per unit of time. The figures stand for (*money values / physical quantities*) of guns and butter. The background factor accounting for such (*upper / lower*) limits on production (given the state of technology) is this: _____

_____

_____ .

11. If all available resources or inputs were devoted to butter production, butter output would be _____ million pounds and gun output would be _____ thousand guns. If the economy wished to have 9 thousand guns per period, butter output could not exceed _____ million pounds.

12. Suppose the community is producing a total of 1 million pounds of butter. It wants to increase this by a further 1 million pounds. The required decrease in gun production would be _____ thousand. If the community was producing 4 million pounds of butter and wanted to increase this by 1 million (to a total of 5 million), the required decrease in gun production would be _____ thousand.

13. Suppose the community is currently producing 15 thousand guns and is considering a reduction to 14 thousand. The change would make possible a butter increase of _____ million pounds. Alternatively, if the community currently produces 9 thousand guns and decides on a reduction to 5 thousand, a butter increase of _____ million pounds would be possible. If gun production were to be increased from 9 thousand to 10 thousand, this 1-thousand increase would call for a reduction in butter output of approximately

_____ million pounds.

---

10. maximum; physical quantities; upper; a limit on the total available supply of resources. 11. 5; 0; 3. 12. 2; 5. 13. 1; 1; ⅓.

The Direction of the Line. There is an obvious similarity between the study-leisure and butter-gun cases. Both illustrate the need for choice and for decision. And the decision must be made in terms of the hard fact that if you want more of the one thing, you must have less of the other.

Graphically, this shows up as a line that falls as it proceeds to the right. The desire for more study time (more butter) is illustrated by a horizontal rightward movement. But to make this desire a reality—to conform to the underlying rule, to stay on the graph line—there must also be a *downward* movement. Some leisure time (some guns) must be given up. The increase in one member of the number pair must be matched by a decrease in the other.

It is highly important for you to notice that we are now trying to describe the graph line in terms of what happens to it as you start at the left and move rightward. *Think of the line as the path traced out by a point which moves toward the right, always satisfying the requirements of the linking rule as it does so.*

In the study-leisure case, the swapping terms between study and leisure are constant. A 1-hour increase in study time always calls for a sacrifice of exactly 1 hour in leisure time. Graphically, this means a *straight* line falling to the right.

In the butter-gun case, swapping terms are not constant. (There is no simple background rule which explains the relationship between the two sets of numbers comparable to the add-up-to-10 rule of the study-leisure case.) Start at the left, at A, and consider the horizontal movement indicating an increase of 1 million pounds of butter. This must be matched by a vertical movement signifying 1 thousand guns. This is the movement from A to B. But at the other extreme, E to F is also indicative of an increase of 1 million pounds of butter. Yet the required vertical movement is 5 thousand guns, or 5 times as large.

This variation in swapping terms shows up in a "nonstraight" line—here, one that is bowed out, or is convex as viewed from above. (For purposes of this discussion, and if you have not yet read Chapter 2, never mind *why* the line is so shaped. It has to do with the "law of diminishing returns," and there is a Study Guide exercise for Chapter 2 to indicate why diminishing returns would have this effect on the underlying linking rule. It is clear that the fact of limited productive resources requires a butter-gun line that falls as it moves rightward. Beyond that, just take it for granted that the exact linking rule is more complicated than in the study-leisure case and need not be exactly stated. What is here important, to

repeat, is this: When the swapping terms vary from point to point, the line curves.)

The common property in the study-leisure and butter-gun cases can be described as an *inverse* relationship. As the graph line is traced out by a moving point, the linking rule requires that the *increase* (positive change) in one magnitude must be accompanied by a *decrease* (negative change) in the other.

Review. Figure 4 contains six different graphs. In each, X signifies the magnitude being measured horizontally, and Y the magnitude being measured vertically. Circle the correct letter or letters below.

14. Diagrams *(a / b / c / d / e / f)* illustrate an inverse relation (positive change in one accompanied by negative change in the other) between X and Y.

15. In one case, Y's response to a change in X is zero, namely in diagram *(a / b / c / d / e / f)*.

16. The X-Y relation is positive rather than inverse (i.e., plus change is accompanied by plus change) in diagram(s) *(a / b / c / d / e / f)*.

17. Among the diagrams illustrating an inverse relation like study-leisure or butter-guns, the swapping terms are constant in diagram(s) *(a / b / c / d / e / f)* and they vary in diagram(s) *(a / b / c / d / e / f)*.

18. To illustrate the relation between an adult's daily food intake in calories (measured along X axis) and his weight (measured along Y axis), the diagram best suited would be (either of two) *(a / b / c / d / e / f)*.

19. The relation between an adult's calorie intake (X axis) and his height (Y axis) would probably be best illustrated by *(a / b / c / d / e / f)*.

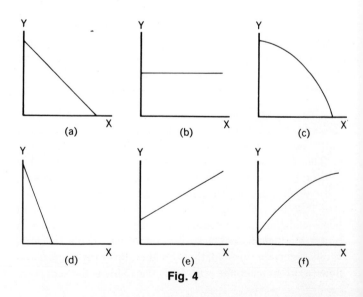

Fig. 4

20. The most probable relation between number of study hours you put in before a given examination (X axis) and examination grade earned (Y axis) is illustrated by (or is supposed to be illustrated by) *(a / b / c / d / e / f)*.

21. In diagram (d), assume the graph line meets the Y axis at measurement 10 and the X axis at 5. (Write these figures on the diagram.) The X-Y swapping terms are then as follows: A 1-unit increase in X must be accompanied by a *(0 / ½ / 1 / 2 / 4 / 10)* unit *(increase / decrease)* in Y. These swapping terms *(are constant / vary according to the position on the line)*.

22. In diagram (b), let the graph line meet the Y axis at measurement 4. Then, when the X value is 0, the Y value must be *(0 / 1 / 2 / 4 / can't tell)*. When the X value is 10, the Y value must be *(0 / 1 / 2 / 4 / can't tell)*.

23. In diagram (e), let one point on the graph line represent the values X = 0, Y = 4. This point on the diagram would be *(at extreme left / near the center / at extreme right)*. Let another point on the graph line represent the values X = 3, Y = 5. These two points indicate an underlying linking rule as follows: For every increase of 1 in the X value, there must be *(an increase / a decrease)* in the Y value of *(¼ / ⅓ / 1 / 3 / 4)*.

NOTE: If you find yourself stuck on any of these questions, or if you have answered incorrectly, do not be too concerned; the unfamiliar is seldom easy. Go back and review earlier material if necessary, until you are reasonably sure you understand why each answer is correct.
14. *a, c, d.* 15. *b.* 16. *e, f.* 17. *a* and *d; c.* 18. *e* or *f.* 19. *b.*
20. *f.* Although *e* would be reasonably correct, presumably the payoff for continued investment in study hours tapers off, as indicated by the bend in *f*'s graph line.
21. 2; decrease; constant. [Start with the point at the Y axis, where X = 0, Y = 10. From here, a 5-unit increase in X (from 0 to 5) would have to be matched by a 10-unit decrease in Y (from 10 to 0). Swapping terms are constant because the line is straight; and 5 for 10 is equivalent to 1 for 2.]
22. 4; 4. A horizontal line means that the Y value stays the same, no matter what the X value is.
23. extreme left; increase; ⅓. (A 3-unit increase in X, from 0 to 3, is matched by a 1-unit increase in Y, from 4 to 5. 3 to 1 is equivalent to 1 to ⅓.)

Summary Thus Far. At this point, you may stop if you wish, for the time being. Save for a few minor points, you have covered all the ground you need with respect to diagrams in Part One of the text. In summary, remember these points:

1. When you meet any graph, always look first to see what is being measured on the horizontal axis and what is being measured on the vertical axis.

2. The line on the graph illustrates some form of relationship between the two items measured. Behind the line are two sets of figures linked together, pair by pair.

3. Which way does the line run? If it rises to the right, it means that as one figure in the pair rises, the other figure rises also. If the line falls as it moves to the right, then the paired numbers move inversely. As one goes up, the other must go down.

This behavior of the line—whether it rises or falls as it moves to the right—is extremely important. Often, for purposes of the idea being illustrated, it is not important to know the exact pairs of numbers corresponding to particular points on the line; on many of the diagrams in the text, actual numbers are not shown on the two axis lines. The specific numbers are often of secondary importance, and the first considerations are these: Is the line rising, or falling, as viewed from left to right? Is it straight, or curved?

You will find a few time-series diagrams in Part One of the text—Fig. 2-9, for example. A time-series diagram simply illustrates a particular period of time in history. One set of numbers consists of dates; one number in each pair is a date. This diagram illustrates how important the question, "Which way does the line run?" can be. The bottom line in Fig. 2-9 falls as it moves rightward, showing clearly how the percentage of the population under age twenty has been dropping. It was just about 50 per cent in 1880; it has fallen more or less steadily since then—save for a sudden jump around 1950, after the rise in marriages which followed World War II.

Slope: Straight Lines. To repeat, a graph is simply a device for illustrating the nature of the relation between two "variables" which happen for some reason to be related or linked together.

One way of indicating what we mean by saying that there is a linking rule which joins the X variable (number of study hours, butter quantity, or whatever) to the Y variable (leisure hours, gun quantity, etc.) is this: X and Y are linked together when any given change in X demands some certain change in Y. That is how in reality things so often present themselves: we start with X and Y occupying some actual positions, and we want to know what would happen to Y if X were to change in its position or value.

In fact, things so often appear in this manner that it is useful to seek an exact measure of the change-in-X-change-in-Y relation. We can put things this way: What change in Y would a 1-unit increase in X require?

In the study-leisure case, an immediate and unqualified answer shows up. The required change in Y would be minus one, or in number symbols, −1. The butter-gun case is more complicated. The answer is always a minus quantity, but whether it is −1 or −2 or −5 depends on whether your starting position is A or B or E. The difference is that one line is straight, the other curved.

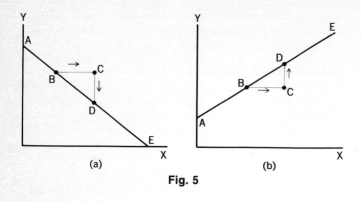

Fig. 5

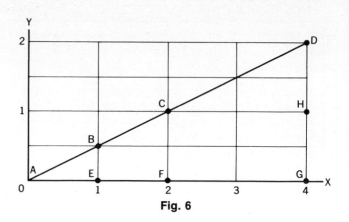

Fig. 6

Consider first the simple straight-line case. Earlier, it was suggested that you think of any graph line (straight or curved) as the path traced by a point which moves to the right, always satisfying the linking rule as it does so. Now again think of the point as making each little movement to the right in two stages. First, a strictly horizontal movement, of sufficient length to indicate a 1-unit increase in the X value (and no change in Y). Second, a vertical movement, up or down; this signifies a change in Y, and the distance moved signifies the amount by which Y must change on account of the 1-unit X increase. For example, in either of the two little diagrams composing Fig. 5, the true path traced out is $ABDE$. But the movement from B to D can be considered as (1) a probing movement from B to C (the 1-unit change in X which takes the point momentarily off its true path), followed by (2) a correcting movement from C to D (the required matching change in Y), as the linking rule tells the point what adjustment it must make to return to the true path.

If BC's length indicates a 1-unit increase in X, then CD's length indicates the rate of change in Y with respect to X change. On the graph, this measure of change is called the *slope* of the line $ABDE$.

Remember these things about slope:

1. Slope is always a number. It is a measure of change. It is a measure of the amount by which Y changes as a result of a 1-unit X change.

2. If the graph line is straight, one single number measures its slope at any and all points thereon. This is just another way of saying that a straight line is one whose direction does not change.

3. The slope number always has a negative value (it is preceded by a minus sign) if the X-Y relation is an inverse one—that is, if a positive increase in X calls for a "negative increase" (a reduction) in Y, as in the study-leisure and gun-butter examples. In graph terms, the slope is negative if the line on the graph falls as it stretches to the right. Slope is a positive number if an increase in X calls for an increase in Y; in graph terms, slope is positive if the line climbs to the right.

Notice that this measurement of slope just means digging more deeply into the matter raised by our earlier question:

Which way does the line run? The first and most elementary step is to note whether the line rises or falls as it runs rightward. Now we want to use a *number* to measure the rate at which it rises or falls (a positive number for any rise, a negative one for any fall).

Now consider a little more fully the technique for measuring or illustrating graphically the slope of a straight line. We have said with respect to Fig. 5 that the slope of the graph line $ABDE$ is measured by the length of CD. This assumes that BC is of a length equal to 1 X unit.

We could equally well have said that slope is measured by the fraction CD / BC, with the lengths of CD and BC representing the numbers for which they stand. Since BC corresponds to the number 1, CD / BC reduces to CD anyhow. The only objection to naming slope as CD / BC is that at first it seems needlessly clumsy.

But measuring slope as CD / BC is a reminder that the Y movement (CD) can be considered only relative to the amount of X movement (BC). Look at Fig. 5. BC and CD form with the graph line itself a right-angled triangle, of which the graph line is the hypotenuse (the side opposite the right angle). Look particularly at diagram (b), in which this triangle is suspended underneath the graph line. If CD / BC is used as the slope measure, *any* right-angled triangle so hung can be used, regardless of the length of its sides. All such triangles hung beneath $ABDE$ would be proportionate, and the relation CD / BC is constant. In Fig. 6, the slope of the line $ABCD$ is ½, and any one of a number of triangles can be used to measure that slope: AEB, AFC, AGD, CHD. The fraction made up of vertical side over horizontal side (if you prefer, the ratio between these two sides) is always ½. The two sides of your triangle which join to make the right angle must of course be exactly in the horizontal and vertical dimensions; but once this requirement is satisfied, the sides of any right-angled triangle can be used to measure the slope of the graph line.

If the graph line falls as its path runs rightward, you can still use a right-angled triangle hung below the line. Or you can use one sitting atop the line, like that in diagram (a) of Fig. 5. The same rule applies: slope is measured by the fraction vertical side over horizontal side. But remember that a falling

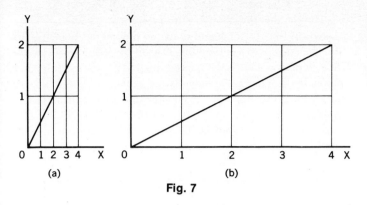

Fig. 7

line means an inverse X-Y relation, hence a negative slope value.

Some people find it helpful to think of slope as "the rise over the run." "The rise" is the vertical distance involved; in Fig. 5 terms, the rise is *CD*. "The run" is the horizontal distance; it is *BC* in Fig. 5 terms. So the rise over the run would in this instance be *CD* over *BC*.

It is tempting to associate the measure of slope with the steepness with which the graph line rises or falls, so that a steeply tilted line is taken as one with a high slope value, positive or negative. And sometimes this conclusion is valid—but don't overlook the fact that the steepness with which a graph line rises or falls depends in part on the scale chosen for the graph. Diagrams (a) and (b) in Fig. 7 both portray exactly the same linking relation, and either is a perfectly respectable illustration. But in (b), the horizontal scale has been stretched out in comparison with that used in (a). The slope of the line in both parts of Fig. 7 is +2. (Note, though, that when you have *two* lines on the *same* graph, so that the same scale applies to both of them, you then can say that the steeper of the two lines has the higher absolute slope value.)

Finally, one small point. We have been talking throughout in terms of a 1-unit *increase* in X. The slope measure would work equally well for a decrease. Suppose that two positions traced by the moving point are these:

	Point A	Point B
X	4	5
Y	10	15

Slope value is 5, since the 1-unit rise in X from 4 to 5 occasions a 5-unit rise in Y. But we could equally well speak of a 1-unit *decrease* in X, from 5 to 4, accompanied by a 5-unit decrease in Y, from 15 to 10. Here again, the convenience of putting things in the form of a fraction (vertical side over horizontal side, or Y change over X change) becomes evident. For the fraction is either

$$\frac{+5}{+1} \quad \text{or else} \quad \frac{-5}{-1}$$

depending on whether you start with an increase or a decrease in X; and the result is 5, or +5, either way.

REVIEW

24. Slope is a measure of the rate at which the Y value—i.e., the magnitude we are measuring along the Y axis—changes for each change of *(zero units / one unit / the same number of units)* in the X value.

25. A graph line has the same slope value throughout when that line is *(curved / rising / straight / falling)*.

26. Graphically, we can illustrate or measure slope in terms of a right-angled triangle below the graph line. Slope is the fraction or ratio obtained by putting the length of the *(vertical / horizontal)* side of the triangle over the length of the *(vertical / horizontal)* side.

27. When the X-Y relation is an inverse one, then its graphical illustration can be considered the path of a point which *(falls / rises)* as it moves to the right. The slope value of such a relation is *(positive / zero / negative)*.

28. In diagram (b) of Fig. 4, the slope of the line illustrated is *(positive / negative / zero / impossible to tell)*.

29. Two positions of X on a straight graph line are 5 and 7. What is the value of slope if the corresponding Y positions are:
a. 5 and 7? . . . . (−3 / −2 / −1 / 0 / 1 / 2 / 3 / infinity)
b. 4 and 2? . . . . (−3 / −2 / −1 / 0 / 1 / 2 / 3 / infinity)
c. 2 and − 2? . . . . (−3 / −2 / −1 / 0 / 1 / 2 / 3 / infinity)
d. 4 and 4? . . . . (−3 / −2 / −1 / 0 / 1 / 2 / 3 / infinity)
e. −2 and −8? . . . . (−3 / −2 / −1 / 0/ /1 / 2 / 3 / infinity)
f. −8 and −2? . . . . (−3 / −2 / −1 / 0 / 1 / 2 / 3 / infinity)

---

24. one unit. 25. straight. 26. vertical; horizontal.
27. falls; negative. 28. zero.
29. *a.* 1. *b.* −1. *c.* −2. *d.* 0. *e.* −3. *f.* 3.

The Slope of Curved Lines. A curved line is one whose direction continually changes. The amount of Y change required by a 1-unit X change varies according to the position from which this change begins.

Consider the curved line *ABCDEF* in Fig. 8. Suppose we are at point B. If we know the exact X and Y values associated with every point on this line—i.e., if we know the underlying linking rule which it illustrates—then we shall have no difficulty in learning what the Y change would be as a result of a shift from B to E. Moreover, we could put the usual right-angled triangle underneath, with corners at B and E, and from it develop a slope value. But this would not in a true sense be the slope of the curved line itself; it would really measure the slope of the straight line running between B and E. We would get a different and somewhat higher slope figure if we

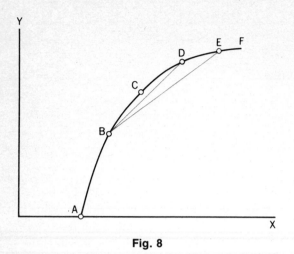

Fig. 8

dealt similarly with a change from *B* to *D*, and a still different figure for a change from *B* to *C*.

For some purposes, it is quite sufficient to know what the actual *Y* change would be in consequence of moving from *B* to *E*, or to *D*, or to *C*. But for other problems it is useful or even necessary to ask: What is the slope of the curved line exactly at some point, such as *B*?

To ask this question is to pose another one: Does it make sense to speak of the slope of a line precisely at a single point?

Certainly point *B*, considered in isolation, has no slope, no direction. But point *B* considered as part of the line *ABCDEF* is another matter. The slope of the line is a measure of the direction in which it runs, reckoned in terms of the scales on the two axes. Think for the moment of *ABCDEF* as the path traced, not by a moving point, but by a moving automobile. The direction of movement of that automobile changes continually, since it follows a curved path. But can we say that at the exact moment when it passes over point *B*, the automobile is headed in some given direction? Certainly we can do so, in the sense that a compass mounted aboard would at that exact moment give an exact reading, such as northeast, or east by north.

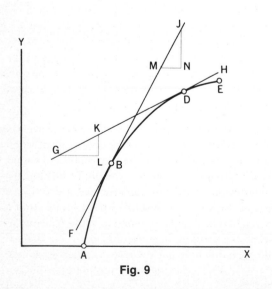

Fig. 9

How is this direction at *B* to be indicated? The accepted answer is this: by a tangent drawn to the curved line at point *B*. The tangent to a curved line is itself by definition a straight line; it does not cross the curved line but touches it only; and it touches it at one point only. By inspection of Fig. 9, it is easy to see how the slope of the tangent line *FJ* is considered as measuring the slope of the curved line at point *B*; and *GH* does the same for point *D*. To each such straight line we can apply our usual right-angle measuring technique.

Review. Circle each correct alternative below.

30. Figure 10 consists of eight separate diagrams, each illustrating a small segment of a graph line. In each, the numbers indicate the length of the adjacent straight-line segment. What is the slope of each *AB* line? Where *AB* is curved, it is the slope at point *C* that is desired.

a. (−4 / −3 / −2 / −1 / 0 / 1 / 2 / 3 / 4 / 10 / *infinity*)
b. (−4 / −3 / −2 / −1 / 0 / 1 / 2 / 3 / 4 / 10 / *infinity*)
c. (−4 / −3/ −2 / −1 / 0 / 1 / 2 / 3 / 4 / 10 / *infinity*)
d. (−4 / −3 / −2 / −1 / 0 / 1 / 2 / 3 / 4 / 10 / *infinity*)
e. (−4 / −3 / −2 / −1 / 0 / 1 / 2 / 3 / 4 / 10 / *infinity*)
f. (−4 / −3 / −2 / −1 / 0 / 1 / 2 / 3 / 4 / 10 / *infinity*)
g. (−4 / −3 / −2 / −1 / 0 / 1 / 2 / 3 / 4 / 10 / *infinity*)
h. (−4 / −3 / −2 / −1 / 0 / 1 / 2 / 3 / 4 / 10 / *infinity*)

---

a. −4. *b.* 3. *c.* 10. *d.* 2. *e.* 0. *f.* −2. *g.* −2. *h.* −1.

Two or More Lines on a Graph. So far our discussion has run in terms of the interpretation of a single line on a graph. But most text diagrams include two lines, usually intersecting at one point on the graph.

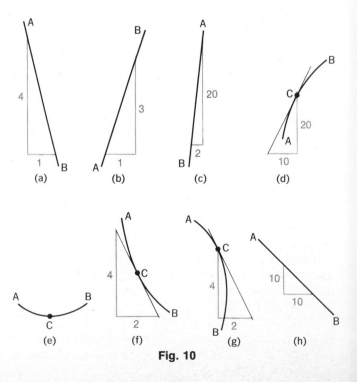

Fig. 10

The supply-and-demand diagram of Chapter 4 is a good example. The demand line, or demand curve, is drawn as usual—from two sets of figures paired together. Here is the schedule of figures used in Chapter 4:

	Price of Wheat per Bushel	Quantity Demanded (Million Bushels per Month)
A	$5	9
B	4	10
C	3	12
D	2	15
E	1	20

This is a "demand schedule." It is a schedule of the quantities of wheat that buyers in some market would demand, i.e., purchase, *if* the price were to stand at any one of five possible levels.

It does not matter whether this is a real market or an imaginary one. The precise figures in the table are not especially important. What this schedule is intended to illustrate is the reasonable (but important) fact that as the price of anything falls, buyers probably will want to buy a larger total amount than they did before. In other words, *quantity* of wheat bought is linked to the *price* of wheat. If price were to change, so would quantity.

Now this schedule indicates what *buyers* of wheat are prepared to do, at various prices. It is also possible to prepare another schedule, indicating what *sellers* of wheat (the producers of wheat, the suppliers of wheat) are prepared to do. In this case, it seems reasonable to assume that if price were to go *up*, thus giving them a greater return, they would try to supply a larger quantity. Alternatively, if price were to fall, they would supply *less*. Below is the schedule from Chapter 4. Note that it illustrates what has just been said—the higher the price, the greater the quantity offered for sale.

	Price of Wheat per Bushel	Quantity Supplied (Million Bushels per Month)
A	$5	18
B	4	16
C	3	12
D	2	7
E	1	0

At this stage, it is not particularly important if you do not understand fully the ideas conveyed by the demand schedule or the supply schedule. So far as the preparation of graphs is concerned, what matters is that you are faced with something already familiar: The demand schedule consists of two sets of figures, neatly paired off one with another. And so does the supply schedule. This means that either schedule can be depicted as a line on a graph.

But note one further fact: There is a fundamental resemblance between these two schedules. Although they represent the attitudes or the intentions of two entirely different

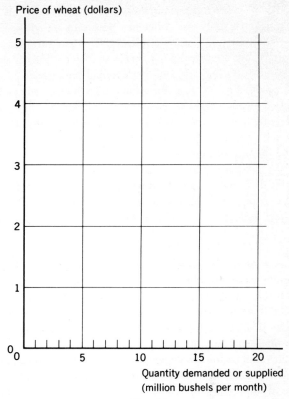

Price of wheat (dollars)

Quantity demanded or supplied
(million bushels per month)

Fig. 11

groups of people, the two schedules *match* one another in that one column refers to *price* and the other to *quantity*. It is only because they match in this respect that both can be depicted on the same graph. If we are to make any sense out of two or more lines on the same graph, these lines must refer to the same kinds of things, measured in the same kinds of units.

In Fig. 11, draw the lines corresponding to these two schedules. (Plot the five points for each schedule and join them with a smooth curve.) Label your demand curve *DD* and your supply curve *SS*.

Your two lines should cross at one point, and one point only. That is the point signifying a price of $3 and a quantity of 12 million bushels. Its significance is that at this level of price, and no other, the intentions of buyers and the intentions of sellers match. In these circumstances, the price of $3 will be called an "equilibrium price," and the quantity of 12 million bushels an "equilibrium quantity."

Once you have grasped the idea of demand schedules and supply schedules, Fig. 11 becomes a very simple illustration, and you can understand it with little trouble. In fact, you may wonder why a graph is necessary at all. If the object is just to find equilibrium price and quantity, and if you have to draw the graph yourself, it would be quicker just to hunt through the two schedules until you found a pair of figures in one that matched a pair of figures in the other.

But the text does not ask you to draw graphs; they are supplied for you. In all cases, a graph is still just an illustration. It will never tell you anything you could not acquire by other means if you were sufficiently determined to do so. But the graph may tell you more quickly! The text supplies you with diagrams at critical points because they are the quickest ways of illustrating points of fundamental importance.

Consider Fig. 11 again, for instance. To the trained eye (by now that means, of course, *your* eye), this diagram tells a good deal more than just the equilibrium price and quantity. It tells how such an equilibrium level is possible. Take any price *above* the equilibrium level, say $4 or $5. At any such price, quantity supplied will not match quantity demanded. More specifically, quantity supplied will *exceed* quantity demanded. But if price is permitted to fall, this excess of supply over demand will grow less. Why? Because, as price falls, the corresponding demand quantity insists on moving to the right (a decreased price means an increased quantity demanded). And as price falls, in order to keep in touch with the collection of points making up the supply curve, it is necessary to move to the left (a decreased price means a decreased quantity supplied). If the demand curve were to climb to the right instead of falling to the right, we might never have an equilibrium price and quantity at all.

The point on the graph at which the two lines intersect is a unique and important point. But to consider it as the only point of importance or interest would be to miss the whole purpose of using graphs as illustrations. Certainly the intersection or "equilibrium" point has no special significance unless there is some tendency for the price which it illustrates actually to become established. And if so established, this is because of the situation that would prevail—and which the graph illustrates with particular clarity—at *other* prices. At prices above the equilibrium level, the graph indicates, the quantity suppliers would like to sell exceeds the quantity buyers are willing to purchase. Now, it is quite possible for such an above-equilibrium price to prevail, at least for short periods, with the actual quantity demanded and bought being less than the potential supply at that price. But if we add to the situation a disposition on the part of buyers and sellers to use *a change in price* as part of the bargaining and competitive process, then it is easy to see why any above-equilibrium price is likely to be pulled down to a lower level.

A similar argument applies to prices below the equilibrium level. Again, such prices *could* prevail, at least temporarily; and once again, we need the rest of the graph as part of the description of actual situations, in order to explain why the intersection point has particular significance.

Conclusion. Graphs were made for lazy people who want to grasp the idea with as little expenditure of time and effort as possible. But if you want to take advantage of this device, you must learn the rules—which (to repeat) are:

1. What does the graph measure on each axis? What are the labels on the axes? Each line on a graph indicates some kind of relation or linking rule between these two sets of numbers.

2. Which way does the line run? Does it fall to the right or

rise to the right? If it falls, then the relation between the two sets of numbers is an inverse one—as one rises, the other falls. If it rises to the right, the two sets of numbers move in the same direction.

3. Is the line straight or curved? If it is straight, the ratio of change in Y to change in X is constant. If the line curves, this ratio varies.

4. If there are two or more lines on a graph, then there are two or more schedules in the background. What kind of relationship is involved in each schedule, and why is it important to bring them together on the same graph? Usually the two lines cross one another at some point, and usually this intersection is important because at this point the two schedules match one another. Why is this matching important?

Review. Complete as before.

31. One point on a graph indicates an X value of 4, a Y value of 10. Another point indicates an X value of 5, a Y value of 8. If these two points are joined by a straight line, the slope of that line is _____.

32. The slope of a straight line is −3. If movement from one point to another along that line results in an increase in Y from 10 to 16, what change in X must have taken place? It will have (*risen / fallen*) by (6 / 3 / 2 / 1 / ½).

33. A line on a graph appears as the upper half of a circle: It starts out at the origin of the graph, rises, and then falls, until finally it drops to the horizontal axis from which it started. Which of the following correctly describes the slope value of this line?

a. It will have a changing slope value, but a figure which is positive throughout.

b. It will at first have a negative slope-value figure (toward the left-hand side) and this slope value will grow larger; then, as the line proceeds to the right, the slope-value figure will become positive.

c. It will at first have a positive slope-value figure (toward the left-hand side) and this slope value will grow larger as the line proceeds to the right; then the slope-value figure will become negative.

d. It will at first have a positive slope-value figure (toward the left-hand side), but this slope value will diminish in value as the line proceeds to the right; it will reach a value of zero, and then become a negative figure.

34. In Fig. 11, the *DD* curve has a (*negative / positive*) slope value. This figure is a (*constant / changing*) one. The *SS* curve in this figure has a (*negative / positive*) slope value. This figure is a (*constant / changing*) one.

---

31. −2. 32. fallen by 2. 33. *d.* 34. negative; changing; positive; changing.

1

BASIC
ECONOMIC
CONCEPTS AND
NATIONAL
INCOME

1 INTRODUCTION

THIS INTRODUCTORY CHAPTER is, above all, one which should be read with a view to *perspective*. Many of the chapters to follow contain concepts which you must study carefully in order to understand, as fully as you can, what they mean and what they do not mean. With a few relatively minor exceptions, this is not true of the present chapter at all. It skims over a great deal of ground so as to give you a rough outline of what the ground is like. Do not worry overmuch about the detail of all this territory. For example, the chapter lists no less than six alternative definitions of economics. Do not try to memorize them or to use them to establish the exact boundaries of economics. Just try to get a rough idea of what this field of study is about.

Because of the nature of this chapter, the Review section which follows is fairly short, and there is no Quiz section. You will find more than enough in the way of Quiz questions in later chapters.

1. It is of some importance to try to understand what economics does *not* try to do. With the text's six alternative definitions of the subject in mind, which of the following seem to you to be correct (C) as to the scope of economic analysis, and which seem incorrect (I)?

a. The first objective of economics as a science is to study human performance in producing and selling goods in order to indicate how business can perform these activities more efficiently. ....*(C / I)*

b. Economics is closely associated with the particular activities in which money is involved—the purchase and sale of goods and of securities, the employment of labor, and so on. ....*(C / I)*

c. Economics is a study of the processes by which a nation acquires a high standard of income and of consumption. ....*(C / I)*

d. In economics, we look at the processes of producing and selling goods, and of buying and consuming goods, in order to develop some theory with respect to such behavior. .*(C / I)*

e. Economics is a study of how people in a society decide what commodities and services they are going to produce, now and in the future, and how those commodities and services are to be distributed among members of the population. ....*(C / I)*

f. The objective of economics, as it strives to become a science, is to indicate the proper goals which human beings ought to pursue with respect to production and consumption. ....*(C / I)*

As a *social* science, the particular concern of economics is the study of people grouped together in a society. The essential characteristic of a society is (in John Donne's words) that "no man is an island, entire of itself; every man is a piece of the continent, a part of the main." No individual and no group within a society can act without that action having its impact, direct or indirect, upon other individuals or groups. It is primarily this quality of *interdependence* that may make the true outcome of behavior difficult to explore, and that calls for a special analysis of that behavior.

---

a. I. *b.* C. *c.* C. *d.* C. *e.* C. *f.* I.

---

2. A basic characteristic of science in any field is its development of *theory*. The nature of theory is overwhelmingly difficult to describe. Yet we can say with some confidence that it is the discovery of *patterns* in behavior. Once the pattern is discovered, behavior which hitherto had seemed incomprehensible or aimless is suddenly revealed as conforming to this pattern.

While the theory may seek to furnish some explanation of why the pattern exists, this is not the first order of business. The essential task is to discover that the pattern is *there*, and to describe it.

This raises the matter of the relation between theory and practice, or theory and reality. Which of the following correctly (C) repeat what the text has to say on this, and which are incorrect (I)?

a. Theory must correspond with reality in the sense of illuminating behavior observed in reality. Failing in this, it is not appropriate theory. ....*(C / I)*

b. In construction of theory, it is necessary to "stand back" from actual behavior a little, much as a referee stands back at a football game, in order to observe what is really happening. This observation involves "abstraction." ....*(C / I)*

c. Of necessity, theory simplifies. It ignores what is irrelevant or unimportant, in order to isolate the *pattern* in behavior. ....*(C / I)*

d. It is the failure of a theory to give a meaningful account of real behavior that marks it as false or incomplete. Yet if it is the best theory available, it may survive. Poor theories are more likely to be killed off by better theories than they are by lack of conformity with facts. ....*(C / I)*

All statements correct (C.)

3. We cannot establish whether or not a particular theory is in accord with reality until we have established what "the facts" of reality are. This is by no means always easy—as the text's Fig. 1-2 (bird or antelope?) is intended to illustrate. This figure is taken from a study of theory in physics, where the basic problem is spelled out: The raw elements of experience which our senses carry to the brain are meaningless until the brain *organizes* them into a pattern (i.e., "theorizes" about them). The brain's disposition is always to fit the material, if possible, into a familiar pattern—even though, in the new situation, that pattern may be a false one.

If this difficulty arises in physics or in chemistry, where controlled experiments are so often possible, it becomes far more acute where the behavior observed is that of human beings.

Where the ordinary business of living requires us to do so, we are forced to develop some workably valid interpretations of the behavior around us. In everyday experience, we can often discover quickly whether or not our conclusions are workably accurate. Interpret a person's behavior falsely, act on your conclusion—and you may soon learn that your interpretation was incorrect. However, there is a broader range of human experience where this element of immediate verification is lacking, or where the degree of verification is uncertain. And here, the final paragraph of the preceding question applies: Where verification of a theory (an interpretation) is difficult, the familiar theory, no matter how unsatisfactory it may be, always survives until it can be supplanted by a clearly superior theory.

Which of the following seem to repeat correctly (C) what the text says on this topic, and which are incorrect (I)?

a. The basic requirement in seeking to develop a theory about observed behavior is ordinary, level-headed common sense. ....(C / I)
b. Common sense is a dangerous starting point, because it really means a reliance on familiar interpretation; on this account, common sense may on occasion be nonsense. (C / I)
c. Study and experience are needed if one is to attempt to construct theory on economic matters. ....(C / I)
d. Long experience is dangerous if familiarity leads to take-it-for-granted interpretations, or if overlong experience from a particular point of view persuades the observer to forget that there are other relevant points of view. ....(C / I)
e. If a participant in the economic world—say a businessman—is to do his job efficiently, he must necessarily do the best he can to understand the relevant economic theory of what he is doing. ....(C / I)
f. The economist's approach and objective differ from that of anyone engaged in business. It is like the referee and the team player at a football game: the good referee would not necessarily make a good player, and vice versa. .....(C / I)

---

a. I. *b.* C. *c.* C. *d.* C. *e.* I. *f.* C.

4. In physics or in chemistry, theory means uncovering the laws which dictate the behavior of inanimate matter, and describing the quantitative properties of those laws. Is the task of economic theory to uncover comparable laws of human behavior—to which people rigidly and mechanically conform?

On this, the text's view is that individuals *(do / do not)* conform exactly to behavior patterns. But people in large groups, *taken as a group, (still do not conform / show considerable conformity, once the pattern is isolated)*.

Sometimes there is a pattern even in nonconformity. The "normal curve"—text Fig. 1-4—is intended to illustrate this point. (It is helpful if you can grasp something of the meaning of "normal" and "skewed" curves, but a detailed understanding is unnecessary at this early stage. These diagrams reappear later in the text.)

---

do not; show considerable conformity.

---

5. The text chapter closes with a short section on "the fallacy of composition." Spend a little time now learning the meaning of this idea, for you will meet it again later. For each statement below, put C in the space if the fallacy of composition seems involved. Put P if the fallacy of *post hoc, ergo propter hoc* (see text footnote 3 in the "Methodology of Economics: Brief Preview" section) may be involved. Put N if neither seems to arise.

a. The American economy remains essentially competitive as a result of diligent application of the antitrust laws. ....( )
b. All theories in social science are forced to simplify the real and complex world; and because of this simplification, the conclusions of any such theory are inevitably distorted and inaccurate explanations. ....( )
c. Workers in any single industry will benefit from higher wages; hence workers in all industries would benefit from a comparable wage increase. ....( )
d. Advertising on a large scale is responsible for the present high standard of living in the United States. ....( )
e. The more the human brain masters a subject in social science such as economics, the less room it has for comprehension of any quite different subject, such as physics. ( )
f. If one firm in an industry benefits from a large-scale advertising campaign, this is an indication that if all firms in that industry were to advertise, they would all obtain comparable increases in sales. ....( )
g. I can gain 15 minutes by driving my car to work instead of using public transportation; if everyone in my community were to follow my example, the total gain in time would run into hundreds of hours each day. ....( )

---

a. P. *b.* N. *c.* C. *d.* P. *e.* N. *f.* C. *g.* C.

2 CENTRAL PROBLEMS OF EVERY ECONOMIC SOCIETY

MOST OF THIS CHAPTER is built on a short series of fundamental ideas. It is essential that you grasp them.

▶ The basic ingredients from which our material wants for goods and services are satisfied are labor, capital goods, and land (alternatively, men, machines, and materials).

These *real* productive inputs—not money—are the items genuinely needed to meet life's material demands. (Money plays a crucial part, which in due course will be considered carefully. But money is only a means for organizing the employment of these real inputs.)

▶ Every society has only a finite supply of these productive inputs. Consequently, there is a limit on the total output of goods and services which that society can produce.

▶ Even in societies relatively well endowed with productive inputs, the total demands of consumers outrun total productive capacity.

In sum, even in rich societies, it is impossible to produce enough to satisfy everybody's desire for everything. Today, many poor economies are still hard-pressed to turn out enough in the way of elemental food and shelter for their populations. The richer societies are easily capable of covering life's basic necessities for all their members. But our interest here is not with necessities alone; it is with consumers' *total* demands. Once necessities have been met, consumer wants pass quickly to comforts and to luxuries. In this sense, even rich societies face *the law of scarcity:* total consumer demands outrun total productive capacity.

1. *a.* The text sets out three basic social problems which arise out of this law of scarcity, namely _____, _____, and _____ goods shall be produced.

b. If the total input stock is limited, then the more of this stock that is devoted to production of good A, the less there remains for production of goods B, C, D, etc. The problem of *how much* of A to produce, *how much* of B, *how much* of C,

and so on (in the light of this limit on the over-all input stock), is the (WHAT/HOW/FOR WHOM) problem.
c. An output restricted by the fact of a limited input supply must somehow be shared out or rationed among society's members; this is the (WHAT/HOW/FOR WHOM) problem.

The problem of HOW goods shall be produced is a little trickier. It is the problem of the exact mix of resources to be used in the manufacture of any given commodity.

It may strengthen your grasp of both WHAT and HOW problems to consider instances in which they would not arise at all. The WHAT problem emerges because resources are versatile, because they have more than one possible use or occupation. Suppose, however, that a particular kind of labor or machine is *not* versatile, that it is useful *only* for producing good A; it is useless for B, C, or D. And suppose (however unlikely) that *all* resources are specialized in this way. Hence there is no opportunity to swap less of A for more of B. Then there is no problem of WHAT to produce, because there is only one bill of goods that *can* be produced.

Similarly, the HOW problem arises because A, B, C, and D can ordinarily be made in more than one way. But suppose there is only *one fixed recipe* for making A: there is no opportunity to substitute more of input X (say, machinery) for less of input Y (say, labor). And suppose this fixed-recipe rule applies throughout. Then there is no problem of HOW goods shall be produced; each good will be made in the one and only way it *can* be made.

The more general situation is that in which there is more than one known productive technique (e.g., men can be substituted for machines, and vice versa). If so, then HOW exists as a social problem. (Typically, the HOW problem appears to students less clear than WHAT or FOR WHOM, or as a problem less vital, less universal. But remember that such a question as "to adopt automatic processes or not to automate" is a particular illustration of HOW. And Chapter 3 will make it clear that in capitalist societies HOW ranks along with WHAT and FOR WHOM as a matter for the pricing system to settle.)

a. WHAT, HOW, FOR WHOM. *b.* WHAT. *c.* FOR WHOM.

2. The nature of the WHAT problem can be illustrated more fully by means of a "production-possibility schedule" and its graphical counterpart, the "production-possibility curve." Because a graph has only two dimensions, the WHAT problem

must then be set out as one involving the choice between *two* goods only (in the text example, the choice between guns and butter). But the principles are the same whether the total number of goods is 2, 20, or 20,000. Ultimately, the problem is that of the terms of choice between a little more of this and a little less of that.

The production-possibility schedule is simply a listing of some of the alternative output combinations which a given input stock could produce weekly, or monthly, or using whatever time unit is convenient.

The production-possibility curve (e.g., Fig. 2-2 in the text) is the graphical illustration of this schedule. (NOTE: If you are weak on graphs, study of the Orientation section in this Study Guide is strongly recommended. The production-possibility diagram is discussed there, on pp. 4–6.)

a. Along the axes of a production-possibility diagram are measured (pick one):
(1) Quantities of productive inputs or resources.
(2) Quantities of finished commodities.
(3) Values of finished commodities.

Each and every point on the entire surface of this diagram (whether on the curve or off it) stands for *some* combination of the two goods involved (e.g., so many guns produced and so much butter produced per unit of time). With a given input stock, some of these points would be attainable, others would not. Specifically, with respect to production, the economy could operate (pick one):
(1) Anywhere on the curve, and only on the curve.
(2) Anywhere on the curve or anywhere inside it (below and to the left).
(3) Anywhere on the curve, inside it, or outside it.

b. In order to operate *outside* the curve (above and to the right of it), the economy would have to (pick one or both):
(1) Somehow increase its stock of inputs.
(2) Discover some new production techniques enabling any given input stock to produce more output than before.

If the economy did somehow add to its input stock, or did discover new production techniques, the production-possibility curve would thereupon (pick one):
(1) Remain unchanged.
(2) Move appropriately inward and to the left.
(3) Move appropriately outward and to the right.

c. If there is a law of scarcity, then the economy will want to make good use of its limited input supply—that is, it will want to operate *on* the production-possibility curve, not inside it. (That is why the text speaks of this curve as the "production-possibility frontier.") Should the economy be operating *inside* the curve, this would be attributable to some inefficiency or breakdown in economic organization. Specifically (pick one or both):
(1) Some part of the input supply must be unemployed.
(2) The input supply, if fully employed, is somehow being

used improperly. The best available production techniques are not being used, or some inputs are in the wrong jobs.

---

a. (2); (2).   *b.* (1) and (2); (3).   *c.* (1) and (2).

---

3. The production-possibility frontier in text Fig. 2-2 is curved. Specifically, it is concave as viewed from the left and below. A full account of the background reasons for this concavity would be complicated, and relatively unimportant at this early stage. However, *one* background factor deserves careful study: the law of diminishing returns.

The nature of this law is most easily illustrated by assuming that only *two* inputs, say A and B, are needed for production of some commodity X. Input A (which in the text example is land) is available in some fixed and limited quantity only. Input B (labor, in the text example) can be varied in quantity employed. The question with which the diminishing-returns law deals is this: We would like to have more of X. The supply of input A, which is essential for X production, is limited. To what extent can we get more X by adding more of input B to the fixed A quantity?

The diminishing-returns law gives the following answer: Up to a point, more B will yield more X. But the cost of getting additional X, in terms of the additional B quantity required, will steadily (*increase / decrease*). Or, to say the same thing differently, the "payoff" from each extra unit of B employed, in terms of the number of extra units of X resulting, will (*increase / diminish*). In fact, a point will ultimately be reached at which—because of the restricted supply of A—the payoff from an extra unit of B employed would be (*zero / infinity*).

Notice that this law runs in physical quantities of A, B, and X—that is, it runs in (*money / "real"*) terms.

For illustrative purposes, it is convenient to use an example involving two inputs only. Most actual productive processes involve more than two (e.g., tools, equipment, and seed grain in addition to labor and land). Where more than two inputs are involved, then, for the diminishing-returns law to apply, (*all the inputs / at least one input, but not all inputs / one input and one only*) must be fixed in available supply.

---

increase; diminish; zero; "real"; at least one input, but not all inputs.

---

4. This question develops more fully the relation between the production-possibility curve, the shape of that curve, and the diminishing-returns law.

A certain economy produces only two consumer goods, X and Y. For manufacture of these goods, it has three kinds of resources: (1) a fixed stock of X resources, useful only in X's production; (2) a similar fixed stock of Y resources; (3) a fixed labor force of 100 men capable of working in either occupation. The following table indicates the amounts of X and of Y producible daily when various quantities of labor work with the specialized resources.

Number of Men	Daily X Production	Number of Men	Daily Y Production	Corresponding X Production
0	0	0	0	600
10	40	10	5	580
20	105	20	12	550
30	200	30	20	500
40	300	40	28	450
50	390	50	36	390
60	450	60	43	300
70	500	70	49	200
80	550	80	54	105
90	580	90	58	40
100	600	100	60	0

The economy's labor force of 100 men—if fully employed—must be distributed between the two occupations: if there are 100 men in X production (yielding an X output of 600), then there must be 0 men in Y production (hence zero Y production); if there are 40 men in X production (producing 300 X), then there must be 60 men in Y production (producing 43 Y). Hence, corresponding to each figure in the "Daily Y Production" column above, there must be an appropriate X-production figure. Fill in the blanks in the extreme right-hand column above with the proper X figures.

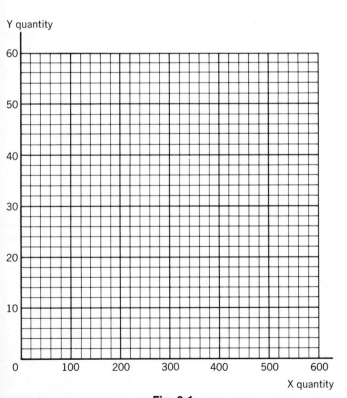

Fig. 2-1

In Fig. 2-1, draw the production-possibility curve—i.e., show the various X-Y combinations which can be produced. (Your curve should have the same "bulged-out" shape as those in the text, with anchor-points at 60 and 600.)

580, 550, 500 etc.—the figures in the "Daily X Production" column inverted.

---

5. *a.* According to the table, diminishing returns first appears in X production when the total of men employed rises to *(10 / 20 / 30 / 40 / 50 / 60 / 70 / 80 / 90 / 100).*

b. The corresponding diminishing-returns point in Y production is at *(10 / 20 / 30 / 40 / 50 / 60 / 70 / 80 / 90 / 100).*

c. This diminishing-returns phenomenon occurs because, as output and employment are increased:
(1) The competence or skill of the men later employed is less than that of the men first employed.
(2) Each man has proportionately less of the fixed or specialized resource to work with.
(3) The product must sell for a lower price.

---

a. 50. *b.* 60. *c.* (2).

---

6. There is no conflict between the law of diminishing returns and the idea of mass-production economies or "increasing returns to scale." A large-scale automobile plant, built to assemble 1,000 cars daily, may be considered as illustrating mass-production economies because, when it is operated at capacity, the dollar cost of each car produced is less than it would be in a smaller plant.

Suppose a heavy rush of orders prompts the company to try to produce daily output in excess of 1,000 cars by hiring more men, running machines a little faster, etc. The probable result will be an output increase that is less than proportionate to the manpower increase. If so, this *(confirms / denies / has no application to)* the diminishing-returns law. The company will find that at some output such as 1,100 cars daily, perhaps even at 1,001 cars daily, further output is impossible no matter how many extra men are hired. If so, this *(confirms / denies / has no application to)* the diminishing-returns law. Here, the limiting input comparable to land in the text example is *(labor / materials / equipment).*

---

confirms; confirms; equipment.

---

7. The law of diminishing returns appraises the cost of getting more and more extra output of a good in terms of the extra inputs (e.g., labor man-hours) required. "The law of increasing (relative) costs," although related to the diminishing-returns law, is different.

Suppose more corn is to be produced, so that more labor

inputs are required on cornland. If resources are fully employed, the needed inputs must be taken away from production of some other good. So the "cost" of getting more corn can be stated not only in terms of the extra inputs needed, but also *in terms of the amount of some other good that must be sacrificed.* That is how the increasing-cost law runs.

Using question 4 data, suppose that production is 600 X units daily and zero Y. If it is decided to produce 5 Y units daily, this requires a sacrifice of *(0 / 5 / 20 / 40 / 600)* X units. Each of the 5 Y units will cost *(4/ 8 / 20 / 40 / 600)* X units.

Suppose, instead, that X output is 500 units, so that Y output can be *(0 / 4 / 5 / 10 / 20)* units daily. To raise this Y quantity to 28 would require reduction of X output to *(0 / 100 / 250 / 400 / 450)*—a drop of *(0 / 10 / 20 / 50 / 100)* units. Each extra Y unit would thus cost *(1 / 5½ / 6¼ / 8 / 10)* X units.

The greater the amount of total Y output happens to be, the *(higher / lower)* would be the cost of obtaining further Y output, measured in terms of X given up.

Whenever a production-possibility curve "bulges out," as in Fig. 2-1, instead of being a straight line, the increasing-cost law automatically applies. Each additional unit of either good will cost slightly more (in terms of sacrifice of the other good) than its predecessor did. Each 1-unit increase in Y means a small, vertical, upward movement on the graph. To stay on the curve, this requires a *(leftward / rightward)* movement to compensate—a *(decrease / increase)* in X. If we want further increases in Y—i.e., if we continue along the curve, moving approximately northwest— these compensating *(leftward / rightward)* movements (the required decreases in X) grow larger.

The curve "bulges out" because of the figures in question 4's table. Had the additional quantity of X per each additional 10 men been *fixed,* with extra Y quantities similarly fixed (i.e., no diminishing returns), the production-possibility curve would have been a straight line. Thus, the diminishing-returns law here accounts for the increasing-cost phenomenon (although it is not the only source of increasing cost.)

20; 4; 20; 450; 50; 6¼; higher; leftward; decrease; leftward.

8. *a.* In question 4, suppose the number of workers rises from 100 to 200 (the fixed amounts of X resources and Y resources remaining unchanged). The production-possibility curve would then move outward (pick one):
(1) Until its end-points indicated 1,200 X, 120 Y.
(2) By a greater amount than stated in alternative (1).
(3) By a much lesser amount than indicated in (1).
(4) Not at all.

b. Suppose X is a necessity (say, food) and Y is a luxury. Every worker (or family) must have at least 3½ units of X daily in order to live. The population still consists of only 100 workers, and they choose to produce 450 of X, 28 of Y. (Mark

this point on Fig. 2-1.) If output is equally distributed, this means each worker gets daily 4½ X units and a little more than ¼ Y unit.

Now let the number of workers rise from 100 to 200. An extended X-production table indicates that 200 workers can produce 700 X. If all workers are to remain alive, what quantities of X and Y will be produced?
(1) 700 X plus about the same amount of Y per worker as before.
(2) 700 X and no Y at all.
(3) More than 700 X and about the same amount of Y per worker as before.
(4) Impossible to tell from information given.

c. If X is food, what idea discussed in the text does this illustrate? _____
_____ .

a. (3). *b.* (2). *c.* Malthusian theory of population growth.

9. For at least two important reasons, the outcome for the world's future indicated by Malthus (that food available per capita may drop to the level of bare subsistence) may not occur. These are:

(1) _____
(2) _____ .

(1) Technological innovations. (2) Population may not increase so fast even when free to do so.

10. Positive checks on population operate by *(increasing / decreasing)* the *(birth / death)* rate. Preventive checks on population operate by *(increasing / decreasing)* the *(birth / death)* rate.

increasing; death; decreasing; birth.

11. Review also two further ideas discussed in the text chapter: economic goods versus free goods, and the net reproduction rate.

QUIZ: Multiple Choice

1. *When production is subject to the influence of the law of diminishing returns—but it is still possible to increase total product—then, in order to obtain successive increases in output of 1 extra unit,* (1) smaller and smaller amounts of the variable input will be needed; (2) adding more of the variable input will do more harm than good, because it must diminish total output instead of increasing it; (3) the cost of hiring each additional unit of the variable input must steadily increase; (4) greater and greater amounts of the variable input will be needed; (5) none of the above is necessarily true.

2. *The three economic problems of* WHAT, HOW, *and* FOR WHOM *goods shall be produced apply* (1) mainly to totalitarian or centrally planned societies, wherein the problem of planning arises directly; (2) only or principally to free enterprise or capitalist societies, wherein the problem of choice is most acute; (3) only or almost entirely to the less developed societies, since development is largely a question of meeting these three problems; (4) to all societies, regardless of stage of development or form of political organization; (5) to none of the above necessarily, since they are problems for the individual business firm or family, not for society.

3. *There cannot be a problem of* WHAT *goods shall be produced if* (1) the supply of productive resources is small, so that it must be devoted to the production of necessities; (2) production has not yet reached the stage at which the law of diminishing returns begins to operate; (3) the supply of productive resources is sufficiently large to make possible the production of some luxury goods; (4) every productive input is so specialized that it can be used only in the production of one good and no other; (5) production can be carried on under conditions of decreasing or constant cost, rather than increasing cost.

4. *If the law of diminishing returns is to apply, the following condition must be satisfied: The increase in output* (1) must come from a proportionate increase in all inputs; (2) comes from an increase in some inputs, but at least one input must remain fixed in quantity; (3) must come from an increase in one input only, all others remaining fixed in quantity; (4) must grow less because of a decline in the competence or skill of inputs later applied; (5) may be proportionate in physical quantity to the increase in inputs, but the *value* of that extra output must decline.

5. *The economic problem of* WHAT *goods shall be produced* (1) may be a problem for any individual firm seeking to make a profit, but is not in any sense a problem for society as a whole; (2) can be illustrated as the problem of choosing a point on the production-possibility curve; (3) is a problem whose nature is illustrated by the law of diminishing returns; (4) arises only when the stock of productive resources is very small, so that it must be devoted to the production of necessities; (5) arises only when all productive inputs are so specialized that each can be used only in the production of one good and no other.

6. *The economic problem of* HOW *to produce goods does not exist* (1) if the required proportions of inputs are fixed for all commodities, so that substitution of input B to replace part of input A in production is impossible; (2) provided production has not been carried to the point where the law of

diminishing returns has begun to set in; (3) where the economy's stock of capital is small relative to its labor force; (4) in a technically advanced society, since proper technology will then have established the best possible method of producing each good; (5) in any circumstances—the problem of how to produce goods is an engineering problem throughout and not an economic problem.

7. *An economy can produce 200 of good X and 300 of good Y—i.e., this is one point on its production-possibility frontier. Another point on this frontier is 240 of X and 290 of Y. The "law of increasing (relative) costs" would be illustrated by the following third point on the frontier:* (1) 280 of X, 270 of Y. (2) 160 of X, 310 of Y. (3) 280 of X, 280 of Y. (4) 160 of X, 315 of Y. (5) 280 of X, 285 of Y.

8. *An economy produces only two goods, X and Y. All the inputs available are entirely "specialized" for producing one good or the other—i.e., the X inputs would be useless in Y production, and the Y inputs useless in X production. Thus there is no opportunity to increase the output of X by transferring resources from the output of Y, and vice versa. Among the five alternatives below, which "production-possibility curve" (illustrating the various X-Y combinations producible) would be most appropriate to this situation?*

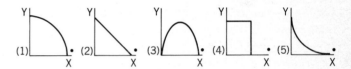

9. *The heavy curved line in Fig. 2-2 at left below illustrates a country's production-possibility curve. A shift in this curve to the position indicated by the line marked 1 would be appropriate to illustrate* (1) a change in the tastes of the population whereby its members want more food produced and less clothing; (2) the appearance of some new resources useful only in the clothing industry; (3) an improvement in

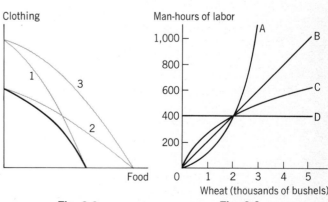

Fig. 2-2　　　　　　　　　**Fig. 2-3**

technology applicable to both occupations; (4) a change in production involving an increase in clothing output and a decrease in food output; (5) the development of a better technology in the food industry.

10. *Which alternative in question 9 would apply had the heavy curve shifted to position 2?* (1). (2). (3). (4). (5).

11. *Which alternative in question 9 would apply had the heavy curve shifted to position 3?* (1). (2). (3). (4). (5).

12. *Figure 2-3 (preceding page) shows outputs of wheat obtainable on a fixed plot of land by varying the input of labor. The curve that would correctly illustrate application of the law of diminishing returns, as the graph is drawn, would be* (1) A; (2) B; (3) C; (4) D; (5) either A or C.

13. *A production-possibility (transformation) curve is intended to show* (1) the exact amounts of two goods that an economy will decide to produce; (2) the most valuable combination of two goods that an economy can produce; (3) the alternative combinations of products available from a given quantity of resources; (4) when the law of diminishing returns first begins to take effect; (5) none of the above.

14. *If, with respect to the guns-and-butter production-possibility diagram used in the text, actual output is marked by a point* inside *(to the southwest) of this curve, this means that* (1) it is impossible to produce more guns without the sacrifice of some butter output; (2) either all available resources are not being fully employed or they are not being employed to the best advantage; (3) the law of diminishing returns cannot be in operation; (4) the diagram illustrates something which could not possibly happen; (5) the phenomenon of "increasing returns to scale" must be in operation.

15. *If all inputs in a productive process are increased in amount by 100 per cent, and the result is an increase in output of 120 per cent, this would* (1) illustrate the law of diminishing returns; (2) contradict the law of diminishing returns; (3) illustrate increasing returns to scale; (4) contradict the principle of increasing returns to scale; (5) contradict the law of scarcity.

3 PRICE FUNCTIONING OF A "MIXED ECONOMY"

1. A "free private enterprise" society permits (for the most part) individual ownership of capital goods and land, so as to encourage initiative and productivity. (Socialist societies bar or sharply restrict such ownership, on the view that it yields such results as an unfair distribution of income.)

The text discusses four principal characteristics of such free enterprise societies, with particular stress upon one of them. List the four below (citing first the major-emphasis one).

(1) _____ .

(2) _____ .

(3) _____ .

(4) _____ .

---

(1) Use of money pricing system; (2) use of an extensive stock of capital goods; (3) specialization, or division of labor; (4) use of money.

Chapter 2 said that the three basic economic problems confronting every society are those of WHAT, HOW, and FOR WHOM. As problems of *choice*, they require *decisions*. The system of markets, money, and prices (in brief, "the pricing system") is the primary mechanism by which a "capitalist" or "free enterprise" system makes these decisions.

The pricing system is essentially one of exchange. Each person specializes (usually in cooperation with others) in producing some commodity or service. Each good thus produced is sold for a money price. These money proceeds are shared among those who helped in production. Each person's money share is his or her claim.

2. *a.* Thus, one vital part of the pricing system is *the market for consumer goods*. But the text speaks of the *two* market fronts on which consuming families face business enterprises. That is, there is a second vital part of the pricing system, a second market with which families must deal. This is the

market for _____ .

b. In the market for finished goods, the individual consumer (or family) is a *(buyer / seller)*. In the market for productive inputs, the individual consumer is a *(buyer / seller)*. By contrast, the business firm whose task it is to manufacture consumer goods or to ready them for sale is a *(buyer / seller)* in the consumer-good market, and a *(buyer / seller)* in the productive-input market.

---

a. Productive inputs (notably labor). *b.* buyer; seller; seller; buyer.

---

3. No society, no matter how much "free-enterprise-oriented," ever relies solely on the pricing system for its decisions on WHAT, HOW, and FOR WHOM. There is always *some* government intervention; that is what makes it a "mixed society." Governments in socialist countries intervene to a greater extent. But these socialist countries also rely heavily upon the pricing mechanism. In this respect, the difference between "capitalist" and "socialist" is one of degree.

The working of the pricing system is best understood by considering a *completely* laissez faire system—i.e., one in which government exists only to provide an outer framework of law and order. In an "ideally competitive" laissez faire world, all monopolistic and other disruptive elements are absent. And prices are notably "flexible"—i.e., responsive to even small changes arising either on the demand (buying) or on the supply (selling) side of the market.

a. Such a system resolves the question of WHAT goods shall be produced by the following process: Consumers use their "dollar votes" (money incomes available for spending) to buy the goods they want most. If they want some of these goods badly enough, they may bid up their prices. Suppliers will be anxious to produce those goods whose prices are high (relative to production costs), and to avoid or cut down on goods whose prices are similarly low. In this way, the problem of *(WHAT/HOW/FOR WHOM)* goods shall be produced is settled. Producers are consciously trying to *(earn profits / satisfy consumer preferences)*—i.e., this is their primary objective—but in so doing, they are also *(earning profits / satisfying consumer preferences)*.

b. The same "ideally competitive" laissez faire pricing system of part *a* operates to settle the question of FOR WHOM goods shall be produced, as follows:

Productive inputs or factors such as labor (skilled or unskilled), land, and machinery also carry prices. These prices—wage rates, salary rates, rental rates, etc.—*(count / do not count)* as part of "the pricing system."

The size of a consumer's money income is governed (pick one):

(1) By the market price(s) of the input(s) and the input quantities the consumer owns.
(2) Only by the price the input commands, not by its quantity.
(3) Only by the input quantity the consumer owns, not by its price.

The FOR WHOM problem is that of distributing (fairly or unfairly) the available consumer-good supply among society's members. The size of *my* money income, relative to *your* money income, settles the FOR WHOM problem as between you and me. And the sizes of these two incomes, as indicated above, are governed by (i) the distribution of input ownership, and (ii) *(input/consumer-good)* prices. Thus, given the ownership distribution, the relation of my income to yours is a matter of the prices my inputs can command relative to yours.

In *my* view, an ideal FOR WHOM solution would give me somewhat more, and give you an inconsequential trifle less. *Your* view might possibly (although unreasonably) differ. When the phrase "ideally competitive" is used concerning a laissez faire distribution system, it means conditions in which my preferences and your prejudices are both set aside, and the outcome is left to the cold, impartial verdict of the marketplace. Overall, in one set of conditions, that verdict might result in substantial inequality of incomes; in another set, in approximately equal incomes. Thus, "ideally competitive" means only the justice rendered by the marketplace—which may or may not conform to other measures of justice. What can be said on behalf of marketplace justice is that—if the market is really free of monopolistic and other imperfections—it is an impartial justice.

c. The "ideally competitive" pricing system settles the question of HOW goods are to be produced as follows: Suppose a given quantity of some good can be made either (*i*) with 2 units of capital and 10 units of labor, or (*ii*) with 10 units of capital and 2 units of labor. For simplicity, assume these two are the only possible combinations.

The HOW problem is that of choosing between these two methods. To make the choice properly, producers must know *(the price of the finished good/which of them is more efficient/the prices of labor and capital).* "The most efficient method," that is, is the method which costs *(less / more)* than any other method. The HOW question persists until *(input/ finished-good)* prices are known, and it is settled by reference to these prices. For example, if capital costs $2 per unit and labor costs $3, then method (*i / ii*) above is preferable. If capital costs $3 and labor $2, then method (*i / ii*) is preferable.

---

a. WHAT; earn profits; satisfying preferences. *b.* count; (1); input. *c.* prices of labor and capital; less; input; ii; i.

In a laissez faire system, producing business firms try to make all the profit they can. But the ability to earn profits is restrained by competition from other firms. Without the discipline of competition, "the profit

motive" cannot be expected to work for the benefit of consumers.

Throughout, the important behavior is marketplace behavior. This governs the interdependent decisions on WHAT, HOW, and FOR WHOM. Suppose a nation puts a tariff on imported oil (departing from laissez faire because it wants to reduce its dependence on such oil). Among other things, this stimulates greater domestic coal consumption. Coal miners have larger money incomes (relative to the rest of the population); the FOR WHOM decision has changed a little. Should the tastes of coal miners happen to be slightly different from those of others in the population, the pattern of overall consumer-good spending changes accordingly; the WHAT decision is altered as production shifts to match demand. And the HOW decision may gradually change as higher oil and coal prices prompt a shift to alternative inputs, such as electricity.

4. *a.* Given the existing supply of any input (a kind of machine, a type of land or labor), the price that input can receive will depend on the demand for it. The strength of this demand, in turn, will depend on (pick one):
(1) The usefulness or "productivity" of that input in producing various kinds of consumer goods.
(2) The price commanded by each of the various consumer goods which the input can help to manufacture.
(3) Both the productivity of the input in making various kinds of consumer goods and the prices for which those consumer goods can be sold.

b. Thus, if input A's productivity in making consumer good X is very high, that will make for a *(high/low)* price for A; if X can be sold only for a very low price, that will make for a *(high/low)* price for A. So consumer-good prices *(have/do not have)* an influence over input prices. The FOR WHOM problem is most immediately settled by the relation between input prices (the fact that some are high and some are low), but because input prices are influenced by consumer-good prices, the disposition of this FOR WHOM problem is also influenced by the relation between consumer-good prices.

---

a. (3). *b.* high; low; have.

---

5. *a.* We can say that the money price system acts as a set of *guideposts* to consumers because (pick one only):
(1) A high price on consumer good X is a persuasion to buy in small quantities or not at all; a low price on Y is a persuasion to buy in large quantities.
(2) If there is only a small supply of consumer good X, it goes to the highest bidders.
(3) A low price on input B is a persuasion to use B as fully as possible; a high price on input A is a persuasion to use A only to the extent necessary.

(4) If there is only a small supply of input A, it goes to the highest bidders.

b. The pricing system also furnishes guideposts to producers, as indicated by alternative *(1 / 2 / 3 / 4)* above.

c. The pricing system also serves to *ration out* whatever supply of consumer goods is available, as indicated by alternative *(1 / 2 / 3 / 4)* above.

d. Similarly, money prices ration out the supply of inputs or factors—see alternative *(1 / 2 / 3 / 4)* above.

---

a. (1). *b.* (3). *c.* (2). *d.* (4).

---

6. *a.* What do the three following have in common?
(1) A minimum-wage law prohibits the payment of any hourly wage rate below $2.30.
(2) A new toll-free highway is built.
(3) Taxation on incomes reduces the spending power of rich citizens.

_____

_____

_____ .

b. Item *(1 / 2 / 3)* of part *a* illustrates an influence directly exerted on the decision as to WHAT goods shall be produced. Item *(1 / 2 / 3)* illustrates a similar influence on HOW, and item(s) *(1 / 2 / 3)* on FOR WHOM.

c. The text suggests that government action influencing WHAT, HOW, and FOR WHOM decisions works mainly through two forms of *coercion*, namely:

(1) _____ ;

(2) _____ .

Item(s) *(1 / 2 / 3)* of part *a* above illustrate(s) such coercion; item(s) *(1 / 2 / 3)* do(es) not.

---

a. Intervention by government in WHAT, HOW, and FOR WHOM decisions. *b.* (2); (1); (1) and (3). (Any of these three moves would probably exert some influence on *all three* of WHAT, HOW, and FOR WHOM; the influences named are simply the most direct ones.) *c.* (1) Taxation; (2) "thou shalt not" rules; (1) and (3); (2).

Section B of the text chapter discusses the subject of *capital*. "Capital" is a word with too many meanings: you must understand the particular meaning here involved. Capital here does *not* mean money. It means man-made productive inputs. It includes durable items like blast furnaces, factory buildings, machine tools, electric drills, tack hammers, and the like. It includes also stocks of semifinished goods; such goods are on the

way to becoming consumer goods, but meantime they are still man-made inputs to be used in later stages of the production process.

Capital is important only because it "pushes back" the law of scarcity; it makes possible the output of more consumer goods. Every nation would like to become "capitalist" in the sense of having a large stock of capital relative to its population. However, there is a cost involved in the production of capital goods. The same resources that make these goods also make consumer goods; there is a choice to be made between capital and consumer goods. *Once the capital goods are finished,* we can have more consumer goods. But if resources are fully employed, then *during the time it takes to make the capital goods, we must give up consumer goods.* The production of capital goods demands *waiting,* the sacrifice of present consumption.

7. *a.* Circle all the following that qualify as "capital"—as the word is used in this chapter.
(1) An oil refinery.
(2) An issue of General Motors stock.
(3) Cash in a businessman's safe.
(4) A screwdriver.
(5) Money borrowed by a business firm from a bank to expand its operations.
(6) A steel-ingot inventory held by a steel company.
(7) Unsold automobiles held by an auto manufacturer.
(8) An inventory of groceries held by a supermarket.

b. Money *(is / is not)* counted as part of "capital" (as the word is used in this chapter) because (pick one):
(1) It is essential to production.
(2) It has no part to play in production.
(3) It is not actually useful in production, although it is essential to have money in order to buy the real inputs that are needed for production.

c. To qualify as "capital" (still using the word as in this chapter), the item in question *(must be / need not necessarily be)* an input that is useful or necessary at some stage of production. And the item must be *(of a type found only in highly developed economies / a primary factor of production / man-made).*

---

a. (1), (4), (6), (7), (8). *b.* is not; (3). *c.* must be; man-made.

---

8. *a.* Remember two elementary but essential things about capital, or "capital goods":
(1) In the final reckoning, only consumer goods are important. Capital goods have no merit in themselves. They are produced only because they are roundabout ways of producing consumer goods.

(2) Because any item of capital takes *time* to make, the effort devoted to making it is production for *tomorrow's* consumption use. The resources employed in constructing that item of capital *could* have been used to satisfy *today's* consumption demands.

Any developed nation, whether "capitalist" or not, possesses a large stock of capital, and much of each day's productive effort goes into maintenance and expansion of that stock. Consequently, in such nations today's productive effort is largely going to satisfy *(yesterday's / today's / tomorrow's)* needs, while the consumer goods actually enjoyed today result from *(yesterday's / today's / tomorrow's)* effort.

b. Circle as many of the following as are correct:
(1) The larger the available stock of capital, the larger the output of consumer goods that is possible.
(2) In terms of Chapter 2's production-possibility curve, additions to the stock of capital push that curve upward and outward.
(3) A decision to produce or not to produce more capital is *not* part of the decision on WHAT goods to produce.
(4) In a fully employed economy, a decision to produce more capital is a decision to produce fewer consumer goods in the immediate future.

c. When reference is made to "a capitalist economy," what is probably contemplated is any economy (pick one or more):
(1) In which most capital goods are privately owned.
(2) In which the stock of capital is large relative to the population of that economy.
(3) Not under communist or socialist direction.

---

a. tomorrow's; yesterday's. *b.* (1), (2), (4). *c.* (1), (2), and (3). [Note that there is room for dispute concerning properties (2) and (3). A dictionary definition of capitalism may not specify that the stock of capital must be large relative to the country's size or population; nevertheless, the "capitalist" countries are typically those in which the stock is large. As to (3), even a communist country may be "capitalist" in the sense of having a large capital stock relative to its population, and wanting to have an even larger stock.]

---

9. Specialization (or division of labor) is resorted to because it increases the output obtainable from a given resource supply. The consequences of specialization include (circle as many as are correct):
a. Exchange of goods.
b. Use of money.
c. Social interdependence.
d. An intensified law of scarcity.
e. Possibly a sense of alienation on the part of members of the society involved.

---

a, b, c, e.

QUIZ: Multiple Choice

1. *Capital (considered as a factor of production, or as one of the trilogy of "land, labor, and capital") means* (1) man-made productive inputs; (2) undeveloped natural resources, such as iron ore not yet mined; (3) the financial assets of producing businesses; (4) the same thing as the nation's total money stock; (5) none of these things.

2. *One vital reason why indirect, or "capital-using," methods of production have not displaced direct methods in economically less developed nations is that* (1) the governments of such nations have not issued enough money to finance indirect production methods; (2) people do not realize that indirect methods would produce more consumption goods; (3) there are no indirect methods that would actually produce more consumption goods; (4) such areas do not have a properly functioning price system; (5) the introduction of such indirect methods would involve a sacrifice of present consumption.

3. *The economic problem of* HOW *goods shall be produced is solved in capitalist societies* (1) through the decisions of consumers in the marketplace, as these appear in the form of finished-good prices; (2) by means of the profit motive impelling producers, which prompts them to try to keep their costs of production at a minimum; (3) by means of extensive use of capital goods; (4) by means of extensive specialization, which may or may not involve large-scale use of capital goods; (5) in none of the above ways, since HOW to produce goods is not a basic problem in capitalist societies.

4. *The economic problem of deciding* WHAT *goods to produce requires or includes, among other things,* (1) the necessity of deciding the degree to which specialization is to be employed in the manufacture of goods; (2) a decision as to the quantity of advertising that should be used to encourage the sale of whatever has been produced; (3) the choice between the production of consumer goods and the production of capital goods; (4) the establishment of a central government, since all decisions on WHAT are ultimately made by such governments; (5) the establishment of a system of perfect competition.

5. *We speak of "land, labor, and capital" as the basic grouping of the factors of production. Which of the following is correct with respect to whether or not money, stocks, and / or bonds should be counted as "capital"?* (1) All three (money, stocks, and bonds) count. (2) Stocks and bonds count, but money does not. (3) Money counts, but stocks and bonds do not. (4) Money and stocks count, but bonds do not. (5) None of the three counts.

6. *A major social problem to which specialization and division of labor give rise is* (1) the need to use paper money; (2) the need to use capital; (3) interdependence; (4) the need to learn economics; (5) none of these.

7. *In economics, the term "imperfect competitor" is applied to a seller who* (1) operates outside the system of specialization and money pricing; (2) supplies a sufficiently large quantity of the good involved to be able to affect its price; (3) seeks to distort the pattern of consumer tastes (through advertising campaigns and the like); (4) knowingly or unknowingly uses inferior production methods; (5) is not correctly described by any of these descriptions.

8. *Figure 3-1 at left below depicts a production-possibility curve involving capital goods and consumer goods. The significance of points A and B is this:* (1) They indicate possible demands for capital goods and consumer goods—*A* representing capital-good demand and *B* consumer-good demand. (2) They represent possible and alternative combinations of output which the economy in question could produce. (3) They indicate the maximum-possible quantities of capital goods and consumer goods which could be produced—*A* indicating maximum-possible capital-good output and *B* maximum-possible consumer-good output. (4) The movement from *A* to *B* indicates the growth of output resulting from the use of capital goods. (5) No significance at all, since production-possibility diagrams refer to consumer goods only, not to capital goods.

9. *In Fig. 3-1, operation at a point such as A indicates production of some capital goods. Assuming this is more than sufficient to replace capital goods currently being worn out, then continued operation at A should result in* (1) an inward movement of the whole curve; (2) no change in the curve, but a move from *A* to *B*; (3) no change necessarily either in the curve or in operation at *A*; (4) no change in the curve, but a move from A to a point inside the curve; (5) an outward movement of the whole curve.

10. *Figure 3-2 at right depicts a production-possibility curve with respect to consumer goods X and Y. The economy involved makes full use of a money pricing system. The significance of such points as A and B is this:* (1) Either is a possible operating point, and if selected, it indicates a verdict on WHAT to produce with respect to X and Y, settled by

consumer preferences as expressed through the price system. (2) Either is a possible operating point, but it will have been reached quite independently of the operation of the price system, since the curve in question refers to production, not prices. (3) If either is chosen as an operating point, it will indicate the combination of X and Y having maximum money value, but it is not necessarily a point in any way related to consumer preferences. (4) Each is a typical point on the curve, and the position of the entire curve (all points thereon) is established by consumer preferences as expressed through the price system. (5) Either is a possible operating point, but a money pricing system is bound to show that *A* is a point preferable to *B*.

11. *In a money-using, capitalist society, the economic problem of* FOR WHOM *goods shall be produced is primarily settled as follows:* (1) Each producer looks for the type of consumer or market most likely to be interested in his product, then tries to tailor that product so that it is particularly appealing to that consumer or market. (2) Consumers bid up the prices of those goods they most want to have, and refuse to bid, or bid only a low price, for goods they find less attractive. (3) Business firms bid for the services of productive inputs according to their usefulness in production, thus giving each input supplier a money income that can be used to buy goods. (4) Competition operates so as to keep down profits, hence to keep prices at a level which consumers can afford to pay. (5) Income is distributed in keeping with the needs of individual consumers.

12. *Which alternative in question 11 best describes the process by which the problem of* WHAT *goods shall be produced is primarily settled, in a society which relies on the mechanism of money and prices?* (1). (2). (3). (4). (5).

13. *If it is true that most of the goods a certain society consumes today were produced in the past, and that most of its production today is intended for future consumption, then from these facts it* must *be true that this society makes extensive use of* (1) specialization and division of labor; (2) money; (3) a money pricing system; (4) advertising; (5) capital.

14. *In a decentralized, capitalist society, the use of a money pricing system is* not *expected to help settle the following economic problem, that of* (1) distributing money incomes among the members of the society; (2) helping a consumer with given tastes and a limited income to decide how best to spend that income; (3) deciding how much of the available resource supply is to be occupied in making any given consumer good; (4) choosing the particular kinds of inputs (factors of production) that should be used for the manufacture of any given consumer good; (5) determining the particular output of goods and services which the society really needs, regardless of the tastes of any or all individual consumers therein.

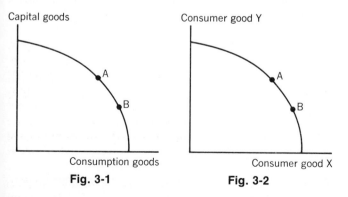

Fig. 3-1   Fig. 3-2

4 SUPPLY AND DEMAND: THE BARE ELEMENTS

MANY FORCES OPERATE to drive the price of any given commodity high or to push it low: people's tastes, the amount of income they have to spend, the prices at which substitute commodities are selling, what it costs to produce that commodity, and so on.

If we are to begin to explain a commodity's actual price, the all-essential starting points are these:

▶ All the multitude of forces which influence the price of a commodity can be clustered into just two groups.

▶ One group of forces operates through its influence on the behavior of *buyers* of the commodity. We sum up what *buyers* want to do through the device of a demand schedule, or demand curve. The demand curve is concerned exclusively with *buyer* attitudes—not with sellers.

▶ The second group of forces operates through its influence on the behavior of *sellers*. This we represent by means of the supply schedule, or supply curve. The supply curve deals solely with *seller* (not buyer) attitudes.

1. *a.* Below are 10 prices (*P*), each one associated with a particular quantity (*Q*). In Fig. 4-1, mark the 10 points corresponding to those 10 *P-Q* pairs.

P:	$10	$9	$8	$7	$6	$ 5	$ 4	$ 3	$ 2	$ 1
Q:	1	2	3	5	8	12	15	20	25	40

Join the 10 points to form a smooth curve.
In this schedule, the lower the price, the *(lower / higher)*

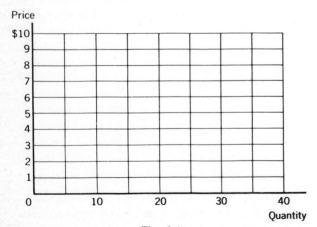

Fig. 4-1

the quantity going with it. Thus these figures suggest a *(supply / demand)* curve.

b. Also record the following 10 pairs in Fig. 4-1.

P:	$10	$ 9	$ 8	$ 7	$ 6	$ 5	$ 4	$ 3	$2	$1
Q:	26	25	24	22	20	18	15	10	0	0

This would represent a *(supply / demand)* curve.

---

a. higher; demand. *b.* supply.

2. *a.* Given the data of question 1, what would be the equilibrium price? ....$*(10 / 9 / 8 / 7 / 6 / 5 / 4 / 3 / 2 / 1)*

b. Why would this be the equilibrium price?
(1) It is about midway in the total schedule of prices.
(2) It is the price sellers have decided should be charged for this commodity.
(3) It is the only price at which the quantity buyers want to purchase just equals the quantity sellers want to supply.
(4) The intersection of two lines on a graph always has to mean something.

---

a. 4. *b.* (3).

3. *a.* If (still using question 1 data) price stood temporarily at a level of $6, what would be the situation?
(1) Quantity offered for sale would exceed quantity demanded, and competition among sellers would drive price higher.
(2) Quantity demanded would exceed quantity offered for sale, and competition among buyers plus seller awareness of shortages would drive price higher.
(3) Quantity demanded would exceed quantity offered for sale, and competition among sellers plus buyer awareness of shortages would drive price lower.
(4) Quantity demanded would be less than quantity offered for sale, and competition among sellers would drive price lower.

b. If price stood temporarily at a level of $3, which alternative in part *a* would apply? .... *(1 / 2 / 3 / 4)*

---

a. (4). *b.* (2).

4. When the text speaks of the "law of downward-sloping demand," it is referring to a particular kind of behavior among buyers with so few exceptions that it is designated as a "law" of behavior. Circle as many of the following as correctly describe or illustrate this law.

a. If the price of X falls, at least some X buyers will increase the quantity they purchase by at least some small amount.
b. When people have more income to spend, they normally increase their purchases of any commodity.
c. Demand curves normally slope downward as they run to the right—i.e., their general direction is between northwest and southeast.
d. The quantity of any commodity bought ultimately tends to decline as it goes out of style or is superseded by something of better quality.
e. When the price of X rises significantly, people tend to reduce the quantity of X that they purchase.
f. If the price of butter falls considerably, the drop will tend to reduce purchases of oleomargarine.

a, c, e. The "law of downward-sloping demand" has to do with the influence of *price* on quantity demanded. Item *b* does not illustrate this law because it refers to an *income* change, not a price change. Similarly, the change in purchases in item *d* is not set off by a price change.

5. When the price of any commodity falls, the quantity buyers want to purchase will increase because (1) new buyers are attracted to the market, and/or (2) old buyers increase the amount they purchase. The text cites two background reasons for this increase in purchases:

a. First, if X's price falls, buyers may substitute X for Y. Even though its price is unchanged, Y is now *relatively* more expensive. This is *(a substitution- / an income-)* effect, and applies *(only to old / only to new / to both old and new)* buyers.

b. The second reason applies only when expenditure on X bulks large in the total budget, so that any rise in X's price provokes a budget crisis, whereas a fall in that price calls for celebration. A fall in X's price resembles an increase in income, for the same amount of X can now be bought, with considerable money left over. With this "increase in income," buyers may want to purchase more of various goods—including more of good X. This is *(a substitution- / an income-)* effect, and it applies *(only to old / only to new / to both old and new)* buyers.

c. These two effects apply *(only for price reduction / only for price increases / for both price reductions and increases).*

a. substitution; both old and new. *b.* income; only to old.
c. both reductions and increases.

6. Put S in the space below if the description suggests the "substitution-effect" of question 5; put I if the income-effect is indicated; put N if neither is appropriate.

a. A family decides its guests cannot tell the difference between butter and oleomargarine; consequently it switches some of its purchases from butter to margarine. .... ( )
b. A sharp increase in rents forces the family to move to a smaller apartment. .... ( )
c. Butter prices go up, and the family switches more of its purchases from butter to oleomargarine. .... ( )
d. The family receives a considerable increase in income and therefore buys, among other things, more butter and more apartment space. .... ( )

a. N. *b.* I. *c.* S. *d.* N. (These two "effects" are intended to apply to the consequences of *a price change* only. In cases *a* and *d*, the behavior change was *not* set off by a price change.)

Remember this essential point:

▶ A demand curve is an "if" schedule. It shows the particular quantity consumers will want to buy *if* the price stands at *this* level; it shows the different quantity they will want to buy *if* the price stands at *any other particular level.*

Thus in Fig. 4-2 (next page) the demand curve indicates that if price should be *AO,* then the quantity consumers would want to buy would be *AF* (or *OC*). Should the price be *BO,* then quantity demanded would be *BG* (or *OE*).

When matters have been worked out, there will be just one actual price. But the essential feature of the demand curve is that it covers *all the possibly relevant prices.* Thus it shows the change in buying that would result from any change in price. If price were to drop from *AO* to *BO* in Fig. 4-2, the resulting increase in quantity demanded would be *CE.*

There is another essential point to grasp:

▶ Price is not the *only* factor which influences consumer decisions to buy. The amount of incomes that people receive, for example, is another factor.

▶ In order to isolate the influence of price, a demand curve is drawn on the assumption that other factors, such as the income level, do not change. Buyer behavior is thus insulated against disturbances arising from such other sources, in order to indicate how such behavior would change solely on account of a change in *price.* This is the "other things equal," or "other things constant," assumption.

▶ These other factors *do* change. Change is recognized by a shift of the entire demand curve to an appropriate new position.

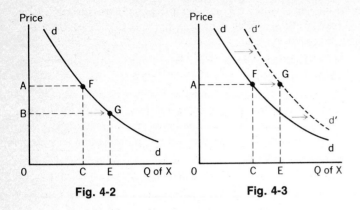

Fig. 4-2   **Fig. 4-3**

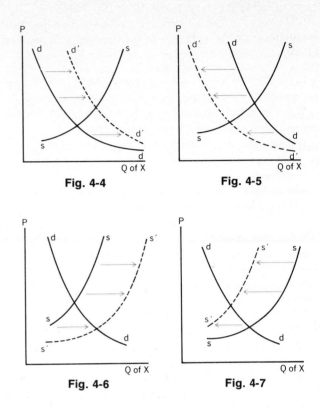

Fig. 4-4   **Fig. 4-5**

Fig. 4-6   **Fig. 4-7**

For example: In Fig. 4-3, the *dd* demand curve is shown as shifting to an entirely new position, *d'd'*. This shift might reflect the fact that (for whatever reason) there has been some increase in consumer incomes. With more money to spend, consumers want to buy more of this commodity X. If its price has been *AO*, they have, until now, been buying in total the quantity *OC*. Now, with higher incomes, they want to increase their purchases by the quantity *CE*, up to a new total *OE*. Mind you, this does not necessarily mean they will *succeed* in buying quantity *OE* at price *AO*, for the supply curve will have something to say about *that*. But our concern for the moment is with *demand*, not supply; it is with what buyers *want* to do. The point is that *at each and any price*, because of the rise in incomes, consumers would want to buy a larger quantity than they would previously have done.

We turn now from demand to supply. What has just been said about the demand curve applies equally to the supply curve:

▶ A supply curve shows how much of the commodity suppliers would want to sell, at each and any price. It shows how suppliers would respond if the actual market price were to change.

▶ Price is not the *only* factor which influences the disposition of suppliers to sell. For example, if costs of production go up, this will change the amount suppliers would want to sell at any given price. For any particular price, they will be disposed to sell less than they did before; at certain low levels of price, they may no longer want to sell any amount at all.

▶ That is, a supply curve, just like a demand curve, is an "other things equal" curve. It assumes all factors which influence supplier decisions, *other than price*, are given or fixed. If any of these "other things" (e.g., production costs) changes, then the entire supply curve must shift to an appropriate new position.

7. Figures 4-4 through 4-7 are intended to illustrate these ideas. In each, *one* curve, demand or supply, has shifted in position because of a change in some influencing factor other than price. The solid line indicates the former position; the broken line, the new. In Fig. 4-4, for example, the demand curve has shifted to the right (or upward) from position *dd* to position *d'd'*.

a. With respect to change in price, the result of each of the shifts indicated by these four figures would be:

(1) In Fig. 4-4, *(and increase / a decrease)*.
(2) In Fig. 4-5, *(an increase / a decrease)*.
(3) In Fig. 4-6, *(an increase / a decrease)*.
(4) In Fig. 4-7, *(an increase / a decrease)*.

b. Each of the seven events outlined below could reasonably be expected to change the position of the demand curve for commodity X, or the supply curve for X, or possibly both the demand and supply curves. That is, each event could be illustrated by one or more of Figs. 4-4 through 4-7. Fit each event into one or more of these figures.

In answering, use "4" as an abbreviation for Fig. 4-4, "5" for Fig. 4-5, and so on. If you think that *both* the demand curve and the supply curve would shift by reason of the event in question, answer by inserting two numbers.

The "leftward" and "rightward" shifts in these figures might equally have been shown as *upward* or *downward* shifts of the demand or supply curve—e.g., in Fig. 4-7, we could equally well say that the supply curve has shifted *upward* to position *s's'*. (HINT: You may find this helpful in item 1 below.)

(1) Costs of manufacturing commodity X increase. .....(   )
(2) Consumer tastes shift away from X and in favor of other commodities. ....(   )

(3) The price of Y, another commodity, one that can readily be produced by the suppliers of X, rises considerably. . ( )
(4) A recession reduces incomes of X buyers. ....( )
(5) A widespread inflation increases both money incomes of X buyers and the costs of producing X. ....( )
(6) The price of Y, another commodity, one which consumers regard as a good substitute for X, rises considerably. ...( )
(7) The government removes a heavy tariff on imports of X so that foreign producers of X are now able to offer supplies on this domestic market. ....( )

---

a. (1) an increase; (2) a decrease; (3) a decrease; (4) an increase. *b.* (1) 7; (2) 5; (3) 7; (4) 5; (5) 4 and 7; (6) 4; (7) 6. [NOTES: As to item *b*(3): The higher price for Y will attract producers into production of Y, and so they will reduce their production of X. As to item *b*(6): If Y is a substitute for X, then X is a substitute for Y, and consumers will switch their buying from Y to X.]

---

8. When either the demand or the supply curve shifts in position, things are thrown "out of equilibrium," and a new equilibrium price and quantity must be established. It's easy to draw supply-and-demand curves upon a page or blackboard—but the market doesn't have such pretty little diagrams laid out for its inspection. The market has to fumble its way toward its new equilibrium. Without knowing the curves, how does it get there? Question 3 has already touched upon this matter; now it is examined in a little more detail.

a. Figure 4-8 reproduces Fig. 4-4—i.e., it depicts one possible shift in one of the two curves. Specifically—note the arrow and the new broken-line position—it shows *(an increase / a decrease)* in *(supply / demand)*.

Before this change, equilibrium price was *AO*, and quantity bought and sold was *OE*. Now demand has increased—again, let's say, because of an increase in consumer incomes. At the *AO* price, buyers would now like to buy the larger quantity *(OE / OF / OG)*. But this buyer wish does not match the supplier wish. To furnish this larger quantity in full,

suppliers would require the price *(CO / BO / AO)*. This in turn does not match consumer wishes. So the new equilibrium must be a compromise in which price is *(CO / BO / AO)* and quantity bought and sold is *(OE / OF / OG)*. This compromise is the new equilibrium position.

b. How is this new equilibrium reached? What the market *can* discern, without the provision of supply and demand curves, is that at the old *AO* price, quantity demanded now *(exceeds / falls short of)* quantity supplied. Buyers find it *(difficult / easy)* to buy all they want to buy; suppliers find it *(difficult / easy)* to sell what they want to sell at the *AO* price. Thus, on both buying and selling sides, the pressure is toward a *(higher / lower)* price. This pressure persists so long as the price holds at any level at which quantity demanded exceeds quantity supplied. This disequilibrium pressure ends when—with the demand curve at its *d'd'* position—price reaches the level of *(CO / BO /AO)*.

In the opposite situation—that of a decrease in demand or an increase in supply—the mechanism just outlined works in reverse.

---

a. an increase; demand; *OG; CO; BO; OF.*
b. exceeds; difficult; easy; higher; *BO.*

---

9. Figures 4-9 and 4-10 show special cases of possible demand or supply curves: a horizontal line in Fig. 4-9, a vertical line in Fig. 4-10. As a demand or as a supply curve, what would such a line mean? (Never mind whether such a curve would be reasonable or not. The question is: What is the information which such a line would convey?)

a. A demand curve indicating desire to buy some fixed quantity at any price (at least within the range of prices indicated by the length of the line drawn), but no intention whatever of buying any greater quantity, no matter how low price might fall, would be illustrated by Fig. 4-*(9 / 10)*.

b. A supply curve indicating that any quantity (at least up to the quantity indicated by the length of the line drawn) would be supplied at the indicated price, but no quantity at all at any lower price, would be illustrated by Fig. 4-*(9 / 10)*.

c. A demand curve indicating willingness to buy any quantity (at least up to the quantity indicated by the length of the line

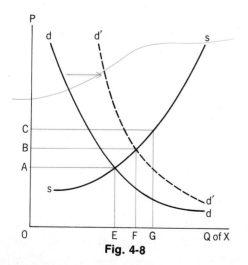

Fig. 4-8

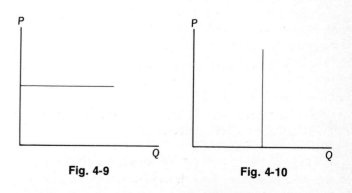

Fig. 4-9   **Fig. 4-10**

drawn) at the indicated price, but unwillingness to buy any quantity at all at any higher price, would be illustrated by Fig. 4-*(9 / 10)*.

d. A supply curve indicating willingness to supply some fixed quantity, regardless of price (even at zero price), but refusal to supply any greater quantity, no matter how high the price (at least within the range of prices indicated by the length of the line drawn) would be illustrated by Fig. 4-*(9 / 10)*.

---

a. 10. *b.* 9. *c.* 9. *d.* 10.

---

10. This chapter explains how "equilibrium price" emerges at the intersection of "other things equal" demand and supply curves. Toward the chapter's close is a discussion of "general equilibrium"—which is distinguished from "partial equilibrium." How does this discussion relate to the principal topic of the chapter? (Choose one or more.)

a. It is a reminder that prices are closely interrelated. It is useful to single out commodity X and explain its price in "partial equilibrium" terms—that is, in terms of "other things equal" demand and supply curves. But in the real world, other things may not stay equal. The demand curve has many strings linking it to other elements in the economy; so has the supply curve. Hence we cannot think of X's price as being determined first, and then Y's price, and after that, Z's price—because the position of X's demand and/or supply curves may be influenced by what Y's price is, and so on.

b. It is a particular way of stating the fact that both supply and demand play their parts in price determination. Equilibrium price must be a "general" equilibrium in the sense that it strikes a balance between demand forces and supply forces.

c. It is an interesting statement about the manner of price determination, but it has no special significance as a warning with respect to topics discussed earlier in the chapter.

---

a. (*b* does not indicate correctly the meaning of "general equilibrium.")

QUIZ: Multiple Choice

1. *The following is a complete and correct definition of the demand curve for commodity X. (Select the best alternative.) It shows, for a given market,* (1) how much of X would be bought at the equilibrium price; (2) how, as people's incomes rise and they have more money to spend, their purchases of X would increase, and by how much; (3) how the amount of money people spend to purchase X changes as the price they must pay for it changes; (4) the amounts of X that would be bought each period, at each and any price, assuming other factors influencing demand (income, tastes, etc.) remain constant; (5) the amounts of X to be supplied in each period, at

each and any price, assuming other factors influencing sale remain constant.

2. *The law of downward-sloping demand says that* (1) an excess of supply over demand will cause a reduction in price; (2) as people's incomes increase, they normally buy more of a commodity; (3) when a demand schedule is illustrated graphically, it runs from northeast to southwest; (4) when price falls, quantity bought normally increases; (5) the quantity bought of any good will ultimately decline as it goes out of style or is replaced by something of better quality.

3. *One reason given in the text for the law of downward-sloping demand is that* (1) when the price of something we buy falls, we are slightly better off; it is as though our incomes had risen slightly, and so we buy a little more; (2) most commodities, over a sufficiently long period of time, tend to lose their markets in favor of newer and more attractive goods; (3) the law of scarcity permits us to consume only so much of a commodity, no matter how much we may wish to have of it; (4) in the case of many commodities, a fall in price will bring in very few new buyers, or none at all; (5) the producers of a given commodity will not offer any quantity for sale at all if its price falls below some critical level.

4. *The government declares that it is prepared to purchase any and all gold supplied to it by domestic gold mines at a price of $175 an ounce. Which—if any—of the four diagrams within Fig. 4-11 below could be used as shown to illustrate this demand situation? (The labels P and Q on the axis lines refer respectively to price and to quantity.)* (1) *a.* (2) *b.* (3) *c.* (4) *d.* (5) None of these diagrams.

5. *A patient must purchase some given quantity of a given drug (but not more than that quantity) and will pay any price, if necessary, in order to obtain it. Which—if any—of the four diagrams within Fig. 4-11 could be used as shown to illustrate this situation?* (1) *a.* (2) *b.* (3) *c.* (4) *d.* (5) None of these diagrams.

6. *I can buy sugar in a supermarket at a fixed price of 50 cents per pound. This price applies to any quantity—1 pound, 5 pounds, 100 pounds. The store is so obliging that it will even sell me fractions of a pound at the same price per pound—e.g., 25 cents for a half-pound. Which—if any—of the four diagrams within Fig. 4-11 can be used as shown to*

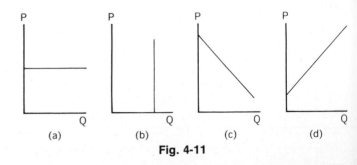

(a)   (b)   (c)   (d)

Fig. 4-11

illustrate this supply situation? (1) *a.* (2) *b.* (3) *c.* (4) *d.* (5) None of these diagrams.

7. *An increase in consumers' money incomes prompts them to demand a greater quantity of consumer good X. Which—if any—of the four diagrams within Fig. 4-11 could be used as shown to illustrate this situation?* (1) *a.* (2) *b.* (3) *c.* (4) *d.* (5) None of these diagrams.

8. *At any given price, the producers of commodity X are willing to supply some given quantity. If they are to supply a larger quantity, they must be persuaded to do so through the offer of a higher price. Which—if any—of the four diagrams within Fig. 4-11 can be used as shown to illustrate this situation?* (1) *a.* (2) *b.* (3) *c.* (4) *d.* (5) None of these diagrams.

9. *If the price of a good is $5 (in a competitive market), and if at that price buyers wish to purchase 4,000 units weekly and sellers wish to sell 5,000 units weekly, then* (1) price will tend to fall below $5 and suppliers will tend to offer less than 5,000 units; (2) price will tend to rise above $5 and suppliers will tend to offer more than 5,000 units; (3) price will tend to fall below $5 and buyers will tend to buy less than 4,000 units; (4) price will tend to rise above $5 and suppliers will tend to offer less than 5,000 units; (5) something is wrong—this could not occur in a competitive market.

10. *If the demand curve for commodity X shifts its entire position to the left (or downward), one reasonable explanation for this shift would be:* (1) The available supply of X has for some reason decreased. (2) The price of X has increased, and in consequence people have decided to buy less of it than they did before. (3) Consumer tastes have shifted in favor of this commodity, and they want to buy more of it than they did before at any given price. (4) The price of X has fallen, and in consequence people have decided to buy more of it than they did before. (5) None of these events.

11. *Four of the five events described below might reasonably be expected to shift the demand curve for beef to a new position. One would not shift that demand curve. The single exception is* (1) a rise in the price of some good which consumers regard as a substitute for beef; (2) a fall in the price of beef; (3) an increase in the money incomes of beef consumers; (4) a widespread advertising campaign undertaken by the producers of a product competitive with beef (e.g., pork); (5) a change in people's tastes with respect to beef.

12. *The phrase "other things equal," or "other things constant," when applied to the demand for commodity X, means this:* (1) The price of X is held constant. (2) Both buyer incomes and the price of X are held constant. (3) Buyer incomes, tastes, and the price of X are held constant. (4) All factors that might influence the demand for X, including the price of X, are held constant. (5) None of the above.

13. *An increase in the cost of materials needed to produce commodity X will affect the demand curve and/or supply curve for commodity X as follows:* (1) The demand curve will move upward (or to the right). (2) The supply curve will move upward (or to the left). (3) Both demand curve and supply curve will move upward. (4) The supply curve will move downward (or to the right). (5) Not at all—no reason why this change need occasion a shift of either curve.

14. *In prosperous times, the price of commodity X may go up, and consumption of X may go up also. This situation* (1) is one of the few recognized exceptions to the law of downward-sloping demand; (2) is precisely what the law of downward-sloping demand says can be expected; (3) is the consequence of a demand curve running from southwest to northeast; (4) cannot be explained by means of ordinary supply-curve and demand-curve analysis; (5) is not correctly described by any of the preceding.

15. *Beef supplies are sharply reduced because of drought in the beef-raising states, and consumers turn to pork as a substitute for beef. In the* beef *market, this would be described, in supply-and-demand terms, as* (1) a leftward (or downward) shift in the demand curve; (2) a leftward (or upward) shift in the supply curve; (3) a rightward (or upward) shift in the demand curve; (4) a rightward (or downward) shift in the supply curve; (5) both a leftward (or downward) shift in the demand curve and a leftward (or upward) shift in the supply curve.

16. *Which alternative in question 15 would be correct with respect to the events described, had that question referred to the* pork *market?* (1). (2). (3). (4). (5).

APPENDIX: Stock-market Fluctuations

1. *a.* "Margin buying" on the stock market works as follows: You want to buy XYZ stock, currently selling at $40 per share; you think XYZ will rise to $50 or higher. You have only $1,000 in cash; this will buy only 25 shares (disregarding the broker's commission and other incidental buying costs). But with a margin requirement of 25 per cent, you can buy a larger number of shares. You do this by borrowing $3,000 from your broker or, via the broker, from a bank or other lending agency. The loan proceeds plus your own cash will buy *(25 / 50 / 100 / 200)* shares. Of course you must put up some security against your loan. But you have this; you can furnish XYZ stock worth *$(1,000 / 3,000 / 4,000)*. This is accepted as adequate security for your $3,000 loan.

b. If XYZ goes to 50, you sell your stock, pay off principal and interest on your loan, and pocket the rest of your profit, happy at having taken an economics course. But if, instead, XYZ should drop below 40—say to 35 or 34—you will get a call from your broker to report that the bank "wants more margin," for the value of the asset you have supplied as collateral is falling. You must put up some more security or else pay off part of the loan. If you fail to come across, the bank will sell your XYZ stock. If it sells at close to 30, the entire sale proceeds go to cover your loan, leaving you with the sad reminder that you should first have read beyond Chapter 4.

Note the unstable quality of a market heavily involved with margin buying. If prices begin to fall, this sets off a *(further wave of selling / wave of buying)*, as borrowers cannot furnish more margin and lenders sell to protect their loans. This pushes stock prices down even more.

---

a. 100; 4,000.   *b.*   further wave of selling.

---

2. *a.* A "bull" market is one in which most expectations are that stock prices are going to *(rise / fall)*. Most people with cash are accordingly inclined to *(buy / refrain from buying)* stocks. Most people holding stocks are inclined to *(continue to hold / sell)* them. The consequence of such expectations is that stock prices generally *(rise / fall)*.

b. A "bear" market is one in which most expectations are that stock prices are going to *(rise / fall)*. Most people with cash are accordingly inclined to *(buy / refrain from buying)* stocks. Most people holding stocks are inclined to *(continue to hold / sell)* them. The consequence of such expectations is that stock prices generally *(rise / fall)*.

---

a. rise; buy; continue to hold; rise.   *b.*   fall; refrain from buying; sell; fall.

---

3. If I buy stock through my broker and through the New York Stock Exchange (NYSE), the seller of that stock (pick one):
a. May have been some private holder, or may have been the corporation whose stock it is (i.e., it may have been stock newly issued by that corporation).
b. Must have been the corporation whose stock it is.
c. Must have been some private holder—i.e., it cannot normally have been the corporation whose stock it is.

---

c. (The NYSE, like other exchanges, is a place where "used" securities are exchanged. A corporation cannot use it to "float" a new issue of stock.)

QUIZ: Multiple Choice

1. *The essential property of margin buying of a stock is* (1) participation in stock buying during a period of price rise by inexperienced investors; (2) trading in a stock in quantities that do not really exist; (3) any purchase of a stock in anticipation of a rise in its price, provided the stock is held for a short period only; (4) a stock purchase financed in part by use of borrowed money; (5) none of the above.

2. *As the result of some favorable news regarding a company, the price of its stock rises. If we were to use supply and demand curves to illustrate the nature of that price rise, we would say that it resulted from* (1) solely a rightward or upward shift of the demand curve; (2) solely a leftward or upward shift of the supply curve; (3) both a rightward demand-curve shift and a leftward supply-curve shift; (4) principally a rightward (or downward) shift of the supply curve; (5) principally a rightward shift of both demand and supply curves.

3. *Some profitable and well-regarded companies whose stocks are listed on the New York exchange pay no dividends at all (e.g., Crown Cork and Seal); profits are used entirely for expansion of plant and operations. As to any such stock, a shrewd investor* (1) might buy it in hope of capital gains, but not otherwise; (2) might buy it in expectation of a "stock split," but not otherwise; (3) might buy it in expectation of a dividend being declared in the near future, but not otherwise; (4) might buy it when he expected stock prices to fall; (5) would not buy it at all.

4. *One group of stock-market investors buys and holds for the long pull, disregarding short-term price fluctuations. This type of investor, according to the text, has the following overall effect on the market: He or she* (1) destabilizes it in that his or her purchases keep tending to push price upward; (2) stabilizes it by refusing to sell on price declines, but destabilizes it by making the market "thinner"; (3) stabilizes it by making it "thinner"; (4) destabilizes it by selling at times which have no relation to the current price of the stock; (5) does none of these things, since his or her group is not of sufficient importance to have any impact.

5. *The contribution of margin buying to the great stock-market crash of 1929 was this:* (1) Owners of stock were forced to sell that stock in order to raise the cash needed to buy the further stock which their margin commitment required them to buy. (2) The small or marginal stock buyers grew panicky and dumped their stock for whatever price they could get. (3) Margin buying had increased the volume of stock trading and thus intensified the fall in prices, but otherwise it played no special part in the crash. (4) The lenders of money sold the stock they were holding as collateral security when stock prices began to fall substantially. (5) Margin buyers made an unsuccessful attempt to stop the decline in stock prices by increasing the amount of their buying.

5 INCOMES AND LIVING STANDARDS

1. The IQs (intelligence quotients) of two separate groups of five people are computed as follows:

Group A	Group B
90	60
92	115
95	117
98	119
160	124

a. The arithmetic mean (i.e., average) IQ for group A is

_____ and for group B is _____.

b. Assuming these IQ figures to be correct for the individuals themselves, we see that if *mean* figures are used to indicate the quality of the typical person in each group, they are to some extent misleading because

_____

_____

_____ .

c. The *median* IQ for group A is _____ and for group B is

_____ . (NOTE: The median is obtained by listing all figures by rank, highest to lowest or lowest to highest, then taking the figure in the exact middle. If the total number of figures is even, so that the exact middle includes two figures, the median is the average of these two.)

d. When groups are very small, as in the two examples above—only five persons in each—it becomes less meaningful to talk about "typical" characteristics of that group. (Small totals were used above to make the overall picture a little easier to grasp.) In such cases, the median probably does a little better than the mean (although this depends on the purpose involved in seeking a "typical" figure). Thus, if it were discovered that the IQ of the fifth person in group A was really 200, not 160, the new figure *(would / would not)* affect the median figure. It *(would / would not)* affect the mean figure.

2. *a.* If, when numbers are listed in rank order, there are some extremely low figures not balanced out by correspondingly high figures, the median will tend to be *(higher than / lower than / the same as)* the mean or average. If the list of numbers is "unbalanced" by a few very high numbers, the median will tend to be *(higher than / lower than / the same as)* the mean. If there is no unbalance in either direction, e.g., if the nontypical person were dropped from group A or B above, the median will tend to be *(higher than / lower than / the same as)* the mean.

b. In terms of the frequency-distribution graph discussed in the text chapter, when there is such unbalance at the high or low end, the distribution involved is said to be *("normally distributed" / a "skew distribution")*, and when such a distribution is illustrated by means of a graph, the result tends to be *(a curve with a long tail at one end / a symmetrical, bell-shaped curve).*

3. Suppose you are given any large group of numbers—say, a list of annual family incomes, or a list of examination grades—and a frequency-distribution table is required. Say the figures are examination grades, ranging from 0 to 100, and a distribution both by number and by per cent is needed. The necessary steps are listed below, but not in the correct order:

a. Compute total for all groups to make sure it equals total number of scores.

b. Prepare a series of groups, say 0–10, 11–20, . . . , 91–100.

c. Record the number of times there is a score falling within each group.

d. Result is a frequency distribution by percentage.

e. Find what per cent of total number of scores the number of scores in each group represents, and check computation by making sure total of all percentages is reasonably close to 100 per cent.

f. Result is a frequency distribution by number.

The correct sequence of the above steps is (1) _____, (2)

————, (3) ————, (4) ————, (5) ————, (6)
————.

---

(1) *b;* (2) *c;* (3) *a;* (4) *f;* (5) *e;* (6) *d.*

---

4. If a Lorenz curve is to be prepared, the steps in question 3 must simply be carried a little further. (A Lorenz curve could be drawn to indicate the degree of inequality in the allotment of grades, but it is usually associated with income distribution.) It is particularly useful when two or more groups are to be compared, as in text Fig. 5-4, since a glance is often enough to indicate the more unequal distribution.

a. Suppose the group consists of 10 individuals; the first receives an income of $1 weekly, the second $2, and so on, the tenth receiving $10. The first is low man on the income totem pole; he represents the bottom 10 per cent of this particular population, and his $1 is about 2 per cent of the total weekly income received by all, which totals $55. Complete the remaining figures below. (For example, the lowest 20 per cent of the population consists of the $1 man plus the $2 man. Their income total of $3 is about 5½ per cent of the combined incomes of all 10—i.e., $3 is about 5½ per cent of $55. So 5½ is the figure to insert in the first blank below.)

Per Cent of Income Received by Lowest

10%	20%	30%	40%	50%	60%	70%	80%	90%	100%
2									100

b. In Study Guide Fig. 5-1, draw the Lorenz curve illustrating this distribution of income. (Note that the Lorenz-curve chart is by nature a square. Most diagrams found in the text are not bounded on all four sides in this way.) Begin by labeling the axes of Fig. 5-1; consult the text for correct labeling of a Lorenz curve.

c. If the distribution of income were more unequal than that indicated at the beginning of this question, the Lorenz curve would (*bulge closer to the lower right-hand corner / draw nearer to the diagonal*); if it were less unequal, the curve would (*bulge closer to the lower right-hand corner / draw nearer to the diagonal*).

---

a. 5½%; 11%; 18%; 27¼%; 38%; 51%; 65½%; 81¾%.
c. bulge closer to right-hand corner; draw nearer diagonal.

---

5. *a.* Suppose we have learned how money incomes are distributed, or how IQs are distributed, among some given group of people or population. We want to illustrate this information by means of a frequency-distribution chart or graph. Which one of the following three alternatives would be measured or indicated on the horizontal axis (i.e., in the between-left-and-right dimension)?

(1) Levels of income (e.g., $0-to-$1,000 group, $1,001-to-$2,000 group, etc.) or level of IQ (e.g., 80-to-85 group, 86-to-90 group, etc.).
(2) Number of people in the population falling into this income category (or IQ category).
(3) Per cent of the population falling into this income category (or IQ category).

b. Which answer to part *a* describes what should be indicated on the vertical axis? .... (1 / 2 / 3)

---

a. 1. *b.* (2); (3) is possible but less usual.

QUIZ: Multiple Choice

1. *In statistics, the difference (if any) between the words "mean" and "median" is this:* (1) Mean is the same as "average," whereas median indicates the exact midpoint in a top-to-bottom ranking. (2) Mean indicates the exact midpoint in a top-to-bottom ranking, whereas median is the same as average. (3) Mean indicates the particular figure or element appearing most frequently, whereas median indicates the exact midpoint in a top-to-bottom ranking. (4) Mean is the same as average, whereas median indicates the particular figure or element appearing most frequently. (5) None—they mean exactly the same thing.

2. *The first person within a group of 10 people receives an income of $1. The second person receives $2, the third person receives $3, and so on (the tenth person receiving $10). If this*

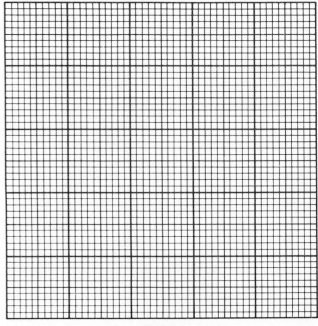

Fig. 5-1

income distribution is illustrated on a frequency-distribution chart, the resulting frequency-distribution line will be (1) a curve with a long tail at one end; (2) a bell-shaped curve; (3) a horizontal line; (4) a right angle; (5) a vertical line.

3. *In a Lorenz-curve diagram, absolute equality in income distribution would appear as* (1) a curved line well bowed out from the diagonal; (2) a curved line close to the diagonal; (3) a right-angled line; (4) a diagonal line; (5) none of these.

4. *If the distribution within any large population of a physical or a mental trait such as the intelligence quotient is illustrated by means of a frequency-distribution (FD) chart or a Lorenz-curve chart, it will most commonly appear as follows:* (1) On an FD chart as a curve with a long tail at one end only, and on a Lorenz chart as a right-angled line. (2) On an FD chart as a symmetrical or bell-shaped curve, and on a Lorenz chart as a right-angled line. (3) On an FD chart as a symmetrical or bell-shaped curve and on a Lorenz chart as a straight line. (4) On an FD chart as a symmetrical or bell-shaped curve and on a Lorenz chart as a curved line. (5) On an FD chart as a curve with a long tail at one end only and on a Lorenz chart as a straight line.

5. *Differences in ability are commonly cited to explain differences in income. In the text's view, this explanation* (1) is only partial because there are so many more instances of skewness in ability than in income distribution; (2) is only partial because the shape of the income frequency-distribution curve is significantly different from that of the ability distribution curve; (3) is only partial because the measured range of individual ability differences is much wider than the range of income distribution; (4) gives a reasonably accurate interpretation of income differences; (5) is almost meaningless because there is no suitable way of comparing ability differences against income differences.

6. *If inequalities of income and of wealth in the United Kingdom (U.K.) and the United States (U.S.) are compared, the following statement emerges (according to the text) as true:* (1) The U.K. has much greater inequality as to both incomes and wealth. (2) The U.S. has much greater inequality as to both incomes and wealth. (3) Wealth inequalities are about the same in both, but the U.K. has much greater inequality of income. (4) The U.K. has much greater inequality of wealth, but income inequalities are about the same in both. (5) There is no significant difference between the two countries as to either income inequality or wealth inequality.

7. *The present (the mid- to late 1970s) level of per capita weekly income in the United States, according to the text, is* (1) over $70 but less than $100; (2) about $100; (3) about $115; (4) about $130; (5) over $200.

8. *There is a sudden and marked change in the distribution of income in a certain population: Income becomes much* more equally distributed than it was before. If this change were being illustrated on a frequency-distribution chart, the resulting change in the position or shape of the line would properly be described as follows: It would (1) more closely resemble a right angle, with its peak at the median income level; (2) become more "squeezed in" (i.e., made taller and thinner) around the median or average income level; (3) become more "flattened out" (i.e., squeezed down vertically), with its top pushed closer to the median or average income level; (4) become more "bulged out," drawing farther away from the diagonal line; (5) become less "bulged out," drawing closer to the diagonal line.

9. *Which alternative in question 8 would be correct had that question, while still pertaining to a move toward greater equality in the distribution of income, referred to a Lorenz-curve chart, not to a frequency-distribution chart?* (1). (2). (3). (4). (5).

10. *With respect to the distribution of incomes in the United States and the relationship between the median and the mean of such incomes,* (1) the mean is higher than the median, owing to the presence of a large number of relatively low incomes; (2) the median is higher than the mean, owing to the presence of a small number of exceptionally high incomes; (3) the mean is higher than the median, owing to the presence of a small number of exceptionally high incomes; (4) the median is higher than the mean, owing to the presence of a large number of relatively low incomes; (5) the median, which used to be lower than the mean, has recently become somewhat higher, owing to the influence of progressive income taxation.

11. *By the "median" family income is meant* (1) the figure obtained by listing all incomes from lowest to highest and taking the one exactly in the middle of the ranking; (2) the income figure that would result if the total of incomes received by all families were divided equally among those families; (3) the income it is estimated a family must have in order to reach the "minimum comfort" level of consumption; (4) the level of income found at the exact midpoint of a Lorenz curve; (5) none of the preceding.

12. *Which alternative in question 11 would be correct had that question referred to the "mean" rather than to the "median" family income?* (1). (2). (3). (4). (5).

13. *If there is any inequality at all in the distribution of income, then the following will be true of the group making up the lowest 20 per cent in the income ranking:* (1) It is just as likely as not that it will receive more than 20 per cent of this total income. (2) It must receive exactly 20 per cent of this total income. (3) It will usually, but not always, receive less than 20 per cent of this total income. (4) It must have received less than 20 per cent of the total income of all groups together. (5) None of the above is necessarily true.

6 BUSINESS ORGANIZATION AND INCOME

BEHIND MUCH OF THIS CHAPTER lies a single idea:

▶ The form a particular business takes—individual proprietorship, partnership, or corporation—is almost always dictated by the amount of money needed to operate in that line of business.

In many industries there is no room for choice, and only a single business form is found: the corporation. If large quantities of money are needed for successful operation in a given line of business, no individual proprietorships or partnerships will be found therein.

Two principal reasons explain why any business demands that money be "tied up" in it. First, it may be necessary to buy expensive, long-lasting machinery, tools, and equipment; perhaps also a building to house them.

But a need for money capital arises quite apart from the necessary investment in such "fixed assets." It arises out of the inevitable *lag between money expenditure and money receipts.* Money must be *spent* to buy materials and hire labor. Money is *collectible* only after the materials have been processed and the resulting finished goods sold. So a growing business needs more "working capital" even when it is not buying more machinery or equipment.

Above all, the corporation is a device for raising money in large volume. This is the key to understanding its characteristics. Ownership shares can be sold to a small number of people or to a large number. The properties of shares of stock are attractive to most holders of money. You can buy 5 shares of stock, or 5,000. You need not "follow your money"; professional managers will tend to the running of the business. "Limited liability" assures you that, at worst, you can lose only the money you spent to buy the stock. You are free to sell the stock at any time without asking the corporation's consent. All such features tend to attract those with money available to put into business enterprise.

1. Five men own a partnership equally among them. For any one of the five, the meaning of "unlimited liability" is this: He is responsible for *(20 per cent of the partnership debts, up to the amount he has invested in the business / 20 per cent of the partnership debts, no matter how large the amount / 100 per cent of the partnership debts, if necessary, in the event his*

partners cannot pay their shares, no matter how large the amount).

---

100 per cent.

---

2. *a.* "Venture capital," or "equity capital," means (pick one):
(1) The excess of assets over liabilities.
(2) Money which typically buys a share of ownership in the business and the chances of gain or loss going with it.
(3) Money loaned to a business involving any form of risk whatever.

b. An advantage of the corporate form of enterprise is this (pick one):
(1) If the company goes bankrupt, the shareholder's liability is limited to contributing a sum equal to the par value of his stock.
(2) As a fictitious legal person, the corporation cannot be sued in its own name.
(3) By separating active management from ownership while limiting shareholder liability, the sources from which money capital can be drawn are greatly broadened.

c. A corporation *(must / may or may not)* have common stock The law which created the corporate form says that a corporation *must* have owners—and the stockholders are its owners.

This stock *(must / may or may not)* be listed on an exchange, such as the New York Stock Exchange. (Actually, only a relatively small number of giant corporations have their stock so listed. Most corporations are "private," in the sense that their stock is not publicly listed for trading. Often this stock is held entirely or almost entirely by members of a single family, only rarely changing hands.)

d. A corporation *(must / may or may not)* have bonds outstanding. The vital difference between stocks and bonds is that bonds are *(certificates of ownership / IOUs).* The corporation is free to borrow (i.e., issue such IOUs) or not to borrow, as it sees fit.

---

a. (2). *b.* (3). *c.* must; may or may not. *d.* may or may not; IOUs.

---

3. Put check marks in the spaces below if the description properly applies to a bond B, a preferred stock P, and/or a common stock C. (Assume each type of security is "normal" in character; e.g., the preferred is ordinary preferred and not cumulative or participating.)

	B	P	C
a. Income therefrom is called interest.			
b. Income therefrom is called a dividend.			
c. Does not pay more than a fixed and stated amount of income to owner			
d. No specified dollar amount of income implied in ownership.			
e. Represents a share of ownership in corporation.			
f. Represents corporation's IOU, not a share of ownership.			
g. Offers complete assurance of steady annual income for owner.			
h. Annual payment to purchaser a fixed obligation of corporation			
i. Offers maximum chance for "capital gain."			
j. May be sold at any time by purchaser to anyone he pleases.			
k. Among these three types, offers greatest assurance of steady annual income.			
l. Corporation will buy it back (redeem it) for stated amount at specified future date.			
m. Must be issued by every business corporation.			
n. Has "limited liability" feature for owner.			
o. Income must be paid to owner whenever corporation earns a profit, but only then.			
p. Income must be paid to owner in all circumstances short of bankruptcy.			
q. Income must be paid to owner before any dividend is paid on common stock.			
r. Income paid to owner only when board of directors decides it should be paid.			
s. Income received therefrom is subject to personal income tax.			
t. Is "equity capital" for corporation.			
u. Is a "fixed charge" for corporation.			

Bond: *a, c, f, h, j, k, l, n, p, q, s, u.*
Preferred: *b, c, e, j, n, q, r, s, t.*
Common: *b, d, e, i, j, m, n, r, s, t.*

Note that the word "debenture" is often used in place of "bond." There are technical differences between the two, but roughly speaking—i.e., for present introductory purposes—"bond" and "debenture" can be taken as one and the same.

4. *a.* Two businesses are identical with one another with respect to size, machinery, competence of working force, cash on hand, etc. They differ *only* in that No. 1 is a newly organized concern, whereas No. 2 has been in business for 20 years and is well and favorably known. If you could buy either of these for the same price, the better buy would be *(No. 1 / No. 2)*. In fact, the worth of *(No. 1 / No. 2)* would exceed that of the other company. The best possible estimate of the extra worth of this company in dollars is called its *(fixed assets / net worth / monopoly power / good will / equity capital)*.

b. Suppose promoters buy such an established company. They then sell stock to the public, and in the process they deliberately exaggerate the money worth of such *(fixed assets / net worth / monopoly power / good will)*, or the worth of other assets, in order to sell the stock at a higher price. This process is called *(watering the stock / incurring fixed charges / obtaining inequity capital / making a capital gain)*. (Note that question 19 in the Appendix to this chapter, p. 48, deals with this type of situation in a little more detail.)

An established and well-regarded company *does* have "good will," and it is a most valuable asset. But its exact money worth is exceedingly difficult—impossible, in fact—to establish. For this reason (and perhaps also because, in the past, grossly exaggerated valuations were sometimes used), today you are unlikely to find "Good Will" listed among the assets on a corporation's Balance Sheet.

Usually it is only when a business is being sold that the good will issue arises. The buyer quite naturally wants to be paid for it. The figure that buyer and seller agree upon may or may not be a good estimate of the worth of good will. All that can be said of it is that this is the bargain they have struck.

a. No. 2; No. 2; good will. *b.* good will; watering the stock.

5. Put an H in the space below if the act in question represents *horizontal integration;* put a V if *vertical integration;* put an N if *neither.*
a. An aluminum-manufacturing company buys a bauxite mine. (Bauxite is the ore from which aluminum is made.) ( )
b. The same company buys a competing aluminum-manufacturing concern. ( )
c. It builds a fabricating plant to process aluminum sheeting into finished aluminum consumer goods. ( )
d. It buys a chain of retail hardware stores in order to market its aluminum products more effectively. ( )
e. It buys a second chain of retail stores to expand its market still further. ( )

a. V. *b.* H. *c.* V. *d.* V. *e.* H.

6. *a.* The function of an investment banking firm is to (pick one):

(1) Accept money deposits from its customers or clientele and to lend out this money to corporations.

(2) Act as intermediary between corporations wishing to raise money by a bond or stock issue and people with money available to purchase such securities.

b. When an investment banking firm *underwrites* a stock or bond issue, this means it gives its assurance to (pick one):

(1) The buyers of the issue that it is of good quality, at the risk of incurring liability to those buyers should trouble later develop.

(2) The sellers of the issue that they will receive a specified price, the bank taking the risk that it may itself have to buy some part of the issue at that price, then sell it later at a lower price.

---

a. (2). *b.* (2).

---

7. Corporations must pay a federal income (profits) tax. It is roughly 50 per cent of income (profit).[1] Unlike the personal income tax, the tax rate does not keep climbing as the income level gets higher.

After this tax is paid, the remaining profit may be paid out as a dividend to shareholders. Usually, only a part is so paid out ("distributed profit"), the balance being retained for expansion of the business ("addition to earnings retained in the business"). (Sometimes no dividend is paid, the entire after-tax profit being retained for expansion.)

a. When a shareholder receives a dividend, the amount *(is / is not)* subject to personal income tax. The personal income tax *(also applies / does not apply)* to profit undistributed by the corporation.

b. Suppose a man is considering incorporation of his business. If income therefrom is very high, and he does not incorporate, he is subject to a high personal-income-tax rate (say 60 or 65 per cent). Incorporation means a maximum tax rate of about 50 per cent. Viewed in isolation from other facts, this is an argument *(for / against)* incorporation.

c. But incorporation means that in addition to the corporate tax, personal income tax applies to all income paid out as dividends ("double taxation"). This is an argument *(for / against)* incorporation.

d. However, *zero* personal income tax is applied to whatever corporation income is *not* paid out in dividends. This is an argument *(for / against)* incorporation.

---

a. is; does not apply. *b.* for. *c.* against. *d.* for.

---

[1]The rate is only 22 per cent on the first $25,000 of profit, but on all profit thereafter it is 48 per cent (these figures applying as of late 1975).

QUIZ: Multiple Choice

1. *The term "limited liability" is frequently used in enumerating the characteristics of a corporation. It means the following:* (1) Any officer of the corporation is strictly limited in his ability to speak for the corporation and commit it to any liability. (2) Once shareholders have paid for their stock, they have no further financial obligation, regardless of how much trouble the corporation gets into. (3) The corporation's liability to pay dividends to its stockholders is a limited one, since it need pay them only if it has earned a profit. (4) There are certain obligations which a corporation can legally refuse to pay. (5) The corporation has only a limited obligation to meet claims made by any single person or firm against it (provided it has acted within the scope of its charter), so that there is some protection for its assets and financial position.

2. *A corporation's obligation to pay interest on bonds it has issued is properly described as follows:* (1) Interest must be paid regardless of whether a profit has been earned or not. (2) Interest must be paid whenever a profit has been earned. (3) Interest need not be paid even if a profit has been earned, but it must be paid before any dividend is paid. (4) Normally, interest ranks ahead of dividends, but there are some circumstances in which a dividend can be paid without payment of bond interest. (5) Interest ranks behind dividends, and is paid only after dividends have been paid in full.

3. *It is probable that the financial statement (in particular, the Balance Sheet) of a corporation will show most, if not all, of the five items listed below. But among these five, the one it absolutely* must *record is* (1) good will; (2) an issue of bonds outstanding; (3) cash in a bank account; (4) buildings and equipment owned; (5) an issue of stock outstanding.

4. *In considering the order or ranking in which a corporation is obligated to pay out various sums of money, payment of dividends on preferred stock takes precedence over (ranks ahead of)* (1) corporation income taxes; (2) local property taxes; (3) salaries of the board of directors; (4) bond interest; (5) none of these obligations.

5. *The primary business of an investment banking firm is to* (1) make loans to small business; (2) sell corporation securities; (3) accept money deposits from its customers; (4) own the shares of a number of corporations—i.e., act as a "holding company"; (5) sell its own securities, using the proceeds to buy stock in other corporations.

6. *A preferred stock is like a* (1) bond, because the dividend must always be paid by the corporation; (2) bond, because the holder of such stock is legally a creditor of the corporation rather than a part owner; (3) bond, since both bond interest and preferred-stock dividend payments are considered operating costs rather than distributions of profit; (4) common stock, because dividends on both stock types ordinarily increase when company profits increase, (5) common stock, since no dividend need be paid on either stock if the board of directors decides it is inappropriate to pay one.

7. *The suggestion of Joseph Schumpeter (quoted in the text chapter) was that "big business" typically yields the following results (when compared with small-business competition):* (1) lower prices and greater improvements in product quality; (2) lower prices but a deterioration in product quality; (3) higher prices and a deterioration of product quality; (4) higher prices but a greater improvement in product quality; (5) no significant difference either in price or in product quality.

8. *A "convertible bond" gives its owner this particular privilege:* (1) It must be exchanged for a given amount of stock at its maturity date. (2) It may be exchanged for a given amount of stock if the owner wishes, on or before maturity date. (3) It may be exchanged for a given amount of stock if the owner wishes, but only at maturity date. (4) It may be exchanged for cash at any of several dates prior to maturity date. (5) It carries an option permitting the owner to buy a given amount of stock at a specified price, up to a specified date.

9. *The term "good will" refers to* (1) a valuation placed on the personal integrity of those who own or operate the business; (2) a fictitious increase in the company's net worth position, created by inflating the value of one or more assets to an exaggerated figure; (3) the earning power of the business; (4) the extra earning power of the business resulting from its established position; (5) providing working capital for established customers by allowing them extra time for settlement of their accounts.

10. *A corporation that is considering "debt financing" (financing via a bond issue) must recognize the fact that* (1) it always involves a fixed annual charge to be paid to debt holders whether the corporation has earned profits or not; (2) issue of debt gives the debt holders a voice in the management of the corporation's affairs, so that they may usurp some part of management's authority; (3) the new debt holders are not necessarily the same group as the original stockholders, so that the ownership shares of those stockholders are diluted by debt financing; (4) it does not actually bring in any additional cash to the corporation; (5) this method of financing first requires an amendment to the corporation's charter.

11. *If a steel-producing company merges with two other companies, one a producer of iron ore, the other a company which fabricates steel into finished or semifinished steel products, this would be an example of* (1) vertical integration; (2) establishing a holding company; (3) the acquisition of venture capital; (4) the development of good will; (5) none of the preceding.

12. *Today's commonest situation with respect to ownership and control of large American corporations (according to the text) is best described as follows:* (1) The professional managers are also the group owning a majority or near-majority of stock, so that they can make all major decisions without real consideration of the wishes of minority stockholders. (2) The professional managers make all major decisions, and the board of directors does not intervene unless it is losing confidence in those managers. (3) The professional managers control the company on all matters of importance except for basic decisions on such matters as production, new plants and new products, these being left to the board of directors as stockholder representatives. (4) The board of directors makes the decisions on all matters of real importance, the role of the professional managers being confined to routine matters. (5) The stockholders rather than the board of directors are increasingly making major decisions, through voting-power control exercised at stockholder meetings.

13. *The application of the federal personal income tax to the shareholders of a corporation, with respect to the income (i.e., profit) of that corporation, applies* (1) in full to the corporation's entire income whether distributed as dividends or not; (2) only to that part actually distributed as dividends; (3) only to that part of income not paid out as dividends—i.e., only to undistributed profit; (4) neither to dividends nor to undistributed profit; (5) both to dividends and to undistributed profit, but with a heavier rate applicable to undistributed profit.

14. *Had question 13 referred to the corporation income tax, not the personal income tax, which alternative in that question would be correct?* (1). (2). (3). (4). (5).

15. *If an investment banking house "underwrites" a stock or a bond issue for some corporation, it* (1) gives its personal guarantee that the interest or dividend promised in this issue will be paid as specified; (2) lends the corporation an amount of money equal to the value of that issue, to be repaid when the issue in question has been fully sold to the public; (3) sells the issue to its customers, with the assurance that, upon request and within a specified time period, it will buy back any part thereof, at a specified minimum price; (4) acts as agent for the corporation, but without any firm guarantee as to the amount of the issue it will sell, or the price it can obtain; (5) guarantees the corporation full sale of that issue at a fixed price, even if the bank has to buy part of the issue itself.

16. *A corporation's obligation with respect to payment of dividends on (ordinary) preferred stock (PS) and on common stock (CS) is correctly described as follows: It* (1) must pay its PS dividend if it has earned sufficient profit to do so, but pays a CS dividend only if the board of directors so decides; (2) must pay dividends on both PS and CS if profits are sufficient to do so, with the PS dividend having priority; (3) must pay its PS dividend regardless of profit earned or loss incurred, but pays its CS dividend only if the board of directors so decides; (4) must pay both PS and CS dividends regardless of profit earned or loss incurred, unless so doing would force it into bankruptcy; (5) need pay no dividend on either PS or CS, regardless of the amount of profit earned, unless the board of

directors decides on such dividend payment, although the PS dividend must have priority.

APPENDIX: Elements of Accounting

Your principal job in this Appendix is to learn about the kinds of information two accounting forms are intended to convey: the Balance Sheet, and the Income (or Profit-and-Loss) Statement.

▶ **The Balance Sheet is a point-in-time statement. Its primary function is to record what the company is "worth," as closely as can be estimated, as of that point in time.**

The Balance Sheet begins by listing the firm's assets: everything it owns—cash, buildings, equipment, inventory, and so on. Each item is given a money value, the best possible estimate of its money worth at that point in time. Sometimes the estimating job isn't easy. There is no problem in figuring the worth of a given amount of cash. But reckoning the true present worth of a factory building or of an elderly machine may be a tough job.

Among these assets, the company can and should include legitimate money claims on others (e.g., money owed by its customers). Sometimes, "intangible" assets are included; but you should disregard these for now. (Good Will, for example, is such an intangible asset; on this, see question 4, p. 39.

The firm's "worth" is not likely to be the same figure as the total of its Assets. Any debts owed to others—its Liabilities—must be deducted. The resulting figure is its Net Worth. Note carefully:

▶ **Net Worth, by definition, is Assets minus Liabilities.**

Now if this is what Net Worth is, because that is how it is defined, then it must be true that:

▶ **Total Assets = Total Liabilities + Net Worth.**

And that's how Balance Sheets are ordinarily drawn up: Assets in one column; Liabilities in an adjoining column; Net Worth below Liabilities.

To say that "the Balance Sheet always balances" is just to say that the Assets column total must be the same as the Liabilities plus Net Worth column total. This *must* be true, because Net Worth *must* be whatever figure is needed to make things come out even; that's how it is defined. (NOTE: Not the way Assets are

defined, nor Liabilities, but the way Net Worth is defined.)

And now the Income (or Profit-and-Loss) Statement:

▶ **The Income Statement is a period-of-time statement. Its primary function is to record how much profit the company earned from its sales during that period (e.g., one year).**

The Income Statement begins by listing the total of goods sold during the period in question, at their sale price. From this sales total are deducted all the expenses which ought properly to be charged as part of the cost of making and selling the goods in question, but *only* the expenses which ought to be so charged. What's left after deduction of these expenses is the company's profit for the period in question.

Watch out for the commonest of Income Statement mistakes: *do not* assume that Income Statements record only *cash* transactions. It is true that the sales total is likely to be matched by a cash inflow of approximately the same amount. But some of the "expenses" listed on an Income Statement did not entail any cash outpayment during the period involved. And some cash outpayments that were made during the period will not show up on the Income Statement at all. (The review questions take you through this set of complications.)

If some items shown on an Income Statement do not stand for cash transactions, and if some cash transactions during the period aren't shown on that statement, then Net Profit (at the bottom of the Income Statement) is certainly not going to be an accurate record of the increase in the company's cash position. It isn't intended to be. Every item on an Income Statement, or on a Balance Sheet, has a money figure appended. But in almost all instances, this is using "money" in its abstract, "estimate of value" sense, and not in the sense of "cash on hand." If you want to know how much cash a company has, its Balance Sheet is a very good place to look. But don't look for it under esoteric categories like Net Worth or Retained Earnings. Just look under Cash on Hand.

1. In December 1975, the Utter Confusion Manufacturing Company was formed, with sale for cash of 5,000 shares of common stock at $10 apiece.

On a separate sheet of paper, show this firm's Balance Sheet as of December 31, 1975, assuming the entire $50,000 stock sale proceeds still held in cash, and no other transactions. Do it in the conventional way: a column headed Assets at left, a column headed Liabilities and Net Worth at right.

Assets		Liabilities and Net Worth		
Cash	$50,000	Liabilities	$	0
		Net Worth:		
		Capital		50,000

2. During 1976 the firm's operations were as follows:

(1) Money received (all in cash):

A. Sales of merchandise manufactured $115,000

B. Bonds sold (100 bonds @ $1,000 each) 100,000

(2) Money paid out (all in cash):

A. Machinery purchased $170,000

B. Raw materials purchased for use 50,000

C. Wages paid to labor 24,000

D. Interest paid on bond issue 10,000

(3) Other facts (not involving cash received or paid):

A. All raw materials purchased were fully used up in manufacturing before the year-end (i.e., closing inventory of raw materials was zero).

B. All finished goods manufactured were sold (i.e., zero finished-goods closing inventory).

C. Depreciation on machinery was estimated at $17,000. (Note that this is just a way of saying that while the machinery was worth $170,000 when bought—say, on January 1—it was estimated as being worth only $153,000 on December 31, having been partly "used up" or worn out by use during the year. It does *not* mean a cash outlay of $17,000.)

a. How much cash did Utter Confusion have on December 31, 1976? (Start with the cash it had when the year began; you have this figure from question 1. Add the money received from sales of merchandise and bonds, listed above; then deduct the various cash outlays also listed). $_____.

b. On a separate sheet, draw up the firm's Balance Sheet as of December 31, 1976. Do this in three steps:

▶ First, run through the information above for Assets held at the year-end, to be listed at their proper value on that date. (HINT: You have already dealt with Cash; you should find only one other asset.)

▶ Second, do the same for Liabilities. (HINT: You should find only one.)

▶ Third, repeat for Net Worth. Remember that Net Worth *must* be whatever figure is needed to prop the Balance Sheet into balance. But follow the convention of dividing Net Worth between Capital and Retained Earnings. Leave Capital at $50,000 (because no more stock was sold during the year). Let Retained Earnings be the line within Net Worth to perform the balancing act.

a. $11,000. *b.* (To save space, the final three zeros have been dropped—e.g., $11,000 is written $11.)

b.

Assets		Liabilities and Net Worth	
Current: Cash ...$ 11		Current Liabilities .....$ 0	
		Long-term Liabilities:	
Fixed:		Bonds	100
Machinery $170		Net Worth:	
Less Dep'n.		Capital $50	
Allowance 17	153	Ret'd. Earnings .. 14	64
	$164		$164

Note that Assets have been divided between Current and Fixed, and Liabilities between Current and Long-term. The original value of Machinery ($170) is shown; then accumulated Depreciation is deducted, in order to reach its proper current value of $153. These are simply accounting conventions; at this stage, it is not important if your answer did not recognize them. But you may as well acquire the habit of following such conventions.

3. Now we develop the firm's Income (or Profit-and-Loss) Statement for 1976, using the information already furnished in question 2. Remember that this statement (1) records revenue earned from sales in 1976, (2) deducts from this revenue the costs of making and selling the goods in question, and (3) shows the income (or profit) remaining after that deduction. It indicates also the disposition of that profit (paid out as a dividend, or retained within the business).

The Sales figure is obviously $115,000. Raw Materials Purchases and Wages are clearly expense items to be subtracted from Sales revenue. But the other items? Ought the Machinery expenditure of $170,000 to be included as a cost to be deducted on the Income Statement? .... *(Yes / No)*

No. Deduct only costs that should be applied against the goods sold. The $170,000 *did not* go into the making of those goods, as witness the fact that at the close of the period, the firm still has something worth $153,000 left out of its initial $170,000 outlay.

4. *a.* Is there, however, any "machinery cost" associated with 1976 production? _____.

b. This Depreciation *(was / was not)* a cash outlay. It *(should / should not)* be recorded as an expense on the 1976 Income Statement *(despite / because of)* this fact.

a. Yes, Depreciation, $17,000. This is an estimate, in money terms, of the extent to which the machinery was "used up" or worn out as a result of its work in 1976. *b.* was not; should; despite. (For comment on this point, see the introductory discussion immediately preceding question 1.)

5. The 1976 bond sale of $100,000 *(ought / ought not)* to appear on the Income Statement. What *must* be recorded on that statement, however, is _____.

ought not; Bond Interest. The fact that the company borrowed $100,000 to buy machinery and the like has nothing to do with the Income Statement. But the *interest* it must pay on borrowed money is a cost of doing business, and as such must be recorded as an expense.

---

6. On a separate sheet, draw up the Income Statement.

Sales		$115
Less Manufacturing Cost of Goods Sold:		
Raw Materials Bought	$50	
Labor Cost (Wages)	24	
Dep'n. on Machinery	17	91
Gross Profit		$ 24
Deduct Bond Interest		10
Net Profit and Addition to Retained Earnings		$ 14

Note the convention of deducting Bond Interest *after* Manufacturing Costs.

---

7. The Addition to Retained Earnings figure on this Income Statement is *(the same as / different from)* the Retained Earnings figure on the year-end Balance Sheet. This *(is / is not)* a coincidence. The Balance Sheet "Earnings Retained in the Business" figure is the total of *all* income (profit) earned, for all years since incorporation, minus *all* dividends paid out throughout that period.

For example, if Utter Confusion's Income Statement for the following year (1977) ended with an "Addition to Retained Earnings" figure of $18.000, the "Retained Earnings" figure on the end-of-1977 Balance Sheet would be $*(14,000 / 18,000 / 28,000 / 32,000)*.

---

the same as; is not; 32,000.

Before continuing, be sure that the points in questions 1 through 7 are reasonably clear. Review them if necessary to make sure you have (at least in terms of the simple example used) a fair perspective on what a Balance Sheet is—what kinds of items go into it, and what do not. Do the same for an Income Statement.

8. Now we tackle a tricky but important Income Statement point. Look at the sample Income Statement in the text Appendix. In general, it resembles that of question 6 above. But—having listed the manufacturing costs incurred (to be deducted from revenue from the year's sales)—it continues with two lines: "Add: Beginning Inventory" and "Deduct: Closing Inventory." (The inventories in question are those of raw materials, goods in process of manufacture, and unsold finished goods.)

Why these two lines? Because without them, the total of "costs incurred in manufacturing the goods sold" would be incorrect, for two principal reasons. The first is this:

▶ The physical quantity of goods a firm *sells* during the year is unlikely to be exactly the same in total as the physical quantity it *manufactures*.

In general, of course, a firm must keep its manufactures in rough correspondence with its sales. It can't provide customers with goods that it hasn't manufactured; it mustn't keep on piling up an inventory of finished goods that it can't sell. Nevertheless (unless the firm produces only custom-made items, with nothing "standard" or "stock"), the total volume of goods manufactured in any period will usually be somewhat different from the total volume the firm manages to sell.

This difference (along with differences in raw-materials inventories, which we'll tackle later) must be recognized on the Income Statement. This is so because:

▶ The Income Statement is expected to report net revenue from goods sold during the year. And it is expected to list as expenses to be deducted from such revenue the cost of the *goods sold*—not the cost of the *goods manufactured*, which is usually a somewhat different figure.

a. We shall now work through a few simple examples to illustrate the point involved. The first: Suppose—with everything otherwise the same as in questions 1 through 7—Utter Confusion ended 1976 with an inventory of unsold finished goods of $6,000. (Its sales were $115,000, as before.) *Note carefully* that this $6,000 is an "at cost" valuation, based on the raw materials, labor, and depreciation that went into those unsold goods. Utter Confusion expects to sell them *next* year, and for *more* than $6,000. But until finished goods are sold, they are always valued "at cost."[2]

Thus in 1976, Utter Confusion *(sold more goods than it made / made more goods than it sold)*. Its total manufacturing expenses for materials, labor, and depreciation were (as before) $91,000. A small part of these expenses went into the making of these *unsold* goods. In fact, since the $6,000 is an "at cost" figure, the cost amount attributable to these unsold goods is *(less than $6,000 / $6,000 / more than $6,000)*.

To repeat the Income Statement rule set out above (in heavy type), in different wording:

▶ As far as possible, charge the goods that were sold with only the costs reasonably attributable to those same goods sold.

That is: *Don't* load costs onto merchandise if those costs are really attributable to the manufacture of *other* goods. With

---

[2]More precisely, the valuation rule is "at the lower of cost or market price." Its purpose is to cover the unhappy situation in which market price has fallen so much (or the goods are so unattractive to customers) that the merchandise cannot be sold even for the basic costs of its manufacture. This complication can be disregarded in an introductory survey.

total Manufacturing Costs of $91,000, and with $6,000 of that total attributable to the unsold goods, the "Manufacturing Cost of Goods *Sold*" in 1976 ought to be *$(80,000 / 85,000 / $90,000 / 91,000 / 97,000)*. This *(is / is not)* the Cost figure that should be deducted from Sales on the Income Statement.

Suppose you list Manufacturing Costs just as in question 6, total them—then continue with a line "Deduct: Closing Inventory, $6,000." The net figure so produced will be *$(85,000 / 91,000 / 97,000)*—which *(is / is not)* the correct "Manufacturing Cost of Goods Sold" amount.

The introduction of this $6,000 closing inventory *(will / will not)* change Utter Confusion's 1976 Net Profit. Specifically, this profit will *(remain at / be changed to) $(6,000 / 12,000 / 14,000 / 20,000)*.

b. A different example: Everything is as it was in questions 1 through 7 (including a *zero* end-of-1976 finished-goods inventory)—except that Utter Confusion began 1976 with a $2,000 inventory of unsold finished goods. It had bought them for $2,000 from a company overloaded with inventory. For convenience, let's say it was a bargain purchase, in that this $2,000 was an "at cost" figure, in the same sense of representing only the labor, materials, and depreciation that went into these goods.

Since the year-end finished-goods inventory was zero, these goods must have gone into Utter Confusion's sales of $115,000. So the $2,000 *cost* of these goods—see the Income Statement rule as to expenses set out above—must go into the Income Statement. (The $91,000 total for labor, materials, and depreciation incurred during 1976 pertains only to the goods manufactured in 1976. It had nothing to do with the stuff in the opening inventory.) Thus the 1976 "Manufacturing Cost of Goods *Sold*" total should be *$(87,000 / 89,000 / 91,000 / 93,000 / 95,000)*.

Suppose you list Manufacturing Costs just as in question 6, total them—and then continue with a line "Add: Beginning Inventory, $2,000." The figure so produced will be *$(89,000 / 91,000 / 93,000)*—which is the *(correct / incorrect)* "Manufacturing Cost of Goods Sold" figure.

The introduction of this $2,000 beginning inventory *(would / would not)* change the 1976 Net Profit figure. Specifically, this profit will *(remain at / be changed to) $(8,000 / 10,000 / 12,000 / 14,000 / 16,000)*.

---

a. made more goods than it sold; 6,000; 85,000; is; 85,000; is; will; be changed to; 20,000.

b. 93,000; 93,000; correct; would; be changed to; 12,000.

---

9. These "Add: Beginning Inventory" and "Deduct: Closing Inventory" lines are needed for a second reason. Again the problem is an inventory one, and the same Income Statement rule is involved, namely: As far as possible, don't charge merchandise with costs that are properly attributable to the manufacture of *other* goods.

The problem now is this:

▶ A firm's inventory of raw materials (and of goods in process of manufacture) is unlikely to be the same in physical quantity or in value at the end of a year as it was at the beginning of that year.

a. Suppose Utter Confusion ended 1976 with a raw-materials inventory of $7,000—i.e., it didn't use up in manufacture all the $50,000 in materials it had bought during that year. (Everything else is as before: sales of $115,000; zero year-beginning raw-materials inventory; zero year-beginning and year-end finished-goods inventories.)

So the value of raw materials that went into the goods sold was *$(43,000 / 50,000 / 57,000)*—and *that* is the amount that should be charged against the goods sold.

Look again at the Income Statement in question 6. After listing and totaling the various Manufacturing Cost items as before, bring in a new line, "Deduct: Closing Inventory, $7,000." This makes the "Manufacturing Cost of Goods Sold" total *$(84,000 / 91,000 / 98,000)*, which *(is / is not)* the correct figure.

Allowing for such a $7,000 closing raw-materials inventory, Utter Confusion's Net Profit for 1976 would become *$(7,000 / 12,000 / 14,000 / 21,000 / 28,000)*.

b. A different and final example: Just after incorporation near the end of 1975 but before commencing operations in 1976, Utter Confusion bought raw materials for $3,000. At the end of 1976, it had a closing raw-materials inventory of $4,000. Everything else is as before: sales of $115,000; raw materials purchased during 1976 of $50,000; zero beginning and closing inventories of finished goods.

In this case, the quantity of raw materials that went into the goods sold must have been (in value) *$(47,000 / 48,000 / 49,000 / 50,000 / 51,000 / 52,000 / 53,000 / 54,000)*. So try the usual add-and-deduct technique—that is, total the Manufacturing Cost on the Income Statement as usual, then follow with "Add: Beginning Inventory, $3,000," and "Deduct: Closing Inventory, $4,000." As before, this *(will/will not)* give you the correct "Manufacturing Cost of Goods Sold" total.

In this case, Utter Confusion's Net Profit for 1976 would be *$(10,000 / 11,000 / 12,000 / 13,000 / 14,000 / 15,000 / 16,000)*.

In ordinary and real situations, these beginning and closing inventories usually involve a mixture of raw materials, goods-in-process (of manufacture), and unsold finished goods. That doesn't matter. To get the inventory total, just add up their values—remembering that unsold finished goods are to be valued "at cost."

Note in passing that a different—and more puzzling—inventory problem is discussed briefly in question 17.

---

a. 43,000; 84,000; is; 21,000. *b.* 49,000; will; 15,000.

---

10. Questions 8 and 9 dragged you (kicking and screaming, no doubt) into problems of beginning and closing inventories. The recognition of such inventory differences affects not only the Income Statement but also the Balance Sheet.

The Balance Sheet is affected in three ways: (1) Any Net Profit change means a matching change in Net Worth (and within Net Worth, in Retained Earnings). (No Net Worth change would be needed if the Net Profit change were just matched by an equivalent change in dividends paid out. But Utter Confusion hasn't paid any dividends as yet.) (2) Any Closing Inventory must be recorded as a Current Asset. (3) If the change described involved an expenditure of money (as it did in two of the four examples), then the Cash Asset must be changed accordingly.

What changes are needed in the end-of-1976 Balance Sheet of question 2, if allowance is made (taking each case one at a time) for the various amendments brought into questions 8 and 9? Specifically, these were (with everything else unchanged):

8a: A closing finished-goods inventory of $6,000.
8b: An opening finished-goods inventory of $2,000.
9a: A closing raw-materials inventory of $7,000.
9b: An opening raw-materials inventory of $3,000, and a closing raw-materials inventory of $4,000.

Write your answers on a separate sheet of paper, remembering (as suggested) that the changes will (or may) involve the Current Asset items of Cash and of Inventory, and the Net Worth item of Retained Earnings.

8a. Add Current Asset (CA): Inventory, $6; change Ret'd. Earnings from $14 to $20. 8b. Change CA Cash from $11 to $9; change Ret'd. Earnings from $14 to $12. 9a. Add CA Inventory, $7; change Ret'd. Earnings from $14 to $21. 9b. Change CA Cash from $11 to $8; add CA Inventory $4; change Ret'd. Earnings from $14 to $15.

---

11. Notice from questions 8 and 9 the difference between "Manufacturing Cost" (manufacturing expenses incurred during the year) and "Manufacturing Cost of Goods Sold" (Manufacturing Cost after adjustment for year-beginning and year-ending inventories).

For example, if Manufacturing Cost exceeds Manufacturing Cost of Goods Sold, this must mean that Beginning Inventory (*exceeds / is less than*) Closing Inventory.

Alternatively, if Beginning Inventory is less than Closing Inventory, then Manufacturing Cost must (*exceed / be less than*) Manufacturing Cost of Goods Sold.

---

is less than; exceed. (On first exposure to these inventory problems, you may find this a very tricky question. If necessary, check the answers by assuming some arbitrary Manufacturing Cost figure; then use the add-and-subtract technique with respect to Beginning and Closing Inventories, in order to obtain Manufacturing Cost of Goods Sold.)

---

12. Suppose question 2's operations were amended as described below. What change (if any) would each of these require in the question 2 Balance Sheet and the question 6

Income Statement? For reasons of space, write your answers on a separate sheet, heading two columns: (1) Balance Sheet Change, and (2) Income Statement Change.

a. The firm also paid (in 1976) a cash dividend of $2,000 to stockholders.
b. The firm's 1976 operations required it to pay corporation income taxes of $3,000 in cash during the year.
c. The firm incurred this $3,000 tax obligation on account of its 1976 operations, but it had not made the payment by the close of the year.
d. Raw materials bought were $50,000 as before, but a $5,000 bill for part of this was unpaid at year-end.
e. Sales were $115,000 as before, but $10,000 of this remained to be collected from customers at year-end.

---

a. *Balance Sheet:* Cash down from $11 to $9; Ret'd. Earnings down from $14 to $12. *Income Statement:* record Dividend Payment at bottom, making addn. to ret'd. earnings $12, not $14.
b. *Balance Sheet:* Cash down from $11 to $8; Ret'd. Earnings down from $14 to $11. *Income Statement:* deduct Taxes after Bond interest, making Addn. to Ret'd. Earnings $11, not $14.
c. *Balance Sheet:* Cash unchanged at $11 but include Taxes Unpaid current liability of $3; answer otherwise same as b.
d. *Balance Sheet:* Cash up from $11 to $16; include Accts. Payable current liability of $5. *Income Statement:* unchanged. (The Income Statement records raw materials bought and used; it doesn't care whether or not they have yet been paid for.)
e. *Balance Sheet:* Cash down from $11 to $1; include Accts. Receivable current asset $10. *Income Statement:* unchanged.

---

13. Use the vast amount of knowledge you have garnered over the past few questions to redo Utter Confusion's end-of-1976 Balance Sheet and its 1976 Income Statement, with a fuller set of transactions. Specifically, the initial Balance Sheet was as in question 1, and 1976 operations were in full as below.

(Developing the Cash figure requires some work. For example, the Sales figure is $115,000, but only $105,000 represents cash incoming; there are year-end Accounts Receivable (sales not yet paid for) of $10,000. A similar adjustment is needed for cash paid out for raw materials.)

For convenience, the final 000s are omitted—e.g., the Bond issue figure of $100 stands for $100,000.

Bond issue (100 @ $1,000) $100
Sales of finished goods 115
Purchases: Machinery 170
            Raw materials 50
            Labor cost (wages) 24

Taxes paid 3
Bond interest paid 10
Dividends paid 2
Accounts payable (raw materials) at year-end 5
Accounts receivable (from customers) at year-end .. 10
Depreciation on machinery for 1976 17
Opening inventories: Raw materials ....zero
                   Finished goods ....zero
Closing inventories: Raw materials 5
                  Finished goods 6

Balance Sheet

Assets			Liabilities and Net Worth		
Current:			Current Liabilities:		
Cash ....$	1		Accts. Payable $	5	
Accts.			Long-term		
Receivable ..	10		Liabilities:		
Inventories ..	11	$ 22	Bonds	100	$105
Fixed:					
Machinery ...	170		Net Worth:		
Less Dep'n.			Capital .... $	50	
Allowance ..	17	153	Ret'd. Earnings	20	70
		$175			$175

Income Statement

Sales		$115
Less Manufacturing Cost of Goods Sold:		
Manufacturing Cost:		
Raw Materials Bought	$50	
Dep'n on Machinery	17	
Labor Cost (Wages)	24	
	91	
Add Beginning Inventory	0	
	91	
Deduct Closing Inventory	11	80
Gross Profit		35
Bond Interest Paid		10
		25
Taxes Paid		3
Net Profit		22
Dividends Paid		2
Addition to Retained Earnings		$ 20

14. *a.* If, in the following year (1977), depreciation on machinery were again $17,000, that would of course be the Depreciation expense to record on the 1977 Income Statement. On the firm's end-of-1977 Balance Sheet, the total of "Allowance for Depreciation" would be $(zero / 17,000 / 34,000 / 51,000). That is, the Depreciation figure on this end-of-1977 Balance Sheet would be (*different from/the same as*) the figure on the 1977 Income Statement. This is so because the Balance Sheet Depreciation figure represents depreciation for the (*year just ended/total for all years since purchase*).

b. The machinery value cited in previous questions has been $170,000 (original purchase value). Each year, a Depreciation expense is recorded for that machinery on the Income Statement. If we were to add up *all* such Depreciation entries on *all* the Income Statements over the whole life of this machinery, the resulting total would be—assuming a scrap value of zero—(*less than $170,000 / $170,000 / more than $170,000*).

---

a. 34,000; different from; for all years since purchase.
b. 170,000.

---

15. The Balance Sheet *always* balances, no matter what, for the reason already indicated in the introductory comments: Net Worth must go up or down, if necessary, by whatever amount is needed to keep things in balance. To use the text's example, if a thief steals all the firm's cash—$5,000, let's say— then Cash (within Assets) drops by $5,000, and Retained Earnings (within Net Worth) drops by the same amount.

Ordinarily, a firm draws up its Balance Sheet only at intervals—once each year, or once each quarter. But it always has a Balance Sheet, as of any point in time, always in balance.

Below are six transactions. Show how each would affect the firm's Balance Sheet. Write your answers on a separate sheet of paper, and use the abbreviations CA and FA, CL and LTL, and NW for Current and Fixed Assets, Current and Long-term Liabilities, and Net Worth, respectively. (Some of these transactions may involve more than two Balance Sheet accounts.)

a. Utter Confusion buys a new factory building for $50,000, using money provided by a local bank on a 15-year mortgage loan.
b. The firm's principal stockholders contribute $25,000 extra cash to the business, for which they receive new shares of common stock of equivalent value.
c. The Internal Revenue Service rules that the company owes an extra $2,000 in corporation taxes for the preceding year. The company pays at once by check.
d. Accounts Payable of $6,000 fall due. The firm is temporarily short of cash, and creditors agree to accept interest-bearing 90-day notes for this amount.
e. The company sells goods for $20,000. Of these sales, $15,000 is paid in cash, and $5,000 still stands as Accounts Receivable. These goods had been valued in the finished-goods inventory ("at cost") at $12,000.
f. A customer owing $2,000 goes bankrupt. Cash of $1,000 is received in full settlement of the amount he had owed.

---

a. (FA) Buildings ....+$50	(LTL) Mortgage ......+$50		
b. (CA)Cash ....+ 25	(NW) Capital ....+ 25		
c. (CA) Cash ....− 2	(NW) Ret'd. Earnings ..− 2		
d.	(CL) Accts. Payable ..− 6		
	(CL) Notes Payable ...+ 6		

e. (CA) Cash ....+ 15   (NW) Ret'd. Earnings..+   8
  (CA) Accts. Rec. ..+ 5
  (CA) Inventory ...− 12
f. (CA) Cash ...... + 1   (NW) Ret'd. Earnings..−   1
  (CA) Accts. Rec. ..− 2

16. If a corporation has issued bonds (or debentures), they must always be recorded on its Balance Sheet within the *(Net Worth/Liabilities)* section. When it issues stock—either common or preferred—the issue must always be recorded on its Balance Sheet within the *(Net Worth/Liabilities)* section.

Liabilities; Net Worth. [Bonds or debentures are debts owed to outsiders, and so must be recorded as Liabilities. The issue of shares of stock is an issue made to the corporation's owners (or part owners); so it must be recorded within the Net Worth section.]

---

17. The text Appendix to Chapter 6 mentions very briefly an inventory problem which becomes acute for many corporations in periods of rapidly rising raw-materials prices (such as in 1974–1976). Suppose, to take an extreme example, a given raw-material item cost you $1 on January 1, and $3 on December 31. You bought such materials throughout the year—at prices of $1, $2, and $3, as the year progressed. What materials cost do you list on your Income Statement for that year, as a charge against the merchandise sold?

This problem has no clear answer. There are simply two conventional rules: FIFO ("first in, first out") and LIFO ("last in, first out"). The FIFO idea is that you first use in manufacture the raw materials you first purchased—in our example, the cheapest ($1) ones. This (by comparison with LIFO) tends to *(lower / raise)* Manufacturing Cost of Goods Sold, and to *(lower / raise)* reported Net Profit.

In contrast, LIFO assumes that you charge the goods sold with the last (and in our example, most costly) materials bought. This *(lowers / raises)* Manufacturing Cost of Goods Sold, and *(lowers / raises)* reported profit. Only if you work down to the bottom of your inventory storage bin do you reach the lower-priced items and apply the lower cost against goods sold.

In an inflationary period, the trend is clearly toward LIFO. Corporations believe that (with high replacement costs for raw materials) FIFO tends toward an overstatement of true net profit.

---

lower; raise; raises; lowers.

---

18. *a.* If a firm deliberately "accelerates" Depreciation entries for its equipment—i.e., records a higher depreciation than the most probable correct figure—this *(increases/decreases)* its recorded profit before tax for that year, and *(increases/decreases)* the amount of income (i.e., profit) tax it must pay in that year. Now, Depreciation as an Income State-

ment expense *(is/is not)* a cash outlay. Hence, although accelerated depreciation causes recorded profit to go *(down/up)*. the fact that it reduces the cash outpayment for taxes means that cash held by the business will be *(decreased/increased)*.

b. In later years, there *(will / will not)* be a corresponding *(increase / decrease)* in taxes due, because (pick one):
(1) The firm can continue to charge this too-high depreciation figure indefinitely.
(2) Depreciation expense must stop once its total for all years reaches original cost.

(NOTE: Students sometimes think that since accelerated depreciation only postpones the evil day, no real gain is involved. Suppose you save $100,000 in taxes this year, but must pay it 5 years hence. If you put the money in a savings bank for 5 years at 8 per cent interest, do you gain? Or if you plow it back into your own firm to earn 15 per cent, do you gain?)

---

a. decreases; decreases; is not; down; increased. *b.* will; increase; (2).

---

19. Two small established corporations, A and B, are bought by a group of promoters, who intend to merge them into one new concern. The combined Balance Sheet of these two firms at time of purchase is:

Assets		Liabilities and Net Worth	
Plant, Equipment, etc. $100,000		Liabilities ...none	
Good Will 50,000		Net Worth ..$150,000	
$150,000		$150,000	

The $50,000 is a fair estimate of the true worth of Good Will—i.e., the "extra earning power" of the two concerns due to their established position. (See review question 4, p. 39, on good will, if necessary.)

The promoters now organize a new firm, corporation C, with 60,000 shares of common stock. Half this stock is to be sold to the public at $10 per share (thus bringing in cash of $300,000). The promoters take the remaining 30,000 shares themselves. In exchange, they give corporation C the assets of the two original concerns. The true worth of these assets is only $150,000; but the promoters inflate this to $300,000 by writing up the value of Good Will from $50,000 to $200,000.

There being no Securities and Exchange Commission to reveal such action, the public innocently buys its 30,000 shares at $10 each, for cash.

a. On a separate sheet, draw up the Balance Sheet of the new concern after all stock has been sold and cash paid in by the public. Use the inflated Good Will figure.

b. The real worth of a share of stock is $ _____ .

c. This process of exaggerating stock values is called _____

_____ .

d. How are stockholders most likely to discover they have paid too high a price for their stock?

_____

_____

a. Assets	Liabilities & Net Worth
Cash $300	
Plant and Equipment . 100	
Good Will 200	Net Worth ..$600

b. $7.50. *c.* watering the stock. *d.* Earnings and dividends below their expectations.

QUIZ: Multiple Choice

1. *In the preparation of an Income Statement for a certain period (in particular, the manufacturing-cost section),* (1) all expenses listed therein must represent cash actually paid out during that period, and all such cash outpayments (pertaining to manufacturing) must be listed; (2) every cash outlay (pertaining to manufacturing) during the period must be listed, and in addition some expenses which did not involve an outlay of cash may appear; (3) some expenses listed may not represent cash outlays during the period, and some cash outlays during the period (pertaining to manufacturing) may not be listed; (4) all expenses listed must represent cash actually paid out during the period, but not all such cash outpayments (pertaining to manufacturing) need be listed; (5) none of the preceding statements is a correct description.

2. *If a manufacturing corporation sells an issue of long-term bonds, then on its Income (Profit-and-Loss) Statement for the period in which the bonds were sold,* (1) both the bond sale and any interest paid thereon during the period will be recorded; (2) the bond sale will be recorded, but not any interest paid thereon; (3) the bond sale will not be recorded, but any interest paid thereon will be; (4) neither the bond sale nor any interest paid thereon will be recorded; (5) only that fraction of the bond sale chargeable to that period will be recorded.

3. *If an Income Statement records no Depreciation expense for particular machinery, even though that machinery was used for production during the year, a reasonable explanation from the accounting viewpoint would be that* (1) the company did not find it necessary to spend any money on maintenance or repair of the machines during the year; (2) Depreciation entries equal in total to the original cost of the machines had already been made on earlier Income Statements; (3) because sales for the year have been below normal, the company has decided not to charge any depreciation cost

for this year; (4) because of an increase in market prices, it is estimated that the money worth of the machinery is unchanged even though it has undergone some depreciation through use during the year; (5) no explanation is needed, since Depreciation entries are properly made on the Balance Sheet, not the Income Statement.

4. *When an Allowance for Depreciation figure is entered in the fixed-asset section of a company's Balance Sheet, its purpose is* (1) to prevent an overstatement of net profit; (2) to reduce the original cost of some asset to an estimate of its true present worth, as closely as can be estimated; (3) to assure that there will be sufficient cash on hand to replace assets when they are worn out; (4) to record the money actually spent in keeping some asset or group of assets in working condition; (5) to record the total amount of money spent on purchase of new assets during the period in question.

5. *Which alternative in question 4 would be correct as to the purpose of listing Depreciation as an expense on a company's Income Statement?* (1). (2). (3). (4). (5).

6. *"A Balance Sheet must always balance" specifically because* (1) total Assets, properly specified, equal total Liabilities, properly specified; (2) Net Profit is defined as total Revenue earned minus total Expenses incurred; (3) the definition of Net Worth is total Assets minus total Liabilities; (4) Current Assets plus Fixed Assets must equal Current Liabilities plus Long-term Liabilities; (5) the definition of Net Worth is Capital Stock plus Retained Earnings.

7. *A company's total Assets at the end of 1976 were $100,000, and its total Liabilities, $70,000. At the end of 1977, its total Assets were $115,000, and its total Liabilities, $75,000. It paid dividends totaling $15,000 in 1977. Assuming no change in its Capital Stock, its Net Profit after taxes for 1977 must have been* (1) $10,000; (2) $15,000; (3) $20,000; (4) $25,000; (5) $30,000.

8. *A "sinking fund" is* (1) another name for the Depreciation account; (2) a liability reserve set up to cover future commitments of fairly certain amount; (3) a special type of surplus reserve; (4) a "pool of liquid assets" found on the Assets side of some firms' Balance Sheets; (5) the special account used to value a firm's Good Will.

9. *A money figure which would appear both on a company's Income Statement for a given year and on its Balance Sheet for the end of that year would be* (1) labor cost; (2) cash on hand at year-end; (3) dividends paid; (4) beginning inventory; (5) closing inventory.

10. *A company's 1976 Income Statement shows a Net Profit earned (after taxes) of $200,000. This means that on its end-of-1976 Balance Sheet, as compared with its end-of-1975 Balance Sheet,* (1) the total of Assets will be up by $200,000, and so will the total of Liabilities plus Net Worth; (2) Retained Earnings will be up by $200,000 minus the total of dividends paid; (3) Current Assets minus Current Liabilities will be up by $200,000; (4) Cash on hand minus expenditures for new Fixed Assets will be up by $200,000; (5) Net Worth will be up by $200,000 minus the total of any bond interest paid.

11. *An Income Statement will not ordinarily record the following transaction:* (1) Sale of goods which must be sold at a price below their manufacturing cost. (2) Amount of expenditure on an advertising campaign. (3) Amount of salary payments to administrative or "overhead" personnel. (4) Any quantity of goods which, although sold during the year in question, were not manufactured during that year. (5) Amount of expenditure to purchase new machinery.

12. *If the term "Retained Earnings" appears on a firm's Balance Sheet, it means* (1) the name of an account on the Assets side, having no connection with Cash on hand; (2) the name of an account on the Assets side, indicating Cash on hand; (3) the name of an account on the Liabilities and Net Worth side, having no connection with Cash on hand; (4) the name of an account on the Liabilities and Net Worth side, indicating Cash on hand; (5) that something is wrong, since "Retained Earnings" is not ordinarily a term used in connection with Balance Sheets.

13. *The use of "accelerated depreciation," or "fast write-off," has, during the period of write-off, the effect of* (1) increasing stated profits but decreasing taxes paid; (2) decreasing stated profits but increasing taxes paid; (3) increasing both stated profits and taxes paid; (4) decreasing both stated profits and taxes paid; (5) none of these.

14. *If, on a company's Income Statement, its Manufacturing Cost is less than its Manufacturing Cost of Goods Sold, its* (1) Beginning Inventory for that period must be higher than its Closing Inventory; (2) profit for the period in question must be lower than its profit for the immediately preceding period; (3) profit for the period in question must be higher than its profit for the immediately preceding period; (4) dividends paid for that period must exceed its addition to Retained Earnings; (5) Beginning Inventory for that period must be lower than its Closing Inventory.

15. *A company's total Assets were $600,000, and its total Liabilities, $400,000, at the end of 1976. At the end of 1977, its total Assets were $550,000, and its total Liabilities, $200,000. During 1977, it (i) paid a dividend of $50,000, and (ii) sold additional shares of its own stock for $100,000. With these figures, its Net Profit after taxes for 1977 must have been* (1) zero; (2) $50,000; (3) $100,000; (4) $150,000; (5) $200,000.

16. *The term "Retained Earnings" as used on a corporation's Balance Sheet ordinarily means* (1) the total of Current Assets minus the total of Current Liabilities; (2) profit for the particular year in question minus dividends paid in that year; (3) the total of Cash on hand minus the total of Accounts Payable; (4) the total of all Assets minus the total of all Liabilities; (5) the total of all net profits earned since incorporation minus the total of all dividends paid.

QUIZ: Other

1. A company's Balance Sheet as of December 31, 1976, in condensed form (the figures showing thousands of dollars) was as follows:

Assets		Liabilities and Net Worth		
Cash	$14	Liabilities:		
Inventory	20	Bonds Issued		$30
Bldgs. and				
Equipment ...	$76	Net Worth:		
Less Dep'n.		Capital Stock	....	$40
Allowance ...	22 54	Ret'd. Earnings ...	18	58
Total	$88	Total		$88

During 1977, its entire transactions were as follows:

a. It sold goods, all for cash, for a total of $80.
b. Manufacturing expenses during the year for wages, raw materials, and miscellaneous costs (excluding depreciation) were $37. Of this, $35 was paid in cash; the other $2 stood as accounts payable at end of 1977.
c. Depreciation on buildings and equipment during 1977 was estimated at $5.
d. Total selling and administrative costs, interest, and taxes were $22, all paid in cash during the year.
e. Dividends of $15 were paid in cash during the year.
f. New equipment costing $18 was bought for cash.
g. The closing inventory was $24.

Prepare this company's Income Statement for year 1977, and its Balance Sheet as of December 31, 1977.

2. As chairman of the board of directors of a company, you are presiding over a stockholders' meeting to review the financial statements of the year. Answer the following questions fired at you by an irritated shareholder:
a. "I happen to know that you spent $20,000 on equipment just before the year's end, and yet you haven't shown that cost on your Income Statement. Why not?"
b. "Are you going to show that $20,000 expenditure on *next* year's Income Statement?"
c. "You show depreciation expense of $15,000 on your buildings and equipment during the year, yet I happen to know that you didn't spend a cent all year on maintenance and repair. What do you mean by showing $15,000 worth of money which you didn't spend at all?"
d. "You have retained earnings of $30,000 on hand, the Balance Sheet says so, right there under the Net Worth section. Why didn't you pay out that money in dividends?"

3. A new manager for a hitherto-unsuccessful business reports at the end of his first year: "We have finally begun to get this firm out of the red. Profit was $8,000.

"Total sales for the year were $100,000, all for cash. Our cash expenses during the year for materials, wages and salaries, advertising, and so on, totaled $82,000. We also allowed depreciation expense of $5,000. We paid property and similar taxes of $5,000.

"One of the firm's troubles has been that it had too much money tied up in inventories. We managed to work inventories down to a much better level: We got raw materials down from $5,000 to $3,000 by the end of the year, and finished goods down from $12,000 to $2,000."

No relevant information has been omitted. Comment.

4. The figures (thousands of dollars) in the two columns alongside, A and B, pertain to two different corporations. Prepare, for company A and for company B, its Income (or Profit-and-Loss) Statement for 1976, and its Balance Sheet as of December 31, 1976. Note that in neither instance is the Retained Earnings figure for December 31, 1976, supplied you; this you must compute. Otherwise, the figures are assumed to be complete.

	A	B
Bonds (or debentures) issued:		
Principal amount owed, Dec. 31, 1976 ...	$ 4,000	$1,000
Interest paid, 1976	300	90
Buildings owned (original cost)	10,000	2,000
Cash on hand, Dec. 31, 1976	800	600
Common stock (original issue price)	3,000	1,500
Depreciation:		
Buildings, all years up to end of 1975	1,000	540
Buildings, 1976 only	200	60
Equipment, all years up to end of 1975 ..	1,000	950
Equipment, 1976 only	200	50
Dividends: Already paid for 1976	225	180
Declared for 1976, not yet paid .	75	70
Equipment owned, original cost	4,000	2,500
Finished and semifinished goods:		
1976 net finished-good sales for cash	6,500	3,750
1976 sales, payment not yet received	600	250
Inventory, Dec. 31, 1975	750	550
Inventory, Dec. 31, 1976	500	600
Labor cost: Wages paid in cash, 1976	1,950	900
Maintenance and repair expense paid, 1976	500	390
Mortgage:		
Principal outstanding, Dec. 31, 1976	2,500	500
Interest paid, 1976	200	50
Note payable to bank:		
Principal outstanding, Dec. 31, 1976	1,000	0
Interest paid, 1976	100	0
Patents owned and good will, Dec. 31, 1976	600	0
Raw materials:		
Inventory, Dec. 31, 1975	500	450
Bought for cash, 1976	1,600	800
Bought 1976, not yet paid for	200	250
Inventory, Dec. 31, 1976	800	300
Retained earnings, Dec. 31, 1975	2,925	620
Selling and administrative costs, 1976:		
Already paid	400	350
Incurred, but not yet paid	50	0
Taxes on profit, 1976, not yet paid	700	450

7 LABOR AND INDUSTRIAL RELATIONS

1. *a.* The *union shop* is correctly described as follows (pick one):
(1) Workers must be union members before they can work on the job.
(2) Workers must join the union after they have been employed for some stated period, such as 90 days.
(3) Workers need not join the union at all if they do not wish to do so, no matter how long they are employed.
(4) By none of the above.
b. Alternative *(1 / 2 / 3 / 4)* correctly describes the *closed shop.*
c. The *open shop* is correctly described by alternative *(1 / 2 / 3 / 4)* above.

---
a. (2). *b.* (1). *c.* (3).
---

2. If all or most workers within a given plant belong to the same union, this would most probably be classified as *(a craft/an industrial)* union. If all or most union members have the same occupation, or closely allied occupations, this would most probably be classed as *(a craft/an industrial)* union.

---
an industrial; a craft.
---

3. *a.* A *jurisdictional* dispute is one between competing unions, in which the employer becomes involved. The question may concern which union has the right to represent a particular group of workers, or whether particular work should be done by members of union A or union B. If union A calls a strike against the employer to compel him to cease dealing with union B, or to compel him to assign certain work to A's members rather than B's members, this is a *jurisdictional* strike. Such disputes and strikes are more likely to arise among *(craft / industrial)* unions. Jurisdictional strikes *(are now / are not now)* illegal. The federal act which stipulates this is the _____ Act.

b. Jurisdictional squabbles obviously weaken the strength of unions in dealing with employers. They have sometimes been a difficult problem for the union movement. The leader who sought to avoid such conflicts by having the national labor movement emphasize the "exclusive jurisdiction" principle was _____.

c. If a union has called a strike against company X, but company X nevertheless continues to operate and to sell its merchandise, the union and the federation may call on union members and the public not to buy X's merchandise. This is a *boycott*, and it *(is / is not)* illegal, according to federal law.

If company Y is a customer of company X (say X produces steel, and Y buys steel from X in order to make and sell steel products), the union and federation may call for a boycott on Y's products, in order to increase the pressure on company X. This is a *secondary boycott*, which at present *(is / is not)* illegal. The federal law which stipulates this is the _____ Act.

---
a. craft; are now; Taft-Hartley. *b.* Samuel Gompers.
c. is not; is; Taft-Hartley.
---

4. In 1890, a federal act was passed which for the next 20 years was used as a weapon against union formation and activity, although this had not been the principal intent of the framers of this legislation. In 1914, another bill was passed, specifically excluding labor unions from application of the first act. The first of these laws was the _____ Act, and the second was the _____ Act.

Sherman; Clayton.
---

5. Are the following statements concerning the National Labor Relations Board true or false?

a. On petition from a union claiming to represent a majority of workers, the NLRB can take a secret ballot of the workers to determine if this claim is valid .... *(T / F)*
b. If a majority vote upholds the union claim in *a*, the NLRB can require the employer to recognize the union as collective bargaining agent and to deal with it .... *(T / F)*
c. In the event of a union-management dispute, the NLRB can enter the dispute and seek to mediate the differences *(T / F)*
d. If no agreement can be reached voluntarily, the NLRB can, on petition to the courts, act as an arbitrator in order to settle the dispute .... *(T / F)*
e. The NLRB can designate an "unfair labor practice," and if necessary take the employer to court to enforce its "cease and desist" order against such practice .... *(T / F)*

a, b, e, True; *c, d,* False.

6. Match each name with the appropriate description below by putting 1, 2, or 3, etc., in the space after each description. The same number may be used more than once (i.e., the same man may satisfy more than one description).

(1) Cesar Chavez (6) John L. Lewis
(2) Calvin Coolidge (7) George Meany
(3) Samuel Gompers (8) Walter Reuther
(4) Sidney Hillman (9) Description fits none of the above
(5) Jimmy Hoffa

a. First president of the CIO. .... ( )
b. Prominent figure in the activity to unionize farm workers. .... ( )
c. First prominent advocate of "business unionism"—i.e., bargaining for better working conditions and higher wages, not political action .... ( )
d. Leader whose union was expelled from AFL-CIO on the charge that it was Communist-dominated or -infiltrated. ( )
e. AFL-CIO president noted for his conservative views on many political issues other than those directly involving labor organization. .... ( )
f. Founder of the American Federation of Labor. ...... ( )
g. Author of statement, "There is no right to strike against the public safety, by anybody, anywhere, any time." ...... ( )
h. Cofounder, along with John L. Lewis, of the CIO federation. .... ( )

a. (6). *b.* (1). *c.* (3). *d.* (9). *e.* (7). *f.* (3). *g.* (2). *h.* (4).

7. Insert the appropriate number, as in the preceding question, to indicate the federal act which contains the provision or prohibition described. Again, the same number may be used more than once.

The main features of the Landrum-Griffin Act, item (3) below, are outlined in footnote 4 in the text chapter. Note also item (8): description may fit none of the acts listed.

(1) Clayton Antitrust Act (1914).
(2) Fair Labor Standards Act (1938).
(3) Landrum-Griffin Act (1959).
(4) Norris-La Guardia Act (1932).
(5) Sherman Antitrust Act (1890).
(6) Taft-Hartley (Labor-Management Relations) Act (1947).
(7) Wagner (National Labor Relations) Act (1935).
(8) No federal act contains this provision.

a. Explicitly stated that workers have the right to form unions, to bargain collectively, and to engage in concerted activities for purposes of collective bargaining; set up machinery to protect exercise of these rights by workers. ( )
b. Included safeguards against misuse of union funds (e.g., prohibited excessive loans to union officers). .... ( )

c. Required unions to file regular financial reports, with stated penalty for noncompliance. .... ( )
d. Prohibited the union shop. .... ( )
e. Provided that the Attorney General may secure a court injunction to suspend strikes in "essential industries." . ( )
f. Established the National Labor Relations Board to act as watchdog against "unfair labor practices" on the part of employers. .... ( )
g. Vastly reduced the power of employers to obtain federal court injunctions as a weapon to break strikes or harass unions. .... ( )
h. Included a union member "Bill of Rights" (e.g., limiting power of unions to discipline their members). .... ( )
i. Stated that union activities were *not* to be considered a "conspiracy in restraint of trade" such as would violate the Sherman Antitrust Act. .... ( )
j. Sharply restricted the closed shop. .... ( )
k. Established an hourly minimum wage for most workers in occupations involving interstate commerce. .... ( )
l. Defined "unfair labor practices" on the part of unions. ( )
m. Prohibited unions from making loans to union officials.( )

a. (7). *b.* (3). *c.* (3). *d.* (8). *e.* (6). *f.* (7). *g.* (4). *h.* (3). *i.* (1). *j.* (6). *k.* (2). *l.* (6). *m.* (8).

8. Review also the following terms discussed in the text: local versus national unions; federation of unions; arbitration.

QUIZ: Multiple Choice

1. *In comparison with the power existing in member national unions, the power position of the AFL-CIO federation is* (1) equal or superior to that of the national unions, since it participates equally in the collective bargaining process; (2) superior to that of the national unions, since in most instances it receives a larger fraction of local union dues than does the national; (3) inferior to that of the national unions, since it relies on the nationals for financial support and does not participate in collective bargaining; (4) superior to that of the nationals, owing to its power to appoint the principal officers of the nationals; (5) not properly defined by any of the above descriptions.

2. *The term "industrial union" means* (1) the same thing as a trade union; (2) a trade union in manufacturing, as opposed to the service trades or agriculture; (3) a union with members in the same craft throughout industry; (4) a union whose membership is drawn from all or nearly all the workers in a given industry; (5) an organization of employers in an industry.

3. *Collective bargaining agreements are usually negotiated by* (1) the federation of national unions; (2) the local union, but increasingly with the assistance of the federation; (3) the local union, but increasingly with the assistance of the national union; (4) the national union, but increasingly with the assistance of the federation; (5) the national union, but increasingly with the assistance of the local union.

4. *In the United States by 1910, according to federal law,* (1) labor organizations were considered legal, provided their purpose or activity could not be construed as an attempt to raise wages; (2) all efforts on the part of labor to organize collectively (i.e., form unions) were still illegal; (3) labor organizations were considered legal, provided their activity did not involve a conspiracy in restraint of trade or a monopolistic restraint of trade; (4) all efforts on the part of labor to increase wages, whether they involved union organization or not, were still illegal; (5) all nonviolent collective bargaining activity was already entirely legal.

5. *"Exclusive bargaining agent" refers to* (1) the craft union principle early adopted by the AFL, whereby each union had complete jurisdiction over workers in its class, and two unions could not conflict in attempting to organize the same workers; (2) the union recognized by the National Labor Relations Board as exclusively entitled to represent all workers within the group concerned, in bargaining with management; (3) a provision in the Taft-Hartley Act which restrains the union from attempting to bargain on behalf of nonmembers; (4) the official who is designated by the union to negotiate with management on behalf of its members; (5) none of these.

6. *One of the important principles by which Samuel Gompers ran the AFL was that* (1) labor must learn to live within a capitalistic system and realize that it was unrealistic to expect "more and still more"; (2) wherever possible, member national unions should be organized by industry rather than by craft; (3) although greater emphasis should be placed on business unionism, pro-union government intervention in collective bargaining was to be sought through political action; (4) the autonomy of each member union with respect to its craft specialty must be clearly recognized; (5) although labor must learn to live with capitalism, in the long run effective business unionism would lay the basis for a philosophy of political action.

7. *The act generally considered the most important piece of legislation in American labor history, in the sense of marking a real turning point in that history, is* (1) the Landrum-Griffin Act (1959); (2) the Wagner Act (1935); (3) the Sherman Act (1890); (4) the Fair Labor Standards Act (1938); (5) the Walsh-Healey Act (1935).

8. *One of the duties of the National Labor Relations Board is to* (1) issue injunctions where needed to prevent strikes in "essential" industries; (2) prevent unions from engaging in "unfair union labor practices"; (3) see that the provision of the Taft-Hartley Act prohibiting the union shop is enforced; (4) enforce the federal minimum-wage law with respect to interstate commerce; (5) hold elections to see which union is entitled to act as collective bargaining agent for workers in a plant.

9. *If the President feels that a strike would endanger the nation's welfare, to suspend this strike he may* (1) apply the "essential industry" provision of the Wagner Act; (2) apply the "restraint of trade" provision of the Clayton Act; (3) apply the court injunction provision of the Taft-Hartley Act; (4) apply the "national emergency" provision of the Landrum-Griffin Act; (5) simply use the prestige of his office to prevent it, since there is no provision in any federal act which gives him any explicit power toward suspension.

10. *The AFL's opposition to the "industrial union" movement was due to* (1) conflict with the AFL business unionism principle; (2) the disapproval of John L. Lewis; (3) a belief that the rise of mass-production industries would make this movement obsolete; (4) conflict with the AFL exclusive-jurisdiction principle; (5) the rise of the Knights of Labor.

11. *The Taft-Hartley Act (1947), among other things,* (1) prohibited non-wage payments to union representatives by employers; (2) required unions to give 60 days' notice before any strike; (3) was for many years used by the courts to curb union formation and activity; (4) removed labor unions from the charge of being a "conspiracy in restraint of trade"; (5) established a Labor Relations Board charged with the duty of making sure that employers did not engage in "unfair labor practices."

12. *Which alternative in question 11 would be correct had that question referred to the Clayton Act (1914)?* (1). (2). (3). (4). (5).

13. *Which alternative in question 11 would be correct had that question referred to the Wagner Act (1935)?* (1). (2). (3). (4). (5).

14. *Which alternative in question 11 would be correct had that question referred to the Sherman Act (1890)?* (1). (2). (3). (4). (5).

15. *Which alternative in question 11 would be correct had that question referred to the Landrum-Griffin Act (1959)?* (1). (2). (3). (4). (5).

8 ECONOMIC ROLE OF GOVERNMENT: EXPENDITURE, REGULATION, FINANCE

1. *a.* Today, the total annual expenditure of the United States federal government—see text Table 8-2—is approximately *$(120 / 205 / 245 / 300 / 350 / 500)* billion annually.

The largest single item within this total, using the kind of summary breakdown employed in text Table 8-2, is *(interest on the public debt / national security / international affairs and finance / health, labor, welfare, and education)*. The present total annual expenditure on this item is approximately *$(60 / 80 / 100 / 120 / 140 / 160 / 180)* billion. Most of this outlay

goes to one program, namely, the _____

_____ program.

b. The second-largest item in this summary breakdown— again see Table 8-2—is *(interest on the public debt / national security / international affairs and finance / health, labor, welfare, and education)*. To reckon the total of outlays for past wars and preparation for possible future wars, we should add to this yearly cost of roughly $95 billion the annual costs of *(i)* veterans' benefits; *(ii)* a considerable part of interest on the public debt; and *(iii)* a considerable part of the expenditure on space research and technology. If we use a rough estimate of $45 billion for the applicable part of the total of these three items, then warfare expenditures—past and possible future— add up to somewhere around $140 billion annually. (It is considered appropriate to include in this total the greater part of interest on the public debt because so much of this debt represents money originally borrowed during, and to finance, World War II.)

---

a. 350; health, labor, welfare, and education; 160; Social Security. *b.* national security.

Some idea of the enormous increase in the size and importance of the federal government, within less than two generations, is to be gleaned by noting that in 1939, just before World War II: *(i)* total expenditure for national security was around $1 billion annually; *(ii)* the federal Social Security program did not exist at all; and *(iii)* other federal expenditures for health and welfare were of trivial importance. In sum, the federal government and its operations meant almost nothing in the everyday life of most people.

World War II changed all that. Ordinary citizens were now required to pay income taxes, to complete income-tax forms (a privilege hitherto reserved for the rich), and to meet a host of federal restrictions. Wartime rationing was temporary. But widespread federal taxation was not.

2. The development of the Social Security system was one important factor accounting for the continuing importance of the federal government in postwar years. The demand for wider coverage has grown: social security benefits—and deductions from wages and salaries to cover Social Security financing—have increased steadily. The "health, labor, welfare, and education" item is not only the biggest in the federal budget today; it is the item that has increased most spectacularly during the past few years. In the eighth edition (1970) of this text, the total for this item was given as $62.9 billion. In the ninth edition (1973), the figure was $99.1 billion. In the current edition (Table 8-2 again), it is $161.4 billion. That is, within a very few years, this outlay has *(almost doubled / considerably more than doubled / more than tripled)*.

The postwar rise in welfare outlays might have been offset by a sufficient decline in national-security expenditures. But this spending category did not fall at the close of World War II to anything like the expected level. Instead, "the cold war" began—and it was fought through the preparation of newly developed and horrendously expensive nuclear weapons. Beginning in the early 1950s, and continuing thereafter, the total of national-security spending persisted at levels that would have been literally incredible by the standards of 1939.

In recent years, this national-security spending has—by comparison with health and welfare—remained relatively stable: it has become institutionalized. It was increased by the Vietnam war—but not by any spectacular amount. Although that war is now ended, expenditures for national security seem more likely to climb gradually than to turn around and begin to decline.

---

considerably more than doubled.

---

3. Comparisons between the growth of the national-security spending total and the health-and-welfare total can be seriously misleading unless an important distinction is made between two kinds of government spending. The distinction is the same whether the level of government is federal, state, or local; but the two spending items just discussed illustrate it.

a. Chapter 2 in the text stressed *the law of scarcity:* the basic scarcity of *(productive inputs / money / consumer goods).* One of the two types of government spending is *that which buys goods and services.* Here, the law of scarcity is directly involved. In its purchases, the government *(competes / does not compete)* with private consumers. It is claiming the use of some part of the limited resource supply. Automobile manufacturers can and do make tanks. When the government places an order for tanks, men and machines must work on that order, whereas they might otherwise have worked to produce privately bought automobiles.

The example just cited—the manufacture and purchase of tanks—is clearly an example of governmental expenditure on *(national security / health and welfare).* Some people regard much of the $95-odd billion spent annually on national security as money largely wasted. Others think differently; but this dispute is not the issue here involved. In principle, *all* goods and services bought by governments are bought for the public's benefit. Nevertheless, when the government buys *any* good, whether a tank or a typewriter for a national park office, it is competing with private consumers by claiming the use of some part of the limited resource supply. Under full-employment conditions, private (nongovernmental) expenditures (for goods and services) and "public" or "social" (governmental) expenditures (also for goods and services) are competing alternatives for the use of the limited resource supply. So the choice between them can be illustrated by a diagram used extensively in text Chapter 2, and again in this chapter, namely the _____ diagram.

b. Much of the government's expenditure on health and welfare falls into a *different* category—and here we reach the distinction between the two kinds of government spending mentioned at the beginning of this question. Such health-and-welfare expenditures are largely *transfer* payments. They are outlays in which the government pays money, because it is considered in the national interest to do so, *without* exacting the supply of any commodity or service in return. An example would be *(purchase of a typewriter / payment of an unemployment benefit).* People within the societies of the Western world have increasingly demanded that government assume at least part of the responsibility for (i) sickness and accident, (ii) unemployment, and (iii) old age. (Moreover, as the text mentions, President Ford's 1975 tax cut for the first time provided payments to poor families with children.) The postwar rise in living standards has evidently prompted a belief that no individual or family should fall below some minimum level of income.

The term "transfer payments" applies because these outlays *(do not increase / increase)* the *total* of claims on the nation's limited productive-resource supply. Instead, they *transfer* some part of such claims from one person or family to another. If you must pay taxes to finance some veteran benefit, part of the claim you would otherwise have had on goods and services is transferred to someone else.

Some of these payments might be designated as charity payments. Most are not. One person may be admitted to a veterans' hospital, not because he or she is destitute, but because of war service in Korea or in Vietnam. Others may receive social security benefits because for years their paychecks were subject to social security deductions. However, these people give no *concurrent* service in return for the benefit claimed. And that is the definition of a government transfer payment—worth noting, for you will meet it again in Chapter 10—a payment for which the recipient gives no *concurrent* service in return.

---

a. productive inputs; competes; national security; production-possibility. *b.* payment of an unemployment benefit; do not increase.

---

4. Pick the *transfer payments* (one or more) from among the following: Payment made to:

(1) An older person in the form of a social security check.
(2) Someone otherwise unemployed for a low-priority, make-work job, such as raking leaves.
(3) A veteran, to finance his or her education, in return for services in the armed forces during an earlier period.
(4) An engineer, for a report considered unacceptable.

---

(1). (3).

---

5. In appraising the changing activities of government in the United States, the text lists five functions:
(1) Direct controls (regulations governing business, finance and banking, minimum-wage and maximum-hour labor laws, pure food and drug acts, etc.).
(2) Social consumption (roads, national defense, public parks, weather forecasting, etc.).
(3) Efforts to control inflation and prevent excessive unemployment through stabilizing fiscal and monetary policy.
(4) Governmental production (post office, hydroelectric-power generation, etc.).
(5) Welfare expenditures (social security, etc.).

Match each one of these five functions with one description below by inserting the appropriate number in the space provided. (Use each number only once.)

a. Never an important function at any level of government, and (except in World War II) hardly increased since the 1930s. .... ( )
b. Always a major governmental function, with one item within this category accounting for much of current federal spending; other items have risen markedly since the 1930s. .... ( )
c. A tiny item in the federal budget before the 1930s; now the single biggest element therein. .... ( )
d. "Policing" in this area expanded since the 1930s, although much had been done earlier. .... ( )

e. Not considered to be a federal governmental responsibility at all before 1932; now considered to be one of its most important responsibilities. ....( )

a. (4). *b.* (2). *c.* (5). *d.* (1). *e.* (3).

6. *a.* A government's "fiscal policy" means its policy as to the nature and money total of its *(expenditures / tax collections / expenditures and tax collections).*

b. Circle each of the following that would be regarded as a decision or action involving fiscal policy:
(1) An increase in the income-tax rate.
(2) A decision to finance an expenditure increase by issuing new government bonds.
(3) A decision to enter the nuclear-energy field by building plants to process uranium ore.
(4) An increase in transfer payments—specifically payments to the aged to cover medical expenses.
(5) A reduction in expenditure on armaments.

a. expenditures and tax collections. *b.* all: (1) through (5).

7. *a.* The choice between "social consumption" and "private consumption" is appropriately illustrated by a production-possibility curve because (pick one):
(1) Both kinds of consumption draw on the same scarce and limited supply of productive inputs.
(2) The kinds of inputs needed for social consumption are basically different from those needed for private consumption.

b. Most items within "social consumption" (government-supplied services) are things it would not be feasible to supply by charging each person a price and letting him buy the quantity he chooses. The factor which the text cites to explain this, and which it regards as common to most or all social consumption items, is this (pick one):
(1) The service is too big to be handled by private business, or if it were so handled, the result would be a monopoly, and the price charged would be too high.
(2) If this service is provided for any single person, it thereby accrues to others as well—the benefit cannot be restricted so as to be available to that person alone.

a. (1). *b.* (2).

8. *a.* If the importance of each level of government is ranked by the total of its expenditures on goods and services, then up until World War I, the three levels of government in the United States would have ranked in this way: federal government *(first / second / third)*, state governments *(first / second / third)*, local governments *(first / second / third)*.

b. Today's ranking would be federal *(first / second / third)*, state *(first / second / third)*, local *(first / second / third)*.

a. second; third; first. *b.* first; third; second.

QUIZ: Multiple Choice

1. *A government's "fiscal policy" would properly be defined as its policy with respect to* (1) the relation between the total of its purchases of goods and services and the total of its welfare payments; (2) the regulation and control of banking and credit; (3) the total and types of its expenditures, and the manner of financing these expenditures—taxation, borrowing, etc.; (4) that part of government operation whose services are sold to the public at a price per unit (e.g., the post office); (5) none of the above.

2. *Government transfer payments made to individuals are basically different from all other types of government expenditure in this respect:* (1) Being fully financed by taxation, they merely transfer money from one person to another. (2) They are always payments for which the recipient gives no concurrent service in return. (3) Receipt of this payment does not increase the recipient's total purchasing power. (4) They involve a "means test" (a check to ensure that without this payment the individual could not survive, or at least would suffer hardship). (5) They have no effect either on private production or on private consumption.

3. *A "production-possibility frontier" diagram can be used with respect to governmental activity to illustrate* (1) the impact on production that will result if a given increase in taxes is levied to finance a given spending program; (2) the choice between quantities of socially consumed goods and privately consumed goods, both of which must be produced out of the same supply of resources; (3) the various means that a government can employ to finance its expenditures, such as the choice between taxation and the issue of bonds; (4) the choice that government must make between its transfer payments and its other purchases of commodities and services; (5) none of the preceding.

4. *The nations which devote the largest fraction of their total national output or product to governmental outlays (according to the text) are* (1) the poorer or less developed nations with a strong orientation toward socialism; (2) the poorer or less developed nations, regardless of their orientation toward socialism; (3) the wealthy or developed nations with the strongest orientation toward socialism; (4) the wealthy or developed nations, regardless of their orientation toward socialism; (5) none of the above, since the fraction seems typically to be the same, regardless of the nation's stage of development or its orientation toward socialism.

5. *By "social consumption," as the term is used in this chapter, is meant specifically* (1) the consumption of goods produced by government factories or agencies rather than by private enterprise; (2) the consumption of goods produced by cooperative effort; (3) the provision of goods from that sector of the economy which has become explicitly socialist in economic organization; (4) the consumption of goods yielding no apparent satisfaction to the individual consumer, yet of immense utility to the whole of society; (5) the consumption of goods not bought through the price-and-market system, but instead paid for through taxation.

6. *The text chapter insists that—by reference to the basic economic principle of resource scarcity—there is a critical distinction to be made between two kinds of government expenditure. The distinction involves* (1) welfare expenditures versus transfer payments; (2) federal expenditures versus state or local expenditures; (3) items with a monetary value versus items that cannot be so valued; (4) transfer payments versus purchases of goods or services; (5) national security outlays versus expenditures for peacetime activity.

7. *The following payment made by a government would be classified as a "transfer expenditure": Payment* (1) of a rental to the owner of a building used for government purposes; (2) made to a consultant for a report, where the recommendations made therein were not adopted; (3) made to a former member of the armed forces, to finance university education; (4) made to a doctor for work in treating charity patients; (5) for shoveling snow made to a worker who has lost his job and would otherwise receive unemployment benefits.

8. *The common element to be found in most or all items included within "social consumption" is (according to the text) that* (1) the individual citizen has no sense of higher satisfaction or improved well-being as a result of them; (2) they have "external effects," and their benefits cannot ordinarily be confined to a single recipient; (3) they are goods or services not produced by private enterprise; (4) they are most effectively produced through specialization or division of labor, rather than by each person's trying to supply them for himself or herself; (5) they are items which, if produced by a private firm, would enable that firm to charge buyers an excessively high price.

9. *The largest single money item in the United States federal government's budget today is* (1) space research and technology; (2) national security; (3) health, labor, welfare, and education; (4) international affairs and finance; (5) interest on the public debt.

10. *The results of a government's transfer-payment program may resemble the results of a new tax program* (1) because it is reasonable to expect that either program would reduce the total output of goods and services; (2) since both activities represent receipts of money by the government and a means whereby it can finance its expenditures; (3) if the tax program falls heavily on the rich and lightly or not at all on the poor, so that it changes the after-tax distribution of income in favor of the poor; (4) because the object of either program may be to cut down on private consumer spending; (5) in no

respect, tax collections being a money inflow and transfer payments a money outflow for the government.

11. *Any highway that is built by the government and made available toll-free to the public furnishes an example of* (1) private consumption; (2) a transfer payment; (3) a welfare expenditure; (4) monetary policy; (5) none of the above.

12. *An area of federal government activity that has increased little or not at all in the United States in the past 50 years has been* (1) direct production of goods and services by government; (2) the use of fiscal policy to regulate the level of overall business activity; (3) the provision of unemployment insurance; (4) transfer payments; (5) governmental control over, and subsidies to, agriculture.

13. *A "welfare expenditure" means* (1) any purchase by government of a commodity or service; (2) a transfer payment; (3) an expenditure by government that results in a useful service being made available to the public; (4) an expenditure by government not financed by tax collections; (5) any payment made by the public to government to cover the costs of social consumption.

14. *A government may reasonably introduce a widespread program of transfer payments in order to* (1) create a surplus in its budget; (2) effect some change in the social decision on the question FOR WHOM goods are to be produced; (3) provide more social consumption; (4) move the economy's production-possibility curve outward and to the right; (5) reduce inflation.

15. *If the term "merit wants" is used in connection with government behavior, it means (according to the text) governmental activity in* (1) reducing or altering the autonomy of consumer choice in a free-market system by deliberately encouraging consumption of certain goods or services, discouraging or prohibiting the consumption of others; (2) framing its expenditure and tax programs so as to encourage individual incentive, thus moving the production-possibility frontier outward; (3) establishing a system of welfare payments to protect the public against the major hazards of unemployment, sickness, and accident; (4) identifying the particular goods and services to be produced via social consumption rather than via private consumption; (5) ranking the priority order in which particular projects are to be undertaken.

16. *A commodity (e.g., a typewriter) produced by a private corporation but bought by a government is counted in the statistics as part of government involvement and outlays* (1) by both capitalist and conventional socialist reckoning; (2) by capitalist reckoning only if that commodity is not freely available for use by any member of the public, although by socialist reckoning it would be counted regardless of such nonavailability; (3) by capitalist but not by conventional socialist reckoning; (4) by socialist reckoning only if that commodity is made freely available for use by any member of the public, and not even then by capitalist reckoning; (5) by neither capitalist nor conventional socialist reckoning.

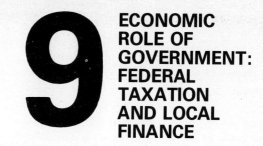

9 ECONOMIC ROLE OF GOVERNMENT: FEDERAL TAXATION AND LOCAL FINANCE

ONE QUESTION DOMINATES all discussion of taxation: *From whom shall taxes be collected?*

If the benefit from some government project accrued entirely to some identifiable group within the population, then it might be fair to argue that taxes collected to finance that project should come from the group that benefits; e.g., taxes for road building should come from those who use the road.

However, results of most expenditures are too diffused to allow application of this "benefit principle." As Chapter 8 pointed out, the essential property of most "socially consumed" goods is that benefit received *cannot* be regarded as flowing only to certain individuals and not to others.

Then what is a fair or equitable basis for distributing the burden of taxation? In particular, how is it to be distributed between rich and poor? This is a chronically recurring question; it explains the significance of the terms *regressive* and *progressive* taxes. You *must* learn the meaning of these two terms. A progressive tax thrusts most of its burden on people of above-average income. A regressive tax bears more heavily on poorer people. However, a tax is *not* progressive simply because it collects more money from a rich man than from a poor one. To establish whether a tax is regressive or progressive, you must (1) find the amount of tax typically paid at various income levels, and then (2) express this tax paid as a percentage of income. If these percentage figures *rise as income rises*—that is, if as income rises, the percentage of income paid in tax rises also—then the tax is progressive. If the percentage figures go *down* as you move to higher income levels, then the tax is regressive. If the percentage figure is pretty much the same at all income levels, then the tax is neither progressive nor regressive: it is "proportional."

1. In order to know whether a tax is progressive or regressive, it is *(essential / not strictly essential)* to know how much money it typically collects from individuals at different levels of income.

One tax is easily classified as to this progressive-regressive distinction, namely, the _____ tax. This tax is *(progressive / regressive)*.

essential; personal income; progressive.

2. *a.* A tax levied as 1 per cent on the first $5,000 of income, 2 per cent on the next $5,000, 3 per cent on the next $5,000, and so on would be *(progressive / proportional / regressive)*.
b. A tax of 10 per cent on all income except the first $1,000—that $1,000 being exempt from tax—would be *(progressive / proportional / regressive)*.
c. If it is true that (among cigarette smokers) people with a yearly income of $8,000 typically buy four packs of cigarettes per week, whereas people with an income of $16,000 typically buy six packs per week, then an excise tax of 10 cents per pack would be a *(progressive / proportional / regressive)* tax.

a. progressive. *b.* progressive. (This one is sneaky. The tax is *almost* proportional; but the tax, expressed as a percentage of income, goes up as income goes up. See the definition of "progressive" in the preceding introduction.)
c. regressive. The tax of 40 cents weekly is a higher fraction of $8,000 than 60 cents is of $16,000.

3. Sometimes it is not an easy matter to conclude whether a tax is progressive or regressive in nature. The tax on corporations' net income (profit) is one such.

Currently, this tax takes 22 per cent of the first $25,000 of corporate profit, and 48 per cent of all further profit. For a big corporation, $25,000 is a minor amount. So it is only a minor simplification to say that the tax is a flat 48 per cent of net income.

If corporations were living people, perhaps this could be designated as a proportional tax, for the rate is the same regardless of the profit amount (ignoring the minor first-$25,000 qualification). But corporations, not being human, do not feel the tax. Those who *do* feel it are their owners—i.e., the *(bondholders / shareholders)*. The tax is levied on earnings which belong to them. (NOTE: We assume, that is, that the corporate tax is a kind of income tax; it is a tax levied on the income accruing to the corporation's owners. There is one important reason why things may work differently; it is discussed in the next question. Here, we assume that the tax really is what it seems to be.)

Now the tax is still "proportional" in the sense that it is 48 per cent of your share of earnings, whether you own 1 share or

10,000. But remember that in taxation, the term "proportional" is intended to mean a tax which takes the same per cent of income at every income level, *right across the entire population.*

The critical point is that *only a fraction of the population owns corporation stock.* So the tax is a tax on a particular segment of the population.

Suppose all corporation stock is owned by poor people. (Never mind the fact that if they owned all that stock, they wouldn't be poor!) As a tax on the incomes of the poor, the corporate tax would be a *(progressive / regressive)* one.

Alternatively, suppose all the stock is owned by rich people. That would make the tax *(progressive / regressive).*

The facts are that some people in the lower income brackets own a little stock; many in the middle brackets do; but the great bulk of corporate stock is owned by people with above-average incomes. So the corporate tax is (subject to the one vital qualification discussed in the next question) held to be, on balance, *(progressive / regressive).*

---

shareholders; regressive; progressive; progressive.

---

4. Suppose the corporate tax rate is raised from 48 to (say) 55 per cent. But corporations respond to this tax increase by raising their prices just enough that their after-tax profit amount is unaffected. If so, they have *shifted* the tax, and the *incidence* of the extra tax falls on the *(corporations / corporations' customers).*

This raises the interesting possibility that most of the corporate tax, possibly even all of it, is not paid out of shareholders' incomes at all. It is passed on to other people via higher prices.

If a corporation's customers happened to consist almost entirely of people in the lower half of the income range, and if it *did* manage to shift the tax via higher prices, this would make the tax (with respect to this particular corporation, anyhow) *(progressive / regressive).*

Conceivably, the tax might be shifted in another way. Corporations, when this tax is loaded upon them, might just possibly manage to *(lower / raise)* the prices they pay for their inputs, such as labor.

There is a fair amount of evidence to suggest that at least part of the corporate tax is shifted via higher prices for the goods corporations sell. But the evidence is not all in; the issue is still being debated and explored.

The words "shifting" and "incidence" are important with respect to taxes; study their meaning. The government may require you to pay a certain tax; but you do not *really* pay it if, through the device of charging a higher price or paying a lower price, you make the tax come out of someone else's pocket. You have *shifted* the tax; and the true incidence of the tax is on the person out of whose pocket the money really comes.

Note how complicated problems of incidence may become, and how difficult it may be to establish what the facts are. A may manage to shift part of a tax to B; B in turn may shift some part of it along to C—and so on. The one tax with respect to which there is almost no problem of identifying incidence is the _____ tax.

---

corporations' customers; regressive; lower; personal income.

---

5. Some people complain that the corporate income tax entails "double taxation." They mean that after this income has been taxed, and part or all of the remainder is paid out in dividends, the dividends *(are / are not)* subject to personal income tax. This complaint assumes, of course, that the corporate tax *(is / is not)* shifted.

Insofar as the "double taxation" argument is valid, it applies *(to all of profit / only to that part of profit paid out as dividends / only to that part of profit which is retained undistributed).*

---

are; is not; only to that part paid out as dividends.

---

6. A tax imposed directly on an individual—i.e., whose amount payable is calculated by some factor such as size of income or value of certain of that person's assets—is designated as *(a direct / an indirect)* tax. A tax levied on a transaction, most commonly on the purchase and sale of a commodity, is *(a direct / an indirect)* tax. Some taxes, such as the corporate income tax, do not fall neatly into either the direct or indirect category.

Problems of determining real incidence are usually more difficult with *(direct / indirect)* taxes.

---

a direct; an indirect; indirect.

---

7. *a.* The "benefit received" taxation principle argues that the distribution of tax levies between citizen A and citizen B should be in proportion to the benefit each receives from the expenditures of government—a "pay for what you get" principle. Which of the following (one or both) may be considered a valid criticism of this principle?

(1) It assumes the particular tax in question can be linked to a particular type of expenditure. Especially where a government's expenditures are large and varied, this is often difficult to determine.

(2) Even if a particular tax can be linked to a particular type of spending (e.g., federal government spending on national defense), it is difficult to decide, in quantity terms, how much benefit rich citizen A derives from it, as compared with poor citizen B.

b. An alternative principle is that tax payments constitute a sacrifice by citizens, and that the distribution of sacrifices should meet certain standards of desirability. It isn't altogether easy to establish what "distribution of sacrifices" really means, but an interpretation outlined in the text is that (pick one):

(1) Every citizen should pay an equal amount of money in taxes, thus equalizing sacrifices.

(2) Taxes should be levied and collected in strict proportion to the amount of income received by citizens.

(3) The tax system should be used to change the distribution of incomes if needed, so that the after-tax distribution more closely approximates what is considered a socially desirable income distribution.

a. both (1) and (2). *b.* (3).

8. *a.* Both of the following are tasks accomplished by taxation. But which, according to the text, is the more fundamental task—(1) or (2)?

(1) Taxes raise the money needed to finance government expenditures.

(2) Taxes reduce private purchasing power and so free for government use the real resources needed to carry out government projects.

b. According to the text, taxation may also accomplish the following purpose(s) (choose either or both):

(1) Taxes may be used to change the pattern of income distribution.

(2) Taxes spread the costs of providing government services as equitably as possible among the people.

a. (2). *b.* both (1) and (2).

9. *a.* Disregarding social security taxes, the two taxes which yield the most revenue for the federal government, ranked in order of their revenue importance, are:

(1) _____ ;

(2) _____ .

b. The most important tax at the level of state government is the _____ tax; the most important tax at the level of local government is the

_____ tax.

c. The single most important expenditure item at the state government level is _____ .

a. (1) Personal income tax. (2) Corporation income tax. *b.* sales; property. *c.* education.

10. The difference between a *sales* tax and an *excise* tax is this: If the tax applies to *all* items sold, omitting only items

specifically named in the law as exempt, it is *(a sales / an excise)* tax. If, on the other hand, the tax applies *only* to commodities or services named in the law (e.g., liquor, cigarettes), it is *(a sales / an excise)* tax.

a sales; an excise.

11. *a.* A "value-added" tax is a tax imposed on each producing firm, on the value added to goods *at that stage of production.* If a textile firm buys $4,000 of yarn and other raw materials, and employs labor to weave these materials into cloth which it sells for $10,000, then the value which it added to its beginning materials was *$(4,000 / 6,000 / 10,000 / 14,000)*, and that is the amount on which the tax is levied.

Suppose another firm—a garment manufacturing firm—bought all of this cloth and paid the full $10,000 for it. It paid a further $2,000 for all its other raw materials, such as thread. It sold the resulting output of garments for $20,000. Then the value added by this firm would be *$(2,000 / 4,000 / 6,000 / 8,000 / 10,000 / 20,000)*.

Note that the "value-added" idea is discussed more fully in Chapter 10.

b. A "turnover tax," by contrast, is levied on each firm's *entire* sales amount. That is, the textile firm above would pay on *$(6,000 / 10,000 / 14,000 / 20,000)*, and the garment firm on *$(6,000 / 10,000 / 14,000 / 20,000)*. So the yarn used by the textile firm is taxed *(once / twice)*—once at the textile-firm level, once (as an ingredient in cloth) at the garment-firm level. This is not all, of course: The firm which spun wool or cotton into yarn must pay the turnover tax, and so must the retail firm which sold the finished garments.

The value-added tax likewise applies at each productive stage—but only on the value added at that stage. The cost of yarn is carefully excluded at the textile firm's stage; the cost of cloth is excluded at the garment firm's stage.

a. 6,000; 8,000. *b.* 10,000; 20,000; twice.

12. The *marginal* tax rate on income means the fraction or per cent*(of the last dollar of income that must be paid in tax / obtained by comparing total tax with total income).* In most countries, including the United States, the marginal personal–income-tax rate *(goes up / goes down / remains the same)* as income goes up.

of the last dollar of income; goes up.

QUIZ: Multiple Choice

1. *The corporation income (profits) tax is defined as a tax levied on* (1) all dividends paid to stockholders; (2) the value added to production by each corporation; (3) the corporation's total net sales; (4) additions to corporate retained earnings; (5) dividends paid plus undistributed profits.

2. *One type of income not subject to taxation at all under United States income-tax law is this:* (1) Income in the form of dividends from stock owned. (2) Income in the form of interest on corporation bonds owned. (3) Real income in the form of housing services from a house occupied by its owner. (4) Real income (i.e., any income not in the form of money) of any and all kinds. (5) Income in the form of capital gains.

3. *An argument made in favor of the corporation income tax is that* (1) it taxes only earnings above the normal return on invested capital; (2) without it, some fraction of corporation income may not be currently taxed at all; (3) on balance, it is a regressive tax; (4) it taxes the income received by bondholders; (5) it means double taxation of corporation earnings.

4. *The tax systems of state and local governments in the United States compare with the federal system as follows:* (1) They are both more progressive. (2) They are both more regressive. (3) The state system is more progressive than the federal, the local system less so. (4) The local system is more progressive than the federal, the state system less so. (5) None of the preceding statements is correct.

5. *The tax yielding the largest annual revenue for the federal government (disregarding social security withholdings from wages and salaries) is the* (1) personal income tax; (2) corporation income tax; (3) value-added tax; (4) excise tax on liquor and tobacco; (5) property tax.

6. *The tax on an income of $20,000 is $4,000. If this income were to rise to $22,000, the tax would rise to $4,800. The marginal rate of tax implicit in these figures is* (1) 20 per cent; (2) about (but not more than) 21 per cent; (3) more than 21 per cent, just under 22 per cent; (4) 40 per cent; (5) none of the preceding.

7. *A government introduces a new and very regressive tax. If a Lorenz curve is used to show the distribution of after-tax income, the effect of this new tax upon the Lorenz curve will be to* (1) push the curve up to a new and higher level; (2) cause it to bulge farther away from the diagonal line; (3) cause it to move closer to the diagonal line; (4) leave the curve unchanged; (5) perhaps do any of the above—impossible to tell from the information given.

8. *A relatively unqualified advantage of the property tax, from the standpoint of the local government imposing it, is this: It* (1) is steady in yield through prosperous and recession periods; (2) is very similar in effect to an income tax, property and income being so closely related; (3) inflicts little hardship upon property owners in a recession; (4) involves few problems of "equity" in taxing different property owners; (5) is not correctly described by any of these statements.

9. *A correct statement with respect to "capital gains" (e.g., profits made in stock-market transactions) in the United States would be that such gains are* (1) not taxed at all under present law; (2) taxed just as though they were any other form of income received; (3) taxed at a heavier percentage rate than other forms of income; (4) taxed as though they were regular income, but with an additional $600 exemption allowed; (5) not properly described by any of the preceding.

10. *A general sales tax, without any exempted commodities, is considered to be* (1) a progressive tax because it applies to luxuries as well as necessities; (2) a regressive tax because wealthy people spend a smaller percentage of their total income on taxed commodities, and hence the proportion of tax payments to income is greater for poor people; (3) a progressive tax because wealthy people spend more than poor people; (4) a regressive tax because more money is collected from a poor man than from a rich one; (5) a proportional tax because everybody pays the same tax percentage on each purchase.

11. *The correct definition of a "proportional" tax would be as follows: It is a tax so formulated that (taking the taxpaying population as a whole, or in terms of the typical taxpayer)* (1) the ratio of money tax amount collected to money income received is approximately the same at all income levels; (2) approximately the same amount of tax money is collected per taxpayer, regardless of that taxpayer's money income; (3) the percentage of money income collected in tax falls as the taypayer's income rises; (4) the total money amount of the tax levy increases as the money income level increases; (5) none of the preceding statements is necessarily correct.

12. *Which alternative in question 11 would be correct had that question referred to the correct definition of a "progressive" tax?* (1). (2). (3). (4). (5).

13. *Which alternative in question 11 would be correct had that question referred to the correct definition of a "regressive" tax?* (1). (2). (3). (4). (5).

14. *By the "incidence" of a tax is meant* (1) its tendency to fluctuate in total amount collected, as between boom and recession periods; (2) its relative importance in the budget of the government involved; (3) the extent to which payment can be avoided through one or more "loopholes"; (4) its burden, in the sense of identifying the people whose real income is actually reduced by reason of that tax; (5) the effect to which its imposition is likely to induce those who must pay it to work less, in an effort to avoid part of such payment.

15. *The essential difference between a value-added tax (VAT) and a turnover tax (TOT) is this: The VAT tax is levied on the firm's* (1) total net sales minus all value added by other firms at earlier production stages, whereas TOT is levied on the total increase in the firm's Net Worth for the period in question; (2) total net sales plus its production costs, whereas TOT is levied on its total net sales only; (3) total net sales minus all value added by other firms at earlier production stages, whereas TOT is levied on the firm's total net sales; (4) total net profit, whereas TOT is levied on its total net sales; (5) total net sales, whereas TOT is levied on its total net sales minus value added by other firms at earlier production stages.

THIS CHAPTER IS IMPORTANT, and must be approached carefully. There is a single basic idea hedged about by complications. The basic idea is simple. Each complication—if taken separately—is fairly easily mastered. The review questions following work accordingly: they start with the basic idea, then tackle the complications one by one. (Of painful necessity, this makes for an unusually lengthy sequence of such questions.)

The basic idea is that of *the national product:* the measure of a nation's total output for a given period (one year, usually).

Every nation uses its limited stock of manpower, machines, and materials to produce commodities and services. The money value of this total output, each item valued at the market price for which it sold or would sell, is the national product for that period. (Never mind about all the difficulties which this computation involves. Your task here is to grasp *the idea*, not to do the counting.)

1. Suppose, for example, that the national output consists of two commodities only: X, a consumer good, and Y, a capital good (some form of machine or tool needed in production). In 1976, just 500 units of X were produced and sold to consumers at a price of $2. Twenty units of Y were produced and sold to business firms, at price $10. Then the national product for 1976 would be $(500 / 800 / 1,000 / 1,200 / 1,500 / 2,000).

1,200.

---

2. Correctly speaking, this figure is *gross* national product. To produce this total output, the nation's existing stock of capital goods must have been to some extent used up or worn out during the year—that is, depreciated. Suppose the nation began the year with a stock of 100 Y-machines (assuming, for simplicity, that there is just this one kind of capital good involved). By the year's end, some few of these machines, the oldest, will have become completely worn out. And all the others will have moved just a little closer to the scrap heap.

Suppose the best-possible estimate of this 1976 depreciation (still using the question 1 example) is $50. (Remember from the Chapter 6 Appendix that depreciation *must* be an estimate; sometimes the best of estimates is not much better than a rough guess. There is no cash expenditure by the producing firm in question in a depreciation figure; it is just

an estimate of the extent of "wearing out" during the year.) The price of a new Y-machine being $10, it is *as though*, to produce the 1976 national product, 5 Y-machines, brand new at the year's beginning, had been completely worn out by the year's end.

The 1976 national-product figure of $1,200 included the value of the 20 new Y-machines produced. But to make these machines, and to make also the 500 units of consumer good X, the equivalent of 5 new Y-machines was totally used up. So the nation was not "better off" at the year's end by 20 machines—only by *(5 / 10 / 15)* machines.

With *gross* meaning "no allowance for depreciation," and *net* meaning "after allowance for depreciation," then this nation's gross national product (GNP) for 1976 was $1,200, and its net national product (NNP) was $*(1,000 / 1,050 / 1,100 / 1,150 / 1,200)*.

In the statistics for national product and national income, the phrase "capital consumption allowances" may be used instead of the word "depreciation."

15; 1,150.

To review:

▶ Gross national product (GNP) is a measure of the total output of goods and services produced in a given time period, usually one year, all valued at their market prices, without any allowance for depreciation.

▶ Net national product (NNP) is GNP minus a suitable allowance for depreciation (capital consumption).

3. There are certain conventional divisions of GNP and NNP figures. Most basic of these is the division between (a) what was not only produced but actually consumed during the year in question, and (b) what was produced during the year, not as goods for immediate consumption, but as an addition to the stock of capital goods.

This is the division between consumption goods (X-goods, in the question 1 example) and investment goods (Y-goods).

The consumption-goods total is the same figure in both GNP and NNP. The investment-goods figure in GNP is *gross* investment: total production of new capital goods *without* depreciation allowance. The investment figure in NNP is *net* investment: value of new capital goods produced *after* a deduction for depreciation. In the example above, the GNP of

$1,200 would divide between consumption of $(200 / 800 / 1,000 / 1,150 / 1,200) and gross investment of $(zero / 100 / 150 / 200 / 250 / 300). The NNP of $1,150 would divide between consumption of $(200 / 800 / 1,000 / 1,150 / 1,200) and net investment of $(zero / 100 / 150 / 200 / 250 / 300).

There are one or two other important divisions of the GNP and NNP totals. In particular, we soon must recognize that both of them include also a "government purchases" figure (the same figure in both). Such matters can be set aside just long enough to gain a little more overall perspective on national-product and national-income measures.

1,000; 200; 1,000; 150.

Like all developed nations, the United States relies overwhelmingly on the price-and-market mechanism. The vast majority of goods and services produced is supplied and bought for a market price. Indeed, that is what makes possible single dollar-value totals for GNP and NNP. In any less developed "subsistence economy," where much of total output does not go through the pricing mechanism, money figures for GNP and NNP are of uncertain value.

There are two notable exceptions:

1. "Social goods," discussed in Chapter 8, are produced through the agency of government. (These are the "government purchases" mentioned above.) They are not sold on the marketplace; instead, people pay for them through taxation.

2. A housewife supplies her family members with goods and services of great value. But ordinarily, even on her more difficult days, she does not think of setting a money price on each service she furnishes.[1]

It is best to begin by setting to one side these and other such exceptions, thinking of a society in which *every* good and service supplied is given a money price, and supplied through the medium of that price.

The price of any such item is the exact amount available for dividing up among all those who helped to produce and sell it. Because incomes are earned by making some contribution to production, the total value of what is produced ought to be the total value of incomes earned. Hence:

▶ To a first approximation, net national product is also national income. The two figures are opposite sides of the same coin.

We must say "to a first approximation," because a particular kind of government taxation causes the national-product and national-income totals to differ

slightly. But we have been setting aside the complications produced by government. And with such complications removed, NNP will equal national income *(NI)*.

This idea needs fuller development. There are just five earning categories within *NI*:

1. Wages and salaries—by far the biggest item.

2. Interest paid by business. (Anyone who has helped to finance a producing firm by lending it money is considered as having contributed to production. The amount of interest paid is the amount of income earned.)

3. Rental income—received by supplying land or other property to producing firms. The principle here is the same as with interest payments.

4. Profit remaining after paying wages and salaries, interest, and rents, consisting of:

(*a*) Corporation profits (belonging to corporation shareholders).

(*b*) Profits from unincorporated businesses—what the statisticians call "proprietors' income."

GNP and NNP can be considered (with government still momentarily left aside) the total output produced and supplied by business firms—"business firm" here meaning anything from a huge corporation to a single individual with a tiny business. The business accounting form which records a firm's output and sales for any given period is its *Income Statement* (Chapter 6 Appendix). The Income Statement reports also its payments in wages and salaries, interest, and so on. So it is helpful to examine the relation between GNP, NNP, and *NI* in Income-Statement terms.

4. *a.* A firm's Income Statement begins with the value of its sales for a given period—say, year 1976, sales amount $800. All costs incurred in making and selling these goods are then listed: depreciation, wages and salaries, interest paid, rents paid. Suppose depreciation to be $25, and the total of the other three items $650. What's left after deducting all such costs from the sales total is profit—in this instance, $(zero / 25 / 50 / 75 / 100 / 125 / 150).

(You are not supposed to notice, drawing on your memory of the Chapter 6 Appendix, that this Income Statement omits mention of "raw materials bought" as an operating cost.[2] This is deliberate: "value added" will be discussed a few questions farther along. For the moment, assume that our firm buys nothing from any other firm. It handles the entire production process, start to finish, by itself.)

The initial sales figure of $800 was this firm's contribution to GNP. Deduct depreciation, and its NNP contribution is $(700 / 725 / 750 / 775). The *NI* figure is the total of wages and salaries, interest paid, rents paid, and profit remaining. So the

---

[1] On this matter of the value of housewives' services, see Appendix question 1a, p. 75.

[2] Also omitted: the "beginning and closing inventory" adjustments. They too will be picked up later. Nor is there any mention of taxes, since we have not yet brought government items into the picture.

NI figure here is $(700 / 725 / 750 / 775)$. Hence *NI* is *(less than / equal to / greater than)* NNP.

b. Notice that *profit is the residual item which makes things come out even.* Had our firm paid out wages, interest, and rents totaling $775, its profit (allowing for depreciation) would have been $(zero / 25 / 50 / 75 / 100)$. *NI* would *(still / no longer)* be $775. That is, *NI* would *(still/no longer)* equal NNP.

---

a. 125; 775; 775; equal to. *b.* zero; still; still.

Our first rapid survey of the national-income and -product accounts is completed. Various complications remain to be recognized—mostly arising out of government expenditure and taxation. With all such government items set aside, what has been said is summed up in Fig. 10-1. Its three columns correspond to the three measures discussed: GNP, NNP, and *NI*. The GNP column divides between Gross investment and Consumption; NNP between Net investment and Consumption; and *NI* divides into the five income categories. NNP differs from GNP only by the measure of Depreciation. *NI* is exactly the same as NNP—although when we come to recognize taxation, we shall find that one set of taxes causes *NI* to fall short of NNP, just as (because of depreciation) NNP falls short of GNP.

Study Fig. 10-1 and the material preceding it until you feel you have a fair grasp of the ideas involved. Now there are complications to master. They can seem painfully difficult unless you recognize them for what they are: necessary adjustments (most of them fairly small) to be made within a framework of basic ideas.

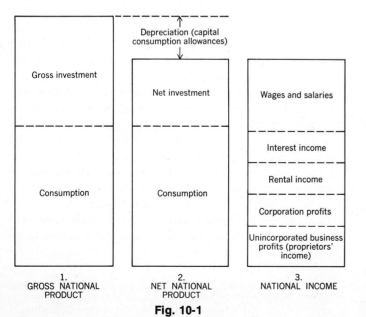

1.
GROSS NATIONAL PRODUCT

2.
NET NATIONAL PRODUCT

3.
NATIONAL INCOME

Fig. 10-1

Figure 10-2 (next page) is an extended version of Fig. 10-1. You have already mastered almost half of this larger (and seemingly involved) diagram: its three left-hand columns correspond to those of Fig. 10-1—save for only two changes: GNP and NNP now include a "Government purchases" block, and *NI* now falls short of NNP by reason of "Indirect business taxes."

5. *a.* All goods and services purchased for the public through the agency of government (federal, state, or local) count in GNP and NNP—assuming they were produced within the year in question. Many such goods will have gone through the market system in that they were produced by a private firm and sold to a government. But—save for a few items like *(national defense / post office services)*—they are not sold to the public for a price per unit. They are Chapter 8's "social goods"; the public *(gets them entirely free / pays for them via taxation)*.

b. All these goods and services enter the GNP and NNP totals *valued at the price the government paid for them.* A judge's legal services are valued at the salary paid that judge; the production of a new typewriter is valued at the price the government paid the typewriter-manufacturing corporation.

Incomes earned via production of such government-purchased goods and services are *(counted / not counted)* in *NI*: as the GNP and NNP columns grow by reason of government purchases, the *NI* column *(grows also / does not grow)*.

You can well argue that GNP and NNP do not need this third component, since every cent of "government purchases" should count either as consumption (e.g., services furnished by a policeman in protecting the public) or as investment (e.g., construction and purchase of some long-lived item like a new highway). But the Government-purchases category is kept separate, largely because government statistics are not kept so as to make possible a meaningful division between consumption and investment within this category. (And it is most helpful analytically to have it kept separate, as we shall see on reaching Chapter 13.)

c. For inclusion in GNP and NNP, there *must* be a good or a service currently produced. Hence, one important category of federal expenditure (and to a lesser degree, of state and local expenditure) is *not* included: payments under the Social Security program and the like. These are "transfer payments" (see Chapter 8, question 3*b*, p. 56). The recipient of such a transfer payment, by definition *(must give something / does not give anything)* concurrently in return.

d. Suppose that, in addition to the $1,200 in private purchases of question 1, we had to recognize government expenditure on goods and services totaling $400, and health and welfare expenditures (payments made to social security beneficiaries) of $100. If depreciation is still $50, then GNP would now be $(1,200 / 1,250 / 1,550 / 1,600 / 1,700)$, and NNP would be $(1,200 / 1,250 / 1,550 / 1,600 / 1,650)$. The required increase

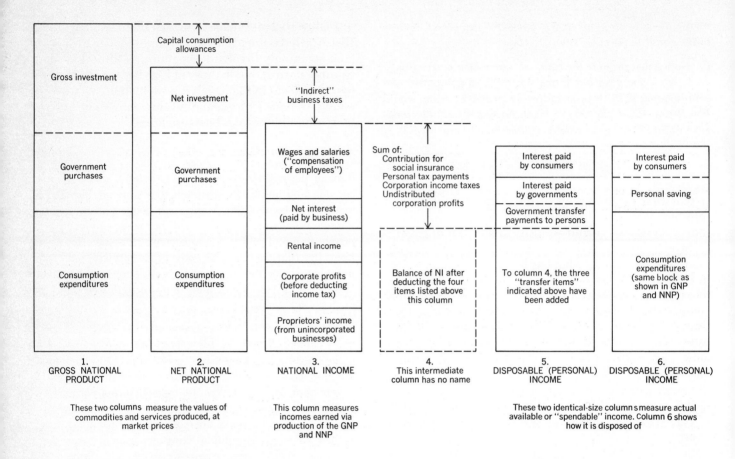

Block

Fig. 10-2

Labels within figure:

Capital consumption allowances

Gross investment

Net investment

"Indirect" business taxes

Government purchases

Government purchases

Wages and salaries ("compensation of employees")

Sum of:
Contribution for social insurance
Personal tax payments
Corporation income taxes
Undistributed corporation profits

Interest paid by consumers

Interest paid by consumers

Net interest (paid by business)

Interest paid by governments

Personal saving

Consumption expenditures

Consumption expenditures

Rental income

Government transfer payments to persons

Corporate profits (before deducting income tax)

Balance of NI after deducting the four items listed above this column

To column 4, the three "transfer items" indicated above have been added

Consumption expenditures (same block as shown in GNP and NNP)

Proprietors' income (from unincorporated businesses)

1.
GROSS NATIONAL PRODUCT

2.
NET NATIONAL PRODUCT

3.
NATIONAL INCOME

4.
This intermediate column has no name

5.
DISPOSABLE (PERSONAL) INCOME

6.
DISPOSABLE (PERSONAL) INCOME

These two columns measure the values of commodities and services produced, at market prices

This column measures incomes earned via production of the GNP and NNP

These two identical-size columns measure actual available or "spendable" income. Column 6 shows how it is disposed of

---

(from the original GNP of $1,200) would be in *(GNP only / GNP and NNP, not NI / all of GNP, NNP, and NI)*, and the amount of this increase would be $*(100 / 400 / 500)*.

---

a. post office services; pays for them via taxation.
b. counted; grows also. *c.* does not give anything.
d. 1,600; 1,550; all of GNP, NNP, and *NI*; 400.

---

6. Consider now the "Indirect business taxes" which, in Fig. 10-2, cause *NI* to fall short of NNP.

There are two kinds of taxes. One is epitomized by the personal income tax. It is levied on, and paid out of, income; and there is little doubt that the burden of this tax rests on the person who must pay it.

But consider another tax: a property tax on business buildings or land. Is this tax ultimately paid by the owners of that business firm, via a reduction in profit earned? More probably, it is paid by the firm's customers via an increase in the price charged for the firm's product.

Consider still another tax: an excise tax on cigarettes. The cigarette-manufacturing firm pays that tax to the government. But cigarette firms "shift" the tax, or at any rate a good part of it, by raising the price of cigarettes.

The important point here is that the items entering into GNP and NNP are valued *at market price*. Most taxes levied on business—property taxes, excise taxes—almost certainly do elbow their way into market price, at least in part, probably in full. The GNP and NNP totals are intended as the measure of a certain volume of real production, valued at its market price. This market-price value must *(be less than / exceed)* the total of money incomes earned from that volume of real production, because of the business taxes which work their way into market price. Apart from depreciation, already taken account of in NNP, it is almost exactly correct to say that such "indirect taxes" mark the only difference between the dollar value of what is produced and the dollar total of what is earned. ("Almost exactly correct," and not "exactly correct," because if you look in the *Survey of Current Business*, the monthly publication in which the Commerce Department reports all the national-product and -income figures, you will find three small items,[3] other than indirect business taxes,

---

[3]They are:
a. The "statistical discrepancy." The Commerce Department collects its figures from both production and earnings sides; they do not come out exactly equal. Considering the obvious difficulties in collecting complete and accurate data, it is remarkable that this

which differentiate *NI* from NNP. They are of minor import-ance, and should be disregarded completely in a first approach to this detail-filled subject.)

The national-income statisticians count *any tax levied on a business firm*—with one important exception—as an "indi-rect business tax" which marks a difference between total NNP and total *NI*. Such taxes are assumed to be "shifted" by the business firm, via an increase in market price.

The one important exception is the corporation income (profits) tax. This is treated as a tax *not* shifted, as a tax on shareholder income.[4] Hence it *(is / is not)* included among the "indirect business taxes."

---

exceed; is not.

National income is a useful concept. For example, the figures within it will give you at least a rough comparison between the total of incomes earned through personal effort and the total of those obtained through ownership of property. But for many purposes, national income is less interesting than *disposable income:*

▶ Disposable income is a measure of the total of in-comes which people can actually dispose of (spend or save) as they wish.

In strict Department of Commerce terminology, it is "disposable personal income" *(DPI)*. But it has become customary to abbreviate this, as the text does, to "dis-posable income" *(DI)*.

DI and *NI* are closely related. But they differ for two reasons. First, *NI* includes only *earned* income (as defined—earned by making some contribution to cur-rent production). There are some other money receipts whose recipients most certainly consider them income. Second, national income is *total* earned income. For several reasons, "take-home pay" (which is roughly the

idea which "disposable income" seeks to convey) is *less than* total income.

The sole task remaining with respect to Fig. 10-2 is to move from *NI* to *DI*. We start with *NI,* and (*a*) make the deductions required to get down to "take-home pay" (question 7), and then (*b*) add the "other forms of income" which *NI* excludes (question 8).

7. The four required deductions are listed above Column (4) in Fig. 10-2. The first two (Contributions for social insur-ance and Personal tax payments) are obvious: your salary check will be less than your total earnings by reason of such deductions. ("Personal tax payments" include not only the federal income tax but other taxes levied on individuals—e.g., local government property taxes.[5])

The third and fourth deductions pertain entirely to corpo-ration profits: they bring such profits down to the level of dividends actually received by shareholders. This dividend total is less than the profits total for two reasons: (*a*) The corporate income tax must be paid out of profit. (*b*) Corpora-tions do not distribute all of their after-tax profit as dividends. (Undistributed profits are the "additions to retained earn-ings" of the Chapter 6 Appendix.)

So if before-tax corporation profits were $100, if the total corporate tax was $50, and dividends were $20, then undistri-buted corporate profits must have been $*(10 / 20 / 30 / 40 / 50)*. Disregarding social insurance contributions and personal tax-es, the amount to deduct from *NI* in moving toward *DI*—that is, the total amount to be deducted from before-tax corporate profits in order to get *DI* in the form of dividends—would be $*(40 / 50 / 60 / 70 / 80 / 90)*.

If *NI* is $600, social insurance contributions are $15, per-sonal tax payments are $120, and corporate taxes and undis-tributed profits are as stated above, then the size of Column 4 in Fig. 10-2 would stand for a figure of $*(285 / 315 / 385 / 420 / 495)*.

30; 80; 385.

---

8. What's left after deduction from *NI* of the four items just discussed is Column (4) in Fig. 10-2. All that remains, in order to reach *DI*, is to add three "nonearned income" items. In Column (5), these three items are stacked on top of Column (4). Column (5) is *DI* [and so is Column (6)].

Think of these three items as being added to Column (4) one by one, starting with the bottom one, "Government trans-fer payments to persons."

a. A typical government transfer payment here would be a $50 social security check paid to a retired worker. Such an expenditure by government *(would / would not)* be included

---

discrepancy should be so small in comparison with the totals involved.

b. "Business transfer payments," to make an allowance for such things as uncollectible debts.

c. "Subsidies less current surplus of government enterprises," an adjustment needed because of such things as the post office, where the price charged for services does not necessarily match the cost of providing those services.

[4]This handling is open to dispute; see Chapter 9, question 4, p. 60, for a brief discussion of possible shifting of the corporation income tax. However, the preparation of statistics cannot be held up until *all* the truth becomes available. The rule here is the rule that must be adopted in any decision-making situation: You balance up the available evidence pro and con as best you can, then you make a decision. All such decisions have their arbitrary element; there is always some contrary evidence that must be ignored.

[5]The Commerce Department also includes in this item some "non-tax payments to government"; these are of minor importance.

in the "government purchases" sector of GNP and NNP. It (*would / would not*) be included in the *NI* total.

Although this $50 does not count as earned income (as earlier defined), the recipient considers it income; most or all of it will be spent on consumption.[6] So it must be included in *DI* (the total of "spendable income") regardless of whether it was earned income or not.

Hence, to the dollar figure represented by the size of Column (4) in Fig. 10-2, we must (*add / subtract*) the total of such government transfers.

b. The second block from the top of Column (5) is "Interest paid by governments." If you own a government bond, you will count interest received thereon as part of your income. In the statisticians' eyes, this is *not* part of *NI*. But it must certainly be included in *DI* (again, because *DI* is the total of "spendable income"). It is handled exactly as the social security payment of part *a* above was handled.

The only interest payments counted in *NI* are those made to individuals *by business firms*. The omission of government-paid interest is open to some dispute. The somewhat paradoxical result which emerges is that if you own a corporation bond or debenture, you are considered as having helped to produce this year's GNP and NNP; your interest is counted in *NI* as your earnings from your help in production. But interest you receive on any government security (*is / is not*) treated as income from production. It is a transfer payment. However, it (*does / does not*) count as part of *DI*.

The reasoning here is that the total amount of governmental debt—hence the amount of interest paid out by governments—bears little relation to the amount of goods and services produced through the agency of government. The best supporting argument is the federal debt. Most of it was incurred during World War II; the debt grew enormously during that war, and doubtless contributed to production at that time. But the war is part of history now. Today, the total output of goods and services produced through the agency of government would presumably be much the same were the public debt much smaller or much bigger.

When statistics must be published, rules must be set for their construction. Sometimes these rules contain an arbitrary element (as already noted regarding the corporation income tax). On your first approach, complications such as this one are of minor importance. Just note that any receipt of interest paid by a business firm (*is / is not*) considered part of earnings from production; if a government pays interest (or if a consumer does—an item still to be considered), it is a transfer payment.

[Notice, though, that government's interest payments are, in the statistics, kept separate from the other government transfer payments: they get a little block of their own in Column (5). It is almost as though the Commerce Department's conscience were not entirely clear on this issue; it segregates such interest payments from the other transfers.]

c. Finally, the top small block in Column (5): "Interest paid by consumers." If someone has borrowed from you in order to finance some consumption purchase, you count any interest paid you on this loan as part of your *DI*. The total of such interest payments is recorded here. NOTE AGAIN: It is exclusively interest *on consumer loans*. As already stated, the Commerce Department handles loans to business firms for the financing of production differently; the total of these business-interest payments is one of the blocks in Column (3); what's left of the total after personal tax payments is in Column (4), and consequently in Column (5)'s large bottom block.

Thus interest on *consumer* loans is ignored up to and including Column (4). But (like items *a* and *b* in this question) it's spendable income. So it must go into *DI*; hence the small block at the top of Column (5).

Exactly this same consumer-interest block shows up at the top of Column (6) as well. One section of the consuming public borrows and pays interest; another section lends, and gets this same interest. *Both* Columns (5) and (6) measure the *DI* total; so this consumer-interest block must go in both. [The difference between the two columns is that (6) records what consumers *do* with their income; this we'll consider in a moment.]

For the consuming public as a whole, this consumer-interest thing is an out-of-one-pocket-and-into-another transaction. The handling is a bit clumsy; again, the item is controversial. (Presumably the Commerce Department wanted to have a record of the total of such consumer-interest payments, and found this the only way to work it in.) But the item is minor, and your policy should be to accept Commerce's decision philosophically and with stern fortitude. (But remember it: it just might be useful to know how such interest payments are handled.)

Question 7 used at its close an example in which *NI* was $600 and the four deductions from *NI* were specified. Using the same figures, and assuming the totals of interest paid by consumers, interest paid by governments, and other transfer payments to be $20, $15, and $25 respectively, then the amount of *DI*—Column (5) or Column (6)—would be $(*445 / 480 / 500 / 505*).

---

a. would not; would not; add.   *b.* is not; does; is.   *c.* 445.

---

9. There are just two things to do with disposable income: Spend it on consumer items, or save it. Personal saving is—by definition—that part of *DI* which is *not* spent on consumption goods or services. So Column (6) in Fig. 10-2 shows what

[6]Don't get mixed up by thinking that if this $50 is spent on consumption goods, the transfer payment really does sneak into GNP and NNP, via the back door of "consumption." Keep your transactions separate. One transaction is the transfer payment by government to the individual; it doesn't count at all in GNP and NNP. *Another* transaction, following this payment, is the consumption expenditure. This *does* count: $50 in GNP and NNP as the purchase of part of the current output of consumption goods; $50 in *NI* as the earnings of those who produced those consumption goods.

people *do* with *DI:* how much in total they spend on consumption, and how much in total they save.[7] (Technically, that "Interest paid by consumers" makes for a third way to dispose of income. But it's a tiny item by comparison with the other two. For almost all purposes, it's sufficient to say that income received is disposed of in just two ways: spent on consumer goods, or saved.)

The "Consumption expenditures" block within Column (6) is exactly the same block as those within Columns (1) and (2)—GNP and NNP.

10. On your first reading, skip this material and move on to question 11. The purpose of the lengthy outline preceding is to take you through national-income and -product material in just enough detail that you can interpret the statistics found in the *Survey of Current Business.* The two items briefly discussed below appear within those statistics; you may wonder what they mean. But both are of rather minor importance, and should be disregarded on a first survey.

Personal Income. The Commerce Department's full name for what we have called disposable income is "disposable personal income." Commerce uses also the term "Personal income"—not quite the same thing. Personal income is a way station on the journey from *NI* to *DI.* It almost reaches *DI;* but it does *not* exclude personal tax payments. *DI* is by far the more useful concept. But there is a quickly published Personal Income statistical series which is often consulted as an indicator of the trend of the more slowly available *DI* series.

Inventory Valuation Adjustment. The *Survey of Current Business* statistics include an "Inventory valuation adjustment" associated with corporate profits. By conventional business accounting methods, a corporation's profit may include a small amount of "inventory profit"—profit not from sales but due to an increase in the market price of raw-materials inventories. The Commerce Department eliminates this ingredient by making the "valuation adjustment" (which is sometimes a negative figure). Do not worry about this item, which is too complicated to consider in the first approach.

11. This question asks you to compute (for three different situations) GNP, NNP, *NI,* and *DI* totals by fitting together bits and pieces of information. The key is Fig. 10-2. Every line in the table following matches an item within that diagram. Your task is to find enough figures that you can build one complete column (GNP, NNP, *NI,* or *DI*), then work to other columns.

The figures are billions of dollars, and refer to some year such as 1976. An "x" opposite any item means that its value is not given you.

[7]The statistics do not record, and are not intended to record, what people *do* with their saving—i.e., buy securities with it, put it in the bank, hide it in the mattress, etc. We shall meet this topic in the next few chapters.

Do at least one of these problems and if your time can possibly permit, do all three. Working this type of problem is most useful in gaining familiarity with national-product and -income figures.

	Problem		
	a	*b*	*c*
Capital consumption allowances	10	25	10
Consumption expenditures	100	180	x
Contributions for social insurance	0	10	5
Corporation income taxes	15	15	10
Corporate profits before taxes	x	x	50
Govt. purchases of goods and services	50	x	50
Govt. transfer payments to persons (other than interest payments)	5	15	15
Gross investment	x	x	55
Indirect business taxes	20	30	40
Interest paid by consumers	10	5	5
Interest paid by governments	5	10	5
Net interest (paid by businesses)	x	x	10
Net investment	50	x	x
Personal saving	x	40	30
Personal tax payments	15	25	20
Proprietor's income (from unincorporated businesses)	x	x	20
Rental income	x	x	20
Undistributed corporation profits	10	5	10
Wages and salaries	x	x	250

For each problem, compute:

	a	*b*	*c*
Gross national product	___	___	___
Net national product	___	___	___
National income	___	___	___
Disposable (personal) income ..	___	___	___

a. The only column you can immediately fill is NNP; for this you have consumption (100), government (50), and net investment (50). The total of these makes an NNP of 200. Add depreciation (10) to reach GNP. The various items needed to move from NNP to *NI* and to *DI* are all given.

b. Here you can start only with *DI;* but you have consumption (180), personal saving (40), and consumer interest payments (5); so *DI* is 225. From here, work backward to *NI,* NNP, and GNP.

c. This one requires you to start with *NI;* you have all the five categories of "earnings" needed to fill out this column.

	a	*b*	*c*
Gross national product	210	305	400
Net national product	200	280	390
National income	180	250	350
Disposable income	160	225	330

12. Using the same data furnished in question 11, compute—if you can—the total of the following (if the data supplied are insufficient and you cannot compute it, put an x in the space):

(1) Personal saving (out of *DI*) in problem *a* . . . . _____

(2) Consumption expenditure in problem *c* . . . . _____

(3) Gross investment in problem *a* . . . . _____

(4) Net investment in problem *b* . . . . _____

(5) Dividends paid out by corporations in problem *c* _____

(6) Government surplus or deficit in problem *c* . . . . . _____

(NOTE: Government's surplus or deficit here is simply the difference between total tax collections and other receipts and total money outlays. Remember that "contributions for social insurance" count as a government receipt.)

---

(1) 50; (2) 295; (3) 60; (4) x; (5) 30; (6) surplus of 5. If part (5) gave you trouble, remember that the total of corporation profits can be divided in three ways only: corporation taxes, dividends, and addition to retained earnings (this last meaning the same thing as "undistributed profits"). So if you know the total and any two of the three, you can compute the third.

---

13. One statistical problem is: How is the dividing line between consumption and investment drawn? What goes into the "Consumption expenditures" category of GNP and NNP, and what into "Gross (or Net) investment"?

Ideally, the consumption figure should measure the goods and services not only produced during that year, but actually consumed during the year (so that they were gone by the year's end). But there is no possible way of measuring this "true consumption." The statisticians must content themselves with recording *what consumers bought*. Clothing, for example, may last much more than a year; but purchase of a new dress or suit is still treated as consumption during the year in which it was made and bought.[8]

Items consumed immediately or almost immediately after purchase (bread, for example) pose no problem. As to those which last (say) 2 or 3 years, the interpretation of consumer purchases as "true consumption" still works fairly well, assuming that what is bought is pretty much a replacement for what is worn out through use. However, one item demands different treatment: *housing*. A house is far and away the longest-lived item a consumer ordinarily buys; it is typically

the biggest purchase a person ever makes. It would be ridiculous to say that a house built in 1976 is fully "consumed" by the end of 1976.

The statisticians handle this by saying: A house is an investment good, not a consumer good. It is a kind of machine for providing consumer services. What *should* be counted as consumption in 1976 GNP and NNP is the *service* which the house supplies—and indeed, if the house is rented, there is a market-price measure of this service.[9]

With every house treated as a service-producing machine, the services supplied by that house are thus counted as consumption within GNP and NNP, valued at the market price of such services (rental value) for each year of its life that it is occupied. In the year it was *built*, the full construction value of the house is counted also—but as an investment item, not as consumption.[10]

a. Suppose a house is built in the first half of 1976 and sold for $30,000. It is rented for the remainder of the year, total rental for the 6 months being $2,000. Depreciation for this same period is estimated at $200. In the 1976 statistics, the proper entries for this house would be: Gross investment, $(*zero* / 200 / 2,000 / 29,800 / 30,000); Net investment, $(*zero* / 200 / 2,000 / 29,800 / 30,000); Consumption expenditures, $(*zero* / 200 / 2,000 / 29,800 / 30,000).

b. Hence the total entries in 1976 GNP and NNP, with respect to construction and use of this house, would be: GNP, $(*29,800 / 30,000 / 31,800 / 32,000*); NNP, $(*29,800 / 30,000 / 31,800 / 32,000*).

---

a. 30,000; 29,800; 2,000 *b.* 32,000; 31,800. (The GNP figure must be gross investment plus consumption; the NNP figure, net investment plus consumption.)

---

14. There are three categories within "investment goods."

[8]Consumer items made during the year but not yet bought are dealt with in question 14.

[9]If the house is owner-occupied, the rental value of its services must be estimated. (This is another exception to the general rule that goods and services go through the market mechanism.) Such an estimate of the total value of housing services for owner-occupied houses goes into each year's "Consumption expenditures" for GNP and NNP.
[10]Is it double counting to include in the figures both the original purchase value of the new house and the value of the services that it supplies? Yes and no. The same is true of any other investment item—a machine or a factory building. (The rent of a factory building works its way into the market price of the item produced therein. The use of a machine inside the factory does the same thing.) The key factor here is *depreciation*. *Gross* national product, which makes no allowance for depreciation, *does* double-count. However, in *net* national product, the original value of the house is gradually subtracted from the national product, year by year, via depreciation, until (at the end of its life) the entire original purchase value of the house has been deducted. All that remains is the total value of the services which that house supplied. (Question 3 in the "Quiz: Other" section covers this point.)

(A fourth category, of minor importance, is left aside for now.[11]) These three are:

(1) New business and industrial buildings, machinery, and equipment produced

(2) New housing constructed (private residences and apartment houses)

(3) Increases in inventories of partially or wholly finished goods.

Category (1) is what we ordinarily think of as "investment goods." Category (2) has been covered in question 13.

If any firm has a bigger physical inventory of its product (partly or wholly finished) at the end of the year than it had at the year's beginning, then the value of its additional inventory must count as part of investment for that year.

Suppose a shirt manufacturer had a $3,000 inventory of shirts on hand at the start of 1976 and a $4,000 inventory at its close. (No problem of style or price change is here involved; the firm just has more shirts on hand, as yet unsold, than it had a year ago.) The fact that its inventory is up by $1,000 means that this firm must have (*sold more than it manufactured* / *manufactured more than it sold*). (In the extreme case, you could think of the firm as, in 1976, making shirts worth $1,000, and not selling a single shirt.)

The essence of investment in *all* its various forms is: production for *future* benefit. A newly finished machine tool yields no direct consumer satisfaction whatsoever. It is built to yield *future* benefit; it is expected to contribute toward consumer-good production *in the future,* throughout its coming 5-year or 10-year life. A new house counts within investment for the same reason.

Our shirt firm's additional inventory must receive the same treatment. It made $1,000 worth of shirts in 1976 which it hadn't yet sold. The shirts it *did* sell count as part of consumption in the regular way. The shirts it made but *didn't* sell must also go into GNP and NNP (because they were made in 1976). But (because they weren't sold) they do not go into consumption. They are included in investment (because they will be consumed *in the future,* presumably *next* year).

This inventory rule must work both ways. Had this firm's beginning inventory been $4,000 and its closing inventory $3,000, then we would include a figure of (*minus* / *plus*) $(*1,000* / *3,000* / *4,000*) within (*consumption* / *investment*).

Note that this is the same "beginning and closing inventory" matter discussed in the course of the Chapter 6 Appendix on business accounting—see questions 8–11, pp. 44–46.

---

manufactured more than it sold; minus; 1,000; investment.

---

[11]This fourth and minor item is "*foreign* investment." The Commerce Department treats this as a separate (and fourth) block within GNP and NNP, calling it "Net exports of goods and services," or "Net foreign investment." As with various other small (and potentially confusing) items, this seems best left to one side for now. It is briefly discussed in the chapter Appendix.

15. *a.* Could a country's net investment for any given period ever turn out to be a negative figure? If you can think of any reason why it could, don't write down the reason; just check the "Yes" box below. If you cannot think of any reason, check the "No" box. .... Yes ( ) No ( )

b. Could a country's *gross* investment ever turn out to be a negative figure? .... Yes ( ) No ( )

Answers are given in question 17's answers. Do 16 and 17 before checking your responses to this one.

---

16. You are given the following data for a certain country, for two different years:

	Year 1	Year 2
New buildings produced	5	5
New equipment produced	10	10
Consumer goods produced	110	90
Consumer goods consumed	90	110
Estimated depreciation on existing buildings during year	10	10
Estimate depreciation on existing equipment during year	10	10
Inventories of consumer goods at beginning of year	30	50
Inventories of consumer goods at close of year	50	30

These figures are complete; there is no government sector of GNP or NNP.

a. The difference, in year 1, between the 110 of consumer goods actually produced and the 90 of consumer goods consumed is explained by _____.

b. The reverse difference in year 2—only 90 produced, 110 consumed—is explained by _____.

c. Compute the following for the two years:

	1	2
Gross national product ....(1) _____	(7) _____
Breakup of GNP into:		
Consumption ....(2) _____	(8) _____
Gross investment ....(3) _____	(9) _____
Net national product ....(4) _____	(10) _____
Breakup of NNP into:		
Consumption ....(5) _____	(11) _____
Net investment ....(6) _____	(12) _____

---

a. increase in inventories on hand at year-end.

b. decrease in year-end inventories.

c. (1) 125; (2) 90; (3) 35; (4) 105; (5) 90; (6) 15; (7) 105; (8) 110; (9) −5; (10) 85; (11) 110; (12) −25.

---

17. To summarize question 16: In the national-product statistics, a negative *net* investment figure *(could / could not)* appear if total depreciation exceeded the total value of new buildings and equipment produced. A negative *net* investment figure *(could / could not)* appear if (leaving depreciation aside) the value of inventory reduction exceeded the total value of new buildings and equipment produced.

A negative *gross* investment figure *(could / could not)* appear if total depreciation exceeded the total value of new buildings and equipment produced. A negative *gross* investment figure *(could / could not)* appear if the value of inventory reduction during the year exceeded the total value of new buildings and equipment produced.

---

could; could; could not; could. Hence the answer to both parts of question 15 is: Yes. (If you were fooled by the gross-investment part, console yourself with the fact that you have plenty of good company.)

---

18. Most commodities go through several "stages of production," each stage handled by a different firm. The text's example is bread, the main ingredient of which starts as wheat grown by a farmer, then becomes flour ground by a milling firm, and finally becomes bread produced in a bakery. The same thing which to one firm is a finished product is to the next firm in line a raw material.

The statisticians count the contribution to production of *every* firm. But the figure counted is "value added"—i.e., the firm's total sales *minus* the value of everything it bought from any other firm. Each other such firm has its own contribution to value added. By counting every firm's contribution, but counting *only* its value added, we just reach the market value of the finished product—as in the text's bread example.

Below is the 1976 Income Statement of the Utter Confusion Manufacturing Company. Its year-beginning and year-end inventories were the same in quantity and value; hence no "inventory adjustment" is needed to obtain the manufacturing cost of goods sold. All sales were made to consumers.

What did this firm contribute to the national-product figures, on a value-added basis? Answer by filling in the blanks following the Income Statement.

Sales $140
Less manufacturing costs of goods sold:
  Raw materials purchased from other firms . $40
  Wages 20
  Depreciation on buildings and machinery .. 10   70
Gross margin 70

Less selling cost:
  Salaries paid to salesmen 10
  Purchases from advertising firm 5   15
                                  55
Less business taxes (indirect) 10
                                  45
Less interest paid on bonds 5
Profit before taxes 40
Less corporation income taxes 20
                                  20
Dividends on stock 15
Addition to retained earnings .... $ 5
Contribution to *NI:*
  Wages and salaries .... *a.*_____
  Interest .... *b.*_____
  Corporation profits .... *c.*_____
  Other, if any:_____ ..... *d.*_____
  Total contribution to *NI* .... *e.*_____
Contribution to GNP on value-added basis:
  Consumption .... *f.*_____
  Investment (if any) .... *g.*_____
  Total GNP contribution .... *h.*_____
Contribution to NNP on value-added basis:
  Computed contribution to GNP ....
  Subtract depreciation (capital consumption) *i.*_____
  NNP contribution .... *j.*_____
The contributions to NNP and *NI* differ by.... *k.*_____
This amount is the total of.... *l.*_____

A breakdown of this firm's contribution to NNP would be as follows:
Consumption .... *m.*_____
Investment .... *n.*_____

To compute the firm's contribution to disposable income, the following two items shown on its Income Statement would have to be deducted from the *NI* figure:
*o.*_____ .... _____
*p.*_____ .... _____

---

a. 30. *b.* 5. *c.* 40. *d.* 0. *e.* 75. *f.* 95. *g.* 0. *h.* 95. *i.* 10. *j.* 85. *k.* 10. *l.* indirect business taxes. *m.* 95. *n.* −10. *o.* corporation income taxes, 20. *p.* undistributed corporation profit, 5.

---

19. A common use of national-product figures is to compare total real output as between two years. But if prices have changed in the interim, the comparison is meaningless unless a proper price adjustment is made.
a. Consider this problem: NNP (in billions) was $500 in 1970, $650 in 1975. The price index was 100 in 1970 and 125 in 1975 (i.e., prices had risen by 25 per cent by 1975). Was 1975's real output higher than 1970's, and if so, by how much?

For the moment, *set aside completely* the question just posed. We'll start with an easier problem, then use it to answer the actual problem. Suppose, instead, that 1975's *real* output had been exactly the same as that of 1970 ($500). That 1975 real output—in 1970 prices—would of course have to be $500. But again, the 1970 and 1975 price indices were 100 and 125—i.e., prices rose by 25 per cent over that period. Allowing for this inflation, the 1975 NNP, expressed in 1975 prices, would have to be

$$\$500 \times \frac{125}{100}$$

That would make the 1975 NNP (in 1975 prices) $*(500 / 550 / 575 / 625)*.

If we wanted to *deflate* this 1975 NNP (in 1975 prices), to get it down to 1970 prices (and so make it comparable with the actual 1970 NNP), we would do *in reverse* what was just done. That is, we would start with the $625 NNP and multiply it by a deflating factor of $^{100}/_{125}$. The result would be $500.

Still assuming, for convenience, a 25 per cent price increase, we can apply this deflating factor of $^{100}/_{125}$ to bring *any* 1975 NNP down to a 1970 price level. (Suppose, for example, real output in 1975 had been *twice* the 1970 NNP of $500. In 1970 prices, 1975 would be $1,000; in 1975 prices, $1,250. The same deflating factor would bring the $1,250 down to $1,000.)

So—to get finally to the problem posed at the start of this question—to get the *actual* 1975 NNP of $650 in terms of 1970 prices and so make it comparable in real terms with the 1970 NNP, we multiply it by $^{100}/_{125}$. The resulting deflated figure is $*(500 / 520 / 580 / 625)*—i.e., real output in 1975 was *(4 / 8 / 12 / 100)* per cent *(higher / lower)* than in 1970.

Another way of making a proper comparison would be to *inflate* the 1970 NNP of $500 by 25 per cent, thus making it comparable with 1975. That is, the 1970 NNP, at 1975 prices, would be $625. Comparing this with the actual 1975 NNP of $650, we get *(a lower increase than / the same 4 per cent increase as / a higher increase than)* before.

b. Sometimes this kind of problem is complicated by asking: What happened to per capita income (income per person, total income divided by total population)? Suppose, for example, that with the same pair of NNPs as before, total population fell by 5 per cent between 1970 and 1975. What was the rise in per capita income?

Real NNPs, in 1970 prices, were $500 in 1970, $520 in 1975. But the latter total was shared among a smaller population. Suppose the 1970 population was 100 people; then, for a 5 per cent drop, it must have been 95 in 1975. If these *were* the two population figures, then real income per person was $5 in 1970 ($500 divided by 100), whereas in 1975 ($520 divided by 95) it was approximately $*(5.0 / 5.5 / 6.0)*. Compar-

ing $5 per person in 1970 with about $5.5 in 1975, the result is that 1975 real per capita income rose by about 10 per cent over 1970. (To compute the percentage change in per capita income, it doesn't make any difference what pair of population figures you use, just so long as they are in the proper ratio. Try it with 200 people and 190, or with 1,000 and 950; you get exactly the same percentage increase.)

---

a. 625; 520; 4 per cent higher; the same 4 per cent increase. *b.* 5.5.

QUIZ: Multiple Choice

1. *In GNP and NNP statistics, "investment" includes* (1) any durable product produced through the agency of government, such as a new road; (2) any purchase of a new common-stock issue; (3) any increase in the amount of year-end inventories over their year-beginning amount; (4) any commodity bought by a consumer but not fully consumed by the year-end; (5) none of these items.

2. *In GNP and NNP statistics, the value of housing services, where the houses are occupied by their owners, is treated as follows: It is* (1) not counted, since property services are not considered "production"; (2) not counted, since such property services are included in the value of the house itself; (3) not counted in GNP or NNP, but is counted in disposable income, using an arbitrary estimate of rental value; (4) counted in both GNP and NNP, using an arbitrary estimate of rental value; (5) counted in GNP, but not in NNP, using an arbitrary estimate of rental value.

3. *To compute a firm's contribution to GNP on a value-added basis, we must deduct from the value at market price of the goods it has produced* (1) all indirect business taxes paid; (2) any undistributed profits; (3) depreciation; (4) all sales to other business firms; (5) none of the above.

4. *In GNP and NNP statistics, a negative gross investment figure* (1) could never occur; (2) could appear if the total of depreciation on buildings and equipment were sufficiently large; (3) would automatically occur if there were no production of buildings or equipment during the year; (4) could be caused by a sufficiently large reduction in inventories during the year; (5) means simply that the economy has produced more than it has consumed.

5. *There would be double counting of GNP and NNP to add together* (1) net value added by the iron-mining industry and net value added by the steel-manufacturing industry; (2) net increase in inventories of flour mills and net increase in inventories of bakeries; (3) total output of iron ore and total output of iron; (4) value added by bakers and value of bread salesmen's services; (5) total of consumer services purchased and total of investment goods produced.

6. *Subtract (a) corporation income taxes and (b) undistributed corporation profit from the total of corporation profit before taxes, and the remainder must equal* (1) indirect business taxes; (2) addition to retained earnings; (3) dividends; (4) bond interest; (5) disposable income.

7. *Among the five items listed below, one is not in the same class as the other four for purposes of national-income accounting, namely,* (1) corporation income (or profits); (2) government transfer payments; (3) net interest payments by business; (4) rental income; (5) wages and salaries.

8. *If you know the NNP figure, and from it want to compute disposable personal income, one thing you must* not *do is to* (1) deduct depreciation; (2) add government transfer payments; (3) deduct indirect business taxes; (4) deduct social security levies; (5) deduct undistributed corporation profits.

9. *In computing the "government" sector of GNP for a particular period,* (1) all governmental expenditures on commodities and services are counted; (2) all governmental expenditures on commodities are counted; those on services are not; (3) all governmental expenditures on final commodities and services are counted; those on intermediate items are not; (4) all governmental expenditures on consumption items are counted, whether commodities or services; others are not; (5) none of the above is correct.

10. *"National Income" (NI), as this term is used in the national-product and national-income statistics, means specifically* (1) NNP (net national product) plus all taxes not considered taxes paid out of income—i.e., NNP plus "indirect business taxes"; (2) NNP minus all taxes that are considered taxes paid out of income, such as the personal and corporation income taxes; (3) NNP plus all taxes that are considered taxes paid out of income, such as the personal and corporation income taxes; (4) NNP minus all taxes not considered taxes paid out of income—i.e., NNP minus "indirect business taxes"; (5) none of the preceding.

11. *If NNP was $360 (billion) in 1975, as measured in 1975 prices, and if the price level had risen by 20 per cent from 1970 to 1975, the 1975 NNP, measured in 1970 prices, would be (in billions)* (1) $300; (2) $320; (3) $340; (4) $360; (5) $432.

12. *In computing the national-income and national-product accounts, it would be* incorrect *to add together the following two items:* (1) Consumption expenditure and Personal saving. (2) Net investment and Consumption expenditures. (3) Corporate profits and Net interest paid by business. (4) Government purchases and Consumption expenditures. (5) Government purchases and Wages and salaries.

QUIZ: Other

1. A storekeeper's sales for the year were $55,000. He paid his father, who had helped set him up in business, $4,000—of which $3,000 represented rent for the store premises and $1,000 interest on borrowed money. His merchandise purchases for the year were $25,000. He paid $2,000 in local business taxes. His help in the store cost him $12,000. He estimated depreciation on his equipment at $500. His merchandise inventory at the year-beginning was $2,000; at the year-end, $2,600.

What did the operations of this man's firm contribute to the national-product and -income accounts, on a value-added basis? Answer by filling in the blanks below.

GNP: Consumption $ _____   NNP: Consumption $ _____
     Investment   Investment
      (gross) $ _____   (net) $ _____
     Total GNP $ _____   Total NNP $ _____
National income:

_____ $ _____
    (type of income)

_____ $ _____
    (type of income)

_____ $ _____
    (type of income)

_____ $ _____
    (type of income)

Total national income .... $ _____
The difference between the NNP and national income totals is explained by _____, $ _____

2. A nation's NNP was $260 billion in 1965 and $325 billion in 1975. Both figures were computed as usual in terms of market prices for the year involved. The index of prices rose from 100 in 1965 to 130 in 1975.

a. As compared with 1965 did real output increase or decrease in 1975?

b. In terms of 1975 prices, what would the 1965 NNP be?

c. In terms of 1965 prices, what would the 1975 NNP be?

3. A house is built and sold in the first 6 months of 1950 for a price of $50,000. It is rented for the next 20 years, beginning July 1, 1950. Annual rent is $3,000 per year ($1,500 for the last half of 1950, $1,500 for the first half of 1970). The house lasts for just 20 years. Depreciation is charged at the rate of $2,500 per year ($1,250 for each of the two half-years involved, 1950 and 1970).

What figures enter the national-product accounts with respect to the building and rental of this house? Answer by completing the columns below.

	1950	1951 or Any Later Year through 1969	1970	Total of All Years Combined
Gross investment	_____	_____	_____	_____
Net investment	_____	_____	_____	_____
Consumption	_____	_____	_____	_____

4. In the table alongside are three sets of statistics relating to national product and income. Some figures have been omitted, but in each case there are just enough to permit computation of the accounts.[12] For each of the three sets of figures:

(1) Compute GNP, NNP, and *DI*, showing your figures in the spaces at bottom of each column.

(2) Fill in all the blanks within each column—e.g., Corporation income (profit) after tax in problem *a*, and so on.

(HINT: These are essentially "jigsaw puzzle" problems. The key diagram for their solution is Fig. 10-2, p. 66. Note that there are just three things to be done with corporation income (or profit): Taxes must first be paid; dividends are paid out of after-tax profit; and what's left is undistributed profit (addition to retained earnings). The total of corporation taxes, dividends, and undistributed profit *must* be corporation income before taxes.)

| | **Problem** | | |
	a	*b*	*c*
Business and industrial plant and equipment constructed......................	105	60	100
Capital consumption allowances (depreciation)	45	___	___
Consumption expenditures..............	380	275	___
Corporation dividends	20	15	25
Corp'n. income (profit) after tax	___	___	___
Corp'n. income (profit) before tax	65	55	___
Corp'n. income (profit) undistributed ...	___	15	30
Government purchases of goods and services	120	___	140
Gov't. transfer payments (excluding interest payments) to individuals	25	10	45
Housing constructed	40	25	60
Increase in inventories of commodities accumulated during year	−10	5	−5
Interest paid: By business (net)	20	25	60
By consumers	10	20	25
By governments	25	10	30
Investment (total gross)	___	90	___
Investment (total net)	___	65	130
Proprietors' income (from unincorporated business)	30	___	50
Rental income	15	30	35
Saving (by consumers, out of *DI*)	___	50	105
Taxes: Corporation income	30	25	45
Indirect business	35	30	30
Personal	90	60	95
Social insurance contributions ...	25	40	40
Wages and salaries	___	300	450
Gross national product	___	___	___
Net national product	___	___	___
Disposable income	___	___	___

[12]In these problems, foreign investment (as discussed in the chapter Appendix) is zero.

APPENDIX: The Official National-Income Data

The ultimate objective of all economic activity is the production of final consumer goods. "Intermediate goods" (like wheat and flour) are en route toward final consumer goods (bread). Capital goods are just a roundabout way of getting consumer goods.

Sometimes it is difficult to decide whether or not a given item belongs in the final-consumer-good category. If you must wear expensive clothes to hold down a particular job, does the purchase of such clothes count as a consumer satisfaction? The statisticians' answer in all such cases is: Make the best decision you think you can that such an item counts or does not count; then ignore any complaints that it is an "arbitrary" rule.

1. *a.* Sometimes the presence or absence of a *money* transaction is a factor in this decision. For example, there is one huge omission in the national product statistics: The services provided for their families by housewives are *not* included in the total. The reason for this is *(male chauvinism / their not being market transactions with a money price, so that estimates of value would be difficult)*.

b. The services provided by a paid housekeeper *(are / are not)* counted. The valuation placed on them is *(zero / the wage or salary paid)*. This practice is *(consistent / inconsistent)* with the handling of housewives' services.

---

a. their not being market transactions with a money price. (As to this answer, add or substitute "male chauvinism" if you are so disposed. After all, the rules for computation of the national-product statistics were mainly developed by men.)

b. are; wage or salary paid; inconsistent.

2. "Foreign investment" is briefly considered in the text appendix. Foreign items were left aside in the chapter: somewhat difficult to handle, their total is fairly small by comparison with magnitudes such as total GNP or NNP.

Suppose a country's 1976 foreign transactions consist *only* of $20 (billion) in merchandise exports and $18 in (consumer) merchandise imports. The $20 in exports will count in 1976 GNP and NNP as part of production. The $18 in imports will count in *DI* as part of consumption expenditures. In effect, this $18 in imports (produced abroad) just replaces $18 (out of the total of $20) in export goods produced at home but sent abroad. The balance of $2 in exports counts in the statistics as "foreign investment."

Why "investment"? Because, as to $2 in export goods produced, there was no domestic consumption payoff this year. *Next* year, or some time *in the future,* the foreign countries which this year incurred a deficit in their trading are expected to make up their debt by supplying $2 in goods or services. So the excess of exports over imports, in the 1976 figures, is production for *future* benefit—i.e., investment.

Foreign transactions extend considerably beyond merchandise exports and imports. However, a twofold distinction can be made as to all of them. There are items which are *like* exports, in that they result in a flow of (foreign) money toward the United States. And there remain items which are *like* imports, in producing a flow of (United States-owned) money toward foreign countries. With *all* transactions sorted into these two "export-like" and "import-like" categories, U.S. foreign investment (or disinvestment) is then handled just as it was above.

Suppose total transactions are these: commodity exports, $30 (billion); commodity imports $45; interest received on bonds issued by foreign companies and owned by residents (export-like items, since foreigners are paying for a service, here the service of the use of money), $10; interest and dividends paid to foreigners, $1; spent by foreign tourists visiting this country, $4. Assuming these to be the only relevant items, then this country's national-income and -product accounts would record foreign *(investment / disinvestment)* of $*(1 / 2 / 3 / 5 / 10 / 15)* billion.

---

disinvestment of $2 billion (export-like items totaling $44, minus import-like items totaling $46).

---

3. At its very close, the text Appendix says that, because of the way terms are defined, net investment *must always* equal the total of three saving items: (1) personal saving (*DI* minus the sum of consumption expenditures and interest paid by consumers); (2) corporation "saving" (undistributed corporate profits); and (3) government "saving"—meaning government's overall budget surplus, or the excess of collections from all taxes, including social security collections, over all governmental expenditures, transfer payments included. Any budget deficit is just a negative surplus, or "negative saving."

a. You can check this equality by reference to the figures in any of the three parts of question 11, p. 69.

b. If you find simple algebra helpful—and ignore this part of this question if you do not—you can use Fig. 10-2, p. 66 to prove this identity. Use symbols for the various items in this diagram: "*Inet*" for net investment, "*C*" for consumption expenditures, "*IBTx*" for indirect business taxes, etc.

Start with Column (2). It consists of: *Inet + G + C.* Subtract from these three items [i.e., from the Column (2) total] enough to get down to the Column (4) total. That is, subtract the indirect business taxes above Column (3), and subtract also the four items above Column (4).

Now take Column (6), and reduce *it* to Column (4) size. This time you begin with the three items within Column (6), and subtract from them the three items at the top of Column (5).

You now have two different expressions, both equal in value to Column (4). Write them down as an equality. Cancel the common items (consumption, and interest paid by consumers). Consolidate all the government items (to get the overall budget surplus or deficit). The result is the equality mentioned.

QUIZ: Multiple Choice

1. *The following is not counted as "investment" in the national-product statistics, namely,* (1) construction of a new machine if it is not actually used for production in the year it was made; (2) the excess of value of goods and services exported over goods and services imported; (3) production of a new house with an estimated 50-year life; (4) production of a new washing machine with an estimated 8-year life; (5) a rise in the amount of inventories during the year.

2. *A widower pays his housekeeper a salary of $4,000 yearly. If he should marry the lady, and pay her an allowance of $5,000 yearly, then (by the "official rules" of counting) the result of the marriage would be that* (1) National income *(NI)* would rise and so would disposable income *(DI);* (2) *NI* would rise, *DI* would fall; (3) both *NI* and *DI* would fall; (4) *NI* would be unchanged, *DI* would fall; (5) both *NI* and *DI* would be unchanged.

3. *"Net foreign investment," in the national-product and -income accounts, means* (1) the excess of goods and services produced by this country and sold to foreigners over goods and services produced abroad and sold to domestic consumers; (2) the total of goods and services produced abroad and sold to domestic consumers; (3) the total value of stocks, bonds, and other such securities purchased from foreigners by citizens of this country; (4) the excess of goods and services produced abroad and sold to domestic consumers over goods and services produced by this country and sold to foreigners; (5) none of these items.

2

DETERMINATION OF NATIONAL INCOME AND ITS FLUCTUATIONS

11 SAVING, CONSUMPTION, AND INVESTMENT

THIS STUDY GUIDE CHAPTER is a long one. Plan to spend time on it, and be patient with all its detail. A firm grasp of the material in this chapter will help you immensely in Chapters 12 and 13. Here—and more fully in 12 and 13—we begin to tackle vital questions: How is it that a capitalist economy may sometimes be afflicted with widespread unemployment? And at other times, with inflationary price rises?

If an economy is to produce at its full-employment level of output, the total of money demand or purchasing power must be at the proper level. If the flow of money spending for goods and services pouring into the marketplace is insufficient to buy what can be produced at full employment (given the prevailing price level), unemployment of men and machines may be expected as a result. If this flow is too large—greater in magnitude than the total available supply of goods (valued at current prices)—then we can expect that prices will rise. This price rise brings the money value of available supply into equality with the too-large money demand flow.

"The flow of money spending" means an expenditure stream with three basic components: consumer spending, investment spending, and governmental spending. If we disregard expenditure by foreigners to buy United States goods (a comparatively minor factor[1]), then every currently produced good or service is supplied to meet one of these three demand categories. The nation's economic well-being requires that their sum total be just right, neither too high nor too low.

In point of fact, this total flow sometimes gets out of hand. It can shrink to produce a recession, or expand to produce an inflation. To understand how these disruptions occur, we must understand the forces that influence and control each of the three flows.

In our first approach, we set government spending and taxation (and also the relatively minor item of foreign transactions) aside. Later, the role of government must be considered at length. But it simplifies the analysis to begin with a situation in which only *private* spending decisions—*C* spending and *I* spending—are important.

[1]In this, the United States is an exception. In Canada and in all European countries, for example, foreign trade is a matter of the greatest importance.

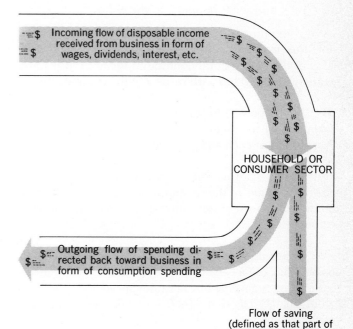

Incoming flow of disposable income received from business in form of wages, dividends, interest, etc.

HOUSEHOLD OR CONSUMER SECTOR

Outgoing flow of spending directed back toward business in form of consumption spending

Flow of saving (defined as that part of income received not spent on consumption)

Fig. 11-1

The *C* Flow. Two factors govern the amount of *C* spending undertaken by a single family, or by a community:

▶ 1. The amount of income received by that family or community.

▶ 2. The way the family or community chooses to divide that income between consumption and saving.

"Income received" means, of course, disposable income—*DPI*, or *DI*. By definition (see Study Guide p. 68), saving ("personal saving") is that part of *DI* not spent on consumption.[2]

Figure 11-1 (above) illustrates this division of

[2]This ignores the fact that, in Department of Commerce terms, part of *DI* goes to interest payments by consumers, now officially regarded as neither consumption expenditure nor saving. This is quite unimportant here; just assume that there are no such interest payments.

The Commerce Department's official wording is "disposable personal income" *(DPI)*. But "disposable income" *(DI)* is shorter and more convenient.

income for a community. The total amount paid out by producing firms in the forms of wages and salaries, rental payments, dividends, and so on appears at top left. It flows to individuals and families as earned income. They divide it between C and S. That part of the income flow used for C spending is obviously directed back toward producing firms. We'll consider in due course what happens to the C flow after it leaves Fig. 11-1—and what happens to the S flow.

We come now to a simple but vitally important concept: *the propensity to consume.* We'll approach it in terms of the single family, although it can be used just as much (and will be) with respect to the community.

▶ The propensity to consume, for any family, is a summing up of the amount of C spending that family will undertake, at each and any level of DI.

In Fig. 11-1 terms, the propensity to consume indicates *how much* of the incoming DI flow (whatever its amount) will be sent through the C spending "loop" at bottom left.

1. *a.* The propensity-to-consume idea needs careful development. Suppose a certain family's monthly expenditure on consumption is governed by this rule: Spend $100 *plus* one-half of monthly DI. Hence its C spending and its saving at various income levels would be (fill in the blanks):

DI	C	S	DI	C	S
$ 0	$ ____	$ ____	$300	$ ____	$ ____
100	____	____	400	____	____
200	____	____	500	____	____

(Remember that S must be the difference between DI and C. So at low income levels, S will be a negative amount.)

b. In Fig. 11-1 terms, should the incoming income flow be $400, the outgoing flow of C spending at bottom left would be $(*400 / 300 / 200*), and the flow through the S "drain" $(*300 / 200 / 100*). Should income rise from $400 to $500, the flow of C spending would rise by $(*200 / 100 / 50*), to $(*500 / 450 / 400 / 350*).

---

a. *C:* 100; 150; 200; 250; 300; 350; *S:* −100; −50; 0; 50; 100; 150   *b.* 300; 100; 50; 350.

---

2. *a.* In Fig. 11-2, plot the points relating C and DI for the six DI values of question 1. Join these points with an appropriate line.

The figures you have completed in question 1 illustrate a propensity to consume. So does the graph you have drawn above. Notice that although the detail of the figures is different, the line you have drawn corresponds in general shape

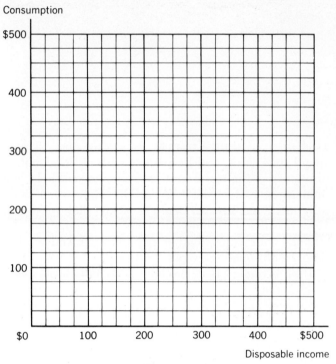

Fig. 11-2

and direction to the propensity-to-consume line in the text's Fig. 11-2. (The text's line has a little curvature, and it is not carried leftward far enough to show consumption at very low incomes. But these differences are unimportant at present.)

b. In Fig. 11-2, draw also a diagonal line from bottom-left corner to top-right corner. (Use, if possible, a different color, to distinguish this line from the propensity-to-consume line.) Note that the text's Fig. 11-2 carries a similar 45° "helping line" or "convenience line."

This particular diagram is used extensively in Chapters 11 through 13 (and indeed in many later places in the text as well). So it is important to grasp the usefulness and significance of the 45° line therein. In this particular diagram—something not done in all or even most graphs—*the same dollar scale* is used on both vertical and horizontal axes. This means that

▶ The 45° line runs through all the equal-value points.

For example, the line you have just drawn on Fig. 11-2 runs through the point marking off $100 of DI and $100 of C; through the point marking $200 DI and $200 C; through $300 DI and $300 C; and so on. *All* the points where DI and C are equal are found on this line, and *only* such points.

One thing the 45° line tells us, then, is the particular DI level at which the family just "breaks even"—spends on C an amount just equal to its DI. This is where 45° line and propensity to consume intersect: in our Fig. 11-2, it is at a DI of $(*100 / 200 / 300 / 400*).

To the *left* of this intersection point, the propensity-to-consume line lies *(above / below)* the 45° line. The significance of this is that within this range of incomes—from $0 to $200—the family spends on *C (more / less)* than its *DI*.

To the *right* of the intersection point, the propensity-to-consume line lies *(above / below)* the 45° line. That is, in this income range, the family would spend *(more / less)* than its *DI*—i.e., it would save part of its *DI*.

---

b. 200; above; more; below; less.

The point made immediately above is a simple one, but be sure you have grasped it: To the *left* of the intersection between the two lines, the family spends *more* than its income; at the intersection, it just "breaks even"; to the *right*, it spends *less* than its income (and saves the remainder).

Now something related to the above, and equally important:

▶ The vertical distance from propensity-to-consume line up to 45° line marks the amount of saving.

This is so because the 45° line marks off equal values horizontally and vertically. (Again, be sure you grasp this; work in terms of the question below.)

3. *a.* For example, at $400 *DI* (at the 400 mark on the horizontal axis of Fig. 11-2), the vertical distance up to the 45° line is $*(500 / 400 / 300)*. The vertical distance up to the propensity-to-consume line is $*(500 / 400 / 300)*; this is the amount of *C* spending. The difference of $100—the vertical distance between the two lines—is the amount of *S*.

b. Similarly, Fig. 11-2 indicates, with the aid of the 45° helping line, that at *DI* of $300 the family would *(save / "dissave")* an amount of $*(0 / 50 / 100 / 150)*. At *DI* of $100, the family would *(save / "dissave")* an amount of $*(0 / 50 / 100 / 150)*. When the propensity-to-consume line is *above* the 45° line, there is "dissaving," or "negative saving." This means simply that if the family's income should happen to be temporarily at a low level such as $100, it would draw on past savings, or borrow, in order to supplement *DI* currently received, for *C* spending.

c. The amount of *S* can of course be plotted directly on a saving-*DI* graph. Record the same six points of question 1 on Fig. 11-3, and join them.

---

a. 400; 300. *b.* save $50; "dissave" $50.

The propensity-to-consume (or "consumption function") idea says this: *income governs spending (and saving)*. It doesn't say income will be the *only* governing factor, since there may be others (size of family, for example). (Typically, such other factors are decidedly less important than income.) It doesn't say that all fami-

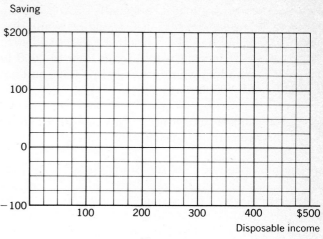

Fig. 11-3

lies are alike: some families would spend more, others less, out of any given *DI* amount. That is, propensities to consume will vary from one family to the next.

We can speak also of the *community* propensity to consume—the community being the aggregate of its individual members. There are one or two analytic problems in aggregating individual-unit consumption functions to get the community propensity to consume; but they are unimportant here. (They arise mainly because spending patterns do vary from family to family.) What is important is that the statistical evidence indicates a fairly consistent pattern between total community *DI* and total *C* spending. (Nobody expects a single family or a whole community to conform with literal precision to some prestated propensity to consume. All we can expect is a reasonable degree of consistency. The text's Fig. 11-5 shows how consistent the relation between consumption and disposable income has been, in the United States.)

From the propensity-to-consume idea, we can say that a given *change* in *DI* is likely to produce a given *change* in *C* spending. Here, we reach a most important concept: the *marginal* propensity. (Again: Be careful. The idea of the marginal propensity is simple, but be sure you grasp what it is and what it is not, for it is used extensively later on.)

Consider the following figures taken from the consumption function in the text chapter's Table 11-2:

Yearly DI	Yearly C	Increase in C
$10,000	$ 9,600	
		$640
11,000	10,240	
		590
12,000	10,830	

These figures say that if this family's *DI* had been $10,000, and rose to $11,000, its *C* spending would rise, not by $1,000, but by $640. (The other $360 would go to extra saving.) If income were to rise from $11,000 to $12,000, *C* spending would rise, not by $1,000 and not by $640, but by $590.

▶ The marginal propensity to consume (MPC) is the ratio between *extra C* spending and *extra DI*.

The next page or so of the Study Guide is devoted fully to this "marginal propensity" idea. If you are puzzled as to why it gets so much space, here is a rough indication: Look again at Fig. 11-1. Suppose the incoming flow of *DI* (at the top of this diagram) rises or falls—rises, let's say. It is the *marginal* propensity, and *only* the marginal propensity, which dictates *how much* of this extra *DI* will go into extra *C* spending, and *how much* of it into extra saving. (And this disposition of extra income, as Chapter 12 will indicate, often turns out to be important.)

Figure 11-1 dealt, of course, with a whole community, whereas the material used above dealt with a single family. But (as already noted) we can use the propensity-to-consume idea (and the marginal-propensity idea also) either for the whole community or for the single family.

Back, then, to the single family. In the case of the figures in the table above, the family's MPC in the $10,000–11,000 *DI* range is .64 (the ratio of $640 to $1,000). Between $11,000 and $12,000, the MPC is .59.

Here are four points to grasp about the MPC (and on which the next set of review questions will drill you):

1. As income rises, in real experience, the MPC typically falls. (Note how it fell from .64 to .59 in the table above.) If we were being very precise, we would not speak of a single MPC figure for an income change as big as $1,000; we would have to recognize the slight change in MPC produced by a *DI* rise of $100 or even $10. But the difference would be almost imperceptible; and so we speak of "the" MPC for an income change of $1,000.

In fact, in text Chapters 12 and 13, a *constant* MPC is assumed—the same at all income levels. For some analytic purposes, this would be an unwarranted distortion of reality. But for others (those the text explores), it is appropriate because it greatly simplifies the approach without significantly altering the conclusions reached.

2. The MPC is concerned solely with the ratio between a *change* in *DI* and the resulting *change* in *C*. In the table above, the family's *C* spending at a *DI* of $10,000 is $9,600. The ratio of $9,600 to $10,000 is .96— that is, the family is spending 96 per cent of its total income on consumption, at this income level. This is the *average* propensity to consume (APC). It is *not* the MPC. The MPC tells us what *extra* consumption spending will go with any *extra* income (i.e., any increase or decrease in income); and the MPC in the vicinity of $10,000 *DI* is about .64 (a little higher, if we allow for the fact that this .64 figure is spread across a full $1,000 income range).

3. Graphically, the MPC is the *slope* of the propensity-to-consume line. (The idea of slope was reviewed in the Orientation on graphs at the beginning of the Study Guide, specifically on pp. 7–10.) If you have had any training in calculus, this will tell you that the MPC is really the derivative of the consumption function; if you have not, you can ignore this sentence.

4. There is also a *marginal propensity to save* (MPS). We know already that a family must always decide to allocate any increase in *DI* (positive or negative) between extra *C* and extra *S*. If the MPC stands for that fraction of an extra dollar of income devoted to *C*, then the remaining fraction (MPS) must go to saving. Always, that is:

$$MPC + MPS = 1$$

4. Review question 1 gave the following propensity to consume: Spend on *C* one-half of monthly *DI* plus $100. Given this consumption function, complete the blanks below to indicate the change in *C* spending resulting from the indicated change in *DI*. Complete also the MPC column (ratio of extra *C* to extra *DI*):

Change in *DI*	Change in *C*	MPC
From $0 to $1 (+ $1)	————	————
From $399 to $400 (+ $1) ...	————	————
From $400 to $401 (+ $1) ...	————	————
From $400 to $410 (+ $10) ..	————	————
From $410 to $400 (− $10) ..	————	————
From $400 to $399 (− $1) ...	————	————

Change in *C:* +50¢, +50¢, +50¢, +$5, −$5, −50¢. MPC: ½ throughout.

5. *a.* What is the slope of the propensity-to-consume line of Fig. 11-2 (the propensity to consume of review questions 1 through 4)? (Recall the rule for slope: fit any right-angled triangle below the line. Slope is the ratio of vertical-side measurement to horizontal-side measurement.) _____.

Slope, as measured by the rule above, would indicate the ratio of *change* in (*DI* / *C* / *S*) to *change* in (*DI* / *C* / *S*). That is, it would measure the value of the (*marginal* / *average*) propensity to consume.

b. The MPC, in this instance, as *DI* rises, *(falls / remains constant / rises)*. Graphically, this propensity to consume is a *(straight / curved)* line. Its slope does not change; hence neither does the MPC.

By contrast, the propensity to consume illustrated in the text's Fig. 11-2 "bends over." Its slope *(increases / remains constant / decreases)* as the *DI* level increases. Correspondingly, the MPC involved *(increases / remains constant / decreases)* as *DI* increases.

a. ½; *C; DI;* marginal. *b.* remains constant; straight; decreases; decreases.

6. Show, for the income levels given, the fraction of total income spent on consumption, and the *marginal* propensity to consume, for the family in questions 1 through 5.

DI	Fraction of DI Spent on C	MPC
$100 ...	_____	_____
200 ...	_____	_____
300 ...	_____	_____
400 ...	_____	_____
500 ...	_____	_____

The figures you have entered in the middle column above represent a series of *(marginal / average)* propensities to consume. They deal with *total DI* and *total C,* whereas the MPC deals with extra or additional amounts.

DI fractions: ³⁄₂, 1, ⁵⁄₆, ³⁄₄, ⁷⁄₁₀. MPC: ½; average.

A final point regarding the propensity to consume—and again an important one in terms of material to follow in the text. If a family increases its *C* spending, a likely explanation—*but not the only possible one*—is that its *DI* has increased. If the imaginary family of the preceding questions were to increase its *C* spending from $300 to $350 monthly, the increase could well be attributable to a rise in *DI* from $400 to $500. But this change could occur for *other* reasons. The family might (with an unchanged *DI*) be changing the distribution of its *DI* between *C* and *S.* It might have decided that its saving for future needs was close to sufficient; or it might be increasing its *C* spending because of greater optimism about the level of its future income. There are plenty of conceivable explanations.

Note this carefully:

▶ If the amount of money habitually spent on consumption changes for any reason other than a change in *DI,* then the propensity-to-consume line has shifted to a new position.

▶ To put the same idea in different words, any nontransitory change in the distribution of *DI* between *C* and *S* means a change in the position of the propensity-to-consume line.

The situation is precisely analogous to the demand-curve analysis of Chapter 4. A demand curve shows how quantity purchased will increase if price falls. But price is not the *only* factor influencing quantity of purchases. Purchases may change because of a change in tastes, a rise in the price of substitute goods, or for other reasons. If some factor such as this—anything *other than* a change in the price of the good involved—is responsible, then we must show the demand curve as moving to a brand-new position.

The same reasoning applies to our propensity-to-consume line. It shows how *C* expenditure will change with any change in *DI*—*other factors held constant.* If some one of these other factors *changes* (thus producing a change in *C* for some reason *other than* a change in *DI*), then we must show the whole propensity-to-consume curve as having moved to an appropriate new position.

7. *a.* The family of earlier questions has a *DI* of $450 monthly (so that its *C* expenditure is $325). One family member now leaves home to get married, and so the propensity-to-consume schedule changes. It now becomes: one-half of *DI,* plus $75.

If family *DI* is unaltered, its monthly *C* spending will henceforth be $*(300 / 325 / 350 / 375)*. On a propensity-to-consume graph such as Fig. 11-2 above, this change would be represented as (pick one):

(1) A movement downward along the existing curve.
(2) A movement upward along the existing curve.
(3) A shift of the entire propensity-to-consume curve *upward* to a new position.
(4) A shift of the entire propensity-to-consume curve *downward* to a new position.

Is the value of the marginal propensity to consume changed? *(No / Yes, it has risen / Yes, it has fallen.)*

b. Suppose the new propensity-to-consume schedule had been: spend two-fifths of *DI,* plus $75. If so, as compared with the previous schedule, the value of the MPC would *(fall / remain unchanged / rise)*.

a. 300; (4); No. *b.* fall. NOTE: When the propensity-to-consume schedule changes, the MPC may change, or may not. The MPC is strictly concerned with a *given* propensity to consume, and with the ratio between extra *C* and extra *DI,* given that propensity to consume.

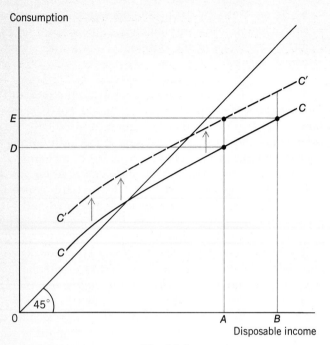

Fig. 11-4

8. *a.* The solid line *CC* in Fig. 11-4 illustrates a community's propensity-to-consume schedule. One possible level of total *DI* is indicated by the horizontal measure *OA*, and total consumption expenditure out of that particular *DI* by the vertical measure *DO*.

The community's total *C* expenditure now rises from *DO* to *EO*. This increase could be the consequence of (pick one):
(1) Only an increase in *DI* from level *OA* to level *OB*.
(2) Only from some factor other than a *DI* increase—a factor causing the propensity-to-consume line to shift upward to a new position indicated by the broken line *C'C'*.
(3) Either of (1) or (2)—an increase in *DI*, or else a decision to spend more prompted by some factor other than an increase in *DI*.

b. A respected economic authority predicts a coming recession. His prediction is influential, and people decide that they should spend less and save more as a precaution against coming hard times (even though *DI* has not fallen—not yet, at any rate). If this decision were to be illustrated in Fig. 11-4 terms, it would imply (pick one):
(1) A movement downward and to the left along a *given* propensity-to-consume line, say the solid *CC* one, to indicate the reduced *C* spending.
(2) An *upward* movement of the *entire* propensity-to-consume line—say from the position indicated by the solid *CC* line upward to the broken *C'C'* line.
(3) A *downward* movement of the *entire* propensity-to-consume line—say from the position indicated by the broken *C'C'* line downward to the solid *CC* line.

a. (3). *b.* (3).

The *I* Flow. Finally, we are able to turn to the second component of the spending flow: investment. In the main,[3] investment spending is spending by business firms for the purchase of new capital goods—new buildings, new machinery, and so on.

We cannot isolate any single factor of dominating importance by which to explain the amount of the *I*-spending flow. Investment spending is undertaken in the hope of profit, and it is influenced by pessimism or optimism regarding the business future, by the quantity of the existing stock of capital goods, by the rate at which new inventions are appearing, by the ease or difficulty of raising money capital, and by many other factors.

As a result, the total flow of *I* spending is far less predictable than the *C* flow. Inevitably, this flow is subject to variations, to sudden increases and decreases. In this simple fact we have one of the keys to disturbances in GNP and NNP. But the full significance of this is not revealed until we reach Chapter 12.

We can begin to put together the pieces of the analysis by joining the two spending flows—*C* and *I*. In Fig. 11-5, *I* spending is shown at the very bottom left corner. It is a money flow toward producing firms, just like the *C* flow. The only difference is that the *I* money flow seeks new capital goods—machinery, buildings, and so

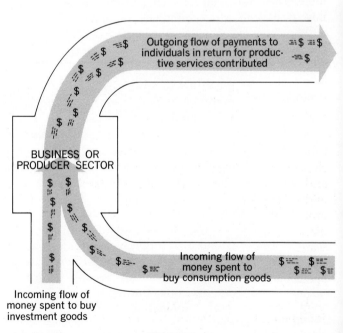

Fig. 11-5

[3]Expenditure on new housing, much of it undertaken by consumers, counts as part of investment—remember Chapter 10. But it is easiest at this stage to think of investment as typically being expenditure to buy new plant and equipment.

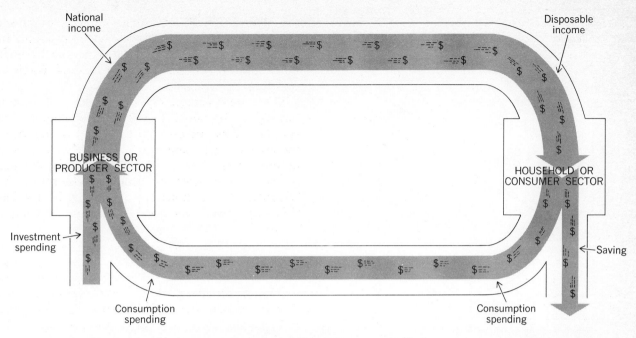

Fig. 11-6

on—whereas the *C* flow seeks consumer goods. But both flows generate employment and production. (We know that the *C* flow comes from consumers. For the moment, never mind about the money source of the *I* flow.)

The *C* flow comes in from bottom right. Together, the two flows constitute the only source of earned income to be paid out in wages, dividends, and the like. (We are assuming provisionally, remember, that government spending is so small that its total can be ignored.)

So we can join Figs. 11-1 and 11-5 to create Fig. 11-6. Study this new figure very carefully indeed. It depicts the central money-flow process of a capitalist economy, and the process on which the analysis of Chapters 12 and 13 depends. It shows a clockwise around-and-around flow of money incomes and spending. This circular flow is continually being depleted by the outward "drain" of consumer saving. It is continually being replenished by the inflow of new investment spending.

Examining Fig. 11-6, you may at first feel a strong inclination to tidy it up or complete it by linking the *S* drain with the *I* inflow, so as to make a closed loop through which saved money flows into investment spending. But be careful! Chapter 11 stresses *the cleavage between saving and investment*—the fact that one group (business firms seeking to buy new capital goods) does most of the investing, while another group (con-

sumers) does much of the saving.[4] In Fig. 11-6 terms, this means we cannot take it for granted that the dollar amount of the *I* inflow (lower left) will automatically equal the dollar amount of the *S* outflow (lower right). Much of the theory of income determination to follow turns on the question of what it means to the economy if the relation between *I* and *S* is disturbed—particularly on account of changes in *I*. Suppose *I* and *S* have been equal in amount. But the *I* flow suddenly grows smaller (because some business firms decide they have added enough new plant and equipment for the time being). The *S* decision makers (households) cannot be expected to change their plans because of a change in *I* decisions about which they were not consulted, and did not even know about. A shrinkage in the planned *I* flow does not occasion an immediate and equal shrinkage in the planned *S* flow. We must allow for the possibility of differences between the two intended flows. (And note that if the *I* inflow shrinks while the *S* outflow remains unchanged, the level of incomes must fall.)

Thus *it would be wrong* to finish off Fig. 11-6 by making a closed loop between the *S* outflow and the *I*

---

[4]Some saving is done by corporations. "Corporate saving" means the same thing as "undistributed corporation profits," or the total of "additions to retained earnings." Since most of this "saving" is used to finance investment projects, it is an exception to the "different groups" idea. Begin by assuming that such corporate saving is zero. It can easily be fitted into the analysis after you have mastered the all-important basic relationships.

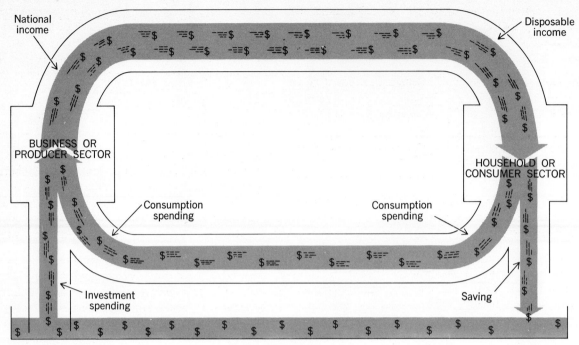

Fig. 11-7

inflow. To do this would be to imply that the *I* inflow *could never be anything different in amount from the S outflow.* It would imply that the *I* flow could never decrease except as the result of a prior decrease in the *S* flow—and similarly for *I* increases.

Yet it is true that personal saving *does* flow into investment, via borrowing or the sale of new corporation stock. An *open* reservoir, as in Fig. 11-7, provides a needed connection between *S* and *I*. But it gives the *I* flow some freedom to increase or decrease without prior change in the *S* flow; and a change in the *S* flow does not mechanically force an identical change in the *I* flow.

Chapter 11 provides the basic tools and background for the analysis of interrelationships between income, investment, consumption, and saving. The actual analysis of these interrelationships follows in Chapters 12 and 13.

9. Investment, as the term is used in economics (as where a firm has a new machine tool built or constructs an addition to its plant), generates employment while the investment item in question is being built, and results in income earned for those so employed. In terms of Figs. 11-6 and 11-7, it is a flow of money expenditure to the firms which produce such investment goods. In this sense, do the following constitute investment?

(1) Having a contractor build a new house for you. *(Yes/No)*
(2) Buying a house built a year ago. ....*(Yes/No)*
(3) Buying Du Pont stock on the stock market. ....*(Yes/No)*

(4) Buying stock in a newly formed corporation, where the money proceeds from stock sale are to be used to build a new factory building. ....*(Yes/No)*
(5) Using money obtained from the bond or stock issue of Item (4) to build a new factory building. ....*(Yes/No)*

---

(1) Yes; (2), (3), (4), No; (5) Yes. [NOTE: The answer cannot be Yes for both (4) and (5), or else there would be double counting. The sale of stock may be a necessary prerequisite to investment, but actual investment takes place only when money is actually spent for the purpose defined as investment.]

---

10. *a.* A firm is considering building a new plant to add to its output capacity. To do this sensibly, it must try to evaluate the future market for its product, to be sure there is likely to be sufficient demand to justify that plant. This requires it to estimate, among other things, the likely degree of competition from rival firms, and coming "general business conditions"—i.e., probable future course of GNP. True or False? ..*(T / F)*

b. This means, then, that the flow of expenditure through the "investment intake" of Figs. 11-6 and 11-7 is governed by many considerations, frequently having to do with forecasts as to the future. ....*(T / F)*

c. A large corporation which has been steadily adding new plant and equipment may stop doing so because it feels it has "caught up" with probable demand for its product for the time being. If it stops, the flow through the "investment intake" of Figs. 11-6 and 11-7 will be correspondingly reduced. *(T / F)*

d. Such investment plans may be postponed or canceled because the firm is fearful of a recession—a drop or pause in GNP. This would again mean a drop in the flow of investment spending. ....(*T* / *F*)

e. If any such reduction in the investment-spending flow occurs, it is reasonable to assume that there will at once be a matching reduction in the flow of personal saving. ...(*T* / *F*)

All true except *e.* Plans to save are in general made quite independently of plans to invest.

---

11. *a.* Money saved by a family and hidden in the family mattress is money withdrawn from the income stream; it creates no income or jobs for anyone so long as it remains in the mattress. ....(*T* / *F*)

b. Money saved by a family and promptly used to buy a new house is money put right back into the income stream. Because (by the definitions of Chapter 10) any consumer expenditure for the construction of a new house counts as investment expenditure, these actions would count as both saving and investment. ....(*T* / *F*)

c. Money saved by a family and promptly used to buy General Motors stock would count as both saving and investment. ....(*T* / *F*)

d. Money saved and deposited in a savings account in a bank counts as saving. This is not investment in the national-income sense. So long as this money stays deposited, it can be used for investment spending only if the bank lends it to some borrower, or if the bank uses the money itself. ......(*T* / *F*)

e. Much investment spending is financed by use of other people's money, i.e., financed by borrowing from a bank or by sale of bond or stock issues. ....(*T* / *F*)

f. Those who are in a position to lend money must consider (1) the honesty of the would-be borrower, and (2) his ability to repay the borrowed money, i.e., the prospects for profitable use of such money. ....(*T* / *F*)

g. If business conditions seem particularly uncertain, people with money to spare may hesitate to lend it, feeling that would-be borrowers are likely to get into trouble and be unable to make repayment. Thus, even though there are mechanisms for converting saving into investment, this does not mean that all saved money is automatically transformed into investment. ....(*T* / *F*)

All true except *c.* [NOTE 1: Money spent to buy a stock or a bond does not count as investment; see parts (3) and (4) of question 9. NOTE 2: When a family spends money to have a new house built, we must think of this money, in Fig. 11-6 and 11-7 terms, as passing through the "saving drain," going at once through the saved-money reservoir, and up

through the "investment-spending intake." It would be easier to think of it as simply passing through the Consumption loop, like any other consumer expenditure. But we can't do that, because the national-product definitions say that any new housing purchase is the one consumer expenditure item which must be classified as investment. No great analytic issue is involved; it's just a matter of respecting the definitions.]

---

12. There are 100 families in an economy. Half have an MPC of ½; half have an MPC of ¾. If this economy's *DI* rises by $10,000, and all this goes to the first group, then *C* spending will rise by $(*zero* / *2,500* / *5,000* / *7,500* / *10,000*). If, instead, all the additional *DI* goes to the second group, then *C* spending will rise by $(*zero* / *2,500* / *5,000* / *7,500* / *10,000*).

Thus, even if we know the exact propensity to consume of each family, we (*cannot* / *can*) predict the exact *C* increase that would follow any given *DI* increase. If different families have different marginal propensities, then for such a prediction, we would have to know how the *DI* increase was distributed—i.e., *which* families got the extra *DI*.

Or suppose every family has exactly the same propensity to consume; but there is some curvature in the propensity-to-consume line, as in text Fig. 11-2. Such a curvature means that MPC (*increases* / *remains constant* / *decreases*) as *DI* increases. If there is some inequality in the distribution of income, then we (*could* / *could not*) predict the exact amount of change in *C* associated with any given *DI* change.

In sum, there are analytic difficulties in moving from an individual-family to a whole-community propensity to consume. But note (see text) that the relationship between *DI* and *C* for the whole economy is still remarkably consistent.

5,000; 7,500; cannot; decreases; could not. NOTE: The text covers this point in its closing "Qualifications" section. If this tricky point bothers you, do not worry too much; it is not essential on your first approach to the fundamentals of this analysis.

QUIZ: Multiple Choice

1. *The "marginal propensity to consume" means this:* (1) At any income level, ratio of total consumption to total income. (2) At any income level, change in consumption-spending total occasioned by a small income change (increase or decrease). (3) For each and all income levels, a schedule showing amount of consumption spending at that level. (4) At any income level, and concerning a small change in that level, the ratio of resulting change in consumption to change in income level. (5) None of these things.

2. *The volume or magnitude of investment opportunities in the American economy (using "investment" in its national-*

product sense), according to the text, is governed primarily by (1) the total amount of saving available for investment users; (2) the level of prevailing interest rates; (3) the state of the stock market; (4) the rate at which new and commercially exploitable inventions are appearing from laboratories; (5) none of the above, there being no such single dominant factor.

3. *The relation between the marginal propensities to consume and to save is that* (1) their total must equal 1, since some fraction of extra income must go to extra consumption spending, and the remaining fraction to extra saving; (2) the ratio between them must indicate the "average propensity to consume"; (3) their total must indicate the current total of disposable income received, since *DI* must divide between consumption and saving; (4) the point at which they are equal must be the "break-even" level of income; (5) none of the above is true, necessarily.

4. *"Personal saving," as the term is used in connection with national-income and -product analysis, means explicitly* (1) the total of all assets held by families; (2) income received within the period in question and not spent on consumption; (3) the total of all assets held by families minus the total of their liabilities; (4) income received within the period in question but used only to buy a security or deposited in a bank; (5) income received within the period in question, not spent on consumption and not used to buy a security nor deposited in a bank.

5. *If people do not consume all their income, but put the unspent amount into a bank or buy a security with it, in national-income and -product terms they are* (1) saving but not investing; (2) investing but not saving; (3) both saving and investing; (4) neither saving nor investing; (5) saving, but investing only to the extent that they buy securities.

6. *The following would be regarded as investment by economists concerned with national product and income:* (1) Any purchase of a corporation bond. (2) Any amount saved out of income and not "hoarded." (3) Any purchase of a new corporation bond. (4) Any productive activity resulting in present consumption. (5) None of the preceding.

7. *The "break-even point" on a family's propensity-to-consume schedule is at the point where* (1) its saving equals its income; (2) its income equals its consumption; (3) its saving equals its consumption; (4) its consumption equals its investment; (5) none of the preceding statements is correct.

8. *In Fig. 11-8, at left above, the solid line CC is the propensity to consume for some family or community. If the total amount of consumption expenditure is EA, the amount of disposable income must be* (1) *AB;* (2) *FD;* (3) *FA;* (4) *DA;* (5) none of the preceding.

9. *Alternatively, given the total amount of consumption expenditure EA in Fig. 11-8, the amount of disposable income must be* (1) *EA;* (2) *GB;* (3) *ED;* (4) *OA;* (5) none of the preceding.

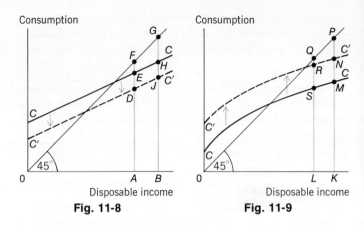

Fig. 11-8   **Fig. 11-9**

10. *In Fig. 11-9, at right above, if the* solid *propensity-to-consume line CC were to shift upward to the broken-line position C'C', this would be appropriate to illustrate* (1) an increase in consumption expenditure resulting from a rise in disposable income; (2) a decision on the part of the family or community involved to consume more and save less out of any given disposable income; (3) a decrease in consumption expenditure resulting from a fall in disposable income; (4) a decision on the part of the family or community involved to consume less and save more out of any given disposable income; (5) none of these events.

11. *The difference between Figs. 11-8 and 11-9, both propensity-to-consume diagrams, is this:* (1) In 11-8, the MPC (marginal propensity to consume) is constant; in 11-9, the MPC decreases as income increases. (2) In 11-8, the MPC decreases as income increases; in 11-9, the MPC is constant. (3) In 11-8, the MPC increases as income increases; in 11-9, the MPC is constant. (4) In 11-8, the MPC is constant; in 11-9, the MPC increases as income increases. (5) In both instances, the MPC falls as income increases, but it falls more rapidly in the case of 11-9.

12. *In Fig. 11-9, if the propensity-to-consume line is the solid line CC, and the amount of disposable income is OK, then the amount of saving out of that disposable income OK must be* (1) *PK;* (2) *MK;* (3) *PM;* (4) *NM;* (5) none of the preceding.

13. *If, again in Fig. 11-9, the amount of disposable income were to change from OK to OL—the solid CC line still indicating the propensity-to-consume line—the amount of saving out of income would become* (1) *SM;* (2) *QR;* (3) *PQ;* (4) *RS;* (5) *QS.*

14. *In Fig. 11-8 (at left above), a change in consumption expenditure from HB to EA would be the result of* (1) a decision to spend more and save less at each level of income; (2) a decrease in disposable income from *OB* to *OA;* (3) a decision to spend less and save more at each level of income; (4) an increase in disposable income from *OA* to *OB;* (5) none of the preceding.

15. *The "propensity to consume" means, or refers to,* (1) the level of income at which consumption spending just equals income; (2) the inclination on the part of some consumers to "keep up with the Joneses" in their consumer spending; (3) the fraction of extra income that will be spent on consumption; (4) a schedule showing the amount a family (or community) will spend on consumption at different levels of income; (5) the fact that, at low incomes, families spend more on consumption than the amount of their incomes.

16. *The statistical evidence suggests that the typical American family behaves as follows with respect to spending out of income:* (1) An increasing proportion of income is spent on consumption as income increases. (2) The same proportion of income is spent on consumption at all except very low income levels. (3) The same proportion of income is spent on consumption at all income levels. (4) A decreasing proportion of income is spent on consumption as income increases. (5) The same proportion of income is spent on consumption at all except very high income levels.

17. *A family saves $2,000 out of a disposable income of $10,000. Its propensity to consume can be represented by the solid line in Fig. 11-8. At the $10,000 income level, its* marginal *propensity to consume should be* (1) less than ⅕; (2) ⅕; (3) less than ⅘, but not necessarily ⅕ or less; (4) ⅘; (5) none of the preceding.

18. *A factor which complicates the determination of the community's overall "propensity to consume" is this:* (1) The amount of consumption expenditure out of any given income total varies very substantially from one year to another. (2) For the whole community, consumption and disposable income must be one and the same thing. (3) Families save more money at higher income levels, which means that they save a larger fraction of their total incomes. (4) Families save more money at higher income levels, which means that they save a smaller fraction of their total incomes. (5) The total of consumption expenditure out of any given income total may vary according to how income is distributed among the members of that community.

19. *Among the following five statements, four repeat ideas stressed in Chapter 11. The fifth is* not *a proper statement of any idea in this chapter. The incorrect one is this:* (1) Much of the saving in today's society is done by one group, and much of the investment by a different group. (2) Undistributed corporation profits (additions to retained earnings) constitute one case in which both saving and investment are undertaken by the same economic unit. (3) The total amount of investment spending is capable of varying considerably from year to year. (4) In today's society, people will not choose to save whenever there are few or no opportunities for investment. (5) The total amount of personal saving is governed by the amount of disposable income and by the propensity to consume.

20. *A family spends $2,000 on consumption when its income is zero, and $6,000 on consumption when its income is $6,000. Graphically, its propensity to consume is a straight line, as in Fig. 11-8. At this family's $6,000 income level, its* marginal *propensity to consume is* (1) ⅔; (2) ¾; (3) ⅘; (4) 1; (5) greater than 1.

21. *"Investment" and "consumption," as these terms are used in national-income and -product analysis, have this feature in common:* (1) Both activities are undertaken by the same group (i.e., households), although not always for the same reasons. (2) Both are demands calling for the current use or employment of the economy's stock of productive inputs. (3) Both are components of disposable income. (4) In both instances, the only factor of major consequence which governs them is the level of national product or disposable income. (5) None of the preceding.

QUIZ: Other

There are 200 families in a community. Each of these families spends monthly on consumption exactly $100 plus one-half its income. (Review question 1 uses this propensity to consume.) Half (100) of these families are "poor"; they each receive monthly incomes of $200. The other 100 families are "rich"; they receive $400 apiece monthly.

It is desired to increase total consumption spending in this community. (Reasons for wishing such an increase can be disregarded.) It is proposed to increase total spending by taxing rich families $100 apiece monthly, giving the tax proceeds to poor families to spend. Thus, each and every family would have a net monthly income of $300.

This proposal is justified as follows: Poor families spend 100 per cent of their incomes on consumption; they receive $200, and they spend $200. Rich families spend only 75 per cent of their incomes; they receive $400, but they spend only $300. So the total of consumption spending would be increased by a redistribution of income.

1. Would such a proposal, if adopted, increase total consumption spending? Explain your answer in terms of the marginal propensity to consume.

2. Are there *any* circumstances in which such a redistribution-of-income proposal would increase consumption spending? Again answer in terms of the MPC.

12 INCOME DETERMINATION: THE SIMPLE MULTIPLIER THEORY

THIS VITALLY IMPORTANT CHAPTER outlines the basic elements of "the theory of income determination." (Remember the comment made at the very beginning of Chapter 11: A good grasp of that chapter will be immensely helpful to you with respect to the fresh material you are now about to tackle.)

The first thing is to grasp the concepts of *equilibrium* GNP and *disequilibrium* GNP:

▶ The characteristic of an equilibrium GNP level is that it is one at which GNP has no tendency to rise or fall in value, because none of its components has any disposition to rise or fall in value.

Next:

▶ The *actual* level of GNP is not necessarily its equilibrium level. But if GNP is out of equilibrium, then it must be rising or falling in value as time proceeds. GNP is thereby seeking out its equilibrium value, and it will continue to rise or fall until it reaches that equilbrium level.

and finally:

▶ Equilibrium GNP does not necessarily mean full-employment GNP.

It is quite possible for GNP to be at equilibrium just at the level where resources are reasonably fully employed, with no undue pressure on prices. But it is also possible for GNP to be in equilibrium at a level *much below* full employment, so that the economy is stuck in conditions of recession or depression.

Similarly, GNP might be *out of equilibrium* even though its current disequilibrium level is one of full employment. It might be trying to reach an unattainable equilibrium, because that equilibrium is above the full-employment-of-resources level, given current prices. The outcome is then an upward price movement.

In sum, there is no automatic tendency for GNP to gravitate to the level which is just what is needed or wanted, and the task of this chapter is to explain why.

Income-determination theory is not easy, and it is most readily outlined by first simplifying things down to essentials. This chapter, like Chapter 11, accordingly assumes that government spending and taxation items are so small that they can be ignored (treated as zero items).[1] It handles depreciation in like fashion. Thus GNP is virtually the same thing as NNP. NNP is made up of C plus I (there being no G.) And (because the items which cause the two totals to differ, mainly government items,[2] have been discarded) NNP is the same thing as *DI* (disposable income). This stripping-down process, clearing away a lot of detail, greatly simplifies the analysis; yet it does not significantly distort the reasoning involved or the ideas to be grasped. (Chapter 13 tackles the same ideas with government brought back in again.)

Chapter 11 noted that C spending is governed primarily by disposable income. In Fig. 12-1 (next page), we show C as varying with GNP rather than *DI*; it is the level of GNP we want to explain, and by the simplifying process just outlined, GNP and *DI* are pretty much the same thing. Figure 12-1's propensity to consume is a straight line (another simplification; it would complicate the analysis to give it a little real-life curvature, but it wouldn't alter the basic conclusions in any significant respect). For the moment, disregard the fact that Fig. 12-1 singles out a GNP (or *DI*) of $100 (billion) and a C of $70 (billion).

Figure 12-2 (to right of Fig. 12-1) refers to investment spending. This I spending is measured vertically, just as C spending is measured in Fig. 12-1. Horizontally, we measure the level of GNP, just as Fig. 12-1 does.

The fact that the I-spending line (the solid line) is shown as horizontal, at a height of 30, signifies that I spending will be $30 (billion) regardless of the GNP level. This is unrealistic: a GNP rise or fall is one of the factors likely to affect I spending. But we start with this assumption for convenience, then change it later on.

Remember what Chapter 11 said: I spending is influenced by many factors. So it can readily change to a different level. For reasons quite apart from the level of GNP, or any change in that level, it may drop to $20

---

[1]Foreign transactions—exports and imports—are also ignored.
[2]This means we also assume undistributed corporation profits to be zero. This item is likewise quite readily picked up at a later stage, when the essentials have been mastered.

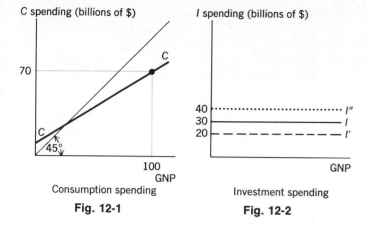

Fig. 12-1 — Consumption spending

Fig. 12-2 — Investment spending

(indicated by the broken *I'I'* line); or it may rise to $40 (the dotted *I"I"* line).

However, we begin with *I* spending of $30 (billion) per period—and we begin, deliberately, with an equilibrium situation. We make GNP $100 (billion) per period. Figure 12-1's propensity to consume says that at this GNP level, the public will want to spend $70 on *C*, and save the other $30.

There are various ways of grasping why these figures fit together to produce "equilibrium." (Always use the way which seems to you to afford the most insight into the way things work in a real economy.) One method is to glance back to Study Guide Fig. 11-7 (p. 86), the circular-income-flow diagram. If the inflow of money expenditure on investment projects is $30, if the outflow of saved money is also $30 (and if $30 is the amount that the public *wants* to save out of a GNP of $100), then nothing is happening that would cause the level of incomes (here, GNP) to change, or the amount of *C*, or the amount of *S*. (Remember, *I* is deliberately being held steady at $30.)

Equilibrium can be identified by the saving-investment equality:

▶ In equilibrium, the total of saving equals the total of investment.

The fact that *S* and *I* are both $30 does not happen automatically, remember. Business firms are doing most or all of the investment; but consumers (a different group) are doing the saving.

The second characteristic by which equilibrium can be identified is less obvious:

▶ The total of incomes earned is just equal to total expenditure to buy goods and services.

Sometimes this second measure of "equilibrium" is more convenient than the first. (Its significance will be

developed more fully in a moment.) However, the two measures are simply alternative ways of identifying exactly the same equilibrium situation.

The interesting thing is that GNP can be pushed "out of equilibrium." (REMEMBER: This is not necessarily undesirable. If equilibrium GNP happened to be a deep-depression GNP, we would *want* it to be pushed out of this equilibrium.) The symptom of an out-of-equilibrium GNP is that *it is changing in value*. It is moving up or down, seeking a new equilibrium at which it can settle.

Only two things (in the simple model we are using) can possibly throw GNP out of equilibrium: *a decision to change I spending, or a decision to change C spending*. In Figs. 12-1 and 12-2 terms, the *I* line must shift, or the *C* line must shift.

Because of the variability of investment, these disturbances are usually (and most easily) outlined in terms of a change in the *I*-spending level. But remember: The propensity to consume can *also* change. (An example of a change in consumer-spending plans and its results follows later in this chapter.)

1. Figures 12-3 (propensity to consume) and 12-4 (investment) below are similar in construction to Figures 12-1 and 12-2.

a. Consider Fig. 12-4. (Disregard for the moment the broken *I'* line at height *RO*.) The solid *I* line at height *BO* is horizontal. To draw this line horizontally is to say that if the level of GNP were to rise, the amount of investment spending would *(rise/remain unchanged/fall)*; if the level of GNP were to fall, *I* spending would *(rise/remain unchanged/fall)*.

b. Consider Fig. 12-3. It says that if the amount of GNP were to be *OE*, the amount of consumption spending would be *(HA / JA / ME / KE)*. With GNP at *OE*, the amount of saving would be *(HJ / JA / MK / KE)*.

If, however, GNP were to be at the lower level *OA*, then *C* spending would be *(HA / JA / ME / KE)*, and *S* would be *(HJ / JA / MK / KE)*.

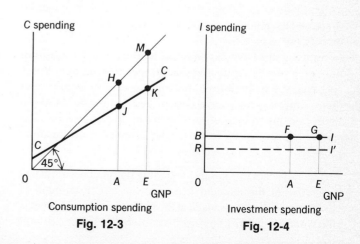

Fig. 12-3 — Consumption spending

Fig. 12-4 — Investment spending

2. If GNP is to be "in equilibrium," the amounts of S and I must be equal. Measure with your eye the two S amounts indicated on Fig. 12-3 (*HJ* and *MK*), and compare them with the investment amount indicated by the solid I line (*BO*, or *FA*, or *GE*) in Fig. 12-4. The S value that would match this I value would be (*HJ / MK*).

That is to say, S and I will be equal when S has climbed to level *MK*. This would call for a GNP level of (*OA / OE*).

Given the I level *BO* (or *FA* or *GE*) then, and *given* the propensity to consume of Fig. 12-3, the equilibrium GNP level must be *OE*. This is the only GNP value at which C-spending plans and I-spending plans "fit together" properly. (Examples of figures which *do not* fit together properly follow in question 3.)

Notice that this equilibrium can be measured in either of the two ways earlier noted:

either as $\quad$ S = I (MK = GE)

or else as $\quad$ GNP = C + I (OE = KE + GE)

3. *a.* Alternatively, suppose the total of investment spending is indicated in Fig. 12-4 by level *RO* (the broken *I'* line) and not by *BO*. What would the equilibrium value of GNP then be? Again measuring with your eyes S amounts versus I amount, it follows that saving would have to be (*HJ / MK*). Saving will be this amount only when GNP is at the corresponding level, namely (*OA / OE*).

Notice in passing one interesting consequence: If the I-spending level were to drop from *BO* to *RO*, then in the resulting new equilibrium, C spending would (*also have dropped / remain unchanged / have risen*). This point will be developed later on.

b. The two equilibrium positions just indicated (each of them corresponding to a different level of I) may help to explain why (as an alternative to S = I) equilibrium can be expressed as: total incomes earned must equal total expenditures (GNP = C + I).

Suppose that GNP has been holding steady at an equilibrium level of *OE*, with investment spending at *BO*. But I spending suddenly drops to the lower level of *RO*, and stays there. (Business firms have become less optimistic about the future; or the volume of just-beginning investment projects simply happens to be less than the volume of just-finishing projects.)

The impact of this cut in I spending does not occur instantaneously. At the moment it occurs, the last installment of GNP income payments made at the older and higher I level is still wending its way toward consumers; and they are still

spending accordingly. So we have a situation in which GNP (*OE*) is *not* equal to the sum of C spending (*KE*) and I spending (*RO*). GNP is out of equilibrium. Because of the drop in I spending, it is going to (*fall / rise*). (This condition of a change in the equilibrium level of GNP is discussed at length below.)

c. Below are three sets of values based on Figs. 12-3 and 12-4. In at least one, the situation is "out of equilibrium." Which one, or which ones?

Case	GNP	C	I	S
(1)	OA	JA	RO	HJ
(2)	OA	JA	BO	HJ
(3)	OE	KE	BO	MK

So investment spending can call the tune, so far as the level of GNP is concerned. Now we must explore more fully what happens when the level of this I spending changes.

For this, we use the figures (in billions) associated with Figs. 12-1 and 12-2. GNP has been in equilibrium at a level of $100, with I spending at $30 and C spending at $70. But, as in question 3 above, I spending drops. It drops from $30 to $20, and it stays at $20. The horizontal I-line of Figs. 12-2 and 12-4 drops to a new and lower position at *I'*.

The flow of money spending directed toward producers has dropped from $100 to $90 because the I-spending component of this flow has dropped. It will take a little time before consumers begin to feel the impact of this. But when business was paying out $100 in wages and salaries, interest and dividend payments, and the like, it was simply passing on money it received from the buyers of consumption goods and of investment goods. When (because of the drop in investment spending) this incoming flow drops to $90, then the earnings flow (wages and salaries, dividend payments, etc.) must drop correspondingly. There is no alternative source which could maintain it at the old $100 level. Some workers will be laid off, or required to work short time; the total of profits earned by incorporated and unincorporated businesses will fall. Specifically, the flow of earned income reaching consumers must likewise drop from $100 to $90. *But note:* This is not the end of the process at all.

4. *a.* When income (which here we are measuring in the form of GNP) drops, C spending will (*drop also/remain constant/rise*); this is what the propensity to consume says.

By how much will C drop, if income (GNP) has dropped by $10? For this, we must know the (*average/marginal*) propensity to consume. [Now you can begin to understand why we lavished so much time on the MPC in Chapter 11. The MPC will tell you the change (rise or fall) in *C* that goes with any given change (rise or fall) in income received.]

Suppose the MPC is 0.6, or ⁶⁄₁₀. This means that the reduction in *C* spending following a $10 reduction in income will be $(*zero / 6 / 10*). That is, with income now at $90 rather than $100, *C* spending, instead of being $70, will be $(*10 / 64 / 70 / 90 / 100*). And the amount saved out of this income of $90, rather than being $30, will be $(*0 / 6 / 10 / 26 / 30 / 36*).

b. Investment spending, remember, has dropped to $20 and stays at $20. After the cut in *C* just reviewed, is *S* = *I*? (*Yes / No*). Is GNP at an equilibrium level? (*Yes / No*).

---

a. drop also; marginal; 6; 64; 26. *b.* No; No.

---

5. We now reach a point in the analysis which *must* be grasped. Although *C* spending has fallen from $70 to $64 on account of the $10 drop in GNP, we are still nowhere near a new equilibrium GNP level. The fact that GNP is still out of equilibrium is evident from the fact that *S* ($26) is not equal to *I* ($20).

The all-important point is that any drop in consumption spending has exactly the same effect on production and on incomes earned as a drop in investment spending has. Consumption spending has fallen from $70 to $64. To producers, this means that the demand for consumer goods has fallen off: a smaller volume of such goods produced and sold means a smaller total of incomes earned.

a. If the total of incomes earned by producing and selling consumer goods drops by $6, this means a drop of $(*3 / 6 / 10*) in GNP. Note that this is *in addition to* the initial drop of $10 set off by the reduction in *I* spending. So GNP, which first fell from $100 to $90, drops further to $(*60 / 80 / 84 / 88*).

To review the sequence of events thus far:
1st event: GNP falls from $100 to $90 on account of the drop in investment spending.
2nd event: Consumption spending falls from $70 to $64 on account of the drop in GNP.
3rd event: GNP falls from $90 to $84 on account of the drop in consumption spending.

But the propensity to consume says that whenever there is any drop in GNP, there will be a drop in *C* spending—equal in our case to six-tenths of the GNP drop. (The only *C* reduction noted in the events above was the drop set off by the *first* GNP cut.)

So *C* spending must fall again: GNP is down by $6. so *C* will be down by 0.6 times $6, or $(*2.0 / 2.6 / 3.6 / 6.0*). That is, *C* falls from $64 to $(*54 / 58 / 60.4 / 64.4*). So we must add:

4th event: Consumption spending falls from $64 to $60.4 on account of the drop in GNP.

Notice in passing that saving is also going down. The most recent GNP drop was $6: the resulting *C* drop is six-tenths of $6; and the drop in *S* is four-tenths of $6—which is $(*1.0 / 2.0 / 2.4 / 3.0*). In summary, *S* first dropped from $30 to $26; then it dropped again from $26 to $23.6.

But saving has not yet reached the investment level of $20. GNP is still out of equilibrium.

b. Next, of course, GNP is hit by the most recent cut in *C* spending:
5th event: GNP falls from $84 to $80.4 on account of the drop in consumption spending.

Now the ball is back in the other court again. If GNP is down by $3.6, *C* must fall (assuming the MPC still to be 0.6) by six-tenths of $3.6—or if you prefer, fall by 0.6 times 0.6 times $6. That is, *C* is down by about $(*2.2 / 2.6 / 3.0 / 3.4*).

And that of course pulls GNP down a little more. But notice that the amounts involved in this around-and-around cycle grow steadily smaller.

Assuming the *I*-spending level to be steady at $20, this process will end, and GNP will be back in equilibrium, when (pick one):
(1) GNP has fallen to zero.
(2) Saving has fallen to zero.
(3) Saving has fallen to $20.

---

a. 6; 84; 3.6; 60.4; 2.4. *b.* 2.2; (3).

Question 5 set out a round-and-round sequence of income reductions. Each reduction is 0.6 times its predecessor (assuming, for convenience, that the MPC remains constant at 0.6).

Mathematically, this kind of sequence is elegantly known as a convergent geometric progression. All you need know about such a progression is that its sum has a finite limit. That is, GNP does not keep dropping until it reaches zero. The sequence 10 + 6 + 3.6 + (0.6 times 3.6) + . . . etc., totals 25. So the total GNP drop will be $25. GNP will fall from its original value of $100 until it reaches a new equilibrium at $75.

Do not worry at this stage about the detail of the mathematics. Instead, try to grasp the general process by which the new equilibrium is reached. You should understand that each drop in *C* spending means a drop in production, in employment, and in incomes earned—which in turn produces a further drop in *C* spending. This is the multiplier process:

▶ Any change in spending which disturbs the equilibrium level of GNP will set off a chain reaction such that the final change in GNP is much larger than—is a multiple of—the initial change.

In our example, equilibrium was disturbed by a cut

in I spending of $10; but in the resulting new equilibrium, GNP had fallen by $25, not just by $10.

It is essential to understand this process. Many students find the circular-flow diagram, Study Guide Fig. 11-7 (p. 86), helpful. The flow of spending through the "investment intake" (at lower left) shrinks by $10; this reduces the flow of incomes through the upper loop by $10. So both C spending and saving must fall. A $6 shrinkage in the money flowing through the lower "Consumption spending" loop means a further reduction in GNP of $6; this means a further cut in incomes of $6—and so on.

Thus GNP can be "out of equilibrium" much of the time (perhaps virtually all of the time, because of continuing changes in I). But the idea of an equilibrium position is still vitally important: If GNP is out of equilibrium, then it is *changing* in value, seeking out its equilibrium goal.

The diagrams typically used to illustrate this analysis are "short-cut" diagrams. They do not bother with the intermediate, out-of-equilibrium process. They show only some original equilibrium GNP level, and the new equilibrium which would result from some change in decisions on the part of I spenders (or C spenders). The saving-investment diagram next used is an example.

6. In equilibrium, saving equals investment. So we can use a saving-investment diagram to illustrate equilibrium GNP.

If we know the propensity to consume, we can develop from it a propensity to save (see review question 3, p. 81), showing the amount *saved* at each GNP level. In Fig. 12-5, the SS line is such a propensity to save; it corresponds to Fig. 12-1's propensity to consume.

The solid II line in this figure repeats that of Fig. 12-2. The intersection of SS and II curves, at GNP = $100, indicates the equilibrium GNP level, *because it is the only GNP level at which S and I are equal.*

a. The broken $I'I'$ line shows what happens if I spending drops from $30 to $20. The new equilibrium GNP must be $(20 / 30 / 60 / 75 / 90 / 100)$, for the same reason as before. If I spending is to be $20, than S must be $20 also; and $75 is the only GNP level at which S is $20.

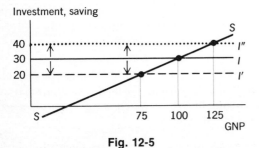

Fig. 12-5

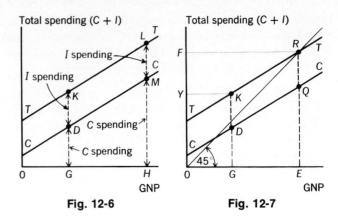

Fig. 12-6   **Fig. 12-7**

b. Also shown on Fig. 12-5 is a dotted $I''I''$ line, at level $40. If I spending were to rise to this level, the diagram indicates that the resulting GNP equilibrium level would be $(75 / 100 / 110 / 125 / 150)$. (CAUTION: Should full-employment GNP happen to be in the vicinity of $100, this equilibrium GNP might be unattainable. Chapter 13 explores this matter.)

---

a. 75. *b.* 125.

---

7. Equilibrium can be identified by the requirement: $S = I$. The saving-investment diagram is accordingly one way of illustrating equilibrium GNP.

Alternatively, equilibrium can be identified by the total-incomes-must-equal-total-spending requirement: GNP = C + I. And there is a diagram which draws on *this* rule. (Remember that to use this diagram is simply to draw on an alternative method of illustrating exactly the same GNP position.)

a. In Fig. 12-6, the line CC is the same propensity to consume we have already used in Figs. 12-1 and 12-3. REMEMBER: The amount of C spending, for any given GNP level, is measured *vertically*. At the GNP level indicated by OG in Fig. 12-6, C spending would be DG. If the GNP level were OH, then C spending would be $(KD / DG / LM / MH)$.

For GNP purposes, our interest is in *total* spending—in C spending *plus* I spending. There is no reason why we cannot *add* I spending on this diagram, thus showing total spending. We draw the line TT above CC, and we make the vertical distance between these two lines the amount of I spending.

To explain more fully: Suppose we take the same level of I spending assumed when Fig. 12-1 was first used, namely, $30. In Fig. 12-6, the vertical distance between TT and CC lines will then be $30. That is, the distance between K and D, marked off by the arrow line, will be $30. So will the distance similarly marked off between L and M.

b. This means that the vertical distance from any point on TT down to the axis line now measures *total* spending, $C + I$. At

GNP level *OG*, the *I* spending would be *KD*, the *C* spending would be *DG*, and total spending, *I* + *C*, would be *KG*—i.e., *KD* plus *DG*.

Similarly, if the GNP level were *OH*, the amount of *I* spending would be indicated by *(LM / DG / MH)*. *C* spending would be measured by *(LM / DG / MH)*. Total spending would be measured by *(LM / KG / MH / LH)*.

This material may be unfamiliar, but it is not complicated. Be sure you understand it reasonably well before you pass on to part *c*.

c. Figure 12-7, alongside and to right of Fig. 12-6, is basically the same as Fig. 12-6. The same *CC* and *TT* lines appear. We have simply added a 45° "helping line."

Now remember the special property of this 45° line (see p. 80): *It marks off all the equal-value points*. Take any point on the 45° line: distances to vertical and horizontal axes will be equal. Take any point *off* this line: distances to the two axes will be *unequal*.

Recall our equilibrium GNP condition: GNP = *C* + *I*.

Pick any GNP at random. Given the particular propensity-to-consume and investment schedules involved, would this GNP be an equilibrium one?

For example, take a GNP of *OG* in Fig. 12-7 (the right-hand figure). Total spending, *C* + *I*, would then be *KG*. But point *K* is *off* the 45° line. So *KG* is *not* equal to *OG*. (That is, GNP would *not* be equal to *C* + *I*.)

Thus the equilibrium GNP level can only be at the point where the total-spending line, *TT*, cuts across the 45° line. This is at point *R*, indicating a GNP of *OE*. Here, total spending of *RE (is / is not)* just equal to GNP of *OE*.

d. If the two equilibrium conditions come to one and the same thing, then it ought to be true that the equilibrium GNP of *OE* depicted in Fig. 12-7 marks an *S* = *I* position.

And it does. Saving at any GNP level is the vertical distance from the propensity-to-consume line up to the 45° line. Hence at GNP of *OE*, saving must be *RQ*. This *(is / is not)* the same as investment.

At any GNP lower than (to the left of) *OE*, *S* would be *(less than/equal to/greater than)* *I*. At any GNP higher than (to the right of) *OE*, *S* would be *(less than / equal to / greater than) I*.

---

a. MH. b. LM; MH; LH. c. is. d. is; less than; greater than.

---

8. Suppose there is a sudden and drastic drop in the level of *I* spending: it falls (say) from $30 (billion) per period to $10. In terms of Fig. 12-7, this would mean a *(rise / drop)* in the total-spending line *TT*.

Figure 12-8 shows this event. The *TT* line drops from its former position (the solid black line) to the level *T'T'* (the broken line). So the new total-spending line will cut the 45° line at point *(X / R / D / Q)*, and the new equilibrium level of GNP indicated will be *(OG / OE)*. That is, the drastic drop in

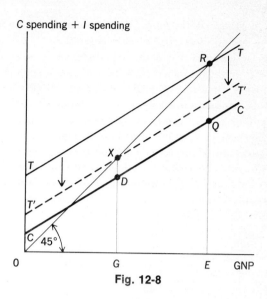

Fig. 12-8

investment spending has produced an even more drastic reduction in incomes and employment.

---

drop; *X*; *OG*.

---

9. *a.* Remember that any such change in *I* spending has a magnified or "multiplied" effect on the GNP level because it sets off a series of *C* changes (as earlier outlined).

If the multiplier figure is 3, and *I* spending rises by $10 billion, then GNP will *(rise/fall)* by *$(10 / 20 / 30 / 40 / 50)* billion. If *I* spending rises by $10 billion with a multiplier of 4, then GNP will *(rise/fall)* by *$(10 / 20 / 30 / 40 / 50)* billion.

The multiplier formula given in the text is:

$$\frac{1}{1 - \text{MPC}} \quad \text{or} \quad \frac{1}{\text{MPS}}$$

This means that if the MPC is 0.6, the multiplier is *(1 / 2 / 2½ / 3 / 3½ / 4)*. If the MPC is 0.8, the multiplier is *(1 / 2 / 2½ / 3½ / 4 / 5)*.

b. Suppose there is a change in investment (either rise or fall) of $10. If the MPC is 0.6, the resulting change in GNP (rise or fall) will be *$(10 / 20 / 25 / 30 / 50)*. If the MPC is 0.8, the resulting change in GNP (rise or fall) will be *$(10 / 20 / 25 / 30 / 50)*.

(NOTE: The multiplier formula given above holds only in the simplified conditions used in this chapter. In Chapter 13, we take account of some complications; and the multiplier formula is changed correspondingly.)

---

a. rise; 30; rise; 40; 2½; 5. b. 25; 50.

---

10. An equilibrium GNP will not be disturbed unless either the *II* line or the *CC* line shifts to a new position. (That is, it will not be disturbed unless there is some change either in investment-spending plans or in consumer-spending plans.

We are of course still assuming the influence of government spending and taxation to be entirely absent.)

Thus far, we have considered only disturbances in equilibrium GNP produced by a change in investment spending (a shift in the *II* line of Fig. 12-2). Changes in GNP are most commonly attributed to changes in *I* spending.

Nevertheless, changes in the propensity to consume *can* occur. Any such change will upset equilibrium GNP just as an *I* change would. Here, you should recall review questions 7 and 8, Chapter 11 (pp. 83–84), which pointed out that the *CC* line (the propensity to consume) can shift up, or down, if for some reason consumers decide to spend more money, or less, out of a given *DI* (here, a given GNP).

We begin with the same set of figures as before: GNP is in equilibrium at $100; *C* spending is $70, and *I* spending is $30. Saving is likewise $30.

For some reason, consumers decide to become more thrifty. They plan to spend $10 less on consumption, and to save $10 more, at each and any GNP level. Since GNP is currently $100, this means they plan to spend $60 on consumption, and to save $40.

Figure 12-9 shows the same propensity to consume we have already used. The consumer decision to save more and spend less will cause the *CC* line to shift downward to the position *C'C'* (the broken line).

But the total-spending line, *TT* in Fig. 12-10 at right, is the sum of *C* + *I*. If *CC* is displaced vertically downward by $10 as in Fig. 12-9 the same must hold for *TT*. It must shift downward to position *T'T'* (also a broken line).

This *(affects / does not affect)* equilibrium GNP. GNP will *(fall / rise)*. The resulting new equilibrium level of GNP indicated in Fig. 12-10 is $ _____ .

(Notice that this initial change in *C* spending has the same multiplier effect as a change in *I* spending would have: an initial change of $10 causes equilibrium GNP to change by $25.)

---

affects; fall; 75.

---

11. The point now to be discussed is a tricky one. Don't tackle it until you feel you have a pretty fair grasp of the preceding material, and don't be discouraged if at first you find it hard going. Others have done so.

The text emphasizes "scheduled" or "planned" investment. It is possible also to have "unscheduled" or "unintended" investment. *Investment of this latter kind is symptomatic of disequilibrium in GNP.*

Consider question 10's reduction in *C* spending. When this first occurs, department stores and other firms involved in retail trade may be taken by surprise. Their inventories pile up as a consequence of reduced consumer buying.

Now Chapter 10 told us that any increase in inventories counts as investment. So—*temporarily*—the drop in *C*

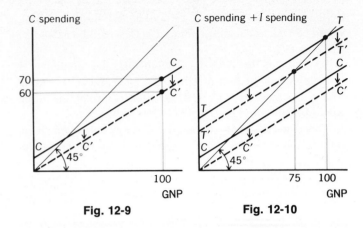

Fig. 12-9   **Fig. 12-10**

spending is matched by a rise in *I*. This makes it *appear* as if GNP were still in equilibrium: the total of *C* plus *I* is unchanged. In fact it is not, because the inventory pile-up (the increase in *I*) was unintended and unwanted. The stores will proceed to work down their inventories by canceling or reducing their orders to their suppliers. That is how the impact of reduced buying spreads to other firms; that is how the drop in incomes begins.

When the new equilibrium is finally reached, there is *(still some / no longer any)* "unscheduled," "unintended," investment.

The same words "unscheduled," "unintended," or "unplanned" may also be applied to saving. Again, the reference is to a situation of disequilibrium GNP, when the various figures for investment, consumption, and saving do not mesh together properly, so that GNP is moving toward a new equilibrium level.

In the *statistical* sense—but not in the analytic sense, which is the important one in this chapter—the statistics for *S* and *I* always show up as equal in total. This does *not* mean that GNP is always in equilibrium; it just means that the statisticians have counted the "unscheduled" *S* or *I* along with the "scheduled" or "planned" *S* and *I*. They have no way of knowing which is which. The important thing about the "unscheduled" figures is that they are about to change in amount, thus affecting the GNP level.

---

no longer any.

QUIZ: Multiple Choice

NOTE: In all the following questions, assume that all types of government transactions (spending and taxation) are absent. Absent also: depreciation, undistributed corporation profits, interest payments by consumers.

1. *Business firms change their plans and increase the total of their spending to have new plant and equipment built. As* *a result, we would expect* (1) no change in GNP, necessarily; (2) GNP to rise, and consumer spending also to rise; (3) GNP to rise but consumer spending to be unaffected; (4) GNP to rise but consumer spending to fall; (5) GNP to fall, but consumer spending to rise.

2. *If, on a graph of the propensity to consume, the entire propensity-to-consume line shifts to a new and different position, above its previous position, this means that consumers have decided* (1) to increase the amount of their saving (S), because of an increase in income; (2) to increase S, because of some factor other than an increase in income; (3) to reduce S, because of a reduction in income; (4) to reduce S, because of some factor other than a reduction in income; (5) to do none of the above necessarily, since a shift in the propensity to consume affects consumption, not saving.

3. *In the circumstances spelled out in this chapter, if the value of the marginal propensity to consume is 0.8, then the value of the multiplier must be* (1) 1.6; (2) 2.5; (3) 2.8; (4) 4; (5) 5.

4. *If the amount of investment (I) spending should suddenly fall, then, other things being equal,* (1) GNP will begin and will continue to fall, but the ultimate fall will be less than the I fall; (2) GNP will fall immediately by an amount much greater than the I fall; (3) GNP will fall immediately by an amount less than the I fall, but will show no further tendency to fall; (4) it is more likely that GNP will rise rather than fall; (5) GNP will begin and will continue to fall, until it has fallen by an amount considerably greater than the I fall.

5. *A change in the total of consumer spending can have the same effect upon GNP (throwing it from equilibrium into disequilibrium, and so changing the GNP value by a multiplied amount) that a change in the total of investment spending would have* (1) only if that C-spending change is set off by some factor other than a change in GNP; (2) only if that C-spending change is itself set off by a change in GNP; (3) regardless of the circumstances that set off the C-spending change; (4) with respect to increases in C spending only, not with respect to decreases; (5) in no circumstances, since disequilibrium GNP results only from changes in I spending.

6. *The "equilibrium" level of gross national product (GNP) is related to the "full-employment" level of GNP as follows: It* (1) is the same thing as full-employment GNP; (2) definitely is not full-employment GNP; (3) normally means full-employment GNP, except in special disequilibrium circumstances; (4) may or may not be the same thing as full-employment GNP; (5) means a future level of GNP above the present full-employment level.

7. *If an equilibrium level of GNP is altered by a decrease in planned investment spending, then we would expect* (1) GNP to fall, but saving (S) to rise; (2) GNP to fall, but no change in S; (3) GNP to fall, and S to fall also; (4) GNP to remain unchanged, but S to fall; (5) none of the preceding.

8. *Which alternative in question 7 would be correct had it spoken, not of a decrease in planned investment spending, but of a decision on the part of consumers to save more and to spend less upon consumption?* (1). (2). (3). (4). (5).

9. *On a 45° diagram, such as is used extensively in both the text and the Study Guide for this chapter, the intersection of the propensity-to-consume and 45° lines has the following significance with respect to GNP: It indicates* (1) the GNP level at which net investment spending (I) first rises above zero; (2) equality of consumption (C) and I; (3) equilibrium GNP; (4) equality of C and saving; (5) nothing in particular, unless I happens to be zero.

10. *We say that GNP is above its equilibrium level whenever* (1) the amount that consumers plan to withdraw from the "income stream" as saving (S) exceeds the amount business firms and others plan to pump into that income stream as investment spending (I); (2) the total of planned consumption spending (C) exceeds the total of planned I; (3) there is no unscheduled or unplanned I; (4) GNP has moved temporarily above the "break-even"point on the propensity to consume; (5) the total of planned I plus the total of planned C exceeds the current level of GNP.

11. *Which alternative in question 10 would be correct had that question referred to a GNP below its equilibrium level?* (1). (2). (3). (4). (5).

12. *Before a particular Christmas, shoppers decide to spend considerably less than retail stores anticipated, leaving those stores with considerable unsold inventories of goods. This situation is an example of* (1) planned investment; (2) unscheduled saving; (3) a rise in GNP; (4) unscheduled investment; (5) none of the preceding.

13. *If GNP falls by reason of a fall in investment spending, we would expect as a consequence that* (1) both consumption (C) and saving (S) would rise; (2) both C and S would fall; (3) C would rise but S would fall; (4) C would fall but S would rise; (5) neither C nor S would necessarily change in value.

14. *One way of specifying the requirement that must be satisfied for an equilibrium level of GNP is to say that* (1) the total of incomes earned must just equal the total that consumers are planning to spend out of that income plus the total they are planning to save; (2) the total of consumer spending must be just equal to the "break-even" level of income; (3) the total of GNP must be just equal to the total of planned saving plus the total of planned investment; (4) the total of incomes earned must just equal the total consumers are planning to spend out of that income plus the total of planned investment; (5) the total of spending must be just enough to bring production to its full-employment level.

15. *The current level of GNP is $500 (billion), and out of this, consumers wish to spend $390 (billion) on consumption. The total amount of investment spending planned is $120* *(billion). These figures indicate* (1) that GNP is out of equilibrium and will fall in value; (2) that GNP is out of equilibrium and will rise in value; (3) that GNP is out of equilibrium, although whether it will rise, fall, or remain at its present level is indeterminate; (4) that GNP is in equilibrium; (5) none of the above necessarily, since, from the information given, GNP may be in equilibrium or out of it.

16. *If the marginal propensity to save is 0.3 (i.e., ³⁄₁₀), and investment spending rises by $6 billion, we can expect this to increase the level of equilibrium GNP by* (1) $2 billion; (2) $6 billion; (3) $18 billion; (4) $20 billion; (5) $60 billion.

QUIZ: Other

1. You are given the following propensity to consume for a community: Consumption spending for each and any level of GNP will be $20 (billion) plus three-fifths of that GNP.

a. What will consumption be if GNP is $40?_____.
If GNP is $60? _____. If GNP is $100?
_____.

b. Draw this propensity to consume in Fig. 12-11.

c. Suppose that investment spending will be $20, at each and all levels of GNP. Draw in Fig. 12-11 a total-spending line (assuming government spending to be zero). What will be the resulting equilibrium value of GNP? _____.

2. Given the following information:
(1) The full-employment level of GNP in a certain economy is estimated at $100 billion.
(2) The amount of consumption spending to be expected at this full-employment GNP level is $80 billion.
(3) The marginal propensity to consume is 0.8.
(4) The amount of planned investment spending will be $10 billion, regardless of the GNP level.

a. Assuming all government items (spending and taxation) to be zero, then the equilibrium level of GNP will be (pick one): (1) $100 billion; (2) $90 billion; (3) less than $90 billion.

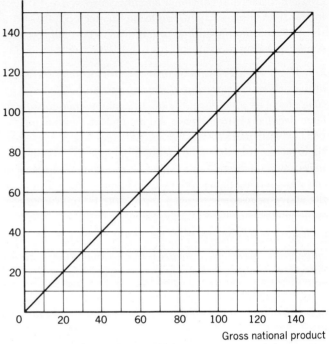

Spending: consumption, investment

Gross national product

Fig. 12-11

b. The increase in investment spending, if any, needed to bring GNP up to its full-employment, $100-billion level would be (pick one): (1) zero; (2) $10 billion; (3) $20 billion; (4) more than $20 billion.

3. The following figures (billions of dollars) indicate an economy's propensity to consume out of GNP:

GNP:	130	150	170	190	210	230	250	270	290	310
C:	112	126	140	154	168	182	196	210	224	238

a. If the amount of investment spending is 60, and if government spending of all types is zero, what is the equilibrium level of GNP? ...._____.

b. If the total of this investment spending should drop by 30, what would be the new resulting equilibrium level of GNP?
...._____.

THIS CHAPTER amplifies and develops the basic analysis of Chapters 11 and 12. Review the material of those chapters, if necessary, before you tackle this one.

1. Chapter 11 emphasized the fact that investment spending is variable because it is subject to many possible influences. One such influence is the level of GNP: *I* spending is likely to be low, perhaps even zero, if the economy is deep in recession, with plenty of unemployed capacity. In contrast, if GNP is close to full employment, investment prospects will seem much brighter, and spending will be correspondingly higher.

In Chapter 12, for simplicity, we assumed *I* spending to be unresponsive to GNP changes. Figure 13-1 below duplicates Fig. 12-2. It shows *II* as *flat:* the *I*-spending amount is the same no matter whether GNP is at level *OG* or *OE*.

In Fig. 13-2 (at right), by contrast, *I* spending is shown as *(falling / constant / rising)* as GNP increases. If GNP is at the level *OG*, *I* spending will be *(LE / HG / OE)*—its total, that is, will be $(15 / 30)$. If GNP is at level *OE*, then *I* spending will be indicated by *(OG / HG / LE)*—that is, an amount of $(15 / 30)$.

In this chapter, we use the same diagrams as those of Chapter 12. But we now recognize that the amount of *I* spending will probably be different at different GNP levels— that a higher level of GNP will "induce" some extra *I* spending. So we make the *II* line in saving-investment diagrams "tilted" (Fig. 13-2) rather than flat (Fig. 13-1).

rising; *HG*; 15; *LE*; 30.

2. We can now examine "the paradox of thrift." The essence of this paradox is as follows: Suppose the community decides to become more thrifty—i.e., decides to save more money out of GNP than is currently being saved. The outcome of this attempt to save *more* may be that *less* is saved.

Figure 13-3 (at left above, a propensity-to-save diagram,

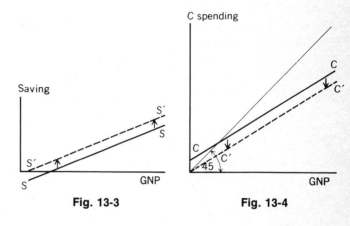

Fig. 13-3   **Fig. 13-4**

illustrates this decision to save more. The *SS* line (the solid line) moves upward to *S'S'* (the broken line).

Now a decision to save *more* means a decision to spend *less*. Figure 13-4 (alongside 13-3) shows the matching *downward* movement in the propensity to consume. (Note that this is exactly the same kind of downward shift in the *CC* line as was illustrated in Fig. 12-9, p. 96).

The components of the paradox of thrift are now assembled. Figure 13-5 (at left, top of next page) shows the GNP equilibrium before the decision to become more thrifty. It is a saving-investment diagram, like Fig. 12-5 (on p. 94), except that the *II* line is tilted.

Figure 13-6 (right-hand figure, next page, repeats Fig. 13-5, but it shows also the upward shift of the *SS* curve to *S'S'*, the same shift indicated in Fig. 13-3.

Examine Fig. 13-6 carefully. The upward shift of the *SS* line has caused GNP to fall. Its equilibrium level has changed from *OE* to *OF*. Be sure you understand why this fall in equilibrium GNP has occurred. It is because *C* spending has dropped (see Fig. 13-4). And *C* spending is one of the components of GNP.

To sum up, by reference to Fig. 13-6:

a. We began with an equilibrium GNP of *(OE / OF)*. The amount then saved out of GNP was *(HF / LE / KL / KE)*. Then consumers decided to save more out of income: their intention was to increase total *S* from *LE* to *(HF / KL / KE)*. The *SS* line shifted upward to position *S'S'*.

But the decision to save more involved also a decision to spend less. This upset the equilibrium level of GNP. GNP fell, and continued to fall until it reached a new equilibrium level at *(OE / OF)*.

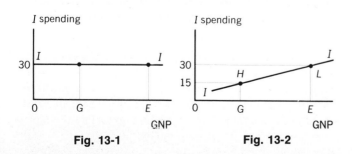

Fig. 13-1   **Fig. 13-2**

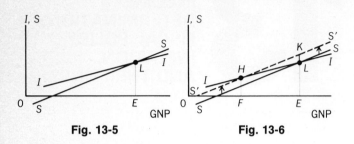

Fig. 13-5   **Fig. 13-6**

b. At this new equilibrium GNP, saving out of income, *S*, is indicated by *(HF / KE / KL / LE)*. This amount is *(less / more)* than was saved in the original equilibrium, when *S* was *(HF / LE / KL / KE)*. Paradoxically, consumers have brought about a result exactly opposed to their intentions.

---

a. *OE; LE; KE; OF.* *b.* *HF;* less; *LE.*

---

3. Question 9, Chapter 12 (p. 95) set out a "simple" multiplier formula—and closed with a warning, namely, that in the form presented there, it applied only in Chapter 12's simplified conditions. Now we must add a complication to this formula.

It's important here to remember something emphasized in Chapter 11 (and already recalled in question 1 for this chapter): *Many* factors can influence investment spending and thus bring about a change in the total level of that spending. One such possible factor is a rise in the GNP level; this is the "induced investment" of question 1 (this chapter). There remain plenty of other possible reasons. To distinguish them from the "induced investment" just mentioned, let these other reasons be lumped together as "autonomous investment" changes.

Now to the multiplier: Its general idea remains exactly as it was in the previous chapter. The idea is that if (say) autonomous investment rises, incomes will increase. When incomes rise, so does consumer (*C*) spending. The rise in *C* spending sends incomes up some more—which means *another* (although smaller) rise in *C* spending, and so on.

When "induced investment" makes its appearance, as in this chapter, we get the same kind of mechanism working on *investment* as on consumption. The paragraph immediately preceding said: If and when autonomous *I* goes up for some reason, then *C* will go up; then (by reason of the further resulting increase in incomes) *C* will go up some more. *Now* we are saying that if, for some reason, autonomous *I* spending goes up, then *C* will rise (just as before)—*and so will I.* Why an *I* rise now, as well as a *C* rise? Because any GNP increase now sets off an *I* increase ("induced investment") as well as a *C* increase (which could be called, although it isn't, "induced consumption"—i.e., induced by a rise in GNP).

a. So "induced investment" elbows its way into the multiplier formula. In Chapter 12, that formula was $1/(1 - \text{MPC})$. Now we have introduced an MPI (marginal propensity to *invest*) as well as an MPC. (The MPC idea, remember, is just

an elegant way of expressing the idea that if GNP changes, *C* will change also, by some specified fraction of the GNP change. Now we are saying the same thing about investment—it *too* will change if GNP changes, by some specified fraction thereof.) The MPC and the MPI are now *both* involved. Since they both push in the same direction (work hand in hand, so to speak), which of the following—look at the preceding formula—seems the most appropriate new multiplier formula? (Pick one.)

(1) $\dfrac{1}{1 - (\text{MPC} - \text{MPI})}$ (2) $\dfrac{1}{1 - (\text{MPC} + \text{MPI})}$

(3) $\dfrac{1}{1 - \text{MPI}}$ (4) $\dfrac{1}{1 - (\text{MPI} - \text{MPC})}$

(Note two small points: (1) Much of the preceding discussion ran in terms of a GNP *increase* set off by an increase in autonomous *I* spending; but of course the process and the formula apply equally to any *decrease*. (2) Footnote 7 in the text chapter discusses this topic of amplifying the multiplier formula.)

b. Suppose each rise (fall) of $10 in GNP induces a rise (fall) of $2 in *I* spending. Then the MPI would be *(.1 / .2 / .5 / 1.0)*. Suppose the value of the MPC is .6. Put these MPI and MPC values into formula (2) (the correct alternative) for the multiplier above. The resulting value of the multiplier proves to be *(1.0 / 2.5 / 4.0 / 5.0)*.

Notice that putting an MPI into the multiplier formula tends to *(increase / decrease)* the value of the multiplier.

---

a. (2). *b.* .2; 5.0; increase.

---

4. The concept of the "deflationary gap" sometimes causes trouble. It need not; the idea is simple. It originates from the fact, stressed in the introduction to Chapter 12, that equilibrium GNP is not necessarily the same thing as full-employment GNP.

▶ A deflationary gap exists whenever equilibrium GNP is significantly below full-employment GNP.

So a "deflationary gap" means primarily a situation in which labor is not fully employed, and plant and equipment are not working close to capacity. The situation is one of "deflation." This is the essential point to grasp, and the only tricky point involves the *quantitative measure* of this deflationary gap.

Two possible measures exist. Suppose (for example) that equilibrium GNP is $60, and full-employment GNP is $100. If the value of the multiplier if 4, then an increase of $10 in *I* spending would be desirable (NOTE: $10, not $40), because it would bring GNP out of recession and up to the full-employment level. (REMEMBER: Rise in GNP = *I* increase × multiplier value.)

So the deflationary gap could be measured either as

(i) the actual difference between equilibrium and full-employment GNPs (in the example, as $40); or
(ii) the increase in "autonomous" spending needed to raise GNP to full-employment level (in the example, $10).

Arbitrarily, the *second* of these possible definitions has been chosen as *the* definition of the deflationary gap.

For example: Suppose equilibrium and full-employment GNPs are $700 and $800 respectively. The multiplier value is 5. The deflationary gap would then be specified as $(5 / 10 / 20 / 50 / 100).

Similarly, if full-employment GNP is $750, the equilibrium value of GNP in deflation is $600, and the multiplier value is estimated at 3, then the deflationary gap would be $(50 / 100 / 150).

Figure 13-7 (below) is a saving-investment diagram. The zone or range of GNPs which could reasonably be considered full-employment GNP is indicated by the rectangular, shaded block. Three different possible I-spending levels are shown, marked 1, 2, and 3. There would be a deflationary gap if the I-spending level were indicated by (I_1 *alone* / I_2 *alone* / I_3 *alone* / *either of* I_1 *or* I_2 / *either of* I_2 *or* I_3 / *any of* I_1, I_2, *or* I_3).

20; 50; I_3 alone.

---

5. An *inflationary* gap is the opposite of a deflationary gap. Again, the beginning point to recall is that equilibrium GNP is not necessarily the same thing as full-employment GNP. There is a deflationary gap when total spending is insufficient to carry GNP to the full-employment level. There is an *inflationary* gap when total spending is so high that it is trying to push GNP *past* the full-employment level.

In Fig. 13-7 terms, there is a deflationary gap if I spending is too low—e.g., at the I_3 level. If I spending were to rise to the I_2 level, things would be just about right. However, if it were to rise still further, to the I_1 level, the problem would now be one of *too much* spending. The region to the right of the full-employment zone in Fig. 13-7 is unattainable, for the

economy's limited stock of resources is not capable of producing any GNP (measured by reference to the existing level of prices) in this region.

If I spending *does* rise to the I_1 level, then there is an inflationary gap. GNP will begin to try to seek out an equilibrium in an unattainable, never-never land to the right of the full-employment region. If not restrained, the pull of demand spending, which cannot call out further real output, will find its outlet in a series of paper price increases.

The basic idea of an inflationary gap, then, is simple: it is a problem of too much spending. The only difficulty (as with the deflationary gap) involves the quantitative definition of this inflationary gap. It is defined in terms which match exactly those used for the deflationary gap.

Suppose GNP is in equilibrium at a full-employment level of $100, with I spending of $20. The multiplier value is 4. This equilibrium is disturbed because I spending rises by $10, to a new total of $30.

This rise in I spending has created an inflationary gap. GNP begins to push upward toward an unattainable and nonexistent equilibrium level of $140.

The inflationary gap would here be defined as $10—not as $40. It would be so defined because a spending cut of $10 would wipe out this gap. Remember that it was a *rise* of $10 in spending that created this inflationary gap.

a. If GNP is in full-employment equilibrium at $700, and I spending (or C spending, for that matter) then rises by $20, the size of the resulting inflationary gap is (*$20 / indeterminate*).

Alternatively, suppose full employment is estimated at $400. Actual equilibrium GNP is $380, so that there is a deflationary gap. The multiplier is 4. An "autonomous" rise in I spending of $10 now occurs. As a result there is (*still a deflationary / now an inflationary*) gap. The amount of this (*inflationary / deflationary*) gap is $(0 / 5 / 10 / 15 / 20 / 25).

b. In grasping the basic ideas of income-determination theory, it is often convenient to assume that a rising GNP puts no upward pressure on prices until "full employment" is reached. But this is by no means always true in reality—as we discovered especially, and to our discomfort, in the 1970s. As spending increases, *some* resources become notably scarce (fully employed), so that their prices rise, while the supply of others may still be readily available. It has not yet been established how close an economy such as that of the United States can approach general "full employment" without generating substantial price increases. Certainly it is true that if a rise in I spending starts to pull the economy out of deep recession, the pressure on prices will then be at its (*minimum / maximum*), while as full employment is more closely approached, this pressure (*decreases / increases*).

---

a. 20; now an inflationary; inflationary; 5. *b.* minimum; increases.

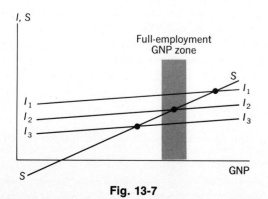

Fig. 13-7

The last major topic in Chapter 13 is the introduction of government spending and taxation—items which thus far we have disregarded.

It is easiest to take these two items separately. First examine the effect of government spending on GNP—without regard for the effect of any taxation levied to finance this expenditure. Then examine the effect of taxation on GNP, ignoring what happens if and when these tax proceeds are spent by government.

6. With respect to its effect on employment and income, government spending on goods and services *(is / is not)* in the same category as *C* spending and *I* spending.

Figures 12-6 and 12-7 (p. 94) showed how, on a 45° diagram, *I* spending could be added to *C* spending to produce a *total*-spending line. *G* spending is handled in precisely the same way: it is added vertically above *I* + *C*—so that the *total*-spending line is now a *G* + *I* + *C* line.

An increase in *G* would *(push up / pull down)* (vertically) the total-spending line. A decrease in *G* would *(push it up / pull it down)* (vertically).

A change in *G* spending *(would / would not)* have multiplier effects similar to any change in *I* or *C* spending.

---

is; push up; pull it down; would.

---

7. Thus far in Chapters 12 and 13, we have been able to work entirely in terms of GNP, using this figure as a measure both of total production and of total income earned from production. But once we get into the matter of taxes, and the effect of taxes on income and spending, we must reintroduce some of the slightly more refined measures employed in Chapter 10. Specifically, we must bring back (i) National Income, which is the measure of total income earned in producing the GNP and NNP, *before* any taxes,[1] and (ii) Disposable Income, which is income earned *after* taxes. (For a review of these differences, see in particular Fig. 10-2, p. 66.)

a. Now suppose that the government suddenly imposes a personal income tax. The immediate effect of this tax will be that National Income *(NI)*—which, remember, is *before*-tax income—is *(unchanged / lowered)*. However, Disposable Income *(DI)*—which is *after*-tax income—will be *(unchanged / lowered)*.

b. When *DI* is reduced, we must expect consumption spending to *(rise / remain unchanged / fall)*. If *C* spending is reduced, then production, and the incomes earned thereby, are likewise reduced. That is, GNP and *NI* will *(rise / remain unchanged / fall)*.

---

a. unchanged; lowered. *b.* fall; fall.

---

8. At least to a first approximation, then, government spending *(G)* and taxation cancel out one another in their effects upon GNP. Any increase in *G* tends to raise GNP; any increase in taxation, to lower GNP.

A curious and interesting thing is that *equal* increases in *G* and in taxation may not exactly cancel out one another at all. (NOTE: The point here is a tricky one—and, on a first approach to the subject, decidedly less important than other topics outlined in this chapter. Do not tackle this question until you have earlier material fairly well under control. And don't be discouraged if at first you find the idea of this question difficult.)

Suppose, say, that *G* and personal taxation are both increased by $30 billion. One's inclination is to say that in combination these two increases would "net out" to zero, leaving GNP unchanged. Not so: A given amount of extra *G* has slightly more *upward* leverage on GNP than the same amount of extra personal taxation has by way of *downward* leverage.

The crucial point involves the exact amount by which such a personal tax increase "pulls down" the propensity-to-consume line on a 45° diagram showing *C* spending at various GNP levels. The tax pulls down the *CC* line all right—but by an amount *less* than the tax increase. This is the point we must explore.

a. We assume that personal taxes are increased by a flat $30 billion.[2] As an immediate result, GNP *(is unchanged / falls by $30)*. (GNP changes only when *C*, *I*, or *G* changes. GNP is going to fall in a moment, to be sure—fall, because higher personal taxes cut the public's disposable income. And *that* will reduce *C* spending. But by how much?—that's the question.)

What *does* happen when the extra $30 (billion) in personal taxes is imposed is that *DI* (disposable income, after-tax income) will *(remain unchanged / at once fall by $30)*.

Now suppose the community's MPC is ⅔, or 0.67. If so, then by reason of the fall in *DI*, consumption spending is going to *(remain unchanged / fall by $20 / rise by $20)*.

So planned consumption is about to drop by $20—*not* because GNP has fallen, but because consumers are being hit by higher taxes, and *even at the old, as-yet-unchanged GNP*, they feel they must cut their spending by $20.

Now, finally, we recognize that when *C* is cut (by $20), GNP will begin to fall. This cut of $20 will have the usual multiplier effects on GNP. *But note carefully:* This multiplier process is going to begin working from a base of $20—not $30. The tax increase was $30. But consumers adjusted to this increase by cutting their consumption by $20—not $30. (The other $10 was made up by a cut in *saving*.)

b. In sum, the initial *C* reduction which starts off the multi-

---

[1]Other than the "indirect business taxes"—see Chapter 10.

[2]For simplicity, we assume the amount of the tax increase to be the same at all income levels.

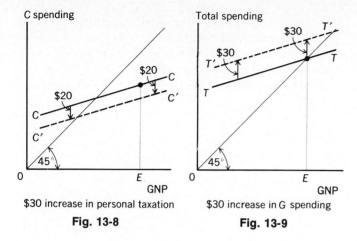

C spending

Total spending

$30 increase in personal taxation

Fig. 13-8

$30 increase in G spending

Fig. 13-9

plier reduction in the level of GNP will be *(less than / the same as / greater than)* the amount of the tax increase.

That is, the public is most likely to adjust to any increase in personal taxes by cutting its C spending (pick one):
(1) By the full tax amount.
(2) By less than the full tax amount, the balance of the adjustment being made by a reduction in saving.
(3) Not at all, the entire adjustment being made in S.

The CC line's downward displacement is illustrated in Fig. 13-8 at left above. Note that the amount by which consumers cut their spending—*even with an unchanged* GNP—equals the amount of the tax cut multiplied by the

_____.

a. is unchanged; at once fall by $30; fall by $20. *b.* less than; (2); MPC.

9. Now consider what happens when the government spends the full $30 (billion) of its tax proceeds for the purchase of goods and services. This will push up the total-spending line—see Fig. 13-9 at right above—by $*(10 / 20 / 30 / 40).*

Finally, combine the two effects: (i) Levying of the tax, and consequent downward shift of the C component of the total-spending line; (ii) Spending of tax proceeds, and consequent upward shift of the G component of the total-spending line.

The overall effect on this total-spending line will be:
(1) To push it up somewhat higher than before.
(2) To pull it down somewhat lower than before.
(3) To leave it in its original position.

30; (1).

10. Chapter 12 set out two alternative "equilibrium conditions" for an equilibrium level of GNP:
i. S = I (made use of in saving-investment diagram).
ii. GNP = C + I (made use of in 45° diagram).

These two conditions are still valid—except that they **must** be amplified to take account of the expansions of **analysis** introduced in this present chapter. For example, the **second** condition obviously now becomes:

$$GNP = C + I + G$$

The *S-I* equality requires a little more amplification. **This** condition really says that for equilibrium, the total **of all** "inflows" to the GNP circuit must just equal the total **of all** "drains" from the circuit. (Inflows and drains are to be **interpreted** in terms of a diagram like Fig. 11-7, p. 86.)

In Chapter 12, there was just one inflow (*I* spending) **and** just one drain (personal saving, *S*).

Chapter 13 has introduced new inflows and drains. **G** spending is an inflow (and so would be government **transfer** payments, although they are not mentioned in this **chapter**). Taxes are a drain. So are undistributed corporation **profits** ("corporate saving").

In an introductory course, there is no reason why you **need** be much concerned about this expansion of the *S-I* equilibrium condition. *But remember:* Don't expect that the equality of *I* spending and personal *S* will necessarily indicate **an** equilibrium level of GNP—not if you are considering **a case** in which elements like taxation and undistributed profits **are** present.

If you are curious about the full expansion of the *S-I* equilibrium condition, it is this:

Personal saving + corp'n saving + tax total
  = G spending + I spending + gov't. transfers

Consolidate the various government items in this equation **to** show that it can be reduced to:

Gov't. surplus + personal saving + corp'n. saving = I

(NOTE: The text chapter mentions this expansion of **the** "equilibrium condition" in footnote 7.)

QUIZ: Multiple Choice

1. *In a certain country (a) full employment implies a GNP of $200 billion; (b) consumption expenditure at this full-employment level of GNP would be $170 billion; (c) total investment and government expenditures will be $20 billion regardless of the level of GNP; and (d) the community's MPC is ¾. Given these facts, the equilibrium level of GNP will be* (1) more than $200 billion; (2) $200 billion; (3) $190 billion; (4) less than $190 billion; (5) impossible to compute from information given.

2. *With respect to the preceding question, the increase in investment spending needed to restore the economy to full employment would be* (1) more than $10 billion; (2) $10 billion; (3) less than $10 billion but a positive amount; (4) zero; (5) impossible to compute from information given.

3. *In the "paradox of thrift," the result of an attempt by the population to increase the total of its saving is as follows:* (1) All of GNP, *C* (consumption), *S* (personal saving), and *I* (investment) unchanged. (2) All of GNP, *C*, *S*, and *I* increased. (3) GNP and *C* unchanged, *S* decreased, *I* increased. (4) GNP decreased, *C* and *I* unchanged, *S* decreased. (5) All of GNP, *C*, *I*, and *S* decreased.

4. *The moral of the paradox of thrift is this:* (1) A decrease in saving during low-employment periods may temporarily increase consumption, but only at the cost of lower GNP later on. (2) An increase in the amount of saving is always a desirable thing in terms of its influence upon GNP. (3) A decrease in the amount of saving is always a desirable thing in terms of its influence upon GNP. (4) Attempts to increase saving may actually increase consumption also, since saving provides the funds to finance investment. (5) None of the above.

5. *The text defines a "deflationary gap" as the amount by which* (1) actual GNP would have to rise in order to reach full-employment GNP; (2) equilibrium GNP would have to rise in order to reach full-employment GNP; (3) the total-spending line, as depicted graphically, would have to rise vertically in order to equate equilibrium and full-employment GNPs; (4) planned investment exceeds planned saving; (5) planned saving exceeds planned investment.

6. *If GNP is in equilibrium, then* (1) consumption must be just equal to investment; (2) business receipts from consumption spending must just equal national income; (3) any increase in spending must result in an inflationary gap; (4) the overall budgets of federal, state, and local governments must be just balanced; (5) none of the above is necessarily correct.

7. *By "induced investment" is meant specifically* (1) investment undertaken by a firm when prompted by the necessity to expand the size of its plant; (2) investment undertaken by business under pressure from government to increase employment; (3) additional investment set off by a rise in the GNP level; (4) investment set off by a new invention or technological development; (5) none of the preceding.

8. *GNP is in equilibrium at its full-employment level. The federal government finds it necessary to increase its expenditures on goods and services by $10 billion. It wants to increase taxes sufficiently so that there will be no more serious threat of inflation—i.e., it wants the net change in the equilibrium level of GNP to be zero. The probable increase in tax collections needed will be* (1) more than $10 billion; (2) $10 billion; (3) less than $10 billion, although not zero; (4) zero; (5) less than zero—i.e., tax collections can be reduced.

9. *An equilibrium level of GNP (below full employment) is disturbed by an autonomous rise in planned investment spending of $10 billion. The marginal propensity to invest is 0.2. The marginal propensity to consume is 0.6. In the new equilibrium resulting from this autonomous investment increase, GNP will have risen (in billions) by* (1) $10; (2) $50; (3) $60; (4) $80; (5) $100.

10. *In the situation described in question 9, when the new equilibrium level of GNP is reached, total investment (autonomous plus induced) will have risen from its previous equilibrium level by an amount (in billions) of* (1) $10; (2) $20; (3) $30; (4) $40; (5) $50.

11. *Which alternative in question 10 would be correct had that question referred to the rise in* consumption *spending produced (in the new equilibrium) by the $10 (billion) rise in autonomous investment spending outlined in question 9?* (1). (2). (3). (4). (5).

12. *The "marginal propensity to invest" means specifically the* (1) ratio of total investment (*I*) to total GNP, no matter what the GNP level; (2) ratio of additional *I* to total *I*; (3) same thing as the marginal propensity to save; (4) ratio of total *I* to total GNP, but only when GNP is at its full-employment level; (5) ratio of rise in *I* to rise in GNP.

13. *Suppose there is "induced investment" as described in the text chapter. If the public should decide to spend less of its disposable income upon consumption, and to save more of that income, the result should be that* (1) investment (*I*) will rise, but saving (*S*) will wind up unchanged; (2) *I* will not change but *S* will fall; (3) both *I* and *S* will fall; (4) *I* will not change, but *S* will rise; (5) *I* will fall but *S* will rise.

14. *The text chapter says that there is a small but significant difference between the multiplier effect of an increase of (say) $10 (billion) in government spending and that of a decrease of $10 in personal taxes levied. This is because* (1) government spending, by increasing income earned, increases consumption spending; (2) a $10 reduction in taxation has a significantly greater effect on the government surplus or deficit than has a $10 increase in government spending; (3) a tax reduction affects consumer income and spending directly, whereas the effect of an increase in government spending on consumers is only indirect; (4) a $10 reduction in personal taxes does not produce a $10 increase in consumer spending, since part of this reduction goes into extra saving; (5) of none of the above reasons.

15. *Whenever total planned investment exceeds the total of planned saving (personal plus corporate), then* (1) GNP will fall, and a deflationary gap will be created; (2) GNP will rise, and an inflationary gap will be created; (3) GNP will rise, but there may or may not be any inflationary gap created; (4) GNP will fall, but there may or may not be any deflationary gap created; (5) there is no reason to expect any change in GNP, either up or down, nor any reason to expect, as a necessary result, any inflationary or deflationary gap.

QUIZ: Other

1. The following annual figures (in billions of dollars) pertain to a particular economy. The three right-hand columns indicate the amounts of planned consumer, investment, and governmental expenditure at the particular GNP level indicated (e.g., if GNP is $200 billion, C spending will be $275, I zero, G $55).

GNP	Consumption	Investment	Government
$200	$275	$ 0	$55
225	285	0	55
250	295	0	55
275	305	0	55
300	315	0	55
325	325	0	55
350	335	4	55
375	345	8	55
400	355	12	55
425	365	16	55
450	375	20	55
475	385	24	55
500	395	28	55

a. What is the equilibrium value of GNP?   ... $ _____.
b. What is the marginal propensity to consume (out of GNP)?

. . . . _____.

c. Suppose the amount of government spending were to drop from $55 to $33 annually. What would be the resulting new equilibrium GNP (assuming no change in the given relations of C spending and of I spending to GNP)? . . . . . $ _____.

d. What is the value of the multiplier? (HINT: See question 3, p. 100.) . . . . _____.

2. Given the following data with respect to a certain economy (the figures being billions of dollars):

i. The amounts of investment spending to be expected at various levels of GNP are:

GNP:$150 160 170 180 190 200 210 220 230 240 250
   I: 17 20 23 26 29 32 35 38 41 44 47

ii. When GNP is $180, consumption spending to be expected is $160.

iii. The community's marginal propensity to *save* (constant throughout the range of GNPs considered) is ⅖.

iv. Government spending and taxation are both zero.

a. In the spaces below, show the community propensity to consume from GNPs of $150 to $250.

GNP:	$150	160	170	180	190	200
C:	_____	_____	_____	_____	_____	_____
GNP:	210	220	230	240	250	
C:	_____	_____	_____	_____	_____	

b. What is the equilibrium level of GNP? . . . . . $ _____.

14 BUSINESS CYCLES AND FORECASTING

1. Chapters 12 and 13 suggested that recessions (or depressions) most commonly arise from a *(drop / rise)* in *(consumption / investment / government)* spending. Owing to the "multiplier effect," this initial *(drop / rise)* has magnified consequences—i.e., total spending drops *(even more / somewhat less)* than the initial drop *(C / I / G)* spending.

___

drop; investment; drop; even more; *I.*

___

2. In terms of the national-product and -income figures of Chapter 10, "the business cycle" means an up-and-down movement of the year-to-year or month-to-month statistics of GNP or NNP. But if any business-cycle movement is to be uncovered in national-product or other statistics, we must adjust the actual recorded figures as follows (one or both may be correct):

a. If using month-to-month data, divide or multiply each item of data by some appropriate figure to remove "seasonal variation."

b. If using year-to-year data, divide or multiply each item of data by some appropriate figure to remove any "secular trend"—i.e., slow long-term growth trend that has nothing to do with the business cycle.

___

a and *b.*

___

3. The production and sales of many business firms are subject to seasonal influence. The sales of department stores, for example, drop off in July and August because people do not buy when they are on vacation; they rise in the Christmas buying rush of November and December. So the stores' owners ought not to be upset just because of a summer sales dropoff; nor should they rejoice just because sales rise toward the year-end. The real questions are these: *How big* must the July-August sales drop be, to provoke concern? *How big* must the November-December rise be, to indicate a true above-normal increase? These are problems in the *elimination of seasonal trend* in sales.

Suppose a store knows that June is typically an average month for sales. July sales are usually 10 per cent below this 12-month average, while August sales are typically 20 per cent below. During 1976, actual sales were as follows: June, $800,000; July, $729,000; August, $664,000. Allowing for seasonal influence, was the real trend in sales upward or downward?

This means: Using June as a measuring base, was the July drop above or below normal? And the same for August? Now if June is average, and July is normally 10 per cent below average (i.e., below June), then a July figure which matched the June figure would be 90 per cent of June, or $*(600,000 / 660,000 / 700,000 / 720,000)*. If we wanted to inflate such a "normal" July total in order to get rid of the normal seasonal drop, we would multiply the July figure of $720,000 by $\frac{100}{90}$. The result would be $800,000—the same as June.

We can use this same "inflating factor," or "seasonal-trend eliminating factor" for *any* July sales figure. In particular, we can apply it to the *actual* July figure of $729,000. That is, we multiply this figure by $\frac{100}{90}$, the result being $*(729,000 / 810,000 / 850,000 / 900,000)*. The fact that this resulting figure is *above* the June figure of $800,000 indicates that July sales, despite their nominal drop as compared with June, were actually moving upward.

We do the same thing for August, which is normally 20 per cent below average. That is, we apply a "seasonal-trend eliminating factor" by multiplying the actual August sales by $\frac{100}{80}$. The actual August total being $664,000, the resulting corrected figure is $*(830,000 / 840,000 / 860,000 / 900,000)*. Because this figure is above *(the June figure / both June and July figures)*, we know that in August the trend was *(again upward / now downward)*.

The set of revised figures ($800,000, $810,000, $830,000) obtained by applying this "correcting factor" is called a ____

___

720,000; 810,000; 830,000; both June and July; again upward; seasonally corrected time series.

___

4. Among the following time series, the greatest cyclical fluctuation is typically found in *(wholesale prices / production of capital goods / production of basic materials such as anthracite coal / expenditure on consumer goods).*

___

production of capital goods.

___

5. If we believe the population level to be in no way influenced by economic conditions, a theory that business cycles result from changes in total population would be an *(external / internal)* theory of the cycle.

If we go to the other extreme, considering population

changes to result entirely from economic conditions (e.g., because people cannot afford to get married during depressions), then such a theory would be an (external / internal) theory of the cycle.

A statistical term sometimes used in place of "internal" is ("exogenous" / "endogenous"), whereas ("exogenous" / "endogenous") may be used in place of "external."

---

external; internal; endogenous; exogenous.

Chapter 13 noted that it is possible to have "induced investment"—that is, I spending may rise when GNP rises. (See, e.g., Fig. 13-2, p. 99.) A higher GNP means more employment and better sales prospects; so business firms may expand their plans to have new plant and equipment built.

The "acceleration principle," which this chapter discusses—and which you must study carefully if you are to grasp it—is another and significantly different view of "induced investment."

▶ The argument of the acceleration principle is that investment spending will take place *when GNP is going up.*

Notice the all-important difference between this view and the simpler induced-investment idea of Chapter 13. The acceleration principle says there will be investment *because GNP is rising.* It is not a *low* GNP that sets off investment, nor is it a *high* GNP. It is the fact that GNP is rising from a lower to a higher level.

Here is the logic behind the acceleration principle: Net investment spending—that is, investment which is more than sufficient to compensate for the current wearing-out of presently existing capital goods—adds to the economy's total capital-goods stock. To produce a GNP of (say) $800 (billion), a certain capital-goods stock is needed. (If you had less than that given stock, you couldn't produce an $800 GNP. If you had more than that stock, you would have *more than enough* for an $800 GNP.)

Similarly, there is a particular capital stock that "just goes" with a GNP of $1,000. Assuming the same price level, this will be a bigger stock than that associated with the $800 GNP.

Once the economy has built the capital-goods stock appropriate to an $800 GNP, and is operating at an equilibrium level of $800, then no further capital goods are needed. That is, net investment spending will be zero so long as GNP remains at $800. The same would be true of a $1,000 GNP: no net investment spending so long as the capital stock appropriate to that GNP has been built, and GNP is in equilibrium at that level.

But if the economy *starts to move* from an $800 GNP toward a $1,000 GNP, then it needs more capital goods—the extra capital goods required for the higher GNP level. So there will be positive net investment spending.

6. *a.* You are a machine-tool salesman. One of your customers is a firm which has 10 machines, identical except for age. Each machine has a 10-year life, and they are nicely staggered in age, so that each year one machine is ready for the scrap heap; there will be one machine 9 years old, one 8 years old, and so on. The plant has just enough business to keep its machines steadily occupied.

As seller of these machines, you visit the plant once yearly, expecting an order for one machine to replace the machine currently wearing out. Assuming, for simplicity, that each new machine costs $10, your order each year will be for $10. In national-product terms, gross investment will be $(100 / 10 / zero), and net investment $(100 / 10 / zero).

Suddenly, the demand for this firm's product jumps. Sales rise by 30 per cent, and stay at this higher level. The firm must expand its equipment (its capital-goods stock) to allow for this extra production. On your annual visit (which is happily timed to coincide with the sales jump), you receive an order for (5 / 4 / 3 / 2 / 1 / 0) machine(s). That is, gross investment (at the $10 price) is $(50 / 40 / 30 / 20 / 10), and net investment is $(40 / 30 / 20 / 10 / zero).

One year passes. Again you visit the plant—knowing in advance that the firm's sales are still holding at their 30-per-cent-higher level. The firm expects them to remain steady at that level. What will your order be *this* time? It will be for (5 / 4 / 3 / 2 / 1 / 0) machine(s). That is, gross investment is $(50 / 40 / 30 / 20 / 10 / zero), and net investment is $(40 / 30 / 20 / 10 / zero).

This is a small-scale example of the acceleration-principle idea. Net investment is not a matter of the absolute level of output. It takes place *when output is rising.*

b. Suppose the level of GNP (or of consumption, which is the major component within GNP) is for 4 successive years as follows: Year 1, $500; Year 2, $600; Year 3, $650; Year 4, $650. The acceleration principle would say that net I spending would be (pick one):
(1) A positive but different amount in each of the 4 years.
(2) Positive between years 1 and 3, zero in year 4.
(3) Zero in the first 2 years, but positive and increasing in the last two.

c. It is hard to say how far the acceleration-principle idea has been verified in experience. Even its most zealous proponents would hardly argue that this principle affords a *complete* account of net I spending. But many economists (not all) think it carries an important element of truth.

Its critics point out that most I spending is undertaken by business firms in the hope of profit. Even if GNP is presently in equilibrium at a certain level, but if business firms think (rightly or wrongly) that that GNP is going to rise, so that there will be an increased demand for output, they *(will / will not)* be encouraged to undertake new investment spending.

Conversely, if GNP is presently rising but if firms are inclined to believe that this rise will be small and of short duration, they *(will / will not)* be encouraged to undertake *I* spending.

---

a. 10; zero; 4; 40; 30; 1; 10; zero. *b.* (2). *c.* will; will not.

---

7. Both the following statements repeat ideas in the text: (1) The level of *C* spending is influenced by the level of *I* spending, because *C* spending depends considerably on the level of GNP, and the level of GNP depends considerably on the level of *I* spending. (2) The level of *I* spending is influenced by *C* spending—specifically, by the rate at which the level of *C* spending is increasing.

a. Which of the above is a statement of the acceleration principle? ....*(1 / 2 / neither)*
b. Which is a statement of the theory of income determination found in Chapters 12 and 13? ....*(1 / 2 / neither)*

In other words, *I* spending and *C* spending interact with one another, each influenced by the other, so that both may be changing as they seek out mutually compatible levels. In the process, GNP (which is principally the sum of *C* and *I* spending) must change also. That is, the ups and downs of GNP that we call the business cycle are to at least some degree the result of this interaction.

When the acceleration-principle idea is introduced, the interaction becomes a complicated one. You should understand the acceleration-principle idea. You should understand that there *is* an interaction between *C* and *I;* you should grasp its general nature. But an introductory course cannot outline in full detail how *I, C,* and GNP would interact in an acceleration-principle world.

---

a. (2). *b.* (1).

---

8. *a.* The National Bureau of Economic Research is a private organization which for years has worked intensively on the statistics of the business cycle. In the 1930s, federal government officials asked the Bureau if there were some figures relating to business activity which, because they turned down (or up) *ahead* of a downturn (or upturn) in GNP, could be used to forecast impending GNP changes. In response, the National Bureau identified certain statistical series called the _____ .

The National Bureau's investigators took all the statistical series they could find, and—from the historical records—

sorted out three categories: leading indicators, coincidental indicators (those which typically kept just about in step with GNP changes), and lagging indicators (those which usually followed GNP in movement).

Unfortunately, any one of the leading indicators (for example, the level of new housing starts, increases or decreases in business inventories) sometimes gives false alarms. Thus at any moment in time, some of them may be turning up while others are steady or turning down. Nevertheless, forecasters study them very carefully indeed, in search of the message they (perhaps) contain.

b. More recently, as elsewhere, computers have moved in. The statisticians will develop, for example, a sophisticated "consumption function" (propensity to consume); this and material from the other components of national product and national income are fed into the computer. The text's verdict is that in performance the best computer forecasts rank *(significantly higher than / at about the same level as / significantly below)* the best noncomputer forecasts.

---

a. leading indicators. *b.* at about the same level as.

QUIZ: Multiple Choice

1. *In the United States, the major business cycle* (1) has been much less pronounced than in European economies, with the single exception of the 1930s; (2) strikes very sharply at certain limited sectors of the economy, but leaves major sectors almost totally unaffected; (3) shows a remarkably uniform and symmetrical pattern in the sequence of prosperity, peak, slump, and depression, once "random" elements have been removed; (4) has been more intense than in European economies, at least with respect to the degree of variation in total employment; (5) is not correctly described by any of these statements.

2. *According to the text, if we look to any particular kind of spending as a key factor in accounting for the major business cycle, we find it in* (1) net investment spending, specifically spending on inventories; (2) net investment spending, specifically spending on durable goods; (3) consumer spending; (4) variations in spending by state and local governments; (5) none of the above, the point stressed being that no single type of spending plays any key role.

3. *The multiplier and the acceleration principle are related in this way:* (1) They both seek to explain how changes in the level of investment spending come about. (2) The multiplier seeks to explain how a condition of full-employment GNP can be maintained, and the acceleration principle seeks to explain how a condition of depression may come about and may persist despite efforts to increase spending. (3) The multiplier shows how a change in the level of GNP, particularly an upward change, may give rise to net investment, and the acceleration principle shows how a given change in spending (e.g., in investment) can result in a larger change in the level of GNP. (4) The multiplier shows how a given change in spending (e.g., in investment) can result in a larger change in the level of GNP, and the acceleration principle shows how a change in the level of GNP, particularly an upward change, may give rise to net investment. (5) In none of the ways described above.

4. *The role of consumer spending in the business cycle, according to United States experience described in the text, is that* (1) changes in consumer durable purchases may occasionally set off an upswing or downturn, and changes in consumer spending will intensify the effect of any disturbance originating outside the consumer sphere, via the multiplier; (2) consumer spending and investment spending seem to have approximately equal parts to play in the cycle, although the two are so intermixed that it is difficult to separate one from the other and to analyze the role of either; (3) changes in consumer spending on nondurables most commonly initiate the downturn in a major business cycle, whereas increases in consumer durable purchases are most likely to start the upturn, as replacement of worn-out durable items becomes necessary; (4) changes in consumer spending are most often the initial disturbing factor, and the impact then spreads to investment spending, thus intensifying the original disturbance; (5) consumer spending has no part to play in the cycle, which (except for wartime disturbances) is almost entirely due to investment-spending changes.

5. *In economics, "capital formation" means specifically* (1) the purchase of any new commodity; (2) net investment; (3) the borrowing of money; (4) the sale of any new stock issue; (5) none of these activities.

6. *According to the acceleration principle, spending on net investment will take place* (1) when GNP or consumption is at a high level; (2) when GNP or consumption is at a low level; (3) when GNP or consumption is rising; (4) when GNP or consumption is falling; (5) perhaps in any of the above situations, since no such link with GNP or consumption is assumed.

7. *The theory of the multiplier* (1) is an external theory of the business cycle; (2) is a theory of the business cycle based on the fact of "replacement waves" in the construction of capital goods; (3) while not a theory of the business cycle, is a useful addition to any cycle theory, since it explains how changes in investment spending can occur; (4) while not a theory of the business cycle, is a useful addition to any cycle theory, since it explains how small fluctuations in spending can have magnified effects on GNP; (5) bears no relationship to the problem of business cycles or their explanation.

8. *The replacement-wave theory of business cycles* (1) is an example of an external theory of the cycle; (2) is considered by most economists to be the most satisfactory internal theory of the cycle yet developed; (3) is particularly useful as an explanation of the major cycle, but has been shown to have limited use with respect to both minor and long-run cycles; (4) is an internal theory which may occasionally explain surges in investment spending, but has too many shortcomings to be of much value; (5) unlike other business cycle theories, puts major emphasis upon consumer spending.

9. *The "acceleration principle" rests on the assumption that* (1) a particular quantity of capital goods is needed for production of any given quantity of output; hence any rise in demand, e.g., an increase in consumer expenditure, will produce a temporary rise in production of capital goods; (2) any increase in spending, e.g., an increase in investment, will be spent and respent by others; hence it will have an accelerated effect on GNP as it spreads through the economy; (3) a short period of increased spending on investment, if large enough, will succeed in "priming the pump" and restoring a low GNP to its previous level; (4) associated with each absolute level of consumer expenditure, a different amount of investment spending can be expected; (5) the accumulated effect of postponed investment spending will ultimately bring an economy out of depression.

10. *When we speak of making a "seasonal adjustment" in statistics, we mean* (1) changing month-to-month or week-to-week figures so as to eliminate the influence thought to result from the season of the year; (2) changing month-to-month or week-to-week figures so as to include the influence resulting from the season of the year; (3) breaking down year-to-year statistics into month-by-month or week-by-week figures; (4) converting week-by-week or month-by-month statistics into quarterly or annual data; (5) none of the above.

11. *Analysis of cyclical fluctuations in business activity usually distinguishes between "minor" and "major" business cycles. In the* minor *cycles, a notably important role has been (and still is) played by* (1) changes in expenditure on housing; (2) investment in new plant and equipment; (3) changes in state and local government spending; (4) swings in total consumer expenditure; (5) changes in inventory investment.

12. *Four of the five following statements are reasonably correct as to the nature of the "acceleration principle." Identify the* incorrect *statement. This theory says, with respect to acceleration-principle induced net investment, that the amount of expenditure thereon* (1) is related to the growth of GNP or of consumption, rather than to the absolute level of either of them; (2) may be very large even though it may be set off by a comparatively small change in GNP or consumption; (3) will be zero if and when GNP reaches an equilibrium level; (4) is explainable in terms of the fact that a particular level of total output requires a particular quantity of capital goods in order to produce that output; (5) tends to increase as more money is injected into the economy through the medium of the banking system.

13. *According to Alvin Hansen's analysis of the business cycle, the movements of GNP therein* (1) are so mixed up that in reality it is impossible to speak of any cyclical movement at all; (2) are not waves at all, but consist rather of movements from steady plateaus of prosperity to steady but lower levels of depression; (3) are revealed as smooth and regular wavelike movements, once the influence of seasonal disturbances has been removed; (4) consist for the most part of seasonal influences and long-term trends, and vanish almost completely when these elements have been removed; (5) actually seem to be a mixture of two or three wavelike movements.

14. *A "time series" means* (1) the period of time from the peak of one major business cycle to the peak of the next; (2) the smooth, wavelike path of GNP or any similar figure that emerges once seasonal and secular influences have been removed from the actual figures; (3) any analysis in which a change in one economic magnitude (*e.g.*, investment) is linked with a change in another (*e.g.*, GNP); (4) data for a period of time (*e.g.*, months or years) for some magnitude such as GNP or consumption; (5) none of the above.

15. *Statistically, the widest swings between peak and bottom of the major business cycle (according to the text) are to be found in* (1) the supply of consumer services; (2) the production of inventories; (3) the production of durables— i.e., capital goods; (4) wholesale rather than retail goods; (5) export and import goods.

15

PRICES AND MONEY

1. Circle each statement which you consider a correct interpretation of what the text chapter has to say about inflation:

a. Issue of new paper money during a period of deep depression is just as inflationary as it would be during a period of full employment.

b. Issue of new paper money in an inflationary crisis normally adds fuel to the flames, but not when the government issues that money in order to purchase gold.

c. Inflation tends to work in favor of the older generation, and against younger people who are just beginning to build up their assets.

d. Inflation benefits the creditor class, because in the resulting social disorganization they can foreclose on debtors and seize real property.

e. Mild inflation actually tends to stimulate investment and production.

f. People who must live on a fixed money income are the only ones who suffer significantly during an inflation.

g. Interest rates typically fall during any period of continuing inflation, because of the decline in the value of money.

h. The inflationary push sends all prices up, but prices rise by about the same proportion, leaving relative prices unchanged.

i. Although all or almost all prices rise, they do not rise proportionally; some rise faster than others. This change in relative prices, which means a change in the distribution of income, provokes social unrest.

j. Interest rates rise during any period of continuing inflation, because an "inflation allowance" gets built into the interest rate.

_____

e, i, j.

_____

2. *a.* In a state of total self-sufficiency, there are (by definition) no exchanges of goods or services of consequence. As soon as specialization in production begins, exchanges begin. Barter, the most obvious exchange method, becomes impossibly clumsy as soon as the variety of items exchanged grows large. You must, for each commodity, work out the swapping terms with every other one (for two commodities, there is just one rate to settle; but for three commodities there are three

rates; for four there are six; for five, there are ten; and so on). And there is a further difficulty: if you have good A, and want to exchange it for B, you must (before even thinking about haggling over terms) find someone who both has B and wants A. The text has a phrase for this; it is called

_____ .

b. So money evolved because money was essential for large-scale exchanges. It began as "commodity money." (This was the transition from barter: people began to measure values in terms of *one* suitable commodity.) In due course, one special commodity often assumed the money role: gold (or in some instances, silver). Now gold has (except for international settlements) lost its association with money.

Today, we have three kinds of money. Ranking them by importance (as measured by total amount within the present money supply), they are:

(1) _____ .

(2) _____ .

(3) _____ .

c. Why do we use three different kinds of money? Why not simplify by having just one single kind?

_____

_____ .

_____

a. the double coincidence of wants. *b.* (1) Demand (or checking) bank deposits; (2) paper currency; (3) coins. *c.* Because each has its particular convenience for particular kinds of transactions.

_____

The text chapter says that today all money is essentially "fiat" money (i.e., the government *decrees* that it is money, and people accept that decree). But what is money? What is it that makes one item money, and another not?

The answer is:

▶ Money is anything that by convention is immediately spendable.

A store will readily give you merchandise in exchange for coins, or for paper bills, or in exchange for part of your checking bank account. (If you propose to pay by check, the only thing the store will want to make sure of is that you really have a bank account of at least the required amount; if you pay by coins or bills, this problem does not arise.)

Anything *not* immediately spendable is *not* part of the money supply, strictly and properly defined. However, there are certain classes of assets which are *very close to being money;* their owners *think of them* as money, because conversion is ordinarily such a quick and simple process. For example: a deposit with a savings and loan association. You can't literally *spend* such a deposit, for (in the United States) the rules governing such deposits specify: no checks. Yet (although it has the legal right to require some specified advance notice), the savings bank will ordinarily exchange your deposit for money right away.

3. *a.* Thus it has become conventional, in tables listing the money supply, to make the distinction between "M_1" and "M_2." (See, for example, text Table 15-1.) Items within M_1 are exclusively the three strictly defined money items. The M_2 category takes account of the close-to-being-money items. It consists of the total of (these "close" items alone / the "close" items plus the M_1 items).

One trouble with the "close-to-being-money" idea is: How close is close? There is a highly efficient market for government bonds, for example; ordinarily they can be sold and so converted into money very rapidly. But if you include such bonds, then why not slightly lower-grade bonds? Why not stocks listed on the New York Stock Exchange?

So, once you move beyond the strict money definition (namely, it's money if you can spend it anywhere within the country), the division tends to become arbitrary rather than functional. The items added to M_1 to make M_2 are exclusively "money deposits" (those on which checks may not be written). Debt securities, even of the highest rating, such as U.S. government bonds, stand just outside of M_2.

There is a general term which the text uses for assets which are close to M_2 even though kept outside; it is

_____ .

b. Which of the following would count as money strictly defined—i.e., as part of M_1?
(1) Any deposit in a commercial bank on which checks may be issued.
(2) Any deposit in a commercial bank, regardless of whether or not checks may be issued against it.
(3) A deposit in a mutual savings account or in a credit union.
(4) A high-grade corporation bond.
(5) A check drawn on a commercial-bank checking account.

---

a. The "close" items plus the M_1 items; near money. *b.* (1) only. [NOTE AS TO (5): One's first inclination is to

count a check issued as money, since you can hand a check across a store counter just as you would a $10 bill. But if you have counted the dollars in the checking account, you mustn't count the check as well. A check is just a piece of paper transferring part of your account to someone else.]

In March, 1975, as text Table 15-1 indicates, the total money stock in the United States (the M_1 stock, consisting of coins, bills, and bank accounts on which checks could be drawn) was $284 billion.

Each dollar of that money stock had, and still has, an owner—an individual, a business firm, a financial institution. Why was this money being held?

If you hold any substantial amount of money, the opportunity is open to you to buy a security with it. This is preferable to holding money in that you can then expect an interest or dividend return. If you reject the idea of buying any security, then you must have some reason for holding onto money instead. (If you buy the security, then you pass your money on to someone else—and the recipient must have some reason for wanting to hold it.)

What are the reasons, then, for holding money as an asset (in preference to other assets that would yield some income return)? Essentially, there are two. The first is a simple one. You need some money on hand because income does not arrive in a minute-by-minute flow. Instead, it comes at discontinuous intervals; wage or salary payments come each week, half-month, or month. Hence, people hold a cash balance which is gradually spent, and gradually declines, until the next installment of income arrives.

The second reason is more complex, and its origins are varied. It is the desire to hold money *as an asset,* *over and above* the ordinary amount needed to tide you over until the next wage or salary payment reaches you. Why? Well, (1) you may want to keep some surplus cash against the possibility of some unexpected and cash-demanding emergency. Or, (2) having acquired your cash illegally, you may be shy about doing anything that would reveal you have it. Or, (3) you may be strongly convinced that security prices are going to fall—so that the *immediate* purchase of any such security would be a bad idea. (This matter of expectations as to future changes in security prices is discussed at length later in the text, notably in Chapter 18.)

Sometimes the reasons for holding money, whatever the purpose, are called "the demand for money." Be careful here. In economics, the word "demand" usually pertains *to the intention of buying something, or the activity of buying it.* Not so here. "The demand for money" means nothing more than has just been said: the decision to hold money in preference to any of the other assets for which money could be exchanged.

4. Above, it was said that there are two principal reasons for holding money. The text puts these in "demand for money" terms, and calls them the _____

demand and the _____ demand.

Students sometimes experience difficulty at first with this matter of the reasons for holding money, or "the demand for money." If you are so troubled, it's worth noting that Chapter 18 in the text explores these matters at greater length. It may help you to turn to review questions 1 and 2 for that chapter (pp. 134–135). There—just to make life a bit more complex for you—the term "liquidity preference" is used. "Liquidity preference" means exactly what was called above the *asset* (or *precautionary*) demand for money. (It means preference to stay liquid in the matter of one's assets; and money is the most liquid of all assets. Thus, "desire to hold money" and "demand for money" mean the same thing; and "liquidity preference" is one of the reasons for deciding to hold money.)

---

transactions; asset (or precautionary).

Often it is important to insist on the distinction between *money* and *income*. Money is a *stock*, such as the $284-billion 1975 stock mentioned above. Income is a *flow of money*, the money total which has flowed into the hands of income receivers for some specified time period.

GNP is simply the measure of a flow of money spent and a flow of income received for some given time period, ordinarily a year. (Strictly, *NI*—national income—is the income concept, but GNP is roughly the same thing.)

Suppose now that GNP was $800 for a given year, and that *M* was a constant $100 throughout that year. Then, on the average, each dollar of *M* must have flowed 8 times around the "income circuit." Look at Fig. 11-7 (p. 86); it may help you understand that money is a *stock* which *flows* as income. Or think of the water in a heating system. That system holds a certain *stock* (a certain physical quantity) of water. A measuring gauge inserted into one of the pipes will record the *flow* of water (a certain quantity per unit of time) through the system, past that point in the pipe.

This introduces the concept of the *velocity* of money—here, its "income velocity." This income velocity—look again at Fig. 11-7!—just means the number of times each dollar, on the average, flows around the income circuit. If the money supply is $100 and GNP is $800, this velocity, *V*, is 8. We can write $MV \equiv GNP$. We use a three-bar symbol rather than a two-bar one because this is not just a simple equality. It is an *identity*, because *V*, by definition, *must be* whatever figure is needed to make things come out equal. *MV* is just another way of writing GNP.

The *MV* definition in turn leads to "the quantity equation of exchange." Any GNP stands for some given quantity of goods and services sold at particular prices. Suppose, for example, that the GNP consisted exclusively of 10 units of A produced and sold at price $3, and 20 units of B produced and sold at $2. Then the GNP would be $3 times 10 plus $2 times 20—total, $70.

So we can write $GNP \equiv PQ$, if by *PQ* we mean the sum of all items produced in the GNP, each recorded at its price. Again we use the three-bar symbol, since *PQ* so defined is only another way of writing GNP. (To write any GNP as *PQ* is simply to draw attention to the price and the quantity components within that GNP.)

In sum, then:

$$PQ \equiv GNP \equiv MV$$

The statement $PQ \equiv MV$ *must* be correct, because its terms are so defined that it could not be otherwise than correct. As an identity, it is not itself particularly interesting or useful. Yet it is the starting point for something that is *not* an identity, but instead a speculation about "the way things are"—the "Quantity Theory of Money."

5. *a.* The "crude Quantity Theory of Money" starts from the "quantity equation of exchange" just noted: $PQ \equiv MV$. This theory asserts (rightly or wrongly) that in real life, in actual behavior, *two* of the elements in this "equation of exchange" are constant or very nearly so. These are (*V and P* / *V and Q* / *P and Q*).

Thus, if we put *k* into the equation to replace the two constants, we get as a result (circle one): (1) $P = kM$; (2) $Q = kM$; (3) $V = kM$.

b. What the "crude Quantity Theory" really says as a result, then, is that the level of prices depends exclusively on the quantity of money existing. Hence, if the quantity of *M* were doubled, that would just exactly double (*velocity* / *the price level* / *real output*), and do only that.

c. The "sophisticated Quantity Theory of Money" asserts (again, rightly or wrongly) that in real life there is *one* element in the equation of exchange that is constant or very nearly so, namely, (*V* / *P* / *Q*). Hence it assumes that $PQ = kM$, or in other words, GNP = *kM*.

The significance of this theory—if correct—is that control over the total quantity of money in existence is by far the most important element in trying to control the level of GNP (i.e., prevent both depressions and inflations). That is, monetary policy is the proper tool, and the most important tool, to use in regulating the progress of the economy. (Monetary policy is discussed in Chapters 17 and 18.)

---

a. V and Q; (1). *b.* the price level. *c.* V.

QUIZ: Multiple Choice

1. *The essential difference between "money" and "near-money" is that* (1) money is directly spendable; near-money is not; (2) near-money includes all deposits in bank accounts; money includes none of these; (3) the velocity of circulation of money is rapid; that of near-money is slow; (4) near-money is "fiat money"; money is not; (5) near-money constitutes anything that can be marketed for a money price.

2. *Which of the following is not a correct statement with respect to gold and its relationship to money?* (1) Convertibility into gold is essential if paper money is to be accepted by the public as valuable. (2) If gold were not used as "money backing" and for settling international accounts, its value today would be less than it actually is. (3) There is no longer any United States money which citizens can present to the government and receive gold in exchange. (4) There is no longer any legal gold "backing" for the paper money which circulates in the United States. (5) The official United States price of gold (as of late 1975) is approximately $42 per ounce, although, unofficially, many governments accord it a much higher price.

3. *The "income velocity of circulation of money" means* (1) the same thing as the "sophisticated Quantity Theory of Money"; (2) the tendency for prices to rise as newly introduced money passes from hand to hand during a period of full employment; (3) the price level multiplied by the amount of money in existence; (4) GNP (or *NI*) divided by the amount of the money stock; (5) the annual rate of increase in the money stock.

4. *By "asset demand for money" is meant* (1) the desire to retain money as an asset in preference to purchasing a security; (2) the amount which businesses will wish to borrow at any given interest rate; (3) the same thing as "transaction demand for money"; (4) the desire to save more money out of a given income, as protection against an uncertain future; (5) the need of business firms for money which they must convert into fixed assets as a necessary part of production.

5. *There is a group of assets which is categorized as "near-money." As to this asset category, the text says that U.S. government bonds are* (1) included to the extent that such bonds were purchased with part of the actual money supply, but not otherwise; (2) excluded, since these bonds do not constitute spendable money; (3) included, since the income from such bonds is paid in cash; (4) excluded, since only assets which count as legal tender are included in the near-money category; (5) included, since people's spending habits are influenced in much the same way, whether their assets are held in such bonds or in actual money.

6. *When a check drawn on a bank account is used as a means of payment, that check counts, or does not count, as part of the total money supply as follows: it* (1) counts, provided it is a valid check, i.e., there are funds in the bank to support it; (2) counts, whether valid or not, provided the person to whom it is given accepts it; (3) counts if used to buy goods and services, but not otherwise; (4) does not count, since no bank account is considered part of the money supply; (5) does not count—to count both it and the deposit account on which it is drawn would be double counting.

7. *If I choose to hold money in preference to buying securities because I expect security prices to fall, my behavior illustrates* (1) the use of money as a medium of exchange; (2) the precautionary demand for money; (3) the principle of "near-money"; (4) the "sophisticated Quantity Theory of Money"; (5) none of the above.

8. *The "quantity equation of exchange" says* (1) that the absolute level of prices is unimportant, the significant factor being the relationship of one price to another; (2) that increases in money GNP are explainable in terms of a proportionate increase in the amount of money in existence; (3) that the "income velocity" of money is constant or approximately so; (4) that the purchasing power of money will be proportional to the amount of gold which each money unit represents; (5) none of the above.

9. *In terms of total value, the largest single component in the United States money supply (what the text calls "narrowly defined money," i.e., excluding "near-money") is* (1) metallic coins; (2) paper bills; (3) bank money (i.e., demand deposits); (4) checks written on demand deposits; (5) none of these items.

10. *The "precautionary demand for money," as the text uses this term, means* (1) the total of bank accounts upon which checks may be drawn; (2) the quantity of securities demanded at any given interest rate; (3) the same thing as the "asset demand for money"; (4) the amount saved by consumers out of income over the period in question; (5) none of the preceding.

11. *The "crude Quantity Theory of Money" asserts* (1) that it is the total volume of money transactions in the economy which dictates the total quantity of money brought into existence; (2) that the velocity of money, not the absolute quantity of money, is the critical factor in price determination; (3) that relative prices—the relationship of one price to another, not the absolute level of prices—is the all-important factor in need of recognition; (4) that the total supply of money should be kept constant even in the face of a rising real GNP; (5) none of the preceding.

12. *The "sophisticated Quantity Theory of Money" asserts* (1) that the velocity of circulation of money, although not necessarily constant, changes only slowly and in small measure over any short time period; (2) that changes in the total quantity of existing money have more influence upon the level of interest rates than they have upon the price level; (3) that the total of bank checking deposits, not the total of coins and paper bills in circulation, is the critical factor in price determination; (4) that the quantity of money in circulation should be kept in proportion to the quantity of gold held by the federal government or by the central bank (Federal Reserve System); (5) none of the preceding.

13. *When money has been deposited in any private financial institution (e.g., a commercial bank, a savings and loan association, etc.), the critical factor in deciding whether that deposit should count as part of the money supply (M_1 or "money narrowly defined") is that* (1) checks can be freely written against the deposit by its owner; (2) the deposit has insurance or backing by the government or some public institution; (3) the institution maintains 100 per cent backing or reserve for the deposit—whether the backing is provided by government or not; (4) the institution has a legal franchise which permits its deposits to be counted as money; (5) so long as the money deposited consists of genuine bills or coins, then the deposit within any such institution must be counted as part of the money supply.

14. *Some recent developments, such as the use of computers and the increasing use of credit cards, have had the effect (according to the text) of* (1) giving increasing support to the "sophisticated Quantity Theory of Money"; (2) raising the free-market price of gold; (3) reducing the absolute total of the quantity of money in existence; (4) increasing the velocity of circulation of money; (5) reducing the velocity of circulation of money.

15. *When the text speaks of "the transaction demand for money," it means* (1) the considerations which prompt the owners of money to insist upon being paid interest if they are to lend that money to others; (2) the desire of any individual to earn money in order to buy the goods and services considered necessary or desirable; (3) the need to hold some money to tide one over during the period between the arrival of one paycheck and the next; (4) the willingness to spend money to buy any desired commodity or service; (5) the same thing as the "asset demand for money."

16. *The "transaction demand for money" described in question 15 will most probably* (1) decline whenever the level of GNP rises; (2) increase slightly should interest rates fall significantly; (3) decline in conditions of inflation, when money becomes less desirable as an asset to be held; (4) decrease slightly should interest rates fall significantly; (5) do none of the preceding.

17. *I decide against the purchase of any government bond because I expect that the government will shortly offer a new bond issue that will promise a higher interest rate than those on the bonds currently available for purchase. In this, I am illustrating what the text calls* (1) a decrease in the velocity of money; (2) the "transaction demand for money"; (3) the "crude Quantity Theory of Money"; (4) the demand for "near-money"; (5) the "asset demand for money."

18. *I decide against the purchase of any government bond because I expect that the market price of government bonds is likely to fall in the near future. Given this decision and the behavior it illustrates, which alternative in question 17 would be correct?* (1). (2). (3). (4). (5).

16 THE BANKING SYSTEM AND DEPOSIT CREATION

AS CHAPTER 15 INDICATED, "bank money"—money in the form of bank accounts on which checks may be drawn—is far and away the most important component of the money supply. Your principal task in this chapter is to learn how such bank money comes into being.

▶ Bank money is created by the activity of banks in making new loans; and any increase in lending by banks creates new bank money.

The money is created out of thin air, so to speak; and its ultimate backing is nothing more than the confidence which the public has in the banking system.

This vital point is most easily grasped by considering first a "banking system" which consists of a single bank. The review questions start with just such a one-bank system; then they go on to *two* banks; and finally, to a system of many banks.

Before starting, turn back if necessary to Chapter 6's Appendix and review the terms "Balance Sheet," "Asset," and "Liability." These simple accounting terms are used throughout this review section, and your grasp of the banking process should not be weakened through uncertainty over their meaning.

1. *a.* Turn to text Table 16-1. What was the total amount of "bank money" (demand deposits) in the United States on

January 1, 1975? . . . .$ _____ billion.
b. Again in Table 16-1: What "Reserves" (i.e., cash on their own premises or deposits with the Federal Reserve) did all

member banks possess as assets? . . . . . .$ _____ billion.
c. In other words, their total "cash reserves" (against deposits) were approximately (*three times* / *equal to* / *one-seventh of*) their demand-deposit liabilities.

---

a. 249.4 *b.* 36.9 *c.* one-seventh of.

---

2. *a.* This total of "demand deposits" in text Table 16-1 (pick one):
(1) Does not count as money.
(2) Counts as money because of its cash backing.
(3) Counts as money because it is spendable.
(4) May or may not count as money—impossible to tell without further information.

b. If this demand-deposit total were for any reason increased—say from $249 billion to $269 billion—that increase (*would* / *would not*) count as an increase in the nation's money supply.

---

a. (3). *b.* would.

The questions to follow begin with a situation in which there is no "bank money." They trace the development of such money through lending activity on the part of banks.

These questions concern an isolated community which uses initially only gold coins as money. The local goldsmith has a storage vault for gold. He is prepared to store money for others in this vault, charging a small fee. He chooses to list such deposits as an asset on his Balance Sheet, matched by a "deposit liability" of equal amount.[1] His Balance Sheet, with respect to such deposits, reads:

Assets	Liabilities
Gold coins in vault $10,000	Deposits—payable to customers on demand $10,000

3. *a.* A. Pennywise, a customer of the goldsmith, is asked for payment by one of his creditors. The goldsmith's shop having already closed for the day, Pennywise gives his creditor a note reading as follows:

To: Ye Gold Shoppe.   Pay B. Poundfoolish $5 from my deposit.   (Signed) A. Pennywise.

What is the name given to such a note?_____.

---

[1]Of course, the goldsmith could omit both Asset and Liability items from his Balance Sheet entirely. If his obligation is to pay back those identical gold coins which the depositor left with him, he doubtless will do so. But if his obligation is simply to pay back gold coins *of equal value*, there is no reason why he should not list them as shown (see the text's section "How Banks Developed out of Goldsmith Establishments"). If he does, it will be one case in which the warning in the Appendix to Chapter 6 against linking up the amount of a particular asset with a particular liability does not apply.

Note that the figures listed do not show the complete Balance Sheet, only the accounts which now interest us.

b. Poundfoolish presents the note the next morning, but instead of taking coins, he asks the goldsmith to keep the money stored in his name. Is any change necessary in the goldsmith's Balance Sheet? If so, explain.

_____

_____ .

_____

a. A check. *b.* Total of deposits unchanged; only ownership of deposits need be changed.

4. *a.* If this practice of writing notes to the goldsmith becomes general, does it involve any increase in the total money supply? .... *(Yes / No)*
b. If we define money as something which can be spent immediately, which should count as money: gold coins in the vault or demand deposits? .... *(Coins / Deposits / Both)*

a. No. *b.* Deposits. (Gold coins must be withdrawn before they can be spent, thus destroying the corresponding deposits.)

5. Suppose (1) *all* money transfers are now handled by such checks, (2) Ye Gold Shoppe is the only place for storage of gold, and (3) all members of the community keep their entire gold supply in this vault, the total being $10,000. Will the asset figure of $10,000 in gold on the Balance Sheet ever change? Why or why not?

_____ .

_____

No, because gold is never withdrawn.

6. Most transactions are now handled by check. Occasionally a depositor withdraws gold to make a payment, but the person receiving payment usually deposits it once again, since the vault is the safest place for gold storage and checks can always be drawn against such deposits.

A responsible businessman now asks the goldsmith for a loan of $2,000. The goldsmith has no gold free of deposit claims, only the $10,000 deposited with him. Is there any reason why he should nonetheless consider making the loan? (See the text's section How Banks Developed out of Goldsmith Establishments—the "anonymity" of deposited money.)

_____ .

_____

Most of the $10,000 gold is not being used.

7. The loan is made. The businessman is given $2,000 in gold. The goldsmith's Balance Sheet (insofar as these transactions are concerned) now reads:

Assets	Liabilities
Gold ..$8,000	Demand deposits ..$10,000
Loans .. 2,000	

Obviously the businessman borrows money in order to spend it for some purpose. What is likely to happen to the $2,000 in gold after he has spent it?

_____ .

_____

It will be redeposited by the person to whom it is paid.

8. *a.* If the person receiving the gold redeposits it with the goldsmith, how will his Balance Sheet then appear?

Assets	Liabilities
Gold ....$ _____	Demand deposits ....$ _____
Loans ... _____	

b. Has the money supply (the total of "spendable stuff") increased? *(Yes / No).* By how much? _____ .

a. Gold 10,000; Loans 2,000; Demand deposits 12,000.
b. Yes; by $2,000.

9. Suppose the borrower, instead of taking $2,000 in gold, simply asks for a $2,000 deposit account against which he can draw checks. How will the Balance Sheet appear before the loan is spent? (NOTE: In actual practice, this is how bank loans are normally handled.)

Assets	Liabilities
Gold ....$ _____	Demand deposits ....$ _____
Loans ... _____	

Same answer as in question 8*a.*

10. After the borrower has spent his $2,000 loan (making payment to people whose custom it is to keep a deposit with the goldsmith), how will this Balance Sheet look?

Assets	Liabilities
Gold ....$ _____	Demand deposits ....$ _____
Loans ... _____	

Same answer as in question 8a.

11. Provided (1) the custom of using checks for payment is followed and people rarely withdraw gold coins from the vault, and (2) we disregard any inflationary consequences of the money-supply increase, what is the limit on the amount of loans the goldsmith could make? (NOTE: There is no *legal* reserve requirement.)

_____

_____ .

_____

Almost no limit, except as an increase in total M tends to increase amount of gold circulating hand to hand.

12. Below is the relevant part of the goldsmith's Balance Sheet after he has made loans of $20,000, at a time when $2,000 of the community's total gold stock is not stored with him but is in hand-to-hand circulation:

Assets	Liabilities
Gold .... $ 8,000	Demand deposits $28,000
Loans ... 20,000	

a. The total money supply *(M)* is now $_____, consisting of $_____ bank money (demand deposits) and $_____ in gold in hand-to-hand circulation.

b. Should the $8,000 gold in vault count as part of M?

_____

_____ .

_____

a. 30,000; 28,000; 2,000.
b. No; it must be withdrawn before it is spendable, and withdrawal would reduce bank money by same amount.

13. When the goldsmith makes such loans, will his action influence I spending or GNP? Why or why not?

_____

_____ .

_____

Yes; borrowers borrow for spending, typically I spending.

14. An increase in the money supply such as this (one or both may be correct):
a. Is presumably desirable insofar as it encourages new investment projects and so adds to the community's stock of real capital, and insofar as expanded credit makes business operations easier.

b. Is presumably undesirable if it adds to spending power at a time when all real resources are fully employed, so that its effect is simply to touch off inflationary price rises.

a and *b*.

We want to examine the situation when the community has grown to accept the use of "bank money," as modern economies have come to do.

We assume, therefore, that the money expansion indicated in question 12 has not had adverse effects: the process of expansion has been gradual, and the extra spending has in the main put unemployed resources to work on investment projects. Hence, the M increase has generally matched as well as having contributed to an expansion of the community's productive capacity.

It is essential, of course, that there be confidence in the goldsmith's establishment. Given this confidence, there is no reason why any large number of the community's members should want to switch from bank money to gold money all at the same moment. The new bank-account money will then function just as effectively as gold money did.

15. *a.* Starting with question 12's Balance Sheet, depositors withdraw $2,000 in gold coins as suitable gifts to students at graduation time. Show the new Balance Sheet.

Assets	Liabilities
Gold ....$ _____	Deposits ....$ _____
Loans .... _____	

b. Does this withdrawal change the total of M? The composition of M?

_____

_____

c. Following the event of part *a*, what is likely to happen to the extra gold in circulation?

_____

_____

a. Gold, 6,000; Loans, 20,000; Demand deposits, 26,000.
b. No, but bank money is now $26,000; coin money, $4,000.
c. It will most probably be spent; and those who receive it in payment for goods will redeposit most or all of it with the goldsmith.

16. Start with question 12's Balance Sheet. The $2,000 in gold in hand-to-hand circulation is deposited with the goldsmith. Show his resulting Balance Sheet. (Loans remain at $20,000.)

Assets		Liabilities	
Gold ....$ _____		Deposits ....$ _____	
Loans .... _____			

Gold, 10,000; Loans, 20,000; Demand deposits 30,000.

17. *a.* From what fear can the goldsmith never fully escape?

_____ .

b. If he were faced with immediate demands for gold in excess of his supply, could he meet the crisis by suddenly demanding repayment from all his borrowers?

_____

_____ .

c. Suppose (with the Balance Sheet as in question 16) a panicky demand for gold develops. Can the goldsmith meet this demand by saying: "Only $10,000 of my deposits stands for true deposits of gold. All the other deposits represent loans. I will pay off the $10,000 in the 'real deposits.' The rest of you are just borrowers and have no right to demand gold." Why or why not?

_____

_____

_____

_____ .

a. From the fear that he will be lynched because people demand more gold than he possesses.
b. No; he will only bankrupt borrowers; gold supply is only $10,000.
c. No; most or all borrowers will have spent their deposits, which thus pass into the hands of other depositors. Most deposits are indistinguishable one from another.

18. As protection against the danger of a panicky demand for gold, the authorities issue this decree: "All deposits with Ye Gold Shoppe are insured. The public's deposits are protected." If the public has confidence in this proclamation (whatever its meaning), this *(will / will not)* lessen the possibility of a bank run.

_____

will.

The authorities now require the goldsmith to maintain a gold reserve of at least 20 per cent of his demand deposits. That is, he is expected to restrain his total loans sufficiently that his total demand deposits are not more than 5 times the gold amount he is holding. For every $1 in gold on hand, he must have not more than $5 in demand deposits.

The community's total gold supply is $10,000. On the average, $8,000 of this is deposited in the bank. The other $2,000 is held by people in "hand-to-hand circulation." This $8,000–$2,000 ratio varies somewhat. People continually withdraw small gold amounts from the bank for one purpose or another; at the same time, others are bringing small gold amounts in for deposit. A few people may prefer gold coins to bank-deposit money; some transactions are perhaps more conveniently made by gold coins. Some gold coins are collected in piggy banks; but this accumulated gold is spent from time to time, thus finding its way back to the bank.

As a consequence of this variation in gold deposited, the 20 per cent gold-reserve ratio is *not* applied on a strict hour-to-hour or day-to-day basis. The goldsmith is expected to hold down his loans and deposits sufficiently that on the average of (say) each week's transactions, his gold on hand is at least 20 per cent of his demand deposits. But he is not in trouble just because, by the accident of one day's withdrawals, he is down to a 15 per cent gold reserve. Next day's deposits will probably restore him to 20 per cent.

If, however, enough gold is withdrawn into hand-to-hand circulation that the ratio between gold and deposits *persists* at a ratio below 20 per cent, then the goldsmith must take action. Perhaps he can persuade the public to deposit more gold with him—but that may not be easy to do. Failing this, he must reduce his loans. He will not be enthusiastic about doing this, for it will reduce the total of his interest earnings. But a reduction in loans will reduce his demand deposits (see question 21*b* to follow). That will bring the required ratio of gold to deposits back into line.

19. *a.* Show the goldsmith's Balance Sheet if he has $8,000 in gold on deposit and is fully "loaned out," allowing for the legal reserve requirement.

Assets		Liabilities	
Gold ....$ _____		Deposits ....$ _____	
Loans .... _____			

b. The community's total *M* at this point is $ _____ , made up of $ _____ in bank money and $ _____ in gold in hand-to-hand circulation.

a. Gold, 8,000; Loans, 32,000; Deposits, 40,000.
b. 42,000; 40,000; 2,000.

20. *a.* The Balance Sheet is as in question 19*a*. A depositor now withdraws $100 in gold. Show the resulting Balance Sheet.

Assets	Liabilities
Gold ....$ _____	Deposits ....$ _____
Loans .... _____	

b. Will this withdrawal force the goldsmith to reduce his loans? .... *(Yes / No)*

---

a. Gold, 7,900; Loans, 32,000; Deposits, 39,900.
b. No. This is a typical day-to-day withdrawal. The same $100, or another $100, will probably be redeposited tomorrow. No loan reduction is needed unless the gold-deposits ratio *stays* below 20 per cent.

---

21. *a.* A storekeeper brings in $500 in gold coin, the proceeds of Christmas sales, for deposit. How does this change question 20*a*'s Balance Sheet?

Assets	Liabilities
Gold ....$ _____	Deposits ....$ _____
Loans .... _____	

b. This storekeeper has a loan of $1,000 outstanding at the bank. By now, he has more than $1,000 in his deposit account. He asks that his loan be paid off. His deposit is reduced by $1,000, and he is given back his IOU. How will the Balance Sheet now look? (Disregard interest on the loan.)

Assets	Liabilities
Gold ....$ _____	Deposits ....$ _____
Loans .... _____	

c. When the loan is paid off, does this affect the community's total money supply, *M*? If so, by how much?

_____ .

---

a. Gold, 8,400; Loans, 32,000; Deposits, 40,400.
b. Gold, 8,400; Loans, 31,000; Deposits, 39,400.
c. Yes, it reduces total *M* by $1,000. NOTE: Any *increase* in the bank's total loans increases *M*; any *decrease* in total loans decreases *M*.

Thus far, we have assumed that there is just *one* goldsmith in town, just one bank. Now an event of crucial importance in the economic history of the community occurs: A second goldsmith sets up business in competition with Ye Gold Shoppe.

There are now two very important points which you must grasp, and which the questions to follow develop:

▶ Neither bank will have as much freedom to increase loans as was true in the one-bank case. If either bank has sufficient reserves to permit a loan increase, it must allow for the fact that any loan increase will cause some of its reserves to "spill over" to the other bank.

▶ Yet "the banking system" (the two banks taken together) has exactly the same power to expand loans, on the basis of any given amount of reserves, as the one-bank system did.

22. The new goldsmith is willing to store gold and to handle checks as a means of transferring deposits from one customer's account to another. But he does not wish to engage in lending.

A few customers of goldsmith No. 1, finding the new location more convenient, transfer their accounts. They do so by issuing checks drawn on their accounts with No. 1, payable to No. 2. How does No. 2's Balance Sheet look immediately after he has received checks for $5,000?

Assets	Liabilities
_____	_____
_____ $ _____	_____ $ _____

Checks drawn on Ye Gold Shoppe, $5,000; Demand deposits, $5,000.

23. *a.* What would you expect goldsmith No. 2 to do with these checks drawn on goldsmith No. 1?

_____

_____

b. Does this produce any crisis for anyone? If so, whom?

_____

c. What must goldsmith No. 1 now do? Does this produce any crisis for the community?

_____

_____

---

a. Demand payment of No. 1 in gold.
b. Yes, for No. 1, who now has insufficient gold to meet legal reserves.
c. Hurriedly call in loans in effort to bring in gold, possibly bankrupting borrowers.

---

24. After protracted discussion between all concerned, the second goldsmith agrees to engage in lending. He is subject to the same 20 per cent legal reserve requirement as goldsmith No. 1. How will the Balance Sheet of either look if each has $4,500 in gold and is fully "loaned up"?

Assets	Liabilities
Gold ....$ _____	Deposits ....$ _____
Loans .... _____	

Gold 4,500; Loans 18,000; Deposits 22,500.

25. A local boy who has made good abroad now returns home, bringing with him $3,000 in new gold coins. These he deposits with goldsmith No. 2. Show the goldsmith's Balance Sheet immediately after this deposit has been made, i.e., before he has had any opportunity to increase loans.

Assets	Liabilities
Gold ....$ _____	Deposits ....$ _____
Loans .... _____	

Gold 7,500; Loans 18,000; Deposits 25,500.

26. *a.* Goldsmith No. 2 now has "excess reserves." By simple application of the 1:5 ratio, it would seem that his $7,500 in gold would support total deposits of $ _____—i.e., he could increase his loans by $ _____.

b. There are still reputable borrowers available. So No. 2—perhaps incautiously—*does* increase his loans by $12,000. He gives the new borrowers deposit accounts, against which they can issue checks. Show his Balance Sheet immediately after this expansion in loans and deposits, but before the borrowers have had time to spend any part of these deposits.

Assets	Liabilities
Gold ....$ _____	Deposits ....$ _____
Loans .... _____	

c. At this stage, No. 2's reserve position is: (*Still has excess reserves* / *Just fully loaned up* / *Overexpanded*).

a. 37,500; 12,000. *b.* Gold 7,500; Loans 30,000; Deposits 37,500. *c.* fully loaned up.

27. When business firms or individuals borrow, they do so in order to use the money for some purpose. So the borrowers issue checks against their deposits. Some of these checks will be made payable to people who keep their accounts with goldsmith No. 1; and so they will be deposited with No. 1. The remainder will go to people who keep their accounts with No. 2. Assume that the split is 50–50; that is, $6,000 in

checks will be payable to customers of No. 1 and will become deposit accounts for No. 1, and $6,000 will go to customers of No. 2. How will the Balance Sheet of No. 2 be affected by the checks payable to his own customers?

_____ .

Not at all, save for redistribution of ownership of deposits.

28. *a.* What will goldsmith No. 1 do with the $6,000 in checks he receives? Does this mean a crisis for anyone?

_____ .

b. Did goldsmith No. 2 overreach himself by this loan expansion? .... (*Yes / No*)
c. If he had been the *only* goldsmith in town, would this have been such an overexpansion? .... (*Yes / No*)

a. Demand $6,000 gold of No. 2—a crisis for No. 2.
b. Yes. *c.* No.

29. Goldsmith No. 2 overreached himself by a $12,000 loan increase. But by how much *could* he have increased loans without being embarrassed by the consequent drain of gold to goldsmith No. 1? If we assume that the total of checks issued by borrowers always divides equally between the two establishments, then goldsmith No. 2 will always incur a drain of gold equal to one-half the loan increase.[2] How much of a loan increase can he stand so that the gold remaining after this drain is adequate to support his deposits? NOTE: You can solve this problem by simple algebra.[3] But do not spend a lot of time on it; it is not of sufficient importance for that. If you dislike algebra, just look at the answer below, and make sure only that you understand that a loan increase of this amount will come out "just right."

a. The loan increase is $(*1,000 / 4,000 / 6,000 / 10,000*).

b. Goldsmith No. 2's Balance Sheet, after making these loans but before any part has been spent, will be:

Assets	Liabilities
Gold ....$ _____	Deposits ....$ _____
Loans .... _____	

[2]Assume that none of this new gold "leaks" into hand-to-hand circulation outside the two banks.
[3]Let X = the loan increase. The gold loss will be $\frac{1}{2} X$. Total gold remaining will be $\$7,500 - \frac{1}{2} X$. Deposits will rise by $\frac{1}{2} X$ because half the depositors keep their accounts with Goldsmith No. 2. And gold retained must equal one-fifth of deposits. Solve the equation thus indicated.

c. After the loans have been spent and gold has been transferred to the other establishment, it will be:

Assets	Liabilities
Gold ....$ _____	Deposits ....$ _____
Loans .... _____	

a. 4,000.
b. Gold 7,500; Loans 22,000; Deposits 29,500.
c. Gold 5,500; Loans 22,000; Deposits 27,500.

30. *a.* Goldsmith No. 2 now is fully loaned up. Does this end the process of loan and money expansion?

_____

_____ .

b. Taking "the banking system" as a whole, i.e., the two goldsmiths together, by how much can lending and the money supply be expanded as a result of the extra reserves of $3,000 in gold? (Assume that both banks abide by the 20 per cent reserve requirement, that both wish to be fully loaned up, and that none of this new gold leaks into hand-to-hand circulation outside the two banks.)

_____ .

a. No, because No. 1 now has excess reserves and can expand on a similar basis; hence there will be a back-and-forth movement of the new gold.
b. Lending can be expanded by $12,000. Including the extra $3,000 gold brought in, this means the total money supply is expanded by $15,000. Hence with respect to increases in lending and in M, the case is no different from the single-bank case.

31. In a one-bank banking system, when that bank receives extra reserves, it can increase its loans without any part of reserves "leaking away" to other banks. In a two-bank system, either bank, upon increasing its loans, will experience a reserve leakage equal to *part* of the loan increase. If the banks are of equal size, the probable loss will be about one-half of the loan increase—as we assumed in the preceding questions. If there were three such banks, the loss would be about two-thirds. And with *many* banks, the loss of reserves will be just about equal to the full increase in loans. This is the case discussed at length in the text.

a. If bank X is one among many banks, its reserve loss will just about equal its loan increase because (pick one):
(1) The number of checks written by borrowers and made payable to X's depositors will be so small it may as well be considered zero.
(2) Practically all the checks are likely to be made payable to depositors of bank X.

b. If goldsmith No. 2 is one among many banks, by how much (if at all) could he increase his loans on the strength of the $3,000 gold deposit described in question 25? (REMEMBER: He must keep a 20 per cent reserve against the $3,000 newly deposited with him.) By $(0 / 200 / 600 / 2,000 / 2,400 / 3,000).

c. Show his Balance Sheet after these loans have been made and loan proceeds spent by the borrowers.

Assets	Liabilities
Gold ....$ _____	Deposits ....$ _____
Loans .... _____	

a. (1). b. 2,400.
c. Gold 5,100; Loans 20,400; Deposits 25,500.

32. Do such loans by goldsmith No. 2, in the many-bank case, terminate the extra lending that can be generated by the extra $3,000 in gold? If not, why not?

_____

_____ .

No; other banks now have excess reserves and can expand loans—up to the same $12,000 total as before.

33. *a.* The combined Balance Sheet (billions of dollars) of *all* commercial banks appears (in part) below. The legal reserve requirement is 20 per cent of deposits. The banks thus have excess reserves of $(0 / 5 / 10 / 15 / 20 / 30) billion.

Assets	Liabilities
Reserves (deposits with Federal Reserve and cash in vaults) $30	Demand deposits . .$100
Loans 70	

b. Show their Balance Sheet after they have taken full advantage of excess reserves to expand loans. All new money remains as demand deposits.

Assets	Liabilities
Reserves ....$ _____	Deposits ....$ _____
Loans .... _____	

a. 10. b. Reserves 30; Loans 120; Deposits 150. When we have many banks, but work in terms of their *combined* Balance Sheet, the reasoning can be the same as in the one-bank Ye Gold Shoppe case.

34. The process of bank-money creation is most easily explained (perhaps can only be explained) in terms of deposit of cash in a bank. But bear in mind that *once the credit expansion process is completed, and banks are fully loaned up, most deposits made with banks do not permit any further loan expansion at all.*

In the two cases following, assume the banking system to be fully "loaned up." The reserve requirement is 20 per cent.

a. I deposit $1,000 cash in my bank. Which description is more correct?
(1) This $1,000 will permit the banking system to expand loans by $4,000.
(2) Unless the $1,000 was a net addition to reserves, no loan expansion by the banking system is possible. The money may have been withdrawn from another bank (or even my bank) a day or two earlier.

b. I deposit a $1,000 salary check in my bank. Again pick the better description.
(1) This $1,000 will permit the banking system to expand loans by $4,000.
(2) *My* bank's reserves are increased, but at the cost of another bank. There has been no net addition to the entire banking system's reserves.

a. (2). *b.* (2).

35. It is frequently said that "banks lend out the money which people deposit with them." Circle as many of the following statements as seem to you correct.

(1) Money deposited with a bank does not necessarily permit any expansion of loans by banks.
(2) If the money deposited is cash, and if it constitutes a net addition to reserves, then the deposit will support a loan increase.
(3) If a deposit *does* constitute a net addition to total banking system reserves, then it will permit a loan increase by the banking system of several times the deposit amount.
(4) If the cash deposit does support a loan increase, the banks do not "lend out" that cash. On the contrary, *they keep it.* They use it as a reserve to support the money they have newly created.
(5) If I deposit $1,000 in my bank, then *I* am the only person who can spend that deposit. If I choose not to spend it, it is as effectively "out of circulation" as if I had hidden the money at home.
(6) If I *withdraw* $1,000 in cash from my bank, and hide it at home, so that there is a net reduction in bank reserves, this will force a multiple contraction of loans. To this extent then, there is a difference between keeping money in a bank and keeping it at home.

All statements correct.

36. In the United States, the public chooses to hold roughly one-fourth of the total money supply in coins and paper bills

(about $61 billion in 1975), and the remaining three-fourths in bank demand (checking) accounts (about $215 billion in 1975).

These two fractions are set by the public in keeping with its needs and convenience. The public holds as much in the way of coins and bills as it finds convenient for the kinds of transactions coins and bills best handle. Usually, each person keeps the *remainder* of whatever money he may possess, after his coin-and-bill need is satisfied, in a bank account. So any excess of coins and bills over the total "convenience" figure would typically be deposited in bank accounts and so converted into bank money (thus adding to the banking system's reserves).

Suppose the nation is recovering from recession. As part of this recovery, bank lending increases considerably. GNP rises, as does the total of deposit-account money. It is likely that the public, wanting to maintain the same convenient ratio between the two kinds of money, will convert some of the newly created bank money into coins and bills.

To the banking system, this means a "leakage" of reserves into hand-to-hand circulation. (This is the first of the "Two Qualifications to Deposit Creation" mentioned near the end of the text chapter with respect to the multiple expansion process: if deposits are expanded significantly, this may cause some part of the reserve base to "leak away.")

If the leakage is sufficiently large, and if the Federal Reserve does not take action to restore bank reserves (on this, see the next chapter), the banking system may be forced to cut back somewhat on loans.

Circle as many of the following as are correct:
a. Any sudden disposition on the part of the public to change the form of its assets in favor of coins or bills and against bank money (i.e., to convert bank money into coins or bills) will reduce bank reserves and may force a reduction in lending.

b. If we recognize "leakage into hand-to-hand circulation" as a consideration, this reduces the multiple factor by which the banking system could convert any amount of excess reserves into loans and deposit accounts.

c. If bank money comes to be used for transactions hitherto reserved for coins and bills (e.g., if gasoline purchases come to be paid for monthly by credit card, rather than by at-the-pump cash payments), this increases bank reserves and makes possible some expansion of loans.

d. The banks cannot significantly alter the fraction of the total money supply which the public wants to keep in the form of coins and bills rather than as bank deposits (except insofar as they succeed in encouraging the use of credit cards and the like).

All statements correct.

37. The reserve which a bank is legally required to maintain against its deposits (*may / must*) consist of (*a deposit* *with a Federal Reserve Bank exclusively / cash held on its own premises exclusively / both a Federal Reserve deposit and cash on its own premises).*

---

may; both an FR deposit and cash on its own premises.

QUIZ: Multiple Choice

1. *In a "fractional-reserve" banking system, such as that of the United States, the reserve requirements imposed on commercial banks* (1) are primarily intended to set a limit on the total money supply rather than to serve as adequate protection against bank runs; (2) are in excess of what is normally required, but are sufficient to cover what would be needed if for any reason people became uneasy over the safety of bank deposits, (3) are essentially an average of the amounts needed to meet the public's demands in good times and bad; (4) are now obsolete, according to the text, and will shortly be replaced by a 100 per cent reserve requirement; (5) are not correctly described by any of the above.

2. *A fractional-reserve banking system is unstable in foul weather because* (1) the system's demand deposits are always somewhat in excess of its loans and discounts; (2) it it impossible to convert assets into cash quickly enough to satisfy all the depositors who want their money; (3) the reserve ratio required for time deposits is higher than that for demand deposits, and banks are legally required to keep much of their cash as a reserve against these time deposits; (4) banks are bound to make some bad loans which cannot be collected, so that their deposit liabilities must exceed their assets; (5) the money in banks' legal reserve with the Federal Reserve must be left there, not used to pay off deposits.

3. *The role of the commercial banking system (all commercial banks taken together) in "money creation" is this: It* (1) creates money in the sense that it creates demand-deposit accounts which borrowers can spend, but the total of these demand deposits does not exceed the total of coins and paper bills it retains as a reserve against deposits; (2) creates money only in the sense that it makes available to borrowers most (but not all) of the coins and bills that have been deposited with it; (3) creates money by creating deposit accounts which borrowers can spend, and the total of these deposits is much greater than the total of coins and bills in existence; (4) cannot properly be said to create money in any sense; (5) creates deposit accounts which depositors can spend, and the total of these accounts exceeds the total of coins and bills in existence, but these deposit accounts are defined as "near-money," not as money.

4. *The economy's money supply will increase whenever commercial banks* (1) increase their deposits with a Federal Reserve Bank; (2) increase their loans to the public; (3) increase their demand-deposit liabilities by receiving coins or

bills from the public as a deposit; (4) withdraw part of their deposit from a Federal Reserve Bank; (5) reduce their demand-deposit liabilities by paying out part of these accounts in the form of coins or paper bills.

5. *The principal assets of a commercial bank are* (1) its Federal Reserve, demand, and time deposits, vault cash, and government securities; (2) its demand deposits, Federal Reserve deposit, capital stock, and government securities; (3) its demand deposits, vault cash, government securities, and Federal Reserve deposit; (4) its Federal Reserve deposit, vault cash, government securities, and capital stock; (5) its Federal Reserve deposit, vault cash, the IOUs of borrowers, and government securities.

6. *I deposit, in Bank X, $10,000 in paper currency which has for a long time been hidden and out of circulation. The legal minimum reserve requirement for banks is 25 per cent of deposits. Bank X is one among many banks. This deposit should enable Bank X, if it wishes, to increase its loans by a maximum amount of* (1) zero; (2) $7,500; (3) $10,000; (4) $30,000; (5) more than $30,000.

7. *Assuming that the loan increase does not set off any increase of coins and paper currency in hand-to-hand circulation, the deposit described in question 6 would enable the banking system to increase its loans by a maximum of* (1) zero; (2) $7,500; (3) $10,000; (4) $30,000; (5) more than $30,000.

8. *In the circumstances of questions 6 and 7, if consideration is given to some increase of coins and paper currency in hand-to-hand circulation, the most probable maximum amount (among the five alternatives listed below) by which the banking system as a whole could increase loans would be* (1) zero; (2) less than $5,000; (3) between $20,000 and $30,000; (4) between $30,000 and $40,000; (5) more than $40,000.

9. *Had Bank X been a "monopoly bank"—i.e., if there were no other banks in competition with it—but with all other circumstances as in question 6 (including zero hand-to-hand circulation leakage), the maximum amount by which this deposit would have enabled Bank X to increase its loans, if so disposed, would be* (1) zero; (2) $7,500; (3) $10,000; (4) $30,000; (5) more than $30,000.

10. *If the legal reserve requirement had been 20 rather than 25 per cent, but with all other circumstances as in question 6, the deposit would have enabled Bank X to increase its loans, if so disposed, by* (1) zero; (2) $2,000; (3) $8,000; (4) $10,000; (5) $40,000.

11. *If the deposit of question 6 had been a $10,000 check drawn on Bank Y, but with all other circumstances as in question 6, this deposit (considered in isolation from all other deposits or withdrawals) would have enabled Bank X to increase its loans, if so disposed, by* (1) zero; (2) $7,500; (3) $10,000; (4) $30,000; (5) more than $30,000.

12. *The deposit of question 11 would enable the entire banking system to increase loans, if so disposed, by* (1) zero; (2) $7,500; (3) $10,000; (4) $30,000; (5) more than $30,000.

13. *Which one among the following five statements is* incorrect *(according to the text) with respect to "bank runs" and bank failures?* (1) The bank's predicament arises from the fact that it has turned most of its cash into "earning assets"— government securities, IOUs, and the like. (2) The bank's depositors are simply trying to convert their assets from one form of money into another form of money. (3) The bank has been operating on a fractional-reserve basis. (4) Membership in the Federal Reserve System is no guarantee against the possibility of a bank run. (5) The bank must have been insolvent, or very nearly so, before the bank run begins.

14. *If the legal reserve requirement is a minimum of 30 per cent of the amount of demand deposits, and if the banking system now has excess reserves of $15 million, then (disregarding any resulting increase in hand-to-hand circulation) the banking system could increase demand deposits by a maximum of* (1) zero; (2) $10.5 million; (3) $15 million; (4) $35 million; (5) $50 million.

15. *The banking system can create deposits which are several times as large as reserves deposited with it. One element which limits the extent of the banking system's power to do this is the legal reserve requirement. Another limiting element is the fact that* (1) no individual bank can really increase the money supply; it can only lend out a major fraction of any money deposited with it; (2) all member banks must maintain a deposit with the Federal Reserve; (3) a substantial increase in loans on the part of any single bank normally causes it to lose cash reserves to other banks; (4) a substantial increase in the quantity of bank-deposit money usually causes part of that money to be converted into coins and bills; (5) cash on the banks' own premises can no longer be counted as part of their reserves.

16. *The Federal Reserve System is owned by the* (1) federal government and operated in keeping with the needs of the federal government; (2) public, through the federal government, and operated in keeping with the needs of the public; (3) commercial banks and operated in keeping with the wishes of the commercial banks; (4) public, through the federal government, but operated in keeping with the needs and wishes of the commercial banks; (5) commercial banks, but operated in keeping with the needs of the public.

17. *The Federal Reserve System has many functions and responsibilities. Which among the following does not correctly describe the Fed?* (1) It seeks to make a system of small-unit banking workable in an advanced economic society. (2) It controls the quantity of commercial-bank demand deposits, which make up the major part of the nation's money supply, in that it controls legal reserve requirements. (3) It seeks to earn a profit for its member-bank owners. (4) It considers itself primarily responsible to Congress rather than to the Treasury. (5) It holds on deposit most of the "Reserves" of member banks.

18. *The "excess reserves" of a commercial bank consist of* (1) assets which, although not money, can be quickly converted into money by the bank should the need arise; (2) money and near-money assets possessed by the bank in excess of 100 per cent of the amount of its demand deposits; (3) cash which must be kept on hand, not because everyday bank needs require it, but because of a legal requirement; (4) money held by the bank in excess of that fraction of its deposits required by law; (5) the difference between the amount of its money assets and the amount of its demand deposits.

QUIZ: Other

1. Suppose we define the total money supply (M) as the total of coins, paper bills, and bank demand-deposit accounts owned by the public, excluding any coins or bills held within the banks as reserves. Now the following events occur:

(1) A single small bank receives a deposit of $1,000 in coins and bills, money which hitherto had been hidden in a mattress.
(2) Out of this deposit it makes a loan of $800 by giving the borrower credit for a deposit (checking) account of $800. (The remaining $200 is retained as a reserve against the original deposit.)
(3) The borrower issues checks in order to spend his $800 loan. The deposit thus passes (via those to whom the checks are made payable) from the original bank to other banks.

a. Did event 1 change (increase or decrease) M? Explain.

b. Did event 2 change M? Explain.

c. Did event 3 change M?

d. If your answer to *b* was yes, how can you reconcile it with the argument that no single bank can create money, since it only lends out part of what was deposited with it? If your answer to *b* was no, how can you reconcile it with the fact that the bank's demand deposits rose by $800?

e. Suppose the bank had given the borrower $800 in cash, instead of a deposit account. How, if at all, would this change your answers to the preceding questions?

2. Assume that (*a*) commercial banks are all subject to a legal reserve requirement of 20 per cent; (*b*) they have no excess reserves of any kind, except that (*c*) they always keep an *extra* 5 per cent of their demand deposits as vault cash or till money, in addition to the legal requirement; and (*d*) the total of demand deposits is $12 billion. If the legal reserve requirement is increased from 20 per cent to 25 per cent, by how much must demand deposits be changed, if at all?

MONETARY POLICY, in essence, means this: policy designed to make the borrowing of money easy or difficult, as conditions require.

Those who borrow money do so in order to spend it. Consequently, if the amount of borrowing can be increased or decreased, so can the total volume of spending. And as spending goes, so goes GNP.

The total of borrowing *can* be manipulated—by the Federal Reserve System. The Fed can control (or at any rate, significantly influence) the borrowing total because of the power it can exercise over the reserves of the commercial banks.

Your first and major task in this chapter is to learn the methods through which the Fed can regulate the total of commercial bank reserves—particularly through "open-market operations."

1. *a.* To understand how monetary policy is operated, it is necessary to have some familiarity with the various accounts on the Federal Reserve Balance Sheet. So begin by writing down the names of the three Asset accounts (omitting Miscellaneous Assets) in text Table 17-1.

(1) _____ .

(2) _____ .

(3) _____ .

b. Omitting Miscellaneous Liabilities and Capital Accounts, write down the four items on the Liabilities and Net Worth side of the Fed's Balance Sheet.

(1) _____ .

(2) _____ .

(3) _____ .

(4) _____ .

---

a. (1) Gold Certificates and Other Cash; (2) U.S. Government Securities; (3) Discounts and Loans.
b. (1) Federal Reserve Notes; (2) Member Bank Reserve Deposits; (3) U.S. Treasury Deposit; (4) Foreign and Other Deposits.

---

2. The Federal Reserve can operate monetary policy primarily because it is a "bank for bankers." Disregarding the smaller banks that are not members of the Federal Reserve System,

commercial banks keep most of their cash on deposit with the Fed. This means that on the Balance Sheet for the commercial banks (combined), there is (*an asset / a liability*) Deposit with Federal Reserve, while on the Fed's Balance Sheet there is a matching (*asset / liability*) account called

_____ .

This corresponds exactly to the relation between me and my commercial bank. The money I have on deposit in a checking account, I count as an asset. Disregarding any checks I have written but which have not yet reached the bank, exactly the same figure shows up on the bank's Balance Sheet as (*an asset / a liability*).

---

an asset; liability; Member Bank Reserve Deposits; a liability.

Commercial banks do not keep a Federal Reserve deposit just as an expression of their faith in the banking principle. They do so because they are legally required to keep a Reserve against their own deposit accounts, and a deposit with the Fed is the most convenient way of keeping most of it, particularly since there are continually accounts to be settled with other banks.

Cash on the bank's own premises—"vault cash," or "till money"—may also be counted as part of this Reserve. But the Reserve must take one of these two forms: either a deposit with the Fed, or cash on hand.

If a bank is deficient in its Reserve requirement—i.e., if its total Reserve is less than the legally required percentage of its total customer deposits—then it must do one of two things: increase its Reserve, or decrease its customer deposits.

Usually a bank can increase its Reserve—temporarily—by borrowing funds from another bank which happens to have excess Reserves. (There is an active market in such transfers. It is the "Federal Funds market," and the interest rate charged is the "Federal Funds rate." But these loans are made strictly on an overnight basis.)

Alternatively, the deficient bank might sell some of its security holdings to another bank with Reserves in excess. Or it might borrow from the Federal Reserve; but, as will be noted in a moment, this is another short-term and limited expedient.

If the Reserve situation is tight throughout the entire

banking system, and some banks are deficient in Reserves, the remedy will almost certainly have to be a reduction in demand deposits.

3. For reasons indicated in Chapter 16, the banks accomplish this demand-deposit reduction by means of a

_____ .

---

reduction in loans made to customers.

---

4. *a.* So a bank that is deficient in Reserves must, if the deficiency persists, curtail its loans. As old loans fall due and are paid off, the bank does not make corresponding new ones.

This loan-contraction process works to remedy a Reserve deficiency because it is the opposite of the loan-expansion process examined in detail in Chapter 16. A business firm accumulates the money needed to pay off its bank loan by means of sales to customers. The checks received from customers, which the borrowing firm deposits in its bank, ordinarily come from other banks; and the receiving bank collects funds in settlement from these other banks. Hence, as funds for loan repayment accumulate, Reserve funds tend to flow *(away from / toward)* the bank which earlier made this loan.

In sum: When a bank is deficient in Reserves, it can remedy the deficiency by cutting its loans. This transfers the deficiency to other banks, and they too must curtail loans, unless they have excess Reserves. A reduction in loans means *(a reduction / an increase)* in total deposits. (For example, see questions 21b and c, p. 120.) So when the banking system reduces total loans, it is reducing deposits to the level which a given Reserve total will support.

b. If total Reserves, in Federal Reserve deposits and cash on hand, are $20 (billion), total demand deposits owned by the public are $110, and the Reserve requirement is 20 per cent, then Reserves are *(in excess / deficient)*. The amount of Reserve *(deficiency / excess)* is $(2 / 10) billion.

c. In such a case, the banks may be able to supplement Reserves by borrowing from the Fed. But there are limitations on this method, on both borrowing and lending sides. Banks are usually reluctant to borrow from the very agency which polices their overall activities. And even if the banks are prepared to borrow, there is no automatic guarantee that the Fed will lend. The Fed's ordinary policy is to grant loans to deficient banks only for enough time to permit the adjustment to be made by other means without disrupting the economy. So ultimately the banking system must *(increase / decrease)* its loans—unless the Fed decides that a credit expansion is desirable, and so increases the Reserve base by one of the methods outlined in this chapter.

Such a loan reduction will *(reduce / increase)* the demand-deposit total. It may also perhaps bring in some coins and bills hitherto in hand-to-hand circulation, which can be added to Reserves.

d. In the situation described in *b* above, assuming no change in coins or bills in circulation, loans and deposits would have to be *(increased / decreased)* by $(1 / 2 / 5 / 10 / 20) billion.

---

a. toward; a reduction. *b.* deficient; deficiency; 2. *c.* decrease; reduce. *d.* decreased; 10.

---

5. Consider the liability on the Federal Reserve Balance Sheet, "Federal Reserve Notes, $70.9 (billion)." Circle all the following statements you think are correct.

a. This liability represents the bulk of the paper money circulating in the United States—in fact, all such money except for some older types (e.g., silver certificates, United States notes) still held by the public to a very limited degree but being withdrawn as they appear in circulation.

b. This figure of $70.9 represents the total of all such Federal Reserve paper money existing outside the Fed itself—i.e., held by commercial banks and by the public.

c. This total of paper money is listed as a liability by the Federal Reserve because, in the last analysis, such bills are simply IOUs of the Fed and must be listed on its Balance Sheet, as any such IOU must be.

d. If any member commercial bank deposits a $10 Federal Reserve note with the Fed, then on the Fed's Balance Sheet the liability Member Bank Reserves rises by $10 and the liability Federal Reserve Notes falls by $10 (since this particular IOU is no longer outstanding).

e. If a Federal Reserve employee receives a brand-new $10 Federal Reserve note as part of his salary, the Fed's liability Federal Reserve Notes must rise by $10.

f. If any commercial bank withdraws $10 from its deposit with its Federal Reserve Bank, and takes this withdrawal in the form of a $10 Federal Reserve note, then the Fed's liability Member Bank Reserves must fall by $10, and its liability Federal Reserve Notes must rise by $10.

g. Federal Reserve notes held by a commercial bank in its own vaults may be counted as part of its legal Reserve.

h. The public can increase its holdings of Federal Reserve notes simply by withdrawing part of its demand-deposit accounts. This action would decrease the deposit-money total and increase the total of paper money held by the public.

All statements are correct. NOTE: Some students have difficulty accepting the fact that any piece of paper money such as a ten-dollar bill is really an IOU. It is; it is an IOU of the Federal Reserve. Like any other IOU, it must appear on the Fed's Balance Sheet as a liability. Any new Federal Reserve notes which the Fed pays out must increase that liability; any notes returned to the Fed (e.g., deposited by a member bank, for credit to its Reserve) reduce that liability.

The questions which follow deal with the operation of monetary policy in terms of Federal Reserve and commercial bank Balance Sheets. Before tackling them, try to be reasonably clear on questions 2 through 5.

In these questions, assume that commercial banks are required to keep a Reserve of at least 20 per cent of their total demand deposits. Ordinarily, each bank tries to keep this Reserve as follows: 15 per cent as a deposit with the Fed, and 5 per cent as cash on its own premises—"vault cash."

We start with the following (incomplete[1]) Balance Sheets (in billions of dollars) for the Federal Reserve and the combined commercial banks.

Federal Reserve

Assets		Liabilities	
Gold certificates .. $10		Federal Reserve notes .. $15	
Govt. securities ... 35		Deposits:	
Loans 5		Government 5	
		Member bank 30	

Combined Commercial Banks

Assets		Liabilities	
Federal Reserve deposits ....$ 30		Demand deposits $200	
Vault cash 10			
Loans 160			

6. This question outlines the working of the principal weapon which the Federal Reserve uses in conducting its monetary policy: open-market operations.

The Fed decides (for reasons that will shortly be evident) to buy government securities from the public. It enters the bond market and buys $10 (billion) of short-term government securities (bidding up the prices of these securities somewhat, if necessary, in order to obtain them).

The Fed pays for these bonds by means of checks drawn on itself. These checks pass through the following sequence: (1) The members of the public who sold the bonds, and to whom the checks are payable, deposit them in their accounts in commercial banks. (2) The banks, to whom these claims on the Fed have now passed, return them to the Fed as increases in their Reserve account deposits.

Hence, as a consequence of this bond purchase by the Fed, two significant account totals have increased: (1) The public now has an additional $10 in its total demand deposits with commercial banks.

[1]Some accounts which are of no interest for purposes of this exercise have been omitted; the remaining accounts have arbitrarily been made to balance between themselves. You can work these exercises just as though they were the complete Balance Sheets.

(2) The commercial banks likewise have an additional $10 in their deposits with the Federal Reserve.

Write out new Balance Sheets for the Fed and the banks, corresponding to those immediately preceding this question, but showing the changes just described. (As yet, the banks have changed neither their vault cash nor their loans.)

Federal Reserve

Assets		Liabilities	
Gold certs. ....$ _____		FR notes ....$ _____	
		Deposits:	
Govt. securities _____		Govt. .... _____	
Loans .... _____		Banks .... _____	

Combined Commercial Banks

Assets		Liabilities	
FR deposits ..$ _____		Demand deposits ..$ _____	
Vault cash .... _____			
Loans .... _____			

Fed: Gold certs., 10; Govt. securities, 45; Loans, 5; FR notes, 15; Govt. deposits, 5; Bank deposits, 40.
Banks: FR deposits. 40; Vault cash, 10; Loans, 160; Deposits, 210.

7. The position of the commercial banks is now that they *(have excess Reserves / are just fully "loaned up" / are deficient in their total Reserve requirement).*

This means that they *(will want to increase / must decrease)* their total loans in order to increase their earnings.

Specifically, their total Reserves are now $*(10 / 20 / 30 / 40 / 50)*, and this is sufficient to maintain demand deposits totaling a maximum of $*(150 / 200 / 250 / 275 / 300).*

have excess Reserves; will want to increase; 50; 250.

8. Show Balance Sheets of both the Fed and the combined banks, after the banks have taken full advantage of this opportunity to increase their loans.[2]

Remember that both FR deposits and vault cash count as

[2]At the close of Chapter 16, it was pointed out that if the banks create a considerable amount of new "bank-account money," as in this case, the public may want to convert some of it into coins and bills. If this happens, the banks must provide the public with such coin and bill money by getting it from the Fed. This of course reduces their own deposits (Reserves) with the Fed. Consequently, this reduces somewhat bank power to increase deposits on the basis of a given amount of new and excess Reserves. But apart from this reduction in their expansion power, the process is unchanged. For simplicity assume (in this and subsequent questions) that the deposit increase causes *no* increase in the quantity of coins and bills held by the public.

Reserves: the banks want to keep them in a 15:5 (or 3:1) ratio. Vault cash is increased by withdrawing part of the FR deposit. Assume that withdrawal is made in Federal Reserve notes.

Federal Reserve

Assets		Liabilities	
Gold certs. . . . .$ _____		FR notes ....$ _____	
		Deposits:	
Govt. securities	_____	Govt.	_____
Loans	_____	Banks	_____

Combined Commercial Banks

Assets		Liabilities	
FR deposits ..$ _____		Demand deposits ..$ _____	
Vault cash	_____		
Loans	_____		

Fed: Gold certs., 10; Govt. securities, 45; Loans, 5; FR notes, 17.5; Govt. deposits, 5; Bank deposits, 37.5.
Banks: FR deposits, 37.5; Vault cash, 12.5; Loans, 200; Deposits, 250.

9. *a.* Assuming that the banks do so increase their loans, then the money supply has *(increased / decreased)*, altogether, by $*(0 / 10 / 20 / 30 / 40 / 50)*.
Would you expect this to affect the level of GNP?

_____

_____ .

b. In sum, if the Federal Reserve were to undertake such a bond purchase, its objective would be to *(raise / restrain)* the level of GNP by making credit *(easier / more difficult)* to obtain. We would expect interest rates (certainly on bank loans) to *(rise / fall)*.

a. increased; 50. Yes, because increased lending by banks means increased spending by borrowers.
b. raise; easier; fall.

10. *a.* Will the increase in the money supply indicated in question 8 happen automatically or inevitably? What would stop it from happening?

_____

_____ .

b. If banks should refuse to increase their loans, at all, will this open-market operation have increased the money supply at all? If so, how, and by how much?

_____

a. No. If banks cannot find satisfactory borrowers, or want to keep excess Reserves because they are uneasy about expanding loans.
b. Yes, by the $10 created when the Fed bought securities.

11. If the Federal Reserve wants to *tighten* credit and to *restrain* the GNP level, then the open-market process outlined in questions 6 to 8 will work in reverse.

a. That is, the Fed will enter the market and *(buy / sell)* government securities. If necessary, it will accept a *(lower / higher)* price for this purpose. The private sellers will pay for these securities with checks drawn on their commercial bank accounts. The Fed will return these checks to the banks involved, and require settlement by *(increasing / reducing)* the Reserve deposit which these banks keep at the Fed.

b. When the Reserves of commercial banks are down, then (unless they have excess Reserves) they must *(increase / decrease)* their loans to customers. So the effect of this tighter-money open-market operation is that the totals of commercial-bank loans and demand deposits go *(up / down)*.

(If you wish, you can work all this out in detail, starting with the same pair of Balance Sheets which preceded question 6, and with a *sale* by the Fed of $10 of its government securities. Remember that if a bank has more Federal Reserve notes than needed to cover its 5 per cent vault-cash requirement, it can return the excess to the Fed, thereby increasing the amount of its Reserve deposit.)

c. Because money loaned by banks is ordinarily spent by the borrowers, and because so much of this spending goes to maintain or increase GNP, the overall effect of this tight-money operation is to *(restrain / increase)* the GNP level.

a. sell; lower; reducing. *b.* decrease; down. *c.* restrain.

12. Should the commercial banks happen to have excess Reserves when the Fed begins a tighter-money open-market operation, then all this operation does is to soak up part of the excess. The banks are *not* under pressure to reduce their loans and deposits because of a shortage of Reserves. The Fed must continue its operation until the banks *do* come under pressure.

Notice a difference between easy- and tight-money policies. When an easy-money policy gives them more Reserves, the banks *(must / may or may not)* then increase their loans to the fullest-possible extent. If they don't like the credit prospects of the would-be borrowers standing in line, they may decide not to become "fully loaned up." Nothing the Fed can do can force them to change this decision.

The Fed can always push a tight-money operation until any excess Reserves have been mopped up. Thereafter, the banks *(do not have any / still have some)* choice. They *(need not necessarily / must)* reduce their loans outstanding.

may or may not; do not have any; must.

13. In a "tight-money" period, interest rates are generally going (*up / down*). In such a period (pick the best alternative):
a. Borrowed money is hard to obtain because the total of loans granted is going down.
b. The total supply of borrowable money is small.
c. The total of loans granted may actually be increasing, but not so fast as the demand for such loans, so that to any borrower, money seems hard to obtain.

up; *c.*

14. *a.* The "discount rate" means the interest rate charged by the (*commercial banks / Federal Reserve*) for loans made to the (*public / commercial banks / Federal Reserve*).

b. As earlier indicated, commercial banks can and do borrow from the Fed. But such borrowing is limited in amount and in scope. The Fed reserves the right to refuse the loan. And it will not permit a bank to maintain continuously part of its loans on the strength of Reserves borrowed from the Fed. Such borrowing is intended primarily to tide the bank over a period of adjustment, since it cannot reduce its loans to customers overnight. Banks themselves are often reluctant to borrow from the Fed; there is a feeling among many banks that such borrowing is unwise or undesirable.

If banks *did* borrow continuously from the Fed as a means of obtaining Reserves to increase their own loan total (which they do not), then an increase or decrease in the discount rate charged by the Fed could reasonably be expected (*to affect / not to affect*) the amount so borrowed. But since such borrowing is limited, a discount-rate change has little immediate effect. Such a change is really a kind of flag raised by the Fed to signal that it is continuing to move toward easier or tighter money and that its open-market operations will be conducted accordingly. Thus, an increase in the discount rate is most likely to indicate continued, or even increased, (*selling / buying*) of bonds by the Fed in the open market; a decrease in the discount rate, greater (*selling / buying*) of bonds.

a. Federal Reserve; commercial banks.
b. to affect; selling; buying.

15. So the total money stock can be changed by deliberate Federal Reserve action. Or it can be changed by an altogether-different factor: foreign trade.
Consider the following sequence of events:

(1) The Volkswagen company has sold $4 billion worth of cars in the United States. These sales are not matched by U.S. sales abroad—i.e., the United States has imported $4 billion more than she has exported. The U.S. buyers have paid for

their cars by check, and the money is now in several Volkswagen-owned dollar accounts in U.S. commercial banks.

(2) As a German company, Volkswagen ultimately wants its own domestic currency, Deutsche marks. So it sells its U.S. dollar accounts to the West German central bank, the Bundesbank, for marks.

(3) The Bundesbank asks the Federal Reserve for gold in exchange for the dollar accounts it now possesses. The United States is still willing, on demand from a foreign central bank or government, to furnish gold in exchange for dollars. So the Fed transfers $4 billion gold to West Germany.

(4) The U.S. dollar bank accounts have changed hands a second time: they are now owned by the Fed. The Fed notifies the commercial banks involved that these accounts are canceled, and that the banks' deposits with the Fed have been reduced by $4 billion.

Start with the same pair of Balance Sheets which preceded question 6. Show below how they will appear after the reductions in gold, in the banks' Fed accounts, and in bank demand deposits. (The $4 billion was part of the original $200 billion.) No change has occurred as yet in vault cash or in bank loans. (NOTE: Treat gold and gold certificates as one and the same. As the text points out early in this chapter, gold certificates are a kind of "warehouse receipt" which the government deposits with the Fed in lieu of the gold itself. For present purposes, the differences between the two are quite unimportant.)

Federal Reserve

Assets	Liabilities
Gold certs. ....$ _____	FR notes ....$ _____
	Deposits:
Govt. securities _____	Govt. .... _____
Loans .... _____	Banks .... _____

Combined Commercial Banks

Assets	Liabilities
FR deposits ..$ _____	Demand deposits ..$ _____
Vault cash .... _____	
Loans .... _____	

Fed: Gold certs., 6, Govt. securities, 35, Loans, 5, FR notes, 15, Govt. deposits, 5, Bank deposits, 26.
Banks: FR deposits, 26, Vault cash, 10, Loans, 160, Deposits, 196.

16. *a.* As matters now stand, the commercial banks (*have excess / are deficient in*) Reserves.
b. Assuming that the Federal Reserve takes no counteraction

of any kind to replenish the banks' Reserves, show in the Balance Sheets below the outcome after the banks have adjusted their loans and deposits.

Remember that the banks can reduce their vault cash, if they consider they have more than enough, by depositing any excess for credit to their Reserve account. This time, unlike question 8, assume that the banks make the vault-cash adjustment via coins rather than Federal Reserve notes. (The asset "Gold certs." on these Balance Sheets is an abbreviation for "Gold certificates and cash." Cash refers to Treasury-issued coin money and to any older bills like silver certificates, originally issued by the Treasury, which the Fed happens to have on hand.)

Federal Reserve

Assets	Liabilities
Gold certs. . . . .$ _____	FR notes . . . .$ _____
	Deposits:
Govt. securities _____	Govt. . . . . _____
Loans . . . . _____	Banks . . . . _____

Combined Commercial Banks

Assets	Liabilities
FR deposits . .$ _____	Demand deposits . .$ _____
Vault cash . . . . _____	
Loans . . . . _____	

a. are deficient in.
b. Fed: Gold certs., 7; Govt. securities, 35; loans, 5; FR notes, 15; Govt. deposits, 5; Bank deposits, 27.
Banks: FR deposits, 27; Vault cash, 9; Loans, 144; Deposits, 180.

17. Notice that the outcome of these events is the same as if the Fed had conducted a *(tight-money / easy-money)* open-market operation in the amount of $4 billion.

The Fed may of course consider this credit contraction undesirable. It can stop matters by keeping in its own name the $4 billion in commercial bank accounts—i.e., it will not reduce the banks' Reserves by $4 billion. However, what it will probably do, if it does not wish a credit contraction, will be to reduce these bank accounts *gradually,* at the same time conducting an *(easier / tighter)* money policy than it otherwise would have done.

tight-money; easier.

18. The Federal Reserve System publishes its Balance Sheet (the Balance Sheet for the 12 Reserve Banks combined)

every week. It is reproduced in such papers as *The New York Times* and *The Wall Street Journal,* and is scrutinized very closely indeed by people in the money and credit markets. They are looking for such clues as it may contain concerning changes in the Fed's monetary policy.

These people look with special care at two items on the Asset side: "U.S. Government Securities," and "Discounts, Loans, and Acceptances." For example, if the total of the first of these two assets has fallen, as compared with the previous week, it means the Fed has been *(buying / selling)* in the open market. Disregarding factors such as required seasonal changes in the money supply, this suggests that the Fed is moving toward *(a tighter / an easier)* money policy.

"Discounts, Loans, and Acceptances" means the total of nongovernment IOUs held by the Fed. Typically, these IOUs will have been bought from commercial banks, in order to give those banks extra reserves. Hence, if this asset has *risen* in total, as compared with the previous week, it suggests a move toward *(a tighter / an easier)* money policy.

The total of these two assets is called "Reserve Bank Credit"—i.e., the credit (IOUs, government and nongovernment) which the (Federal) Reserve Bank is currently holding.

selling; a tighter; an easier.

QUIZ: Multiple Choice

1. *"Open-market operations" means specifically* (1) the activity of commercial banks in lending to business firms and to consumers; (2) the activity of the Federal Reserve in making loans to commercial banks; (3) the effect on the level of interest rates caused by an increase or a decrease in the total of commercial-bank loans; (4) the total operations of the Federal Reserve designed to increase or to decrease the total of member-bank demand deposits; (5) the activity of the Federal Reserve in buying or selling government securities.

2. *The principal assets on a Federal Reserve Balance Sheet are* (1) gold certificates and cash, deposits by banks, and deposits by government; (2) Federal Reserve notes, government securities, and loans; (3) gold certificates and cash, member-bank deposits, and loans; (4) gold certificates and cash, loans, and government securities; (5) Federal Reserve notes, gold certificates and cash, and member-bank deposits.

3. *The text speaks of five steps in the process by which the Federal Reserve can affect the level of GNP. If the Fed seeks to increase GNP, one of the following is* not *among these steps, namely, to* (1) increase investment spending so as to raise the level of total spending; (2) increase interest rates to make lending more attractive to holders of cash; (3) increase bank Reserves so as to encourage the banks to increase their noncash assets; (4) increase demand deposits; (5) increase the availability of credit.

4. *Which among the following five combinations constitutes the tools of monetary policy used by the Federal Reserve in "day-to-day" or routine operations (i.e., excluding tools that might be employed in exceptional situations)?* (1) Discount-rate policy, control over stock-buying margin requirements, and moral suasion. (2) Moral suasion and legal Reserve requirement changes. (3) Open-market operations and discount-rate changes. (4) Discount-rate policy and legal Reserve requirement changes. (5) Open-market operations, legal Reserve requirement changes, and selective controls over consumer and mortgage credit.

5. *The total of Federal Reserve notes held by business and the public appears on the Federal Reserve Balance Sheet* (1) as a liability, because these notes are IOUs of the Fed; (2) as an asset, since these notes constitute part of the money supply; i.e., they are cash; (3) as a liability, because these notes are part of Reserves; i.e., they represent deposits made by commercial banks; (4) within the Capital Accounts section, since this represents the money by means of which the Federal Reserve is financed; (5) not at all—only notes *not* held by business or the public appear on this Balance Sheet.

6. *If the Federal Reserve System raises the discount rate, this act should be interpreted as part of a general policy intended, among other things, primarily to* (1) reduce the total of commercial bank Reserves; (2) increase the amount saved out of income by the public; (3) encourage increased borrowing from the Fed by commercial banks; (4) increase the total of commercial bank Reserves; (5) do none of the preceding.

7. *Suppose the Federal Reserve System conducts a large-scale open-market purchase of government securities from the public. Which alternative in question 6 would be correct as to the primary objective of this act?* (1). (2). (3). (4). (5).

8. *The "monetarist school" (as led by economists such as Milton Friedman) holds that* (1) essentially all effort to control cyclical fluctuations in GNP should be undertaken by control of the money supply, and not by fiscal policy; (2) changes in the level of prices are ultimately traceable to changes in the available supply of gold; (3) changes in the money supply produce changes in the level of interest rates much more than such changes affect the price level; (4) monetary policy should be implemented primarily by means of appropriate changes in the price of gold; (5) as to control of the level of GNP, fiscal policy is more important than any activity which could be undertaken by the Federal Reserve System.

9. *Opponents of the "monetarist school" referred to in question 8 may of course hold many divergent views. But most of these opponents tend to agree upon one point, mentioned in the text, and opposed to the monetarist doctrine, namely, that* (1) the business of the Federal Reserve should be to increase the money supply by a fixed percentage each year, and that activity it undertakes beyond that objective

probably does more harm than good; (2) fiscal policy can affect the absolute level of real GNP as well as its distribution between the public and private sectors of the economy; (3) open-market operations by the Federal Reserve have little effect upon the total money supply; (4) the monetarist-school argument that commercial banks should be held to a Reserve requirement of 100 per cent against deposits is impossible to attain in practice; (5) the size or value of the gold stock has nothing like the importance attributed to it by the monetarist school.

10. *If a commercial bank deposits with the Federal Reserve a $20 Federal Reserve note, the Federal Reserve Balance Sheet will be affected as follows:* (1) The asset Discounts and Loans will rise. (2) The liability Commercial Bank Demand Deposits will fall. (3) The asset U.S. Government Securities will rise. (4) The liability Federal Reserve Notes will rise. (5) None of the preceding is correct.

11. *One reason why a reduction in the discount rate has limited effectiveness as a tool of monetary policy is the fact that* (1) the Fed, although it can increase the quantity of money held by the public, cannot force the public to spend that money, which is what is needed to increase GNP; (2) the Fed no longer has the same statutory power it once had to change the discount rate; (3) the Fed cannot control the quantity of discount borrowing, since banks borrow only in whatever amounts they choose; (4) such a reduction is likely to be offset (have its effect canceled out) by an increase in member bank Reserves; (5) such a reduction is likely to drive down the prices of stocks and bonds.

12. *If the Federal Reserve sells a large quantity of U.S. government securities to the public, it would be reasonable to conclude that this action is intended to* (1) increase the total of personal saving; (2) decrease the total of loans made by commercial banks to their customers; (3) increase the total of deposits of member banks with the Federal Reserve; (4) decrease the general level of interest rates; (5) increase the volume of Federal Reserve notes in circulation.

13. *If the Federal Reserve buys a large quantity of U.S. government securities from the public, then* (1) the Federal Reserve liability Deposits: Member Bank Reserves will go up; (2) the commercial bank liability Demand Deposits will go down; (3) the total quantity of money held by the public will go down; (4) the Federal Reserve asset Discounts, Loans, and Acceptances will go up; (5) the commercial bank asset Loans and Discounts will go down.

14. *If the Federal Reserve wants to restrict the growth of the total money supply, its task is made more difficult if* (1) it lacks legal power to reduce the Reserve requirements of commercial banks; (2) commercial banks are holding large excess Reserves; (3) the amount of personal saving out of income is very high; (4) gold is being exported to other countries in large quantities: (5) business firms and the public are anxious to buy more government bonds than they now hold.

15. *The "discount rate," as this term is used in monetary-policy discussion, means* (1) the degree of reduction in price required by the Federal Reserve when it purchases any government security; (2) the degree of pressure exerted by the Federal Reserve upon commercial banks to reduce their loans to customers; (3) the interest rate charged by the Federal Reserve on loans made to commercial banks; (4) the extent to which the Federal Reserve is acting so as to increase the money supply and the level of GNP; (5) none of the preceding.

16. *A large-scale "easier credit" operation conducted by the Federal Reserve through open-market operations will* (1) raise the price of government securities; (2) reduce the total of commercial bank Reserves; (3) lower the level of prices generally; (4) lower the price of government securities; (5) raise the legal Reserve requirements imposed upon commercial banks.

17. *If the Federal Reserve sells a large quantity of government securities in the open market, one of its purposes is normally to* (1) make credit generally more easily available; (2) discourage the public from buying government securities; (3) increase the level of investment spending; (4) decrease the discount rate; (5) decrease the total quantity of money in circulation.

18. *An increase in the discount rate will ordinarily* (1) cause both stock and bond prices to rise in value; (2) cause stock prices to rise but bond prices to fall in value; (3) cause stock prices to fall but bond prices to rise in value; (4) cause both stock and bond prices to fall in value; (5) have none of these results.

18 SYNTHESIS OF MONETARY ANALYSIS AND INCOME ANALYSIS

BECAUSE OF THE ROLE of the commercial banks in money creation, monetary policy is most easily and fully outlined in banking terms, as was done in Chapter 17. But monetary policy can also be described almost without reference to the role of the banks; that is what this present chapter does. This approach brings out some further aspects of monetary policy; among other things, it is an outline which draws closer to the "income-determination theory" of Chapters 12 and 13. And fiscal policy, although more fully treated in Chapter 19, is also discussed, to make the point that monetary policy and fiscal policy have a common objective with respect to GNP.

Note especially the importance of text Fig. 18-1 in this chapter's monetary policy discussion. Monetary policy, in its simplest and most elemental outline, is expected to work as follows:
(a) The volume of money influences the interest rate and credit availability. (Specifically, the greater the volume of money, the lower is the interest rate and the easier are credit conditions.)
(b) The interest rate (and credit availability) influences investment spending. (Specifically, the lower the interest rate, the higher such spending tends to be.)
(c) The level of investment spending governs the level of GNP. (By the analysis of Chapters 12 and 13, the higher investment spending is, the higher is GNP.)

The three parts of text Fig. 18-1—(a), (b), and (c)—match the three stages of the sequence just outlined. The sequence is not a hard one to grasp, and your most difficult task is to master two technical terms used: "liquidity preference," and "the marginal efficiency of investment."

1. The concept of liquidity preference is probably most easily grasped by pushing aside temporarily all thoughts of monetary policy in order to focus on the idea behind this concept.

▶ Liquidity preference means the disposition to hold money as an asset in preference to any form of interest- or dividend-yielding security.

So liquidity preference is exactly the same thing as what in Chapter 15 was called "the asset demand for money."

The point now of importance is that the extent of this "liquidity preference" or "asset demand for money" *will be influenced by the level of interest rates.*

The disadvantage of holding money as an asset is that it yields no interest or dividend return. However, money is easily portable, immediately spendable, and (when held as cash rather than as a bank checking account) anonymous. For several reasons, these virtues may be sufficiently important to persuade you to hold at least part of your assets in the form of money. You may hold it as insurance against the appearance of some cash-demanding emergency. If your circumstances are such that you think you may one day have to leave town in a hurry, money is a particularly useful asset to hold.

Motives such as these may be little influenced by any change in interest rates. But there is an altogether different reason for holding money: the *risk* involved in purchase of any interest- or dividend-yielding security. Its market price may fall.

The market price of *any* security will fluctuate. If you buy a 7 per cent government bond in 1976 for $1,000, that bond will pay you $70 annually in interest, and you will get your $1,000 principal back at maturity in (say) 1986 or 1993. Meantime—if it is a marketable bond, as most issues are—you may sell it on the open market at any time you wish. You may get $1,000 for it; you may get more; you may get less. Suppose that for some reason you want to sell your bond just 6 months after its purchase. But credit conditions have changed. There has been an increase in borrowing, so that the market rate has been pushed from 7 per cent up to 8 per cent. You will then get *less than* $1,000 for your bond if you sell it on the open market. Nobody is going to pay you $1,000 for a security yielding $70 annually, if $1,000 will buy another such security yielding $80 yearly.

So the risk you took when you bought the bond was the risk that its market price would *(rise / fall)*. Or to say the same thing in different words, your risk was the risk that the market interest rate would *(rise / fall)*. In the circumstances just described, you would have done better to sit on your $1,000 for 6 months, sacrificing the interest return for that period (or better yet, put it into a short-term "note" paying some interest, although usually a lower rate than that offered by longer-term issues), and *then* buy a bond—one paying $80 yearly in interest.

Of course, even when you buy this higher-interest bond, you run the risk that the market rate may rise to 9 per cent, in which case your bond likewise takes a beating in market price. But it is also possible for this rate to drop back to 7 per cent—in which case your bond's market price will rise *above* $1,000, and you can smugly congratulate yourself on your acumen as a speculator.

(Notice in passing that all aspects of risk in security buying can be summed up as market-price risk. One such aspect is the risk that the borrower might default. If a borrowing firm defaults, the market price of its IOUs will fall—all the way to zero, if there is no prospect that the default will later be made good, even in part.)

---

fall; rise.

---

2. The significance of the foregoing is this:

▶ If people think that security prices are going to fall, then they have a rational motive for holding money as an asset (a strong liquidity-preference motive).

▶ The total of this asset or liquidity demand for money will be significantly influenced by the interest-rate level.

(Since the term "liquidity demand" is sometimes used, recall the point made in Chapter 15, p. 112, that "demand" here does *not* mean the intention to *buy* something. It just means the decision to hold money in preference to any other asset.)

If the market interest rate goes up, then the market price of securities falls. (Remember what happened to your 7 per cent bond when the market rate rose to 8 per cent.) It is this fear of such a security-price fall (alternatively, this fear of a rise in interest rates) that accounts for the particular aspect of liquidity preference we are now considering.

However, if and when security prices *do* fall—when the worst has happened, so to speak—then the purchase of securities becomes more attractive. Their yield has risen. (If you can now buy a bond that will pay you $70 yearly for $900 rather than $1,000, your return will be close to 8 per cent.) So the sacrifice you make if you insist on retaining zero-interest money has become (*greater / less*).

To be sure, if you think security prices are going to fall *still more* (i.e., that interest rates are going to *rise* still more), then you will deem it preferable to continue to hold money as your asset, and to sacrifice any interest return for the time being. But the higher that interest rates rise within what can be considered their normal up-and-down range, the stronger becomes the argument that they are next going to fall instead of rising further—i.e., the stronger the pressure (*to hold money in preference to securities / not to hold money, but to buy securities*).

---

greater; not to hold money, but to buy securities.

---

3. This, then, is the background of the *LL* curve in text Fig. 18-1(a):

▶ The higher the interest rate, the less the asset demand for money (the preference to remain liquid) normally becomes.

With the *LL* (liquidity-preference) curve drawn as it is, this diagram says that if the interest rate were to go *up*, some people would decide that they ought to (*use some of their "idle" money to buy securities / sell some of their securities and hold money as an asset instead*).

Alternately, if the interest rate goes *down*, then the total quantity of money which people will want to hold as an asset will (*increase / decrease*).

In sum: Interest is the reward paid you for parting with money (parting with liquidity). If the interest rate falls, that reward is less, and the attractiveness of parting with money decreases—i.e., "liquidity preference" becomes a stronger force.

---

use some of their "idle" money to buy securities; increase.

---

4. At last we can consider how monetary policy works, in liquidity-preference terms. Text Fig. 18-1(a) shows how the Federal Reserve will seek to push the economy out of a recession, raising the GNP level.

We start, in terms of this diagram, at point *A*. The Fed now undertakes a large-scale open-market operation: it enters the securities market and buys government securities from the public—bidding up their price to the extent needed to persuade the public to sell them.

Suppose these open-market purchases have increased the total of the public's "asset money" from *A* to *B*. But *B*, in the text diagram, indicates a lower interest rate.

This interest-rate reduction comes about as follows: Having more "asset money" than before, people begin to look for other interest- or dividend-yielding securities to replace those sold to the Fed; they look for corporation bonds and the like. When this money enters the market seeking securities (other than the government issues whose price the Fed has already bid up), its effect is to cause the prices of those other securities to go (*up / down*). If the market price of securities goes up, then, for reasons already indicated in question 2, the market interest rate goes *down*.

So the sequence, in summary, is this: In an easy-money operation, the Fed enters the market to (*buy / sell*) government issues. This bids up their price, thus sending the effective interest rate on these issues (*up / down*). The sellers of these issues look for other securities to buy with their newly acquired cash. This sends the prices of such securities (*up / down*) and their effective interest yield (*up / down*). With (*lower / higher*) interest rates and easier credit conditions, borrowers with real investment projects in mind are *(discouraged / encouraged)* regarding them.

---

up; buy; down; up; down; lower; encouraged.

---

5. Look once again at the *LL* curve in text Fig. 18-1(a). Suppose it were much steeper (closer to being vertical) than as drawn. Such a steeper curve (as compared with the one drawn) would mean that any given change in interest rates—say, the reduction from 8 per cent to 4 per cent indicated—would produce a *(larger / smaller)* change in the "asset demand for money."

That is, starting from point *A*, but with a steeper *LL* curve than that shown, the Federal Reserve would have to pump a *(smaller / larger)* amount of extra money into the economy, to get the interest rate down from 8 to 4 per cent.

Conversely, if the *LL* curve were flatter (closer to being horizontal) than shown, the Fed's task (for any desired reduction in interest rates) would be *(easier / more difficult)*.

If the *LL* curve were flatter, it would mean that asset holders were highly sensitive to interest-rate changes. Even a fairly modest reduction in interest rates would "turn them off" securities; they would want to sell securities in large quantities and to hold money instead.

Should the *LL* curve be very close to horizontal (i.e., highly elastic with respect to interest-rate changes), monetary policy may prove ineffective—for we then have what the text describes as "the depression model." In depression conditions, people are fearful of the risk which security holding involves; they dread the possibility of a calamitous price drop. (And when buyers are few, security prices quite naturally *do* drop.) In seeking to produce easier money conditions, the Fed always must battle against "liquidity preference." But this struggle is at its worst when the *LL* schedule is highly elastic. In such conditions, when the Fed raises the prices of government securities, the public sells them readily. But they hold the cash proceeds as cash; they do not look for other securities to buy, because they are uneasy about the entire securities market.

So the extra money pumped into the economy does no good. The Fed wants to see this money move out of the hands of asset holders and into the hands of borrowers who will spend it. But in the depression model, the cash remains with the asset holders; it is idle, inactive money.

---

smaller; smaller; more difficult.

---

6. All the preceding discussion of "liquidity preference" and "asset demand for money" has dealt with the attitudes and behavior of *lenders* of money, *buyers* of securities. That is, we have been considering people and financial institutions holding money saved out of income, interested in exchanging this money for securities (bonds or stocks) if the terms seemed sufficiently attractive.

Now we pass to the other side of the market—to the attitudes and behavior of *sellers* of securities.

Some of these sellers may be people wanting to dispose of securities they bought earlier. Perhaps they want to sell because they need cash for some expenditure; perhaps their "asset demand for money" has risen—i.e., thinking security prices are likely to fall, they want to switch to money.

But the sellers consist also of business firms wanting to borrow money (to sell new IOUs) because they need financing for new investment projects. And this brings us to the "marginal efficiency of investment."

This "marginal efficiency" is an interest rate.

Any sensible firm contemplating a new investment project—say, the building of a new plant—must do its best to estimate (1) what it would cost to build that plant, and (2) what this plant would yield in the way of net income (income over and above operating costs), if built. Such estimates or forecasts, being clouded with uncertainty, are exceedingly difficult. But an intelligent decision requires the firm to make the best estimate it can.

This topic is discussed much later in the text (in Chapter 30). All you need know at this stage is that such an estimate can be summed up in the form of an interest rate. The firm must be able to say: We think the cost of building and establishing this projected new plant would be approximately X dollars. By a conservative estimate of the net income it would bring in, if and when built, the plant would yield us (say) 10 per cent on the X dollars that would be tied up in it.

If money can be borrowed at 9 per cent, and if the firm has been conservative in its cost and revenue estimates, then the plant *(would / would not)* be worth building. Even after paying the interest charges on borrowed money, there would be income left over. If money can be borrowed only at 12 per cent, that plant *(still would / would not)* be worth building.

Suppose the market interest rate has been 12 per cent. The plant will not be built. Then the market rate drops to 9 per cent. It will now be worth borrowing the money to build this plant. It is a "marginal" investment project, worth building only if and when the market interest rate falls significantly below 10 per cent.

Similarly, it can be expected that there will be other new investment projects to be tackled if—but only if—the market interest rate drops from 9 per cent to 8 per cent, or from 6 per cent to 5 per cent.

---

would; would not.

---

7. This, then, is the background of part (b) of text Fig. 18-1—the "marginal efficiency of investment" schedule.

▶ The "marginal efficiency of investment" schedule is one showing, for some given point in time, the amount of investment that would be undertaken, at different possible interest rates.

▶ This "marginal-efficiency" schedule indicates that if the interest rate falls, the total of such investment spending will increase.

In sum: If the market interest rate decreases, some investment projects hitherto considered "extra-marginal" (just outside the boundary of profitable undertakings) will become (more / less) attractive to business firms, since their financing will have become (cheaper / more expensive). Conversely, if the market rate rises, some planned investment projects will be (undertaken / canceled).

Note that "the market interest rate" is here taken as a kind of symbol for the general availability of credit. Sometimes credit becomes more freely available without much change in this market rate, so that firms who previously found they could not borrow as much as they wanted at the prevailing rate now find that they can do so.

Note also that this discussion of the background of investment spending ties in with earlier material. Chapter 11 said that such spending is affected by many factors. Chapter 13 cited the level of GNP as one such; Chapter 14 cited *changes* in the GNP level. Now we are considering still another: the cost of borrowing money and credit availability.

---

more; cheaper; canceled.

---

8. In some few instances, supplying firms can make fairly close estimates of the likely "efficiency" of a proposed investment project. (For example, a power company can often make pretty good estimates of the likely increase in demand for electricity in its community over the next 10 years.) More commonly, there are so many uncertainties over future marketing conditions and the like that these "efficiency" estimates are very rough even at best—so that the firm will include a big "safety factor" in its estimate before it goes ahead with an investment project.

Because precise estimates are difficult or impossible, some economists argue that the marginal-efficiency schedule, as in text Fig. 18-1(b), will not show much responsiveness to any moderate change in interest rates. That is, a small change in the market rate will produce (a very large / only a very small) change in the total of investment spending.

Insofar as this is true, it would make the *me* curve of Fig. 18-1(b) very (steep / flat). And it would make the Fed's task of altering the GNP level via changes in the money supply (easier / more difficult).

Note one further qualification mentioned in the text as to the power of monetary policy. Insofar as big corporations finance their projects, not by going to the money markets, but instead out of their own undistributed profits, changes in money markets are (likely / unlikely) to affect their plans.

---

only a very small; steep; more difficult; unlikely.

---

9. The key diagram in this text chapter is Fig. 18-1—a three-part diagram—and the preceding review questions have been framed accordingly. Questions 1 through 6 dealt with "liquidity preference"—i.e., with part (a) of Fig. 18-1. Questions 7 and 8 covered "the marginal efficiency of investment"—part (b) of this diagram.

Part (c) of Fig. 18-1 requires less attention, for it simply repeats material dealt with earlier in the text. It shows the relationship between investment and GNP: the higher investment spending is, the (higher / lower) will be GNP. Any rise or fall in investment spending will have a magnified effect upon GNP, by reason of the multiplier process outlined in Chapter 12.

---

higher.

QUIZ: Multiple Choice

1. *A reduction in interest rates engineered by the Federal Reserve can reasonably be expected to* (1) encourage investment (*I*) spending because it makes lending of money more attractive; (2) discourage *I* spending because it makes borrowing of money less attractive; (3) have little or no effect on *I* spending, since that is not its purpose—interest-rate changes are intended to alter security prices, not *I* spending; (4) discourage *I* spending because it makes lending of money less attractive; (5) encourage *I* spending because it makes borrowing of money more attractive.

2. *The "marginal efficiency of investment" schedule means* (1) a schedule showing how the total volume of investment spending will change with changes in the interest rate; (2) a schedule showing how the true rate of interest on an interest-bearing security will vary as its market price varies; (3) an indicator of the extent to which changes in investment spending will change the level of GNP; (4) an estimate of the rate of profit which any given investment project will yield to its owners; (5) none of the above.

3. *By "liquidity demand for money" ("liquidity preference") is meant* (1) the desire to hold securities which can readily be converted into money at a fixed or near-fixed price if necessary; (2) the amount which businesses will wish to borrow at any given interest rate; (3) the desire to save more money out of income as protection against the uncertainties of the future; (4) the same thing as "asset demand for money"; (5) the same thing as "transactions demand for money."

4. *According to the text, extensive use by corporations of undistributed profits ("retained earnings") to finance expansions of their operations affects monetary policy as follows: Because* (1) the amount of such retained earnings is highly responsive to interest-rate changes, it makes monetary policy easier to conduct; (2) the flow of such retained earnings is unresponsive to interest-rate changes, it makes monetary policy harder to conduct; (3) such retained earnings flow automatically into investment, it makes monetary policy easier to conduct; (4) such retained earnings constitute increases in the "asset demand for money," it makes monetary policy harder to conduct; (5) the Federal Reserve can strongly influence the level of such undistributed profits, it makes monetary policy easier to conduct.

5. *Which of the following is* not *a correct statement of a point made (directly or indirectly) by the text with respect to the problem of automation and unemployment?* (1) In the short run, automation may increase rather than decrease employment, provided the new machines cannot be built solely from the depreciation allowances of old machines, but, rather, call for new net investment spending. (2) The displacement of some workers from established jobs is a regrettable but necessary development if the economy is to increase its per capita real income by means of technological change. (3) It is possible for a firm which successfully adopts automation processes to employ as much labor as, or more than, before, even though it continues to produce the same level of output. (4) Insofar as automation does tend to produce unemployment, adoption of proper expansionary monetary and fiscal policies can expand demand for goods and services and thus increase employment opportunities. (5) The belief has often been expressed that there is only a fixed amount of output to produce, so that every time a machine displaces a man, there is one less job for labor, but this is a misleading and unwise belief on which to base any policy toward automation.

6. *Monetary policy and fiscal policy differ in this way:* (1) Monetary policy is deliberately operated in an effort to keep GNP in the full-employment region, whereas fiscal policy cannot have anything but minor effects on the GNP level. (2) Monetary policy deals with the amounts of money spent and collected by the government whereas fiscal policy deals with interest rates. (3) Monetary policy seeks to encourage or discourage investment (I) spending and consumption (C) spending by business firms and private citizens by influencing interest rates and credit availability, whereas fiscal policy operates directly upon incomes through spending and taxation. (4) Fiscal policy works principally through changes in the level of I spending, whereas monetary policy affects I spending little or not at all. (5) There is no essential difference between them at all, since both objectives and techniques of operation are the same—they differ only in that they are administered by two different agencies.

7. *Monetary policy is made somewhat less effective in restraining a period of excessive spending insofar as* (1) the "marginal efficiency of investment" schedule is highly elastic; (2) corporations rely heavily upon internal financing for their investment projects; (3) the "liquidity preference" schedule is highly inelastic; (4) changes in interest rates tend to bring with them changes in the market value of securities; (5) investment spending responds more to changes in credit availability than to changes in interest rates.

8. *In terms of the "saving-investment" diagram used extensively in Chapters 12 and 13 of the text, the introduction of a tight-money policy by the Federal Reserve would be intended to* (1) lower both the investment (I) and saving (S) schedules, hence lower GNP; (2) raise the I schedule, hence lower GNP; (3) raise the I schedule, hence raise GNP; (4) lower the S schedule, hence raise GNP; (5) lower the I schedule, hence lower GNP.

9. *If the Federal Reserve conducts a large-scale easy-money open-market operation,* (1) government security prices will rise and interest rates will fall; (2) interest rates will fall, but government security prices need not be affected; (3) both government security prices and interest rates will fall; (4) government security prices will fall and interest rates will rise; (5) interest rates will rise, but government security prices may or may not change.

10. *The Federal Reserve should slow down or halt a tight-money policy* (1) as soon as interest rates have reached a sufficiently low level; (2) when investment spending has been sufficiently increased; (3) whenever the equilibrium level of GNP has been reached; (4) when prices begin to rise sharply; (5) in none of these situations.

11. *The effectiveness of monetary policy in a recession will be reduced or destroyed if* (1) interest rates cannot be forced down much because the level of borrowing is highly responsive to small changes in the level of the interest rate; (2) the Fed finds that security prices start to go up as soon as it begins its easy-money operations; (3) interest rates cannot be forced down much because money holders prefer to retain money rather than buy securities at any lower rate; (4) the "asset demand" or "liquidity demand" for money is very low: (5) the value of the "multiplier" is very high.

12. *The effectiveness of monetary policy in a recession will be reduced or destroyed if* (1) the public is principally interested in holding securities rather than money as assets; (2) the Federal Reserve does not wish the prices of government securities to fall below their maturity value; (3) the Federal Reserve is determined to maintain an easy-money rather than a tight-money policy; (4) the current level of interest rates is very high; (5) potential borrowers do not respond to reductions in the interest rate or to greater availability of credit.

13. *If the Federal Reserve conducts a large-scale open-market sale of government securities, then we would expect* (1) the marginal efficiency of investment to increase; (2) the federal government's budget to move into surplus or at least into balance; (3) the total quantity of money in circulation to increase; (4) liquidity preference to decrease; (5) none of the preceding to occur.

14. *The saying quoted in the text, "the central bank can pull on a string, but it can't push on a string," is intended to illustrate the following fact about monetary policy:* (1) The Federal Reserve cannot conduct a tight-money open-market policy without lowering the market price of government bonds. (2) The Fed's power to keep the price level from rising too rapidly is greatly weakened if strong trade-unions keep pushing up the level of wages. (3) The Fed's power to bring out spending in a period of depression is considerably greater than its power to hold back inflationary price rises at a time when people are beginning to lose confidence in money. (4) The Fed's anti-inflationary powers are much greater than its powers to persuade more people to lend and borrow during a recession. (5) Through much of its history, the Fed has been reluctant to apply tight-money policies at times when such policies were needed.

15. *When fiscal policy and monetary policy are being operated in concert in order to combat a recession, we are likely to observe (according to the text) a combination of a* (1) budget deficit and open-market security purchases; (2) budget surplus and open-market security purchases; (3) budget deficit and open-market security sales; (4) budget surplus and open-market security sales; (5) balanced budget and open-market security sales.

16. *A government bond is marketable; i.e., its owner may sell it freely in the bond market. The holder of this bond gets* $70 per year in interest; the government will also pay back the principal amount of $1,000 ten years from now. An increase in demand for these bonds engineered by the Federal Reserve drives up their price in the bond market to $1,050. To a person who has paid this price, the "yield" (effective interest rate earned) is (1) zero; (2) less than 7 per cent but not zero; (3) 7 per cent; (4) more than 7 per cent but less than 10 per cent; (5) 10 per cent or more.

17. *The impact, if any, of the bond price change described in question 16 on new bonds being offered for sale by the federal government and by corporations will be as follows:* (1) Both new government and new corporation bonds must be offered for sale at a somewhat higher interest rate. (2) New government bonds can be offered for sale at a lower interest rate, but new corporation bonds must be offered at a higher rate. (3) Both new government and new corporation bonds can be offered for sale at a somewhat lower interest rate. (4) New government bonds can be offered for sale at a somewhat lower interest rate, but new corporation bonds will not be affected at all. (5) There is no reason why the sale of either new government or new corporation bonds should be affected at all.

APPENDIX: Mechanisms of Monetarism and Income Determination

Some of the material in this Appendix is difficult; so do not be discouraged if at first you find it hard going. It contrasts the older "classical" view of the way in which a capitalist economy operates with the newer "Keynesian" view. Subtle distinctions are involved, and the conflicting ideas require careful sorting out.

1. An all-important prop in the classical view of things was Say's Law: "The total money demand for goods is always just equal to the total money value of goods produced for sale." Say's Law asserts, that is, that there can never be a recession due to insufficient $C + I + G$ spending.

Behind Say's Law lies the belief that money exists only to be spent. Say's Law theorists saw no logical reason why people should choose to *hold* money for any significant length of time.

This law would automatically be correct if all income received were spent without delay on consumer goods. Then (assuming no diversions of income on account of taxation or undistributed profits), total demand for goods would just be equal to total incomes earned.

The trouble with Say's Law arises over *saving.* Say's Law reasoning is that money not employed to buy consumer goods or services will be used without significant delay to buy securities yielding an interest or dividend return. Thus the saved money works its way back (via investment) to the producer sector.

This reasoning, in terms of Study Guide Fig. 11-7 (p. 86), results in a *closed* pipe from S to I. Total money demand is the total of the C flow and the S flow—which becomes an I flow. Money is never "sidetracked" in the passage from S to I.

a. Clearly, money saved must flow through more tortuous channels to reappear as I spending than to reappear as C spending, where the flow is direct. So any weakness in Say's Law must lie in the *(consumption / saving-investment)* sector.

b. An emphasis on liquidity preference (see questions 1 and 2, pp. 134–135) means a view that some S may be withheld from the income stream, perhaps for a significant time period, because the holder chooses to retain that money as an asset. This is a *(reaffirmation / denial)* of Say's Law.

While it is far from being the whole of Keynesian theory, the liquidity-preference idea is sufficient to break the view that there is never a reasonable motive for not converting S into I through security purchases. Large-scale liquidity preference is most likely to be found at the onset of or during a recession. If business prospects look gloomy, it may be widely believed that security prices will fall. Money is then withheld just at the time when its withholding upsets a full-employment economy.

In broader terms, the clash is this: Say's Law implicitly argues that the interest-rate mechanism is adequate to maintain a smooth full-employment relation between S and I. The Keynesian view is that the interest rate cannot sustain this burden alone, and that the S-I equilibrium gets a strong assist from income and employment changes. Thus, if I drops, incomes drop and unemployment develops before S and I are once again equated. The interest rate may help by dropping;

but it cannot drop far enough or fast enough to do the job unassisted. It might have to drop to a negative figure if it had to operate without assistance; and lenders are not notably enthusiastic about negative interest rates.

c. While denying the possibility of a deficiency in *overall* purchasing power, Say's Law theorists fully recognized that there could be, in a sense, insufficient demand for *any particular good.* If consumer tastes shift away from good X, the money flow toward X will dwindle—but the flow toward some other good or goods, Y, will increase.

Prices then have a role in the economy's smooth operation: X's price must fall; Y's price must rise. Such price changes will remove the deficiency of money demand for X, and the excess demand for Y. Smooth operation of the economy (in Say's Law terms) requires *(flexible / rigid)* prices.

In consequence, a defender of Say's Law would reply to the liquidity-preference argument thus: The law is still valid. If part of the returning money flow *is* blocked because money is being held as an asset, this simply puts most or all goods in good X's position. All or most prices must *fall;* if they fall sufficiently, the reduced money flow will still be adequate to buy the full-employment output of goods and services. ("Prices" here include all production costs such as wages. Finished-good prices can hardly be expected to fall if their production costs do not.) Absolute prices will have fallen, but relative prices need not have altered (i.e., the general relation of wages to the prices of consumer goods will not be changed).

Defenders of Say's Law thus say that if the adjustment to a new equilibrium produces widespread unemployment, it is because prices are *(flexible upward / flexible downward / inflexible downward).*

In point of fact, for whatever reasons, the real-life price system does not seem to have the required flexibility to a sufficient degree. And if prices *are* sufficiently inflexible, there *can* be unemployment due to a deficiency of overall demand.

---

a. saving-investment. *b.* denial. *c.* flexible; inflexible downward.

---

2. At this stage in the debate, Say's Law critics argued that even if prices *did* have (or could be given) downward flexibility, this *still* might not restore full employment. (The issue is important, for behind it is the question, Ought we to consider adopting public policies designed to make prices more flexible?)

The argument here is essentially "liquidity preference" again—but this time applied to *commodities* rather than to securities. If prices generally are falling, it makes sense to hold back on purchases (to hold money rather than to spend it). Falling prices mean that you can buy what you want more cheaply just by waiting. Hence, downward price flexibility

might be offset by an increased asset demand ("liquidity preference") for money. If so, then flexible and falling prices do *not* bring the full-employment output of goods or services back into line with total money demand for this output, because as prices fall, money demand for output keeps falling as much or even more.

A. C. Pigou—batting, so to speak, for the opposing or Say's Law team—complicated further an already-complicated argument by introducing a new consideration. He insisted that price flexibility *would ultimately* restore full employment because of a "wealth effect" or "Pigou effect." The *total* money stock still exists unchanged and still has owners, even though a smaller fraction is being spent. As the price level falls, the owners of this money stock are bound to feel wealthier. This greater sensation of wealth will—with a sufficient fall in prices—prompt them to spend more.

That is, the Pigou effect depends on the fact that as prices fall, total *M (falls in relation to the price level / grows in absolute terms / remains unchanged in absolute terms, hence rises relative to the price level).*

---

remains unchanged in absolute terms.

---

3. If Say's Law is accepted (and it once was widely accepted), it is just a short step to the "crude Quantity Theory of Money" (discussed in text Chapter 15, and also in this Appendix). In the Say's Law world, all resources are fully employed and all money is "active"—i.e., there is no liquidity preference.

Suppose the quantity of *M* is somehow doubled. (Don't ask *how* this extra *M* appears. Actually, the manner in which it made its appearance probably would make a considerable difference in the results it produced. But that is not the issue we want to explore at the present stage. Just assume that everybody wakes up some morning with twice as much money as he or she had before).

By the reasoning underlying Say's Law, the only thing to do with this newly acquired *M* is to *(spend / save)* it. But this rise in money purchasing power cannot elicit any rise in real output, for resources are already fully employed. So all the impact of the increased *M* must be on *P*—i.e., prices will be *(doubled / halved).*

Such quantity-theory reasoning assumes a very "frictionless" world, where the fact of *moving* from one price level to another does not set off unwanted side effects. In actual experience, a particular price level may grow familiar, and people may grow uneasy if it doubles, even with a doubling of money incomes. So they might start spending more rapidly, fearing that money is about to lose more or even all of its value—the doubling of prices being a warning of an even more drastic price increase in the future. Such a velocity increase would upset the quantity-theory view that prices would just double.

spend; doubled.

4. *a.* To some extent, the Pigou "wealth effect" case discussed in question 2 assumes a similar "frictionless" world. But this case does *not* assume the operation of the crude quantity theory. On the contrary, Pigou's "wealth effect" arises because, as prices fall, M *(remains constant / increases / decreases).* With prices falling, this assumption *(is contrary to / agrees with)* the crude quantity theory of money.

b. The text points out, however, that we can use the Pigou model in order to make a small correction in the crude quantity theory. Strictly speaking, if there is a large public debt, then a doubling of M and a consequent doubling of P will not leave everything in the same proportion as before. The public owns government bonds, which it thinks of as assets. Unless the dollar total of these bonds is also doubled when prices and incomes are doubled, the public will not feel as well off as it did before. This time the "wealth effect" pertains to bonds, not to M, and since prices now go up rather than down, the effect is the *(opposite of / same as)* that described in question 2. (NOTE: Do not spend much time on this matter if it causes you difficulty. The point involved is of minor importance in an introductory survey.)

a. remains constant; is contrary to.   *b.* opposite of.

5. *a.* Figure 18-4 in the text (the "Hicks-Hansen synthesis") seeks to show, in the simplest possible form, the overall relationship between the money supply, the interest rate, investment spending, and equilibrium GNP. Its background is quite complicated, even though, of necessity, it simplifies a great deal. For example, it assumes that I spending is governed *only* by the level of the interest rate, i. This i-I relation is summed up in the "marginal efficiency of investment" schedule—see text Fig. 18-1(b) and Study Guide questions 6 and 7, p. 136. Such a schedule is drawn on the assumption that all the many other factors which can influence I spending are held constant. A change in any one of them would cause the marginal-efficiency curve to shift to a new position.

Thus we can say that (1) given any certain i, we know from the marginal-efficiency schedule what I spending will be; (2) given I spending and a certain propensity to consume, we know from Chapter 12 how equilibrium GNP will be determined.

Consolidating (1) and (2) above, we can say: If we know what i is, we know what equilibrium GNP will be. This is what the IS curve in text Fig. 18-4 says. It runs northwest to southeast, indicating, as it should, that the lower i is, the *(lower / higher)* will be I spending, and so the *(lower / higher)* GNP will be.

In a sense, this IS curve is a "demand for money" curve. The lower i is (the more readily available credit is), the higher the quantity of money demanded for GNP purposes.

b. If IS is a demand curve, then there must also be a "supply curve" before we can determine the equilibrium levels of i and of GNP (the two magnitudes measured on the axes of this diagram).

The LM curve is just such a supply curve. But it needs careful explanation. Remember the two purposes for which any money supply (M) can be used:

(1) "Active" or "transactions" use—money needed just to sustain GNP at any particular level (given the price level). A higher GNP would require more "active" M; so the needs for active M depend on the GNP level.

(2) "Precautionary demand," "asset demand," or "liquidity preference" (again see questions 1 and 2, pp. 134–135)—a disposition to hold money inactive, the amount of which increases as i falls.

How is the LM curve in Fig. 18-4 constructed? Take any GNP, at random. Take any M—but one large enough to more than cover the needs for active M, given the GNP chosen. The *remaining* M is available for liquidity preference. There is some interest rate i, just low enough that people will wish to hold that quantity of M inactive, given that i.

We started with some given GNP; now we have reached a particular i which is associated with that GNP. This means we have established one point on the LM curve. Other points are derived similarly.

Remember that the LM curve is drawn on the assumption of some given total M (this point is essential). An increase in M would shift the LM curve to the *(right / left).* The curve runs in a generally southwest-northeast direction because (with a given M), if GNP were to increase, that would call for *(less / more)* active money. This would leave *(less / more)* M remaining for liquidity purposes. If people are to be persuaded to part with this inactive money, i must *(rise / fall).* This relation between GNP and i calls for a curve running toward the northeast.

a. higher; higher.   *b.* right; more; less; rise.

QUIZ: Multiple Choice

1. *Say's Law* (1) was used in the "classical" analysis of economic behavior, and asserts that the deficiency in a capitalist system which results in unemployment lies in the tendency for the amount of investment to run ahead of the amount of saving; (2) is part of the "Keynesian" analysis of economic behavior, and asserts that (contrary to classical analysis) people may wish to hold "inactive" money; (3) was used in the "classical" analysis of economic behavior, and asserts that overproduction or unemployment resulting from a deficiency of total purchasing power is impossible; (4) is part of the "Keynesian" analysis of economic behavior, and asserts that prices that are excessively flexible (i.e., that overrespond to small changes in demand or supply) may drive the economy into recession or into inflation; (5) is not correctly described by any of these statements.

2. *The "Pigou effect" says that if* (a) *there is some departure from full employment in a capitalist society and* (b) *all prices are flexible downward, then* (1) the velocity of circulation of money will decrease in proportion to the fall in the price level; (2) the propensity to consume will decrease because the fall in prices will give some asset holders an increased sense of wealth; (3) expectations of a still further decrease in prices may decrease the amount of total spending; (4) the propensity to consume will increase because the fall in prices will give some asset holders an increased sense of wealth; (5) the reduction in costs of production will provide a new incentive for investment spending, thus reversing the departure from full employment.

3. *The text says that there is a "transactions demand" (T-demand) for money, and a "liquidity demand" for money as well. These two "demands" ordinarily behave as follows: The liquidity demand falls as the interest rate* (1) rises, whereas the T-demand rises as GNP rises; (2) rises, whereas the T-demand rises as GNP falls; (3) falls, whereas the T-demand rises as GNP rises; (4) falls, whereas the T-demand rises as GNP rises; (5) rises, whereas the T-demand is unaffected by changes in GNP.

4. *If Say's Law is to be an accurate description of the manner in which the economy functions, the economy must have this property:* (1) The prices of government securities must be stable. (2) There must be no strong asset (liquidity) demand for money. (3) Prices must be fairly unresponsive to small or moderate changes in demand or in supply. (4) The velocity of money must increase or decrease as GNP increases or decreases. (5) The public's tastes must not shift from the purchase of one good to the purchase of another.

19 FISCAL POLICY AND FULL EMPLOYMENT WITHOUT INFLATION

A GOVERNMENT'S FISCAL POLICY is its policy with respect to the money it plans to spend (amount and form of its expenditures) and the money it expects to receive (amount and form of its taxation, and borrowing, if any).

The basic facts on which this chapter depends are in the fiscal-policy section of Chapter 13—namely:

1. An increase in government spending, without a matching increase in taxes, pushes up the total-spending $(C + I + G)$ schedule. Consequently, it increases GNP.

2. GNP will be similarly increased by a tax reduction (provided there is no matching decrease in government spending).

3. The reverse effect occurs from a decrease in government spending, or from an increase in taxation.

Chapter 13 simply noted these facts. Now we consider the government's deliberate attempt to order its tax and expenditure programs so as to keep GNP at a desirable level—at or near full employment, but not so high as to pose a serious inflationary threat.

Monetary policy (discussed in Chapters 17 and 18) and fiscal policy are alike in that they are both weapons by which the authorities may try to avoid undesirable swings in GNP. Disregarding foreign exchange problems (later discussed), this stabilization is the principal objective of monetary policy. But fiscal policy has wider goals. A government spends money on a project because it deems that project necessary or desirable. It does not (or should not) spend money just because the effect will be to increase GNP. And yet, whenever money is spent or taxes are levied, GNP *is* affected, and people's incomes *are* affected. A *positive* fiscal policy is one which recognizes this fact, and tries to organize taxes and spending so that GNP will not be undesirably affected, but rather, will be kept on the right course.

1. The two weapons by which the government can operate a "positive fiscal policy" are _____ and _____.

government expenditures; tax receipts.

2. *a.* Suppose full-employment GNP is $800 billion, and— in terms of the 45° total-spending diagram used in the text

(e.g., Fig. 18-2)—the $C + I + G$ schedule cuts the 45° line so as to indicate an equilibrium GNP of $900 billion. If the goal is to maintain full employment without inflation or deflation, total $C + I + G$ must be *(increased / decreased)*.

b. This could be undertaken by means of *(monetary policy / fiscal policy / both monetary and fiscal policy)*. For example, Congress could pass legislation to *(increase / decrease)* tax rates and / or to *(increase / decrease)* government spending. If government spending alone were changed, it should be *(increased / decreased)* in billions by *($100 / $100 times the multiplier / $100 divided by the multiplier)*.

a. decreased. *b.* both monetary and fiscal; increase; decrease; decreased; $100 divided by the multiplier.

3. The government's fiscal system has some features whose effect is to check any upward or downward movement of GNP without the President or Congress taking deliberate action. They are termed *(discretionary fiscal policies / built-in or automatic stabilizers)*. Examples would be (pick one or more):

a. A change in tax receipts due to a change in GNP, without change in tax rates.

b. An increase in spending on military goods.

c. Payments of unemployment compensation benefits.

d. A decrease in personal-income-tax rates.

built-in stabilizers; *a, c*. Neither a military-spending increase nor a personal-tax-rate decrease would be automatic.

4. This question is intended to illustrate the *automatic stabilizing* effect of the personal-income-tax system. Suppose the economy has been just comfortably at the full-employment level of GNP. Investment suddenly drops by $20 (billion).

Consider first a case in which there is *no* personal income tax. GNP and national income *(NI)* promptly drop by $20. So does disposable income *(DI)*. GNP starts to move downward toward its new equilibrium level. If the MPC is 4/5, the $20 drop in *DI* results in a drop of $16 in consumption spending *(C)*. The multiplier process has begun, and GNP will fall until it reaches a new equilibrium level which is below its old level by several times $20, because of the operation of the multiplier.

a. Consider now a situation which is the same except that a

25 per cent tax has been levied on all earned income (on all *NI*). Once again, investment spending drops suddenly by $20, and consequently so do GNP and *NI*.

The important difference is that *DI* (which is *after*-tax income) will *(still / not)* drop by $20. Suppose, for example, that GNP and *NI* had originally been $200. The income tax, at 25 per cent, would have taken $50, leaving a *DI* of $150. As soon as the drop in investment occurs, GNP and *NI* will drop to $180—and the tax bite will drop to $45. So the amount of *DI* will now be $*(90 / 125 / 130 / 135 / 150)*—i.e., it is down by $*(5 / 10 / 15 / 20 / 25)*.

With the same MPC of ⅚, this drop in *DI* will produce a drop in *C* spending of $*(4 / 5 / 12 / 15 / 20)*.

The significant thing is that, comparing the two situations, the drop in *C* spending will be *(less / more)* in the 25 per cent tax case. It is because *C* spending drops that the original investment drop has a multiplied effect on GNP.

b. Thus, as compared with the no-tax case, the percentage tax case (pick one):
(1) Will stop the drop in *NI* completely.
(2) Limits the GNP drop to the amount of the drop in *I*, i.e., reduces the multiplier to 1.
(3) Cushions the fall in GNP, reduces the size of the multiplier, but does not reduce it to 1.

c. A critical factor which distinguishes the 25 per cent tax case from the no-tax case is this (pick one):
(1) Tax collections drop by $5 when *NI* drops; hence *DI* does not drop by the full $20.
(2) The initial drop in *I* spending is reduced.
(3) The marginal propensity to consume out of *DI* is increased because of taxation.
(4) Taxes cause people to spend more in order to maintain the same level of real income.

d. The "automatic stabilizers" stabilize GNP, then, because they *(increase / reduce)* the size or value of the multiplier.

Notice that, although these stabilizers *reduce* the degree of fall in GNP, they do not *stop* that GNP fall completely. They are important; but they should not be credited with powers which in fact they do not possess.

---

a. not; 135; 15; 12; less. *b.* (3). *c.* (1). *d.* reduce.

---

5. *a.* If the government, in the situation described above, were to cut the tax rate from 25 per cent to 10 per cent, this would be *(another automatic stabilizer / an instance of discretionary fiscal policy)*.
b. Corporations would provide a built-in stabilizing function insofar as they pay *(the same annual dividend regardless of their earnings / a dividend which is a constant percentage of earnings)*.
c. Consumers would provide a built-in stabilizing function insofar as they *(quickly adjust their living standards to decreases in their income / save in booms, dissave in depressions / save as much as they can all the time)*.

---

a. discretionary fiscal policy. *b.* same annual dividend.
c. save in booms, dissave in depressions.

---

6. In the 1940s and 1950s, when careful study began of the effects of government spending and taxation on GNP, the automatic stabilizers were praised because of the braking effect they exert in the event GNP should begin to fall, or begin an inflationary rise. At first it was not fully realized that they can also brake *desirable* GNP rises—those noninflationary rises that are possible owing to expanded capacity. This is particularly true of the progressive income tax. As GNP rises from year to year, money incomes gradually become larger. But as money incomes rise, the percentage rate of tax applicable to those incomes grows *(larger / smaller)*.

This increasing tax bite restrains the growth of consumer spending. Sometimes this restraint is desirable—but not necessarily always. Unless tax rates are lowered, it would be possible for the tax system to prevent total spending from rising to the full-employment level warranted by expanded capacity. The name applied when this undesirable effect occurs is _____.

---

larger; fiscal drag.

---

7. *a.* As an antirecession fiscal policy, the amount of each person's income exempt from income tax is raised from $600 to $750. As a result, tax collections fall by $10 (billion) annually. Assuming this to be the only change in fiscal policy, we would expect the components of GNP to have changed as follows in the resulting new equilibrium: *G* spending *(down by $10 / unchanged / up by $10)*: *C* spending *(up by less than $10 / up by $10 / up by more than $10)*.

b. For the tax reduction of part *a*, substitute an increase in expenditures on highway construction of $10 (billion) annually. Changes in the new GNP equilibrium would then be: *G* spending *(unchanged / up by $10 / up by more than $10)*; *C* spending *(unchanged / up by $10 / up probably by more than $10)*.

---

a. unchanged; up by more than $10.
b. up by $10; up by more than $10. (In both *a* and *b*, the fact that *C* rises by *more* than $10 is of course attributable to the "multiplier effect" discussed in Chapters 12 and 13.)

---

8. If total spending becomes excessive, and fiscal policy is deliberately made contractionary, this would most probably mean *(an increase / a decrease / no change in)* *G* spending, *(an increase / a decrease / no change in)* tax rates, and the budget *(balanced or in surplus / in deficit)*.

---

a decrease; an increase; balanced or in surplus.

9. A concept recently developed with respect to fiscal policy is that of the "full-employment budget surplus."

The all-important fact here to be grasped is this: *The total of tax dollars collected varies with the* GNP *level.* Should GNP *fall,* then total tax collections will *(fall / remain unchanged / increase)*. By their nature, personal income taxes are linked directly to the GNP level: lower incomes, lower taxes. The same is true of corporation-profits tax collections, since profits almost invariably fall when GNP falls.

Suppose GNP is and has been in equilibrium at its full-employment level. The federal government has a budget *surplus* of $5 billion. Now a drop in investment spending causes GNP to fall to a recession level. Assume for simplicity that total federal spending is unchanged (although in recession it is likely to rise somewhat). The budget surplus will be *(reduced / increased)*. Unless the recession is a very minor one, the surplus may well in fact be converted into a deficit because of the resulting drop in tax collections.

Looking at the figures, we might then say: The government is doing its part to remedy the recession. The budget change from surplus to deficit has checked the GNP fall.

The "full-employment budget surplus" reply would be this: *The deficit is not big enough.* The federal government is not doing its full part to remedy the recession.

The supporting argument is this: In the old equilibrium situation, investment spending was sufficiently high that the government had to apply the brakes slightly (run a $5 billion surplus) in order to keep GNP at an appropriate equilibrium level. But now investment has fallen off. We have no indication that it will surge upward to its old level again. What we *do* have is a system of tax rates geared to the old investment-spending level. If GNP were to begin to revive, the deficit would shrink. And a budget surplus would begin to reappear *before* full employment was reached. Budget policy would begin to apply the brakes too soon.

Even those who (rightly or wrongly) attach importance to a balanced budget must recognize that the same tax structure which yields a deficit in recession might yield a surplus at full employment. In recession, this structure should be changed: taxes should *(increased / reduced)*.

fall; reduced; decreased.

10. Often it is convenient to say that a government budget deficit "stimulates" GNP, whereas (as in question 9), a surplus "applies the brakes." These expressions *can* be misleading. The mere fact that the budget is in deficit or in surplus *(must / does not necessarily)* mean that GNP is "out of equilibrium," and consequently moving upward or downward.

What *can* be said correctly is that (other things equal) an *increase* in the government surplus (via increased tax collections or reduced expenditure) will throw GNP out of equilibrium, pushing it toward a new equilibrium level which will be *(higher / lower)* than the former one.

Similarly, an *increase* in any deficit will likewise disrupt any previously-established equilibrium. A deficit increase would push GNP toward a new and *(higher / lower)* equilibrium level.

does not necessarily; lower; higher.

11. In 1976, the national or public debt of the United States (the total of IOUs issued by the federal government) was approximately $*(100 / 310 / 622 / 780 / 1,100)* billion.

A debt figure such as this is meaningless unless it is measured against some production or income figure such as GNP. That is, this debt figure should be compared against a 1976 GNP of approximately $*(490 / 850 / 1,000 / 1,120 / 1,650)* billion. This means that the debt total was *(somewhat less than one-half of / roughly equal to / about twice)* annual GNP. (In 1945, at the close of World War II, it was about 1⅛ times GNP.)

Annual interest charges on this debt were approximately $37 billion in 1976. This was roughly *(2 / 4 / 5 / 7)* per cent of GNP. However, both debt and interest totals are somewhat misleading because more than one-third of the debt is held by governmental and quasi-governmental agencies. Interest paid on this part of the debt is simply an "internal transfer" from one government unit to another. In 1976, about $250 billion was held by various federal agencies (e.g., the Social Security system) on "investment account" and by the Federal Reserve System, leaving approximately $370 billion in the hands of the public.

622; 1,650; somewhat less than one-half of; 2.

12. *a.* An objection often raised with respect to the public debt, or to increases in that debt, is that it postpones trouble: it leaves a burden which the next generation must shoulder. The text's view is that—if the public debt is an internally held one—this objection is *(valid / fallacious)*.

If we really wanted to leave a burden for the next generation, then we should (pick one):
(1) Increase the internal public debt substantially.
(2) Let the present stock of capital goods become run down or depleted.
(3) Increase substantially the size of the economics textbooks which the next generation must read.

b. If a public debt is externally held (i.e., if it is owed to foreigners), then the "burden on the next generation" argument is *(valid / fallacious)*.

a. fallacious; (2). *b.* valid.

13. The text says that the public debt *(ought / ought not)* to be evaluated on the same basis as private debt—say, the debt incurred by a large corporation. That is, the matter of possible bankruptcy *(is / is not)* of much relevance.

The problems genuinely associated with a public debt are discussed in the Appendix. However, the chapter reviews briefly five possible consequences of a large debt: (1) the "transfer effect" or "redistributional effect"; (2) the possible "distorting-incentive effect"; (3) the possible "wealth effect"; (4) the possible "higher-interest-rate effect"; and (5) the possible "investment effect."

The first two of these arise from the fact that taxes must be levied to pay interest on the debt. Those who pay the taxes are not necessarily (dollar for dollar) those who receive the interest payments. So the existence of a large debt may significantly alter the distribution of after-tax income. This is the "transfer effect."

The possible "incentive effect" arises because some people, in order to avoid extra taxes, may work *(fewer / longer)* hours. Part of taxation goes to cover interest on the debt. So the existence of a large debt may *(reduce / increase)* total productive effort.

The possible "wealth effect" emerges because people hold the debt in the form of government bonds. If I hold many such bonds, which I consider an asset and part of my wealth, that may persuade me to spend on consumption *(more / less)* than I would if I did not own those bonds.

If the debt is steadily increasing, the government must enter the bond market from time to time to sell new issues—that is, enter as a *(borrower / lender)*. This means that interest rates may be *(higher / lower)* than they otherwise would have been—hence the "higher-interest-rate effect."

If businessmen think that the country is on the road to damnation because of a large public debt, and if on this account they reduce their investment spending so that GNP slips to a recession level, then this "investment effect" could be serious. If a belief governs behavior, the fact that this belief may be a foolish one is irrelevant. (The possibility that there might be behavior so affected was probably taken more seriously a few years ago than today.)

---

ought not; is not; fewer; reduce; more; borrower; higher.

---

14. The effects of changing government expenditure and tax collections can be illustrated by means of simple algebra. (If simultaneous equations cause you trouble, disregard this question. Its purpose is to clarify material in the text for you, not to complicate it.) The dollar figures below represent billions of dollars.

(1) Assume the community's propensity to consume is ¾ of disposable income *(DI)* plus $100. In algebraic form, $C = \frac{3}{4} DI + \$100$.

(2) Total gross investment *(I)* is $50.

(3) Government expenditure on goods and services *(G)* totals $40.

(4) Taxes *(Tx)* total $40. (For simplicity, taxes are treated as a fixed amount, rather than varying in amount according to the size of GNP.)

(5) *DI* equals GNP minus taxes. In algebraic form, $DI = GNP - Tx$.

a. Start with the equation $GNP = C + I + G$. Substitute into it the values given above. Solve for the equilibrium value of GNP. What is it?

_____ .

Suppose the full-employment level of GNP is $700. Then if GNP is at the equilibrium level just computed, there is *(an inflationary / a deflationary)* gap.

b. With taxes held constant at $40, to what level must *G* be raised in order to reach full-employment GNP? (Use a GNP value of $700 in the equation of *a*, and solve for *G*.) _____

_____ .

c. With *G* held constant at $40, by how much must taxes be reduced to reach full-employment GNP? _____

_____ .

d. If *G* is raised, as in part *b*, what happens to the total of *G* and to the total of *C*—by comparison with their values in the original deflationary level of GNP? How large is the government deficit? What are the corresponding results if instead taxes are lowered, as in part *c*? _____

_____

_____

---

a. $640; a deflationary. *b.* To $55, up $15. *c.* To $20, down $20.
d. *G* raised: *G*, $40 to $55; *C*, $550 to $595; deficit, $15. *Tx* reduced: *Tx*, $40 to $20; *C*, $550 to $610; deficit, $20. (NOTE: Tax reduction brings all the increase in private *C* spending, but it incurs a somewhat larger deficit, since tax changes have slightly less "leverage" on GNP than *G* spending. Chapter 13 discussed this topic. See question 8, p. 102.)

QUIZ: Multiple Choice

1. *The text cites a viewpoint with respect to the national debt that is held by a majority of professional economists. This view is that* (1) the debt question is moving toward an immediate crisis, and recognition of this crisis must be given high priority in fiscal policy; (2) the debt at its present level is a problem of major importance, but there is no occasion to believe that (short of war) its total will increase significantly in future years; (3) the importance of the debt is usually exaggerated by the public, and there is no need for concern over a debt that grows no faster than the economy's potential GNP; (4) although the debt problem poses no immediate crisis for the economy, positive fiscal policy must aim toward a reduction of its present total; (5) the debt poses no significant problem of any kind, despite public beliefs to the contrary, and the prospect of major increases in its total should be viewed without concern.

2. *The meaning of the statement, "Every government has a fiscal policy, whether it realizes it or not," is best expressed by the following:* (1) Every government is forced to do something about depression and inflation, whether it wants to or not. (2) Every government must decide on a tax and expenditure program, and these decisions are bound to have effects upon the economy and upon GNP. (3) In many cases, decisions to spend money must be made even though the expenditure runs contrary to the policy indicated by positive fiscal policy. (4) Every government must make decisions about the quantity of money in the economy, and hence it must influence credit conditions and the rate of interest. (5) Even if government expenditures are kept constant, the tendency for tax collections to rise and fall with the level of GNP confronts every government with problems of deficits and surpluses.

3. *One difference between monetary policy and positive fiscal policy is that monetary policy* (1) is specifically intended to influence the level of money GNP, whereas fiscal policy has no such objective; (2) has to take into account many objectives other than the regulation of the GNP level, in contrast to fiscal policy, which has almost no other objective; (3) is intended to control the level of the money supply, not the level of GNP, whereas the reverse is true of fiscal policy; (4) has less direct influence on GNP, since it operates through its influence on money borrowing, whereas fiscal policy operates more directly on money spending; (5) has more direct influence on GNP, since its influence is exerted directly on money spending, whereas fiscal policy can exert very little direct influence on money spending.

4. *The role of "positive fiscal policy" in increasing or decreasing the amount of the public debt would be correctly described by saying that* (1) it may result in an increase, and possibly a long-term increase, as the result of policy to offset recession; (2) it may result in an increase, and possibly a long-term increase, as the result of policy to offset inflation; (3) an increase resulting from such policy is possible and even likely, but it can only be a short-term increase; (4) there can be no increase, even in the short term, if positive fiscal policy is properly conducted; (5) although a short-term increase is conceivable, a primary goal of long-term positive fiscal policy is to reduce the amount of the public debt.

5. *If a government increases its expenditures on goods and services (without increasing its tax rates) as an antirecession weapon, we could reasonably expect the component parts of GNP to be affected as follows:* (1) The G (government) component of GNP will rise, but there will be a partial offsetting reduction in the C (consumption) component. (2) G will rise, but there is no assured reason for expecting C to rise or to fall. (3) G will rise, and so will C. (4) C will rise, but there is

no assured reason for expecting G to rise or to fall. (5) both G and C will fall.

6. *The federal government amends the personal-income-tax law such that the percentage of tax levied is reduced by 2 percentage points at each income level specified in the law. This would be an example of* (1) discretionary fiscal policy; (2) a built-in stabilizer; (3) contractionary fiscal policy; (4) a deliberate destabilizer; (5) none of the preceding.

7. *If GNP falls from a higher to a lower equilibrium level because of a decrease in investment spending, then (by the reasoning of this chapter)* (1) the total amount paid out in government transfer payments (other than interest payments) will decrease; (2) there will be a decrease in the government's total tax receipts; (3) the government's budget will tend from deficit toward balance, from balance toward surplus, or from surplus toward increased surplus; (4) total consumer saving will almost certainly increase; (5) the size of the multiplier will increase.

8. *Suppose the federal government changes the personal income tax law so that taxes become more "progressive" (as that term was defined in Chapter 9). The effect of this would be, among other things, to increase the* (1) total of welfare expenditures; (2) size of the government's deficit; (3) strength of the "automatic (or built-in) stabilizers"; (4) marginal propensity to consume; (5) total of the public debt.

9. *The exercise by the government of a positive fiscal policy directed toward full employment would have the following impact on the balance of the government's budget:* (1) Properly conducted, it would lead to an annual balancing of the budget. (2) It would necessarily entail budget deficits in most years, but these deficits are less important than is generally supposed. (3) It would entail budget deficits in some years, but the budget would be balanced over the entire business cycle. (4) It would lead to surpluses rather than deficits in most years (in the view of a majority of economists). (5) None of the preceding statements is necessarily correct.

10. *"Positive fiscal policy" means a policy* (1) whereby both government expenditures and taxation are allowed to fall whenever GNP rises and to rise whenever GNP falls; (2) in which the budget is planned to balance over the whole business cycle but not annually; (3) whereby the public debt rises and falls as GNP rises and falls; (4) in which tax rates are changed so as to keep total tax collections approximately equal to total governmental expenditures; (5) not correctly described by any of the above.

11. *GNP is in equilibrium below its full-employment level. The federal government's budget is balanced. Private investment spending rises. If there is no change in federal expenditures or in rates of taxation, we would expect the balance in the federal budget to* (1) change to a deficit if the tax system is progressive but not if it is proportional; (2) change to a deficit regardless of whether the tax system is progressive or proportional; (3) change to a surplus if the tax system is progressive but not if it is proportional; (4) change to a surplus regardless of whether the tax system is progressive or proportional; (5) remain in balance.

12. *A good example of a built-in (or automatic) stabilizer would be* (1) a system of welfare payments which is increased in prosperous periods to give recipients an opportunity to keep up with increases in the cost of living; (2) a decision by the federal government to reduce its public-works program at a time when inflation seems to threaten; (3) a tax system which collects approximately the same amount of revenue from the public in prosperity and depression; (4) the decision of a state government to maintain its financial standing in recession by cutting its less essential expenditures; (5) none of the above.

13. *One of the following is* not *correct with respect to built-in (or automatic) stabilizers, namely:* (1) The decision by corporations to pay out in dividends an amount greater than their earnings, in a time of depression, would be a legitimate example of such stabilizers. (2) The progressive personal income tax is among the most effective of the automatic stabilizers. (3) Their effect is to increase the size of the multiplier. (4) They go into effect at the onset of inflation or recession without the need for deliberate action or decision on the part of any authority. (5) Such stabilizers reduce the extent of any downswing or upswing, but do not iron out such swings completely.

14. *Which of the following kinds of behavior by the private sector would be most likely to increase the "automatic stability" of the economy?* (1) A corporation policy of increasing dividend payments when corporate earnings increase. (2) A corporation policy of decreasing investment when corporate savings increase. (3) A consumer policy of increasing consumer debt when disposable income increases. (4) A consumer policy of spending out of past savings when tax collections increase. (5) A consumer policy of increasing household expenditure only slowly when income increases.

15. *Economist Alvin Hansen spoke of the possibility of a period of "secular stagnation," by which he meant a period in which* (1) governmental emphasis on a balanced budget and refusal to accept the concepts of positive fiscal policy would lead to increasing fiscal difficulties; (2) GNP, although always at or near the full-employment level, would not increase, or would increase only minimally, from year to year; (3) a continuing increase in the public debt might induce ever-increasing pessimism and a refusal to shoulder the burden of ever-increasing taxes; (4) the public would persistently refuse to respond to the stimulus provided by an increase in government spending or by a reduction in taxation; (5) investment opportunities would be chronically insufficient to keep GNP at or near its full-employment level.

16. *The text chapter evaluates public works, as a weapon of discretionary fiscal policy, as follows: They* (1) should be undertaken on their own merits, and not used for fiscal policy purposes, save perhaps for advancing or postponing the date of an agreed-upon program; (2) are still the major component of fiscal policy for the short term, even though it is sometimes difficult to find such programs with a high social priority; (3) are still the major component of fiscal policy, whenever a recession-level GNP needs to be increased; (4) remain the major weapon within fiscal policy, both short-term and long-term, because of their rapid impact upon the employment level; (5) are of little value for short-term fiscal policy due to the long "lead time" typically involved, but they are invaluable for long-term stabilization of GNP.

APPENDIX: False and Genuine Burdens of the Public Debt

1. Much of the present U.S. federal debt was incurred during World War II. Taxes were increased during that period, but the government feared that further increases might produce "disincentive effects" (refusal to work extra hours because of heavier income taxation). So it resorted to borrowing for part of its financing. But for the psychological effects, further tax increases might have been used instead. The major intent of both devices, taxes and borrowing, was the same: *to cut down on consumer purchasing power during the war period.* Part of the required economic "sacrifice" was made during the war in the form of reduced availability of consumer goods. Part came after the war, in that much of the nation's capital stock had been depreciated (run down) to meet the heavy demands of wartime production.

Money transfers (tax payments and loans to government) are important, then, only insofar as they affect *real* output and the distribution of that real output, now or later. This is where the true "burdens" imposed by a large public debt are to be sought.

When such a debt exists, there are interest payments to be made, and the money to make them is ordinarily raised by taxation. (If it is raised by borrowing, the lender has an engraved government IOU instead of a tax receipt. From that lender's standpoint, such an IOU is a valuable asset, and something entirely different from a mere tax receipt. But for fiscal purposes, the immediate effect is the same, IOU or tax receipt: the suppliers of the money received by government have parted with cash they might otherwise have used for their own consumption needs.)

The interest payments made to bondholders are, as money, a claim on the currently produced output of real goods and services. Thus the debt entails a real burden insofar as it is held by *(foreigners / the nation's own citizens)*. The same reasoning *(applies / does not apply)* with regard to repayment of the principal on the loan.

If all interest payments went, dollar for dollar, to just those people who had paid taxes to finance the interest payments, then in money terms (and disregarding handling costs), things would just cancel out. But this is most unlikely: ordinarily A gains and B loses from the combination of tax collection and interest payment. This is the *(transfer / incentive)* effect.

Even if things *did* cancel out in money terms, real output might still be reduced, insofar as people tried to avoid taxes by working fewer hours. This is usually termed the *(incentive / wealth)* effect (see question 13, this chapter, pp. 145–146). However, the text Appendix includes it as part of the transfer effect (i.e., part of the effect caused by tax levies).

foreigners; applies; transfer; incentive.

2. A large debt *might possibly* make the application of anti-inflationary monetary policy more difficult. In a period of threatening inflation, the Fed should apply *(a tight / an easy)* money policy; it should *(buy / sell)* government securities. So market interest rates go *(up / down)*.

Each year and each month, some part of the public debt—government bonds and shorter-term IOUs—reaches its maturity date. Unless it wants to reduce the debt, the Treasury must sell a renewal IOU, offering an interest rate sufficiently attractive to persuade the holder of the maturing IOU (or someone else) to buy it. However, the Fed's tight-money policy has *(increased / decreased)* the rate the Treasury must offer. The Treasury, worrying about higher tax collections needed to finance higher interest payments, might conceivably try to bring pressure on the Fed to relax its policies; at any rate, there is some clash of interest between two public agencies.

a tight; sell; up; increased.

QUIZ: Multiple Choice

1. *The burden of a large, internally held public debt is properly described as follows:* (1) There is no burden at all.
(2) The burden is essentially comparable to that of an externally held debt. (3) There is no direct burden to be borne by future generations, although such generations may have to bear an indirect burden. (4) Although there is an indirect burden, it will not be borne by future generations. (5) By none of these.

2. *Which of the following is not a correct or defensible statement with respect to the public debt?* (1) Any increase in the debt incurred through the exercise of positive fiscal policy is more likely to occur in recession than in full-employment periods. (2) If ownership of the debt were equally distributed throughout the population, it could then have no "disincentive" effects causing people to work less hard than they otherwise would. (3) In Alexander Hamilton's view, the debt furnished a desirable asset for business firms and families to hold. (4) Payment of interest on the debt is likely to have much the same redistributive effects that a regressive tax would have. (5) Possession of such debt in large quantities by families can reasonably be expected to increase their propensity to consume at any level of disposable income.

3. *The "transfer effect" of a large public debt, as that effect is described in the text Appendix, refers to* (1) the necessity of sending goods to foreigners which would not be sent in the absence of such a debt; (2) the burden imposed upon future generations by the presence of an internally held debt; (3) the possibility of an increase in the community's propensity to consume; (4) the possibility that people may in consequence allocate their time differently as between work and leisure; (5) the extra taxes which must be levied in order to pay interest and principal upon that debt.

4. *Which alternative in question 3 would be correct had that question referred to the "wealth stimulus" effect?* (1). (2). (3). (4). (5).

5. *Which alternative in question 3 would be correct had that question referred to the "external-debt burden"?* (1). (2). (3). (4). (5).

3

THE
COMPOSITION
AND PRICING
OF NATIONAL
OUTPUT

BEFORE YOU START, go back if necessary to the Review Questions for Chapter 4. This earlier chapter covers the fundamentals on which Chapter 20 is based.

Chapter 20 has two major topics: (1) elasticity, and (2) changes in demand and supply.

The concept of elasticity was devised to indicate the degree to which quantity demanded (or supplied) would *respond* to any price change. Compare the two demand curves D_1 and D_2 (drawn to the same scale) in Fig. 20-1. Both curves satisfy the ordinary "law of demand": any price reduction would yield an increase in quantity bought. But D_2 is the *more elastic* of the two: if price were to fall from p_a to p_b, the increase in buying would be greater in the D_2 case. If price were to rise from p_a to p_c, the reduction in purchases would be greater in the D_2 case.

1. *a.* Thus, if we say that "demand in this situation is highly elastic with respect to price," we mean that any price reduction would produce a *(large / small) (decrease / increase)* in purchases, and that a price rise would yield a *(large / small) (decrease / increase)* in buying.

b. Although the elasticity idea is more commonly used concerning demand, it can be used also as to the responsiveness of supply. To describe supply as "decidedly inelastic with respect to price" would mean that any price increase would call out a *(large / small) (increase / decrease)* in quantity offered for sale, and that any price reduction would produce a *(large / small) (increase / decrease)*.

2. Such terms as "highly elastic" or "decidedly inelastic" are imprecise. The task now is to give a more exact meaning to elasticity. For this purpose, use the figures below to draw a demand curve in the upper part of Fig. 20-2. (Disregard for the moment the column headed "Revenue.")

Price	Quantity	Revenue	Price	Quantity	Revenue
$10	0	_____	$5	20	_____
9	4	_____	4	24	_____
8	8	_____	3	28	_____
7	12	_____	2	32	_____
6	16	_____	1	36	_____

Associated with each possible quantity bought (and hence with each possible price) will be a certain amount of revenue received by sellers (i.e., expenditure by buyers). If price is $9, so that 4 units are bought, revenue will be $36. Show the proper revenue amounts in the 10 blanks above. Then complete the lower part of Fig. 20-2 to show the quantity-revenue relation (e.g., with quantity 4, revenue is $36, etc.).

3. *a.* Notice the interesting behavior of revenue as we move down the length of this straight-line demand curve. As price falls, revenue (or expenditure):
(1) Remains the same at all quantities purchased.
(2) Falls throughout the entire price range.
(3) First rises, reaches a peak, then falls.
(4) First falls, reaches a minimum, then rises.

b. If price falls from $7 to $6, buyer expenditure (i.e., seller revenue) *(rises / stays constant / falls).* Any price fall brings with it a reduced-expenditure tendency, since the quantity that was bought at the higher price can now be had for less money. If price falls from $7 to $6, the 12 units which formerly cost $84 can now be bought for $72. But the price fall also produces a countertendency: a disposition to buy more. The rise in this case (from 12 to 16) *(is / is not)* sufficiently great to more than offset the reduced-expenditure tendency.

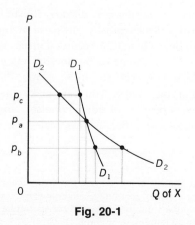

Fig. 20-1

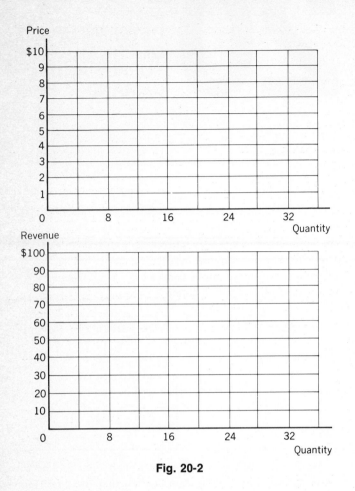

Fig. 20-2

c. If price falls from $4 to $3, the increased-expenditure tendency (*again wins over / loses to*) the reduced-expenditure tendency.

---

a. (3). *b.* rises; is. *c.* loses to.

---

4. "Price elasticity" means the responsiveness or "stretch" of quantity for any given price change. We can reach a more explicit statement of what demand elasticity with respect to price means just by using the phenomenon noted in question 3—that revenue may, for a given price change, go up, go down, or remain constant.

If there is enough "stretch" in quantity demanded when price goes *down* to cause revenue to go *up*, then we designate this section of the demand curve as *elastic* (or as price-elastic). If revenue stays constant, it is *unit-elastic*. If revenue falls, it is *inelastic*. This means the demand curve of question 2 is elastic for prices from $_____ to $_____, and inelastic for prices from $_____ to $_____.

It happens that this demand curve does not conveniently illustrate unit elasticity. But the curve would be unit-elastic between prices $5 and $4 if the quantity associated with price $4, instead of being 24, were _____.

$10 to $5; $5 to $1; 25.

5. If we say this demand curve is elastic between prices of $10 and $5, we speak of *that segment of the demand curve*, not just of one-way movements down the curve. As we go *down* the curve in this region, revenue increases. If we go *up* it from price $5 to price $10, revenue decreases. The degree of stretch (in this case, contraction) in quantity is here sufficiently powerful to cause revenue to decrease with any increase in price.

An elasticity definition must be a two-way street. If demand is elastic because the revenue associated with price $8 is $64 and that with price $7 is $84, then we must say it is elastic if either:

A price decrease brings a revenue increase, or
A price increase brings a revenue decrease.

The same applies to unit-elastic and inelastic sections of the demand curve. (A quick rule is: Demand is inelastic if price and revenue go in the same direction.)

Put E (elastic), U (unit-elastic), or I (inelastic) in each space below, as appropriate to each demand situation:

(1) Price falls from $6 to $5, and consumer expenditure falls from $60 to $55. ....( )
(2) When price falls from $6 to $5, consumer expenditure on this commodity remains the same. ....( )
(3) Price rises from $5 to $6, and quantity purchased falls from 80 (@ $5) to 60 (@ $6). ....( )
(4) Price drops from $6 to $5, and there is no increase in quantity purchased at all. ....( )
(5) Price rises from $5 to $6, and there is no decrease in quantity purchased at all. ....( )
(6) As the result of a certain price increase, revenue received by suppliers goes up from $2,000 weekly to $2,010. ...( )
(7) Because of a price increase from $5 to $5.10, buyers stop buying the commodity entirely. ....( )

---

(1) I; (2) U; (3) E; (4) I; (5) I; (6) I; (7) E.

---

6. Instructors in economics *always* illustrate "inelastic demand" on the blackboard by means of a steeply sloping (near-vertical) line. There is no recorded instance in history to the contrary. There seems to be no convenient alternative means of illustration. Yet, strictly speaking, this method is deceptive. For one thing, you can make the very same demand curve appear "very steep," or else "almost flat," just by manipulating the horizontal-axis scale (see Study Guide Fig. 7, p. 9).[1]

---

[1]If you change the scale, you do not, however, change the *slope* of this line in the sense of its numerical slope value (see p. 9). A line has the same slope value regardless of the particular illustration of that line you may employ on a graph.

For another thing, any straight-line demand curve, as question 2 illustrates, does *not* have uniform elasticity. It is true that the question 2 demand curve always reports the same "responsiveness" to each $1 price change: an increase (or decrease) of 4 in quantity demanded. But in percentage terms, the drop in price from $10 to $9 is *(far more / much less)* drastic than the drop from $2 to $1, for the latter reduction cuts the price in half. That is why the elasticity of this demand curve is different in different regions.

This means that if you take any straight-line demand curve, no matter how steep its slope, you can *always* find a section that is elastic with respect to price if you move *(up / down)* it to sufficiently *(high / low)* prices. *(Exception:* A perfectly vertical line. On this, see question 8*b.)*

much less; up; high.

7. Whether or not demand is elastic, unit-elastic, or inelastic with respect to a price change depends on the response in quantity. But as the preceding questions indicate, a uniform quantity response to a series of price changes which are uniform in the sense of being the same in absolute amount does *not* mean a uniform (constant) elasticity. To repeat question 6, the $1 price cut from $10 to $9 is *in percentage terms* a much smaller reduction than the cut from $2 to $1. Similarly, if the various 4-unit quantity responses are expressed as percentages of total quantity demanded, they are no longer uniform.

This means we can develop a more precise measure of elasticity than the three-way division of question 4. We can get a quantitative demand-elasticity measure by (1) putting the quantity change in percentage terms, (2) putting the price change in percentage terms, and then (3) making these two percentage figures the two halves of a fraction or ratio in order to compare them.

The result is the *elasticity coefficient:* per cent change in quantity divided by per cent change in price. (Note that we put quantity first; we make it the numerator in the fraction, because the bigger the percentage quantity response, the higher the elasticity coefficient should be.)

a. Using question 1 data, compute price-elasticity coefficients between the prices indicated below. (To figure the base for percentage change in price, use the average of the two *P*'s. Thus, with respect to the $1 change between $7 and $6, $6.50 is the base, or 100 per cent, and $1 is about 15.4 per cent of this base. Similarly, with respect to *Q*, take the average of the two *Q*'s, so that the 4-unit change from 12 to 16 is to be expressed as a per cent of 14.)

(1) Between price $8 and price $7 _____

(2) Between price $5 and price $4 _____

(3) Between price $3 and price $2 _____

b. This elasticity-coefficient idea is just an extension of the three-way system of division outlined in question 4. For example, in the unit-elastic case, the two percentage changes just cancel one another out—they are equal. In this case, what should the elasticity-coefficient figure be?

(1 / greater than 1 / less than 1)

c. In the price-elastic case, quantity wins the battle of the percentage changes. What should the elasticity coefficient then be? ....*(1 / greater than 1 / less than 1)*

d. In the inelastic case, what should the elasticity coefficient be? ....*(1 / greater than 1 / less than 1)*

a. (1) 40.0 / 13.3, or 3.0; (2) 18.2 / 22.2, or 0.82; (3) 13.3 / 40.0, or 0.33. *b.* 1. *c.* greater than 1. *d.* less than 1.

8. *a.* A "perfectly elastic" demand curve is illustrated as a horizontal line. Such a line illustrates the ultimate in elasticity (i.e., "infinite elasticity") because it means (pick one):
(1) No matter what the change in price might be, within the range indicated by length of this line, there would be no response in quantity purchased.
(2) The slightest increase in price above the level at which this horizontal line runs would cause purchases to respond—i.e., to decrease—to the point of falling to zero.

b. "Perfectly inelastic" demand signifies a vertical line, or zero elasticity. Which alternative above correctly indicates why such a demand curve would represent the ultimate in inelasticity? ....*(1 / 2 / neither)*

Notice that the two extreme cases of perfectly elastic and perfectly inelastic demand constitute exceptions to the point made in question 6. When a demand curve is illustrated as *perfectly* horizontal or *perfectly* vertical, that slope *does* tell you what the elasticity of the demand curve is.

a. (2). *b.* (1).

9. The idea of responsiveness to a price change applies just as much to supply curves as to demand curves. With respect to supply, however, we can't use question 4's three-way distinction (elastic, unit-elastic, inelastic), because the revenue associated with supply rarely if ever has the either-way behavior which questions 2 and 3 indicated may be characteristic of demand.

But for supply we can use exactly the same elasticity-coefficient measure of question 7, in the same way.

a. In this sense, "perfectly inelastic" supply would be represented by a *(vertical / horizontal)* line, and "perfectly elastic" supply by a *(vertical / horizontal)* line.

b. Perfectly elastic supply appears as a *(vertical / horizontal)* line because that indicates the "ultimate" in responsiveness. It indicates simply a particular *price;* it says that any desired quantity is available at that price; it says that if price were to drop even slightly below this level, quantity supplied would *(fall to zero / become infinitely large)*.

When you enter a supermarket and find you can buy as little or as much as you wish of any given item at its fixed price, in effect you are facing a perfectly elastic supply curve.

---

a. vertical; horizontal. *b.* horizontal; fall to zero.

---

10. If there should be an increase in demand (a shift of the demand curve upward or to the right), price will rise, and suppliers will want to increase their supply offers. But the extent to which they can do so depends on the amount of time they are given in which to increase production. This is the basis for Alfred Marshall's distinction between time periods, on the supply side (see text).

a. If the demand increase is sudden and suppliers have no reserve inventories on hand, it may be that no greater quantity can be offered immediately, despite the price rise. If so, the supply curve must be shown as *(perfectly elastic / perfectly inelastic)*; this is what the text refers to as the new *(long-run / short-run / momentary)* equilibrium.

b. Given a little time, suppliers can adjust to the demand increase by working their plant and equipment more fully (e.g., by adding an extra shift of workers); the result of this increase in supply quantity is the new *(long-run / short-run / momentary)* equilibrium.

c. If this demand increase is sustained and suppliers have still further time, enough to build new plant and equipment, there will be a still further increase in supply quantity offered. Finally, then, an equilibrium price that indicates *(long-run / short-run / momentary)* equilibrium may be reached.

d. Note carefully that all this is just a statement about price elasticity of supply. It says that the degree of responsiveness of supply to a price change will depend on the amount of adjustment time suppliers can have. The longer this time period, the *(higher / lower)* will be the price elasticity (or elasticity coefficient) of supply.

---

a. perfectly inelastic; momentary. *b.* short-run. *c.* long-run. *d.* higher.

The second major topic in this chapter is one that was introduced in Chapter 4: changes in demand or supply. To review the underlying idea in terms of demand: Price is *one* important factor influencing the quantity of good X that will be bought—but it is by no means the *only* influencing factor. Others include the level of consumer incomes, consumer tastes or preferences for X, and the prices at which goods competing with X are selling.

The demand curve for X does not ignore these fac-

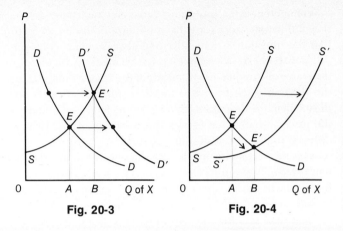

Fig. 20-3   Fig. 20-4

tors other than X's price—but it assumes them *held constant*. If any such other factor *changes*, then the demand curve must be redrawn in an appropriate new position. If consumer incomes rise, for example, it is likely that the demand curve for X will shift to the right (or upward), as in Fig. 20-3 at left above. This is just a particular way of saying that if consumers have more spendable income, they will want to buy more of X, at any given price, than they did previously. (For a review of such shifts in demand—and supply—curves, see particularly Chapter 4, question 7, Study Guide p. 30.)

Thus in the Fig. 20-3 case, quantity bought and sold rises from *OA* to *OB*; and price goes up. Now here is a point you must watch carefully. In Fig. 20-4, alongside Fig. 20-3, there has also been a change in the equilibrium position. Purchases have again risen from *OA* to *OB*—but price has fallen, not risen. This change was initiated by a shift of *the supply curve*.

▶ Figure 20-3 illustrates an "increase in demand"—a shift of the entire demand curve to a new position.

▶ Figure 20-4 illustrates an "increase in quantity demanded"—a movement *along* a demand curve from one point thereon to another. The *position* of the demand curve does not change.

Thus the phrases "increase in demand" and "increase in quantity demanded" have significantly different meanings. An "increase in demand" (Fig. 20-3) occurs when *some factor other than the price of good X* changes, causing buyers to change their decisions; the entire demand curve shifts. An "increase in quantity demanded" (Fig. 20-4) occurs when more of X is bought because its price fell. (Price fell because some background factor caused the supply curve to shift in position.)

11. *a.* A "change in quantity demanded" means precisely (pick one):
(1) A shift in the schedule of quantities that producers will

offer for sale at each and any possible price, due to some change in background conditions such as an increase in production costs.
(2) A shift in the particular quantity which producers offer for sale, due to a change in market price.
(3) A shift in the particular quantity which consumers buy, due to a change in market price.
(4) A shift in the schedule of quantities that consumers will buy at each and any possible market price, due to some change in background conditions such as a change in tastes or consumer incomes.

b. Which alternative properly describes a "change in supply"? .... *(1 / 2 / 3 / 4)*
c. Which alternative properly describes a "change in demand"? .... *(1 / 2 / 3 / 4)*
d. Which alternative properly describes a "change in quantity supplied"? .... *(1 / 2 / 3 / 4)*

---

a. (3). *b.* (1). *c.* (4). *d.* (2).

---

12. *a.* As already noted, Fig. 20-3 (the left-hand figure preceding) illustrates "an increase in demand." This figure illustrates also an *("increase in supply" / "increase in quantity supplied")*.

Barring the exceptional case of a perfectly flat (perfectly elastic) supply curve, this increase in demand will *(always / sometimes / never)* set off a price increase.

Notice that the "increase in quantity supplied" in Fig. 20-3 does not bring about any price reduction. It is just the supplier response to a higher price. All we can say is that insofar as there is some elasticity to the supply curve (i.e., insofar as a higher price elicits a larger supply quantity), it makes the price increase set off by the increase in demand less than it would otherwise have been.

Thus "an increase in quantity supplied" will *(always / sometimes / never)* result in a price reduction.

b. In contrast, Fig. 20-4 (the right-hand figure) depicts "an increase in quantity demanded." This increase came about only because of an *("increase in supply" / "increase in quantity supplied")*. Such an increase in quantity demanded *(will always / might / would never)* be the reason for a price increase. It is simply the buyer response to a lower price.

This difference in the effect upon price in large part explains why all the tedious distinction between the two kinds of "increases" and of "decreases" is necessary.

c. An example framed in terms of decreases: Production of good X is disrupted by lengthy strikes. The supply quantity available is much reduced, and price rises in consequence. This would be an instance of *(a decrease / an increase)* in *(quantity supplied / supply)*, followed by *(a decrease / an increase)* in *(quantity demanded / demand)*. The price rise was set off by the decrease in *(demand / supply)*, and not by the decrease in quantity *(demanded / supplied)*.

---

a. "increase in quantity supplied"; always; never.
b. "increase in supply"; would never.
c. a decrease; supply; a decrease; quantity demanded; supply; demanded.

---

13. *a.* Record the following supply schedule in the upper part of Fig. 20-2 (question 2), using the Q_1 supply figures, (The Q_2 fill-in blanks are for part *b* of this question.)

P	$1.00	$2.00	$3.00	$4.00	$5.00
Q_1	0	12	20	24	26
Q_2					

P	$6.00	$7.00	$8.00	$9.00	$10.00
Q_1	28	29	30	31	32
Q_2					

With the demand curve previously drawn, the equilibrium price indicated is $*(3 / 4 / 5 / 6)*.

b. A tax of $1 per unit sold is now levied on the suppliers of this commodity. (NOTE: Such a tax is an increase in cost per unit of $1; so the suppliers will now sell only at $5 the particular quantity they were formerly willing to sell at $4.) In the Q_2 line above, enter the new supply-schedule figures. Then record the new supply curve in Fig. 20-2. Make it a broken or dotted line, to distinguish this supply schedule from the one previously drawn.

The new equilibrium price will be approximately $*(3.00 / 3.10 / 3.60 / 4.00 / 4.50)*.

---

a. 4. *b.* 0, 0, 12, 20, 24, 26, 28, 29, 30, 31; 4.50.

---

14. The text's discussion of the "incidence of a tax," a tax such as the one in question 13, is interesting because it shows how the greater part of a tax may be paid by buyers or by sellers. But the very first thing to recognize is that this case is simply a particular instance of *a change in supply*—in this instance, a decrease in supply. It is a reduction in the quantity that suppliers will offer for any given price, because of a change in a factor which affects suppliers—in this instance, a tax levied upon them for each unit sold.

Notice that the decrease in supply can be described either as a *leftward* or as an *upward* movement. In terms of the preceding paragraph, it is a leftward movement; in terms of question 13, an upward one.

a. In the case of such a per unit commodity tax, whether price to the consumer rises by approximately the full amount of the tax or by a much smaller amount depends on the shapes of the demand and supply curves. Which of the following (one or more) would make for a price rise very close to the amount of the tax (i.e., a tax whose incidence falls mainly on buyers)?
(1) Highly elastic demand.
(2) Highly inelastic demand.

(3) Highly elastic supply.
(4) Highly inelastic supply.

b. Which alternatives in part *a* (one or more) would make for a very small price rise, i.e., a tax borne mainly by suppliers?
.... (*1 / 2 / 3 / 4*)

_____

a. (2), (3).   *b.*   (1), (4).

_____

15. "The price of any commodity is determined by the amount it costs to produce that commodity." Circle all the following statements which seem to you correct observations with respect to this cost-of-production theory of price.

a. It is the most satisfactory explanation yet furnished as to how prices are determined.
b. It makes no allowance for the influence which demand—i.e., forces from the buying side—can exert on the level of price.
c. The level of production costs is one highly important factor influencing the position of the supply curve—i.e., quantity to be offered for sale at various prices—although not necessarily the only such factor at work.
d. As a theory of price determination, the cost-of-production view is unsatisfactory, since production costs are themselves prices—the prices of productive factors—and it fails to explain how these prices are determined.
e. The existing supply of a commodity will sell at a price below its production cost if demand is insufficient to generate any better price, even though suppliers will not continue to produce the commodity if they know it cannot be sold at a price above costs.

_____

b, c, d, e.

_____

16. Review also the following ideas discussed in the text: the "immutability" of supply-and-demand laws; minimum floors under price and maximum ceilings on price.

QUIZ: Multiple Choice

1. *Consumers have budgeted a fixed money amount to buy a certain commodity. Within a certain range of prices, they will spend neither more nor less than this amount on it. Their demand in this price range would properly be designated as* (1) in equilibrium; (2) perfectly elastic; (3) perfectly inelastic; (4) highly inelastic but not perfectly so; (5) unit-elastic.

2. *The price-elasticity coefficient of demand equals* (1) amount of price decrease divided by amount of quantity increase; (2) percentage change in revenue divided by percentage decrease in price; (3) percentage change in revenue divided by percentage increase in quantity demanded; (4) percentage change in quantity demanded divided by percentage change in price; (5) none of the above.

3. *When the words "total revenue" are used in any discussion of demand curves, their meaning is* (1) the profit, after deduction of costs, which the suppliers of the commodity involved earn from selling it to consumers; (2) the total amount of money consumers will spend on the commodity at any particular price; (3) the income suppliers will receive from sales if they sell the quantity they hope to sell; (4) the quantity of the commodity that is associated with any particular price; (5) no meaning at all—the words "total revenue" cannot have any meaning in relation to demand curves.

4. *Alfred Marshall's concepts of "momentary," "short-run," and "long-run" supply curves were intended to bring out this fact:* (1) Over a long period of time, gradual increases in skill and improvements in the art of production tend to bring down the price of any commodity. (2) Price increases as cost of transport to any given market increases. (3) The extent to which quantity supplied will respond to a given price or demand change depends on the amount of time given producers to adjust their operations to this change. (4) In order to make the supply-curve idea meaningful, it is necessary to speak of the quantity that will be supplied per period of time. (5) Although demand may exert some short-run influence, ultimately the price of any commodity must be determined by the cost of its production.

5. *The market price of a commodity and its costs of production are related in this way:* (1) If price is below cost of production, there will be a shift in the demand curve. (2) Costs of production influence the quantity of goods that producers will offer for sale at each and any possible price. (3) Price can never fall below costs of production. (4) Price can never rise above costs of production. (5) There is no significant relationship between price and production costs at all.

6. *If a demand curve is such that a 10 per cent reduction in price brings a 5 per cent increase in the amount of money people spend to buy that commodity, then in this region of the demand curve, demand is (with respect to price)* (1) elastic; (2) unit-elastic; (3) inelastic, although not perfectly so; (4) perfectly inelastic; (5) perhaps any of these—information given is insufficient to determine elasticity.

7. *If a demand curve is such that a 10 per cent reduction in price brings a 5 per cent increase in the quantity of the commodity that people buy, then in this region of the demand curve, demand is (with respect to price)* (1) elastic; (2) unit-elastic; (3) inelastic, although not perfectly so; (4) perfectly inelastic; (5) perhaps any of the above—information given is insufficient to determine elasticity.

8. *If I can buy any quantity I please of a commodity at a fixed price, this means that the supply curve which confronts me is* (1) perfectly inelastic; (2) perfectly elastic; (3) unit-elastic; (4) elastic, but not necessarily perfectly elastic; (5) none of these things, necessarily.

9. *The government levies an excise tax of 5¢ per unit sold on the sellers in a competitive industry. Both supply and demand curves have some elasticity with respect to price. This tax means that on the supply-and-demand diagram,* (1) the entire supply curve shifts leftward by an amount indicating 5¢, but (unless demand is perfectly elastic) price will not rise; (2) the entire supply curve shifts upward by an amount indicating less than 5¢, but (unless demand is highly elastic) price will rise by the full 5¢; (3) the entire supply curve shifts leftward by an amount indicating less than 5¢, but (unless demand is highly inelastic) price will rise by more that 5¢; (4) the entire supply curve shifts upward by an amount indicating 5¢, but (unless supply is perfectly elastic) any price rise will be less than 5¢; (5) the entire demand curve shifts upward by an amount indicating 5¢, and price will rise by 5¢.

10. *The change brought about by the tax levy described in question 9 would be designated as* (1) a decrease in supply followed by a decrease in quantity demanded; (2) a decrease in quantity supplied followed by a decrease in quantity demanded; (3) a decrease in supply followed by a decrease in demand; (4) a decrease in quantity supplied followed by a decrease in demand; (5) none of the above.

11. *A perfectly inelastic supply curve would be shown on the ordinary supply-and-demand graph as* (1) a vertical line; (2) a horizontal line; (3) a straight line, but neither horizontal nor vertical; (4) a curved line; (5) perhaps any of the above.

12. *Which alternative in question 11 would be correct for the similar graphical portrayal of a perfectly inelastic demand curve?* (1). (2). (3). (4). (5).

13. *A change in quantity demanded, as distinct from a change in demand, means* (1) that buyers have decided to buy more (or less) than they did before, at the existing price; (2) that the elasticity of demand with respect to price has increased or decreased; (3) simply that the quantity of purchases has changed, regardless of the factor which brought about this change in buying; (4) that the market price has fallen or risen, and buyers have changed their total purchases accordingly; (5) an increase in total purchases, but not a decrease.

14. *Which alternative in question 13 would be correct for a change in demand, as distinct from a change in quantity demanded?* (1). (2). (3). (4). (5).

15. *If a demand curve is described as being elastic with respect to price, the exact meaning of this is that any increase in price would bring about* (1) an increase in quantity purchased by buyers; (2) a decrease in quantity purchased by buyers; (3) an increase in total expenditure by buyers; (4) a decrease in total expenditure by buyers; (5) a shift of the demand curve to a new position.

16. *If a demand curve is unit-elastic throughout its entire length, this means, with respect to (a) graphical appearance of the demand curve and (b) total expenditure by buyers to purchase the commodity, that* (1) the demand curve is a straight line, and total expenditure by buyers is the same at all prices; (2) the demand curve is not a straight line, and total expenditure by buyers falls as price falls; (3) the demand curve is a straight line, and as price falls total expenditure by buyers first increases and later decreases; (4) the demand curve is not a straight line, and total expenditure by buyers rises as price falls; (5) none of the above is correct.

17. *An increase in demand for a certain product occurs. In Alfred Marshall's analysis, a new short-run and a new long-run equilibrium price will emerge. In the normal case, these would be related to the original price as follows: long-run equilibrium price will be* (1) higher than both short-run and original prices; (2) lower than short-run but higher than original price; (3) the same as original price but lower than short-run; (4) lower than both short-run and original prices; (5) related to short-run and original prices in a manner not indicated by any of the above.

18. *Suppose the demand curve for wheat is perfectly inelastic. A tax of 50¢ per bushel sold is imposed on suppliers. Then* (1) price will rise, but by less than 50¢, and there will probably be some reduction in the quantity bought and sold; (2) price will rise by the full 50¢, but there will be no reduction in the quantity bought and sold; (3) price will rise, but by less than 50¢, and there will be no reduction in the quantity bought and sold; (4) price will rise by the full 50¢, and there will definitely be a reduction in the quantity bought and sold; (5) none of the above is correct.

19. *A crop failure reduces the amount of wheat available, and so the price rises. In precise terms, this is* (1) a decrease in quantity supplied followed by a decrease in demand; (2) a decrease in supply followed by a decrease in demand; (3) a decrease in quantity supplied followed by a decrease in quantity demanded; (4) a decrease in supply followed by a decrease in quantity demanded; (5) none of these things.

20. *One way to distinguish an increase in quantity demanded from an increase in demand is to say that the former* (1) could result in an increase in price, whereas the latter could not; (2) could not result in an increase in price, whereas the latter could; (3) refers to the short-run increase in quantity purchased and the latter to the long-run increase; (4) brings an increase in total expenditure by buyers, whereas the latter does not; (5) is basically the same as the latter, except for a difference in price elasticity of demand.

APPENDIX: Cases on Supply and Demand

Proposition 1(*a*) in this Appendix is, "As a general rule an increase in demand—supply being constant—will raise price." Be very clear on this: *This is a proposition about supply curves.*

"An increase in demand" means a shift of the whole demand curve to the right, as in Fig. 20-5 below. If the supply curve does not shift (i.e., "supply being constant"), and if the outcome is that price is raised (e.g., from *CO* to *FO* in Fig. 20-5), then there is a strong likelihood that the supply curve must run in the southwest-northeast direction illustrated by *SS* in Fig. 20-5.

Of course, price would increase if *SS* were vertical. But note part (*b*) of Proposition 1: "Probably also, but less certainly, it will increase the quantity bought and sold." If *Q* is to increase as well as *P* (in Fig. 20-5, it increases from *OA* to *OB*), then *SS* *must* run in the southwest-northeast direction.

So Proposition 1 could be reworded: "In general, supply curves run in the southwest-northeast direction." The way to find out the nature of the supply curve is to change the position of the demand curve (i.e., allow demand to increase or to decrease), and then see where the new equilibrium point lies.

1. *a.* The significance of a supply curve which runs generally in the southwest-northeast direction, then, is that in the event of an increase in demand, we would expect quantity bought and sold to (*increase / remain unchanged / decrease*) and price to (*increase / remain unchanged / decrease*).

b. There are numerous exceptions to this general rule. Supply curves can be flat or vertical, for example. And (just possibly) there can be falling supply curves (i.e., the supply line points downward rather than upward if you run your eye along it from left to right). Most of this Appendix is taken up with the reasons behind the general rule for supply curves and the reasons for the exceptions.

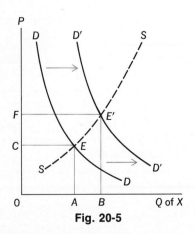

Fig. 20-5

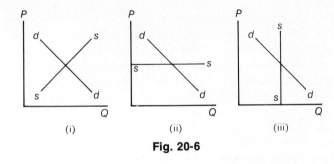

Fig. 20-6

Figure 20-6 shows three different supply-curve situations: i, ii, and iii. Its parts illustrate different "cases" discussed in the text.

(1) The constant-cost case is illustrated by (*i / ii / iii*).
(2) The perfectly inelastic supply case is (*i / ii / iii*).
(3) The increasing cost case is (*i / ii / iii*).
(4) The perfectly elastic supply case is (*i / ii / iii*).
(5) The "economic rent" case is (*i / ii / iii*).
(6) The case in which quantity supplied would respond neither to a price rise by increasing nor to a price fall by decreasing is (*i / ii / iii*).
(7) The case in which suppliers are ready to sell, at the prevailing price, a greater quantity or a smaller quantity than they now sell is (*i / ii / iii*).

c. Suppose an increase in buyer incomes pushes each of the demand curves of Fig. 20-6 to the right. The result will be a change in price and / or quantity bought and sold. Circle *one or more* letters, as appropriate. Letter *N* signifies that the outcome described fits none of the three cases of Fig. 20-6. Given this increase in demand:

(1) Price will rise in case(s) (*i / ii / iii / N*).
(2) Quantity bought and sold will increase in case(s) (*i / ii / iii / N*).
(3) Both price and quantity will increase in case(s) (*i / ii / iii / N*).
(4) Price will not rise in case(s) (*i / ii / iii / N*).
(5) Quantity will not increase in case(s) (*i / ii / iii / N*).
(6) Neither price nor quantity will increase in case(s) (*i / ii / iii / N*).

---

a. increase; increase. *b.* (1) ii; (2) iii; (3) i; (4) ii; (5) iii; (6) iii; (7) ii. *c.* (1) i, iii; (2) i, ii; (3) i; (4) ii; (5) iii; (6) *N*.

---

2. The term "economic rent" was first used because it was thought the rental of undeveloped land illustrated the case involved. The owners of such land might receive a high rent if the demand were sufficiently high; but they would have been willing to rent the *same* amount of land for a low rent if necessary. Such a case would signify:
a. A perfectly elastic supply curve.

b. A perfectly inelastic supply curve.

c. A supply curve neither perfectly inelastic nor perfectly elastic.

d. A backward-rising supply curve.

(NOTE: There is a fuller discussion of economic rent in Chapter 28.)

---

b.

---

3. *a.* There is one case in which an increase in price might *decrease* the amount offered for sale. This is the *(backward-rising supply / economic-rent / increasing-costs / inelastic supply)* case.

b. With the supply of what kind of commodity or service is this case most commonly associated?

_____ .

c. The explanation for this backward-rising case (discussed more fully in Chapter 29) is that with a higher price:

(1) It will be impossible for the supplier to furnish the same amount of the service as before.

(2) Fewer people want to supply this service.

(3) The supplier can enjoy the same or more income *and* more leisure time.

(4) The supplier wants to reduce the amount of income obtained from supplying this service.

---

a. backward-rising supply. *b.* labor service. *c.* (3).

---

4. Economists blithely recognize rising supply curves, horizontal supply curves, vertical supply curves, even some special backward-bending curves (as in the case of labor supply). But they suddenly become cautious if *falling* supply curves are suggested—i.e., any supply curve which goes beyond the perfectly horizontal stage into the northwest-to-southeast region.

Given such a supply curve, then an increase in demand would lower price, not raise it. Economists' caution as to this possibility derives from their awareness of the law of scarcity. If resources are scarce, then an increased pressure of demand on any part of those resources is most likely to *raise* price, not lower it.

The explanation that at once comes to mind with respect to falling supply curves is that of "economies of scale," or mass-production economies. It would be foolish to try to deny that such opportunities for lower per unit cost at larger outputs sometimes arise. But insofar as they appear, firms will try to exploit them by expanding their output—until the economies no longer exist for *further* increases in output. The firms which fail to seize such opportunities may be driven from business—as were many small carriage builders who had entered the automobile business, when Henry Ford began mass-production techniques.

Thus, if the industry in question is even approximately competitive, economies of scale will not show up as falling supply curves, since such economies of scale will already have been exploited. (This is explained more fully in later chapters on "the theory of the firm.") If demand is not sufficient to absorb all the resulting output, some firms are driven from the market, thus reducing total potential output. So mass-production economies tend to be, so to speak, to the *left* of the supply-and-demand equilibrium point.

If mass-production economies extended over a very large output scale for each and any firm, the driving-out-of-firms process might conceivably be pushed to the point where the industry had only one very large firm, which would be called

a _____ .

Moreover, the text points out that many actual cases in history which *look* on the surface to be falling supply-curve cases are actually cases of

_____ .

---

monopoly; shifts of the supply curve to the right.

Proposition 2 in this Appendix is, "An increase in supply, demand being constant, will almost certainly lower price and increase the quantity bought and sold." This is an assertion about demand curves (just as Proposition 1 was an assertion about supply curves). It is illustrated by Fig. 20-7 at left below: an increase in supply (a shift of SS to position $S'S'$) produces a lower price and a larger quantity bought and sold *because* the demand curve runs northwest-southeast.

Notice that Proposition 2 is much firmer about the probable consequences than was Proposition 1; hence the Appendix spends no time discussing any exceptions to this general characteristic of demand.

5. *a.* Thus, Proposition 2 is just a restatement of (pick one):

(1) The law of supply and demand.

(2) The law of downward-sloping demand.

(3) The principle of demand elasticity.

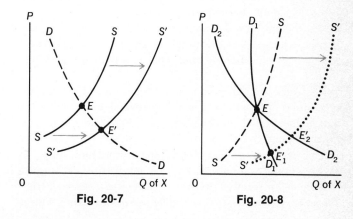

Fig. 20-7   **Fig. 20-8**

b. The text does pause for a moment to note that the *extent* to which price will fall with any given supply increase (or rise with any given supply decrease) will be governed by demand elasticity with respect to price.

Figure 20-8 (preceding page) illustrates the point. It shows two different demand curves: D_2 is more elastic than D_1. (Figure 20-1, Study Guide p. 153, illustrates the same elasticity difference between two demand curves.) If supply were to increase in the manner indicated by the shift of SS to position $S'S'$, the price fall would be greater if the demand curve were (D_1 / D_2) than if it were (D_1 / D_2). (NOTE: Remember that it is dangerous to associate price elasticity with the slope of the demand curve—see question 6, Study Guide pp. 154–155. But it is safe to say that for any given price and quantity, the flatter the demand curve, the more elastic it is.)

In terms of a *decrease* in supply, the price rise associated with such a supply decrease will be greater, the more *(elastic / inelastic)* demand is with respect to price.

---

a. (2). *b.* D_1; D_2; inelastic.

---

6. The "dynamic-cobweb" case indicates that if equilibrium price is for some reason disturbed, so that some other price prevails temporarily in the market, the consequences may be a series of oscillations, with price swinging first above, then below, the equilibrium level.

The cobweb case really involves *two* supply curves. First, there is the "true" supply curve—i.e., the schedule of quantities producers would *want* to supply, given various possible prices. If this true supply curve were the only one involved, there would be a simple price equilibrium, as in the ordinary supply-and-demand case. What complicates matters is that the producers are assumed to have to make their decision on the quantity to be produced and shipped for sale *before* they know what price will actually prevail in the market. They have to estimate what this price is going to be; and in the cobweb case, they estimate wrongly.

In the text example, it is assumed that all suppliers estimate that next period's price will be the same as last period's price. So they produce the quantity they would like to sell at that price (according to their "true" supply curve); and they ship that quantity to the market.

It is when this fixed quantity reaches the market and is sold that the wrongness of this producer guess is revealed. Price turns out to be different from what it was in the previous period.

Next time around, producers are again forced to estimate what future price will be; again they assume it will be what it was in the period immediately preceding; and again they guess wrongly.

This case assumes that once producers send their supply to market, there is no holding back on any part of that supply. This means a supply curve that *(is perfectly price-elastic / has some price elasticity / is perfectly price-inelastic).* This is

the *second* supply curve. In contrast, the "true" supply curve is assumed to *(be perfectly price-elastic / have some price elasticity / be perfectly price-inelastic).*

---

is perfectly price-inelastic; have some price elasticity.

QUIZ: Multiple Choice

1. *An increase in supply will lower price unless* (1) supply is perfectly inelastic; (2) demand is perfectly elastic; (3) it is followed by an increase in quantity demanded; (4) demand is highly inelastic; (5) both demand and supply are highly inelastic.

2. *An increase in demand will not raise price if* (1) the case is that of "pure economic rent"; (2) demand is highly elastic; (3) supply is perfectly elastic; (4) it is followed by an increase in quantity supplied; (5) demand is perfectly inelastic.

3. *Which diagram in Fig. 20-9, if any, depicts the pure economic-rent case?* (1) *a.* (2) *b.* (3) *c.* (4) *d.* (5) None of them.

4. *Which Fig. 20-9 diagram, if any, depicts the perfectly inelastic supply case?* (1) *a.* (2) *b.* (3) *c.* (4) *d.* (5) None of them.

5. *Which Fig. 20-9 diagram, if any, depicts the constant-cost case?* (1) *a.* (2) *b.* (3) *c.* (4) *d.* (5) None of them.

6. *If an industry is competitive (in the text's usage of this term), the situation with respect to mass-production economies, or reductions in per unit cost for the individual firm due to larger-scale output, will be as follows:* (1) There may be plenty of known economies which individual firms can still exploit, or there may not. (2) Firms will have expanded their output sufficiently to have taken advantage of all known economies. (3) Insofar as unexploited economies exist, the industry supply curve will be a falling one—i.e., will have some northwest-to-southeast inclination. (4) Insofar as unex-

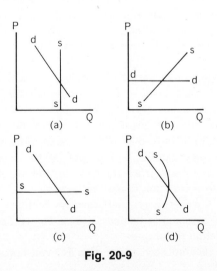

Fig. 20-9

ploited opportunities exist, the supply curve will be a rising one. (5) None of the above.

7. *The results observed in the dynamic-cobweb supply-and-demand case depend in large part on the assumption that* (1) the supply curve for the commodity is inelastic; (2) the commodity involved can be stored and kept in inventory, so that sellers can withdraw part or all of their supply from the market if they do not like the price that prevails; (3) the demand and supply curves intersect at a price that is satisfactory neither to suppliers nor to buyers; (4) suppliers decide on the quantity they will send to market in this period on the basis of an earlier-period price; (5) both demand curve and supply curve are highly inelastic, so that any shift in either curve results in a large change in price.

8. *The dynamic-cobweb supply-and-demand case refers to the following:* (1) A situation in which there is an interaction between supply and demand curves, so that a shift in one curve may set off a shift in the other, thus making it difficult for a stable equilibrium price to develop. (2) The tendency of price to be pulled toward the critical point at which supply and demand curves intersect. (3) A situation in which any disturbance of equilibrium price may set off a series of price oscillations, possibly with the swings growing wider as they continue. (4) The case in which consideration is given to the quantity that will be demanded and the supply offered per period of time, instead of the time factor being disregarded, as it is in ordinary supply-and-demand analysis. (5) A situation in which both demand curve and supply curve are highly elastic, so that any price fluctuations caused by a movement of either curve tend to be extremely wide.

9. *"Increasing costs" (as the term is used in the text) means* (1) the same thing as perfectly inelastic supply; (2) that at any higher price a larger quantity will be supplied; (3) any upward shift in a supply curve due to an increase in input prices; (4) any leftward shift of the supply curve following an increase in demand; (5) none of the above, necessarily.

10. *If the revenue received by a factor of production is classed as a "pure economic rent," and if the demand for this factor declines,* (1) the price of this factor will fall, but the quantity bought and sold will remain unchanged; (2) the price of this factor will fall, and the quantity bought and sold will decline; (3) the price of this factor will remain unchanged, but the quantity bought and sold will decline; (4) both the price of this factor and the quantity bought and sold will remain unchanged; (5) none of these is true.

11. *"Perfectly elastic supply" indicates* (1) constant cost; (2) increasing cost; (3) decreasing cost; (4) that revenue received by suppliers is designated as economic rent; (5) that a certain fixed supply will be offered no matter what price may be.

12. *If a commodity's return is in the nature of a pure economic rent and a tax is imposed on the commodity, then* (1) the incidence of the tax is borne wholly by the suppliers, and price to the buyers will not change; (2) the incidence is borne wholly by the buyers; (3) the incidence will be shared between the suppliers and the buyers; (4) the output of the commodity will fall and its price will rise; (5) the output of the commodity will not fall but its price will rise.

13. *The law of diminishing returns plays the following background part in demand and/or supply curves:* (1) It explains, at least in part, the increasing-cost case. (2) It explains why an increase in supply will almost certainly lower price. (3) It accounts, in part, for the fact that price must be lowered if a greater quantity is to be sold. (4) It explains, at least in part, the backward-bending supply curve case. (5) Its part is not correctly indicated by any of these statements.

14. *In the circumstances usually cited to explain the phenomenon of the backward-rising supply curve, it follows that* (1) continual decreases in demand will continually increase the quantity of the service supplied; (2) the supply curve will not bend back to such an extent that with increased price the total revenue received by the supplier or suppliers actually decreases; (3) any increase in demand will tend to be followed by an increase in quantity supplied, but not by an increase in supply; (4) the supply curve may ultimately climb to the point where it touches the vertical (price) axis; (5) the return received by the supplier or suppliers will be known as pure economic rent.

15. *If the land suited for growing wheat is fixed in quantity, the supply curve for wheat* (1) should still have some price elasticity—i.e., indicate that as price rises, supply quantity offered would increase; (2) must rise vertically, i.e., be perfectly inelastic; (3) may in consequence be backward-bending; (4) might be perfectly horizontal, since the supply of wheat and the supply of wheat-growing land are two different things; (5) will not be influenced by the price offered for wheat.

16. *If a good is produced under "constant-cost" conditions, the effect of a $1 tax on each unit sold would normally be* (1) to raise price to consumers by $1; (2) to raise price to consumers by less than $1, if demand is elastic; (3) to require the entire tax to be paid by producers, unless demand is perfectly elastic; (4) to raise price to consumers by less than $1, if demand is inelastic; (5) none of these.

21 SUPPLY AND DEMAND AS APPLIED TO AGRICULTURE

THREE IMPORTANT BACKGROUND FACTS need to be grasped for an understanding of the behavior of farm prices and of governmental support of farm prices.

The first of these facts is that agricultural products are usually sold on an entirely different type of market from that on which industrial goods are sold. A farmer typically ships his produce to a central market and accepts the price which it brings; he has no control over that price. The market is constructed so as to yield a price that will clear away (or ration out) the supply quantities shipped to it, large or small, in the given demand conditions. Thus the farm-product market is likely to be one with notably "flexible" prices: any change in demand or in supply shows up at once as an increase or a decrease in market price.

This property of agricultural prices makes them an admirable introductory illustration of the working of supply and demand forces. Farmers themselves are rather less enthusiastic about the situation: they dislike price gyrations which they cannot control and (usually) cannot predict. The simple fact of the "flexibility" of unregulated farm prices is one important reason behind the demand of farm producers for regulated prices. They feel that the gains they enjoy when price is high are more than offset by the losses they suffer when it is low.

The second fact is that both farm demand and farm supply seem to be decidedly price-inelastic. (On the demand side especially, there are exceptions. Demand for meats and fruits seems much more elastic. It is worth noting that government support programs are far less evident with respect to these products.)

1. *a.* The result of this combination of an inelastic demand curve and an inelastic supply curve is that a *(small / large)* shift in *(the demand / the supply / either)* curve is apt to result in a *(small / large)* shift in price.

The effect of this elasticity combination revealed itself with special force in the 1930s, when depression caused the consumer demand curve to move leftward. Farm prices fell calamitously. As a result, the government began its large-scale venture into farm price and production control.

b. The *(elasticity / inelasticity)* of demand for farm products generally has a further implication. When farm prices fall because of some increase in supply, farm income goes *(up /*

down). When a support program is introduced to push the price back up again, farm income goes *(up / down)*.

---

a. small; either; large. *b.* inelasticity; down; up.

The third basic fact is that the long-run trend in farm prices in the present century has been downward. This trend has not been a steady one. It was interrupted, for example, by both the world wars, each of which meant a big surge in demand for food, as production in war-ravaged areas was disrupted. There was another jump in world food demand in the early 1970s. Until this proves itself to be an enduring phenomenon, we must continue to say that the long-run trend in farm prices has been a downward one. Again, this calls for explanation in supply and demand terms.

2. *a.* During this century, the demand curve for farm products in the United States *(has / has not)* moved rightward. This results from the fact that (pick one):
(1) Consumers have not been interested in buying more farm products.
(2) Real incomes and living standards have gradually increased, and people want to consume more farm products than they formerly did.
(3) Tastes have shifted away from industrial products and in favor of farm products.

b. These real-income increases have prompted American consumers to increase their buying of farm goods *(less than proportionately / just about in proportion / more than proportionately)* to the increase in their incomes.

c. Concurrently, and mainly because of much greater use of farm machinery and vastly improved technology, the supply curve for farm products has likewise moved *(rightward / leftward)*.

Combining these demand and supply factors, it transpires that the rightward movement of the supply curve has *(failed to keep up with / just matched / outrun)* the rightward movement of the demand curve. Thus the tendency of farm prices has been to drift *(upward / downward)*.

d. Technology and the increased use of machinery have been the principal governing factors on the farm supply side. But the text mentions another contributing supply factor, namely:

_____.

a. has; (2). *b.* less than proportionately. *c.* rightward; outrun; downward. *d.* a higher rural birth rate, adding relatively to the farm labor force.

---

3. *a.* Which of the following is most nearly correct in summarizing productivity advances and farm-size trends in American agriculture?

(1) Save in a few products such as hybrid corn, there have been no truly impressive increases in output per man-hour and per acre, and this relative backwardness in productivity is one of the root causes of the farm problem.
(2) There have been remarkable increases in output per man-hour and per acre, appearing to such an extent among large farm units that small and medium-sized family farm units have almost completely vanished.
(3) There have been such remarkable increases in output, and they have appeared most prominently among the large farm units; but there are still very many small low-productivity farm units.
(4) Productivity increases have been distributed equally among large and small farm units, so that farm size is no indication of productive efficiency for that unit.

b. As a result of the situation indicated in part *a*, the major benefit of government-maintained price support programs has accrued to the *(large / small) (efficient / inefficient)* producers, only a much smaller part to the *(large / small) (efficient / inefficient)* producers.

---

a. (3). *b.* large, efficient; small, inefficient.

---

4. *a.* When farmers began to demand government regulation of farm prices, they insisted that the important thing was a proper relation between farm prices and industrial-good prices: they wanted the price of what they sold to go up by as much as did the prices of the things they had to buy. In the 1930s, they looked back to the 1910–1914 period as a "golden age," in the sense that the relation then existing between these two sets of prices was considered satisfactory and equitable.

This "parity" idea was worked into the price support program. Suppose, for example, that the 1910–1914 price of wheat was $1. The index of prices of industrial goods was 100 in 1910–1914; today it is 300. What should wheat's price be today, for "100 per cent parity"? ...._____.

b. A declared parity or support price above the current market level will have no effect whatever on that market price— unless the government influences either the supply curve or the demand curve. It can reduce supply (through some form of output restriction). Or it can enter the market as demander.

If the government becomes a demander, the shape or position of the demand curve is altered. Text Fig. 21-4 can illustrate this. A support price is set at the level indicated by height *BO*. The Agriculture Department enters the market as buyer to establish this price. This means that the demand curve, formerly *dd'*, now becomes *(dCEF / dCB' / dCB)*. The total demand curve now has a "kink" at point *C*.

c. Notice that this new demand curve (kinked at *C*) (pick one):
(1) has the same elasticity with respect to price as it did before.
(2) has now become perfectly price-elastic at price *BO*.
(3) is now less price-elastic than it was before.

That is, the part of the original demand curve below point *C* has now disappeared. The newly-introduced flat section of the demand curve extending rightward from *C* says that the government will buy *(no quantity / some limited quantity / any quantity)* at price *BO*. So the demand at prices less than *BO* no longer has any economic significance.

---

a. $3. *b.* *dCB'*. *c.* (2); any quantity.

---

5. The trouble with a price support program such as that indicated by text Fig. 21-4 is that the government must store (or else destroy) what it buys. Many stored food products deteriorate; storage can be costly. Worst of all, goods which took real effort to produce are not made available to consumers.

Hence, there was proposed a "two-price plan"—what the text calls a "subsidized producer-consumer price differential." Basically, this was a proposal to pay farmers the parity price—and then sell to the public the goods so bought at whatever lower price would dispose of them.

This proposal involved an interesting little economic question. Would the two-price plan have cost more than the ordinary storage plan? You can answer this question if you have mastered Chapter 20's elasticity discussion. On text Fig. 21-5, draw a vertical line from point *C* down to the axis. Mark *H* at the point where it crosses *AE*, and *K* where it reaches the axis. Recall from Chapter 20 that rectangle *BCKO* indicates total consumer outlay when the price is *BO*. At price *AO*, consumer outlay would be rectangle *AEsO*. Which outlay is bigger? That depends on price elasticity. The taller rectangle *BCKO* will be bigger if demand is price- *(elastic / inelastic)*.

Now, clutching this piece of information, turn back to the main problem. Which is bigger—the tall rectangle of Fig. 21-4 (storage plan cost), or the flat one of Fig. 21-5 (two-price plan cost)? Just manipulate these two rectangles until they correspond to the two described above, which we *do* know how to compare. The small rectangle *CFEH* is common to both, so the answer to the which-is-larger question will be unchanged if we take *CFEH* away from both. Similarly, it does no harm if we add rectangle *AHKO* to both. But we then have as a result the two rectangles described in the preceding paragraph. So we can say the two-price plan would cost more if consumer demand is price- *(elastic / inelastic)*.

___

inelastic; inelastic.

___

QUIZ: Multiple Choice

1. *Four of the five items below are factors cited in the text as contributing to the economic problems of United States agriculture. The one exception (the one not so cited) is this:* (1) In this century, technological progress has greatly increased the total supply of farm goods that can be produced. (2) With increases in real income, a smaller fraction of the consumer's dollar has come to be spent on food. (3) Birth rates have been higher in rural than in urban areas, thus adding relatively to the farm population. (4) The improvement in technology has, via the law of diminishing returns, reduced the man-hour productivity of farm labor. (5) Small changes in demand or in supply tend to bring about large changes in prices of farm goods.

2. *Under U.S. Public Law 480,* (1) a low-income country may buy surplus farm goods with its own currency, and the United States will spend the proceeds only on projects which put a minimum of strain on that country's limited resources; (2) a limit is imposed on the maximum payment that may be made to any one farmer under the price support program; (3) the government may buy farm goods from producers at a "parity" price which may be substantially above the free-market price; (4) the government is empowered to restrict the acreage farmers may plant, in return for a price support program; (5) the government is empowered to sell surplus farm goods on the market at prices that may be below the prices it paid farmers to buy them.

3. *From the standpoint of the economist who stresses the importance of the price mechanism for maintaining a proper allocation of the factors of production, the most serious objection to the parity-pricing program for farm goods has been that* (1) most of the benefit accruing from the program of price increases has gone to farmers with higher-than-average incomes who are not in need of such assistance; (2) the restrictions on acreage to be cultivated constitute an undesirable interference with the decisions and behavior of individual producers; (3) there is a gross inconsistency between government's policy of improving farm technology and output through research and its policy of purchasing and storing excess farm output; (4) maintenance of prices above the market or competitive level has encouraged resources to stay in agriculture instead of moving toward industry; (5) the price support program has converted an elastic demand curve for farm products into an inelastic one.

4. *One reason for the decline in the relative importance of the agricultural sector in the United States is the fact that* (1) the birth rate is lower in the rural regions; (2) there are still so many people engaged in agriculture that the law of diminishing returns is operating, and output per man-hour is lower than it should be; (3) parity prices have kept farm output from increasing as much as it otherwise would; (4) as people's incomes increase, their demand for agricultural products increases less than their demand for industrial products; (5) since the end of World War II, farm prices have risen considerably less than industrial prices.

5. *A parity-price farm program has been likened to a minimum-wage law. But there is this difference between maintaining a parity price of $2 on a farm commodity and maintaining a $2 minimum wage: The* (1) government makes the parity price effective by working almost entirely on the demand side of the market and makes the minimum wage effective by working almost entirely on the supply side; (2) parity price is necessarily set at much above the equilibrium level of price, whereas the minimum wage is necessarily set at the equilibrium level; (3) parity program gives suppliers revenue from quantities not bought or wanted by consumers at the parity price, while a minimum wage does not; (4) parity program is really intended to affect the incomes of those who benefit from this program, and this is not true of the minimum-wage program; (5) minimum-wage program operates by changing the total demand and/or supply curves, whereas the parity program does not affect either demand or supply curves.

6. *Farm prices (when not maintained by a government support program) swing more widely than industrial prices; they usually climb higher in boom periods and fall lower in recessions. These swings can in part be explained by* (1) the high degree of price elasticity of both demand and supply curves; (2) the high degree of price inelasticity of both demand and supply curves; (3) the high elasticity of supply curves but not necessarily high elasticity of demand curves; (4) the combination of highly price-elastic demand and highly price-inelastic supply; (5) none of these conditions, since price elasticities are unrelated to price changes.

7. *A plan to increase farm incomes by means of crop restriction or acreage restriction programs has best prospects for success if* (1) the demand for farm products is inelastic with respect to price; (2) the supply of farm products is inelastic with respect to price; (3) the demand for farm products is unitelastic with respect to price; (4) the supply of farm products is elastic with respect to price; (5) the demand for farm products is elastic with respect to price.

8. *The basic idea of a parity farm price, and one reflected in the manner of its computation, is a farm price that* (1) is based on the costs of production of an efficient farm; (2) is sufficiently high to yield farmers a fair return yet avoids a piling up of farm surpluses; (3) will rise in proportion to any rise in industrial prices; (4) is steady, and avoids the changes which occur in the prices of things farmers buy; (5) will reflect the improvements in farm technology.

9. *A valid criticism of the "100 per cent of parity" method of computing a "fair" price for any farm product is that it ignores the fact that* (1) improved technology may have reduced the cost of producing each unit of that product; (2) the supply of farm products is highly responsive to any small change in the level of price; (3) the prices of things a farmer buys, taken together, are as important to him as the price of the thing he sells; (4) the prices of things a farmer buys, although in fact they have risen, could also fall; (5) supply and demand curves for that product may not intersect at the level indicated by that parity price.

10. *One proposed solution to the problem of farm prices and farm surpluses has been what the text calls the "subsidized producer-consumer price differential plan" (or the "two-price plan"). A basic consequence of implementing this plan would be that* (1) existing surpluses of farm goods would gradually be sold off in order to push farm prices down to their natural supply-and-demand level; (2) the Agriculture Department would buy only a limited quantity of farm output for storage, and any balance would have to be sold by farmers at an unsupported price; (3) the price paid by farm-product users would reflect the relation between farm operating costs and the level of prices paid by farmers for the industrial goods they need; (4) the price paid by farm-product users would fall to whatever level was needed to dispose of the entire current supply; (5) the price paid to farmers by the Agriculture Department would be adjusted to take account of improvements in farm technology.

11. *Question 10 referred to the "two-price plan." Another arrangement has been the "parity-price loan-or-purchase plan." With respect to the government expenditure required to maintain them, the two plans compare as follows:* (1) If demand for farm goods is elastic with respect to price, the two-price plan would be more costly. (2) If demand for farm goods is inelastic with respect to price, the two-price plan would be more costly. (3) The two-price plan would be the more costly in all circumstances. (4) The two-price plan would be less costly in all circumstances. (5) The government's expenditure would be virtually the same in both plans, regardless of circumstances.

12. *In terms of farm income, the difference between the two plans cited in Question 11 (assuming the same supply curve in both instances) would be* (1) higher farm revenue under the two-price plan; (2) higher farm revenue under the parity plan; (3) greater income stability under the two-price plan; (4) greater income stability under the parity plan; (5) no real difference at all.

13. *Whenever a drop in consumer demand occurs (e.g., in a recession), farm output behaves as follows, by comparison with industrial output: Usually (according to the text)* (1) it is substantially reduced, and the reduction approximately matches that in industrial output; (2) it is substantially reduced, so that its reduction exceeds that of industrial output; (3) it is little reduced, just as industrial output is little reduced; (4) it is little reduced, the reduction in industrial output being considerably larger; (5) it is little reduced, and the reduction matches quite closely the reduction in industrial output.

14. *One reason for the behavior of farm output, mentioned in the text and referred to in question 13, is the fact that* (1) farm labor is unionized to a much lesser extent than industrial labor; (2) farmers are trying to maintain farm prices at a level proportionate to that of industrial prices; (3) agricultural technology and productivity are being steadily improved; (4) when farm prices drop, many farmers decide to leave their land idle; (5) reductions in output do not result in a major reduction in farm operating costs.

APPENDIX: Economics of Speculation, Risk, and Insurance

1. *a.* Suppose a commodity such as wheat or cotton is traded at more than one location. Markets for such commodities are ordinarily well organized, and this results in a particular geographic price relationship. We would expect prices at the various trading points to *(be the same at all points / vary according to local demand and supply forces / vary by no more than the amount of transport cost between points).*

Any disturbance of this "equilibrium price relationship" will persist only for the briefest period of time, owing to the activity of professional speculators. This activity is known as *(hedging / selling short / arbitrage).*

b. Suppose, for example, the commodity is wheat and the trading points are Chicago and Seattle. A surge of demand drives up the price in Seattle. Speculators promptly *(buy / sell)* in Seattle and *(buy / sell)* in Chicago. This pushes the Seattle price *(up / down)* and the Chicago price *(up / down).* That is, prices at the two cities draw *(closer together / farther apart)* as a consequence of this arbitrage activity.

---

a. vary by amount of transport cost; arbitrage. *b.* sell; buy; down; up; closer together.

---

2. *a.* In a well-organized competitive market, there is also a definite pattern of prices over time. If a crop is harvested once a year but is in demand throughout the year, the monthly price pattern to be expected, starting with the after-harvest month, is one of *(constant / gradually falling / gradually ris-*

ing) prices. Price must *(fall / rise / remain constant)* because of

_____ .

b. This mechanism works as follows: In the immediate after-harvest period, cash-hungry producers tend to throw much of their crop on the market at once. Assuming no activity by speculators, this makes for a *(low / high)* price—whereas, later in the year, the supply offered will tend to be much *(lower / higher)* and the price consequently much *(lower / higher)*. The informed speculator, realizing this, *(buys / sells)* in the early after-harvest period, and *(buys / sells)* in later months.

The effect of this speculative activity is to cause the immediately-after-harvest price to be *(higher / lower)* than it otherwise would be, and later prices to be *(higher / lower)*.

a. gradually rising; rise; storage and interest costs.
b. low; lower; higher; buys; sells; higher; lower.

3. *a.* More generally, speculators stabilize prices for all *foreseeable* fluctuations—of which the seasonal is simply the most obvious. Suppose, for example, that reports begin to drift in from coffee-producing countries that the next crop to be harvested is likely to be unusually large—which means the coffee price will fall when this crop appears on the market. This will set off activity in the coffee "futures market." For reasons explained more fully in question 4, "futures contracts" are widely used on the commodity exchanges.

A futures contract is simply one in which buyer and seller agree on price and quantity *now*; but actual delivery of the commodity by the seller (and payment by the buyer) does not take place until an agreed *future* date. The seller may own none of the commodity at the time he makes the contract; he may well buy it only on the required delivery date (and, it is hoped, at a price below the price at which he has agreed to sell).

So in the coffee example, speculators will begin to *(buy / sell)* coffee for future delivery. They anticipate, of course, that when the large crop arrives, the price will be *(lower / higher)* than it currently is, so they can *(buy / sell)* the coffee they must deliver at a price *(above / below)* that in their futures contracts.

b. As news of the impending large crop spreads, and more and more sales offers are made in the futures market, the price in that market will naturally decline. So you now can buy coffee, for delivery some months ahead, at a lower price. Buyers of coffee for present use, noticing this, will *(moderate / intensify)* their bids for immediate-delivery coffee. Sellers of coffee will be a little *(more / less)* disposed to sell their stocks right away. This *(increases / decreases)* today's price, and so *(increases / decreases)* today's purchases. This *(increase / decrease)* in present consumption, and consequent reduction in present stocks, tends to *(moderate / enhance)* the

price disturbance to be expected when the large new coffee crop arrives.

c. When the time arrives to make delivery on their futures contracts, the speculators *(buy / sell)* the coffee they must supply in the "spot" market (on-the-spot delivery). The risk they run is that the price they then must pay may be *(higher / lower)* than they anticipated.

d. Note, then, that speculators do not *eliminate* price fluctuations. If a coffee crop is unusually large, coffee price will almost certainly fall. What speculators do is to spread over a *(narrower / wider)* span of time the impact of this large crop on coffee price. Today, well before the new crop has appeared, coffee's price has fallen and consumption has increased. Prices will be low when the new crop arrives, but not so low as they would have been if some of the impact had not been absorbed earlier.

Similarly, in the example of question 2, the effect of speculative activity is to *(moderate / widen)* the amplitude of the up-and-down seasonal price swing.

Of course, if speculators anticipate the future incorrectly, they create *unnecessary* price swings. The common view which associates speculation with this type of price movement doubtless comes from speculative activity in the stock market, since the future price of a stock is probably more difficult to forecast accurately than the future price of a commodity.

a. sell; lower; buy; below. *b.* moderate; more; decreases; increases; increase; moderate. *c.* buy; higher. *d.* wider; moderate.

4. Although speculators trade on the "organized exchanges," they are by no means the only participants. There are exchanges for purchase and sale of many farm products and metals, including coffee, cocoa, sugar, eggs, hides, lead, tin, and mercury. These exchanges originated from a desire on the part of both buyers and sellers to avoid unnecessary and sometimes chaotic price changes. The uncertainty generated by these price fluctuations was considered undesirable, and it was found that much of this week's high price and next week's low price could be eliminated by "averaging them out" over time. The use of futures contracts developed, not for the convenience of speculators, but because there were both commodity producers and commodity consumers who found these contracts desirable.

a. Suppose, for example, you are a manufacturer of soft drinks. Your product retails for 25 cents per bottle. A major change in costs might drive up the price of all soft drinks to 30 cents. But such changes come infrequently, and for practical purposes you must think of the 25-cent price as beyond your power to alter.

You are a buyer of sugar, a major ingredient in soft drinks.

Sugar is traded throughout the world, and its price is *not* fixed. You are thus haunted by the fear of being squeezed between a rising raw-material price and an unchangeable sales price. The windfall profit you would earn if sugar's price should *fall* is hardly sufficient compensation for the fact that a large price rise could push you into bankruptcy. So, to cover your future needs, you *(buy / sell)* a specified amount on the sugar exchange (in sugar, the unit for each "contract trade" is 112,000 pounds). Delivery is to be made at a specified future date. Price is settled *(at time of delivery / immediately)*. In this transaction, you are a *(hedger / speculator)*.

b. In this contract, you have *(bought / sold)* futures. You *(have / have not)* settled in advance what the cost of your sugar needs will be. If it turns out at time of delivery that sugar's price has risen, you *(are / are not)* squeezed.

c. The man who sold you your sugar may have been an agent for a sugar producer, or he may have been a speculator. If he was a speculator, his estimate has been that he can buy sugar for delivery to you at a price *(below / above)* the price he has quoted you. Professionally, his job is to assume the risk involved in sugar price fluctuation.

d. The example used in the text Appendix involves a firm which is uncertain about the price of corn it will *sell* at some future date. Such a firm will hedge by *(buying / selling)* futures.

Not all commodity speculators are professionals. If you are shrewd (or lucky), you can make a lot of money quickly by trading in commodities; if not, you can lose it just as fast. The key factor here is that margin requirements on the commodity exchanges are usually much lower than they are on the stock exchanges; typically, they run from 10 per cent to 20 per cent. (For an exercise on margin buying, see Study Guide p. 33.)

A 10 per cent margin requirement allows you, with your own stake of (say) $10,000, to borrow $90,000 and buy or sell accordingly. If you buy, and your commodity goes up in price by just 10 per cent, you have doubled your $10,000 (disregarding incidental costs). The margin system then allows you to operate on a $200,000 scale. Unfortunately, a 10 per cent drop in price wipes you out; you retire to the sidelines, certainly sadder and possibly wiser.

---

a. buy; immediately; hedger. *b.* bought; have; are not.
c. below. *d.* selling.

---

5. *a.* Gambling can be criticized on economic grounds if one assumes the validity of the law of *(diminishing marginal / increasing marginal / diminishing total)* utility. (Note that Chapter 22 contains a fuller discussion of marginal utility.) Briefly, the view here is that as income increases, the "utility" or satisfaction derived from each extra dollar goes *(down / up)*. The first dollars of income go toward highest-priority needs; lower-priority requirements are met as income

increases. If you bet $100 on an even-chance outcome, you have a 50 per cent chance of gaining $100 and a 50 per cent chance of losing $100. If the marginal utility of money really decreases, the utility of the $100 you could win is *(more / less)* than the utility of the $100 you could lose.

b. Insurance companies insist, sometimes vehemently, that you do not "gamble" by taking out a policy with them. To gamble on the outcome of an event is to assume a risk of loss that would not have existed but for the decision to gamble. In contrast, you can insure only against *(a new / an already-existing)* risk. You can insure only if you have an "insurable interest"—i.e., if you *(are creating a new / already face the)* risk.

---

a. diminishing marginal; down; less. *b.* already-existing; already face the.

QUIZ: Multiple Choice

1. *In an ideal competitive market for a crop harvested once a year, the monthly price pattern over one year will show* (1) constant prices; (2) gradually falling prices as demand becomes satiated; (3) gradually falling prices because of storage and interest costs; (4) gradually rising prices because of storage and interest costs; (5) none of these patterns.

2. *The effect caused by speculators on market price is* (1) always to cause price to be more stable over a period of time than it would otherwise be; (2) always to cause price to be less stable over a period of time than it would otherwise be; (3) to accentuate upswings in price, but to prevent downswings from being as violent as they otherwise would be; (4) to accentuate downswings in price, but to prevent upswings from being as violent as they otherwise would be; (5) not properly described by any of these.

3. *The law with respect to property insurance requires the existence of an "insurable interest" for the insurance policy to be legally valid. This means specifically that* (1) the policy must specify the particular kind of event that must occur for the insurance proceeds to be paid; (2) the policyholder must apply for the insurance in good faith and must accept all conditions stipulated in the policy; (3) because of the speculative or uncertainty element which such a contract involves, it must satisfy the prevailing laws concerning gambling; (4) the person insured must face some genuine economic risk which is removed or partly removed by the policy; (5) the person insured must be the owner of the property insured.

4. *A commodity futures contract is one in which* (1) delivery is to be made over a series of future dates, typically monthly, with the contract typically extending over one year; (2) the price exceeds the current market price by an amount which covers interest and storage charges for the period up to the specified future date; (3) a specified quantity is to be delivered at a specified future date, the price to be the market price prevailing at that future date; (4) delivery and payment are not to be made until a specified future date, but price and quantity are settled now; (5) the buyer may require the seller to retain possession of the commodity, and require its delivery at any time within a specified future period.

5. *If we know that a firm has entered the futures market as a seller of some commodity in order to "hedge," then we know that this firm* (1) estimates that the "spot" price is going to rise, and that it deliberately assumes the risk involved by acting on this estimate; (2) wants to protect itself against the possibility that there will be a later drop in the "spot" price; (3) estimates that the "spot" price is going to fall, and that it deliberately assumes the risk involved by acting on this estimate; (4) wants to protect itself against the possibility that there will be a later rise in the "spot" price; (5) will concurrently buy for "spot" delivery at a lower price in some other market, and consequently will earn a profit on the two transactions combined.

6. *Which alternative in question 5 would be correct had the firm entered the futures market as a buyer, and had bought as a speculator?* (1). (2). (3). (4). (5).

7. *The term "selling short" with respect to some commodity or security means specifically* (1) any sale made in the expectation that the price of that commodity or security is going to fall; (2) any sale made in the expectation that the price of that commodity or security is going to rise; (3) a sale made for future delivery, when the seller does not now possess the commodity or security he is selling; (4) a sale made at a price which it is agreed shall be the price prevailing at some future date; (5) an attempt to "corner the market" on that commodity or security.

8. *If news suddenly reaches speculators that there is likely to be an exceptionally large crop of some commodity appearing in the market a few months from now, we would reasonably expect the following results to occur in the market for that commodity:* (1) The "spot" or current market price will fall, but the futures price will be unaffected. (2) The "spot" or current market price will be unaffected, but the futures price will fall. (3) The "spot" or current market price will be unaffected, but the futures price will rise. (4) Both the "spot" or current market price and the futures price will rise. (5) Both the "spot" or current market price and the futures price will fall.

9. *The activity known as "arbitraging" involves* (1) buying in the futures market, deliberately assuming the risk that the price of the commodity in question may fall; (2) selling in the "spot" market, buying in the futures market, as protection against the possibility that the price of the commodity in question may rise; (3) buying in one geographic market and selling in another, by reason of a price difference between them; (4) selling in the futures market as protection against the possibility that the price of the commodity in question may fall; (5) none of the above.

"DEMAND THEORY" means an analysis of the background of demand curves. Thus it explores the factors that are important in consumer buying decisions. The main factors involved are: (1) income, (2) prices, (3) choice according to personal tastes.

Ordinarily, as a consumer, you have only a limited amount of money to spend in each period on the things you need, and that please you. Each good has a market price; usually you cannot alter these prices. You must decide which goods to buy, and how much of each to buy, knowing that each purchase will take up part of your limited income or budget total.

If your budget were so large that you could buy all you wanted of all the goods that interested you, there would be no problem of choice. Ordinarily—alas!—that is not the case. You must *decide*—decide, for example, whether to buy two more units of good A (price $1), or instead to buy one more unit of good B (price $2). Each purchase would entail the same $2 outlay, and a limited budget says you can't have both. So you must carry inside your head some personal measuring scale which says that buying the one unit of B would yield you more satisfaction than would purchase of the two units of A (or vice versa). Tastes differ, of course. The person next to you, with the same income, might well make the opposite choice.

This small A-or-B choice illustrates the more general problem of how to make the best use of a limited income. There are thousands of different assortments of goods, each one a little different from the next, which could be bought with a given income (and given prices). Which among them is the "best" choice?

It is easy to understand that decisions must be made in buying. And prices and incomes are objective, easily understood concepts. But tastes are more difficult. We have to devise some analytic concept—and it isn't easy! —to represent what we mean by personal "tastes," "preferences," or "needs."

This chapter uses the "utility" idea: Each consumer measures commodities by his or her personal quantitative standard of satisfaction or utility. A certain buyer may reckon, for example, that buying one unit of A would yield 50 utility units ("utils"); two units would yield a total of 120 utils; and a third A unit would raise the satisfaction meter to 180 utils.

In real life, nobody is conscious of putting exact numerical values on each quantity of each good he consumes. The utility notion represents the consumer as being a lot more precise than buyers actually are. Don't be too impatient with the utility idea on this account. It says that consumers must do something at least *approximating* this, even if only intuitively, if they want to make the best-possible use of a limited income.

This quantitative utility idea is employed because it is a way of showing how a consumer will go about "maximizing satisfaction"—i.e., making the best-possible use of a limited income in the light of his or her own set of preferences.

The very first step is to distinguish carefully between *total* utility and *marginal* utility. In the example above, the buyer derived a *total* utility of 50 utils from consuming one unit of A, 120 utils from two units, and 180 utils from three units. Marginal utility is the *extra* utility contributed by the *last* unit consumed (the unit that is just at the edge or margin of consumption, so to speak). The marginal utility of the first unit of A must be 50 (because its consumption raised total utility from 0 to 50); that of the second unit, 70 (because total utils rose from 50 to 120); that of the third unit, 60 (from 120 to 180).

1. Thus, if the *total* utilities associated with consumption of 1, 2, and 3 units of B were to be respectively 100, 160, and 200, the corresponding marginal utilities would be (*100, 260, 460 / 0, 100, 160 / 100, 60, 40 / 200, 360, 500*).

100, 60, 40.

The second step is to note the principle of *diminishing marginal utility*. This principle says that as consumption of any single good increases, the total utility therefrom will increase (up to a point)—but marginal utility gradually decreases. The third ice-cream cone (or the third martini) may add to your satisfaction, but not so much as the first one did; the fifth one may add still a little more satisfaction, but not so much as the third one did. In these circumstances, your total satisfaction is still rising, but the payoff from each additional (marginal) unit consumed is becoming less and less.

2. *a.* The following set of *total* utility figures (for 1, 2, 3, and 4 units consumed) illustrates the idea of diminishing marginal utility: *(200, 300, 400, 500 / 200, 450, 750, 1,100 / 200, 400, 1,600, 9,600 / 200, 250, 270, 280).*

b. The following set of *marginal* utility figures (again for 1, 2, 3, and 4 units consumed) would likewise illustrate the diminishing marginal utility principle: *(200, 150, 100, 50 / 200, 300, 400, 500 / 200, 200, 200, 200 / 200, 250, 270, 280).*

c. Behind the notion of diminishing marginal utility is the simple idea that we can have too much of *any* good thing. Ultimately, enough of anything is enough. Diminishing marginal utility means that this point of satiation *(is being approached / has been reached).*

If and when the satiation point is actually reached, the following utility situation will prevail (pick one):
(1) Total utility and marginal utility will be one and the same figure.
(2) Total utility will be zero, marginal utility will have reached its maximum.
(3) Total utility will have reached its maximum, marginal utility will be zero.
(4) Both total utility and marginal utility will be zero.
(5) Both total utility and marginal utility will have reached their maximum values.

a. 200, 250, 270, 280. *b.* 200, 150, 100, 50. *c.* is being approached; (3).

Now we use the ideas of total and marginal utility to illustrate the idea of "maximizing satisfaction," or making the best-possible use of a given income. We deal with a consumer with a fixed weekly budget, buying three goods only, A, B, and C. Table 22-1 shows his personal schedule of total utility for these three goods.

The consumer wants to spend his fixed income *so as to obtain that particular ABC combination yielding the maximum attainable number of utility units.* Note that the utility units for A are of the same kind as those for B and C. For example, if he bought 2 units each of A, B, and C, his total satisfaction would be 950 utility units (120 plus 700 plus 130).

In this table, the three sets of utility values are assumed to be independent of one another. That is, the amount of utility the consumer gets for any given quantity of A is not affected by the amount he happens to be consuming of B or of C. This is not necessarily true in real life—for example, if A and B happen to be substitutes. But this assumption is made for greater clarity and convenience.

3. In the selection of a "utility maximum," the idea of *marginal* utility proves to be crucial. First of all, then, use the information in Table 22-1 to record, in Table 22-2, marginal utilities of A, B, and C. To speed things up, a few of the marginal utility figures are already entered.

A: 18, 10, 7, 5, 5, 4, 4, 3.
B: 100, 20, 10, 8, 6, 4, 2, 1, 1.
C: 50, 45, 40, 35, 28, 20, 12, 6, 4, 3.

4. The consumer of question 3 has $52 per week to spend on commodities A, B, and C. (These are the only commodities available, or the only ones that interest him.) A's price per unit is $1; B's is $2; C's is $4.

How much of A, B, and C should he buy, for maximum satisfaction?

There are plenty of ABC combinations that $52 would just buy. *But which combination buys the maximum number of utility units?*

One possible combination is 12 of A, 10 of B, 5 of C (yielding a total of 1,611 utility units). Does this "maximize utility"? No, for if you cut A purchases by 4 units, that allows purchase of 1 extra C unit, and the utility gain from increasing C will outweigh the utility loss from reducing A (by 19 utility units).

So *marginal* utility is the critical factor in measuring utility losses and gains. The last units of A purchased are not "utility bargains" as compared with C, even though C's price is higher. But of course prices are important. What you must ask is really this: Are the three commodities offering equally good "utility bargains per dollar of outlay"—at the margin? If they are, then utility is maximized.

a. This means dividing each *MU* by the price of the commodity. Do this in Table 22-3.

b. Remember this:

▶ The *problem* is to find the highest attainable total of utility units which, given the stated ABC prices, $52 will buy.

▶ The rule for solving the problem is to find that ABC combination which makes marginal utility per dollar the same for all of A, B, and C.

Table 22-3 has several such equal-utility combinations. For example, circle the *MU*-per-dollar figures in this table for 6 of A, 5 of B, and 5 of C. Each figure circled is 10.

Now do the same for 8 of A, 6 of B, 8 of C (a common *MU* / $ of 5). Repeat for 12 of A, 8 of B, 9 of C (a common *MU* / $ of 3).

Only one of these ABC combinations satisfies the further requirement that it can be bought for just $52. Which one?

c. To summarize: Given the specified ABC prices, and this particular consumer's utility schedules, the best-possible

Table 22-1. Total Satisfaction, Measured in Utility Units, Derived from Consumption of:

	1 Unit	2 Units	3 Units	4 Units	5 Units	6 Units	7 Units	8 Units	9 Units	10 Units	11 Units	12 Units
A	50	120	200	240	258	268	275	280	285	289	293	296
B	400	700	900	1,000	1,020	1,030	1,038	1,044	1,048	1,050	1,051	1,052
C	70	130	180	225	265	300	328	348	360	366	370	373

Table 22-2. Marginal Satisfaction or Utility, Measured in Utility Units, When Consumption Is:

	1 Unit	2 Units	3 Units	4 Units	5 Units	6 Units	7 Units	8 Units	9 Units	10 Units	11 Units	12 Units
A	50	70	80	40								
B	400	300	200									
C	70	60										

Table 22-3. Marginal Utility Units per Dollar of Outlay (MU Divided by Price of the Commodity), When Consumption Is:

	1 Unit	2 Units	3 Units	4 Units	5 Units	6 Units	7 Units	8 Units	9 Units	10 Units	11 Units	12 Units
A	50	70	80	40								
B	200	150	100									
C	17.5	15										

ABC combination for an expenditure of $52 is 8 of A, 6 of B, and 8 of C. Table 22-1 indicates that the total number of utility units attained from this ABC combination is (1,030 / 1,658 / 3,050) units.

In the given circumstances of budget and prices, this is the maximum attainable number of utility units. Suppose, e.g., that the consumer experiments by cutting his C purchases from 8 units to 7. This saves him $4, which he uses to buy 2 extra units of commodity B. Combining the reduced total utility from lower C purchases with the increase from higher B purchases, the net change in total utility would be (an increase / a decrease) of _____ unit(s).

a. A: same as Table 22-2; B: 50, 10, 5, 4, 3, 2, 1, 0.5, 0.5; C: 12.5, 11.25, 10, 8.75, 7, 5, 3, 1.5, 1, 0.75. *b.* 8 of A, 6 of B, 8 of C. *c.* 1,658 units; a decrease of 6 units.

5. *a.* Formally stated, the ABC maximum-utility consumer-satisfaction rule given in the text is:

_____ .

b. In the equilibrium of question 4, the ratio of MU / p would be for A _____ / _____, for B _____ / _____, and for C

_____ / _____. Hence (disregarding any drop in marginal utility occurring within fractions of a commodity unit), the number of utility units bought by the very last dollar spent on each commodity would be the same for all, namely, _____ units per dollar.

a. $\dfrac{MU_A}{p_A} = \dfrac{MU_B}{p_B} = \dfrac{MU_C}{p_C}$ *b.* 5/$1; 10/$2; 20/$4; 5.

6. *a.* This consumer suffers a cut in his spendable income from $52 to $36 per week. In the table below, fill in the details of his new equilibrium position. The heading "MU / $," in the right-hand column, means "number of utility units bought with the marginal or last dollar of expenditure."

Quantity Purchased	Price	Expenditure	Marginal Utility	MU/$
A _____	$1	_____	_____	_____
B _____	2	_____	_____	_____
C _____	4	_____	_____	_____

b. The price of commodity C falls from $4 to $3. The other prices are unchanged. The consumer again spends $52 weekly. Show his equilibrium position.

Quantity Purchased	Price	Expenditure	Marginal Utility	MU/$
A _____	$1	_____	_____	_____
B _____	2	_____	_____	_____
C _____	3	_____	_____	_____

a. A: 6 units, $6, 10, 10; B: 5 units, $10, 20, 10; C: 5 units, $20, 40, 10.

b. A: 11 units, $11, 4, 4; B: 7 units, $14, 8, 4; C: 9 units, $27, 12, 4.

7. *a.* The income cut of question 6*a* illustrates in part the "leftward shift" of the consumer demand curve caused by an income drop. Formerly this consumer bought _____ units of A. After his income drop, even though A's price is unchanged, his purchases are only _____ units. In Chapter 20 language, this is a decrease in *(demand / quantity demanded)*.

b. The reduction in C's price in question 6*b* illustrates, with respect to C, an increase in *(demand / quantity demanded)*.

That is, out of the utility background, we can identify consumer demand curves. For example, with a budget of $52, and with A's and B's prices $1 and $2 respectively, this consumer will buy _____ units of C if its price is $4, and _____ units if its price is $3. Other points on the C demand curve would be derived by taking other C prices.

a. 8; 6; demand. *b.* quantity demanded; 8; 9.

8. The relation between utilities of commodities B and C in Table 22-1 illustrates something of Adam Smith's "paradox of value." Smith was interested in the fact that commodity prices often are poor indicators of the true relative usefulness of commodities. Thus water, which is essential for life, is cheap; diamonds, which have no such status, are expensive.

Our consumer, in the equilibrium of question 4, is buying _____ units of B and _____ units of C. In this position, the *total* utility of B is _____ units, and the *total* utility of C is _____ units. Measured in terms of total utility furnished, B is the more useful or desirable of the two commodities. Yet the market sets a higher price per unit on C.

The explanation is that market prices are influenced by *(marginal / total)* utility. The *(marginal / total)* utility of extra units of a commodity such as B declines sharply after a certain total quantity is consumed. If the supply offered is sufficiently large, consumers will bid a price for extra units of B reckoned only in terms of its low *(marginal / total)* utility, and this price will hold for the entire supply. If B's supply were sufficiently reduced, its price *(would rise very sharply / would rise a little but not much / would·fall)*. The "utility bargain" consumers

get from purchasing a commodity with high *total* utility at a low price is termed:

_____ .

6 of B; 8 of C; 1,030; 348; marginal; marginal; marginal; would rise very sharply; consumer's surplus.

9. *a.* Back in Chapter 4, the text spoke of the two "effects" which explain why, if the price of a commodity falls, more of it is bought (or why less is bought if price rises). (See Study Guide p. 29, question 5.) These "effects" are introduced once again in this chapter. Specifically, they are (i) the *(substitution / institutional)* effect, and (ii) the *(envy / income)* effect.

In this question and the one following, we use the idea of marginal utility to examine in more detail the nature of these two effects. The table below is similar in general construction to Tables 22-1 and 22-2. It shows the levels of marginal utility *(MU)* and total utility *(TU)* associated with different quantities of commodities X and Y, measured in satisfaction units, as some particular consumer measures satisfaction. (Commodities X and Y are the only ones this consumer can buy, or the only ones in which she is interested.)

No. Units Consumed	MU of X	TU of X	MU of Y	TU of Y
3	32	348	20	130
4	28	376	18	148
5	24	400	16	164
6	20	420	14	178
7	16	436	12	190
8	12	448	10	200
9	8	456	8	208
10	5	461	5	213
11	3	464	3	216

b. Suppose that the prices of X and of Y are $2.40 and $1.00 respectively, and that the consumer has just $20 per period to spend. What will be her equilibrium or maximum-satisfaction X-Y choice? (Look in the table for an X-Y combination with MUs which stand in the 24:10 or 12:5 ratio. When you find such a combination, see if it can be bought for just $20. If not, look for another one which can be so bought.) In this situation, our consumer will buy _____ units of X and _____ units of Y. The total of satisfaction units she obtains, from X and Y combined, will be _____.

c. Now let the price of X drop from $2.40 to $1. The price of Y is still $1, and our consumer still has $20 to spend. What will be her new "equilibrium position"? (Since the prices of X and Y are now equal, look for an X-Y combination with equal MUs, purchasable for just $20.) The consumer will now buy _____ units of X, as compared with 5 previously, and will now buy _____ units of Y, as compared with 8 previously.

Thus in the new situation, the X quantity has *(increased / decreased)*. This is not surprising, since X's price has fallen. The Y quantity has *(increased / decreased)*. Why this should happen is not so immediately obvious. Y's price has not fallen; indeed in relative terms—relative to the price of X—that price has risen.

d. What has happened is that our consumer was spending considerably more than half her income on X. Thus a reduction in X's price had an effect similar to a substantial rise in her income—as witness the rise in her total satisfaction level, from the original total of 600 units to *(620 / 664 / 670 / 674)* units. With what is equivalent to a larger income, our consumer buys more of X—and more of Y.

When X's price falls, there are thus *two* resulting effects which operate upon Y purchases. Insofar as X and Y are substitutes, the consumer will be disposed to buy *(more / less)* of Y. But countering this is the "income effect" just discussed, which inclined her to buy *(more / less)*. In this case, the "income effect" won out over the "substitution effect." Had X and Y been to a greater extent substitutes, the Y quantity would have fallen instead of rising.

a. substitution; income. *b.* 5; 8; 600. *c.* 10; 10; increased; increased. *d.* 674; less; more.

10. (If you find this question puzzling or difficult on your first approach to this chapter, disregard it.) Insofar as X and Y are substitutes, we would expect any reduction in X's price to *reduce* purchases of Y. But as question 9 has just indicated, this "substitution effect" may be blurred or concealed by an "income effect"—the rise in the consumer's real income, as indicated by the rise in her satisfaction level. To get at "the pure substitution effect," uncomplicated by any income effect, we would have to (i) give our consumer the reduction in the price of X, but concurrently (ii) lower her money income by just enough to permit her (with the lower X price) to just maintain her original satisfaction level. This we now do.

a. The price of X drops from $2.40 to $1—and concurrently, the consumer's budget or income drops from $20 to $12. (The price of Y remains at $1 throughout.)

The top and bottom lines in the table below summarize the two situations discussed in question 9. In the blank spaces in the middle line, fill in the detail of the "equilibrium situation" required by the conditions just outlined.

Budget	X Price	Y Price	X Quantity	Y Quantity	Satisfaction Units
$20	$2.40	$1.00	5	8	600
$12	$1.00	$1.00	___	___	___
$20	$1.00	$1.00	10	10	674

Compare the top line with the one you have just completed. X's price has fallen, but so has income. The consumer

adjusts her purchases as best she can to the new conditions. When she has done so, her satisfaction level *(has risen / is unchanged / has fallen)*. There is no "income effect" arising from the lower X price, because the consumer's money income is deliberately (if temporarily) squeezed by just enough to keep her real income constant.

Compare purchases in these two situations. Purchases of X *(rise / fall)* from 5 to *(3 / 7 / 10)*. This is the "pure substitution effect" (of the reduction in X's price) upon X purchases. Purchases of Y *(rise / fall)* from 8 to *(5 / 7 / 10)*. This is the "pure substitution effect" on Y purchases. We get what we would expect if X and Y are substitutes and X's price falls: *(an increase / a reduction)* in Y purchases.

b. Now we return our consumer to her $20 income (with the reduced price of X still in effect). This means we compare the middle line in the table with the third line. Purchases of X rise from 7 to 10; those of Y, from 5 to 10. These are the "income effects" of the reduction in X's price. All we have done is to "break apart" the price reduction of question 9. First we observe the results of the pure substitution effect (comparing top line with middle one); then the results of the income effect alone (comparing the middle line with the bottom one). In question 9, we went straight from the top to the bottom line (the two effects combined) without any intermediate pause.

To summarize, with matters still put in terms of a reduction in the price of X: Given such an X-price reduction, the substitution effect tends to *(increase / leave unchanged / decrease)* X purchases, and to *(increase / leave unchanged / decrease)* Y purchases. The income effect of such a price reduction (with a small qualification noted below) tends to *(increase / leave unchanged / decrease)* X purchases, and to *(increase / leave unchanged / decrease)* Y purchases.

The qualification mentioned concerns "inferior goods." By definition, a "normal good" is one of which the consumer wants to buy *more* as his or her income increases; an "inferior good," to buy less. Thus, as to the small category of inferior goods, the income effect works in the opposite direction. The implications of all this are discussed more fully in intermediate price-theory texts.

a. 7; 5; 600; is unchanged; rise; 7; fall; 5; a reduction.
b. increase; decrease; increase; increase.

11. A consumer has $50 per week to spend, all of it on commodity X (price $5) and commodity Y (price $4).

For each of the four cases below, indicate, if you can, whether or not this consumer is "at equilibrium," i.e., if he is deriving the maximum attainable satisfaction. If you lack sufficient information to answer, explain why. If you know he is not at equilibrium, indicate the direction in which he should move, e.g., buy more of X and less of Y, less of X and more of Y, more of both, etc. (Any increase in purchases of either commodity would increase total utility but would decrease *MU*—

i.e., the utility schedules follow the same general pattern indicated in Tables 22-1 and 22-2.)

a. He now buys 2 of X and 10 of Y. Total utility of X at this level is considered to be 500 utility units; total utility of Y, 400 units.

_____ .

b. He now buys 6 of X and 5 of Y. Total utility of X at this level is considered to be 400 utility units; marginal utility *(MU)* of X, 60 units; total utility of Y, 800 units; *MU* of Y, 30 units.

_____ .

c. He now buys 6 of X and 5 of Y. *MU* of X at this level is considered to be 25 units; *MU* of Y, 20 units.

_____ .

d. He now buys 6 of X and 4 of Y. *MU* of X at this level is considered to be 25 units; *MU* of Y, 20 units.

_____ .

a. Impossible to tell; *MU*s are not given. *b.* Buy more of X, less of Y. *c.* Now at equilibrium. *d.* Buy more of both. *MU*s are balanced with prices, but not all income is spent.

QUIZ: Multiple Choice

1. *By the "marginal utility" of a commodity is meant* (1) an indication of the last use to which the commodity has been put, or the use to which it would next be put if more were available; (2) the same thing as the price of that commodity; (3) the relationship which the total utility of that commodity bears to the total utility of all other commodities that are consumed; (4) the extra utility yielded by each successive last unit consumed of that commodity; (5) the same thing as total utility.

2. *The "paradox of value," with respect to prices and consumer purchases, refers to the following:* (1) Prices of commodities are not always proportional to the total satisfaction they give us, as witness the fact that some absolute necessities of life are cheap. (2) It is impossible to explain the price of a commodity either in terms of demand factors alone or supply factors alone. (3) It is impossible to explain why people's tastes are what they are, or why they vary from one person to the next. (4) Some consumers tend to value commodities according to their price, even to the point of buying more if price goes up. (5) None of the above.

3. The *"income-effect"* as used in explaining the law of *downward-sloping demand means that* (1) if people's money incomes fall, they will normally purchase less of any given commodity; (2) any fall in price of a good purchased has an effect similar to a small rise in people's incomes, and this may prompt them to buy a little more of that good; (3) the amount purchased of certain goods known as "inferior goods" may

actually decrease as people's incomes rise; (4) as people's incomes rise, they save proportionally more out of income; hence they actually spend a smaller fraction of their income; (5) if the price of a good drops, it is as though the prices of all other goods had risen, in relative terms; hence slightly less of those other goods will tend to be bought.

4. *An "inferior good," by definition, is one* (1) which consumers will not buy, except at a very low price; (2) whose quantity purchased would decrease if its price should fall; (3) whose marginal utility is either zero or negative; (4) whose quantity purchased would decrease if the consumer's income should rise; (5) not properly described by any of the preceding.

5. *The meaning of "equilibrium position," as this term is used with respect to consumer behavior, may properly be described as follows: It is* (1) that position at which, given existing prices, the consumer would need a larger income in order to reach a higher satisfaction level; (2) always that position which the consumer is actually occupying; (3) the position to which the consumer would wish to move if only he had sufficient extra income; (4) that position at which the consumer has no desire to have any more of any commodity; (5) that position at which the consumer has no desire to have any more of any of the commodities he is now buying.

6. *When the consumer "equilibrium position" discussed in question 5 is attained, then (with "satisfaction" measured in the consumer's own personal measure of satisfaction units)* (1) the total satisfaction derived from each commodity must equal the total satisfaction derived from every other commodity; (2) the ratio between total satisfaction derived from any commodity and the price of that commodity must be equal for all commodities; (3) the satisfaction derived from the last tiny unit of each commodity bought must be equal as among all commodities; (4) the ratio between total satisfaction derived from any commodity and the total expenditure on that commodity must be equal for all commodities; (5) none of the preceding descriptions is necessarily correct.

7. *A consumer's demand curve for any given commodity is most likely to shift to the right (or upward) with* (1) a rise in the price of substitutes, or a fall in the price of complements; (2) a rise in the price of either substitutes or complements; (3) a fall in the price of substitutes, or a rise in the price of complements; (4) a fall in the price of either substitutes or complements; (5) none of these cases.

8. *A consumer has $20 per week available to spend as he wishes on commodities A and B. The prices of these commodities, the quantities he now buys, and his evaluation of the utility provided by these quantities, are as follows:*

	Price	Units Bought	Total Utility	Marginal Utility
A	70¢	20	500	30
B	50¢	12	1,000	20

For maximum satisfaction, this consumer should (1) buy less of A, more of B; (2) buy same quantity of A, more of B; (3) buy more of A, less of B; (4) buy more of A, same quantity of B; (5) remain in his present position, since that position is the best-attainable one.

9. *The price of good X falls. The income-effect (if any) of this price change* (1) will normally cause X purchases to be increased; (2) will normally cause X purchases to be decreased; (3) may cause X purchases either to increase or to decrease, there being no "normal" consequence; (4) by definition, neither increases nor decreases X purchases; (5) will not apply, since income-effects refer to changes in spendable income, not to price changes.

10. *If the marginal utility of a commodity is zero, then* (1) total utility for this commodity has reached a maximum; (2) the commodity in question has no utility, i.e., it is not one that consumers want to use; (3) the paradox of value must be involved; (4) the consumer has reached his equilibrium position with respect to purchase of this commodity; (5) total utility for this commodity must be zero also.

11. *Four of the following five statements are reasonably accurate in the sense of conforming to what the text says regarding "utility," "total utility," and "marginal utility." One is false—i.e., it runs counter to the text's ideas. Which one?* (1) Two different consumers may place quite different utility measures upon the same commodity, or upon the same quantity of that commodity. (2) When total utility reaches its maximum, marginal utility must be zero. (3) The "utility" idea is an attempt to indicate how the consumer evaluates the satisfaction derived from commodities purchasable. (4) Total utilities may differ from one consumer to the next, but marginal utilities must be the same for both. (5) Utilities as here employed must be "additive"—i.e., for any one consumer you can add together the total utilities derived from particular quantities of goods X and Y.

12. *A consumer gradually increases the quantity of good X which he consumes per period of time, until finally he reaches the level at which he is satiated with respect to X. Through this sequence of increases,* (1) total utility from X always remains constant, whereas marginal utility gradually falls; (2) both total and marginal utility remain constant, up to the satiation level; (3) total utility always rises, whereas marginal utility gradually falls; (4) total utility may fall, but if so, marginal utility rises; (5) both total and marginal utility may fall.

13. *The price of good X is $1.50 and that of good Y $1. If a particular consumer considers the marginal utility of Y to be*

30 units, and he is in equilibrium with respect to purchases of X and Y, then he must consider the marginal utility of X to be (1) 15 units; (2) 20 units; (3) 30 units; (4) 45 units; (5) none of the above necessarily—information given is insufficient to tell.

14. *If, in question 13, the figure of 30 units had been the total (rather than marginal) utility of Y, which alternative would be correct with respect to the total utility of X?* (1). (2). (3). (4). (5).

15. *A consumer regards goods X and Y as substitutes. If the price of good X rises and there is some "income effect" from the price rise, that effect must (barring the special case of an inferior good) incline the consumer to alter his purchases of good Y as follows: to* (1) increase them; (2) decrease them; (3) leave them unchanged; (4) increase them if the price of X exceeds that of Y, otherwise to decrease them; (5) do none of the above necessarily, since there is no rule as to the consequence of an income effect.

16. *Which alternative in question 15 would be correct had that question referred to an increase in the price of X and to the resulting effect upon the consumer's purchases of Y—but to the "substitution effect," not to the "income effect"?* (1). (2). (3). (4). (5).

17. *An individual shifts to a new equilibrium position as a result of some change either in market prices or in her income. In this new equilibrium situation, marginal utilities are all lower than they were in the old situation. Her tastes or preferences are (in utility terms) unchanged. This means that* (1) she is definitely worse off in her new situation; (2) she is definitely better off in her new situation; (3) she is definitely worse off than in her old situation if her income has changed, but not otherwise; (4) she is definitely better off than in her old situation if prices have changed, but not otherwise; (5) she may be better off or worse off in her new situation—no information given points to either one or the other.

18. *The idea of "consumer's surplus" pertains to the fact that* (1) in some purchases, the gain consumers obtain from buying exceeds the gain suppliers obtain from selling; (2) the purchase of many goods is an immense bargain to consumers, for, if necessary, they would pay far more than they actually do in order to get them; (3) the marginal utility of the first units of a product consumed may considerably exceed the total utility which this product supplies; (4) total utility increases either when consumer incomes rise or when the prices they must pay for goods fall; (5) when demand is inelastic with respect to price, buyers can obtain a larger quantity for the expenditure of less money.

APPENDIX: Geometrical Analysis of Consumer Equilibrium

This Appendix deals with the same central problem discussed in the chapter: How a consumer must go about trying to make the most of a given budget or

income if he or she is faced with a given set of consumer-good prices and has given tastes.

Only the illustrative method is different. Here, it is

the "indifference-curve" approach. By this method, the whole problem of "maximizing satisfaction" (when dealing with tastes, prices, and income) can be illustrated on a single graph. To be sure, the graph deals with a very simple case, one in which only *two* goods are involved. But this still reveals with clarity the nature of the *general* problem, where choice is between many goods and services. (The indifference-curve approach is not limited to simple two-good cases. But this case is the only one you need worry about here.)

Indifference-curve treatment has a further advantage. It avoids the assumption that consumers put numerical "utility values" onto each quantity of each commodity, an assumption which many economists (not unreasonably) dislike.

1. "Indifference curves" are intended to portray a consumer's tastes.

a. Any single indifference-curve line, such as that in text Fig. 22-5, is made up of a series of points. Each point on such a line stands for a different *(amount of money / level of satisfaction / combination of two commodities)*. What these points— all the points on any one line—have in common is that they all represent the same *(amount of money / level of satisfaction / combination of two commodities)*, in the eyes of this consumer.

b. We can draw on a consumer's "indifference map" *(only one / a few / an infinite number of)* indifference lines. As to any two such indifference curves, the one lying farther from the graph's origin—i.e., farther to the northeast—must stand for the *(higher / same / lower)* level of satisfaction. [On text Fig. 22-6, draw lightly a 45° line from the origin (bottom left-hand corner) of the graph. The four points at which this line crosses the four indifference curves mark four different clothing-food combinations. The farther out the indifference curve, the bigger is the clothing-food combination on that line.]

c. If two *different* clothing-food combinations lie on the same indifference curve—i.e., if they indicate the *same* satisfaction level for a consumer—the second must represent more food and less clothing (or vice versa) than the first. (You cannot be at the same level of satisfaction as before if you have more food *and* more clothing, or if you have less food *and* less clothing.) This is indicated by the fact that any single indifference curve runs in a generally *(northeast-to-southwest / northwest-to-southeast)* direction.

a. combination of two commodities; level of satisfaction. *b.* an infinite number of; higher. *c.* northwest-to-southeast.

2. *a.* Now set aside for a moment the indifference-curve idea—i.e., the representation of a consumer's tastes. Turn, instead, to what the consumer *could* buy (regardless of his

tastes), if possessed of a given income and faced with a particular set of prices.

In the simple two-good case here discussed, all the possible combinations purchasable (with a given income and with given prices) can be represented by a straight line on a graph—the "budget line" or "consumption-possibility line" in the text's Fig. 22-7.

Be sure you understand the information which this budget or consumption-possibility line is intended to convey. Each and any point on this line stands for a different *(amount of money income / level of satisfaction / combination of the two commodities)*. The combinations are all different, but they all have one thing in common, namely that, given the prices specified, they all *(are purchasable for the same money income amount / stand for the same level of satisfaction)*.

b. So the consumer can move up or down this budget line as he wishes; all points thereon are equal so far as the expenditure of money income is concerned. Which point should he choose? That is a matter of his tastes. In the matter of the satisfaction they yield, the various food-clothing combinations on the budget line are *not* equal. The consumer should pick the combination which he likes most—or in more elegant terms, which " maximizes his satisfaction."

The mention of tastes pulls us back to indifference curves again. The task of moving back and forth along the budget line, seeking the maximum-satisfaction food-clothing combination, is just a matter of finding the point on this budget line which reaches the *(highest- / lowest-)* attainable indifference curve. This is illustrated in text Fig. 22-8. The highest-attainable indifference curve is always the one which lies farthest to the *(northeast / southwest)* on an ordinary graph.

a. combination of the two commodities; are purchasable for the same money income. *b.* highest-; northeast.

3. Studying text Fig. 22-8, you will see that point B therein, the consumer's equilibrium or maximum-satisfaction point, is one at which the indifference curve is just tangent to the budget or consumption-possibility line. That is, equilibrium is a situation where the slope of the one line matches the slope of the other. (As to the meaning of "slope," turn back, if necessary, to Study Guide p. 7.)

It happens that the slope of the budget line is a matter of the prices of the two commodities involved. This question explores the matter more fully. (If it causes you difficulty on your first survey, leave this question aside.)

The slope of the line in text Fig. 22-8 (neglecting its negative sign) is 6/4, or 1½. At the two extreme positions, the consumer could have either 6 of C and zero F (point N), or 4 of F and zero C (point M). If he moves any distance down the line from point N, he finds that this 6/4 (or 3/2) swapping ratio applies. If he moves from N to the middle dot on NM, he must give up 3 units of C, but he gains 2 units of F.

The prices of F and C govern this swapping ratio. Giving up 3 units of C (price $1) recovers $3 of his budget. This he can use to buy 2 units of F (price $1.50). So, whether measured as 6/4, 3/2, or $1.50/$1, the slope measures market swapping terms. (But note that when we switch from quantities to prices, C and F change places. You can buy the commodity with the *lower* price in *greater* quantity.)

If the budget is $40, with prices of C and of F as indicated below, show the slope of the consumption-possibility line first as a ratio C/F, then as a ratio p_F/p_c. F (food) is the horizontal-axis commodity, as in the text. (All slope values are assumed to be preceded by a negative sign.)

	Ratio C/F	Ratio p_F/p_C
a. p_C = $1, p_F = $4	____ / ____	____ / ____
b. p_C = $5, p_F = $2	____ / ____	____ / ____
c. p_C = $2, p_F = $10	____ / ____	____ / ____

a. 40 / 10, $4 / $1. *b.* 8 / 20, $2 / $5. *c.* 20 / 4, $10 / $2.

4. The text chapter Appendix concludes with a brief survey of the effects of a change in income or in price upon the consumer's equilibrium position.

a. Consider income changes first. If the consumer's income is halved (as in the text example), he must cut down on his purchases. The income cut means—look at text Fig. 22-9—a shift of the budget line to the *(northeast / southwest)*. The new half-the-income budget line *(is / is not)* parallel to the old one.

Note that in his new and painful income situation, our consumer will not necessarily buy food and clothing in the same proportions as before. He must cut his purchases, and may indeed cut each of them by 50 per cent. (In the text illustration, he does just this.) But the point he picks upon his new budget line will be governed, as before, by his tastes. He may wind up buying relatively more food and less clothing, or vice versa.

b. An increase in the price of food or of clothing works somewhat like an income reduction: It pulls the consumer down to a lower satisfaction level. But compare text Fig. 22-10 (illustrating an increase in the price of food) with text Fig. 22-9 (income reduction). In both instances, the budget line shifts in position. But in Fig. 22-10, unlike 22-9, the new budget line *(is / is not)* parallel with the old one. The point is that if the consumer wanted to spend *all* his income on clothing, a food-price increase would not affect him. Point N (text Fig. 22-10) is still attainable. At the other extreme, if he wanted to spend all his income on food, a doubling of the food price would *(leave him unaffected / require him to halve his purchases)*.

That is why the budget line shifts as it does. And as before,

the consumer picks the best-attainable position on the new budget line, as his tastes dictate.

There is much more to be said on these topics, but it must be left for more advanced texts.

a. southwest; is. *b.* is not; require him to halve his purchases.

QUIZ: Multiple Choice

1. *The position and shape of any indifference curve for any particular consumer are governed* (1) by his tastes and by the amount of his income; (2) solely by the prices of the goods he is buying; (3) by his tastes, by the amount of his income, and by the prices of the goods he is buying; (4) by the prices of the goods he is buying and by the amount of his income, not by his tastes; (5) solely by his tastes.

2. *Which alternative in question 1 correctly names the factor or factors governing the consumption-possibility line?* (1). (2). (3). (4). (5).

3. *On his indifference-curve map, a consumer's approach to his equilibrium position is properly described as follows: He* (1) moves to that point on his consumption-possibility line representing the combination of goods having the highest money value; (2) moves to that point on the consumption-possibility line whose slope equals the ratio of the two prices; (3) moves along the consumption-possibility line until the extra utility supplied by one good is just equal to the extra utility supplied by the other; (4) picks the highest-valued indifference curve which his consumption-possibility line will permit him to reach; (5) picks the highest-valued consumption-possibility line which his indifference curve will permit him to reach.

4. *One of the following statements with respect to indifference-curve analysis of consumer behavior is incorrect, namely, that* (1) each point on an indifference curve stands for a different combination of two goods; (2) each point on a consumption-possibility line stands for a different combination of two goods; (3) all points on an indifference curve stand for the same level of real income in the sense of satisfaction; (4) all points on a consumption-possibility line stand for the same level of money income; (5) all points on an indifference curve stand for the same level of money income.

QUIZ: Other

In the upper part of Fig. 22-1, the line AB_0 is a consumer's "budget line," and E_0 is his equilibrium point thereon. The curved line is an indifference curve for this consumer, and it is tangent to the budget line at this E_0 point. (The two other curved lines are also indifference curves.) The price of good X is $4.

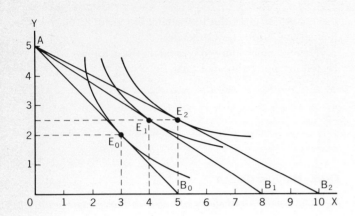

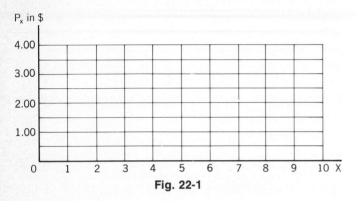

Fig. 22-1

1. The price of good Y must be *(a)* $1; *(b)* $2; *(c)* $3; *(d)* $4; *(e)* $5; *(f)* impossible to tell from diagram.

2. The consumer's income or budget must be *(a)* $50; *(b)* $20; *(c)* $10; *(d)* $5; *(e)* $2; *(f)* impossible to tell.

3. The "budget" or consumption-possibility line shifts from position AB_0 to position AB_1. Such a shift could only be caused by *(a)* a fall in the price of X; *(b)* a rise in the price of X; *(c)* a rise in the price of Y; *(d)* a fall in the price of Y; *(e)* an increase in income.

4. Quantitatively, what change is indicated by the shift from AB_0 to AB_1? That is, whether it is price of X, price of Y, or income that has changed, what is its new value? *(a)* $50; *(b)* $20; *(c)* $10; *(d)* $5; *(e)* $2.50; *(f)* $2; *(g)* $1.

5. If a further shift in the AB line occurs, from AB_1 to AB_2, which alternative in question 3 explains it? *(a / b / c / d / e)*

6. Which alternative in question 4 indicates the new value of the magnitude which has changed? ....*(a / b / c / d / e / f / g)*

7. Use the lower part of Fig. 22-1 to show the demand curve of the consumer in the preceding questions for commodity X. This demand curve is to be drawn given the particular level of income and price of good Y indicated by the preceding questions. Plot three points on this curve, correctly indicating the consumer's demand for X in these circumstances. (HINT: What price or prices of X must go with the three consumption-possibility lines illustrated? What quantity or quantities of X does he buy?) Join these three points with a smooth curve.

23 COMPETITIVE SUPPLY

CHAPTER 22 dealt with the background of the demand curve. This present chapter begins discussion of the factors which influence supply.

It is essential for you to understand that this chapter deals exclusively with one case: that of "pure" or "perfect" competition. In this very special situation:

▶ The firm is faced with a market price over which it has no control. It is too small in relation to the market in which it sells to be able to affect that price.

▶ It can sell as much or as little as it pleases at that price. It has no selling problems and no selling costs (only production costs).

▶ Its task as a "profit maximizer" is to select that particular output for sale which will yield it the highest-attainable profit (at the given market price).

1. *a.* The text refers to both "the firm" and "the industry"; the difference between these terms is important. The individual unit producing and selling output in the hope of making a profit for its owners is the *(firm / industry)*, and its supply curve shows what this unit would offer for sale at each possible price. The total of all individual units together is the *(firm / industry)*, and the supply curve of this aggregate shows total quantity that will be offered for sale by all these units combined.

b. A "competitive firm," as the term is used in this chapter, means one operating under the special conditions of pure (or perfect) competition. Remember carefully what was said above: *In these conditions, the firm can choose the quantity of output it is going to produce and sell, and it is assumed to choose the quantity which (given the market price offered) yields it the highest-attainable profit.*

"Profit" here means (pick one):
(1) Total Cost incurred in producing output minus Total Revenue or income from selling that output.
(2) Total Revenue or income from selling output, without regard to costs incurred.
(3) Total Revenue or income from selling output, minus Total Cost incurred in producing that output.

"Profit" means, then, the revenue that you take in from sales of your product, minus the costs incurred in producing that product.

a. firm; industry. *b.* (3).

2. The terms "revenue" and "cost" are used extensively in the next few chapters; so this question reviews them carefully.

Revenue, or Total Revenue, means total number of units sold, multiplied by the market price at which they were sold. In Income Statement terms (Appendix to Chapter 6), it is Net Sales.

Total Cost means all costs incurred in producing and selling that output. Total Cost has two parts:

(1) Variable Costs—meaning *those costs whose total amount varies with the amount of output produced.* For example, direct labor cost is a cost whose total amount will rise as the amount of output rises; this is a Variable Cost.

(2) Fixed Costs—meaning *those costs which are fixed in amount regardless of the level of output* and which would accordingly have to be paid by the firm *even if its output were zero.* Interest on a bond issue is a cost the firm must pay whether it is operating at zero output or at maximum capacity; this is a Fixed Cost.

The distinction between Fixed and Variable Costs turns out to be important and interesting. (Note that the text chapter discusses these concepts in the section Total Cost and Short-run Shutdown Conditions.) Sometimes you cannot understand a firm's situation and problems until you have grasped the distinction between these two kinds of cost.

In each space below, put V if you think the item would be a Variable Cost; put F if a Fixed Cost.
a. Cost of raw materials. ....( )
b. Depreciation on machinery, when quantity of output produced is considered to be the factor responsible for the amount of this cost. ....( )
c. Annual fire-insurance premium on buildings. ....( )
d. A sales tax levied on the firm on each unit of output sold. ....( )
e. Depreciation on machinery, when time rather than quantity of output produced is considered to be the factor principally responsible for the amount of this cost. ....( )
f. Salaries paid to supervisors on an annual basis. .....( )
g. Local property taxes on buildings. ....( )
h. Cost of electric power for machines. ....( )
i. Cost of maintaining the research department. ....( )

j. A royalty paid for the use of certain machines, paid according to number of units produced. ....( )

k. Extra pay for overtime work by labor. ....( )

a. V. *b.* V. *c.* F. *d.* V. *e.* F. *f.* F. *g.* F. *h.* V. *i.* F. *j.* V. *k.* V.

3. In Table 23-1, the figures in Columns (1) and (2) indicate the estimated Total Cost incurred in producing quantities of output from 0 to 20 units weekly for a particular firm. Fixed Cost is $50 per week.

a. In Column (3), complete the missing figures for Average Cost—i.e., cost per unit of output, or Total Cost divided by number of units produced. (Note that the text discusses Average Cost more fully in Chapter 24.)

Table 23-1

(1) Output	(2) Total Cost	(3) Average Cost	(4) Increase in Total Cost	(5) Marginal Cost
0	$50.00			
			$10.00	$5.00
2	60.00	$_____		
			10.00	5.00
4	70.00	17.50		
			10.00	5.00
6	80.00	13.33		
			_____	_____
8	90.00	_____		
			10.50	5.25
10	100.50	10.05		
			11.00	_____
12	111.50	_____		
			13.00	6.50
14	124.50	8.89		
			_____	_____
16	140.50	8.78		
			_____	11.00
18	162.50	_____		
			40.00	_____
20	202.50	10.13		

b. Table 23-1 indicates that, for this firm and this product, Average Cost reaches its minimum level at an output in the vicinity of *(10 / 12 / 14 / 16 / 18 / 20)* units.

c. In Column (4), complete the missing figures for increase in Total Cost—i.e., the rise in cost resulting from an increase from 0 to 2 units, from 2 to 4, etc. Notice that these figures are not lined up opposite 0, 2, 4 units, etc. Instead, they are set *between* 0 and 2, between 2 and 4, etc., to indicate that each figure marks the cost of moving from one output figure to the adjacent one. If output is increased from 2 units to 4, Total

Cost rises by $10; if it is reduced from 4 units to 2, Total Cost falls by $10.

The text emphasizes the importance of the concept of Marginal Cost. Column (4) is leading up to Marginal Cost for this product. But this column dealt with *two-unit* changes in output and cost—whereas Marginal Cost is a *per unit* cost figure.

▶ Marginal Cost is the *increase* in Total Cost resulting from a one-unit increase in output. Or it is the *decrease* in Total Cost resulting from a one-unit decrease in output.

d. Hence, to obtain Marginal Cost, the figures in Column (4) must be divided by 2. Complete the missing Marginal Cost figures in Column (5).

Note carefully that Marginal Cost, even though it is also a per unit cost measure, is not the same thing at all as Average Cost. Marginal Cost measures only the *change* in Total Cost resulting from the last unit produced, or that would result if one more unit were produced.

Because this table deals with two-unit output changes, Column (5) is not precisely accurate as a measure of Marginal Cost. If the table were enlarged to show unit-by-unit (rather than two-unit) changes, then, for example, the 8-to-9 Marginal Cost figure in Column (5) would be a little below $5.25, and the 9-to-10 figure a little above. But $5.25 is a reasonably close estimate for both.

a. $30;$11.25;$9.29;$9.03. *b.* 16. *c.* $10;$16;$22. *d.* $5; $5.50; $8; $20.

4. *a.* In Fig. 23-1, plot the Total Cost curve, using Columns (1) and (2) of Table 23-1 (i.e., plot the several points indicated by these columns; then join them with a smooth curve).

b. In Fig. 23-2, use Columns (1) and (3) to plot the Average Cost *(AC)* curve. Also in Fig. 23-2, use Columns (1) and (5) to plot the Marginal Cost *(MC)* curve. (Because the *MC* values are in-between points, record them opposite odd-numbered quantities of output—1, 3, 5, 7, etc.) Mark your two curves on Fig. 23-2 as *AC* and *MC* respectively.

c. Figure 23-2 indicates that (pick one or more):
(1) The *AC* curve, as it moves to the right, cuts through the bottom point of the *MC* curve.
(2) The *MC* curve, as it moves to the right, cuts through the bottom point of the *AC* curve.
(3) The *MC* curve, as it moves to the right, cuts through the *AC* curve, but not at its bottom point.
(4) The *AC* curve, as it moves to the right, cuts through the *MC* curve, but not at the *MC* curve's bottom point.

c. (2) and (4). (Note that this property of the *MC* curve—that it always cuts through the bottom point of the *AC* curve—is discussed more fully later on.)

Total cost in $

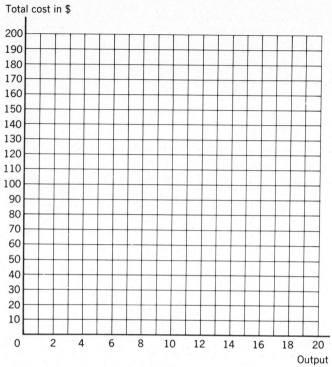

Fig. 23-1

AC, MC in $

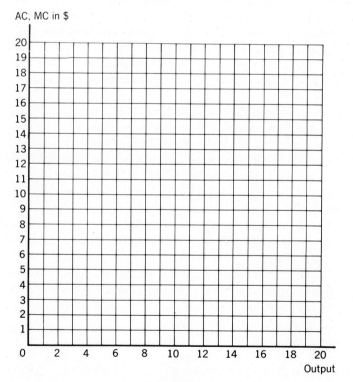

Fig. 23-2

5. Table 23-2 turns from Average and Marginal Costs to revenue from sales. It deals with two possible prices, $11.20 and $8.80. It shows the total income or revenue that would accrue at each of these two prices if various quantities of output (from 10 to 20) were produced and sold. (Revenue is price per unit multiplied by number of units sold.) Table 23-2

shows also Total Cost (from Table 23-1) of these outputs. And it shows the profit (Total Revenue minus Total Cost) that would result from each of these outputs.

Complete the blank spaces in this table.

Table 23-2

Quantity	Price: $11.20			Price: $8.80		
	Revenue	Total Cost	Profit	Revenue	Total Cost	Profit
10	$ ____	$100.50	$11.50	$ ____	$100.50	−$12.50
12	134.40	111.50	____	105.60	111.50	____
14	156.80	124.50	32.30	123.20	124.50	−1.30
16	179.20	140.50	____	140.80	140.50	____
18	201.60	162.50	39.10	158.40	162.50	−4.10
20	____	202.50	____	____	202.50	

Revenue at $11.20: $112, $224; Profit: $22.90, $38.70, $21.50.

Revenue at $8.80: $88, $176; Profit: −$5.90, $0.30, −$26.50.

6. *a.* Table 23-2 says that at price $11.20, Maximum-profit output quantity would be *(12 / 14 / 16 / 18 / 20)* units. At this output (from Table 23-1 or Fig. 23-2), Average Cost is

$_____. Figure 23-2 indicates that at this output *MC* would be approximately $_____. (NOTE: The fact that *MC* here *exceeds* $11.20 indicates that the true Maximum-profit output would be slightly less—say about 17¼ units. Tables 23-1 and 23-2 lack sufficient detail to indicate Maximum-profit output as precisely as this.)

b. At price $8.80, Maximum-profit output is *(12 / 14 / 16 / 18 / 20)* units, Average Cost is $_____, and *MC* is $_____, approximately.

a. 18; 9.03; 13. *b.* 16 units; 8.78; 8.80.

7. *a.* That is, at Maximum-profit output, price (P) and *(Average / Marginal)* Cost are equal. Think of the firm as expanding weekly output from 10 units to 11, from 11 to 12, and so on. As output quantity changes, the *AC* figure changes, and so does the *MC* figure. For maximum profit, the firm should halt output expansion when *(MC has fallen / AC has fallen / MC has risen / AC has risen)* to a level equal to price.

b. At price $8.80, it does not pay to produce and sell the seventeenth and eighteenth units that could be sold profitably at price $11.20. This is so because the firm has a plant of fixed size, and when its capacity output is approached, per-unit costs begin to rise. Specifically (see Table 23-1), Total Cost will rise by $(6.50 / 8 / 11 / 20) for each of the seventeenth and eighteenth units. The simple but basic point involved is this: In profit terms, it pays to produce and sell an extra unit of output only if the extra revenue that unit brings in (here, the price of that unit) exceeds the extra cost (Marginal Cost, the rise in Total Cost) which was incurred in producing and selling that extra output unit.

---

a. Marginal; *MC* has risen.   *b.*   11.

---

8.   *a.* To review: We have thus far established that if market price were $11.20, the firm would wish to supply *(10 / 12 / 14 / 16 / 18 / 20)* units weekly; if the price were $8.80, it would supply *(10 / 12 / 14 / 16 / 18 / 20)* units.

b. At the $11.20 price, its profit would be $_____, and at the $8.80 price, $_____.

[NOTE: Do not shed too many tears for the owner of this firm over his tiny profit at price $8.80. This figure does not reflect the total return for his effort. Table 23-1 listed costs of $140.50 incurred in producing output of 16 units weekly. These costs properly include (1) an interest return on such money as he has tied up in the business, and (2) an appropriate salary for his work in managing it. (See the text's discussion in Chapter 24 of "implicit-cost elements.") That is, he is doing slightly better than he would if he loaned his money elsewhere and sold his entrepreneurial services to someone else. Specifically, he is doing better by the princely sum of 30 cents weekly.]

---

a.   18; 16.   *b.*   39.10; 0.30.

---

9.   The relation between revenue, costs, and profit is most directly illustrated by a diagram such as Fig. 23-1. On it, draw the Total Revenue line for price of $11.20. (Just show the point that would indicate revenue from 2 units sold at $11.20 each, from 4 units so sold, etc. Then join your points.)

Total profit for any output is the distance vertically downward from the Total Revenue line *(TR)* to the Total Cost line *(TC)*. The search for Maximum-profit output is the search for the output level at which this distance is greatest.

Draw a similar *TR* line for price $8.80—and note that at most outputs, *TC* is then higher than *TR*, meaning that at any such output, a loss would be incurred. For identification, mark your first line $11.20 and your second $8.80.

Then draw two more lines for prices of $7 and $4.

Your four *TR* lines should be four straight lines radiating out from the origin, with $11.20 highest, $4 lowest.

---

10.   Clearly, if price falls much below $8.80, there will be no output at which the firm can do as much as to break even. In such circumstances, ought the firm to shut down (supply zero output) rather than incur a loss?

As preliminary to exploring this question, complete the missing figures in Table 23-3, showing *TR*, *TC*, and "negative profit" for various outputs at prices $7 and $4.

Table 23-3

Quantity	Price: $7			Price: $4		
	Revenue	Total Cost	Profit	Revenue	Total Cost	Profit
10	$70.00	$100.50	-$30.50	$40.00	$100.50	-$60.50
12	84.00	111.50	_____	48.00	111.50	_____
14	98.00	124.50	-26.50	56.00	124.50	-68.50
16	112.00	140.50	_____	64.00	140.50	_____
18	126.00	162.50	-36.50	72.00	162.50	-90.50
20	140.00	202.50	-62.50	80.00	202.50	-122.50

At $7: -$27.50; -$28.50. At $4: -$63.50; -$76.50.

---

11.   The point now to be stressed is this: Our firm cannot escape loss just by shutting down its operations. It has Fixed Cost of $50 (e.g., the interest which must be paid on a debenture issue), and it is stuck with this cost even when shut down—until or unless it goes bankrupt.

The all-encompassing profit-maximizing rule is this: *Do the best you can.* Pick the output that maximizes your profit. If market price is so low that there is no output yielding a positive profit, then minimize your loss. The worst that can happen is that you will incur a loss equal to your Fixed Cost—by shutting down. But if you can find an output level which, even though it incurs a loss, means a loss *less than* that Fixed Cost—then operate at that output.

a. Specifically, if market price is $7, application of this rule means that the firm should (pick one):
(1) Shut down.
(2) Operate at output 10, since a loss of $30.50 is preferable to a loss of $50.
(3) Operate at output 14, since loss at that output ($26.50) is lowest among the figures listed in Table 23-3, and is preferable to a $50 loss.

b. If market price were to be $4, the firm should *(operate at output 10 / operate at output 14 / shut down)*.

c. The general rule which emerges out of these considerations is the following (pick one):
(1) If there is some output at which loss would be less than the amount of Fixed Cost, produce and sell that output; shut down operations if loss exceeds Fixed Cost at all (non-zero) outputs.
(2) Shut down whenever there is no output at which it is possible to earn a profit or at least to break even.

(3) If there is some output at which loss would be greater than the amount of Fixed Cost, produce and sell that output; shut down operations if loss is less than Fixed Cost at all (nonzero) outputs.

So in summary, the two profit-maximizing rules are:

▶ Pick the output at which $MC = P$. This is the best possible (nonzero) operating output.

▶ If this best possible (nonzero) output yields a loss, compare this loss with Fixed Cost. If loss is less than Fixed Cost, operate at that output. If loss exceeds Fixed Cost, disregard the $MC = P$ rule, and shut down.

(WARNING: The first of these two rules, as stated above, applies only in the special case of pure or perfect competition taken up in this chapter. It is a special instance of a more general rule. When we turn to non-perfect competition, in Chapter 25, the same general reasoning applies; but the profit-maximizing rule is restated in a different and more general form.)

---

a. (3). *b.* shut down. *c.* (1).

---

12. An example may illustrate more fully the nature of the "Shutdown rule"—the second of the two rules above. Figure 23-3 depicts two different situations. The height of each block indicates the dollar value of revenue or of cost, when the firm is at its best-possible operating position. The two situations are *exactly* alike in respect to Total Revenue, Total Cost, and operating loss incurred. They differ only in the distribution of costs as between Fixed and Variable. The amount of Fixed Cost is larger, and that of Variable Cost is smaller, in situation *(1 / 2)*.

The Shutdown rule says the firm should cease production in situation *(1 / 2)*, and continue to operate despite loss in situation *(1 / 2)*. The reasoning behind this rule is just that set out at the beginning of question 11. You are stuck with a loss no matter what you do. The worst that can happen is that you incur a loss equal to Fixed Cost. But if you can find an operating level at which the revenue earned from sales more than covers your Variable Cost, then some part of that revenue remains to be applied against Fixed Cost—so that your loss is then less than Fixed Cost. The $P = MC$ rule is then *(still / not)* useful, because it *(will / will not)* indicate the minimum-loss operating level.

2; 1; 2; still; will

---

13. Figure 23-3, along with the discussion which ended the preceding question, suggests an alternative statement of the Shutdown rule. It is this: Shut down when Total Revenue (at the best-possible operating position) is *(less / greater)* than total Variable Cost.

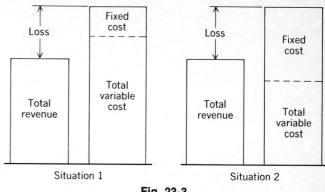

Situation 1   Situation 2
Fig. 23-3

There would be no great point in developing a second version of the Shutdown rule, were it not that this leads to a *third* version, and one that is often very useful. The blocks in Fig. 23-3 stand for *TR* and *TC* at some particular quantity of output (the one indicated by the $P = MC$ rule). Divide *TR* by that quantity of output, and we get price (since $TR = \text{price} \times \text{quantity}$). Divide total Variable Cost by quantity, and we get Average Variable Cost, or Variable Cost per unit of output.

So we could frame the Shutdown rule in a still different way: Shut down when market price *(exceeds / is less than)* Average Variable Cost.

The special significance of this alternative is that it is framed in *price* terms. It indicates the *particular price which is just sufficiently low that the firm then decides to stop supplying anything to the market.* A price which is *just equal* to Average Variable Cost is the razor's edge. The firm's supply curve "breaks" at this price. Below it, the firm shuts down.

---

less; is less than.

---

14. This question is a quick review of ground covered. The terms introduced in this chapter (Total Revenue, Total Cost, Fixed Cost, Variable Cost, Marginal Cost, etc.) have been used principally to establish one idea: how the supply curve of the individual producing firm will be determined, assuming the firm operates under conditions of pure (or perfect) competition and wants to maximize its profit.

a. The firm's primary profit-maximizing rule is: Pick the output level at which $MC = P$. This means that the firm's supply curve (i.e., the schedule of quantities it will want to sell at various possible prices) will be the same as its *(Marginal / Average)* Cost curve. (Study Fig. 23-2, if needed, to be sure you grasp this point.)

Under the specified conditions of pure (or perfect) competition, the firm has no control whatever over market price. But it can sell as much as it wishes at that price. In other words, *(price / quantity of output)* is the "variable" on which it can make a decision. The $P = MC$ rule is applied to this choice of *(price / output)*, since (when the firm's output is sufficiently increased) MC rises as output quantity rises.

b. The firm's second profit-maximizing (i.e., loss-minimizing) rule is: If, at the level of output at which $MC = P$, P turns out to be less than Average Variable Cost, then shut down operations—i.e., supply zero output. This means that the firm's supply curve—the schedule of quantities it will supply at each and any possible price—will correspond to the MC curve *(only down to / even beyond)* the critical minimum price.

c. So the bottom point on the firm's supply curve is at the price just equal to Average Variable Cost. This is the firm's "shutdown price" (see question 13). Run your eye *upward* from that bottom point on the supply curve, and you first pass through a range at which the firm would lose money if it had to sell at any of them. Nevertheless, *faced* with any such market price, it *would* sell, for the loss so incurred would be *(greater / less)* than the Fixed Cost loss which a shutdown would entail. In due course, you reach the "Break-even price," where price is just equal to Average Cost, and losses are zero. At any price *above* this Break-even level, the firm will earn a *(positive / negative)* profit.

---

a. Marginal; quantity of output; output.   *b.* only down to.
c. less; positive.

---

15. The underlying factor mentioned in the text which explains why Marginal Cost rises as production is increased

is: _____ .

If we are talking about production in a manufacturing plant, the "fixed" element which principally accounts for this effect is *(land / labor / plant and equipment / raw materials).*

The firm can of course plan for a different size of plant—perhaps in particular a larger plant, if there are "economies of scale" whereby with such a larger plant per unit costs could be lowered. This topic, which takes us from "short run" to "long run," is discussed in Chapter 24.

The law of diminishing returns; plant and equipment.

---

16. The text chapter closes with a discussion (beginning with the section Synthesis of Marginal Cost and Marginal Utility) moving far beyond the problems of the single firm. Bear in mind that this material rests squarely on the ideas of Chapter 2: the law of scarcity, and the three socioeconomic problems arising from this law (WHAT, HOW, and FOR WHOM goods shall be produced). The focus in these sections is with an "efficient" decision on WHAT to produce.

In a Robinson Crusoe situation, the dimensions of the problem are easily grasped. Crusoe understands that his material welfare depends on his available resources (his labor, tools, and the land around him). However, if Crusoe is going to allocate these resources sensibly among the various goods they could produce, his decisions must really be made in *marginal* terms: the *marginal* utility to him of each com-

modity, the *marginal* cost of turning resources toward the production of the particular commodity. (The real cost is the sacrificed alternative: if more of X is to be produced, then some of Y must be sacrificed.)

In a many-individual society, the problems become far more complicated, but the fundamentals persist. If resources are to be sensibly employed, Marginal Utility is still the all-important consideration on the consumer side, and Marginal Cost on the supply side. (These topics are explored at greater length in Chapter 32 and its Appendix.)

QUIZ: Multiple Choice

1. *The profit-maximizing rule for a firm in pure (or perfect) competition is: Price to equal Marginal Cost. The meaning of this rule is:* (1) Keep increasing output quantity (Q) until price (P) has risen to equality with Marginal Cost (MC). (2) Keep increasing Q until P has fallen to equality with MC. (3) Keep increasing Q until MC has fallen to equality with P. (4) Keep increasing Q until MC has risen to equality with P. (5) Keep decreasing P until P reaches equality with MC.

2. *The supply curve of a firm in pure (or perfect) competition is the same thing as* (1) its Marginal Cost curve; (2) a part of its Marginal Cost curve; (3) its Average Cost curve; (4) that entire part of its Average Cost curve in which AC rises or remains constant as output increases; (5) none of these.

3. *Fixed Cost for a firm's operating plant means* (1) any cost whose amount is established at the time the input is purchased; (2) the minimum cost of producing any given quantity of output under the most favorable operating conditions; (3) any cost whose per unit amount has been settled for some considerable future period, such as a long-term wage contract with a labor union; (4) the amount of cost that must be incurred even if zero output is produced; (5) none of these things.

4. *Marginal Cost for a firm's operating plant means* (1) the increase over normal cost that must sometimes be paid to obtain output, such as the extra amount of overtime pay; (2) cost incurred even if the firm produces zero output; (3) the difference between the amount of Total Cost actually incurred to produce any given output and what is considered to be the minimum-possible Total Cost of producing that output; (4) the increase in Total Cost that accrues from an increase in quantity produced of one unit; (5) the increase in Total Cost that accrues from any increase in quantity produced, whether one unit or more.

5. *The property taxes a firm must pay on its plant are increased—i.e., its Fixed Cost is increased. On a graph illustrating this firm's cost curves, the Marginal Cost curve would be affected by this Fixed Cost increase as follows: It would* (1) move to the right; (2) move to the left; (3) move upward; (4) move downward; (5) not move at all.

6. *Four of the five statements below repeat statements made in the text chapter concerning pure (or perfect) competition. Among these five, the one the chapter does* not *make (the one incorrect statement) is:* (1) The single firm is able to sell as much or as little as it pleases at the prevailing market price, without sales effort. (2) In order to secure the maximum-attainable profit, each firm will seek a level of output at which Average Cost has fallen to equality with market price. (3) With some qualifications, this competitive situation is held to yield the maximum-attainable output from a given resource supply, in given conditions of technology. (4) The single firm's supply curve is obtained from its Marginal Cost curve. (5) The single firm in this competitive situation is too small and unimportant to be able to influence market price.

7. *A firm operating in circumstances of pure (or perfect) competition faces a market price of $10. It is producing 2,000 units of output daily, at a Total Cost of $19,000. This firm,* (1) to improve its profit position, should increase the amount of its output; (2) to improve its profit position, should reduce the amount of its output; (3) to minimize its loss, should shut down; (4) although making some profit, may or may not be at the output level yielding maximum profit—the information furnished is not sufficient to cover this point; (5) from the information given, is apparently now at its maximum-profit position.

8. *If the firm described in question 7 were to increase its output to 2,001 units, Total Cost would thereupon become $19,010. Would this additional information change your answer to that question? The correct alternative would then (or still) be:* (1). (2). (3). (4). (5).

9. *Figure 23-4 illustrates two different situations. In each, the blocks indicate amounts of Total Revenue and Total Cost for a firm when it is in its best-possible operating position (for any output other than zero). According to this diagram (and by the Shutdown rule set out in this chapter), the firm, to minimize its loss, should* (1) shut down, whether in situation 1 or situation 2; (2) continue to operate, whether in situation 1 or situation 2; (3) shut down in situation 1, continue to operate in situation 2; (4) continue to operate in situation 1, shut down in situation 2; (5) perhaps do any of the above—the diagram omits the essential information needed for decision.

10. *Total Cost in a certain plant, at an output level of 1,000 units daily, is $4,900. If production were to be reduced by 1 unit (to a total of 999 units), Total Cost would become $4,890. Within the output range thus indicated,* (1) Average Cost (AC) would exceed Marginal Cost (MC); (2) AC and MC

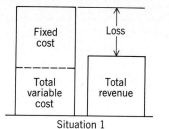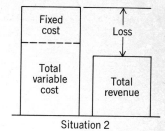

Situation 1   Situation 2

Fig. 23-4

would be approximately equal; (3) MC would exceed AC; (4) no comparison between MC and AC is possible, since the information given is not sufficient to determine MC; (5) no comparison between MC and AC is possible, since the information given is not sufficient to determine AC.

11. *The firm operating the plant described in question 10 operates in conditions of pure (or perfect) competition, and is producing an output of 1,000 (or 999) units daily. The market price is $8. This firm, if it wants to maximize its profit, should* (1) increase its price; (2) reduce its price; (3) increase its output; (4) reduce its output; (5) perhaps do any of the above, since the information furnished is insufficient to tell.

12. *A firm operating in circumstances of pure (or perfect) competition finds that, at its best-possible operating position, its Total Revenue does not cover its Total Cost, although this Revenue is more than sufficient to cover Fixed Cost. This firm* (1) is incurring a loss, and would improve its position by shutting down; (2) is incurring a loss, but minimizes that loss by continuing to operate at its present position; (3) is incurring a loss, but could reduce or perhaps remove it by increasing its production and sales; (4) is incurring a loss, but the information given is not sufficient to indicate whether it would minimize that loss by continuing to operate or by shutting down; (5) may be incurring a loss or earning a profit—the information furnished is insufficient to tell.

13. *Which alternative in question 12 would be correct had that question specified that the firm's Total Revenue (although still insufficient to cover Total Cost) was more than sufficient to cover its Total Variable Cost?* (1). (2). (3). (4). (5).

14. *A firm which operates in conditions of pure (or perfect) competition, and wants to earn as much profit as the situation will allow, must* (1) try to set a price equal to Average Cost; (2) try to produce an output at which its Average Cost is at the lowest-attainable level; (3) try to produce an output at which Average Cost is just equal to market price; (4) try to make its Total Revenue just equal to its Fixed Cost; (5) take none of these actions, necessarily.

THIS CHAPTER explores more fully the idea of Marginal Cost, already discussed in Chapter 23, particularly in its relation to the other cost measures. You may find it helpful to run over questions 1 through 4 in Chapter 23 (pp. 181–182).

1. From Chapter 23: Total Cost of production can be separated into two parts: Fixed Cost and Variable Cost. Fixed Cost is the cost that would be incurred even at zero output.

Divide each of these three *aggregate* cost measures (Total, Fixed, and Variable) by the quantity of output being produced, and you get three corresponding *per unit* figures: Average Cost *(AC)*, Average Fixed Cost *(AFC)*, and Average Variable Cost *(AVC)*.

In addition, there is the per unit cost measure already discussed at length: Marginal Cost *(MC)*.

Note one point: Because Total Cost is made up of Fixed Cost and Variable Cost, it *must* be true that *(AC = AFC — AVC / AC = AFC + AVC / AFC = AC + AVC)*.

AC = AFC + AVC.

---

2. *a.* Table 24-1 in the column alongside uses the same figures as did Study Guide Table 23-1. From it, compute a few

AFC figures. When output is 4, *AFC* would be $_____$;

when output is 8, *AFC* would be $_____$; when output is

12, *AFC* would be $_____$.

Notice that the mathematical computation involved is not overwhelmingly complicated. As we move to higher outputs, we are just dividing $50 by successively larger figures. On a graph such as the text's Fig. 24-1(b), which shows what happens to per unit costs as output is increased, *AFC* would *(fall / rise)* continuously. *AFC* simply keeps dropping all the time because a fixed money cost is being spread over more and more units of output, and that's all there is to *that*.

b. To compute *AVC* for any output, you must first establish (total) Variable Cost, by subtracting *(Marginal / Fixed / Variable)* Cost from Total Cost—i.e., in the case of Table 24-1,

subtracting $_____$ from Total Cost.

Complete Table 24-1 by writing in the three missing *AVC* figures, those for outputs of 4, 8, and 12.

c. Using the *AFC* and *AVC* figures you have already worked out in this question for outputs 4, 8, and 12, check to make sure the rule is satisfied: *AFC + AVC = AC*.

Table 24-1

Output	Total Cost	Average Cost	Marginal Cost	Average Variable Cost
0	$50.00			
			$5.00	
2	60.00	$30.00		$5.00
			5.00	
4	70.00	17.50		——
			5.00	
6	80.00	13.33		5.00
			5.00	
8	90.00	11.25		——
			5.25	
10	100.50	10.05		5.05
			5.50	
12	111.50	9.29		——
			6.50	
14	124.50	8.89		5.32
			8.00	
16	140.50	8.78		5.66
			11.00	
18	162.50	9.03		6.25
			20.00	
20	202.50	10.13		7.63

a. $12.50; $6.25; $4.17; fall. *b.* Fixed; $50; $5; $5; $5.12.

3. *a.* In Table 24-1, for outputs from 0 to 9, *AVC* is a *(rising / constant / falling)* figure. On a per unit cost graph, such as Fig. 24-1(b) in the text chapter, it would be illustrated as a *(rising / flat / falling)* line.

Often *AVC* is described as *falling* (rather than constant) for outputs that are small relative to plant capacity. [In text Fig. 24-1(b), for example, *AVC* falls slightly until an output slightly in excess of 3 units is reached.] It is not altogether clear which of these two behaviors (flat or falling) is typical of actual cost performance. But the point is of minor importance here. What *is* important is that as output is increased, *AVC* in due course begins to *(rise / fall)*.

b. In Table 24-1, for outputs up to 10, *AVC* is *(the same as / different from)* MC. (This is because *AVC* is assumed constant up to that output level.) At output 12—and indeed at all outputs including and beyond 10—*AVC* and *MC* are *(the same / different).* Specifically for any output such as 12 or higher, *MC* is *(greater / less)* than *AVC.*

It is not difficult to see the relation between *MC* and *AVC.* Marginal Cost is nothing but the variable cost of the last unit produced; it is the extra cost occasioned by producing that last unit. Average Variable Cost is the average of all these separate *MC* figures, from the first unit of output right up to the particular quantity of output in question. So if *MC* starts to rise (and as plant capacity is approached, it *will* rise—remember Chapter 23), *AVC* will in due course rise also. But because *AVC* is an average of *all* per unit Variable (or Marginal) Costs, it cannot change as rapidly as *MC.* Being held back by all the other figures of which it is the average, *AVC* will rise more *(rapidly / slowly)* than *MC.*

---

a. constant; flat; rise. *b.* the same as; different; greater; slowly.

---

4. *a.* Suppose we had used a case in which (unlike Table 24-1) *AVC* initially *falls.* If *AVC* is an average of all the previous *MC*s, and if *AVC* falls as we move from output 2 to output 3, from 3 to 4, and from 4 to 5, this must mean that the *MC* for outputs 3, 4, and 5 is *(greater than / the same as / less than)* the corresponding *AVC* figure. It is the inclusion of that extra figure *(MC)* which pulls down the average. In sum, if *AVC* is falling, *MC* must be *(less / greater)* than *AVC.*

b. This point can be illustrated by an example involving classroom grades. In a given class of students, the average examination grade is always 70. Now we add, one by one, a few new students (some extra or "marginal" students) to this class. They are weaker students; they always score between 50 and 55 on examinations. And so, when added to the class, they *(increase / pull down)* the class average from 70 to (say) 65. (When marginal value is below average value, the marginal pulls down the average.)

c. We add a few more students. They are a little better; they score from 60 to 63. But they are likewise below the new class average of 65. So that average is *(pulled down / increased)* just a little more—say from 65 to *(64 / 66).*

d. We add one more student; he always scores 64. His addition does not change the class average. (When marginal equals average, average does not change.)

Finally we add a few students who always score *above* 64. Their addition will accordingly *(increase / decrease)* the class average. (When marginal exceeds average, marginal pulls up average.)

---

a. less than; less. *b.* pull down. *c.* pulled down; 64. *d.* increase.

---

5. The implications of the preceding question need to be considered carefully. To grasp them, look at Fig. 24-1 (next page), showing the per unit cost curves for a firm with a plant

of some given size. The Average Cost (*AC*) curve is approximately U-shaped. If output is gradually expanded from a zero level, *AC* will initially *(rise / fall),* because Fixed Cost is being spread over increasingly *(larger / smaller)* outputs. However, as plant capacity is approached, *AC* must ultimately *(rise / fall)* because of the influence of *(Fixed Cost / the law of diminishing returns.)*

In these circumstances, the Marginal Cost (*MC*) curve *must always cut through the exact bottom point of the AC curve.* (It may take you a little time to think this through, but it follows from the reasoning of question 4. If *AC* is falling, it must mean that *MC* is below *AC.* If *AC* turns around and begins to rise, it can only be because *MC* has risen *above AC.*)

Exactly the same conclusion applies with respect to the *AVC* curve: *the MC curve must cut through its bottom point. AVC* is exactly the same kind of average as *AC.* The only difference between them is that *AC* includes the unchanging figure of Fixed Cost, whereas *AVC* does not.

So Fig. 24-1 illustrates the general relationship that must exist between the three most important per unit cost measures. *AC* must be, at least approximately, U-shaped, and *MC* must cut through its bottom point. *AVC* may or may not be U-shaped, but it most certainly will rise as plant capacity is approached. If it *is* U-shaped, and if it has a unique bottom point, then *MC* will cut through that point.

---

fall; larger; rise; law of diminishing returns.

Chapter 23 set out the rules for Maximum-profit output, in the special circumstances of pure (or perfect) competition. To review those rules:

▶ To earn maximum-possible profit, the firm will produce and sell that output at which its Marginal Cost has risen to equality with market price.

▶ That price must be greater than (or in the very limiting case, just equal to) Average Variable Cost; otherwise, the firm would do better to shut down.

6. *a.* This question reviews the application of these rules in terms of Fig. 24-1 [which corresponds to the text's Fig. 24-1(b)]. The three horizontal lines indicate the demand curves corresponding to three possible levels of market price. (Remember that the firm in pure or perfect competition has no selling problems. It can sell as much or as little as it pleases at the prevailing market price, without advertising or other sales cost.) For example, if price is *HO,* the firm can move anywhere along d_1d_1. The point at which *MC* has risen to equality with *that* market price is *N*—i.e., if *HO* were the market price, the firm would produce and sell quantity *(OF / OE / OG).* Note carefully that in this position, price is *above AC*—i.e., the firm is *(earning a profit / just breaking even / incurring a loss).*

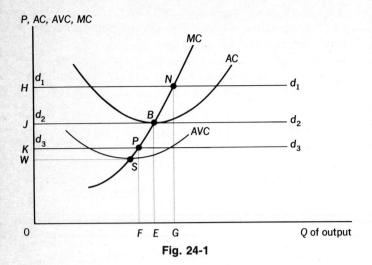

Fig. 24-1

b. If price happened to be *JO*, then the firm's demand curve would be (d_1d_1 / d_2d_2 / d_3d_3), and its Maximum-profit output would be (*OF* / *OE* / *OG*). It would then be (*earning a profit* / *just breaking even* / *incurring a loss*).

c. If price were *KO*, the firm's best-possible position would be to produce (*nothing* / *output OF* / *output OE*). In this position, its loss would be (*less than* / *equal to* / *greater than*) the amount of its Fixed Cost.

d. If price becomes so low that it does not even cover Average Variable Cost, then the firm would do better to shut down operations entirely. (REMEMBER: if price does not cover Average Variable Cost, then operating loss exceeds Fixed Cost—questions 12 and 13, p. 185.) On Fig. 24-1, the boundary of this shutdown price zone is marked by price (*HO* / *JO* / *KO* / *WO*). This price is (*greater than* / *just equal to* / *less than*) the minimum level of (*Average Variable* / *Average Fixed*) Cost.

The equilibrium position of the firm, as discussed in review question 6 above, was for the most part covered in Chapter 23. In the present chapter, the text stresses that there are some *long-run* equilibrium considerations still to be taken into account. Specifically, there are *three* such long-run considerations, and questions 7 through 11 examine them.

7. The market price which each firm in pure (or perfect) competition must accept is the price resulting from the intersection of industry demand and supply curves. At any moment of time, it could be any of Fig. 24-1's prices—*HO, JO, KO,* or even *WO*. However, it is argued that there is a *long-run* tendency for price to gravitate toward level *JO*, the (*Break-even* / *Shutdown*) price.

The reasoning behind this argument is not difficult to grasp. Suppose price is *below JO*. This means that all supplying firms are losing money. (For convenience, think of every firm as having the set of cost curves indicated by Fig. 24-1, because they all produce the same product with the same technology, all paying the same prices for their inputs.) If price persists below the *JO* level, some firms are bound to drop out. Either they will leave voluntarily as some of their fixed-cost obligations come up for renewal and give them an opportunity for exit, or they will be forced out through bankruptcy.

When these firms leave, industry supply will be (*increased* / *decreased*), and market price will thereupon (*rise* / *fall*).

Suppose, on the other hand, that price happens to be *above JO*. This means that the firms presently in the industry are earning profits. These profits will attract new firms to the industry. (Remember from question 8, p. 184, that even at Break-even price *JO*, the typical firm is earning a "normal" return on its invested capital.) If new firms enter, this will mean (*an increase* / *a decrease*) in industry supply. So price will thereupon (*rise* / *fall*).

In sum, whenever price happens to be *below JO*, the tendency is for price to *rise*. If it is *above JO*, the tendency is for price to *fall*. This is strictly a *long-run* tendency: enough time must be allowed for new firms to enter, or for old firms to depart.

The *JO* price is a goal toward which things are gradually trending. That *JO* level would be reached if enough time were allowed for conditions to work themselves out. In actual experience, this is unlikely to happen, because other factors typically change before this long-run equilibrium goal is reached. Thus suppose that price is gradually moving toward *JO*, but is still above that level because new firms have not had sufficient time to enter. Then a change in input costs, or in technology, causes the Fig. 24-1 cost curves to shift to new positions. The long-run *JO* goal toward which things were gravitating is destroyed. A new long-run goal is set up—which in turn may be destroyed before it is realized.

8. Notice that a firm bent on profit maximization has no special incentive to try to produce that output at which its *AC* is lowest. With its given plant, the lowest *AC* it can attain is indicated in Fig. 24-1 by *BE*. This is obtained only when output is (*OF* / *OE* / *OG*). But the firm will want to produce that output if and only if market price happens to be (*HO* / *JO* / *KO* / *WO*).

However, there is the long-run tendency outlined in question 7 for price (*P*) to gravitate to the *JO* level, where market price, *AC*, and *MC* all are equal, and *AC* is at its minimum level; hence the "long-run equilibrium condition" stated in the text for the firm:

$$P = MC = \text{minimum-level } AC$$

Note carefully that in this phrase "long-run equilibrium condition," the word "equilibrium" is being used in a somewhat different and fuller sense.

The firm's basic profit-maximizing rule is: Pick the output at which $P = MC$. But now we also have $P = AC$ in the "equilibrium requirement," and $P = AC$ is *not* ordinarily a profit-maximizing rule. Any firm which hopes to make a lot of money by picking a level of output at which price and AC are one and the same is going to be terribly disappointed. In this position, the firm by definition is *(earning a profit / just breaking even / losing money).*

The firm with profit maximizing as its goal will *deliberately pick* the $P = MC$ position. But there is a long-run tendency for it to be *pushed* to a position where $P = AC$. (Thus, if P exceeds AC, the chance of profit attracts new firms, and the increase in supply resulting from their entry pushes down P. Through the mechanism of changes in market price, each firm is pushed toward the $P = AC$ position.) The $P = MC$ part of the long-run equilibrium condition refers to the firm's profit-maximizing goal. The $P = AC$ part refers to the fact that things will not have completely "settled down" for the industry or for any firm therein until this $P = AC$ condition has been pretty well satisfied. (Remember the point made at the close of question 7: This long-run position may never be reached, but it is still a goal toward which things are trending.)

OE; JO; just breaking even.

9. In the present context, "short run" means generally a situation in which (1) the industry is made up of a *given* number of firms, and (2) each of those firms has a *given* amount of plant and equipment. Hence, in the short run, industry supply quantity can only be changed when the given total of firms use their given plant and equipment more intensively or less so.

"Long run" correspondingly means (1) for the industry, that enough time is allowed to elapse for old firms to exit or for new firms to enter; and (2) for the firm, that enough time is allowed for it to plan and build a larger or a smaller plant, if it decides to do so.

These two factors are the first and second of the three "long-run equilibrium considerations" mentioned in the paragraph preceding question 7. (Question 11 covers the third.) We have covered the matter of entry or exit of firms; now we turn to possible changes in the size of the firm's plant.

Short-run cost curves such as those of Fig. 24-1 answer this type of question: *With the plant we now have* (and with input prices at their present levels), what would be the AC, or the MC, for any particular output level?

The firm can ask a different question: What would be the *very lowest cost* of producing any given output (no matter how large or how small)—*if we had the plant most appropriate for that output?* (The "most appropriate" plant is defined

as the one that would produce the output quantity in question at lowest possible AC, given the existing state of technology and input prices.)

When a firm asks this question, it is clearly transcending the limitation of its present fixed size of plant. It is thinking in terms of complete freedom to build any size of plant.

When such questions of considering or planning for a plant of different size are involved, we move into the area of Long-run Average Cost (*LRAC*, or *LAC*). The graph illustrating *LRAC* for a firm or plant is structurally the same as that for the short-run situation: AC is measured on the vertical axis; quantity of output is measured horizontally. But on the long-run diagram—in the text, the diagram is Fig. 24-4—we show *all* possible short-run AC curves. There is one such short-run AC curve for each possible plant size. (We exclude, of course, any plants that would not be efficient for producing *some* output quantity.) The "bottom edge" resulting from this accumulation of short-run curves is the long-run curve.

This long-run curve is sometimes called (borrowing a mathematicians' term) the "envelope curve," or the "planning curve."

So the firm's long-run AC curve for commodity X could be used to indicate (pick one or more):
a. The lowest-possible AC at which any quantity of X could be produced, and the particular size of plant needed in order to obtain that AC.
b. The level of output at which it would be most profitable to produce X.
c. The particular quantity (or quantities) of X at which the very lowest per unit cost (AC) of all would be possible, and the plant size (or range of plant sizes) required for that minimum AC.
d. The price the firm ought to charge in order to obtain the maximum profit from sale of X.

a and *c*.

10. *a.* The long-run AC curve is usually depicted as a saucer-shaped curve—first falling, then flat, then rising. (Sometimes it is depicted as having a unique bottom point, like the short-run AC curve, rather than having a flat "bottom region." The two *LAC* curves in text Fig. 24-4 have a single bottom point.)

The falling region is that of "increasing returns to scale," where, as the size of plant is increased and the scale of operations expanded, the result is a *(higher / lower)* short-run AC. The flat region (or the bottom point) represents minimum-attainable AC (given present technology and input prices).

At some level of output (perhaps very large), presumably some inefficiencies of too-large size set in, so that *LRAC* will ultimately begin to turn up, even if only slightly. (Particularly as a consequence of recent developments in communication methods, such as computers, it is clear that a firm can often become very large indeed without incurring inefficiencies of large size that are of sufficient importance to offset the economies of large-scale operation.)

b. Question 7 discussed the "long-run" tendency in pure (or perfect) competition for new companies to enter or old ones to depart. Notice now that this long-run adjustment may involve also some *change in the size of plant* for existing firms. If there are economies of scale to be obtained from increasing plant size, then businesses—given sufficient time—will gravitate toward those larger plants.

This fact uncovers one of the paradoxes of pure (or perfect) competition in its relation to contemporary economic life. The argument for such competition is its presumed *efficiency* (in the sense of using a given resource stock to the best advantage). Each firm is too *(small / large)* to be able to exert any "monopolistic" control over price. And there is the presumed tendency for price to gravitate in the long run toward minimum-possible *AC*.

Yet if the *LRAC* curve is such that minimum-level *AC* requires a large output and plant size, the firm needed to operate that plant may be too *(small / large)* for the requirements of pure competition. Pure competition then becomes inefficient. Hence the discussion, in text Chapter 24 (and in the Appendix to Chapter 20), of cost patterns and market imperfection.

At least one noted economist, Joseph Schumpeter, was highly skeptical of the virtues of pure (or perfect) competition in modern economic life; see the Schumpeter quotation near the end of the text's Chapter 6.

---

a. lower. *b.* small; large.

---

11. We now reach the third and last of the "long-run" considerations. "The long run" means allowing enough time for firms to exit or enter, and enough time for firms to pick a different plant size if necessary. So it allows for the maximum-possible supply response, in terms of quantity change, to any change in industry demand. Suppose there *is* a big change in supply output. What will this do to input prices?

Let us start with a competitive industry in full long-run equilibrium. For each and every firm, $P = MC$ = minimum long-run *AC*. Suddenly there is a big increase in industry demand for the product. The upper-left-hand diagram in Fig. 24-2 shows this shift of *dd* to a new position *d'd'* (broken line). Price consequently rises from *JO* to *KO*.

The *ss* supply curve in this diagram is short-run supply. The rise in industry output from *OA* to *OB* is consequently the extra supply that the *given* total of firms can produce by employing their *given* plant and equipment more intensively.

Because price has risen, all firms are now making profits. This will attract new firms; and the *ss* curve will begin to shift to the right as this new supply is added to industry supply. (In the top left-hand diagram of Fig. 24-2, sketch in lightly, in pencil, a new *ss* curve to the right of the present one.)

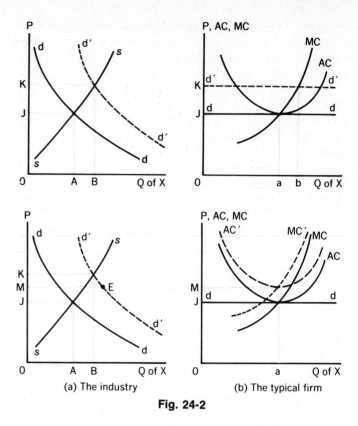

(a) The industry   (b) The typical firm

Fig. 24-2

Industry output has now risen for two reasons: the already-existing firms are producing more, and new firms have entered. This calls for greater employment of inputs. And this may raise input prices.

a. For the moment, we deliberately assume that this input price rise does not happen. The firms in the industry can get all the extra labor, materials, power, and so on, *without* raising the price of any such input. *If* such is the case, then the industry's *long-run* supply curve will be a horizontal line. In the upper-left part of Fig. 24-2, draw a horizontal line to the right from the intersection of *dd* and *ss*. Carry it far enough to intersect *d'd'*.

This is the "constant-cost" situation (see Appendix to Chapter 20). New firms enter and add to supply until price has (in the long run) returned to its old level of *JO*.

The situation of the typical firm in this constant-cost situation is indicated by the upper-right diagram. When market price rose from *JO* to *KO*, the firm expanded its output from *Oa* to *Ob*. But as new firms enter, market price reverses itself and begins to *(fall / rise)*. Finally, the firm is back at its original position, with output *Oa*, at price *JO*.

b. Suppose, however, that input prices *are* affected as the demand for inputs increases. The normal expectation would be that input prices will *(rise / fall)*. And it is to be expected that this rise in production costs will work its way into the price of the finished product.

We now have two effects working on the price of this finished good. Entry of new firms, by increasing industry supply, is pushing price *(down / up)* from its new short-run level *KO*. But higher input cost is tending to push price *(down / up)*.

The long-run outcome must be one in which price has *(fallen / risen)* somewhat from its *KO* level, but has *(fallen / risen)* somewhat from its original *JO* level. In the bottom-left part of Fig. 24-2, illustrate this by drawing a long-run supply curve from the intersection of *dd* and *ss* upward through the point *E* on *d'd'*.

This is the "increasing-cost" case. What it really says is that if people want more of a particular good in the face of a limited stock of resources, they may have to pay a higher price to get it, even in the long run, when supplying firms have had all possible opportunity to adjust to the demand increase.

c. The situation of the typical firm, in the increasing-cost case, is shown in the bottom-right diagram. In general, the sequence of events will begin as it did in the constant-cost case: the increase in industry demand will push up market price, and the firm will therefore expand its output (just as the constant-cost firm expanded its output from *Oa* to *Ob*). However, the rise in input prices complicates matters. This rise is brought about because (i) existing firms want to produce more output, and (ii) new firms are entering.

The individual-firm *AC* and *MC* curves, such as shown in the two right-hand diagrams, are drawn on the assumption of *given* input prices, because the quantity of input bought by any one firm will not be sufficiently large to affect that input's market price. But when *all firms together* demand more inputs, those input prices *do* rise. This is depicted as an *upward shift* of the entire *AC* and *MC* curves for the individual firm, as indicated by the broken lines in the bottom-right diagram.

The process of adjustment to a new long-run equilibrium is considerably more complicated when input prices change. We can, however, state the most basic characteristics of this new equilibrium. The individual firm's cost curves must rise. And market price will be as suggested by *MO* (bottom-left diagram). It must be *(higher / lower)* than the original *JO* level.

(NOTE: The matter of changing input prices is quite complicated at a first approach, and you should not be discouraged if you find it difficult to follow. The basic idea is simple enough: If people want more of something, they probably will have to pay a higher price to get it. But the detail of the adjustment process for the individual firm is tricky.)

---

a. fall. *b.* rise; down; up; fallen; risen. *c.* higher.

12. The economists who worked out the theory of pure (or perfect) competition were aware that in actual experience, the per unit costs of the various firms in an industry sometimes go *down,* not *up,* as that industry develops and expands. Pure-competition theory tries to recognize this through the concept of *external economies.*

Before you proceed, notice that this is the same topic which was discussed in review question 4 for the Appendix to Chapter 20. And it is the exact *reverse* of the situation discussed in question 11 above. Question 11 dealt with *rising* supply curves. Now we consider the possibility of a *falling* supply curve, one with some northwest-to-southeast inclination, one that would point to *lower* prices in the event of an increase in demand.

It is highly unlikely that an increased demand for any particular input would push down its price. But it is just possible that an expansion of the industry's scale of output *might* generate some production economies for each of the member firms comprising that industry. If so, this would be an *external economy.*

Remember that this external economy must be the *reverse* of the situation depicted in the bottom-right part of Fig. 24-2. The individual firm's *AC* and *MC* curves shift *downward,* not upward, if there is a rise in industry output.

A valid external economy must be "reversible." That is, if industry output were subsequently to contract, each firm's *AC* and *MC* curves would shift back up again. So an external economy is *not* just a technological, cost-reducing development which, although it was originally prompted by expanded demand for the product, would remain even if demand were later to contract. (For *this* kind of cost reduction, see text Fig. 20-14.)

a. An external cost economy is designated as "external" because it is external to the activity of any single firm. If a firm's output is not pressing hard against plant capacity, the firm may find that some increases in output reduce *AC*. A firm may find that if it built a larger plant equipped for mass production, its per unit costs would fall. These are *internal* economies, not external. On the firm's per unit cost diagram, such internal cost economies would be illustrated by an *AC* curve which *(has some northwest-to-southeast inclination / shifts downward to a new position).*

(NOTE: This topic of external economies is a complicated one. You should not be expected to do more than glean a general idea of the problems and issues involved, in an introductory course.)

b. Which of the following suggests an *external* economy? (Pick one or more.)
(1) A mine in northern Canada must rely on diesel engines for power. More mines spring up in the area, and as a result, a dam is built to generate hydroelectric power for all mines.
(2) General Motors introduces a new mass-production automobile plant which significantly reduces the per unit cost of automobile assembly.
(3) Expansion of the electronics industry in a particular area bring more engineers to that area, thus somewhat reducing the acute shortage of (and exceedingly high salaries paid to) engineers in that area.

c. In sum, for any single firm, an external economy means (pick one):

(1) An Average or Marginal Cost curve that falls as it moves toward higher outputs—i.e., runs southeasterly.
(2) A reduction in an input's per unit cost when the firm buys that input in sufficiently large quantities.
(3) A reduction in per unit cost occurring when the size of the firm's plant is expanded.
(4) A downward shift or displacement in the position of the industry supply curve.
(5) None of the above.

---

a. some northwest-southeast inclination. *b.* (1), (3). Note that neither is a valid example unless you agree that the economy would reverse itself if the industry subsequently contracted in size: the dam would not be maintained; most of the engineers would leave. *c.* (5).

---

13. The text mentions that "opportunity-cost" elements may have to be included in the firm's costs. I run my own business. In reckoning my · Average and Marginal Costs, I should include the cost of my own labor. (On this point, see the Note in question 8, Chapter 23, p. 184.) I include my own labor as a cost—at $2 per hour. Now I learn I can get a job down the street at $4 per hour. The fact that this opportunity is open to me means that I should include in costs my labor at *(zero / $2 / $4 / $6)* per hour. (Of course, I may prefer to run my own business, and if so, I may be quite happy to run it at what appears to be a slight loss when this full opportunity cost is counted.)

$4.

QUIZ: Multiple Choice

1. *The "long-run" equilibrium condition, "price equal to minimum per unit (average) cost," used in pure (or perfect) competition theory,* (1) is a rule which the firm need not consider in the short run, but must obey in the long run if it wants to choose the output level that will maximize its profit; (2) is a rule the firm must obey in the short run only if it wants to choose the output level that will maximize its profit; (3) is not a rule any profit-maximizing firm need consider either in the short or the long run, but indicates a situation toward which it is said all firms will be pushed in the long run; (4) is a rule any profit-maximizing firm must respect in both the short and the long run; (5) has no status either as a profit-maximizing rule or as a situation toward which firms will tend to be pushed, whether in the short or the long run.

2. *A firm is operating in circumstances of pure (or perfect) competition. It is producing that quantity of output at which Average Cost is at its minimum level. This firm* (1) must be at its Maximum-profit output level, but may or may not be charging the best price it could get for that output; (2) must be at its Maximum-profit output level and need not reconsider its price, since this is a market price over which it has no control;

(3) is not at its Maximum-profit position, and should increase its output; (4) is not at its Maximum-profit position and should decrease its output; (5) may or may not be at its Maximum-profit position—the information furnished is insufficient to tell.

3. *If the term "opportunity cost" is used in connection with any of a firm's costs, it means* (1) including as a cost of any input the market price or return that input is offered in any other occupation; (2) certain nonrecurring or once-and-for-all costs involved in getting production under way; (3) costs which would be incurred even at zero output but which do not increase in amount as output is increased; (4) any cost incurred which does not involve an actual outlay of cash; (5) nothing at all, since the term would not be used with respect to production costs.

4. *A firm operates under conditions of pure (or perfect) competition. At its present level of output, all the following have a value of $1: price it is charging, Marginal Cost, Average Cost. Marginal Cost would rise with any increase in output. This firm* (1) definitely is at its Maximum-profit position; (2) definitely is not at its Maximum-profit position; (3) may or may not be at Maximum-profit position; Average Variable Cost would have to be known before answering; (4) may or may not be at Maximum-profit position; Total Cost and Total Revenue would have to be known before answering; (5) may or may not be at Maximum-profit position; total Fixed Cost would have to be known before answering.

5. *At the quantity of output where Average Cost has reached its minimum level,* (1) Average Variable Cost will equal Fixed Cost; (2) profit must be at its maximum level for the firm; (3) Marginal Cost will equal Average Variable Cost; (4) Marginal Cost will equal Average Cost; (5) none of the above is necessarily true.

6. *A firm operating in conditions of pure (or perfect) competition is producing a daily output such that its Total Revenue is $5,000. That output is its profit-maximizing output. The firm's Average Cost is $8, its Marginal Cost is $10, and its Average Variable Cost is $5. Its daily output is* (1) 200 units; (2) 500 units; (3) 625 units; (4) 1,000 units; (5) impossible to tell from the information furnished.

7. *The Fixed Cost for the firm described in question 6 is* (1) $10; (2) $100; (3) $500; (4) $1,500; (5) impossible to tell from the information furnished.

8. *The daily profit earned, or loss incurred, by the firm in question 6 (profit being the excess of Total Revenue over Total Cost, and loss the excess of Total Cost over Total Revenue) must be* (1) a loss of $500; (2) neither profit nor loss, for the firm just "breaks even"; (3) a profit of $500; (4) a profit of $1,000; (5) impossible to tell from the information furnished.

9. *If Marginal Cost exceeds Average Cost (AC) within a certain range of plant outputs, then, with respect to any* increase in output within that range, (1) *AC* must rise; (2) *AC* must fall; (3) *AC* must either rise or fall; (4) *AC* must remain constant; (5) *AC* may rise, fall, or remain constant.

10. *The text refers to the "Break-even point" for a firm in pure (or perfect) competition. This Break-even point occurs at the output level where two cost magnitudes are just equal, namely,* (1) Marginal Cost (*MC*) and Average Cost (*AC*); (2) Average Variable Cost (*AVC*) and Average Fixed Cost (*AFC*); (3) *MC* and *AVC*; (4) *AC* and *AVC*; (5) *MC* and *AFC*.

11. *The text refers also to the "Shutdown point" for a firm in pure (or perfect) competition. Which alternative in question 10 would be correct had that question referred to the Shutdown point?* (1). (2). (3). (4). (5).

12. *In a certain plant, Marginal Cost is $2 at 400 units of output weekly, and it is $2.50 at 500 units of output. Referring to output increases within this 400-to-500 range, Average Cost* (1) must rise; (2) must fall; (3) must remain constant; (4) may rise, may fall, or both, but cannot remain constant throughout this output range; (5) may rise, may fall, or may remain constant throughout this output range.

13. *A firm operating in circumstances of pure (or perfect) competition produces and sells 200 units of output daily at a price of $7. Its Average Cost is $4.99. If it were to increase output and sales to 201 units daily, Average Cost would rise to $5. To maximize its profit, and from the information supplied, this firm should* (1) increase its output, since Marginal Cost (*MC*) is approximately $6; (2) reduce its output, since *MC* is approximately $6; (3) remain at its present output, since *MC* is approximately $7; (4) certainly not reduce its output, and probably increase it, since Average Cost is approximately $5; (5) increase its output, since *MC* is approximately $5.01.

14. *A firm must sell its product at a market price of $1.90. Its present operating figures are as follows: Average Cost, $2; Marginal Cost, $1.50; Average Variable Cost, $1.50; total Fixed Cost, $500 per period. To maximize its profit, this firm should* (1) definitely increase its present output level; (2) definitely reduce its present output level; (3) remain at its present output position; (4) shut down; (5) perhaps increase, perhaps decrease its output—the one critical figure needed to make this decision is lacking.

15. *The text chapter discusses the firm's "Long-run Average Cost curve" (also described as the "Long-run planning envelope curve"). This curve is intended to show (referring to given conditions of technology)* (1) the minimum cost of producing any given output quantity, if the firm can select, for each such output, the plant most economical for producing that quantity; (2) the minimum cost for the profit-maximizing output, using the particular plant best suited for that particular output; (3) the minimum cost of producing any given output quantity, using a plant of one given size only for all such outputs, but the plant which yields the lowest-attainable Average Cost figure; (4) the minimum cost of producing any given output quantity, using a plant of one given size only for all such outputs, but the plant which yields the lowest-attainable Marginal Cost figure; (5) the future increase or decrease in Average Cost that can be expected as the number of firms entering the industry increases or decreases.

16. *In this chapter, as in Chapter 23, the text presents a basic "Maximum-profit rule" for firms in pure (or perfect) competition. The essence of that rule is the following:* (1) Look for the output at which Average Cost of production is at its minimum level, in given conditions of technology. (2) Produce and sell until the extra cost which more output would entail begins to exceed market price. (3) Move to the minimum-cost point on your long-run Average Cost curve. (4) Set a price at which the excess of price over Average Cost is at its highest attainable level. (5) None of the above.

17. *Four of the five items cited below are relevant in discussing the approach toward the "long-run equilibrium position" in pure (or perfect) competition. One of the five is not relevant in that it refers to a different topic. The nonrelevant item is this: In the movement toward that equilibrium goal,* (1) an increase or decrease in demand may suddenly set a new goal; (2) input prices may change as a consequence of this movement; (3) new firms may enter or existing firms may leave; (4) existing firms may decide to build new plants of a different size; (5) the long-run average cost curve may be such that only a few firms can survive.

18. *Because of a city tax reduction, the total Fixed Cost a firm must pay is reduced by $500 monthly. The firm operates in conditions of pure (or perfect) competition. Variable Cost is not affected by this Fixed Cost change. If the firm seeks to maximize its profit, this cost reduction should (at least in the short run) result in* (1) a reduction in price; (2) an increase in output; (3) an increase in price; (4) a reduction in output; (5) no change in output or in price.

QUIZ: Other

1. You find that when you operate your plant, the Marginal Cost of daily production of the 9th, 10th, . . . , and so on up to the 20th unit is as indicated below:

Unit	9th	10th	11th	12th	13th	14th
Marginal Cost	$4.10	$4.10	$4.11	$4.13	$4.16	$4.20

Unit	15th	16th	17th	18th	19th	20th
Marginal Cost	$4.30	$4.50	$4.90	$6.30	$7.00	$9.00

a. If your product sells at a market price of $4.50, how many units would you want to sell daily to earn the maximum amount of profit? _____.

b. If Total Cost of producing the first 8 units is $36 (of which $4 is Fixed Cost), how much profit or loss accrues daily from selling part *a*'s quantity? _____.

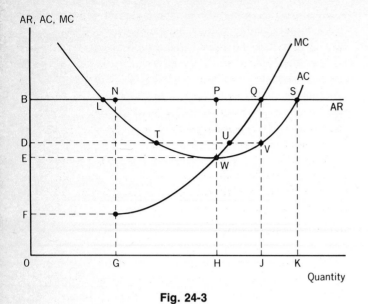

Fig. 24-3

c. If you sold 2 units more than this quantity daily, how much profit or loss would accrue? _____.

d. If price were $4.11, how many units should you sell, and how much profit or loss would accrue? _____.

e. With price at $4.11 (and Total Cost as in *b*), would you continue operations? Why or why not?

_____.

2. Figure 24-3 shows Marginal Cost, Average Cost, and Average Revenue (per unit revenue) for a particular firm operating in circumstances of pure (or perfect) competition. The firm wishes to operate so as to maximize its profit.

a. At what level of output will the firm operate? (1) *OG*; (2) *OH*; (3) *OJ*; (4) *OK*; (5) *BO*.

b. Which of the following correctly indicates the price at which it will sell its product? (1) *OG*; (2) *DO*; (3) *BF*; (4) *OK*; (5) *NG*.

Table 24-2

Case	Price	Q of Output	Total Revenue	Total Cost	Total Fixed Cost	Total Variable Cost	Average Cost	Average Variable Cost	Marginal Cost	With Increase in Output, *MC* Would	Answer
a.	$2.00	10,000		$16,000			At minimum level				
b.			$10,000		$2,000		$4.00	$3.00	$6.00		
c.	2.00	2,000			2,000	$5,000			2.00	fall	
d.			6,000	6,000		4,500	At minimum level	0.75			
e.	5.00	2,000						5.25	5.00	rise	
f.			20,000	18,000			3.60		4.00	rise	
g.		4,000	16,000	16,000			At minimum level	5.00	3.00	fall	
h.	4.50				9,000	12,000	5.25	At minimum level			
i.		3,000	9,000						3.25	3.00	rise	
j.		2,000	16,000		3,000				7.00	8.00	rise	

c. Which correctly indicates the level of Average Cost at this Maximum-profit output? (1) *PH;* (2) *VJ;* (3) *SK;* (4) *DV;* (5) *EW.*

d. Which correctly indicates the level of Marginal Cost at the Maximum-profit output? (1) *OG;* (2) *DO;* (3) *BF;* (4) *OK;* (5) *NG.*

e. Which rectangle correctly indicates the amount of Total Cost of producing the Maximum-profit output? (1) *DVJO;* (2) *BQJO;* (3) *BPHO;* (4) *BSKO;* (5) *EWHO.*

f. Which rectangle in part *e* correctly indicates the firm's Total Revenue at Maximum-profit output? (1); (2); (3); (4); (5).

g. Which rectangle correctly indicates Total Profit earned at this output? (1) *BQJO;* (2) *DVJO;* (3) *BQVD;* (4) *BPHO;* (5) none of the preceding four.

3. You are a consultant on profit maximization. What do you recommend in each of the ten cases listed in Table 24-2, p. 196? Each firm operates in circumstances of pure (or perfect) competition, and wants to maximize its profit (or minimize its loss).

NOTE: These problems are not easy. They require you to know the profit-maximizing rules for the firm in pure (or perfect) competition (price to equal marginal cost; marginal cost to be rising with any increase in output; production to be shut down in the event of a loss exceeding the fixed-cost amount), and to know the relationship among the various cost curves as illustrated, for example, by text Fig. 24-1(b).

Enough information is supplied in each case, despite the blanks, to provide an answer. But note that there is at least one "nonsense" case among the ten, in which the figures are inconsistent and could not all be correct.

Answer for each case by putting *one* of the numbers 1 through 7 from the code below into the extreme right-hand column of the table. (The same number may of course be used for more than one question.)

(1) Firm is now at correct position.
(2) Firm should increase price.
(3) Firm should decrease price.
(4) Firm should increase quantity of output and sales.
(5) Firm should decrease quantity of output and sales.
(6) Firm should shut down operations.
(7) A nonsense case—figures supplied are inconsistent and could not all be correct.

25 MAXIMUM-PROFIT EQUILIBRIUM: MONOPOLY

1. If an industry is to be classed as one of pure (or perfect) competition, there are said to be two basic requirements, namely:

(i) _____ ;

(ii) _____ .

It is argued that when these two conditions are satisfied, the result is, for the individual firm, a demand curve that is virtually horizontal—i.e., perfectly or almost perfectly elastic with respect to price. This is the situation of Chapters 23 and 24: the firm can sell as much or as little as it pleases at a market price over which it has no control.

Few real-life firms find themselves in this position. The text chapter says that this is because of failure to satisfy one or both of the two basic requirements for perfect competition. In real life, that is, the number of firms may be too *(large / small)* for perfect competition. In addition, the products sold by the various firms may be *(identical among all firms / differentiated from one firm to the next)*.

(i) many small firms, (ii) All selling identical products; small; differentiated from one firm to the next.

2. These two characteristics—a too-small number of sellers and/or the differentiation of the competing products—are said to have "monopolistic" consequences.

Notice that this word "monopolistic" does *not* mean that the firms involved are monopolies. The conventional definition of a monopoly situation is this: (i) only one firm in the industry, and (ii) no close substitutes available for the product of that one-firm industry.

Except in a few special areas such as public utilities, cases approximating genuine monopoly are almost as difficult to find as are cases of perfect competition. Monopoly is a kind of extreme instance of competitive imperfection. Economist Edward H. Chamberlin, who did much to develop the ideas set out in the first part of this chapter, argued that the typical real-life situation is one of "monopolistic competition." Each firm finds that it must reckon with the competition of close substitute products (so that it is not a monopoly); and yet its situation is not that of pure or perfect competition.

The word "monopolistic" is used because it is argued that there is one monopoly-like characteristic to be found in all such cases of monopolistic or imperfect competition. It has to do (see the text section Imperfect Competition Defined) with

the demand curve facing each individual firm: that demand curve is

_____ .

less than perfectly elastic with respect to price—i.e., it is "tilted" rather than horizontal.

3. If the number of selling firms is small, the name given the resulting situation is _____ .
If the number of selling firms is large but competition is not perfect, this must be (in the language of the text) a situation of

_____ .

oligopoly; many differentiated sellers.

In its opening sections, this text chapter describes the circumstances of imperfect or monopolistic competition. But it does not attempt to explore these situations in any real detail. Instead, after its introductory outline, the chapter turns to an examination of the profit-maximizing behavior of a *monopoly* firm. Analytically, this monopoly case is decidedly easier than the so-called "intermediate" cases—those not perfectly competitive, and yet not completely monopolistic. It would be unwise to tackle these more intricate cases before having mastered the elementary ideas of monopoly pricing.

The terms and diagrams involved in a description of monopoly pricing may seem complicated at first. Yet the basic idea involved is simple. The monopoly firm is assumed to behave so as to "maximize its profit"— which is exactly what the firm in pure (or perfect) competition was assumed to do in Chapters 23 and 24. The monopoly firm simply operates in rather different circumstances.

To review the basic ideas of "profit maximization":

1. "Maximizing profit" means making as much money as market conditions will permit.

2. To "maximize profit," there must be something the firm can *do* that will influence its profit. There must be some variable which changes profit, and which the firm can control.

3. This chapter assumes that the monopoly firm can control the quantity it sells, just as the firm in pure (or perfect) competition can do. (In real life, this control is

at best indirect and incomplete; there are other and more complex decisions to be made. But this chapter tackles a simple case.) So the variable which the monopoly firm can control is sales quantity: it looks for the particular quantity that will maximize its profit.

4. The monopoly firm is assumed to have control over its sales quantity because it knows the demand schedule for its product—i.e., it knows the sales quantity that goes with each and any price it might charge.

5. From this demand schedule, it is easy to develop a *revenue* schedule (Total Revenue being quantity sold multiplied by price per unit)—i.e., a schedule showing revenue associated with each possible quantity sold.

6. The firm must know also the Total Cost of each and any output quantity. By bringing together the revenue and cost schedules, it can then identify that output quantity at which the excess of revenue over cost (profit) is greatest. (And it can tell the price to charge for this Maximum-profit output just by consulting the demand schedule once again.)

To repeat, the essential thing to grasp about this sequence of ideas is that *it is simple*. It is only when the monopoly firm's profit-maximizing "equilibrium position" (with respect to sales output and price) is outlined in *marginal* terms that it may seem complicated. But these marginal terms are essential analytic tools when one moves on to more complex situations. Hence the emphasis on Marginal Revenue and Marginal Cost in the text chapter and in the review questions here.

4. Columns (1) and (2) of Study Guide Table 25-1 represent a demand schedule. This schedule has been computed or estimated by a firm as indicating the quantities it can sell daily at various prices.

This firm must operate under conditions of *(perfect / imperfect)* competition, since as the output to be sold increases, price *(remains constant / must be reduced)*.

---

imperfect; must be reduced.

---

5. We treat the first two columns of Table 25-1 as representing a monopoly firm's demand schedule. The question: What price will this firm charge, and what output quantity will it sell—if its objective is Maximum-profit?

a. Column 3 of Table 25-1 shows Total Revenue—price times quantity. As a small exercise, complete the four blanks in this column. (Disregard for the moment the three right-hand columns in Table 25-1.)

b. Then use the figures in Columns (2) and (3) to illustrate Total Revenue in Fig. 25-1—i.e., show the Total Revenue associated with various output quantities. Join the points with a smooth curve. (Disregard momentarily the Total Cost *(TC)* curve already drawn on Fig. 25-1.)

Table 25-1

(1) Price	(2) Quantity	(3) Total Revenue	(4) Extra: Quantity	(5) Extra: Revenue	(6) Marginal Revenue
$14.00	10	$140			
			7	$64	$9.14
12.00	17	204			
			8	46	5.75
10.00	25	___			
			___	29	___
9.00	31	279			
			8	33	4.13
8.00	39	312			
			11	___	3.45
7.00	50	___			
			___	14	___
6.50	56	364			
			7	14	2.00
6.00	63	378			
			8	13	1.63
5.50	71	391			
5.00	80	___			
			10	5	0.50
4.50	90	405			
			11	___	−0.09
4.00	101	___			
			___	−5	−0.38
3.50	114	399			

c. Notice that this demand schedule becomes price-inelastic (Chapter 20, Study Guide p. 153) when price is sufficiently lowered—specifically, when price reaches $(8 / 7 / 6 / 5 / 4).

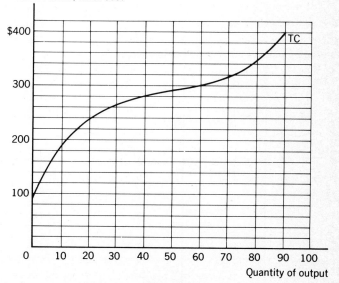

Fig. 25-1

6. *a.* Table 25-2 shows the firm's Total Cost and Marginal Cost for production of the commodity whose demand curve is detailed in Table 25-1. Table 25-2 is similar in construction to Table 23-1 (p. 182)—but just to refresh your memory on the process of computing extra cost, complete the four blanks in Columns (3) and (4) of Table 25-2 with the proper figures.

The graph of Columns (1) and (2) of Table 25-2 is already drawn on Fig. 25-1 as a Total Cost curve *(TC)*. (Mark the curve you drew in question 5 as *TR*, to distinguish it from the cost curve.)

b. It is now possible to see at once why the profit-maximizing process outlined here is a simple one. The firm is doing nothing more than to search for the output at which the

Table 25-2

(1) Output	(2) Total Cost	(3) Extra Cost	(4) MC per Unit
0	$90		
		$60	$12.00
5	150		
		35	7.00
10	185		
		30	6.00
15	215		
		___	___
20	235		
		15	3.00
25	250		
		12	2.40
30	262		
		10	2.00
35	272		
		8	1.60
40	280		
		6	1.20
45	286		
		5	1.00
50	291		
		4	0.80
55	295		
		5	1.00
60	300		
		___	___
65	308		
		10	2.00
70	318		
		12	2.40
75	330		
		15	3.00
80	345		
		20	4.00
85	365		
		35	7.00
90	400		

vertical distance between *TR* and *TC* is greatest. This distance, for any output, is *(fixed cost / price / profit or loss)*. (If *TR* is above *TC*, it is profit; if *TC* is above, it is loss. So it is preferable to look for "greatest vertical distance" with *TR above TC*. The greatest distance with *TC* on top marks the maximum-possible loss, which is somewhat less desirable as an operating position.)

7. *a.* Figure 25-1 is too small to indicate quickly the precise Maximum-profit position. But even a glance is sufficient to indicate that this best-possible position is approximately *(45 / 65 / 85)* units of output.

The firm can be thought of as *gradually* increasing its output and sales, pausing at each increase to see if its profit position is improved. Each extra unit of output brings in a little more revenue (provided demand has not yet moved to the price-inelastic range); and each extra unit incurs a little more cost. The firm's profit position is improved if this small amount of extra revenue *(exceeds / is equal to / is less than)* the small amount of extra cost.

b. More elegantly put, output should be increased, for it will yield an increase in profit, if Marginal Revenue *(MR)* *(exceeds / is equal to / is less than)* Marginal Cost *(MC)*. The firm should cut back its output and sales if it finds that *MR* *(exceeds / is equal to / is less than)* *MC*.

And so the "in-balance" position is where *MR* is *(less than / equal to / greater than)* *MC*.

8. Now we develop the idea of Marginal Revenue more carefully. Column (4) in Table 25-1 shows the extra number of units sold if price is reduced. Column (5) shows extra revenue (positive or negative) accruing from that price reduction. Complete the blanks in these two columns to familiarize yourself with the meanings involved.

Column (6) shows extra revenue *per unit*—Marginal Revenue. Note three things about Marginal Revenue: *(a)* It is precisely analogous to the Marginal Cost of Chapters 23 and 24. Marginal Cost in those two chapters was the *extra* cost resulting from the *last unit of output produced*. Similarly, Marginal Revenue is the *extra* revenue yielded by the *last unit of output produced and sold*. *(b)* *MR falls* as quantity of sales is increased; it can even become a negative figure. *(c)* The *MR*s of Column (6) are not precisely accurate, for Table 25-1 records only price changes of $1 or 50 cents. A true *MR* table would show extra revenue from *each separate* extra unit, not an average of anywhere from 6 to 11 extra units. Table 25-1 would have to include much smaller price changes to show *MR*'s true unit-by-unit performance.

Complete the blanks in Column (6) in Table 25-1.

Column (4): 6, 6, 9, 13.   Column (5): 38, 9, −1.
Column (6): 4.83, 2.33, 1.

---

9.   The general profit-maximizing rule is: Expand your output until you reach the output level at which $MR = MC$—and stop at that point.

Chapter 23 gave a profit-maximizing rule for the firm in pure (or perfect) competition: $P = MC$. This is nothing but a particular instance of the $MR = MC$ rule. It is assumed in pure (or perfect) competition that the demand curve facing the individual firm is perfectly horizontal, or perfectly price-*(elastic / inelastic)*. That is, if market price is $2, the firm receives *(less than $2 / exactly $2 / more than $2)* for each extra unit that it sells. In this special case, MR (extra revenue per unit) is *(greater than / the same thing as / less than)* price per unit (which could be called Average Revenue, or revenue per unit). So in pure (or perfect) competition, $P = MC$ and $MR = MC$ are two ways of saying the same thing.

---

elastic; exactly $2; the same thing as.

---

10.   *a.* In imperfect competition, the firm's demand curve is *(tilted / flat)*—and things are different. From inspection of the figures in Table 25-1 [compare Columns (1) and (6)], it is evident that with such a demand curve, MR at any particular output is *(greater than / the same thing as / less than)* price for that output.

b. Why is this so? Suppose, at price $7, you can sell 4 units; at price $6, 5 units. Revenues associated with these two prices are respectively $28 and $30. Marginal Revenue from selling the fifth unit is accordingly $(2 / 5 / 6 / 7 / 28 / 30). It is the difference in revenue obtained as a result of selling the one extra unit. Why only $2—when the price at which that fifth unit sold was $6? Because to sell that fifth unit, price had to be reduced. And that lowered price applies to *all* 5 units. The first 4, which formerly sold at $7, now bring only $6. On this account, revenue takes a beating of $4. You must subtract this $4 from the $6 which the fifth unit brings in. This leaves a net gain in revenue of $2—Marginal Revenue.

c. Notice also that MR and price elasticity are related. Recall from Chapter 20 (questions 2 through 4, pp. 153–154) that demand is price-inelastic if, when price is reduced, revenue goes *(down / up)*. This means that when demand is inelastic with respect to price, MR is *(negative / zero / positive)*. At elasticity of unity, MR is *(negative / zero / positive)*. When demand is price-elastic, MR is *(negative / zero / positive)*.

---

a. tilted; less than.   *b.* 2.   *c.* down; negative; zero; positive.

---

11.   To return to the fortunes of the firm in Tables 25-1 and 25-2: The tables do not provide sufficient unit-by-unit detail to show the exact Maximum-profit output level. But Table 25-1 indicates that between sales outputs of 63 and 71, MR is

$1.63. The MR figures fall as sales are expanded, so that the $1.63 would apply near the midpoint of this range, say at output 67. MR would be somewhat higher between 63 and 66; somewhat lower between 68 and 71.

Similarly, MC (Table 25-2) would be about $1.65 at output of 67 units. So the Maximum-profit position would fall very close to 67 units produced and sold per period.

To sell this output, the firm would charge a price (see Table 25-1) of about $(7 / 5.75 / 4 / 1.60). Its Total Revenue [look for nearby figures in Column (3)] would be roughly $(380 / 580 / 780). Total Cost (Table 25-2) would be roughly $(310 / 510 / 710), leaving profit per period of about $70.

5.75; 380; 310.

---

12.   The text notes that in geometric terms Marginal Revenue can be depicted as the *slope* of the Total Revenue curve. [See, e.g., text Fig. 25-3 (b).]

a. This can be illustrated by looking more carefully at the Total Revenue curve you have drawn in Fig. 25-1. Study Guide Fig. 25-2 shows an enlargement of a small segment of that curve: that part of the curve between output quantities of 25 and 31. If 25 units are sold, the price is $10 and Total Revenue is $250. This is point A on Fig. 25-2. If price is reduced to $9, that increases sales by 6 units, from 25 units to 31 units. Thus Total Revenue becomes $279 (31 multiplied by $9). So, if the firm reduces price from $10 to $9, in effect it moves from point A to point B.

Figure 25-2's heavier, curved line is the smooth curve used to join points A and B. It is an approximation of the points that would be obtained if we had quantity and revenue data on prices such as $9.90, $9.80, and so on.

There is also a *straight* line (the thin line) joining A and B. It is close to the probable true Total Revenue curve although it is not likely to be the exact curve.

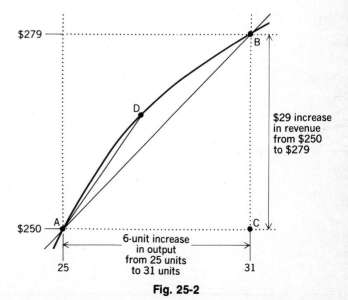

Fig. 25-2

The *slope* of any *straight* line is, as always, the ratio of the two sides of a right-angled triangle drawn beneath it. Here, the slope of the straight line AB is BC / AC. But BC stands for the $29 rise in revenue; AC stands for the 6-unit increase in output. So BC divided by AC is $_____. It is the _____ figure found in Column (6) of Table 25-1.

b. Instead of dropping from price $10 all the way to $9, suppose we had moved only to (say) $9.60. That would have produced (roughly) a 2-unit increase in quantity demanded. In this way, we would move closer to the true *MR* figure than our previous 6-unit approximation supplied. In Fig. 25-2 terms, we would be moving from A only to D, not from A to B. Notice that the straight line (the thin line) joining A to D becomes a (*better / poorer*) approximation of the presumed true Total Revenue curve than was the case when the points involved were A and B.

In sum, the closer we move point B to point A (for example, if we make it D rather than B), the closer the slope figure comes to being a measure of the true *MR* figure. Strictly speaking, we have true *MR* (the rate of change in revenue as measured in terms of 1-unit output changes) only when the line whose slope is being measured to indicate *MR* is actually *tangent to* the Total Revenue curve.

---

a. 4.83; Marginal Revenue. *b.* better.

---

13. In its near-closing section "Bygones and Margins," the text chapter emphasizes that if a firm is setting its price and output according to *MR = MC* principles, *it will disregard Fixed Cost.*

This does not mean that Fixed Cost is unimportant to the firm. But the all-important curves, for profit-maximizing purposes, are Marginal Revenue and Marginal Cost. [See text Fig. 25-4(a), where Maximum-profit output is marked by intersection of these two curves.]

Recall the Total Cost discussion in Chapter 24 (Study Guide questions 1 and 2, p. 188). Average Cost is the sum of Average Fixed Cost and Average Variable Cost.

a. Suppose a firm's Fixed Cost is increased (e.g., by a flat tax levied on a monopolist, as in the text section mentioned above). Will the effect of this tax be to raise the firm's AC curve? . . . .*(Yes / No)*
b. Will the tax affect the monopolist's Variable Cost, or the AVC curve? . . . . *(Yes / No)*
c. Will the tax affect the monopolist's Marginal Cost curve? (REMEMBER: *AVC is* the average of all *MC*s, from zero up to the output in question.) . . . . *(Yes / No)*
d. If the *MC* curve is unaffected, will such a flat tax change the Maximum-profit output? (Presumably the tax will not affect demand for the product, so it will not affect Marginal Revenue.) . . . . *(Yes / No)*

e. If the tax does not affect *MC*, *MR*, or Maximum-profit output, will price be changed? . . . . *(Yes / No)*

---

a. Yes. *b.* No (because the tax affects only Fixed Cost and the *AFC* curve). *c.* No. *d.* No. *e.* No.

QUIZ: Multiple Choice

1. *If a firm's Marginal Revenue exceeds its Marginal Cost, Maximum-profit rules require that firm to* (1) increase its output in both perfect and imperfect competition; (2) increase its output in perfect but not necessarily in imperfect competition; (3) increase its output in imperfect but not necessarily in perfect competition; (4) decrease its output in both perfect and imperfect competition; (5) increase price, not output, in both perfect and imperfect competition.

2. *Whenever a firm's demand curve is horizontal or "perfectly elastic,"* (1) the firm cannot be operating under conditions of perfect competition; (2) the profit-maximizing rule of *MR*-equal-to-*MC* does not apply; (3) price and Marginal Revenue must be one and the same; (4) price and Marginal Cost must be one and the same; (5) none of these conclusions is necessarily correct.

3. *A basic difference between the firm in perfect (or pure) competition and the monopoly firm, according to economic analysis, is that* (1) the perfect competitor can sell as much as he wishes at some given price, whereas the monopolist must lower his price whenever he wishes to increase the amount of his sales by any significant amount; (2) the monopolist can always charge a price that brings him a substantial profit, whereas the perfect competitor can never earn such a profit; (3) the elasticity of demand facing the monopolist is a higher figure than the elasticity of demand facing the perfect competitor; (4) the monopolist seeks to maximize profit, whereas the perfect competitor's rule is to equate price and Average Cost; (5) none of the above.

4. *"Oligopoly"* means (1) the same thing as imperfect competition; (2) a situation in which the number of competing firms is large but the products differ slightly; (3) a situation in which the number of competing firms is small; (4) that particular condition of imperfect competition which is just removed from monopoly, regardless of the number of firms or type of product; (5) none of these.

5. *When a monopoly firm seeking to maximize its profits has reached its "equilibrium position," then* (1) price must be less than Marginal Cost; (2) price must be equal to Marginal Cost; (3) price must be greater than Marginal Cost; (4) price may be equal to or below Marginal Cost, but not above it; (5) none of the above is necessarily correct since equilibrium does not require any particular relation between price and Marginal Cost.

6. *The text, in this chapter, sets out a general rule which a firm supposedly should follow with respect to maximizing its profit. The essence of this rule can be stated as follows: Its purpose is to identify* (1) that output at which Total Revenue is at its maximum; (2) that output at which the excess of price over Average Cost is greatest; (3) that output at which the excess of Total Revenue over Total Cost is greatest; (4) the highest-obtainable price; (5) that output at which Average Cost is at its minimum.

7. *"Marginal Revenue" means* (1) the price that can be obtained for the very last unit sold; (2) Total Revenue divided by quantity of units sold; (3) Total Revenue minus the price received for the very last unit sold; (4) the amount of increase in Total Revenue brought in by the very last unit sold minus the increase in Total Cost which that unit occasioned; (5) the amount of increase in Total Revenue brought in by the very last unit sold.

8. *"Monopoly" exists, according to the economist's definition of this term,* (1) whenever there is only one seller of a particular product; (2) whenever the seller has at least some degree of control over the price he can charge; (3) whenever profit earned by the seller exceeds the amount that should properly be earned as interest on money invested, plus an allowance for risk undertaken; (4) whenever a seller manages to maintain his position through successful advertising; (5) in none of these situations, necessarily.

9. *A firm operating in a situation of imperfect competition finds that at its present output level, Marginal Revenue is $2 and Average Cost is $1.75, which is the minimum value of Average Cost. For Maximum-profit, this firm should* (1) increase price; (2) decrease price; (3) decrease output and sales; (4) leave price and output unchanged; (5) perhaps do any of these things—information given is insufficient to tell.

10. *Which alternative in question 9 would be correct had it specified that price rather than Marginal Revenue was $2?* (1). (2). (3). (4). (5).

11. *The essential characteristic of (or "acid test" for) all cases of imperfect competition, according to the text, is that the single firm's* (1) demand curve has a downward tilt; (2) Marginal Revenue exceeds the price it charges; (3) Average Cost curve falls over a substantial or large range of outputs; (4) product is "differentiated" from one firm to the next; (5) Average Cost curve rises over a substantial or large range of outputs.

12. *If the price a firm obtains for its output exceeds the Marginal Cost associated with that particular output, Maximum-profit rules would require that firm to* (1) increase its output in both perfect and imperfect competition; (2) increase its output in perfect but not necessarily in imperfect competition; (3) increase its output in imperfect but not necessarily in perfect competition; (4) decrease its output in both perfect and imperfect competition; (5) increase price, not output, in both perfect and imperfect competition.

13. *Which alternative in question 12 would be correct had that question said that price is* less *than Marginal Cost?* (1). (2). (3). (4). (5).

14. *To explain why imperfect competition is far more prevalent than perfect competition, the text lays considerable emphasis upon the fact that, for the firms in many industries,* (1) advertising has now become more powerful than price as a sales weapon; (2) Marginal Revenue tends to equal or even to exceed price; (3) Average Cost continues to fall until a large output has been reached; (4) a high price charged to consumers has become the most effective method of maximizing profits; (5) Marginal Revenue tends to fall significantly below price.

15. *A correct statement of the relationship between Marginal Revenue (MR) and elasticity of demand (with respect to price) is this: When MR is* (1) negative, demand must be inelastic; (2) zero, demand must be inelastic; (3) positive, demand must be inelastic; (4) negative, demand must be unit-elastic; (5) positive, demand must be perfectly elastic.

16. *Among the five statements below, one must be false with respect to any firm operating under conditions of imperfect competition. Which one?* (1) The number of competing sellers offering similar (although differentiated) products can be large. (2) Other firms may sell products which are identical or almost identical with this firm's product. (3) The number of competing sellers offering similar (although differentiated) products can be small. (4) The firm's Marginal Revenue will be less than the price it obtains. (5) The demand curve facing the firm can be perfectly horizontal.

17. *If a firm discovers that demand for its product is inelastic with respect to price, in the price-and-output range in which it is selling, and if it seeks to maximize its profit, it should* (1) remain at its present position; (2) always lower its price and seek to increase its sales; (3) always raise its price, even at the cost of a sales reduction; (4) raise its price, but only if that price reduction will not reduce its sales; (5) perhaps do any of the above—the information given is not sufficient for any change in decision.

18. *Which alternative in question 17 would be correct had it specified "elastic with respect to price," not "inelastic"?* (1). (2). (3). (4). (5).

QUIZ: Other

1. Figure 25-3 shows the per-unit cost and revenue measures confronting a firm which operates under conditions of monopoly or imperfect competition. The *AR* line is Average Revenue—price obtainable per unit. *MR* is Marginal Revenue; *MC* is Marginal Cost; *AC*, Average Cost.

Revenue per unit in $
Cost per unit in $

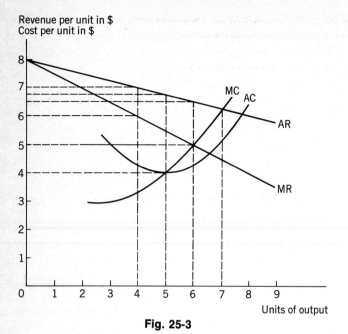

Fig. 25-3

a. Which line indicates the demand curve? .... _____

b. If output is 4, what must price be? .... _____

c. What is Marginal Revenue with output 4? .... _____

d. At what level of output does Average Cost fall to its minimum level? .... _____

e. What would price be with output at this minimum *AC* level? .... _____

f. What would Total Cost be (at this level)? .... _____

g. What would Total Revenue be? .... _____

h. What would profit be? .... _____

i. At what output would profit be maximized? ..... _____

j. What is Marginal Revenue at this output? .... _____

k. What is Marginal Cost at this output? .... _____

l. What is Average Cost at this output? (Assume it is 20 cents above minimum level.) .... _____

m. What is price at this output? .... _____

n. What is Total Profit at this output? .... _____

2. You are a consultant on profit maximization. What do you recommend in each of the seven cases listed in Table 25-3? Each firm is a monopoly, or operates in circumstances of imperfect competition, and wants to maximize its profit (or minimize its loss).

Enough information is supplied in each case, despite the blanks, to provide an answer. Note that there is, among the seven, at least one "nonsense" case in which the figures are inconsistent and cannot all be correct.

Answer for each case by putting *one* of the numbers 1 through 5 from the code below into the extreme right-hand column of the table. (The same number may of course be used for more than one question.)

(1) Firm is now at correct position.

(2) Firm should increase price and reduce quantity produced and sold.

(3) Firm should reduce price and increase quantity produced and sold.

(4) Firm should shut down operations because loss at best-possible operating position exceeds Fixed Cost.

(5) A nonsense case—figures supplied are inconsistent and could not all be correct.

Table 25-3

Case	Price	Marginal Revenue	Quantity of Output	Total Revenue	Total Cost	Fixed Cost	Average Cost	Marginal Cost	Answer
a.	$8.00	$4.00	2,000			$2,000	$4.00	$3.00	
b.	5.00	4.00	1,000		$4,000	1,000	At minimum level		
c.			4,000	$8,000			1.80	2.00	
d.	8.00	zero		32,000		5,000		4.00	
e.	1.00	2.00	10,000			2,000	2.00	2.00	
f.	3.00		2,000		6,000		At minimum level		
g.	2.50	2.00	10,000			4,000	3.00	2.00	

APPENDIX: Monopoly Regulation and Exploitation; Game Theory

1. Suppose a firm to be in a monopoly position with respect to some product or service considered as a necessity. The demand for this product or service is sufficiently strong that the monopoly firm, setting its price by the profit-maximizing rules of this chapter, is able to obtain very substantial profits. If for some reason there is no prospect of competition bringing the price down, the authorities may intervene and set up a commission to regulate this firm's price. The problem, then: If price is not to be set by the standard of Maximum Profit, by what rule or standard *ought* it to be set?

a. If the evil in the original situation is thought to be the amount of profit the monopoly firm earned, the commission may decide to set a price which brings the enterprise only a reasonable return on the capital invested. In terms of the per unit demand-and-cost diagrams used in this chapter, this means a price identified by the intersection of the *(Marginal Revenue / demand)* curve and the *(Marginal / Average Variable / Average)* Cost curve.

Economic theory tries to probe a little deeper for "the correct price." The past three chapters have emphasized the importance of having the price of each and every good just equal to the *(Average / Marginal / Total)* Cost of producing that good. The underlying idea is that it is only when prices *do* reflect these *(Average / Marginal / Total)* Costs that we can get the right balance with respect to quantities of goods produced. The resource supply out of which they are produced is limited; if these resources are fully employed, then more of good A means less of B, or of C, or of D. An overall Price-equals-Marginal Cost situation means that we have just the right quantity of good A, just the right quantity of B, and so on. The quantities are "just right" in the sense that any rearrangement would worsen rather than improve the community's welfare. (This reasoning is subject to a number of qualifications, but they need not be considered here.) The concluding sections of text Chapters 23 and 25 discuss this material in more detail, and it is tackled again in Chapter 32.

b. Applying this principle to the regulated-monopoly situation, it follows that the regulated price ought to be set equal to *(Average / Marginal / Total)* Cost. In diagram terms, it would be identified by the intersection of the *(Marginal Revenue / demand)* curve and the *(Marginal / Average Variable / Average)* Cost curve.

Suppose, for example, that Average Cost is $1, Marginal Cost is 50 cents, and price has been set at the $1 Average Cost figure. The consumer then pays $1 for each unit he buys, including the last unit. Yet that last unit added only 50 cents to total production cost; and it would cost only another 50 cents, or just slightly more than 50 cents perhaps, to produce one further unit. Why shouldn't consumers be able to buy that unit for what it would cost to produce it? A resource is not

being used to its best advantage if consumers, reckoning in terms of the price they must pay for an additional unit, halt their purchases at a point where the extra cost of using the resource to produce that additional unit is significantly less than price. The situation is as it was in monopoly: Price is *above* Marginal Cost.

c. The complication, of course, is that the total revenue yielded by a Marginal Cost price will be insufficient to cover total cost when Marginal Cost is *(less / higher)* than Average Cost. In terms of text Fig. 25-6, the Marginal Cost pricing principle produces this difficulty when the demand curve for the product or service cuts through the Marginal Cost curve to the *(left / right)* of the point where this *MC* curve passes through the bottom point of the Average Cost curve.

The Appendix to text Chapter 25 indicates that in such circumstances, the proper solution would be to set:
(1) A price just sufficient to cover costs, including a reasonable rate of return on capital invested.
(2) A Marginal Cost price and to provide a subsidy to the firm sufficient to cover its resulting loss.
(3) A Marginal Cost price and to make the firm pay its loss out of profits obtained earlier.

d. What if the demand curve cuts through Marginal and Average Cost curves in the region to the right of the intersection of these two cost curves? A Marginal Cost price would then mean *(profits / losses)* for the supplying firm. The text argument is that in this situation:
(1) A principle of pricing by Average Cost should be adopted.
(2) The Marginal Cost pricing principle should be retained, and the excess profit taken away via taxation.
(3) The Marginal Cost pricing principle should be retained, and the firm allowed to retain the profit thus earned.

The subsection in the text Appendix on "Monopoly exploitation of labor" (at the close of its "Ideally Regulated Pricing" section) is a brief mention of the same Marginal Cost principle applied in a quite different situation.

---

a. demand; Average; Marginal; Marginal. *b.* Marginal; demand; Marginal. *c.* less; left; (2). *d.* profits; (2).

---

2. Oligopoly (a small number of sellers) is one of the forms of imperfect competition mentioned in the text chapter. Although oligopoly is a common situation in contemporary business life, the analysis of oligopoly pricing and oligopoly behavior is one of the most poorly developed of all aspects of economic theory. "The theory of games" is one attempt to break new ground in this area. (Game-theory proponents say that their analysis is useful also in such other areas as the analysis of politics and of warfare.)

Two vital concepts in the theory of games are those of *conflict* and of *strategy*. The two (or more) players in a game are in *conflict*. Each strives to beat the other (or the others), and devises a *strategy* for that purpose. (A strategy is simply a decision as to what you are going to *do* in the game. You have devised a strategy when you say, "If my opponent does *this*, then I am going to do *that*.") In principle, even in a game as complicated as chess, it is possible for you to work out the best-possible strategy in response to each move your opponent might make—although with a long sequence of moves, and with a wide variety of alternative strategies at each move, the process in chess and other such games becomes so complicated that even a computer cannot handle it.

Game theory relies on the evident parallels between oligopoly and games. Oligopoly firms are in competition—i.e., in conflict—with one another. The essence of oligopoly is interdependence: the number of competitors is small, and "what you do affects me, and what I do affects you." Thus (up to some point, at least), each of us is fighting to win over the other for a share in the consumer's dollar. My strategy will be governed (or at least influenced) by what you do competitively, and your strategy will similarly be affected by what I do. (Critics of game theory will say that this parallel between games and oligopolistic behavior can be pushed too far, and that in other important respects the two situations are quite different.)

The Macy's-Gimbel's example in the text is an elementary instance of game theory applied to a duopoly situation. (When the number of competitors is reduced to two, oligopoly is reduced to duopoly.) Gimbel's strategy is: We will match Macy's price or any other. Macy's strategy is: We will sell at 10 per cent below any other price, including Gimbel's. If both firms hold rigidly to these strategies, regardless of consequences, the ultimate result must be a price equal to (*Marginal Cost / zero / Average Cost*).

So if each firm were to stick grimly to its original strategy, the outcome would be disaster for both. This outcome is produced by *the two strategies in combination*. When through experience the two firms come to realize this fact (that the outcome is one of strategies in combination), one firm or both will switch to a different and less short-sighted strategy. In the example above, it seems probable that the onus for a change in strategy would rest primarily with (*Macy's, the price cutter / Gimbel's, the price matcher*).

Particularly if the products sold by the two firms are the same, or virtually the same, so that they must charge the same price, it is evident that the outcome will be a price set by some form of tacit agreement, if not by collusion. (Figure 25-7 in the text yields no information as to what that price will be.)

---

zero; Macy's, the price cutter.

---

3. In the Macy's-Gimbel's example, the final outcome (that of a zero price for both, assuming no change in either firm's

strategy) would be realized only after an infinite series of moves and countermoves. Other elementary presentations of game theory show the outcome of *one single move* on the part of each of the two participants. Text Table 25-4, where the participants are Orange and Brown, is an example. Each has just one move to make: Orange can set his price either at $2 or $1; Brown has the same alternatives. So each must pick between two possible moves; and the result—"the payoff"— is a consequence of *the two choices combined*.

a. Put yourself in Orange's position: If you (Orange) set your price at $2, and Brown sets *his* price at $2 also, then, by reference to text Table 25-4, your (*profit / loss*)—the orange figure at the bottom left-hand corner of the cell marked A— will be $(9 / 6 / 2 / 0), and Brown's (*profit / loss*)—the brown figure at the top right-hand corner of the same cell—will be $(9 / 6 / 2 / 0). However, if Brown instead sets his price at $1 (with yours at $2), your resulting (*profit / loss*) will be $(9 / 6 / 2 / 0).

b. Your alternative choice (as Orange) is to pick price $1. If Brown concurrently chooses price $2, your (*profit / loss*) will be $(9 / 6 / 2 / 0). If, instead, Brown has picked price $1, your profit will be $(9 / 6 / 2 / 0). (The two of you must move at the same time. You are not allowed to have Brown make his move first, and *then* make your move.)

c. For you (Orange), the best of all worlds would be to land in cell (*A / B / C / D*), since your profit would then be $(9 / 6 / 2 / 0). This outcome (*would / would not*) be a happy one for Brown, for his (*profit / loss*) would be $(9 / 6 / 2 / 0). You cannot pick price $1 in confidence that you will reach cell C, since Brown may set his price at $1 also, in which case you both reach the zero-profit position of cell D.

d. If, however, your choice (as Orange) is to set a price of $2, you can wind up with a loss of $(9 / 6 / 2 / 0) if Brown sets his price at $(2 / 1). Hence, on both "best-possible outcome" and "play it safe" grounds, price $(2 / 1) is your better choice. Since, in this particular model, Brown's situation is identical with yours, he too will want to set his price at $(2 / 1). Thus cell (*A / B / C / D*) is a "stable equilibrium position."

Alternatively, cell D is an equilibrium position because if you take any of the other three cells, one firm or the other can always better its position by altering its choice. If the two firms land in cell B, for example, (*Orange / Brown*) will thereupon change his price from $2 to $1, thereby moving from a (*profit / loss*) of $(9 / 6 / 2 / 0) to a loss of $(9 / 6 / 2 / 0). This moves them both to cell D: note in text Table 25-4 the orange arrow crossing from cell B to cell D.

e. But note one further point: Just as in the Macy's-Gimbel's model, the possibility of collusion exists. If you (Orange) conspire or collude with Brown, then the cell you choose together will be (*A / B / C / D*), since your profit will be $(9 / 6 / 2 / 0), and Brown's will be $(9 / 6 / 2 / 0).

Bear in mind that this particular model is, as it were, rigged toward an outcome of collusion. Other models could be used in which the two firms, even if they wanted to conspire, could not agree in selecting a cell because there is no "best for both" cell. Moreover, this is a two-firm model. As the number of firms is increased, even, say, to four or five, the possibility of successful, outright collusion to reach an "exploit the buyer" price diminishes. A more likely outcome would be tacit agreement on a "satisfactory" price, which is not necessarily the same thing.

---

a. profit; 6; profit; 6; loss; 2. *b.* profit; 9; 0. *c.* C; 9; would not; loss; 2. *d.* 2; 1; 1; 1; D; Orange; loss; 2; 0. *e.* A; 6; 6.

Game theory is a comparatively recent development, and economists disagree as to the extent to which it can be made useful in analysis of pricing behavior. But it brings out one point of great importance. The pure competitor of Chapters 23 and 24 and the monopolist of Chapter 25 are exactly alike in one respect: Each is assumed to know exactly the courses of action he can follow and exactly what the outcome will be; there is no uncertainty. A real-life businessman is unlikely to find himself in this happy position; he is forced to decide and to act without knowing just what the outcome of his action (the payoff) will be. Game theory brings out this condition with special force by presenting a situation in which you do not know the outcome of your move because your opponent is trying to stop you from reaching your desired goal. "The prisoner's dilemma," discussed at the end of the text Appendix, depicts precisely the same problem of deciding under conditions of uncertainty. (The "uncertainty" in these simple models is of course limited, since there are only two possible outcomes to each move, and the payoff from each outcome is known.)

Whether or not game theory is the proper vehicle to use, price theory needs to be able to depict situations in which decisions must be made under uncertainty; and it must isolate the economic circumstances which produce this uncertainty. As yet, it has not progressed very far in this direction.

QUIZ: Multiple Choice

1. *The "ideally regulated price" for the monopoly situation described in the text Appendix would be one set equal to* (1) Marginal Cost, in the event such Marginal Cost should fall with any increase in output, otherwise to Average Cost; (2) Marginal Cost, in the event such Marginal Cost should rise with any increase in output, otherwise to Average Cost; (3) Marginal Cost, regardless of whether such Marginal Cost would rise or fall with any increase in output; (4) Average Cost; (5) either Marginal or Average Cost, whichever of the two would be lower at the output level involved.

2. *Including in production cost a normal or reasonable rate of return on capital invested, the "ideally regulated price" of question 1 would result in a loss for the regulated monopoly* (1) if Marginal Cost should fall in value with any increase in output, but not otherwise; (2) if demand is inelastic with respect to price; (3) if Marginal Cost should rise in value with any increase in output, but not otherwise; (4) if Marginal Cost should fall in value with any increase in output, and to some extent if it should rise; (5) in no circumstances.

3. *Insofar as game theory is useful in price analysis, it is most likely to be applicable in cases of* (1) oligopoly; (2) monopoly; (3) many differentiated sellers; (4) pure (or perfect) competition; (5) industries where speculation plays a dominant role.

4. *In game theory, a "game-payoff matrix" is* (1) an outline of that particular strategy which would produce the maximum payoff for either player; (2) a table or figure showing alternative strategies and their payoffs; (3) an outline of that strategy by means of which the winner of the game reached his victory; (4) that combination of strategies which would produce the maximum payoff for the two players combined; (5) none of these things.

5. *In "the prisoner's dilemma," two persons, A and B, have been arrested for a crime (of which they are both guilty). They are kept separate, and the dilemma for A is whether or not to confess, not knowing whether or not B will confess. The text uses this situation to illustrate the clash between "altruism" and "selfishness." In this situation, the altruistic decision for A is to* (1) confess, assuming that B will likewise confess; (2) refuse to confess, but assuming that B will confess; (3) confess, but assuming that B will refuse to confess; (4) confess, regardless of whether B confesses or not; (5) refuse to confess, assuming that B will likewise refuse.

26 IMPERFECT COMPETITION AND ANTITRUST POLICY

1. In his books *The New Industrial State* (1967) and *Economics and the Public Purpose* (1973), John Kenneth Galbraith has argued that microeconomic price theory does a poor job of describing contemporary economic life, mainly because of its neglect of the development of the large corporation. Price theory says that supplying firms work through the price-and-market mechanism. Galbraith says that big corporations increasingly dislike the uncertainties of this mechanism, and try to avoid the market by private contracts or by merger with other firms. Price theory has little to say on the subject of advertising. Galbraith says advertising is among the most important weapons available to big corporations; they use this weapon to manipulate consumer tastes and to force unnecessary goods upon the public. Price theory says that supplying firms seek to maximize their profits. Galbraith says the goal of big corporations is *growth,* not profit maximization, because those who control the corporation have no great interest in such maximization. (This view on profit maximization was expressed with little qualification in the original edition of *The New Industrial State.* Later, Galbraith amended it somewhat, conceding that any company which neglects its profit opportunities unduly is in danger of takeover by another corporation.)

Galbraith thinks society's direction is passing increasingly into the hands of *(shareholders / professional administrators / technically trained experts)* through the control which this group exerts within each corporation. He thinks this process is *(confined to the United States / worldwide).* In this development, he *(puts / does not put any)* emphasis on the significance of different political systems.

---

technically trained experts; worldwide; does not put any.

---

2. Galbraith is by no means the only critic of the theory as presented (for example) in Chapters 23 through 25 of the text. That theory says that business firms must pay strict attention to "marginalist" rules if they want to maximize their profits. Opponents of the theory insist that business executives in fact pay little attention to such rules—partially because they lack the detailed information on costs and on revenues required for application of these rules, partially because the environment in which they must operate is in other respects markedly different from that assumed in the theory. The typical real-life price (so these opponents argue) is a "markup price," not a marginalist one. That is, it begins with *(marginal / average)* cost, and to this figure some markup is added.

The text's verdict on such criticism is (pick one):
(1) The idea that prices are really built on markups proves on careful examination to be factually incorrect.
(2) The markup idea is pretty vague, but insofar as the markup amount can be interpreted in terms of marginal revenue and cost, the theory as previously outlined is still valid, in broad terms.
(3) The whole theory of pricing may have to be rewritten in the light of such attacks.

---

average; (2).

---

3. The case of *pure oligopoly* illustrates with special clarity the problems confronting the firm in imperfect competition. In this situation, the number of firms engaged in close competition is *(large / small, or comparatively small),* while the products they sell are *(uniform / differentiated).*

The important consequence of this uniformity or "homogeneity" of product is that *all firms must charge the same price.* If any one company tries to raise its price, and the others do not follow suit, that company will most probably *(gain / lose some of its / lose all or practically all its)* customers. On the other hand, if this company *reduces* price, it is most likely that all rivals will be forced to follow suit. Thus, each firm has some influence over the price buyers must pay, particularly because of its ability to reduce price.

The knowledge that "we're all in the same boat" may produce a tacit agreement among the firms to abide by some given price, and to use competitive weapons *other than price* to try to secure business, such as advertising.

One interesting consequence of this handling of competition is that even though the products are essentially homogeneous (i.e., no customer is disposed to pay a higher price for the product of any one firm), each firm may try hard to persuade the buying public that its product is "different," in order to retain or expand its share of the market. This may make it difficult to decide whether the various products sold by the firms comprising this industry are really differentiated or homogeneous.

---

small; uniform; lose all or practically all.

---

4. Text Fig. 26-2, showing a "kinked" demand curve, illustrates the pure-oligopoly predicament. Point *G* indicates the established price and the quantity the firm is now selling at that price. If the firm were to raise price, its sales would fall off drastically (unless, of course, rival companies do likewise—on this, see below); so the demand curve will be horizontal or almost so with respect to any price *increase*.

If, on the other hand, the firm *cuts* price, its rivals usually have little alternative but to follow suit. The best single assumption (not necessarily always correct) is that in the event of such an all-around price cut, each company will continue to retain the same percentage share of the total market for the product. So with respect to price *reductions*, the firm's demand curve is *(horizontal or highly price-elastic / a smaller-scale version of the industry demand curve)*. Consequently, there is a "kink" in the demand curve at point G.

This outline of oligopoly pricing leaves some unsettled questions which economic theory is as yet unable to answer. For example, it was mentioned above that if one firm raises its price, its sales will be cut drastically unless rival firms follow suit. When *will* they follow suit? The underlying question is this: What are the principles or rules by means of which oligopoly firms decide on a mutually acceptable price? (Quite possibly, average cost—the cost which must be covered if any profit is to be made—is prominent in these considerations.) Another question: Is it possible to explain all this in the same $MR = MC$ profit-maximizing terms outlined in Chapters 23 through 25?

a smaller-scale version of the industry demand curve.

5. In each space below, put I if the description suggests a firm operating in one of the categories of *imperfect* competition. Put P if it is typical of a firm in *perfect* competition. Put B if it applies to firms in *both* situations; put N if it applies to *neither* situation.

a. Any decline in industry demand normally causes price charged by this firm and by its competitors to fall. .....( )
b. In some circumstances, the firm is willing to sell at price below *AC*. ....( )
c. Any excess of price over *AC* is temporary; entry of new firms will push price down to equality with *AC*. ......( )
d. The firm seeks an output level at which $MR = MC$. ( )
e. Industry of which it is a member consists of only six or seven firms, which, however, compete vigorously with one another for business. ....( )
f. It operates at an output where price = *MC*. ....( )
g. It finds it necessary to reduce price if it wants to increase the quantity of its output and sales. ....( )
h. It may reach price-fixing agreements or understandings with other firms out of a fear that price competition will result in excessive losses. ....( )
i. When demand declines, it does not change price. ...( )
j. The product it sells is somewhat differentiated from that sold by its competitors. ....( )
k. In the long run, it can be expected to operate at an output where *AC* is at its minimum level. ....( )

l. It operates at an output where *MC* is well above price. ( )
m. It has some degree of choice, some alternatives, as to the price it may charge for its product. ....( )
n. It operates at an output where *MC* is well below price. ( )

---

a. P. *b.* B. *c.* P. *d.* B. *e.* I. *f.* P. *g.* I. *h.* I. *i.* I. *j.* I. *k.* P. *l.* N. *m.* I. *n.* I.

6. The text, in the section "Many Differentiated Sellers," leaves oligopoly, moving on to the different case in which sellers are many in number but where each firm's product is "differentiated" to some degree from those of the other firms—a situation which is said to give each firm some degree of "monopoly power"—i.e., power to set its own price.

The fact that there are *many* sellers suggests that it is fairly easy for new firms to enter the industry in question. And new firms *will* be tempted to enter, insofar as those already therein are earning profits. This entry may of course take time; by the convention mentioned in Chapter 24 (Study Guide question 7, p. 190), entry (or exit) of firms is a "long-run" consideration.

a. Insofar as new firms *do* enter, they take over some part of the market of already-operating firms. This means that, for any one of such older firms, its demand curve tends to be pushed *(to the right or upward / to the left or downward)*. This *(reduces / increases)* the profit of the older firm. If the entry tendency persists, the firm's demand curve will wind up just *touching*, or tangent to, the Average Cost curve. Such a tangency situation means that the firm in question can *(still earn a profit / just break even / operate only at a loss)*.

When this tangency point is reached for the typical firm—i.e., for most, if not all, firms—the profit feature which attracted new entrants *(still / no longer)* exists.

b. Each firm's demand curve, in this "differentiated seller" situation, is assumed to be a *(tilted / flat)* one, because the fact of product differentiation supposedly *(gives some / does not give any)* degree of monopoly power to the firm. But *if* the demand curve is tilted, and *if* things wind up with this demand curve just touching the Average Cost curve, the tangency point thus produced *(must / cannot)* occur at the very bottom of the *AC* curve. (A tangency point is one at which the two curves involved have the same slope. If the demand curve is tilted at the point in question, so must be the *AC* curve.)

c. Thus our hypothetical firm winds up earning no profit, yet operating at an output level which is *(less than / equal to / greater than)* its minimum-*AC* output. In the sense that a larger output would reduce its *AC*, this firm has "excess capacity." Economists were much occupied with these ideas when Edward H. Chamberlin first introduced them. They suggested that "competition" might not work quite as pure (or perfect) competition theory had suggested it would. In squeezing out profits, it might not work toward minimum Average Cost. The argument of pure competition theory had been that—if only in the long run—we would get the best of all the worlds: minimum Average Cost of production, and zero profits.

(Chamberlin would have insisted that any such comparison between the supposed "long-run" results of pure and of monopolistic competition must not be used to condemn monopolistic competition. He was convinced that monopolistic competition was the near-universal and inevitable situation. Pure competition theory might point to an "ideal" situation; but it was an unattainable ideal in real-life circumstances.)

---

a. to the left or downward; reduces; just break even; no longer. *b.* tilted; gives some; cannot. *c.* less than.

---

7. When a regulating commission is given the task of setting the rate or price that a "regulated monopoly" (e.g., an electric power company or similar public utility) may charge, its first consideration is likely to be: Find a price that will just yield the company a "fair rate of return"—for example, 8 per cent on the company's invested capital.

The problem then becomes one of deciding what the invested-capital amount really is. What is the money value of the company's plant, equipment, and similar assets? On what money amount is it to be allowed to earn 8 per cent? The text mentions three methods of computation: original cost of fixed assets, replacement cost of fixed assets, and capitalized market value of fixed assets.

Capitalized market value says that assets should be valued, not by their cost, but by the net income or return they bring in. Asset A's original (or replacement) cost may be much above that of asset B; but if A and B both earn the same income (and are expected to continue to do so), A and B have the same capitalized value.

Elsewhere, capitalized value is considered (see Chapter 30) the most appropriate method of computing asset values. Yet the text here rejects it. Which of the following (one *or* more) properly explains why?

a. If the utility is just beginning operations, it has no history of revenue or income earned; and such figures are essential for the computation of a capitalized value.
b. The purpose is to determine the rate, or price, the utility should properly charge. If in the past it has earned a very high income by charging exorbitant rates, the capitalized-value method will point to a correspondingly high asset value and so can be used to justify the rates charged.
c. Suppose the regulating body has been overly harsh and has allowed only rates that are much too low. If revenues are low, the capitalized-value method will indicate that the utility's assets have only a low value, and so will justify the rates that have been imposed.

All: *a*, *b*, and *c*.

---

8. The first antitrust act, passed in 1890, was the *(Sherman / Clayton / Celler)* Act. An unusually short act in wording, it forbade two things: (1) contracts, combinations, or conspiracies in restraint of trade or commerce, and (2) monopoly or attempts to monopolize.

These two provisions received very different treatment by the courts. Conspiracy is a well-understood term in law, and the crime of conspiracy was identifiable. From the beginning, the Sherman Act was applied firmly in opposition to attempts to set price and parcel out markets, *when such attempts were made by separate and independent firms meeting together—* i.e., "conspiring."

The courts had no such well-established tradition as to what constituted a monopoly. Nevertheless, two notable monopoly convictions were obtained (at the Supreme Court level) in 1911: against the American Tobacco Company and the Standard Oil Company. These companies had employed highly ungentlemanly behavior toward their competitors. Both were ordered broken up into smaller units.

In both cases, the Supreme Court enunciated "the rule of reason." Only *unreasonable* restraints on competition, the Court said, should constitute violations of the Sherman Act. In effect, this was a complaint against the vagueness of that act, especially with respect to the meaning of monopoly. And it suggested that *the courts* would decide what was reasonable and what was not.

Congress, feeling that the rule-of-reason provision would allow the courts to specify the meaning of the law, passed the *(Celler / Robinson-Patman / Clayton)* Act in 1914. This was in effect an amendment to the Sherman Act, spelling out in more detail what constituted a violation of that act. But the new act did not answer two vital questions: What is a monopoly? What is an attempt to monopolize?

In 1920 came a famous landmark monopoly case, the

_____ case, which was dismissed primarily because the company—unlike American Tobacco and Standard Oil—had carefully refrained from aggressive action against its competitors. "The law," said the Court, "does not make mere size an offense."

The paradox which now arose was this: If officials from a group of independent firms meet together to set price, this violates the Sherman Act (under the conspiracy section). Suppose now that these firms merge to form one large-sized company. The same officials meet again, this time as vice-presidents of the new concern. Is their meeting a violation of the Sherman Act (under the monopoly section, as interpreted by the U.S. Steel case)? No.

The Great Depression of the 1930s provoked considerable antibusiness sentiment, and it was argued that the U.S. Steel decision did not reflect antitrust's true intent. When Thurman Arnold was appointed director of the Justice Department's Antitrust Division, a broadside of new prosecutions began. A notably successful "monopoly" conviction was upheld by the

Supreme Court in 1945: the _____ case. Another antitrust success was the "Big Three" Cigarette case—seemingly of greater potential importance because it struck at a more prevalent phenomenon: (*oligopoly / monopolistic competition / monopoly*).

But Arnold's influence was gone; and the pendulum swung back. Since Arnold's day, antitrust policy has never displayed any comparable willingness to challenge the big-corporation status quo.

For a brief period in the 1960s, there was a strong antitrust attack on "conglomerates" (the common control of corporations without obvious marketing or production links). But the crusade faltered when some of the larger conglomerates disintegrated, more because of their own weight than because of antitrust pressure.

In the mid-1970s, two huge antitrust suits are pending: against IBM, and against AT&T. It will probably take years before final decision is reached upon either of them.

One paradoxical aspect of antitrust is this: Its intent was to encourage competition. Yet acts such as Robinson-Patman and Miller-Tydings, ostensibly amendments to the Sherman Act, actually operate *against* competition in the form of price competition. Both these acts were passed in the 1930s, and they reflect the painful consequences that competition can produce under the abnormal conditions of serious depression.

Sherman; Clayton; U.S. Steel; Alcoa; oligopoly.

QUIZ: Multiple Choice

1. *Four of the five statements below more or less repeat ideas to be found in John Kenneth Galbraith's books* The New Industrial State *and* Economics and the Public Purpose. *One statement runs counter to the ideas in those books. Which one?* (1) The primary goal of big corporations is growth rather than profit maximization. (2) Big corporations prefer a climate of uncertainty to one of stability, since growth is more easily attained in such a climate. (3) The tendency toward a "meritocracy" is apparent as much in Communist as in Western societies. (4) Big corporations find advertising preferable to price cutting as a weapon for increasing sales. (5) The control of big corporations is increasingly being taken over from shareholders by technically trained experts.

2. *In a period when competition is usually keen, business firms may lower their "full cost" prices in efforts to secure more business. Ordinarily, there is a "rock bottom" price. Except in highly unusual circumstances, price will never be reduced below the level of* (1) average cost; (2) minimum average cost; (3) average fixed cost; (4) average variable cost; (5) total fixed cost.

3. *In deciding the rate that a public-utility company should be permitted to charge, the method of "capitalized value of earnings" should not be used, because* (1) it is based on past earnings, and so could be used to justify any level of rates, whether too high or too low; (2) it fails to take account of the increase in costs of replacing equipment due to higher prices, so that it usually points to rates that are too low; (3) it is a mechanical formula which always yields the current rate of interest, a figure which could be obtained without going to all the trouble of using the formula; (4) it puts all emphasis on the cost of replacing assets, even though actual expenditures to replace long-lived assets may lie many years in the future; (5) of none of these reasons.

4. *One major intent of both the Robinson-Patman Act and the Miller-Tydings Act was to* (1) encourage mergers, to enable small firms to compete more effectively against large firms; (2) break up the development of conglomerates; (3) restrict the use of price as a competitive weapon; (4) extend the definition of "conspiracy" to include tacit agreements and parallel action; (5) encourage a freer use of price competition.

5. *The text outlines certain "overcrowded" and "sick" industries characterized by "overentry." Which one of the following statements is* false *by reference to this material in the text?* (1) Jobs created by new firms persistently entering the industry largely represent a waste of resources. (2) Most firms tend to have considerable unused capacity most of the time. (3) Probably many or most firms in the industry earn no profit, or very little. (4) Competition keeps price at or below its purely competitive level, even though it bankrupts some firms. (5) New firms tend to enter the industry at about the same rate as old ones leave.

6. *An "administered price," as the text uses this term, means a price* (1) typically found in the conditions of "many differentiated sellers"; (2) set so as to yield the firm in question no profit over and above a reasonable return upon its invested capital; (3) set usually in conditions of oligopoly, and not subject to frequent change; (4) imposed by some regulatory authority; (5) other than that found at the "corner" or "kink" of a "kinked" demand curve.

7. *The idea of a "kinked" or "cornered" demand curve is particularly associated in price theory with the situation of* (1) differentiated products; (2) regulated monopoly; (3) oligopoly; (4) "sick" industries, characterized by overentry; (5) none of the above.

8. *The argument that a "kinked" demand curve may be typical of certain imperfectly competitive situations is based on the reasoning that (with respect to the firm involved)* (1) the entry of new firms will gradually push this firm's demand curve downward or leftward, until its profit is eliminated; (2) competing firms will almost certainly match any price reduction it may make, but are much less likely to match any increase; (3) in imperfect competition, the demand curve facing this firm cannot possibly be one of perfect price elasticity; (4) the markup price the firm sets may in fact reflect a considerable miscalculation of the true demand for its product; (5) the fact that the firm's product is to some degree differentiated from those of competing firms imparts to it a certain degree of monopoly power.

9. *Insofar as it is true that the demand curve facing a firm is "kinked" (as described in the text) and the firm is operating at this kink, that firm will be more inclined (than if faced with an ordinary demand curve)* (1) to lower price, but less inclined to raise it; (2) to raise price, but less inclined to lower it; (3) both to raise price and to lower it; (4) neither to lower price nor to raise it; (5) to do any of these things, perhaps; in the matter of attitude toward price changes, the kinked curve is no different from a regular one.

10. *All the following acts are classed as antitrust laws, but one of them is frequently described as an act which violates the essential spirit of the antitrust laws, namely,* (1) the Federal Trade Commission Act (1914); (2) the Robinson-Patman Act (1936); (3) the Sherman Act (1890); (4) the Clayton Act (1914); (5) the Celler Act (1950).

11. *According to the text, if we have an industry of many sellers of differentiated products, and if entry into this industry is free, the long-run equilibrium position of the typical firm will have these properties:* (1) Average cost (AC) will be at its minimum-possible level, and price charged (P) will be equal to that AC. (2) AC will be at its minimum level, and P will be above that AC. (3) AC will be above its minimum level, and P will be above that AC. (4) AC will be above its minimum level, and P will be equal to that AC. (5) None of the above, necessarily.

12. *One reason why a firm operating under conditions of imperfect competition is likely to want to use an administered or markup price is* (1) lack of sufficient knowledge of marginal revenue at various levels of output; (2) lack of sufficient knowledge of marginal cost at various levels of output; (3) desire to have a break-even point occurring at a high level of output; (4) that it fears the charging of any higher price would attract new competition into the field; (5) that this price indicates the most efficient plant output level.

13. *The "rule of reason," as enunciated by the Supreme Court with respect to antitrust law, in effect said this:* (1) "Tacit collusion," or parallel action, with no meetings or conversations among the parties involved, may be a violation of the law. (2) The deliberate use of price discrimination to damage or destroy a competitor is a violation of the law. (3) Trade unions may be guilty of illegal conspiracy, just as corporations may be. (4) Any merger between corporations which gives the merged firm control over a substantial percentage of the market may be a violation of the law. (5) The fact that a corporation is big is not of itself an offense; there must be evidence of actual coercion or attacks on rivals.

14. *Which alternative in question 13 is the critical one with respect to the decision reached in the "Big Three" Cigarette case (1946)?* (1). (2). (3). (4). (5).

4

**DISTRIBUTION
OF INCOME:
THE PRICING
OF THE
PRODUCTIVE
FACTORS**

27 THEORY OF PRODUCTION AND MARGINAL-PRODUCTS

THIS CHAPTER has two principal topics. One is *income distribution*—the manner in which the real product produced is shared out among different groups. In an interdependent society, various kinds of labor and capital must *cooperate* in order to turn out the national product. How is the fruit of a *cooperative* process to be shared out among those who helped produce it? Shared equally? According to ability? (If so, how is ability to be measured?) Is labor exploited by capital owners in the distribution of this product?

Such questions are largely meaningless unless we have first tried to identify scientifically the rules by which the national product *is* divided. Both Marxist and non-Marxist economists have puzzled over this issue. Unfortunately, the theory of income distribution is still in an incomplete and unsettled state.

The first step in this theory, regardless of your political orientation, is to recognize that the share you and your group get is largely a matter of the price you are paid for the productive service you supply (relative to the prices other groups are paid). So it is a supply-and-demand problem. Income-distribution theory requires you to dig into the factors behind the demand for, and the supply of, such productive inputs.

This chapter concentrates on *the demand for inputs*. A producing firm must hire labor and buy raw materials and machinery. So it is a demander of productive inputs. We must expect it *to try to keep its costs of production for any given output at a minimum*. Thus the inputs it buys, and the quantity of each it buys, will be strongly influenced by this rule of cost minimization. (Its purchases will be influenced also by the price it can get for the commodity it produces.)

Thus, from the general subject of income distribution, the text chapter proceeds to its second major topic: how a firm seeks to keep its production costs at a minimum.

The first concept to learn is that of *the production function*.

We deal with some given product X, requiring inputs A, B, and C (e.g., labor, materials, machinery) for its production.

▶ The production function is a statement of the quantitative relation between inputs A, B, and C and output X, in given conditions of technology.

So the production function may say, for example, that if you have 10 units of input A, 30 units of B, and 20 of C to use, the most you can get from them is 200 units of X (in the given conditions of technology).

▶ The production function will tell you, for any ABC combination, what maximum quantity of X producible to expect from that combination.

▶ The production function will also tell you, for any given quantity of X, the various and different ABC combinations that could produce that X quantity.

This last point is especially important. In some cases, the production function may specify *fixed* proportions between inputs: thus, it takes just one man to drive a truck, and a second driver is more of a hindrance than a help. In this fixed-proportions case, there is *one and only one* ABC combination appropriate for any given quantity of X.

The more general case is that in which (within limits) you can substitute one input for another. (If the truck driver is given a larger vehicle, the labor-capital proportions have been changed.) This means there will be *more than one* ABC combination possible for any given X quantity. A production function sums up *all* the possible ABC combinations, for *each and any* X quantity.

In this more general case—assuming each of inputs A, B, and C to have a market price per unit—*different ABC combinations, all alike in that they are just capable of producing some given X quantity, will involve different total costs.* ("Total cost" means total A quantity multiplied by its price per unit, *plus* the same for B, *plus* the same for C.)

▶ When the text speaks of "minimizing cost," it means choosing that particular ABC combination that would cost least (given the prevailing prices of A, B, and C) for the particular quantity of X involved.

In the special fixed-proportions case mentioned above, there is no problem of "minimizing cost": there being only one ABC combination possible, there is only one total dollar cost possible for producing any given X quantity (given the ABC prices). The "cost-minimizing rule" developed in the text chapter is meaningful *only when there is a choice between alternatives to be made.* It is simply a rule used to make sure that the particular ABC alternative selected is—given the prevailing ABC prices—the minimum-cost one.

1. *a.* Note particularly that the production function itself will *not* tell you the minimum-cost ABC combination, for it is just a summing up of all the physical relationships between inputs and output. You *also* need input prices. But you must begin with the production function, which (to review) indicates:
(1) What it will cost to produce any given quantity of X by using A, B, and C.
(2) What the prices of A, B, and C are.
(3) For each and any X quantity, the various combinations of A, B, and C which could produce that X quantity.

b. Suppose it is true that 10 units of A, 30 units of B, and 20 of C, used in the best-known way, could just produce 200 units of X. This is (pick one):
(1) An example of a production function.
(2) Not an example of a full production function, but rather of the kind of information a production function is typically expected to supply.

---

a. (3). *b.* (2).

There are two reasons why a producing firm might incur a too-high production cost for the output it is turning out. One has already been mentioned: It might be using the wrong ABC combination, since another combination would be cheaper.

The second reason is that the firm might use its inputs foolishly, or without adequate supervision, so that the ABC combination employed produces less output than it could turn out in the given conditions of technology.

▶ The output figure which the production function will link with any given ABC combination is the *highest* figure attainable. That is, it assumes the inputs are used to the best advantage and not wasted.

2. For example, suppose 10–30–20 is a workable ABC combination for 200 X (when these inputs are used to the best advantage). If these input quantities were to be doubled to 20–60–40, then this higher combination could certainly produce more than 200 X—perhaps 400 X. (The figure 400 assumes "constant returns to scale"; but that is a qualification we need not worry about here.)

a. Except in the special fixed-proportions case, the production function will indicate *other* ABC combinations, in addition to 10–30–20, for 200 X. The combination 20–60–40 *(could / could not possibly)* be among them. If 10–30–20 is sufficient for 200 X, then the use of 20–60–40 would be

wasteful—and the production-function figures assume that inputs are *not* used wastefully. The 20–60–40 combination will be found within the production function all right—but associated with an X-output figure *(lower / higher)* than 200, a figure such as *(150 / 200 / 400)* of X.

b. Still assuming that 10–30–20 is an ABC combination for 200 X reported by the production function, then *only one* of the four alternatives below could be *another* 200-X figure. Which one? (NOTE: Be sure you understand why only the one alternative could be correct; if stuck, consult the explanation in the answer.)
(1) 20 A, 40 B, 30 C.
(2) 10 A, 35 B, 20 C.
(3) 8 A, 25 B, 19 C.
(4) 10 A, 28 B, 21 C.

c. From the information in part *b*, it follows that if 200 X is being produced with the 10–30–20 ABC combination, this output level could be maintained by:
(1) Replacing 1 A unit by 2 extra B units.
(2) Replacing 2 B units by 1 extra C unit.
(3) Replacing 1 B unit by 2 extra C units.
(4) Replacing 2 A units by 2 extra C units.

---

a. could not possibly; higher; 400. *b.* (4). Combination (1) won't do, for the same reason that 20–60–40 won't do. Combination (2) is the same as 10–30–20, except that the B units are up from 30 to 35. With those extra 5 B units, it ought to be possible to get slightly more than 200 X units. Combination (2) thus suffers from the same defect as combination (1), on a smaller scale. Combination (3) has *less* of all three inputs than 10–30–20. If it *did* belong in the production function (for 200 X), it would automatically evict 10–30–20, for the same reason that 10–30–20 evicts 20–60–40, 20–40–30, or even 10–35–20. Combination (4) is the only one in which (compared with 10–30–20) there is *more* of one input and *less* of another. That is, there has been a swap of inputs to maintain the same output level. *c.* (2).

---

3. *a.* The text stresses marginal-physical-product (MPP) as the critical measure in cost-minimizing decisions. Marginal-physical-product of factor A is defined as:
(1) Change in quantity of X resulting from increasing or decreasing A by 1 (small) unit, with inputs B and C held constant.
(2) Change in quantity of X resulting from increasing or decreasing A by 1 (small) unit, with inputs B and C increased or decreased in proportion.
(3) Change in quantity of X resulting from increasing or decreasing B and C by 1 (small) unit each, with quantity of input A held constant.
(4) Total quantity of X produced, divided by total quantity of A used.

b. Suppose the production function says:

X output is 200 units with a 10–30–20 ABC combination, and X output is 203 units with a 10–31–20 ABC combination.

This means that at this point in the production function (pick one):
(1) The MPP of X is 3 units.
(2) The MPP of B is 3 units.
(3) The MPP of A and C is 3 units.

---

a. (1). *b.* (2) Here, the only difference between the two ABC combinations is that in the second, the B units have been increased from 30 to 31. This 1-unit increase in B results in a 3-unit increase in X output (quantities of A and C held constant); so the MPP of B is 3 units.

---

4. *a.* If the MPP of input B is said to be 3 units of finished good X, this means specifically that output of X will *rise* by 3 units if the employment of B is *(increased / decreased)* by 1 unit, and the employment of all other inputs, such as A and C, is *(increased proportionately / held constant)*. It means also that output will *fall* by 3 X units if the employment of B is *(increased / decreased)* by 1 unit, and the employment of all other inputs is *(increased proportionately / held constant)*.

b. If the quantity of input B employed is *increased,* with employment of other inputs, such as A and C, held constant, we would expect the MPP of B gradually to *(increase / decline)* due to the *("law of diminishing returns" / relative scarcity of B that would develop)*. Similarly, if the B quantity is *reduced* (with A and C quantities held constant), we would expect the MPP of B gradually to *(increase / decline)* due to the *("law of diminishing returns" / relative scarcity of B that would develop)*.

---

a. increased; held constant; decreased; held constant.
b. decline; "law of diminishing returns"; increase; relative scarcity of B that would develop. Be sure you understand these answers. B's MPP is defined as the change in output (increase or decrease) of X resulting from a 1-unit change (increase or decrease) in quantity of B employed, the quantities of all other inputs being held constant. (For an accurate indication of MPP, this B unit should be small in relation to total quantity of B.) B's MPP is not an absolute or unchanging thing. It depends on quantity of B employed, and also of quantities of A and of C employed.

---

5. *a.* Suppose that 200 units of X could be produced, as in question 2, by either of two ABC combinations: 10–30–20, or 10–28–21.

Suppose further that the prices of A, B, and C are respectively $2, $1, and $3. In terms of minimizing cost, the preferable combination would be the *(10–30–20 / 10–28–21)* one.

Change the ABC prices to $2, $2, and $1. The minimum-cost combination would then be the *(10–30–20 / 10–28–21)* one.

b. The text provides a rule whose use enables the firm to look at any ABC combination and—*without any reference to the costs of other possible combinations*—to say: This combination is (or is not) at Least-cost one, for the output in question.

Write down the Least-cost rule given in the text:

_____ .

---

a. 10–30–20; 10–28–21. *b.* $MPP_A / P_A = MPP_B / P_B = MPP_C / P_C$.

---

6. *a.* Suppose that the quantity of X produced is 200 units. The quantities employed, prices, and MPPs of inputs A, B, and C are as follows:

	A	**B**	**C**
Quantity employed ..	10	30	20
Price	$2	$1	$3
MPP	2	3	1

Total cost incurred for the 200-unit output is $*(90 / 100 / 110 / 120 / 130)*. The Least-cost rule of question 5 *(is / is not)* being satisfied.

Leave input A to one side in order to compare B and C. The last unit of B employed added *(1 / 2 / 3 / 4)* unit(s) of X to output. Since B's price is $1, each of these units cost approximately *(10 / 25 / 33 / 39 / 75)* cents. In contrast, the last unit of C employed added *(1 / 2 / 3 / 4)* unit(s) of X. Since C's price is $3, that unit cost $*(1 / 2 / 3 / 4)*.

b. This means that Total Cost could be reduced by increasing the employment of *(B / C)* and decreasing that of *(B / C)*. What will be the X output if we reduce employment of C by 3 units and increase employment of B by 1 unit? (Assume for convenience that C's MPP remains constant over this 3-unit change in employment.) It will be *(196 / 197 / 200 / 201 / 203)* units of X. As a result, Total Cost would *(rise / fall)* from $110 to $*(100 / 102 / 106 / 108 / 112)*.

c. As employment of B is increased, we would expect B's MPP (see question 4*b*) to *(rise / fall)*. As employment of C is reduced, we would expect C's MPP to *(rise / fall)*. Thus, as we make the changes indicated, we would be *(approaching / moving away from)* the Least-cost position of question 5*b*.

d. Reverse the MPPs of B and C given at the beginning of this question: make them 1 and 3 respectively. That *(would / would not)* be a Least-cost position.

Make the MPPs of A, B, and C respectively, 4, 2, and 6. The prices of A, B, and C are as before. This *(would / would not)* be a Least-cost position.

---

a. 110; is not; 3; 33; 1; 3. *b.* B; C; 200; fall; 102.
c. fall; rise; approaching. *d.* would; would.

7. It is important to try to relate the ideas set out in this chapter to those discussed earlier. Chapters 23 through 25 dealt at length with the firm's choice of its profit-maximizing output, the basic rule being *MR = MC*. In this chapter—thus far, at any rate—we have not considered the profit-maximizing output. Our concern has been with the rule which tells the firm, for *any* output, whether or not that output is being produced at minimum-attainable cost.

Why bother with *any* output, if the firm's real interest lies in the one profit-maximizing output? Because the Total Cost curve (from which Marginal Cost is obtained) is an essential ingredient in the *MR = MC* profit-maximizing choice. This Total Cost curve indicates minimum-attainable cost for *all* possible outputs. The Least-cost rule is needed in order to develop the Total Cost curve; the Total Cost curve is needed in order to identify the *MR = MC* profit-maximizing output position.

a. Thus, in summary: When the firm establishes a Least-cost output position, it has established (pick one):
(1) The Total Cost Curve.
(2) One point on the Total Cost curve, in any and all circumstances.
(3) One point on the Total Cost curve, given the existing production function and the existing ABC prices.

b. If the firm wants to maximize its profit, it will go about it in this way (pick one):
(1) It will pick the maximum-profit quantity of X, then find the Least-cost ABC combination for that X.
(2) It will find Least-cost points for all possible X outputs (i.e., develop the Total Cost curve), then use this information in conjunction with the Total Revenue curve to establish maximum-profit output.

---

a. (3). *b.* (2).

---

8. With this link between the Least-cost rule and the Total Cost curve established, we can now draw the idea of the Least-cost rule closer to the *MR = MC* idea discussed earlier.

a. If we say that A is an input, X is the product produced, and the MPP of input A is 2, then the 2 refers to (*units of A / units of X / dollars*). This MPP is, so to speak, the "payoff" in X output resulting from employment of the last unit of A. But payoff is more commonly thought of in money terms. To know what this MPP payoff will bring in dollars, we must know what revenue the sale of the additional X units will bring in—i.e., we need to know the (*price of A / marginal revenue accruing from sale of X*).

b. If the marginal revenue accruing from sale of 1 additional X unit is $3 (the MPP of input A being 2), then the dollar payoff resulting from hiring the last unit of A is $(*2 / 3 / 5 / 6 / 10 / 12*). (We disregard the slight drop in *MR* that might come from selling the second of these two X units.)

c. The technical name for this dollar payoff is the "marginal-revenue-product" (MRP). That is, the MRP of (say) factor input A is specifically (pick one):
(1) MPP of A multiplied by marginal revenue accruing from sale of X, or MPP of A × *MR*.
(2) MPP of A multiplied by price of A.
(3) MPP of A not multiplied by anything.

d. In the special case of pure (or perfect) competition—but *only* in that case—this MRP of A could be defined as the MPP of A multiplied by the price of X. But "marginal revenue from X" is more general. It takes in all the cases, pure competition included.

Barring the special case of pure (or perfect) competition, as the firm increases its output and sales, the marginal revenue from sale of X will (*rise / remain constant / fall*).

This means that the MRP of each input, and of all inputs, will, as employment is increased (*rise / remain constant / fall*).

---

a. units of X; marginal revenue accruing from sale of X.
b. 6. *c.* (1). *d.* fall; fall.

---

9. Suppose our firm is in a "balanced" position with respect to input employment—i.e., it is satisfying the Least-cost rule with respect to inputs A, B, and C. Now it wants to find out if it is at its maximum-profit output level.

To do this, it can look at any one of its inputs—say input A. A's price is (say) $4 per unit. A's MPP is 3. The marginal revenue from sale of X is $1.

a. This means that A's MRP—the dollar payoff from employing the last unit of A—is $(*1 / 2 / 3 / 4 / 7 / 12*).

It cost $(*1 / 2 / 3 / 4 / 7 / 12*) to buy that last unit of A services. So its employment (*added $1 to / subtracted $1 from / did not change*) total profit.

Our firm, remember, is in a "balanced" position with respect to input employment. Thus the same conclusion would have been reached had we looked at input B or input C. So, in the given circumstances, the firm (*definitely is / definitely is not / may or may not be*) earning maximum possible profit. For that maximum profit, it should (*reduce / increase*) its output—i.e., (*reduce / increase*) its employment of inputs.

b. A different example, to illustrate the point more generally: The MPPs of A, B, and C are respectively 12, 8, and 2. Their prices are respectively $6, $4, and $1. So the firm (*is / is not*) producing its current output at mimimum cost.

The marginal revenue from sale of X is $1. Thus input A's MRP is $(*12 / 10 / 8 / 6 / 4 / 2*). Input B's MRP is $(*12 / 10 / 8 / 6 / 4 / 2*). Input C's MRP is $(*12 / 10 / 8 / 6 / 4 / 2*).

This firm (*is / is not*) operating at maximum-profit output. For such a maximum, it should (*increase / decrease*) its output, by (*increasing / decreasing*) the employment of (*input A only / B only / C only / all inputs*).

c. As employment is so changed, input MRPs will *(fall / rise).* The increase in input employment should be halted when each MRP has *(fallen below / reached equality with / risen above)* the price of the *(input / finished product).*

---

a. 3; 4; subtracted $1 from; definitely is not; reduce; reduce. *b.* is; 12; 8; 2; is not; increase; increasing; all inputs. *c.* fall; reached equality with; input

---

10. The process just described is really nothing more than an elaboration of the *MR = MC* maximum-profit rule set out in earlier chapters. Think of the firm (as we did in those earlier chapters) as gradually approaching this *MR = MC* output level, starting from an output where *MR exceeds MC.* As output is expanded, *MR* gradually falls (unless the situation is one of pure or perfect competition), and *MC* gradually rises.

The output increases needed for this *MR = MC* equality are obtained by increasing the employment of A, B, and C. However, as this increase is undertaken, things must be kept "in balance"—i.e., the minimum-cost rule of question 5 must be satisfied. If it is not, the output in question could be produced at lower cost. The firm is "above" its true Total Cost curve rather than "on" it.

With the "in-balance" rule watched, expanding output moves toward the *MR = MC* maximum-profit position. That position can be described in MRP terms, as well as *MR = MC* terms. As output is increased, MRPs fall (see question 8*d*). When they have fallen to equality with input prices, for all inputs employed, (1) the "in-balance" rule is automatically satisfied, and (2) so is the *MR = MC* maximum-profit rule.

a. Take the MPPs for inputs A, B, and C of question 9*b* (12, 8, and 2 respectively). If you know that ABC prices are $6, $4, and $1 respectively, and that the firm has reached its maximum-profit output, what must be the *MR* from the sale of the last X units? *($8 / $6 / $2 / $1 / 50¢).*

b. Change to different figures. If *MR* is $2, if ABC prices are $8, $4, and $10, and if the firm is at maximum-profit output, A's MPP must be *(1 / 2 / 3 / 4 / 5)* units of X, that of B must be *(1 / 2 / 3 / 4 / 5)* units, and C's is *(1 / 2 / 3 / 4 / 5).*

---

a. 50¢. *b.* 4; 2; 5.

---

11. In everyday terms, the explanation of the maximum-profit rule for input employment (namely, equate the MRP of that input with its price) is this (pick one):

(1) The price of the factor input should equal the price of the output X.
(2) The marginal-physical-product of each and all inputs should be the same amount.
(3) Any extra unit of an input is worth hiring or buying so long as the extra revenue it brings in (via extra production and extra

sales) exceeds what it costs to hire or buy it; the buying process should be halted only when the extra revenue falls to equality with the extra cost.
(4) The price of each factor input should be equal to marginal revenue from the last unit of X sold.

---

(3).

---

12. The preceding questions have tried to indicate the considerations that are most important to a firm in deciding how much of an input A it will want to buy, given some price of A. If A's price were to rise or to fall, the calculations would have to be redone. In sum, we are trying to isolate the considerations that lie behind a firm's demand for any input, at various possible prices of that input.

The demand for any input is sometimes called a "derived demand." People want a finished good, such as X, for the satisfaction it provides them. Nobody wants an input such as A for *that* reason. Nevertheless, A is wanted, because it is useful in X production. The demand for A is "derived from" the demand for X.

A highly important factor in this derived demand for A is its "productivity" in producing X—more specifically, its MPP. The value of this MPP is strongly influenced by the quantity of A employed. It *(depends also / does not depend)* on the quantities of inputs B and C employed. We cannot speak of the "productivity" of A, or of the demand for A, without assuming something about the extent to which B and C are available to work cooperatively with A.

Moreover, demand for A will be affected by the price of X, the finished good which A helps to produce. The higher X's price, the greater will be the demand for A.

So the demand for A must assume given quantities of B and C employed. It must likewise assume given prices of X and of inputs B and C, since a change in any of these prices would require all Least-cost and Best-profit positions to be recomputed.

In sum, the demand for an input is very much an "other things equal" demand. Alternatively, and in the language of the text, it is a

"_____ demand."

---

depends also; jointly interdependent.

---

13. Finally, we return to the puzzling and difficult question with which the chapter began: that of income distribution. What are the forces which settle the manner of division of a cooperatively produced output? How much can any one contributing input expect to receive?

Clearly, the demand for that input (as discussed in the preceding question) is important in settling this question. Demand (together with available supply) determines the price per unit of input services. And if you know relative input prices, you know something about how those inputs are likely to share in the total of goods produced.

The "marginal productivity" analysis outlined in this chapter first began to emerge late in the nineteenth century. Economist John B. Clark, who did much to develop it, felt that this analysis pointed strongly toward the underlying laws which governed the distribution of real income (goods and services) among the inputs which had cooperated in the production of those goods and services.

Clark pointed out that if each input is paid a price just equal to its MPP, there will (in the right circumstances) be just enough product to distribute.

Suppose that total output is 200 units of X, produced with a 10–30–20 ABC combination. Suppose the MPPs of A, B, and C are 9 of X, 3 of X, and 1 of X, respectively. Suppose further that inputs are paid not in money, but "in kind"—i.e., in units of product X. Then payments to inputs will be as follows (complete the blanks):

Quantity of Input		MPP of Input		Total Payment to Input	
_____	units of A ×	_____	=	_____	units of X
_____	units of B ×	_____	=	_____	units of X
_____	units of C ×	_____	=	_____	units of X
	Total payment			_____	units of X

It is here assumed that A, B, and C are the *only* inputs contributing to X's production. When each is paid according to its MPP, the total payments *(are less than / just equal / exceed)* the total amount of X produced.

There were two seemingly attractive features about this method of approach. First, payment according to MPPs just "exhausts the product"—i.e., there is just enough to go around, with no surplus of product and no deficit. Second, there is a suggestion that this distribution is "fair" or "just," each input being paid according to its marginal) productivity.

Today, it is conceded that the business of income distribution is much too complex for treatment in simple terms. Opinions differ sharply as to the meaningful content of this "marginal productivity" approach. And in any event, Clark's analysis works as outlined here only in the right circumstances. Those circumstances include a "constant returns to scale" production function. If the production function lacks this property (and there is no reason why all should have it), a distribution by MPPs will not necessarily just exhaust the product; total payments may exceed or fall short of total product. (A constant-returns production function is one wherein, no matter what the quantity of inputs, doubling of all input quantities just doubles product quantity, neither more nor less. Halving all the input quantities just halves the prod-

uct. The explanation why such a production function has the product-exhaustion property is mathematical, and it is not explored in the text or here.)

---

10 of A × 9 = 90 of X. 30 of B × 3 = 90 of X. 20 of C × 1 = 20 of X. Total payment 200 of X. Just equal.

QUIZ: Multiple Choice

1. *If inputs A, B, and C together produce product X, the marginal-physical-product of input A is defined as* (1) the extra output of X resulting from the employment of one extra unit of A, inputs B and C being increased proportionately; (2) the amount of input A required to produce one extra unit of X, amounts of inputs B and C being held constant; (3) the extra output of X resulting from the employment of one extra unit of A, amounts of inputs B and C being held constant; (4) the amount of input A required to produce one extra unit of X, amounts of inputs B and C being increased proportionately; (5) none of the above.

2. *When a firm has employed all its inputs in such quantities that the ratio of input price to input MPP is the same for all inputs, this means that the firm* (1) is operating in such a way that it has made the marginal-revenue-product of each input equal to its price; (2) is operating at maximum-profit output and is producing that output at minimum cost; (3) is operating at maximum-profit output, but may or may not be producing that output at minimum cost; (4) may or may not be operating at maximum-profit output, but is producing its present output at minimum cost; (5) may or may not be at maximum-profit output and may or may not be producing its present output at minimum cost.

3. *The production function will tell a firm* (1) what it will cost to produce any given quantity of output; (2) the maximum-profit level of output; (3) the various combinations of inputs that should be used in order to produce any given quantity of output most efficiently, i.e., at least money cost; (4) the various combinations of inputs that could be used in order to produce any given quantity of output; (5) none of these.

4. *According to John B. Clark's theory of income distribution, if 10 units of a particular input are employed, the price paid to each of those units should be an amount equal to the value of* (1) the average of the MPPs of each of the 10 units; (2) its own MPP; (3) the MPP of the tenth unit; (4) the APP (average-physical-product) of the 10 units; (5) none of the above.

5. *The text chapter cites some findings as to changes in the productivity of labor and capital in the American economy, and as to the payments made these two inputs. One statement among the following five is* false *as to those findings. Which one?* (1) The share of national income going to labor is approximately three times the share going to property. (2) The productivity of both labor and capital has increased because of new technologies and skills. (3) The growth in the capital stock has exceeded the growth in the labor force. (4) The total return to capital has increased because of growth in its size, but the return per unit of capital has fallen. (5) A small percentage increase in the labor input seems to increase output more than a corresponding increase in capital.

6. *The marginal-revenue-product of input A, used to produce product X, is defined as* (1) the marginal-physical-product (MPP) of X multiplied by price of X; (2) the average-physical-product (APP) of A multiplied by price of X; (3) the MPP of X multiplied by quantity of X; (4) the APP of A multiplied by marginal revenue of X; (5) none of these things.

7. *A, B, and C are inputs employed to produce good X. If the quantity of A used is increased, we would ordinarily expect A's marginal-physical-product to* (1) increase, in all circumstances; (2) increase if the quantities of B and C have been left unchanged, but not necessarily to increase if the B and C quantities are increased in the same proportion; (3) decrease, in all circumstances; (4) decrease if the quantities of B and C have been left unchanged, but not necessarily to decrease if the B and C quantities are increased in the same proportion; (5) decrease if B and C quantities are increased in the same proportion, increase if B and C quantities have been left unchanged.

8. *A firm operates in conditions of imperfect competition. The price of one of its inputs, A, is $10, and the marginal-physical-product of A is 5 units of finished product X. If this firm is at its maximum-profit output position, then the marginal revenue from sale of X must be* (1) $1; (2) $1.50; (3) $2; (4) $5; (5) $10.

9. *The marginal-revenue-product of input A, in the circumstances of question 8, must be* (1) $1; (2) $1.50; (3) $2; (4) $5; (5) $10.

10. *A firm operates in conditions of imperfect competition. The price of one of its inputs, A, is $10, and the marginal-physical-product of A is 5 units of finished product X. The price of X is $2. The firm has satisfied the Least-cost rule for input employment. From the information given, this firm* (1) cannot be at its maximum-profit position, and to reach that position should decrease its output; (2) cannot be at its maximum-profit position, and to reach that position should increase its output; (3) is at its profit-maximizing position; (4) is at its maximum-profit position but should employ less of input A and more of other inputs; (5) may or may not be at maximum-profit position—one essential item of information is lacking.

11. *Given the data of question 10, if the marginal-revenue-product of input A must be one of the five following dollar amounts, that marginal-revenue-product is* (1) $1; (2) $2; (3) $3; (4) $4; (5) $5.

12. *Change the information of question 10 in one respect only: The firm operates in conditions of pure (or perfect) competition. Which alternative in question 10 would then be correct?* (1). (2). (3). (4). (5).

13. *When a firm has satisfied the Least-cost rule for input employment, then its situation must be as follows: It* (1) cannot be at its maximum-profit position; (2) may or may not be at its maximum-profit position, but must be operating at the particular output level which yields lowest-attainable Average Cost; (3) must be at its maximum-profit position; (4) may or may not be at its maximum-profit position, but will have equated the marginal-physical-product of each input with marginal revenue; (5) may or may not be at its maximum-profit position—the information furnished is insufficient to be able to tell.

14. *One of the following is not a correct statement of the relationship between the total product of an input or factor and the marginal-physical-product (MPP) of that factor. Which one?* (1) Total product at any output level equals the sum of all MPPs up to that level. (2) MPP at any output level multiplied by that output quantity equals total product. (3) Graphically, the slope of the total product curve at any output level equals MPP at that level. (4) Graphically, the area under the MPP curve for any quantity of the input or factor equals the total product associated with that input quantity. (5) MPP is defined as the increment in total product resulting from a 1-unit increase in the factor (other factor quantities being held constant).

15. *A firm employs such quantities of inputs A and B that the marginal-physical-product of A is 60 units, and that of B is 40 units. Prices of A and B are $4 and $2 respectively. Assuming A and B to be the only inputs involved, this firm is* (1) producing its present output at minimum cost, but definitely is not earning maximum-possible profit; (2) not producing its present output at minimum cost, and is not earning maximum-possible profit; (3) producing its present output at minimum cost, but may or may not be earning maximum-possible profit; (4) not producing its present output at minimum cost, but nevertheless is earning maximum-possible profit; (5) possibly in any of the positions just described—information furnished is insufficient to tell.

16. *In question 15, change the price of input A from $4 to $3, all other information remaining as before. Which alternative in that question is then correct?* (1). (2). (3). (4). (5).

17. *In a simple one-product economy, such as the example used in the text chapter, the demand curve for labor is really* (1) labor's total revenue curve; (2) the residual left after payment of rent; (3) labor's total product curve; (4) labor's marginal-physical-product curve; (5) none of the preceding.

18. *In the simple one-product economy mentioned in question 17, with two factors or inputs, one fixed in supply and the other variable, it is correct to say that* (1) each factor earns a return based on its average productivity; (2) the return to the factor in variable supply is a "pure economic rent"; (3) the sum of the two factor shares equals total product; (4) the area under the total product curve of the variable factor equals national product; (5) none of these statements is correct.

QUIZ: Other

You are a consultant on cost minimization and profit maximization. What do you recommend with respect to each of the six cases listed in Table 27-1?

In all of them, product X is made through the employment of inputs A and B (and there are no other inputs involved). In all of them—*note carefully*—the marginal-physical-product of A is 3 units of X, and the marginal-physical-product of B is 9 units of X.

"*MR* from X Sale" in the table means marginal revenue of the current level of output and sales; "*P* of A" and "*P* of B" indicate the market prices (in dollars) the firm must pay for A and B respectively.

The questions to answer are:
(1) Is this firm at its maximum-profit position? Answer by writing Yes or No in the column indicated.
(2) What, if anything, is wrong with the firm's present position? Answer by putting *one* of the numbers 1 through 5 in the right-hand column, according to the following code:

Table 27-1

Case	MR from X Sale	P of A	P of B	At Maximum Profit?	Answer
1	$1	$2	$10		
2	2	6	18		
3	3	12	18		
4	4	9	18		
5	5	21	54		
6	6	12	63		

1. Present position is the correct one.
2. For present output, A-employment is too high, B-employment too low.
3. For present output, A-employment is too low, B-employment too high.
4. Output should be reduced by employing less of both A and B.
5. Output should be increased by employing more of both A and B.

APPENDIX: Graphical Depiction of Production Theory

Here is a good illustration of the power of a graph to illustrate ideas clearly and simply—once you have mastered the basic elements of reading graphs. This Appendix deals with the same topic which the chapter discusses: how to choose among input combinations so as to obtain that particular alternative which costs the least. If we limit the number of inputs to two (e.g., labor and land), the idea of the "production function" can be illustrated by a series of *equal-product* lines. On the same diagram, we may easily draw any number of *equal-cost* lines. Taken in combination, equal-product and equal-cost lines readily outline the whole business of cost minimization.

1. From Table 27-1 in the text, show on Fig. 27-1 the various land-labor combinations that will produce an output of 346 units. Join these points with a smooth curve. Repeat (also on Fig. 27-1) for outputs of 490 and 282. For identification, label the three curves *q* = 282, *q* = 346, and *q* = 490.

Each of the three resulting curves in Fig. 27-1 is an equal-product curve. It is correctly described as follows (pick one):

(1) Each and every point on the curve stands for a different combination of labor and land quantities; these combinations all have the common property that they can be bought for the same total dollar outlay.

(2) Each and every point on the curve stands for a different quantity of output; these quantities all have the common property that they can be bought for the same dollar outlay on labor and land.

(3) Each and every point on the curve stands for a different combination of labor and land quantities; these combinations all have the common property that they can produce some given quantity of output.

_____

(3).

2. *a.* Equal-cost lines may also be drawn on Fig. 27-1. Suppose labor costs $2 per unit, and the rental of a unit of land costs $3. Pick, at random, any dollar amount that would be sufficient to buy a few units of land and of labor at these prices—say, $12. Now you must draw a line which shows all

Units of land

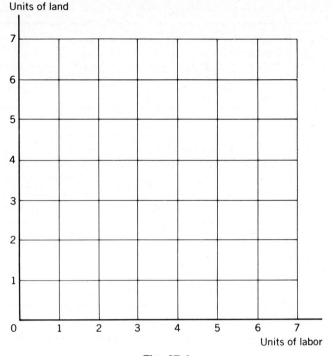

Fig. 27-1

the possible combinations of land units and labor units which (given these prices) $12 would just buy.

If, for example, the entire $12 were spent on land, it would buy *(1 / 2 / 3 / 4 / 5 / 6)* units. So *one* point on the $12 equal-cost line would, on Fig. 27-1, be on the *(vertical / horizontal)* axis—the one measuring land units—at value 4.

Another possibility would be to spend all the $12 on labor units. If so, it would buy *(1 / 2 / 3 / 4 / 5 / 6)* units; and *another* point on the $12 equal-cost line would be on the *(vertical / horizontal)* axis at value 6.

The full $12 equal-cost line is a straight line joining these two end-points. (Draw this line on Fig. 27-1.) Take *any* land-labor combination that $12 will just buy (given the two prices specified)—for example, 2 land units and 3 labor units. You will find that the point on the diagram corresponding to these two values falls on the line just drawn. That is, this line sums up *all* the possible land-labor combinations which $12 will just buy.

b. Which of the equal-product curves drawn earlier does this $12 equal-cost line just touch? *(The 282 line / The 346 line / The 490 line / None of them).*

a. 4; vertical; 6; horizontal. *b.* the 346 line.

3. *a.* One point on this equal-cost line is 1½ labor and 3 land. What output, approximately, would be produced with this combination, according to Fig. 27-1?
(1) Less than 282—probably about 250.
(2) Between 282 and 346—probably about 300.

(3) Between 346 and 490—probably about 420.
(4) More than 490—probably about 530.

b. Would it be sensible to spend $12 to buy the combination described in part *a*, given these factor prices and this production function?
(1) Yes—it is just as good as any other combination.
(2) Not if the object is to get as much output as possible for the $12 outlay.
(3) Yes, if the firm wants to produce an output of 300.

a. (2). *b.* (2).

4. *a.* Which alternative in question 1 correctly describes the equal-cost line you have drawn? .... *(1 / 2 / 3 / 4)*

b. Remember that the cost figure of $12 was picked at random. There is nothing to indicate that it is the amount of cost the firm will actually incur, or should incur; it is just some figure convenient for illustration. (There are plenty of other cost figures that could be used, and plenty of other equal-cost lines that could be drawn; we'll come to this in a moment.) But suppose we assume arbitrarily that the firm did have just $12 to spend, and wanted to spend it to the best advantage. Expressing this $12 as an equal-cost line, what would the firm seek to do?
(1) Move up or down that line seeking the highest-attainable equal-product curve the line encounters.
(2) Find the point on the equal-cost line which represents the lowest dollar outlay for the labor and land inputs.
(3) Move up or down that line seeking the lowest-attainable equal-product curve the line encounters.
(4) None of these.

c. Still assuming land and labor prices of $3 and $2 respectively, draw on Fig. 27-1 the equal-cost line signifying total expenditure of $6—another cost figure picked at random. Now note the properties of the two equal-cost lines. They are *(parallel / not parallel).* The line for $12 cost lies *(below and to the left / above and to the right)* of the $6 cost line.

Thus, given a fixed pair of input prices, the higher the cost figure selected, the *(higher and farther to the right / lower and farther to the left)* the corresponding equal-cost line will be. If the input prices are the same for any two or more such lines, then they will be parallel—i.e., have the same slope. Given such fixed input prices, the swapping terms between land and labor (the rate at which you could exchange a little less of one for a little more of the other) are fixed, regardless of the amount available to be spent.

a. (1). *b.* (1). *c.* parallel; above and to the right; higher and farther to the right.

5. Draw a third equal-cost line parallel to the previous two, but this time so drawn that it just touches your 282 equal-product curve. Drawing this line parallel to the other two implies that (pick one):

(1) The dollar expenditure on inputs is the same.
(2) It touches the same equal-product curve as did the other two.
(3) The prices of land and of labor are again $3 and $2.

The equal-cost line you have just drawn stands for a dollar outlay of approximately $(5 / 10 / 12 / 15 / 18). (HINT: Use the same device employed in question 2a. Go to either one of the line's two end-points, where all the money is spent on one of the two inputs. How much does it cost to buy that particular quantity?)

---

(3); 10.

---

6. *a.* As you study these equal-product and equal-cost curves, it becomes evident that *the points of tangency between them*—the points where an equal-cost curve just touches an equal-product curve—are important. As to any one of these tangency points, why? (More than one of the alternatives may be correct.)
(1) Because for any given level of output it indicates the lowest-possible equal-cost line that can be reached—i.e., it indicates minimum cost for that output.
(2) Because for any given level of outlay on factors it indicates the highest-possible equal-product line that can be reached—i.e., it indicates the maximum output that can be obtained for that dollar outlay.
(3) Because it indicates maximum-profit output level.
(4) Because it indicates the minimum-possible level of output that can be attained for any given dollar outlay.

b. You now have drawn three equal-cost curves, and two of them are tangent to equal-product curves. (An equal-product curve indicating somewhere around 140 units of output, had you drawn it, would be tangent to the third equal-cost curve, that tagged with cost $6.)
Studying carefully these tangency points, you will notice that each such point has a pair of figures going with it. Thus, for the two tangency points here involved, there are two pairs of figures, as follows (pick one):
(1) Output 282, cost $12; output 346, cost about $10.
(2) Output 282, cost about $10; output 346, cost $12.
(3) Output 346, cost $12; output 490, cost $15.
(4) Output 282, cost $12; output 490, cost $15.

c. You must think through the significance of these pairs of figures. Given the specified prices of land and labor, an output of 282 units cannot be produced for less than $(6 / 10 / 12 / 15 / 20), and an output of 346 units cannot be produced for less than $(6 / 10 / 12 / 15 / 20). The significance of these two pairs of figures, then, is that:
(1) One of them is maximum-profit output.
(2) They are two points on the total cost curve.
(3) They discourage anyone from studying economics.

d. Thus, given the production function and input prices, the firm can develop its total cost curve—that is, the minimum

cost of production, in the given circumstances of technology and input prices, for each and any level of output. (We have here developed the minimum cost for two levels of output. The cost for the many other possible levels would be obtained by consulting *other* tangency points between equal-cost and equal-product curves.)

Students frequently make the mistake of assuming that the firm *first* settles on its maximum-profit output level, and *then* finds the cost of producing that output. Not so: Cost is one of the elements in profit, and you can't settle on your maximum-profit output until you know the total cost of each and all possible outputs. So the sequence is to (pick one):
(1) First pick maximum-profit output, then find the minimum cost of producing that output.
(2) First establish the minimum cost of producing any and all outputs, then combine cost and revenue data to pick maximum-profit output.

---

a. (1) and (2). *b.* (2). *c.* 10; 12; (2). *d.* (2).

---

7. Any point where equal-cost and equal-product lines are tangent to one another (i.e., just touch, do not cross) is a minimum-cost point. At this point, they have the same slope. Using E (earth) and L as symbols for land and labor, then the slope of the equal-(cost / product) line is always $-P_L / P_E$. Slope of the equal-(cost / product) line is always $-\text{MPP}_L / \text{MPP}_E$. A point at which the two slope values are equal is always a minimum-cost point.

Do not be too disturbed if these matters of slope cause you difficulty. The essential point, which is not too hard to grasp, is that a Least-cost point must be one where an equal-product line is just tangent to an equal-cost line. When we go on to express this tangency point in terms of the slopes of these two lines, we are just trying to state the nature of this Least-cost position in more precise (and mathematical) form.

In particular, you may have trouble understanding why the slope of any equal-product line must be $-\text{MPP}_L / \text{MPP}_E$. Here is a rough explanation: Slope is always the ratio of the two changes needed to move from one point on the line to another point very close by. Suppose land is reduced by 1 tiny unit and that labor must be increased by 2 tiny units to compensate (stay on the equal-product line). That would make the slope of the equal-product line $-\frac{1}{2}$.

When land was reduced, output fell—by an amount dictated by MPP_E. The amount of labor needed to make up that output loss was dictated by MPP_L. Since it took the addition of 2 L units to compensate for the removal of 1 E unit, labor's MPP must be only ½ that of land. So slope can be measured by the ratio of MPPs as well as by the ratio of input quantity changes.

---

equal-cost; equal-product.

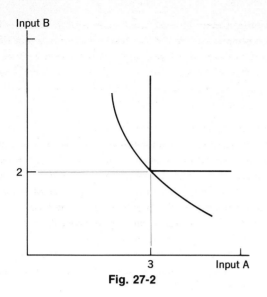

Fig. 27-2

There is considerable dispute over the extent to which the fixed-proportions case is found in reality. (In part, it may be a question of what you mean by "input" or "factor." If you speak in general terms of "labor" or "capital," substitution is certainly possible. But the more specific you become as to *type* of labor or capital, perhaps the more likely fixed proportions may become.)

---

a. (3); different input combinations are; is not. *b.* an upward; unchanged; zero.

QUIZ: Multiple Choice

1. *On an equal-product-curve diagram involving product* X *and inputs* A *and* B, *any equal-cost line indicates.* (1) different quantities of X, showing the increase in X that would entail an equal increase in cost; (2) the various quantities of A and B that would be equally costly at various prices of either A or B; (3) all the various combinations of A and B (in physical quantities of each) that could just be bought for some given money outlay; (4) different combinations of A and B (in physical quantities of each), all such combinations having the common property that they could just produce some given quantity of X; (5) none of the above, there being no such line on an *equal-product line*? (1). (2). (3). (4). (5).

2. *Which alternative in question 1 correctly describes any equal-product line?* (1). (2). (3). (4). (5).

3. *The equal-product-curve diagram illustrates* (1) the total cost curve; (2) the separate marginal-physical-products of the inputs involved; (3) the point of maximum profit; (4) the production function; (5) different quantities of the product involved that would be equally profitable to produce.

4. *The slope of an equal-cost line is a measure of* (1) the ratio of the price of the factor on the vertical axis to the price of the factor on the horizontal axis; (2) the ratio of the price of the factor on the horizontal axis to the price of the factor on the vertical axis; (3) the various outputs which may be produced at a given cost; (4) the total cost of producing a given output; (5) the marginal-physical-productivity of one of the factors.

5. *If factor or input proportions are fixed, this affects the value of the marginal-physical-product (MPP) of these inputs as follows:* (1) MPPs must be zero. (2) MPPs will be higher than if proportions were not fixed. (3) It makes no difference—MPPs will be the same as if proportions were not fixed. (4) MPPs of all inputs must be equal, but they will not be zero. (5) None of the above is correct.

6. *In Fig. 27-3, the line GH is an equal-cost line, with respect to employment of inputs or factors A and B. A shift of GH to a position such as GJ would be caused by* (1) a fall in the price of input A; (2) a rise in the price of both inputs; (3) a fall in the price of input B; (4) a rise in the price of input B; (5) a fall in the price of both inputs.

8. *a.* If the conditions of production are such that for any given output level there is only one possible input combination, then (pick one):
(1) There is no production function.
(2) There are no equal-product curves.
(3) This is a case of fixed proportions.

Figure 27-2 contrasts this case (also described in the text appendix as "the fixed coefficients case") with that assumed up to this point. Both curved and right-angled lines illustrate equal-product curves for some given output quantity. (You can of course draw as many of these equal-product curves as you wish, one for each possible output level. Figure 27-2 shows only one illustrative curve for each situation.) A curved line implies that *(different input combinations are / only one input combination is)* possible for the output in question. A right-angled line implies that substitution of one input for another (thus producing a different input combination) *(is / is not)* possible.

b. In Fig. 27-2, the inputs are A and B, and in the fixed-proportions case, the required "mix" has (arbitrarily) been made 3 to 2. If B inputs were to be increased from 2 to 3 (with A inputs at 3), this would mean *(a rightward / an upward)* movement away from the "corner" on the right-angled equal-product line. With B inputs increased to 3, total output would be *(increased / unchanged / decreased)*, for we would still be on the same equal-product line.

This means that in the fixed-proportions case, the marginal-physical-product (MPP) of each input must be *(positive / zero / negative)*. So the Least-cost marginal-product rule set out in the chapter cannot be applied. But then there is no need for it, since there is no longer any problem of choice. Given input prices, there is only one possible cost figure associated with each possible output level, assuming the inputs are used to the best advantage.

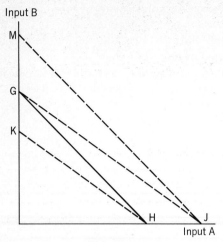

Fig. 27-3

7. *Suppose, in Fig. 27-3, that the equal-cost line GH had instead shifted to position MJ (there being no change in the total-cost figure assumed). Which alternative in question 6 would correctly explain this shift?* (1). (2). (3). (4). (5).

8. *Suppose, in Fig. 27-3, that the equal-cost line GH had instead shifted to position KH. Which alternative in question 6 would correctly explain this shift?* (1). (2). (3). (4). (5).

9. *When an equal-cost line such as GH in Fig. 27-3 is drawn, it is assumed with respect to that line that the following is given or held constant: The* (1) total expenditure on input A; (2) total expenditure on input B; (3) quantity of the product produced; (4) total expenditure on either A or B, but not both; (5) total expenditure on the two inputs combined.

10. *Had question 9 referred to an equal-product rather than an equal-cost line, which alternative in that question would then be correct?* (1). (2). (3). (4). (5).

11. *Equal-product lines and equal-cost lines have this property in common: Any point on either of these two lines is intended to mark some* (1) quantity of finished-product output; (2) figure of total revenue in dollars; (3) combination of physical quantities of inputs; (4) pair of input prices; (5) figure of total cost in dollars.

12. *When the difference between the "fixed proportions" (FP) and "variable proportions" (VP) cases (with respect to the use of inputs in production) is illustrated by means of equal-product curves or lines, it shows up as follows: The* (1) FP case is a straight line, the VP case is a right angle; (2) FP case is a right angle, the VP case is a curved line; (3) FP case is a curved line, the VP case is a right angle; (4) FP case is a right angle, the VP case is a straight line; (5) FP case is a curved line, the VP case is a straight line.

QUIZ: Other

Figure 27-4 illustrates a production function involving the employment of inputs X and Y. The two curved lines are

equal-product lines for outputs of 300 and 420 units. *AB* and *CD* are equal-cost lines. *AB* marks a cost outlay of $36.

1. From examination of *AB*, the price of X must be $(2.50 / 4.50 / 5.50 / 6.00 / 8.00), and the price of Y must be $(2.50 / 4.50 / 5.50 / 6.00 / 8.00). The minimum total cost of producing 300 units of output is $(36 / 45 / 54 / 100 / 160). Average cost is (5 / 10 / 12 / 15 / 60) cents.

The quantities of X and Y used to produce 300 units of output at minimum cost would be (2¼ of X, 5 of Y / 4 of X, 3 of Y / 5 of X, 9 of Y / 8 of X, 6 of Y).

Given the above prices of X and Y, equal-cost line *CD* must indicate a total outlay of $(36 / 45 / 54 / 100 / 160).

2. Suppose the firm is operating at point *F*. This *(is / is not)* a minimum-cost point. Operating at *F*, the quantity of output produced would be *(100 / 300 / 360 / 400 / 420)*. Total cost of that output would be (approximately) $(36 / 45 / 54 / 100 / 160). Average cost would be (approximately) (5 / 10 / 12 / 15 / 60) cents. For this expenditure amount, the maximum output quantity that *could* be produced would be (approximately) *(100 / 300 / 360 / 420 / 500)*.

3. Suppose equal-cost line *CD* (still signifying the same total cost amount as before) were to shift to position *CE*. This would indicate *(a decrease / an increase)* in the *(price of X / price of Y / quantity of output produced)*.

Specifically, the price of *(X / Y)* would have *(risen / fallen)* to $(3.50 / 4.00 / 6.00 / 7.80 / 10.80).

This shift in *CD (would / would not)* require a comparable shift in line *AB*.

4. Given question 3's price change, the minimum cost of producing 300 units of output would now become $(36 / 45 / 54 / 100 / 160). The X and Y quantities needed to produce that 300-unit output would be (2¼ of X, 5 of Y / 4 of X, 3 of Y / 5 of X, 9 of Y / 8 of X, 6 of Y).

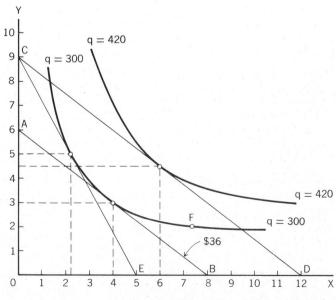

Fig. 27-4

28 PRICING OF FACTOR INPUTS: LAND RENTS AND OTHER RESOURCES

MUCH OF THIS CHAPTER deals with the concept of "economic rent." Unless the ideas surrounding this concept are carefully sorted out, they can be confusing. The basic first points to grasp are these:

▶ "Economic rent" is always associated with the payment made to an input or factor of production—typically, but not necessarily, land.

▶ The term "economic rent" is used if, and only if, the supply curve of that input is perfectly inelastic with respect to price.

1. *a.* As between Figs. 28-1 and 28-2, the one which illustrates the perfectly price-inelastic situation is *(28-1 / 28-2)*. A supply curve such as Fig. 28-1 implies that if price should drop, say, from p_1 to p_0, the quantity offered for sale will *(increase / decrease / remain the same as before)*. Sketch on Fig. 28-1 a demand curve passing through the point on SS corresponding to p_1. Then sketch another to indicate a leftward shift of demand reducing price to p_0.

b. The significance of economic rent is best understood by considering an input supply curve having the more customary shape, as in Fig. 28-2. Here, if price drops from p_1 to p_0, quantity offered for sale will *(increase / decrease / remain the same as before)*. Sketch two corresponding demand curves on Fig. 28-2.

c. In Fig. 28-2, why does a price drop cause part (or all, if the drop is large enough) of supply to be withdrawn? What happens to the quantity of input services AB if they disappear from supply offered?

To answer this question, we need to spell out more carefully the nature of the supply curve we are discussing. Suppose

it is specifically the land supply offered for rental to farmers who want it for growing corn.

In these circumstances, a fall in price from p_1 to p_0 will persuade the landowners to rent part (or all) of their land to *other* demanders—say, farmers who want land for barley growing. This would explain why—in the corn market—there is the reduction in supply quantity AB, in Fig. 28-2. If the demand of corn growers for land decreases, thereby reducing the land rental price from p_1 to p_0, the AB quantity is transferred to farmers who want more land for barley production. Note carefully that this assumes the land in question has one or more alternative uses—i.e., it can be used for barley production as well as for corn production.

If, however, the land has no alternative use, if it is literally useful only in corn production, then any decrease in demand for land by corn growers will reduce its price. And the quantity of land supplied will *(increase / decrease / remain the same as before)*, so that Fig. 28-1 is the relevant illustration. The landowners would not be happy over the price reduction, but they could not do anything about it.

---

a. 28-1; remain the same. *b.* decrease. *c.* remain the same.

We can now identify "economic rent" more precisely:

▶ Economic rent, strictly interpreted, is the return paid to an input which has just one single occupation: it is useful in production of one single commodity only. Because its employment is so limited, the input's supply curve with respect to that occupation is perfectly price-inelastic.

The problem here is: Just what does "one single occupation" *mean?* Land suited for corn production could almost certainly be used for other grain crops. The idea of "economic rent" was developed by British economists in the nineteenth century. (One of them was David Ricardo, and the reason for interest in this question is more clearly indicated in question *2c* below.) When these economists spoke of "corn production," they really meant "grain production," or "food production"—i.e., they interpreted the words "occupation" and "commodity" rather broadly. And we can speak of Iowa farmland in the same broad sense: If

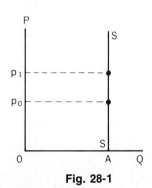

Fig. 28-1

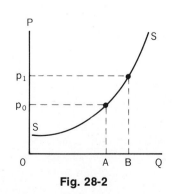

Fig. 28-2

we say it has only a single occupation, we mean that its effective usefulness is pretty much limited to grain or food production, so that the only effective demand of significance is that of farmers who want to use it for this purpose.

Nevertheless, this land is not a "single-commodity" input unless the word "commodity" is used loosely. Thus the term "rent" is often used with reference to *any* input whose *total* supply is perfectly inelastic with respect to price even though it may have several occupations. You will notice that this is how the text chapter uses the term, even though it also discusses "single-occupation" rent cases.

2. *a.* When an input does have only a single employment, then the supply curve facing demanders who want to use it in that employment will be perfectly inelastic with respect to price because the suppliers have no alternative to which to turn should price be low. They would have to supply the same quantity, if necessary, even at a very low price. If the market for this input is competitive, *will* the price be low? (Pick one.)
(1) Yes, if competitive forces are operating.
(2) It is impossible to tell. Price will be set where the demand curve crosses this perfectly inelastic supply curve; this may be a very high price, if the demand for this limited supply is sufficiently great.

b. The single-occupation case illustrates how fallacious a "cost of production" theory of price can be. Suppose that the input is cows, and that cows are useful only for giving milk. Demand for milk has driven up its price to a high level. The resulting "derived demand" for cows has driven up *their* price to a high level. In this situation, it is *not* correct to say (pick one) that:
(1) The price of cows is high because the price of milk is high.
(2) The price of milk is high because the price of cows is high.

In short, you *(can / cannot)* in this case give a meaningful explanation of the price of milk in terms of the costs involved in producing milk.

c. The cows-and-milk example illustrates the more general issue which produced the term "economic rent." This term arose out of David Ricardo's exploration of changes in the prices of food and of land in early-nineteenth-century England. As in the cows-and-milk instance, a higher demand for food had driven up the rental price of land. Analytically, the proper conclusion was this: The increased price of food cannot be blamed on the higher rental price of land. Land's price has risen only because the demand for food has increased.

Remember that this conclusion holds only for a single-occupation, perfectly inelastic supply input. Suppose that "land" has many uses *other than* food production. Demand in

some of those *other* uses has driven up the rental price of land. Food producers must now pay a higher price for that part of the total land supply which they use, even though this price rise has nothing to do with the demand for food. In this instance, the higher price of food *(could / could not)* legitimately be blamed on the higher cost of inputs required to produce food.

---

a. (2). *b.* (2); cannot. *c.* could.

---

3. Economists' interest in the case of the single-occupation, perfectly inelastic supply input led them to ask another question: Does the payment made to such an input constitute a cost of production?

At first, this may seem an odd question. Each separate user of that input must pay the money price, high or low, for the quantity of that input which he buys, and to that buyer his outlay most certainly *is* a cost of production.

But money cost is supposed to be only the surface manifestation of *real cost to society*. The text's Chapter 2 pointed out that you can look at *real cost* in this way: The cost of getting more guns is the sacrifice of butter which (when resources are fully employed) is necessary if more guns are to be produced. The way to get more guns is to switch some of those inputs which are useful in either occupation from butter production to gun production.

Economic-rent inputs, by definition, are those which have only one occupation and so cannot be switched. By the real-cost definition just outlined, their employment *(still entails / does not entail)* a cost to society. When such inputs are put to work, their employment does not entail any sacrifice of an alternative commodity.

---

does not entail.

---

4. From the perspective of a single farmer, one among many such farmers, the supply curve of single-occupation land will not appear perfectly inelastic. If the rental market for land is a competitive one, each farmer sees only the market price of land, at which price he can rent as much or as little as he wishes. To him, land supply appears *(perfectly elastic / somewhat elastic / perfectly inelastic)*.

Consider now the case of an input which happens to have several widely differing possible occupations, and whose *total* supply curve (the schedule of supply quantities offered to all buyers taken together) is perfectly price-inelastic. To *any one class of buyers*, the supply curve of this input will *not* be perfectly inelastic.

To illustrate: Suppose the input in question can be used for making any of goods X, Y, or Z, so that there are three classes of buyers. For some reason, the demand for this input on the part of those who use it for making X declines sharply. Because this demand is part of total demand, the input's price should *(fall / rise)*. Consequently, the producers who use it for making Y and Z will be disposed to buy *(more / less)*. That is, the input's total fixed supply will be redistributed: more goes toward Y and Z, and less toward X. Thus, to X producers, supply *(will / will not)* be perfectly inelastic, for when their demand decreases (and the input's price consequently falls), the quantity supplied to them decreases.

---

perfectly elastic; fall; more; will not.

---

5. Henry George's "single-tax" movement drew on the idea of perfectly inelastic supply. In his famous book *Progress and Poverty,* George argued that the main explanation for continuing poverty in the midst of economic progress was high land rent. Landlords were exacting large incomes from land which they (or their ancestors) had been shrewd (or lucky) enough to acquire before the present need for such land had evolved. The price of such land was high because (1) the demand for land was now exceedingly high, and (2) supply, being fixed, had not expanded to match the increase in demand. Hence the single-tax movement—the single tax proposed being, of course, a tax on land. (Remember that this is not strictly a "pure economic rent" case. George was talking about land and land rental; but the land he discussed was not necessarily single-occupation land.)

Regardless of the merits or demerits of Henry George's single-tax movement, instances of perfectly inelastic input supply—if they can be found—have interesting implications for taxation policy.

As illustration, consider the case in which supply is *not* perfectly price-inelastic. Figure 28-2 (p. 227), for example, might illustrate the fact that labor will work longer hours only if it is offered a higher price (for all hours supplied) for so doing. If an increased demand for labor were to push the price up from p_0 to p_1, that higher price would accomplish two things: (1) It would coax out the additional quantity supplied AB, which would not have been forthcoming at price p_0; and (2) it would ration out the total available supply OB to those willing to pay the higher price.

Suppose now, with price at p_1, a tax is levied on the sale of this input. (For illustration, refer back if needed to text Fig. 20-6.) Its effect would be to reduce the after-tax return received by labor to, say, p_0. And as a consequence, market quantity supplied would be reduced from OB to OA. The tax thus has the unfortunate effect of "distorting production incentives"—i.e., people decide to supply somewhat less labor in order to escape paying part of the tax.

By contrast, consider the case of perfectly inelastic supply—Fig. 28-1. Here, a price rise from p_0 to p_1 (brought about by an increase in demand) would accomplish *(neither / only one / both)* of the results in the Fig. 28-2 case. It *(would / would not)* coax out an additional supply quantity. It *(would / would not)* ration out the available supply.

Moreover, if a tax were to be levied on the sale of this input, results would be different in the inelastic-supply case. The important thing is that if such a tax were to reduce the after-tax return of suppliers from p_1 to p_0, this would produce *(a large / a small / no)* reduction in supply quantity. Imposition of this tax *(would / would not)* cause any reduction in GNP, since there would be no reduction in quantity of work hours supplied.

---

only one; would not; would; no; would not.

---

6. Even if you favor taxing economic-rent inelastic-supply cases because taxation does not reduce supply quantity, you still must find them. They are not so widely available as might be thought; and mistakes can be made in picking them out.

a. This is true even of land. Ricardo spoke of land as "the original and inexhaustible gift of nature." But there are initial costs of clearing nature's gift for cultivation; there are continuing costs of keeping it drained and fertilized. The greater the derived demand for land, the greater the incentive to bring into cultivation land with higher maintenance costs. To the extent that this is true, there will be for each piece of land a critical rent below which it will ultimately disappear from cultivation. This makes the supply curve for land *(completely / less than completely)* inelastic.

b. Some highly specialized machinery has been built for rental to manufacturers. The costs of servicing this machinery and keeping it in good running order for rental are negligible. Will the supply curve (short-run) for this machinery be perfectly inelastic, and ought the return received by its owners to be termed "economic rent," from the information thus far supplied? . . . . *(Yes / No)*

Suppose, however, that the equilibrium price established is below the level needed to cover replacement costs plus interest on the money tied up in this machinery. This indicates that the *long-run* supply curve *(will / will not)* be perfectly price-inelastic. Consequently, we *(ought not to / should still)* designate the income received by suppliers of this input as "economic rent."

(The text calls this an instance of "quasi rent": see footnote at conclusion of the section Factor-Price Determination by Supply and Demand.)

---

a. less than completely.   *b.* Yes; will not; ought not.

QUIZ: Multiple Choice

1. *One characteristic of an economic-rent situation is that* (1) price will increase with an increase in demand but will not decrease with a decrease in demand; (2) total quantity supplied will increase with an increase in demand but will not decrease with a decrease in demand; (3) total quantity supplied will not change if price falls; (4) price will not change with an increase in supply; (5) none of the above.

2. *If land is fixed in total supply but has many alternative uses (one of which is tobacco production), then normally a 50 per cent tax on rental price of any land used for tobacco production will result in* (1) a 50 per cent increase in the rent which tobacco producers must pay; (2) a 50 per cent decrease in the rent paid by users of such land; (3) a 50 per cent decrease in the rent received (net) by owners of such land; (4) no change in amount of rent paid or received; (5) none of these occurrences.

3. *If supply is perfectly inelastic with respect to price, and if there should be a decrease in total demand (a leftward shift of the supply curve), then* (1) quantity supplied will not be reduced, thus causing price to fall more than it otherwise would; (2) quantity supplied will not be reduced, thus causing price to fall less than it otherwise would; (3) quantity supplied will fall, thus causing price to fall more than it would otherwise; (4) quantity supplied will fall, thus causing price to fall less than it would otherwise; (5) none of these results will occur.

4. *If a productive input has just one single employment or use (i.e., there is only one commodity it can help to produce), then (according to the text chapter), the price paid to it* (1) will tend to fall below the normal competitive level, because of the absence of competitive bidding; (2) will be a cost to each of its separate users, but not a cost to the whole community or society; (3) should not be counted as a cost by each of its separate users, although it will still be a cost to the whole community or society; (4) will be a cost both to its separate users and to the whole community or society; (5) will not be a cost either to its separate users or to the whole community or society.

5. *It would be correct to say that economic rent is not a cost of production, in the following sense:* (1) It is not a payment to a factor of production that actually makes a contribution to the output of finished goods. (2) The suppliers of the input in question can receive the same price for employment in occupation A as they can in occupation B. (3) The rent payment in question is really a payment for buildings or improvements to the land, not for the use of the land itself. (4) If, when this factor is used for the production of good A, this employment does not entail any sacrifice of any other good B. (5) Competition among the suppliers will continually tend to push the price of this factor toward zero.

6. *Henry George's "single-tax" explanation of the prevalence of poverty* (1) assumes that the land supply curve is perfectly or almost perfectly inelastic with respect to price; (2) finds the explanation of poverty in the multiplicity of taxes imposed on the poor by the capitalist class through the agency of government; (3) is essentially the same as the Marxist analysis of the exploitation of workers by capitalist manufacturers; (4) is based on the assumption that supply curves for many scarce inputs are "backward-bending," so that increased quantities of these inputs will be supplied if prices are *lowered,* not raised; (5) is not correctly described by any of these statements.

7. *A tax levied on a factor of production* (1) must always be borne entirely by the suppliers of that factor; (2) will be shifted forward to buyers if the factor supply is perfectly inelastic; (3) will be partly shifted forward to buyers if supply is perfectly elastic; (4) must always be borne by the buyers of that factor; (5) will be shifted forward to buyers the more any price fall reduces quantity supplied.

8. *If the return to a productive input is classed as one of economic rent, this means that the supply curve of that input which confronts any one of its demanders must be* (1) perfectly inelastic; (2) perfectly elastic; (3) nonexistent; (4) highly inelastic; (5) not necessarily any one of the above.

9. *The verdict of the text chapter on rent payments is (in part) that* (1) unless competitive rent payments are made, society's resources cannot be allocated into employment properly; (2) the more elastic with respect to price an input's supply is, the more its rental payments should be taxed; (3) it still is correct, broadly speaking, to say that rent does not enter into the cost of production; (4) the allocation of resources tends to be distorted by the fact that certain input supplies are inelastic with respect to price; (5) the more inelastic with respect to price an input's supply is, the more its rental payments should be taxed.

10. *If we say that "the supply curve of input A is perfectly inelastic with respect to price," we are most likely to mean, if speaking correctly, that its supply curve will be perfectly inelastic when set against the demand curve of* (1) any single user only; (2) any single class of users (i.e., any single industry) only; (3) all its users combined only; (4) any single user or of any single class of users, but not when set against the demand curve of all users combined; (5) any of the above— i.e., it will be perfectly price-inelastic no matter what demand curve it is set against.

29 COMPETITIVE WAGES AND COLLECTIVE BARGAINING

AS YOU READ THIS CHAPTER, keep in mind the type of background question with which it is really concerned. For example, why is it that the level of real wages in the United States is so much higher than it is in many other parts of the world? Is it simply because the American worker has more equipment and tools with which to work? Or are there other factors which need to be taken into account in a reasonably comprehensive explanation?

1. *a.* By the term "real wages" is meant (pick one):
(1) The same thing as money wages.
(2) Money wages after allowing for tax and other withholdings deducted from such wages.
(3) Money wages in relation to the consumer price level—i.e., what money wages can buy in real goods.

b. The idea of the "general wage level" (pick one):
(1) Is so imprecise, because of the enormous variation in wages or salaries between unskilled and highly skilled labor, as to be quite meaningless.
(2) Although imprecise, is still meaningful when we deal with such problems as the general level of wages in America versus that prevailing in other countries.
(3) However imprecise it may seem, can actually be worked out with considerable precision.

c. Between 1950 and 1970 in a certain country, money wages tripled. During that period, the consumer-goods price index rose from 400 to 600. It follows that *real* wages (*did not rise at all / rose by a factor of 1½ / doubled / tripled / more than tripled*).

d. We say that, other things equal, an increase in population would lower wage rates, owing to operation of the diminishing-returns law. We mean by this that an increase in the labor force would lower wage rates (pick one):
(1) Even if there were a corresponding increase in the available supply of other inputs such as raw materials and capital goods.
(2) With the supply of capital goods held constant.

a. (3). *b.* (2). *c.* doubled. *d.* (2).

2. The text speaks of the "optimum population" for any given country, meaning the population level at which the amount of real income per capita would reach its (*maximum / minimum*).

Behind the optimum-population idea is the reasoning that *two* forces are at work on the real-income level. One tends to raise real incomes as population increases, the other to lower them.

The income-raising force derives from the fact that the population is the consumer market. Producing firms must be faced by a sufficiently large consumer market before they will invest in the capital equipment and producing techniques which take full advantage of the economies of large-scale production. The countertendency results from the fact that the population is in effect the labor force; and a too-large labor force may suffer from

_____ .

That is, if population pushes too far in excess of the country's existing supplies of (*land / capital equipment / land and capital equipment*), per capita income will (*rise / fall*).

maximum; the law of diminishing returns; land and capital equipment; fall.

3. The idea of "the iron law of wages" evolved in the arguments of both Thomas Robert Malthus and Karl Marx (although for quite different reasons). The essence of the iron-law idea is that wages tend to be pushed to the (*competitive / minimum-subsistence / marginal-product*) level. (Malthus' argument—recall Chapter 2—rested on the belief that population would increase until this level was reached; Marx's, on the belief that this outcome was part of capitalist exploitation of the labor force.)

The text expresses (*agreement / qualified agreement / disagreement*) with the iron-law idea.

minimum-subsistence; disagreement.

4. *a.* The hourly wage offered a worker rises. He has some freedom of choice as to the number of hours he works per day or per week. In these circumstances, he can, if he wishes, work (more than one may be correct):

(1) The same number of hours and earn more daily or weekly income.
(2) More hours and earn more income.

(3) Fewer hours and earn the same income.

(4) Fewer hours and earn more income.

b. The fact that the worker may choose any one of the four alternatives of part *a* indicates the opposite and conflicting pulls of substitution-effect and income-effect.

When the worker is offered a higher wage for each hour worked, he is then sacrificing more money income than before for each hour he does *not* work. The higher hourly wage is an inducement to work *(more / fewer)* hours per day or week because "leisure (not working) has become more expensive." This by itself is the substitution-effect. It inclines the worker to give up some *(working hours in favor of leisure / leisure hours in favor of work).*

c. However, leisure time is (for most people) a desirable thing: as real incomes rise, they want more of it. The offer of a higher hourly wage makes possible more leisure *(with / without)* the sacrifice of any of the commodities that wage income will buy. The pull of the income-effect is toward *fewer* working hours and *more* leisure.

d. For example, suppose that at $4 hourly, the worker decides to work 40 hours weekly and to earn $160. At $6 hourly, he would choose to earn $210—that is, he would work *(35 / 40 / 45)* hours weekly. In this instance, the *(substitution- / income-)* effect has dominated.

---

a. All four are correct. *b.* more; leisure hours in favor of work. *c.* without. *d.* 35; income.

---

5. The term "economic rent" (see Chapter 28) is not usually applied with respect to labor. But in instances like the Babe Ruth case (see the text chapter section Rent Elements in Wages of Unique Individuals), it applies. Babe Ruth was paid the fantastic sum (for the 1920s) of $80,000 annually for playing baseball. Had diminished competition among baseball-club owners forced him to do so, he would probably have played for $10,000 annually. His unique skill seems to have been in baseball alone, not in any other occupation; so it is highly unlikely that any alternative employment open to him would have paid him anything like $80,000. (If Babe Ruth played today, he could earn substantial supplementary income by extolling the joys of shaving cream or hair tonic on TV commercials, but that fact does not alter the reasoning. He would be paid this *only because of* his status as a baseball player earning $80,000 annually.)

This means that Babe Ruth's labor supply curve to baseball clubs would be perfectly inelastic with respect to wage or salary prices (pick one):

a. From $80,000 annually to zero annually.

b. From $80,000 annually to some figure such as $5,000 annually.

c. Only at $80,000 annually; it would be less than perfectly inelastic at *any* lower figure.

In sum, the Babe Ruth case *(illustrates / does not illustrate)* the situation of economic rent.

---

b; illustrates.

---

6. Job A is exactly like job B in terms of skill required, hours of employment, etc.; but A pays a higher wage than B because it is more dangerous. The excess of the A wage over the B wage is called, in the language of the text, *(an equalizing difference / a qualitative differential).* If the A wage were higher because the job called for greater skill, the excess would be called *(an equalizing difference / a qualitative differential).*

---

an equalizing difference; a qualitative differential.

---

7. Ever since the days of classical economics, it has been customary to speak of "the three categories of productive inputs: land, labor, and capital." While often convenient, this division can become a misleading oversimplification. It can, for example, lead to the tacit assumption that within any one of the three categories there is substantial "homogeneity" or uniformity—which is not the case. Thus, "labor" includes everything from unskilled manual labor to high-level managerial or intellectual competence, corresponding to which there are many different wage and salary rates.

The classical economists used the land-labor-capital distinction as an analytic tool because it corresponded to the political realities of the day (see Study Guide p. 245). But they had to reckon with the fact that there are many different types of labor, and consequently many different wage rates. One elementary device introduced to account for this was the concept of "noncompeting labor groups."

The text's verdict on this concept is that (pick one):

a. It is the best way to account for the fact of differing labor groups.

b. It is convenient as an introduction to the problem, but is misleading, in part because it suggests there is no competition between adjacent groups.

c. It has no real meaning at all.

---

b.

The first half of this text chapter discusses the factors that would govern the labor market if it were perfectly competitive. In point of fact, it is not perfectly competitive either on the demand or on the supply side. The second half of the chapter accordingly turns to some of the labor market's imperfections. But note that it is "imperfectly competitive" only by reference to the strict standards of perfect competition. The market is still subject to strong competitive pressures.

8. One of the four methods (see text) by which a trade union may try to raise wages is through a direct attempt to increase the wage rate. If a union seeks to follow this path, the most desirable situation from its standpoint (to minimize any unemployment effect arising out of the wage increase) would be to have the derived demand for labor (*elastic / inelastic*) with respect to price, and the supply of labor (*elastic / inelastic*) as to price.

inelastic; inelastic.

9. Which of the following union practices operates primarily by shifting the labor supply curve to the left, and which by moving the derived demand curve for labor to the right? After each, put S for supply curve or D for demand curve.
a. Inserting featherbedding rules into local building codes.
.... ( )
b. Setting long apprenticeship periods for entrants into the occupation. .... ( )
c. Asking consumers to buy only union-made products.
.... ( )
d. Imposing high initiation fees upon entrants into the occupation. .... ( )
e. Limiting use of labor-saving tools and equipment. .. ( )
f. Agitating for tariff protection. .... ( )
g. Agitating for limitations on immigration. .... ( )

a. D. *b.* S. *c.* D. *d.* S. *e.* D. *f.* D. *g.* S.

10. When the text speaks of the possible "shock effect" of trade-union activity for higher wages, it is referring to (pick one):
a. The discovery by unions that higher wages may mean unemployment for some of their members.
b. The fact that a firm or industry may be galvanized out of complacency and forced to look to new methods for using labor more efficiently.
c. The fact that higher wages in a unionized industry tend to raise wages in nearby nonunionized industries.
d. The inclination of a firm to shut down completely under the pressure of excessive wage demands.

b.

QUIZ: Multiple Choice

1. *The concept of "noncompeting groups in the labor market" is considered useful in seeking to explain* (1) structural unemployment; (2) wage differentials among different categories of labor; (3) the lack of mobility among older workers; (4) the impact of wage increases in unionized sectors of the economy upon nonunionized sectors; (5) why wage rates in certain industries have risen faster than the average.

2. *A situation which (according to the text) is an indicator of an imperfect labor market would be one in which* (1) certain firms must make a decision on the wage policy they are going to adopt; (2) different wages are paid for different jobs in order to compensate for differences in risk; (3) different wages are paid for different jobs on the grounds that the jobs have different requirements; (4) the wages paid for certain jobs fall into the category of economic-rent payments; (5) the excess of one wage rate over another is an "equalizing difference."

3. *The idea of an "optimum population" refers to* (1) a population experiencing diminishing returns; (2) a population experiencing increasing returns; (3) a population of the highest-possible quality; (4) a population that maximizes the total output of a country; (5) a population at the point where the gain from increasing returns to scale is just counterbalanced by the effect of diminishing returns.

4. *According to Malthus' analysis of wage determination,* (1) it is impossible for either employers or unions to fix wage rates at anything but the competitive level; (2) employers will be able to force wages down to the equilibrium level by maintaining a high degree of unemployment; (3) the long-run supply curve of labor is a horizontal line at the wage level where workers will just be able to maintain and reproduce themselves; (4) the money wage received by workers must always equal the real wage; (5) employers will be able to force wages down to the subsistence level by maintaining a high degree of unemployment.

5. *It can properly be said that labor can be exploited, and will be, in the wage it is paid (particularly by the standard of a competitive market), if* (1) the union imposes restrictions on labor supply; (2) the derived demand for labor is highly inelastic; (3) increased wages reduce the marginal-physical-product of labor; (4) the supply curve of labor is backward-bending; (5) the employer is in a monopsony position.

6. *Four of the following five statements more or less repeat ideas discussed in the text chapter. One of the five runs counter to what is said therein. Which one?* (1) A wage increase in a single industry may have particular effects upon labor's real income and employment, but it is dangerous to apply the same conclusions when reasoning as to a wage increase applicable to the whole economy. (2) The facts make it clear that unions have managed to raise real incomes for their members. (3) The average wage in unionized industries is decidedly higher than that in nonunionized industries. (4) The percentage differential between wages in unionized and nonunionized occupations has been narrowing over the past 40 years. (5) Unionized industries, as compared with nonunionized ones, tend to be made up of large-scale firms and of firms using labor of higher-than-average skills.

7. *The so-called "substitution-effect," as applied to a worker's decision to change or not change the number of hours he*

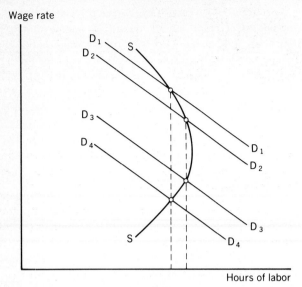

Wage rate

Hours of labor

Fig. 29-1

or she works daily when offered a different price per hour of labor, refers specifically to the following fact: (1) If the price offered labor rises, the worker's disposition is to buy better but more costly goods, hence to work longer hours. (2) A general increase in wages tends to produce a general rise in consumer prices, which cancels out the worker's real-income gain. (3) Because leisure (nonwork) time is desirable, a worker's normal inclination is to choose more leisure as part of any rise in real income. (4) The cost of working is leisure (nonwork) time sacrificed, hence if the wage offered labor falls, leisure becomes relatively less expensive. (5) Any labor cost increase prompts employers to try to substitute capital for labor in production.

8. *Which alternative in question 7 would be correct had that question referred to the "income-effect," not to the "substitution-effect"?* (1). (2). (3). (4). (5).

9. *The "lump of labor" viewpoint is essentially a belief that* (1) the quality of a hand-crafted product is inherently superior to that of a machine-made product; (2) the supply of labor will not vary significantly with the price that is offered for it—i.e., the labor supply curve is almost perfectly inelastic; (3) labor effort is the ultimate measure of value, and the prices of goods should reflect the amount of labor effort that went into making those goods; (4) any commodity embodies a fixed quantity of labor (direct or indirect) in its manufacture, regardless of the production technique used; (5) there is only a finite and fixed amount of useful work to be done.

10. *The viewpoint referred to in question 9 arose principally out of* (1) the experience of workers in depression periods; (2) the clash between income-effects and substitution-effects; (3) the experience of workers in inflationary periods; (4) the fact that the total labor supply curve is highly inelastic with respect to price; (5) the belief that the total fund of money out of which wages must be paid is essentially fixed in amount.

11. *Figure 29-1 illustrates a backward-bending or backward-rising labor supply curve and four possible demand curves. If the demand curve were to change from position 1 to position 2,* (1) the substitution-effect would dominate over the income-effect; (2) the substitution-effect and income-effect would cancel one another out; (3) the income-effect would dominate over the substitution-effect; (4) the income-effect and the substitution-effect would work in the same direction; (5) none of these statements would be correct.

12. *Referring to the same figure, if the demand curve were to move from position 2 to position 3, which alternative in question 11 would be correct?* (1). (2). (3). (4). (5).

13. *Again referring to this figure, if the demand curve were to move from position 3 to position 4, which alternative would be correct?* (1). (2). (3). (4). (5).

14. *Still referring to this figure, if the demand curve were to move from position 4 to position 3, which alternative would be correct?* (1). (2). (3). (4). (5).

15. *To say that there is an "economic rent" element in a person's income means that* (1) this income comes at least in part from property ownership rather than labor supply; (2) this income exceeds what it would be were the labor market perfectly competitive; (3) if the price offered for this person's labor were increased, he or she would want to reduce the number of daily hours worked; (4) this income is much above average, but is the result of some natural talent; (5) this person's labor supply curve is perfectly inelastic with respect to price, at least within some range of prices.

16. *Between two periods, the index of money wages fell from 600 to 540. The index of consumer prices fell from 400 to 300. This means that, between the two periods, real wages* (1) rose by 50 per cent; (2) rose by 20 per cent; (3) rose by 10 per cent; (4) did not change; (5) fell by 20 per cent.

17. *A trade union which is struggling to raise wages for its members and at the same time to maintain as much employment as possible for them will be encouraged in its efforts by* (1) an elastic derived demand for labor; (2) an elastic supply of labor; (3) an inelastic demand for the finished product; (4) a perfectly competitive market for labor; (5) an imperfectly competitive market for labor.

18. *If everyone in the labor force were exactly alike (i.e., no difference in skills or competence), and if the labor market were perfectly competitive,* (1) any wage-rate differences would have to be explained as "qualitative differentials"; (2) there would still be a considerable range of different wage rates, with several different reasons to explain them; (3) any wage-rate differences would have to be explained as equalizing differences; (4) any wage-rate differences would have to be explained in terms of the differing wage policies adopted by different firms; (5) there would be only one wage rate.

30 INTEREST AND CAPITAL

THE WORD "CAPITAL" has two different meanings: *money* capital, and *real* capital. *Money* capital means simply borrowable money. The amount subsequently returned by the borrower is ordinarily greater than the original amount, and we refer to this excess as "interest." Interest is the *price* that must be paid for the use of money capital for some specified period of time. We can think of this price as being set by the interaction between demanders (borrowers) and suppliers (owners of such capital, willing to part with it if offered sufficient interest as an inducement). Notice that *time* is an essential ingredient if we are talking about the interest which money capital can earn.

Real capital means any "capital good" which is "productive" in the sense that it can contribute to production of finished goods. A house is a capital good because of the consumer services it can provide in the form of shelter. A machine tool is a capital good.

Time is likewise an essential ingredient with respect to real capital. If we could somehow press a button on any real capital item, with the result that it instantaneously yielded its entire outflow of services in one enormous heap, then it would be a consumer good, not a capital good. The essence of a capital good is that it "pays off" slowly. You must wait until tomorrow for at least part of the output it can produce. (Inventories of semifinished and wholly finished goods also count as capital goods. Such goods do not "pay off" slowly, in the sense that a machine tool does. But it is the fact that they are not to be consumed until tomorrow that explains their being included in capital goods.)

If time is involved, then *the idea of an interest rate is also involved.* Suppose a given capital good would cost you some given money amount to build. If built, it would yield a stream of output (some commodity or some service) stretching into the future. Each item of that output would have some money value. (Because it is a future item, you have to *estimate* what that value would be. But if you are thinking of building this capital good, you must make this estimate, just as you must estimate how far into the future this output stream will extend—i.e., how long the capital good will last.)

This expected stream of future incoming revenue is the capital good's "money payoff." And note carefully:

▶ There is always an interest rate which will just equate the capital good's money cost with its total stream of expected future money revenues.

▶ That interest rate—the interest rate which investment in this capital good would yield—is called the capital good's "net productivity."

1. Consider an asset that will cost you $100, right now, to construct. If you construct it, there will be no payoff for 2 years. But 2 years from now, this asset will pay you $121—nothing before that, and nothing after. This $121 is free of any incidental costs or expenses; it is the net return on your $100 outlay. The $121 return is safe; there is no uncertainty about its arrival.

This capital asset has an annual net productivity of 10 per cent. Ten per cent is the annual interest rate at which a loan of $100 will just "grow," with annual compounding of interest, into $121 in 2 years. At the end of year 1, the principal amount of $100 will earn $10 interest. This interest is left to become extra principal for year 2, so that in the second year the loan is $110, not $100. At the end of year 2, the interest for that year is $11. So the total repayment at end of year 2 will be $121—$110 principal, plus $11 interest.

a. Two dollar figures are involved: in the example, a cost figure of $100 today, a revenue figure of $121 just 2 years from today. An interest rate (10 per cent annually, in the example) "matches up" the two differing dollar figures. So the "net productivity" of a capital asset is expressed as *(a dollar figure / an interest rate).*

b. If you had to borrow $100 to construct the asset of part *a,* and could borrow this money in the money capital market at 5 per cent annually, would you do so? *(Yes / No).*

c. Would you borrow the money at 9 per cent annually? *(Yes / No).* At 11 per cent annually? *(Yes / No).*

---

a. an interest rate. *b.* Yes, for you would be ahead of the game financially even after paying your interest. *c.* Yes, for the same reason (remember that there is no uncertainty about your $121 return). No; you would be out of pocket after paying interest.

More typically, a capital good promises a *series* of future revenue figures, strung out over time, rather than the single $121 payoff of the example above. And it may entail a series of cost figures (an initial cost, then some later outlays). This complicates the algebra, but it does not upset the principle that there is always an interest rate which matches a cost (or set of costs, at specified dates) with a set of revenues (also at specified dates, coming somewhat later in time than the first of the cost dates). Don't worry about the details of the algebra (there is more on this in the chapter Appendix). Just note that there is always an interest rate which is the "net productivity" of an asset with given cost and revenue figures.

2. Suppose you have money available to lend, or to use in the purchase of some revenue-yielding asset. The market interest rate is 10 per cent annually. The borrowers in this market are of such good credit standing that the risk of any borrower defaulting on his loan is virtually nonexistent.

The owner of an asset such as that described in question 1 (i.e., guaranteeing a single return of $121 at the end of 2 years) offers to sell it to you.

a. If this asset could be bought for $90, would you buy it? *(Yes / No).* If you did, the interest rate you would be getting on your outlay would be *(less than 10 per cent / 10 per cent / more than 10 per cent).*

b. If the asset could be bought for $100, then it would be *(an unusually good buy / an unusually poor buy / as good as, but no better than, other available alternatives).*

c. Would you pay $102 for this asset? *(Yes / No).* If you did, the interest rate you would be getting on your outlay would be *(less than 10 per cent / 10 per cent / more than 10 per cent).*

---

a. Yes; more than 10 per cent. *b.* as good as, but no better than. *c.* No; less than 10 per cent.

---

3. *a.* Suppose the market rate of interest is 4 per cent annually, not 10 per cent. Would you now buy this asset for $102, if you had the opportunity? *(Yes / No).* If you did, the interest rate you would be getting would be *(less than 4 per cent / 4 per cent / more than 4 per cent).*

b. Actually, with a market interest rate of 4 per cent annually, i.e., if the return generally available for "investing" money capital is 4 per cent per year, the market price of this asset would stand at about $112 (more precisely, $111.85). Why? (Pick one.)

(1) Because $112 is the amount which, if lent out for 2 years at 4 per cent annually, would "grow" to $121.
(2) Because the interest return or net productivity of this asset is 10 per cent regardless of the amount of money laid out to build or buy it.

---

a. Yes; more than 4 per cent. *b.* (1). (This asset's net productivity is 10 per cent *only* if it can be bought or built for $100.)

To repeat: An asset's "net productivity" is an interest rate. If, concerning an asset, you are asked, "What is its net productivity?" you need two pieces of information:
(1) Amount it would cost to build or buy this asset now.
(2) Amounts of future net revenue it is expected to bring in—and the expected dates of their arrival. (*Net* revenue means revenue after allowing for any costs incurred in using the asset or collecting the revenue.)

Given this information, there is always one interest rate that indicates the "rate of return" on (net productivity of) the asset in question.

Question 3 took you to a different—but closely related—question: What is the maximum amount you should pay for a given asset? What is its present value?

To reply, again you need two pieces of information:
(1) As before, amounts and dates of the future revenue the asset is expected to bring in.
(2) The *market* interest rate.

From this information, you can compute the asset's present market value—more precisely, its *capitalized* present value. Thus, in question 3, the asset yielding $121 just 2 years from now has a capitalized present value of $100 if the market interest rate is 10 per cent. Its capitalized present value is about $112 if the market rate is 4 per cent. (Again: Don't worry over the algebra needed for this kind of computation.)

To "capitalize" an asset is to value it as it should be valued: in terms of the future net revenues it is expected to bring in. This stream of *future* revenues is reduced to a single *present* value by means of the market interest rate.

4. After you have computed an asset's capitalized value, suppose you find this figure is different from the asset's actual construction cost. If so, then this asset's net productivity (which is an interest rate, remember) is different from the market interest rate.

Suppose actual cost is *less than* capitalized value. Then it *(would / would not)* be profitable to borrow money to construct it. This asset's net productivity is *(less than / equal to / greater than)* the market interest rate.

If capitalized value is less than construction cost, the asset *(would / would not)* be worth building. The market value of such an asset already constructed would be *(less than / equal to / greater than)* its construction cost.

---

would; greater than; would not; less than.

To capitalize an asset's future revenues is to *discount* them. (The chapter Appendix has a fuller discussion of discounting.) To discount is to determine the *present* value of some *future* sum, using the market interest rate. If that rate is 10 per cent annually, then $121 due 2 years from now discounts down to a present value of $100. If the market rate is 4 per cent annually, that $121 would discount down to a present value of approximately $112.

Suppose an asset promises income at the ends of years 1, 2, and 3. Then we discount each of these revenue items separately to obtain their present values. The *sum* of all such discounted figures is the asset's present value.

Note the sequence: *First* discount each item of future income separately. *Then* add the resulting discounted values to obtain capitalized (or discounted) value. *Do not* try to add together revenue figures accruing at different points in future time, before discounting them. The farther away in future time any money amount lies, the lower will be its present discounted value.

Summarizing:

▶ Discounting is the process of cutting any expected *future* money figure down to a lower present value by means of the market interest rate.

▶ The farther away in future time this money amount lies, the deeper the discounting knife cuts.

For example, if a revenue amount of $121 is expected 2 years from now, its present value, given a market interest rate of 10 per cent, is $100; if expected 4 years from now, its present value is about $83.

And note also:

▶ The higher the market interest rate, the sharper the discounting knife.

If the market interest rate should rise from 10 per cent to 12 per cent, the present discounted value of $100 due 2 years from now is cut from $100 to about $96.

5. This means, then, that if market interest rates *rise*, the present discounted value of any sum expected at some date in the future will (*rise / remain unchanged / fall*). And if the market interest rate should *fall*, an asset's capitalized value (assuming no change in its expected future receipts) must (*rise / remain unchanged / fall*).

fall; rise.

6. *a.* You own a piece of land which brings you net rental income (after allowing for maintenance cost, etc.) of $500 yearly. You expect annual rental to continue at this figure. The capitalized value of this land would be (pick one):
(1) $500.
(2) The sum of all expected future receipts of $500.
(3) The sum of all expected future annual receipts, each "discounted" down to a present-value figure by means of the market interest rate.

b. Suppose the asset in part *a* is expected to yield $500 yearly and keep on doing so throughout the future—i.e., it represents a "perpetual income stream." Each $500 can then be thought of as the interest yield on a loan which has no maturity date (date for repayment of principal). Or it can be thought of as the yield on a loan which has a finite maturity date but which is automatically renewed once again at each such date.

What is the amount of principal that would have to be involved if its interest yield is $500 annually and the interest rate is 4 per cent annually? (If $500 is 4 per cent, what is 100 per cent?) .... $_____.

c. The text gives a simple formula for computing the capitalized value of such perpetual-income assets. Write it down, and make sure the formula works for the case of part *b*.

_____ .

d. Is this formula consistent with the rule that capitalized values are reckoned as the sum of the discounted values of all expected future revenues? (Pick one.)
(1) No—the perpetuity case has to be handled by means of a different formula, because of the infinite number of expected future revenue items.
(2) Yes—in this special case, the sum of all discounted values forms a convergent geometric progression.
    (NOTE: If you don't know what a convergent geometric progression is, don't brood over it. The point is simply this: Even though the number of discounted $500s to be added together is *infinite*, their total is still a *finite* sum when you allow for discounting. The convergent geometric progression is just the mathematical concept used to make this point.)

a. (3). *b.* $12,500. *c.* $V = \$N / i$, or $12,500 = $500 / 0.04. *d.* (2).

All this discussion of capitalized values and discounting is a lead into the problem of *the determination of the level of interest rates*. ("Interest," remember, is the income received by those who supply money capital to borrowers.)

We must begin by thinking of the interest rate as a rate determined by the demand for loanable money and the supply of such money. But talk of "supply and

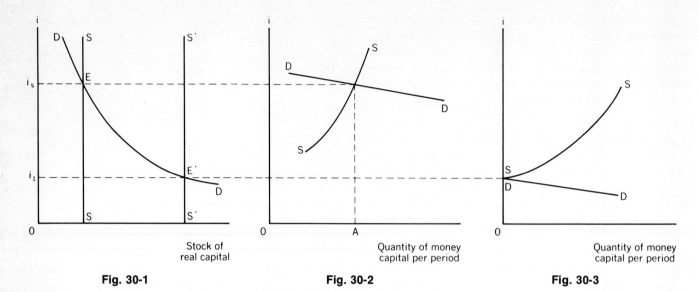

Fig. 30-1   Fig. 30-2   Fig. 30-3

demand" is empty unless we probe for the factors lying *behind* the demand curve, *behind* the supply curve. Prominent among the demanders of money capital are business firms with investment projects (the building of capital goods) to undertake. Their decisions as to whether or not to borrow, and how much to borrow, will be influenced by the level of the interest rate because some projects will be worth undertaking at low interest rates, and not worth undertaking at high ones. Why? Because the "net productivity" of such projects (and remember that this productivity is expressed as an interest rate) will be below a high market interest rate, and above a low market interest rate.

In sum, computations of net productivity must lie behind the demand curve for loanable money. The suppliers of such money are largely those who have saved (or who are handling the money which other people have saved and entrusted to them). From here, we work our way into the traditional—and simplified—version of capital and interest theory outlined in the chapter.

Figures 30-1 through 30-3 illustrate this theory. On all three diagrams, the interest rate (a percentage figure per annum) is measured vertically, with zero interest at bottom.

Figure 30-1 corresponds to the text's Fig. 30-1. It is assumed in this case that all capital goods are exactly alike, so that we can add them together in physical units and get a meaningful total, just as we can add dollar figures together. The SS line in Fig. 30-1 indicates the economy's *total* stock of capital at some particular period of time. It stands for some figure such as 400 units of capital. SS is vertical because the present capital stock is 400 units no matter whether the interest rate is 2 per cent, 10 per cent, or any other figure.

The *DD* curve is the "demand" of business firms for such capital goods. It intersects SS at point E, indicating an interest rate of i_s. To grasp the meaning of this *DD* curve, suppose i_s indicates an interest rate of 8 per cent. Then *DD* intersects SS at the 8 per cent level because the firms estimate that the last (or marginal) units of that 400 capital stock have a net productivity of 8 per cent. This estimate is based on the cost of producing more capital goods and on the estimated net revenues capital goods will bring in.

7. *a.* To further grasp what *DD* means and why it intersects SS where it does, suppose the situation is a little different. With the capital stock at 400, business firms are more optimistic about the payoff of capital goods. Specifically, they think that the last units of a 400 stock have a net productivity of 10 per cent. Then if the interest rate is not 10 per cent but 8 per cent, they will want to have (*more than 400 / just 400 / less than 400*) units of capital. The interest rate must be 10 per cent before their disposition to use capital goods is limited to 400. That is to say, *if* business firms were more optimistic about the net productivity of capital, the *DD* curve in Fig. 30-1 would lie (pick one):

(1) Farther to the right than is now indicated.
(2) Just where it is now.
(3) Farther to the left than is now indicated.

It would intersect the SS curve at a point indicating (*less than 8 per cent / 8 per cent / more than 8 per cent*).

And so, given the existing stock of capital and its net productivity, the interest rate in this economy, at this period of time in its history, is i_s.

But the people in this economy are still saving money. Moreover, in the traditional account, people save *because of* the interest rate. And they are willing to lend this saved money to business-firm borrowers.

The SS curve in Fig. 30-2 illustrates this situation. Its southwest-to-northeast direction illustrates the assumption that people will save and lend more if the interest rate is increased. Note that in Fig. 30-2 the horizontal axis measures *money* (not real capital units, as in Fig. 30-1).

There is also a *demand* for this money, or money capital. Business firms are willing to pay 8 per cent on borrowed money because there are still some projects on which new capital goods (additions to the present total stock) would have a net productivity of 8 per cent. Of course, large additions to the capital stock would lower its net productivity because of diminishing returns, but that comes later. For the time being, business firms are willing to borrow (in each period of time) the amount of money indicated by OA in Fig. 30-2 at 8 per cent because they think there is still useful employment for this amount of money at this rate. DD in Fig. 30-2 is close to being flat at rates even a little above 8 per cent, unless there are many would-be borrowers who see projects with a payoff in excess of 8 per cent. But if the rate were to drop a bit below 8 per cent, that might produce a substantial increase in the quantity of money capital demanded (i.e., demand might be highly elastic with respect to interest rate changes, if there are plenty of unexploited projects with net productivity a little below 8 per cent).

b. That is, OA in Fig. 30-2 indicates, per period of time (pick one):
(1) The number of units of capital to be added to the capital stock.
(2) Nothing whatever with respect to the capital stock.
(3) Money which will be spent to purchase additional units of capital.
The effect of the borrowing and lending process in each period (Fig. 30-2) will be, in terms of Fig. 30-1, to (pick one):
(1) Move the vertical SS curve a little to the left.
(2) Move the vertical SS curve a little to the right.
(3) Move the DD curve a little to the right.
(4) Move the DD curve a little to the left.

c. Accordingly, as time goes by (in this traditional account), if the situation is not disturbed by technological change or the like, the stock of capital goods will *(fall / remain constant / increase)* and the interest rate will *(fall / remain constant / increase)*.

But (again according to the traditional account) as the interest rate falls, the public's disposition to save decreases. At rates below i_s (see the SS curve in Fig. 30-2), the amount saved (and loaned) decreases. And at a sufficiently low rate, nothing will be saved; all of incomes will go to consumption. This is shown in Fig. 30-3 by the fact that SS is zero at i_l.

That is to say, after a sufficiently long period of time and a sufficient increase in the capital stock, the process of capital accumulation comes to an end. In terms of Fig. 30-1, the economy's capital stock has then increased to the level indi-

cated by _____, and the interest rate is _____.

In terms of Fig. 30-3, the DD curve begins at interest rate i_l because (pick one):
(1) There are no more projects worth undertaking at i_l, only those at rates below that level.
(2) People will supply money only at rates below i_l.

---

a. more than 400; (1); more than 8 per cent. *b.* (3); (2).
c. increase; fall; OS';i_l; (1).

---

8. At least twice in this chapter, the text mentions two fundamental elements lying behind demand for and supply of capital, hence behind the level of the interest rate. What are they?

(1) _____ .

(2) _____ .

---

(1) Technical net productivity of capital; (2) Willingness of public to save rather than consume part of its income.

---

9. The text mentions a number of qualifications that must be made in the traditional theory of capital and interest if that theory is to accord with reality.

a. For example, it is doubtful if people's consumption-saving decisions are greatly influenced by the level of the interest rate. At least, those decisions do not seem to be altered by moderate changes therein.

Suppose (1) the decision to save out of income is quite unresponsive to any change in the interest rate, and (2) whatever amount people *do* save, they are willing to lend it out at any positive interest rate. In Fig. 30-2, this would affect the *(DD / SS)* curve; it would in consequence become *(vertical / horizontal / a diagonal line)*.

However, the second of the assumptions above is probably unsound. While the amount people *save* may be unresponsive to interest-rate changes, the amount they *lend* probably *is* responsive. That is, at lower interest rates, they will lend *(more / less)*. The SS curve now shown in Fig. 30-2 *(indicates / does not indicate)* such an attitude.

b. If real and money incomes gradually rise over time, people can and do save more money out of incomes. This affects the *(DD / SS)* curve in Fig. 30-2. Such income increases shift that curve to the *(right / left)*.

c. If you try to compute the income accruing from any proposed capital project, you must look into the future, and the future is always uncertain. You must make the best estimate you can of the net revenues it is likely to earn, but—particularly if you are going to borrow money to finance the project—you must recognize that this estimate may prove too high.

Hence the net productivity figure actually used in investment decisions will almost certainly be (above / below) that which a "best-possible" or "single most likely" estimate of future revenue would yield. In brief, it is a conservative measure to (cut down / increase) your revenue estimates to allow for uncertainty.

This factor of uncertainty surrounding the future is so important that it is unwise to think of business firms typically changing their investment plans on account of small-to-moderate changes in market interest rates. Uncertainty makes their estimates of net productivity rough even at best.

d. Estimates of probable net productivity are influenced also by a quite-different factor: the climate of optimism or pessimism. If business firms, looking into the uncertain future with respect to projected capital plans, suddenly become more pessimistic, this will shift the (DD / SS) curve in Fig. 30-2 to the (right / left).

Similarly, if lenders, trying to decide whether or not borrowers will really be able to make good on their borrowing obligations, suddenly become more pessimistic on this score, this will shift the (DD / SS) curve in Fig. 30-2 to the (right / left).

e. The net productivity of capital may be altered by technological change. We would ordinarily expect such changes to (increase / decrease) capital's net productivity. In Fig. 30-2, such technological change would shift the (DD / SS) curve to the (right / left).

a. SS; vertical; less; indicates. b. SS; right. c. below; cut down. d. DD; left; SS; left. e. increase; DD; right.

10. With respect to interest which a rich man charges a poor man for a loan to finance the latter's consumption needs, the text evaluates its morality (or immorality) as follows (pick one):
(1) It is immoral.
(2) Provided the interest market is competitive, it is neither more immoral nor less immoral than any other transaction between a rich man and a poor man, since the rich man provides a valuable service in return for the money he is paid.
(3) There is no question of immorality involved.

(2).

11. What role, if any, should the interest rate play in a centrally planned socialist economy?
(1) It would still exist to the extent that borrowing and lending would still exist, e.g., the state might wish to make loans to its citizens. But if borrowing and lending are ended, then there is no role for the interest rate.
(2) The state must still decide how much of its resources should go into investment (capital accumulation), and it must still decide which investment projects have highest priority.

For this computation of "highest net productivity," the interest rate is still essential.
(3) It would have no role whatsoever to play.

(2).

QUIZ: Multiple Choice

1. The "net productivity of capital" is (1) an amount of time; (2) a dollar figure; (3) a figure in dollars per unit of time; (4) an interest rate or percentage; (5) a figure in units of output per period of time.

2. By the "capitalized value" of an asset is meant specifically (1) its original cost plus an estimate of maintenance expense throughout its lifetime; (2) the same thing as its original cost; (3) the sum of all its discounted net earnings; (4) the sum of all its net earnings, without discounting; (5) the rate of interest at which the asset would just become worth purchasing or constructing.

3. If the "net productivity" of any capital asset is to be computed, several items of information are needed. Which among the following is not required for proper computation of net productivity? The (1) original cost of purchasing or constructing the asset; (2) rate of interest that must be paid if money is borrowed to finance the original cost; (3) estimated maintenance or operating cost that must be incurred in order to keep the asset in satisfactory operating (revenue-earning) condition throughout its life; (4) estimated revenue that the asset will produce throughout its lifetime; (5) degree of "riskiness" surrounding estimated revenue, i.e., the degree of uncertainty as to whether revenues in the estimated amounts will really appear or not.

4. The law of diminishing returns plays the following part in interest-rate determination, according to traditional theory: (1) As capital goods accumulate relative to supplies of land and labor, the net productivity of increments to the capital stock must fall. (2) The cost of producing additional capital goods must necessarily increase (in the absence of innovation). (3) A steady increase in the output of whatever consumer good a particular capital good produces must lower the price of that consumer good and thus lower the net productivity of the capital good. (4) It explains why innovation cannot continually check the long-run tendency of the interest rate to fall. (5) It must be used if the net productivity of any capital good is to be computed.

5. In traditional interest-rate theory, the rate of interest is determined by (1) the estimated net productivity of capital; (2) the extent to which the public wishes to use the income it receives for consumption; (3) both the estimated net productivity of capital and the extent to which the public wishes to use the income it receives for consumption; (4) the estimated net productivity of capital and the size of the capital stock; (5)

the estimated net productivity of capital and the rate of technological development.

6. *Traditional interest-rate and capital theory held a particular view regarding a "long-run equilibrium" position for the economy, namely, that there is* (1) a tendency toward such an equilibrium, in which the market interest rate would be zero; (2) a tendency toward such an equilibrium, in which gross investment would be zero; (3) a tendency toward such an equilibrium, in which net investment would be maintained at a steady and non-zero rate; (4) a tendency toward such an equilibrium, in which saving out of income would be zero; (5) no tendency toward any such long-run equilibrium.

7. *The traditional theory described in question 6, the text points out, neglected the fact that* (1) the amount saved out of income might be influenced by the interest rate; (2) it is necessary to discount future items of income in order to establish their present value; (3) while the interest rate may approach zero, it cannot actually reach zero; (4) technological change might continually increase the net productivity of capital; (5) people are typically impatient to consume now, rather than accumulate for future consumption.

8. *A further shortcoming in the traditional theory mentioned in question 6, also referred to in the text, was that it* (1) ignored the role of the diminishing-returns law in gradually pushing down the rate of return on new capital projects; (2) failed to incorporate properly into its analysis the concept of the net productivity of capital; (3) failed to recognize that changes in real income, by changing the quantity of saving, would affect the interest rate; (4) neglected the fact that the amount saved out of income might be affected by the interest rate; (5) neglected the role of indirect or roundabout methods in the matter of capital-good production.

9. *In a centrally planned socialist state, the rate of interest would (or should) play a role as follows (according to the text): It would* (1) reflect the public's decision as to the allocation of the national product between consumption and investment; (2) govern the state's decision regarding the allocation of the national product between consumption and investment; (3) rank proposed capital-good projects according to their net productivity; (4) serve to indicate the attainable increase in national product to be expected over future years; (5) do none of these things, interest being essentially a capitalist phenomenon.

10. *A certain asset is expected to yield a steady net income (i.e., after allowing for all costs or expenses) of $100 annually, from now until eternity. If the market rate of interest is 8 per cent per annum, the market value of this asset ought to be* (1) $800; (2) $1,250; (3) $8,000; (4) $10,000; (5) infinity.

11. *Should market interest rates generally fall, this would affect the "present discounted value" of any given capital-good asset as follows: That value would* (1) fall, since lower interest rates indicate that revenue amounts accruing at any future date are now given a higher present value; (2) fall, since lower interest rates indicate that revenue amounts accruing at any future date are now given a lower present value; (3) remain unchanged, except insofar as any relevant cost or revenue item is thereby changed; (4) rise, because lower interest rates indicate that revenue amounts accruing at any future date are now given a lower present value; (5) rise, because lower interest rates indicate that revenue amounts accruing at any future date are now given a higher present value.

12. *Which alternative in question 11 would be correct, had that question referred to the asset's "net productivity," not to its "present discounted value" (still referring to a fall in market interest rates)?* (1). (2). (3). (4). (5).

13. *In a period of deflation (i.e., of generally falling prices), the "real" rate of interest obtained by any lender on money lent* (1) will exceed the stated rate; (2) will become a negative figure; (3) will fall below the stated rate, although not to the extent of becoming a negative figure; (4) will become a meaningless or incalculable figure; (5) is not correctly described by any of the preceding.

14. *If a nation deliberately introduces a "tight" fiscal policy and an "easy" monetary policy, then its purpose in choosing these alternatives (in addition to the maintenance of full employment) would presumably be to* (1) attain the highest-possible level of consumption; (2) keep the government's budget balanced; (3) avoid inflationary price increases; (4) produce a high level of growth in the capital stock; (5) restrict investment to projects with high net productivity.

15. *With respect to the monetary rate of interest and the net productivity of capital, which of the following is true?* (1) Although both are expressed as percentages per annum, they are never the same thing. (2) Since both are expressed as percentages per annum, they are always the same thing. (3) Given any rate of interest, society should undertake all investment projects whose net productivity exceeds that rate of interest. (4) Given any rate of interest, society should undertake all investment projects whose net productivity is less than the rate of interest. (5) An economy must be in long-run equilibrium whenever net productivity of capital equals the monetary rate of interest.

16. *The "net productivity" of any capital good could reasonably be described as* (1) that particular rate of interest at which the capital good would just be worth buying or building, i.e., revenues would just be matched by costs (including interest); (2) the dollar amount of profit that would accrue if that capital good were bought or built; (3) the same thing as the market rate of interest; (4) the physical increase in output (as distinct from the money value) that would accrue if that capital good were bought or built; (5) the percentage figure obtained by adding up all net revenues that would accrue from the capital good and dividing this total by its cost.

17. *In the traditional interest-rate theory described in the text, there is a long-run tendency for the interest rate to* (1) rise, owing to the law of diminishing returns, unless checked by technological change; (2) rise, owing to an increasing amount being saved out of higher real incomes; (3) fall, owing to an increasing amount being saved out of higher real incomes; (4) fall, owing to the law of diminishing returns, unless checked by technological change; (5) reach an equilibrium level from which there would be only short-run departures, even though the stock of capital goods may steadily increase.

18. *If business firms generally become more optimistic regarding the revenues that would accrue from the investment projects that they are planning, the net productivity of capital* (1) will increase, since revenues enter into the computation of net productivity; (2) will decrease, since the net productivity is an interest rate, and the interest rate goes inversely to the value of the investment project; (3) will not change, since the net productivity is governed by technical considerations, not by expected revenues; (4) will probably fall, although there is a special case in which it would rise; (5) may do any of the above, since the effect of a change in expected revenues upon net productivity is unpredictable.

APPENDIX: Theoretical Aspects of Interest

Throughout much of the text chapter preceding its appendix, it was assumed that "capital goods" are homogeneous, uniform, standardized. This makes it much easier to assert that as more and more capital is produced, its net productivity will fall—that is, the law of diminishing returns will operate as capital is increased relative to labor and to land.

1. This assumption of homogeneity is convenient but false. Capital goods are in fact heterogeneous in the extreme. In the text appendix, it is asserted that when this fact of nonhomogeneity is recognized, the tendency of capital's net productivity to fall *(still / no longer)* applies.

To put it briefly and nonrigorously, the best projects are usually undertaken first, leaving the lower-productivity items for later. Of course, technological change can shake things up, producing a "new deal" as to productivities. Projects which benefit from new technology will become more attractive. Their net productivity, that is to say, will be *(raised / lowered)*.

---

still; raised.

---

2. Classical economists often regarded the interest rate as the device by which people choose between present and future consumption. If the rate if 5 per cent per annum, and you have $100, you may choose between $100 consumption today or $105 consumption a year from now. Or you may pick $50 today and $52.50 next year, or any such intermediate combination. The point is that insofar as you pick "next year," you *save* and you *lend* (in order to get the extra 5 per cent). It follows from this reasoning that a different interest rate would produce a different consumption-saving distribution.

All economic theory is an attempt to describe "the way things really are." Reasoning such as that above faces one difficulty: It assumes that what people reasonably *ought* to do, they *will* do. Unfortunately, people are sometimes perverse enough, in their actual behavior, not to conform to the analysis. And they are not necessarily being unreasonable. The trouble instead may be that the analysis fails to recognize considerations that are important in accounting for actual behavior.

It seems to be true that interest-rate changes do *not* significantly alter consumption-saving decisions. People save against life's uncertainties, and they save for specific future goals. The interest rate is probably a minor consideration in most saving decisions.

In the classical view, there is a long-run interest-rate "floor," established when the rate falls sufficiently that people feel the extra return is not worth waiting for. But if saving persists regardless of the interest-rate level, will that rate drift down toward zero?

For two reasons, any such tendency seems unlikely. First, technological innovation should persistently *(increase / decrease)* the net productivity of new capital projects. Second, the lending process is always haunted by some uncertainty or risk that the money loaned will not come back, or will not come back in full. So if there is an interest-rate floor, it will be set by refusal to *(save / lend)* anything at rates at or below this floor.

---

increase; lend.

---

3. Note that this interest-rate floor has already been discussed (in Chapter 18). It is the floor resulting from "liquidity preference"—meaning preference to hold money as an asset in preference to securities if the interest return on the latter is considered too low. Conceivably, this might pose a problem for antirecession monetary policy. As an antirecession move, the central bank would want to *(raise / lower)* interest rates in order to encourage *(investment spending / saving)*. It does this by entering the securities market and *(buying / selling)* government securities. The effect is to push up the price of such securities and so to *(increase / decrease)* the effective interest rate thereon. In principle, this interest-rate change will spread to nongovernmental securities. But if people refuse to buy these nongovernmental securities at such lower interest rates because they consider the rates too low in the light of the uncertainty involved, then the "easy money" operation is blocked, and some other antirecession device must be adopted.

---

lower; investment spending; buying; decrease.

---

4. In the preceding question (as in Part 2 chapters), it was assumed that through open-market operations you can change the money quantity, M, and the interest rate, i. To at least some degree, these ideas clash with the "traditional" view that the principal i-determining forces are the net productivity of capital and the disposition of people to save.

Many classical economists insisted that i's level is set only by these "real" (nonmonetary) forces; some of them vehemently denied the idea that i can be influenced by changing M. (In the background is the "Quantity Theory of Money"—Chapter 15—which asserts that changes in M have their effect on *prices*, not upon interest rates. So implicit in the quantity theory is the idea that anything changing M will not change i.)

Today, as the text points out, economists generally agree this view was too narrow. At least in the *(short run / long run)*, an increase in M can *(lower / raise)* i. It is, however, true—and this is the truth the classical view sought to express—that this extra M may and should, in due course, become "active money." As it is thus soaked up by the economy, its effect is to increase production, or prices, or both. As GNP rises, the need for active money may rise to the point where i rises again—i.e., the extra M's impact on i was short run only.

---

short run; lower.

---

5. *a.* You must decide whether asset A or asset B has the higher market value. A promises to make four income payments of $1,225 each at the end of years 1, 2, 3, and 4. B promises to make five payments of $1,000 each at the end of years 1, 2, 3, 4, and 5. The confidence with which payments can be expected is the same in both. The valuation rule to follow is to choose the asset which (pick one):
(1) Has higher total income payments, regardless of the date on which these accrue.
(2) Pays income for the longer period of time.
(3) Pays off more quickly.
(4) Yields the higher capitalized value—determined by discounting all income items by means of the market interest rate and summing all such discounted values.

b. Thus (to repeat something already said in the chapter), do not try to value assets by what they would cost, or did cost, to construct. Value them instead in terms of the future revenues they are expected to bring in. But *discount* these revenues.

The basic discounting formula is simple. Take any one item of expected future revenue, N. It is due to arrive t years from now. The market interest rate, expressed as a fraction (e.g., 5 per cent = $5/100$) is i. The discounted value (the present value) of that expected future revenue item is $N / (1 + i)^t$.

The capitalized values of assets A and B accordingly depend on the market interest rate. The higher this rate (see the discussion preceding question 5, pp. 237, the sharper the discounting knife. The farther away in time any revenue item is, the more deeply it cuts. So the higher the interest rate, the more probable that asset *(A / B)* will have the higher capitalized (discounted) value.

---

a. (4). *b.* A. A and B have equal capitalized values when the interest rate is approximately 4½ per cent annually. At any lower rate, B has the higher value; at any higher rate, A has.

---

6. In the text's brief discussion of "reswitching," it is assumed that two alternative methods of producing one unit of some finished product exist. Both require the input of some labor *now;* then you must *wait* until the finished product matures. Specifically (assuming 1 year as the "waiting period" unit):

Method A: 7 labor units now, then wait 2 years.
Method B: 5 labor units now, then wait 3 years.

Which method would be more attractive to producers? That depends on the interest rate. In this example, you can say unequivocally that A would be preferable at any rate above 40 per cent annually; at 40 per cent there would be no difference; below 40 per cent, B would be preferable.

Suppose the market interest rate is 40 per cent annually; and let the finished product be worth $10. Since it accrues in the future, you must discount this $10 to get its present value. Discounted from 2 years ahead (see the formula in question 5b) at the 40 per cent rate, $10 becomes $5.11; discounted for 3 years, $3.65.

Now suppose labor costs 73 cents per unit. It makes absolutely no difference whether you use method A (spend $5.11 on labor now and wait 2 years) or method B (spend $3.65 on labor now and wait 3 years). Either way, your payoff will be $10, and the return on your investment will be 40 per cent—just the market rate.

Now suppose the market rate is only 20 per cent annually. Given the same input and output prices as before, both method A and method B would now be highly attractive. In both instances, their net productivity would still be 40 per cent—twice the new market rate of return.

But now raise the input price to make them less profitable.

It becomes apparent—and this is the point made in the text—that *method A will cease to be profitable (cease to earn the market rate) while method B is still profitable.* At 20 per cent annually, $10 discounts down to $6.95 for 2 years, $5.79 for 3 years. Let labor's price be $1 rather than 73 cents. It *(would still / would not)* pay to spend $7 (method A) to get a return with a present value of $6.95. It *(would still / would not)* pay to spend $5 (method B) to get a return with a present value of $5.79.

In this sense, then, it is said that "rich" societies (those with low interest rates) can afford more "roundabout" production methods (those with long waiting periods); poor societies (with high interest rates) incline toward more hand-to-mouth methods.

The "switching" argument (among other things) challenges part of this view; it says you cannot necessarily rank methods by their roundaboutness, as was possible with A and B above. The dispute is a complicated one. Rather than try to grasp its detail, you should take the brief outline in the text appendix as indicative of the fact that capital theory is still highly incomplete, and that there is plenty of disagreement among economists studying this intricate subject.

would not; would still.

QUIZ: Multiple Choice

1. *If a fall in interest rates does not reduce the amount people save out of their incomes, then* (1) "liquidity preference" may still provide an interest-rate "floor," below which the rate will not fall; (2) a decrease in the net productivity of capital may still provide an interest-rate floor; (3) the consequence of unreduced saving will be that the fall will be checked, and interest rates will begin to rise; (4) only a fall in GNP—i.e., recession—can stop this interest-rate fall; (5) attempts to stimulate GNP by means of "easy money" policies have little hope of being effective.

2. *An increase in the quantity of money will not affect interest rates* (1) if the amount of saving is unresponsive to interest-rate changes; (2) if it is part of an antirecession policy; (3) if the quantity theory of money strictly applies; (4) if

investment spending is unresponsive to interest-rate changes; (5) in any circumstances.

3. *If the market rate of interest rises, other things equal, the present discounted value of any given capital asset should* (1) rise, and the more the asset's expected revenues extend far into the future, the more it will rise; (2) rise, and the more the asset's expected revenues accrue in the immediate rather than the remote future, the more it will rise; (3) fall, and the more asset's expected revenues accrue in the immediate rather than more it will fall; (4) fall, and the more the asset's expected revenues accrue in the immediate rather than the remote future, the more it will fall; (5) not be changed.

4. *Those who invest in any new capital good always face some degree of uncertainty as to the future revenues which that good will bring in. In interest-rate theory, the effect of this uncertainty factor is* (1) fully recognized in the traditional account of capital and interest; (2) to set an effective ceiling or maximum level for the market interest rate; (3) to make the task of establishing an "easy" monetary policy an easier one; (4) to make the task of establishing a "tight" monetary policy a more difficult one; (5) to set an above-zero floor or minimum level for the market interest rate.

5. *The present discounted value of $500 payable one year from now, at a market interest rate of 9 per cent annually, is* (1) $545; (2) $500; (3) a little more than $455, but less than $500; (4) $455; (5) a little less than $455.

6. *Implicit in the text's discussion of capital and interest is a rule for the proper method of deciding what the "worth" or "value" of any asset is and how this value should be determined. This rule is to* (1) value assets according to original cost of construction or purchase, deducting from this cost figure an appropriate depreciation figure to arrive at present value; (2) value assets according to the net revenue they are expected to yield in the future, capitalized value being the sum of all such expected future revenues; (3) value assets according to the net revenue they are expected to yield in the future, capitalized value being the sum of all such expected future revenues after each has been discounted to present value by means of the interest rate; (4) determine the dollar figure which represents the net productivity of the asset and then discount that net productivity figure by means of the interest rate, should such a procedure be necessary; (5) do none of the preceding.

31 PROFITS AND INCENTIVES

EVER SINCE THE DAYS of Adam Smith and the British classical economists, it has been conventional to speak of three "basic" classes of factors of production: land, labor, and capital. (The topics of the three chapters immediately preceding reflect this classification.) This tripartite division must have seemed especially appropriate in the England of classical economics, for there were then two important political groups: the landowning aristocracy, and the rising "capitalist" class of merchants and industrialists. And then, of course, there was "the working class."

This division suggests three classes of income: rent, wages, and interest. But what place is there, then, for profit? Is profit just a particular form of interest?

There is a distinction which says that interest is the return on *loaned* money, and that money put up to buy a share of ownership in a corporation is *not* loaned money: it earns profit, not interest. Although this distinction is important for legal and accounting purposes, it does not establish a *functional* distinction between interest and profit comparable to the distinction between income earned through the sweat of one's brow and that earned from owning property. Can profit be established as a *fourth* income category by isolating some difference between what money supplied by bond sales *does*, and what money put up to buy stock *does?*

1. *a.* If we attempt this, we at once find that *part* of what is customarily called "profit" vanishes, swallowed up by one of the other categories. Suppose a man runs a roadside stand situated on his own land. Typically, he will describe his net income as his "profit." But part of that profit should properly be considered as (*rent / interest*) earned by his land, and another part as (*wages / profit*) for the labor he supplies.

Similarly, it is possible to think of at least part of a corporation's earnings as interest on money which the shareholders put up.

When someone is self-employed, those parts of his income which he calls "profit" but which can be fitted into one of the other three categories may also be called (*"implicit" / "unearned" / "surplus"*) wages, interest, or (*income / rent / surplus*).

b. However, economists are usually persuaded that it is impossible to translate *all* of profit into factor earnings of the other three types, except in the very special—in fact, impossi-

ble—situation of (*monopoly / perfect competition / imperfect competition*), where everything has worked itself out to a full equilibrium level. In that situation, which in consequence is characterized by (*extremely settled and stable conditions / changing conditions / self-employment of all factors / no obligation to learn economics*), there will be implicit wages, interest, or rent, but there will be no "profit" by the interpretations of the term cited in questions 2 and 3.

---

a. rent; wages; "implicit"; rent. *b.* perfect competition; extremely settled and stable conditions.

If, in situations other than perfect competition, there is some part of profit which cannot be converted into implicit wages, implicit rent, or implicit interest, then it is necessary to answer the question: What useful function is performed or undertaken by the individual who receives a profit? Profit is the reward for *doing what?*

As to this, there are two major—and conflicting—viewpoints.

2. *a.* The first viewpoint, associated particularly with economist Frank H. Knight, regards profit as the return for dealing with an unavoidable fact, namely (*scarcity / the competition of self-employed factors / entrepreneurship / uncertainty*). Profit, or at least part of profit, is the reward society gives to those who shoulder the burden of uncertainty successfully. The only circumstances in which this profit-or-loss uncertainty would not exist would be those of perfect competition. The conditions of perfect competition are (*a goal we should strive for / unlikely to be attained / quite unattainable*).

b. A more restricted and developed version of this same view was set out by Joseph Schumpeter, who said that profit is the reward for doing new things successfully, such as introducing new goods or new production methods. Schumpeter called this process _____, and the person undertaking it, an _____.

In his book *Capitalism, Socialism and Democracy,* Schumpeter argued that the innovating process lay historically at the very heart of capitalism, and that it was the real justification for a "profits system." He felt that most of the gains in real income that have accrued under capitalism have come, not from more careful allocation of a given stock of resources, but from the creation of *new* goods and *new* productive techniques.

Innovation, in the Schumpeterian view, is a risky and uncertain business, and the majority of would-be innovators *(fail / succeed)*.

In this Schumpeterian view, situations of "monopoly" and of "innovation" are *(inextricably mixed / completely separate)*. A firm may be in a monopolistic position; and yet that monopoly position may have resulted from successful innovation. Schumpeter thought we should be cautious in our monopoly-opposing public policies; he was afraid that too-harsh policies might destroy the very incentive to innovate on which truly significant gains in real income depend. Schumpeter thought that most monopoly situations acquired through innovation are in due course toppled by other successful innovations originating elsewhere—producing what he called "the process of creative destruction."

---

a. uncertainty; quite unattainable. *b.* innovation; entrepreneur (or innovator); fail; inextricably mixed.

---

3. *a.* By the second major view, profit is considered unnecessary and undesirable; it is a _____ return resulting from a "_____ scarcity."

b. The point is that when a good is offered for sale by a monopoly firm, price will be *(higher / lower)* and output will be *(higher than / lower than / the same as)* it would be under conditions of *(pure or perfect competition / oligopoly)*.

---

a. monopoly; contrived. *b.* higher; lower; pure or perfect competition.

---

4. The monopoly view of profits is complicated by the fact that a genuine "monopoly return" may at the same time be a legitimate rent or interest return. Suppose that the original monopolist has an asset which for some reason is protected against competitive inroads and so is earning a large monopoly return. He sells this asset at its full capitalized value (i.e., value as established by its total discounted future earnings, calculated by the method indicated in Chapter 30). The purchaser must charge *(the same price as / a higher price than / a lower price than)* the original monopolist did in order to receive *(the normal competitive return / a monopoly return)* on the money he has invested.

---

the same price as; the normal competitive return.

---

5. The Marxian theory of surplus value uses altogether different terminology from the monopoly-return view; but these two views share a hostility to profit in the belief that it is *wrong*.

In the Marxian view, there is only one input which should be rewarded for its effort, that input being *(land / labor / capital)*. It is labor which readies Nature's basic endowment of land for cultivation; it is labor which makes capital in the form of tools and machines; hence it is labor which should receive the reward in the form of the finished product.

By this Marxian view, then, if 10 men work with land and machines to produce a product, then (pick one):
(1) All that product would go to those 10 men; or they would be paid an amount equal to its total product.
(2) Part of that product would go to the 10 men; part would go to repay the labor effort which preparing the land and building the machines entailed.

Machines can be used (in cooperation with labor) to build machines; the resulting machines may be used to produce still other machines—and so on. Thus the meaning in actual application of Marxian labor theory becomes sometimes difficult to follow. But it is a device to express the idea that labor is exploited, that it creates *(more / less)* value than the value it is paid.

---

labor; (2); more.

---

6. *a.* If my earnings come from the sale of a vastly improved product, something which my competitors have not yet succeeded in imitating, they will count as profit in the view of:
(1) Joseph Schumpeter, but no other.
(2) Both Schumpeter and Frank Knight.
(3) Schumpeter, Knight, and the "monopoly-profit" view.
(4) Nobody.

b. One of the following would *not* be counted as profit no matter which of the definitions discussed in this chapter is used, namely, money received from:
(1) Successfully producing and selling a revolutionary new can opener.
(2) Selling water at a high price, from the only well in the district which has not dried up.
(3) Selling a security on the stock market at a higher price than was paid for it.
(4) Selling wheat at a higher price than was paid for it, the result of accurately foreseeing a crop failure and shortage.

c. Monopoly profit comes whenever:
(1) Quantity offered for sale can successfully be limited in order to raise price.
(2) The demand curve facing the seller is horizontal.
(3) The commodity sold is limited in total available supply.
(4) Sales can be increased through advertising.

---

a. (3). *b.* (3). (This "profit" is not the return from producing and selling any commodity or service.) *c.* (1).

7. Answer as true (T) or false (F), according to the information furnished in the text chapter:

a. In Joseph Schumpeter's theory, the "innovator" is not the man who invents something new, but the man who undertakes to put that something new on the market. ..... *(T / F)*

b. It is possible for a given profit to be both the return from a monopoly position and the return from having successfully dealt with uncertainty. .... *(T / F)*

c. The distinction between a "natural scarcity" and a "contrived scarcity" is often difficult to make. .... *(T / F)*

d. Any talented singer whose services command a high price enjoys a monopoly position, according to the accepted definition of the term. .... *(T / F)*

e. Even in perfect competition, with all-around equilibrium reached, profit in the sense of something other than implicit wages, rent, or interest would still persist. .... *(T / F)*

f. In the national-income statistics, the total of corporation profits after taxes is at present about 35 per cent of total corporation wage payments. .... *(T / F)*

g. According to Frank Knight's interpretation of profit, the total of profits earned in some particular year might turn out to be a negative figure. .... *(T / F)*

h. A clear distinction should be made between hostility toward extreme inequality in the distribution of income and hostility toward profit in general. .... *(T / F)*

---

a. T. *b.* T. *c.* T. *d.* F. *e.* F. *f.* F. *g.* T. *h.* T.

QUIZ: Multiple Choice

1. *In the view of Frank H. Knight, "profit" should be regarded as* (1) the return received by an entrepreneur who faces a downward-sloping demand curve for the product in question, and who seeks maximum profit in pricing that product; (2) essentially a random distribution of profit among business firms—i.e., a distribution settled by chance, over which no firm has any control; (3) the return received by someone for activity in which some element of uncertainty is involved, so that loss cannot be ruled out as a possible outcome of this activity; (4) only the return received by someone who engages in a particular form of uncertainty-involving activity, namely "innovation"; (5) none of the preceding descriptions.

2. *If the economist named in question 1 had been Joseph Schumpeter, which of the alternatives listed would have been correct?* (1). (2). (3). (4). (5).

3. *If profit is regarded as the return earned by successful innovators, it would be correct to say that in equilibrium under perfect competition, there would be no profit (other than the implicit returns to labor or property) because* (1) all profit, properly seen, is always an implicit return to labor or property; (2) all demand curves, those of industry as well as those of individual firms, would be infinitely elastic; (3) earnings on invested capital would be too low to encourage innovation; (4) in such a situation, losses would have to balance gains exactly; (5) if innovations were occurring, the situation would no longer be one of equilibrium in perfect competition.

4. *If profit is regarded as a monopoly return, it would be correct to say that in equilibrium under perfect competition, there would be no profit (other than the implicit returns to labor or property) because* (1) all profit, properly seen, is always an implicit return to labor or property; (2) if profit existed, it would immediately be competed away by entry into the industry involved; (3) owners of labor and property would hire their services out to other employers in preference to being in business for themselves; (4) such an equilibrium would involve the removal of all scarcities; (5) the rate of interest would have dropped to zero.

5. *If our concern is for the best-possible employment of a given stock of productive resources, we would want to see "profit" eliminated* (1) as Knight defines profit, as Schumpeter defines it, and as it is defined in both contrived-scarcity and implicit-return views; (2) as Knight and Schumpeter define it, but not as it is defined in the contrived-scarcity and implicit-return views; (3) not as Knight and Schumpeter define it, but as it is defined in both the contrived scarcity and implicit-return views; (4) only as it is defined in the contrived-scarcity view, not in any of the others mentioned above; (5) only as Knight defines it, not in any of the other views mentioned.

6. *In the view of Joseph Schumpeter, an "entrepreneur" is* (1) any individual engaging in activity in which any risk, uncertainty, or speculation is involved; (2) the individual (or group of individuals) furnishing the risk-taking money capital by which any enterprise is financed; (3) one who invents a new product or process; (4) that individual (or group of individuals) responsible for making the major operating decisions within any business; (5) none of the above.

7. *Four of the five statements below repeat statements in the text chapter concerning monopoly influence and "contrived scarcity." The fifth statement is false by reference to the text. Which one?* (1) If there are no production costs, the rule for exploitation of a contrived scarcity is to try to sell at a level of output where marginal revenue is zero. (2) The payment of rent to landowners whose land is available in perfectly price-inelastic supply is evidence of a contrived scarcity. (3) Contrived scarcities cannot be fully equated with high profit, for the monopolistic return obtained in such conditions of scarcity may be no higher than the return that would obtain under perfect competition. (4) If property earning a monopoly-profit return is sold, the income received by the buyer may become rent or interest, and so may cease to be identifiable as a monopoly-profit return. (5) Contrived scarcity is always associated with a demand for the product or service involved which is less than perfectly price-elastic.

8. *One of the following would not be a good example of profit earned according to the "uncertainty" definition of profit, namely, income earned by* (1) a firm which gambles successfully on the introduction of a new product; (2) a speculator in wheat; (3) a firm now operating at a profit after a long investment of time and money in developing new cost-saving machinery for its production line; (4) an insurance company which protects its policyholders against the risk of property damage by fire; (5) a farmer who successfully grows a crop on land hitherto considered impossible or unsatisfactory for that crop.

9. *Four of the five statements below more or less repeat the text's statements describing the conditions of equilibrium in static perfect competition. Which one statement is not made in the text, and is false with regard to that equilibrium?* (1) Profit, in the sense of something other than implicit wages, rent, or interest, would no longer exist. (2) Price would be equal to marginal cost for each good produced. (3) There would be no uncertainty concerning the level of future prices. (4) Inequalities of income resulting from ownership of property would be competed away and vanish. (5) A new competitor would find it easy to enter any industry if he chose to do so.

10. *A "contrived scarcity" is to be expected whenever* (1) the seller of a product faces a horizontal demand curve; (2) the seller of a product faces a downward-sloping demand curve; (3) the entrepreneur undertaking the activity in question faces more than a usual degree of risk or uncertainty; (4) profit can be considered an "implicit" factor return; (5) heavy taxes are imposed in such a way as to discourage the undertaking of risky projects.

11. *Joseph Schumpeter felt that the status of profits in a capitalist economy ought to be evaluated primarily as follows: They* (1) arise mainly out of monopolistic distortion of prices, and should be eliminated insofar as elimination is possible without undue disruption of the economy; (2) are largely illusory, since the reported figures are in the main disguised wages, interest, or rents; (3) have a positive contribution to make, since continuing profit opportunities are the true driving force behind further expansion of real output; (4) would continue to exist even under conditions of static perfect competition; (5) are essentially what is elsewhere described as "economic rent."

12. *With respect to the profits referred to in question 11, Schumpeter's further view was that* (1) in a full reckoning, they will be exactly balanced by the losses of other participants in the economy; (2) in most instances, they can and should be eliminated by taxation; (3) they have equal status in a socialist economy; (4) usually, they will in due course be competed away as further innovations appear in the economy; (5) the distortions in income which they produce may ultimately destroy the capitalist system.

13. *Four of the following five statements more or less repeat statements made in the text chapter concerning Frank Knight's theory of profits. One statement runs counter to Knight's views. Which one?* (1) Successful innovation cannot be regarded as a valid instance of profit arising out of the acceptance of uncertainty. (2) The operation of an insurance company cannot be regarded as a valid instance of the acceptance of risk. (3) If profit is considered the reward for assuming risk, the net total of profit in any given year might be a negative figure. (4) Profit is a necessary component in national income if people by and large dislike risk and are prepared to pay in order to avoid risk. (5) Profit, or a large part of it, is society's reward to those who shoulder the burden of uncertainty.

14. *Karl Marx's view of profit (expressed in outlining the properties of his ideal society) was essentially as follows: It is by nature "surplus value" and should be eliminated,* (1) whether called profit, rent, or interest; (2) whether called profit or interest, although rent payments have a valid role; (3) whether called profit or rent, although interest payments have a valid role; (4) but distinguished from rent and interest payments, both of which have a valid role; (5) except where it is a payment for the assumption of risk, in which case it has a valid role.

1. *a.* "Microeconomics" (see text), in its purest form, is (for example) analysis focusing upon the individual consumer seeking to maximize satisfaction, given a pattern of tastes, a limited income, and a set of consumer-goods prices. Study of the single business firm seeking to maximize profit is also microeconomics.

Analysis of the price of a single commodity is likewise termed microeconomics. But in this instance we make the first step toward "macro" analysis, since we lump together all individual buyers on the demand side and all individual sellers on the supply side.

Macroeconomic analysis deals explicitly with *aggregates*—e.g., net national product, total consumer spending. The income-determination theory in Chapters 12 and 13 is *(microeconomic / macroeconomic)* analysis.

b. There is a gap between "micro" and "macro." You cannot take ordinary "micro" analysis and use each bit of it as a building block toward a "macro" whole. Suppose there are only three goods in the economy—X, Y, Z. You *cannot* first develop supply-and-demand analysis for X, then turn to Y, and then to Z—finally lumping them into an "aggregative" or "macro" supply-and-demand whole.

The reason for this difficulty is that "micro" analysis uses an "other things equal" approach. The demand curve for X is drawn on the assumption that *all factors other than the price of X* which might affect the demand for X (the level of buyer incomes, the level of the price of Y, and so on) are held given and fixed. To some extent, we can handle changes in these "other variables." If Y's price changes, or if the level of buyer incomes changes, we say that the demand curve for X must be shifted to a new position in order to reflect this change.

For some problems, this method is useful and appropriate. For others, it breaks down. Suppose, for example, that we deal with just two commodities, butter and margarine. Initially, prices of both are in equilibrium. Now a technical development sharply reduces the cost of margarine production. In supply-and-demand terms, we say the margarine supply curve shifts downward (or to the right), establishing a new and *(higher / lower)* "equilibrium" price.

But the butter demand curve is drawn on the basis of the *former* margarine price. The two goods being substitutes, the fall in margarine's price causes the butter demand curve to shift *(leftward / rightward)*—producing a new "equilibrium" butter price.

The margarine demand curve, unaffected up to this point,

is drawn on the basis of the original butter price. So *it* shifts, producing a new margarine price—which throws the disturbance back to the butter market.

Ultimately the two prices will settle down at mutually compatible levels once again. But the point is that the levels of butter and margarine prices are *(mutually interdependent / independent)*.

Using the ordinary supply-and-demand diagram to illustrate a price change means deliberately ignoring the impact which that change will have on other prices—and the possible "feedback" effect which *those* price changes may have on the price first altered.

Until (and unless) prices establish a "general-equilibrium" relationship with one another, some prices will continually change and so will provoke changes in other prices. This idea of the mutual interdependence of prices is not too difficult to grasp intuitively (it was mentioned as early as Chapter 3; see review questions 3 and 4, pp. 23–24. But there is no simple device for illustrating it comparable to the ordinary supply-and-demand diagram.

Notice that the GNP equilibrium cases of Chapters 12 and 13 are simple "general-equilibrium" models. They do not deal with prices, but they do deal with *mutually compatible* levels of GNP, consumption spending, and investment spending.

---

a. macroeconomic. *b.* lower; leftward; mutually interdependent.

---

2. *a.* The text has emphasized the special case of "perfect competition" because (more than one may be correct):

(1) It has special significance with respect to the "best" use of a given but limited stock of resources or inputs.
(2) With a few monopoly exceptions, the structure of the real-life American economy corresponds reasonably well to the requirements of perfect competition.
(3) Although structurally the American economy does not satisfy the requirements of perfect competition, it is still highly "competitive" in many other senses. This prompts some economists to think that analysis built as though perfect competition applied can still give useful results (in some cases) when applied to the American economy.

b. Perfect competition has special significance from a "welfare" standpoint. If we take as given the stock of resources, the

conditions of their ownership, and the state of technology, then the set of prices which would emerge under perfect competition would yield (pick one):
(1) The most efficient allocation of all such resources among their various possible allocations.
(2) The most desirable distribution of income among the people who make up the population in question.

c. The table below is intended to illustrate the meaning of "efficient resource allocation." It assumes that the economy produces only three goods, X, Y, and Z. A general equilibrium has been reached; as part of this, XYZ quantities produced are as in line 1 and XYZ prices as in line 3.

	X	Y	Z
1. Total quantities of goods produced and bought	3,000	4,000	5,000
2. Marginal utilities of goods for a typical consumer	100	50	200
3. Price of good	$2	$1	$4
4. Marginal cost of good	$2	$1	$4

Given the XYZ prices of line 3, the "typical consumer" *(has / has not / may or may not have)* reached his maximum-satisfaction position.

If supplying firms operate under conditions of perfect competition, then, with prices as in line 3 and marginal costs as in line 4, they *(have / have not)* reached maximum-profit positions.

(Note the general-equilibrium quality of this. Consumers reach maximum-satisfaction positions by juggling their XYZ purchases. Producers adjust the level of their marginal cost by varying the quantity of X, Y, or Z that they produce and sell. The quantities in line 1 and the prices in line 3 must be such as to satisfy *both* consumers and producers. The situation must be one in which neither consumers nor producers can see any advantage in any change of position.)

The significant property of this situation is indicated by comparing line 2 with line 4. Here, prices are an accurate indication of marginal costs. And marginal cost is a money indicator of the *real* cost of getting another unit of X, Y, or Z.

d. Now suppose all figures—save one—in the table above are unchanged. But the case is now a different one. Good X in this new case is produced under conditions of imperfect competition. This means that each producer of X will equate marginal cost with the *(price of X / marginal revenue from X)*. In imperfect competition, marginal revenue is *(the same as / greater than / less than)* price. The price of X is still $2; but its marginal revenue to producers is, say, $1.20. The *MC* figure for X in line 4 above must then be $1.20. All other figures are unchanged, and general equilibrium prevails.

Note that the producers of X, by equating *MR* and *MC*, produce and sell a quantity of X which is *(the same as / less than / more than)* the quantity they would have produced by equating *MC* with price.

In this new case, consumers are still at equilibrium. But the prices they must pay are no longer a true indicator of real underlying marginal cost—since X's *MC* is $1.20, not $2.

Here there is a contrived scarcity of X which buyers must accept as though it were a real scarcity—i.e., as though it would really cost $2 in real resources to produce one more unit of X. It is evident that if the price of X were to fall to $1.20, a new general equilibrium would have to be worked out, with new XYZ prices and quantities. And it can be shown—although it is not easy to show—that the new XYZ quantities would represent a slight gain in the community's real income.

---

a. (1); (3). *b.* (1). *c.* has; have. *d.* marginal revenue from X; less than; less than.

---

3. "Welfare economics" (see text) has nothing necessarily to do with improving the status of the poor. It means only that branch of economics in which the words "better" and "worse" are used—i.e., in which it is said that some situation A is more desirable than some alternative situation B.

The statement that A is preferable to B demands some value scale. Since individual preference scales differ, this makes welfare economics a difficult and dangerous area. However, the following statement seems fairly safe: Situation A is preferable to B if, in the course of a change from B to A, some people would be made better off while nobody would be made worse off.

Unfortunately, there are probably not too many of these convenient nobody-worse-off changes. The next step in welfare economics is to a situation in which there are losers as well as gainers—but the predicted gain of the gainers exceeds the predicted loss of the losers. So the gainers could "bribe" the losers to make the change. Or the gainers could be taxed by a sufficient amount to compensate the losers and still have some part of their gains left.

It is in this sense that the equilibrium of perfect competition is declared to be "efficient." When this equilibrium is reached, it is impossible to find any alternative attainable combination of goods and services in which those who gain by the change could *(fully / less than fully)* compensate the losers and still be better off.

Note particularly that *this is ultimately a matter of the "efficient" allocation of a given and limited resource stock*—limited in the particular sense that it cannot yield enough output to satisfy everybody's demands for everything he or she would like to have. Perfect competition (so it is argued) allocates this resource stock into employment in the best-possible way—allocates it, that is, so that the combination of goods and services produced meets the requirement set out in the preceding paragraph.

This "efficiency" definition is acceptable only insofar as the assumptions underlying perfect-competition theory are acceptable. The theory assumes that there *(are / are no)* significant economies of large-scale operations. There *(are / are no)* "external diseconomies." (There is an external diseconomy if a plant pollutes the air or water and is not required to bear the cost which this pollution imposes.) The distribution of income, equal or unequal, is *(declared to be the most appropriate / accepted without comment on its desirability)*. The stock of resources is assumed to be *(fixed / increasing)*. The state of technology is assumed to be *(given / improving)*. (Schumpeter, for example, insisted that assumptions such as the last two miss the whole point of the "efficiency" of competitive capitalism—see review question 2, pp. 245–246.

---

fully; are no; are no; accepted without comment; fixed; given.

QUIZ: Multiple Choice

1. *In general equilibrium and in a situation of perfect competition,* (1) for each consumer, the marginal utility of each good consumed is equal to the price of that good; (2) for each consumer, marginal utilities of all goods consumed are proportional to the marginal costs of those goods; (3) the marginal-physical-product of each input is equal to the price of that input; (4) the marginal-revenue-product of each input is equal to the price of the finished good it produces; (5) none of these statements is necessarily correct.

2. *The profit-maximizing motive in perfect competition differs from the profit-maximizing motive in imperfect competition in this respect:* (1) The perfect competitor tries to equate price and average cost, which does not lead to maximum profit. (2) The perfect competitor tries to equate price and marginal cost, which does not lead to maximum profit. (3) The perfect competitor tries to equate marginal revenue and marginal cost, which does not lead to maximum profit. (4) The imperfect competitor tries to equate price and marginal cost, which leads to a larger profit than the equating of marginal revenue and marginal cost. (5) In none of these ways, the firms in both situations being equally interested in earning as much profit as possible.

3. *The theory of perfect competition, according to the text chapter,* (1) gives a reasonably accurate description of real performance, even though it cannot be used to evaluate the efficiency of that performance; (2) describes real performance in rough outline despite competitive imperfections, and is most important for appraising the efficiency of that performance; (3) is most important for appraising the efficiency of real performance, even though it is not even approximately correct in describing that performance; (4) bears almost no resemblance to real performance, and cannot be used to evaluate its efficiency, but is most important because its material is a lead into the theory of imperfect competition; (5) with relatively minor monopoly exceptions, gives a closely accurate outline of real performance, and can be used to identify the monopoly exceptions.

4. *Four of the following five alternatives state conditions which* must *be satisfied if the equilibrium conditions of all-around perfect competition are to be satisfied. One alternative states a condition* not *so required—i.e., one which perfect competition would* not *necessarily produce. Which one?* (1) Price is equal to average cost. (2) For each individual, and for each good he or she consumes, the ratio between marginal utility and price is the same for all such goods. (3) Price is equal to marginal cost. (4) There is no significant inequality in the distribution of income among individuals. (4) Price is equal to minimum average cost.

5. *Four of the following five alternatives state conditions which indicate that the conditions of all-around perfect competition are* not *satisfied. One alternative states a condition which* must *be satisfied, to meet the requirements of perfect competition. Which one?* (1) Market prices are steady in the sense of being unresponsive to short-run changes in demand or in supply. (2) Price is equal to average cost but not to marginal cost. (3) Different wage rates are paid in different geographic locations for work whose requirements are exactly the same in both locations. (4) Product differentiation yields a price that equals average cost, but not minimum-attainable average cost. (5) Marginal cost is equal to average cost.

6. *The theory of perfect competition began by recognizing two facts, namely, that resources are scarce and that the price system is a mechanism for allocating the use or employment of those resources. From here, the theory gradually developed a set of rules which, if satisfied (it was believed), would indicate that the scarce resources were being utilized "optimally"—i.e., to the best-possible advantage, in terms of the output they produced. These rules were stated with special regard for one kind of influence that might drive results away from the perfectly competitive equilibrium. That disrupting influence was* (1) laissez faire pricing activity; (2) activity over time; (3) interdependence among the inputs employed; (4) the presence of monopoly or of monopoly elements; (5) space, or geographic, differences.

7. *Perfect competition theory's equilibrium requirements, as indicated in question 6, set out rules for the "optimum" allocation of scarce resources. Yet the result, even with these rules fully satisfied, may not be "optimal," insofar as it is true that* (1) price is equal to marginal cost; (2) external economies or diseconomies are present; (3) monopoly or monopoly elements are present; (4) price is equal to average cost; (5) it is possible to substitute one input or resource in place of another.

8. *A criticism of the supposedly "optimal" results produced in the equilibrium of perfect competition (and a criticism mentioned in the text) is that this theory* (1) assumes each individual's demands in the marketplace reflect that individual's true well-being; (2) assumes the complete absence of governmental activity or presence; (3) emphasizes almost to excess the importance of distributing income in an "ethically optimal" manner; (4) assumes that people's money incomes are limited to a degree which is not actually the case; (5) takes no account of investment (i.e., production for the future), putting its entire emphasis upon present consumption.

9. *On behalf of the equilibrium of perfect competition, it is said that it includes this "welfare" property, namely, that it produces a situation in which* (1) the marginal utilities derived from all commodities are equal; (2) every individual involved is better off than he or she would be in any other situation; (3) the total utilities derived from all commodities are equal; (4) no one individual could be made better off without, in the process, making somebody else worse off; (5) no outside "efficiency property" can or need be applied in order to declare the results as good or as bad.

APPENDIX: Review of Commodity and Factor Pricing: General Equilibrium and the Parable of Ideal Welfare Pricing

1. Chapter 2 said that any economy's stock of resources is always "scarce" in the sense that there are not sufficient inputs to meet everybody's wants fully. Even with inputs fully employed to the best advantage, there are always some unsatisfied wishes. And Chapter 3 said that the pricing system is important in making the best of this problem of scarcity.

After a lengthy survey of price and price making in Parts 3 and 4, we can now look more carefully at the tasks which a properly functioning price system is expected to perform.

This matter is illustrated conveniently by considering an authoritarian, centrally directed society, since the people in control of such a society must consciously think about the role prices are to perform.

In that situation, there might be a completely arbitrary decision as to how inputs are to be used to produce particular goods in particular quantities, and a comparable decision as to how they are to be distributed. But it may alternatively be decided, in order to avoid resentment and unrest against such arbitrary decisions, to give the population some opportunity to exercise *choice*. This entails a resort to money—whether the word "money" is used, or some other name. Money is a device whereby people *vote* for the goods they want to be produced and supplied to them.

Suppose we deal only with goods X, Y, and Z. The state has produced some quantities of X, Y, and Z, and has given the people money to buy them. It has made a guess as to proper XYZ prices and will use these "guess prices." Clearly, the money supply *(M)* distributed must bear some relation to these prices. If *all* the M distributed is to be used in buying the available XYZ quantities, then the following relation must hold:

———————————————————————————— .

If this relation is not satisfied, then either the state winds up with unsold goods or else the people wind up holding M which (at least for the time being) can buy *(goods / nothing)*.

$X \times p_x + Y \times p_y + Z \times p_z = M$; nothing.

2. *a.* The next problem the state will face is that—unless the planners were very farseeing indeed in their guesses— the relation between the three prices will need adjustment. People will decide that, at the prices asked, say, X and Y are the most desirable goods. So they buy X first, then Y, and turn to Z only when the shelves are empty of X and Y. All Z will ultimately be sold—if there is no other way to spend the money. But the fact that X and Y vanish so quickly should be a signal to the state to (pick one):
(1) Raise X and Y prices; leaving Z price unchanged.
(2) Increase the supply of money.
(3) Raise X and Y prices; lower Z price.
(4) Lower X and Y prices; raise Z price.

b. Suppose the state continues, period after period, to produce the same XYZ quantities. But it experiments with prices until all three goods seem to disappear into consumer hands at about the same rate. This is at least a rough indication that for consumers the marginal utilities of X, Y, and Z are *(equal / proportional to XYZ prices)*.

a. (3). *b.* proportional to XYZ prices (see Chapter 22).

3. *a.* The state has now developed a set of XYZ prices which are most appropriate to consumer tastes for X, Y, and Z—given the *fixed* XYZ quantities produced each period. But the state should now examine those quantities; specifically, it should compare XYZ prices with XYZ marginal costs. Suppose the prices of X and Y are $2 and $1 respectively. Their *MC*s are just reversed; they are $1 and $2. This means that the state is *(overcharging / undercharging)* the public in its price for X. To produce one more unit of X would involve an additional cost of only $1; yet the public pays $2 for each unit.

By the same reasoning, the public was (*overcharged* / *under-charged*) for the last unit of Y sold.

b. The point of this is that the XY prices are not true indicators to the public of XY costs of production. Money marginal cost is the surface indicator of real input cost. Here, the quantity of X produced should be (*increased* / *decreased*) and the quantity of Y (*increased* / *decreased*) by a transfer of resource employment. This will (*raise* / *lower*) X's *MC* and (*raise* / *lower*) that of Y. As a result of these changes in quantities offered for sale, X's price will (*fall* / *rise*) and Y's will (*fall* / *rise*). This in turn will move price and *MC* (*closer together* / *farther apart*).

---

a. overcharging; undercharged. *b.* increased; decreased; raise; lower; fall; rise; closer together. (Notice especially that *marginal* cost, not average cost, is the true cost criterion which prices ought to reflect.)

---

4. A farmer owns two equal-sized plots of land, A and B. His sons have a total of 800 man-hours in the crop season to work them. Results of five different allocations of this manpower are shown below. (In each instance, the man-hour total over A and B combined is 800.) "Marginal-product" means the extra yield from the very last man-hour worked.

Situation	Plot A				Plot B			
	Man-hours	Total Bushels	Marginal-product	Product per Man-hour	Man-hours	Total Bushels	Marginal-product	Product per Man-hour
1.	400	3,900	8.5	9.8	400	2,300	2.0	5.8
2.	500	4,700	7.5	9.4	300	2,000	4.0	6.7
3.	600	5,400	6.0	9.0	200	1,500	6.0	7.5
4.	700	5,900	4.0	8.4	100	840	7.5	8.4
5.	800	6,100	1.0	7.6	0	0	—	—

a. In situation 1, manpower is equally divided between A and B. The resulting crop is (*2,300* / *3,900*) bushels from A and (*2,300* / *3,900*) from B. Since the plots are of equal size, (*A* / *B*) is consequently the more fertile of the two.

The object is to get the maximum total crop from A and B. This occurs in situation (*1* / *2* / *3* / *4* / *5*), where the total of bushels from A and B combined is (*3,900* / *6,000* / *6,900* / *10,000*).

b. Suppose, however, that the sons are actually in situation 4: 700 man-hours on A, 100 on B. They have not bothered to look at the increase in crop that would come from switching to situation 3. They simply justify 4 by pointing out that the "payoff per man-hour worked" (product per man-hour) is exactly the same on both plots, namely (*6.0* / *7.5* / *8.4* / *9.2*).

If the objective is a maximum quantity of bushels, this rule

of thumb of equal product per man-hour is (*correct* / *incorrect*). The proper maximum-product rule is to distribute the labor so as to equate (*marginal* / *average*) products on the two plots. In this instance, correct manpower allocation would yield a marginal-product of (*4.0* / *6.0* / *7.5* / *8.0*) on each plot.

c. Suppose the labor is correctly distributed (situation 3). But the sons assigned to plot B feel humiliated because their product per man-hour is lower than that of the sons working plot A. They complain that they could raise their productivity if only Papa would let them join their brothers on A. The father could equate the returns to labor on the two plots by imposing a "rent" of (*1* / *1½* / *3* / *5* / *6*) bushels for each man-hour spent on more fertile plot A. This would underscore the fact that the higher man-hour return on A is attributable to A's greater fertility, not to better-quality labor. This illustrates the (*phenomenon of general equilibrium* / *necessity of setting a price, if only an "accounting price," on any scarce resource*).

---

a. 3,900; 2,300; A; 3; 6,900. *b.* 8.4; incorrect; marginal 6.0. *c.* 1½; necessity of setting a price.

QUIZ: Multiple Choice

1. *Which of the following would* not *be determined by the forces of supply and demand under an "ideal" socialist system?* (1) The accounting prices of intermediate goods. (2) The amount of the social dividend each individual receives. (3) The price of labor (wage rates). (4) The prices of consumer goods. (5) None of these.

2. *A socialist state wants to use its scarce resources to the best advantage. It uses a pricing system for distribution and sale of consumer goods. The state should instruct the manager of each consumer-good plant to try to set price at a level equal to* (1) marginal cost of production (*MC*), provided *MC* is rising; (2) *MC*, provided *MC* is falling; (3) *MC*, whether *MC* rises or falls; (4) average cost of production (*AC*), provided *AC* is rising; (5) *AC*, whether *AC* is rising or not.

3. *In terms of "efficient resource allocation," if grain is to be grown on two adjacent plots of land, A and B, A being naturally more fertile or productive than B (and both owned by the same landlord), then, quite apart from the landlord's desire to get maximum rent for his land,* (1) the same (non-zero) rent should be charged for both plots; (2) no rent should be charged for either plot; (3) a higher rent should be charged for B than for A; (4) a higher rent should be charged for A than for B; (5) plot A should be used intensively, plot B not at all.

4. *The use (if any) of an interest rate in a fully socialist state would be* (1) to regulate or at least influence the amount of money saved by its people; (2) to regulate the total amount of investment undertaken; (3) to regulate the amount of the social dividend available for distribution; (4) to establish or at least influence the priority order in which investment projects were undertaken; (5) not applicable at all.

5

INTERNATIONAL TRADE AND FINANCE

1. *a.* In essence, foreign transactions are the same as domestic transactions. Typically, one party gives money in exchange for a commodity, service, or security supplied by the other party.

The major difference is that in the foreign transaction, *two* monies are involved, directly or indirectly. If an American firm sells machinery in France, the French buying firm will want to pay in francs, since that is the currency in which it ordinarily deals. But the currency needed by the American firm in order to buy raw materials and to pay wages and dividends is the *(dollar / franc).*

b. Suppose the American firm is paid in francs. Suppose also that a French firm has sold wine in the United States, for dollars. The French firm has accumulated dollars which it would like to exchange for francs. And so the two sellers can swap the currency they have for the currency they want. The American firm is *(a supplier of dollars and a demander of francs / a supplier of francs and a demander of dollars).* The French firm is *(a supplier of dollars and a demander of francs / a supplier of francs and a demander of dollars).*

c. This dollar-franc exchange is a _____

_____ transaction. The rate at which the

currencies exchange is the _____ rate.

In practice, of course, the French seller of wine and the American seller of machinery almost certainly will not make a direct exchange. If the American firm is paid in francs, it will most probably sell them to its American bank for dollars, and the bank, rather than the exporting firm, will be the supplier of francs on the foreign exchange market.

d. Suppose the French wine exporter insisted on payment directly in francs. How (if at all) would this change the currency swap indicated above? (Pick one.)
(1) No exchange transaction would be needed.
(2) It would make no difference, except that the party appearing on the exchange market would be the American importer (or his bank); there would still be a demand for francs and an offer of dollars in exchange.
(3) The transaction would be reversed—the American wine importer would appear on the exchange market wanting to buy dollars and sell francs.

a. dollar. *b.* supplier of francs; supplier of dollars. *c.* foreign exchange; foreign exchange. *d.* (2).

2. *a.* The earliest exchanges in man's history were barters—goods exchanging for goods. These were succeeded by what we ordinarily call "money transactions"—those everyday swaps in which goods exchange for money. But now we are discussing transactions in which one money exchanges for another money—so in a sense, we are back to barter again. If we refer to the exchange market between dollars and pounds, we can speak equally of the price of the pound sterling in *(dollars / pounds sterling),* and of the price of the dollar in *(dollars / pounds sterling).*

b. Suppose, for example, that the rate of exchange between U.S. dollars and British pounds sterling is £1 = $2. This means that (pick one or both):
(1) The price of the pound sterling is $2.
(2) The price of the dollar is £0.50, or one-half a pound sterling.

c. As a further consequence of the money-for-money property of foreign exchange transactions, note that the participants can be identified as "demanders" or as "suppliers" only by identifying one of the two monies as the good that is bought and sold. If you want to buy pounds sterling, you think of yourself as a demander of pounds. But it would be equally correct to describe you as a *(supplier of pounds / demander of dollars / supplier of dollars).*

a. dollars; pounds sterling. *b.* (1) and (2). *c.* supplier of dollars.

3. Left to its own devices, a foreign exchange rate will move up and down under the pressure of supply-and-demand forces. It is a price, subject to the same influences as any other price. However, governments rarely leave the foreign prices of their own currencies entirely free to "float." To a greater or lesser degree, they try to *control* foreign exchange rates. Any nation heavily engaged in exporting and importing finds the price which its currency can command on the foreign exchange markets to be a matter of the highest importance.

Until very recently, governments have usually tried to keep the prices of their own currencies in foreign monies fixed, or very nearly so. That fixed rate has been altered only under the strongest pressure for change.

The great advantage of a fixed exchange rate is that you then know exactly what a foreign purchase will cost you and what a foreign sale will bring you, in domestic money. And the demands for a fixed rate (commonly heard among bankers and business firms especially) are bolstered by the fact that in the past, nations have often relied on a particular technique for maintaining fixed rates: the gold standard.

You go on the gold standard by declaring that gold is the basis or standard for your currency unit—and you say how much gold. Thus the United States may say that the gold "content" of its dollar is 1/100 of an ounce. And it backs up this statement by a declared willingness to buy or to sell gold freely at $100 per ounce.

a. Suppose further that the United Kingdom, also on the gold standard, will buy or sell gold at £50 per ounce. This implies a pound-dollar exchange rate of (*£1 = $7 / £1 = $5 / £1 = $3 / £1 = $2*).

This £1 = $2 algebraic equality means nothing to exporters or importers unless it affects the rate at which they can buy or sell a currency. But the gold standard does just that, since a further requirement of this standard is that the country must not restrict the export or import of gold.

In such circumstances, if you owe a British firm 100 pounds sterling for goods imported, it will never cost you much more than $200 to pay your bill. If necessary, you can get your £100 via gold. You *(buy / sell)* gold for $200. You send that gold to Britain, and sell it to the British government, receiving *(pounds / dollars)* in exchange. (In practice, of course, banks and other such agencies would handle the gold part of the transaction in bulk, but the effect is the same as if you did it yourself.)

b. If pounds happen to be selling at $2 on the foreign exchange market, payment via gold is unnecessary. The gold route will cost you a little more than $200, because of the cost of shipping gold. Nevertheless, this payment route *will* be used if supply-and-demand forces drive the price of the pound sterling sufficiently *(above / below)* $2.

There is a critical exchange rate, in practice only slightly above the "par value" of $2—say, $2.02—above which demanders of pounds will not go. If the rate climbs to that $2.02 point, they leave the foreign exchange market and obtain their pounds via gold instead. This rate is known (see text) as "the upper gold point."

c. There is similarly a "lower gold point"—at, say, $1.98. On the foreign exchange market, the sterling-dollar rate will not fall below that figure. Nobody holding £1 would be likely to sell it for $1.97—not if $1.98 is to be had by using that £1 to *(buy / sell)* gold in Britain, taking that gold from *(the United States to Britain / Britain to the United States)* and selling it there for *($2 / £1)*.

The 2-cent differential on either side of "par value" represents the cost of shipping 1/100 of an ounce of gold from one nation to the other.

---

a. £1 = $2; buy; pounds. *b.* above. *c.* buy; Britain to the United States; $2.

---

4. Suppose a widespread taste for Scotch whiskey develops in the United States. This means an increase in demand for *(dollars / pounds sterling)*. If the United States is on the gold standard, and if this demand increase is sufficiently large, there will be a flow of gold *(away from / toward)* the United States. If this demand increase persists without countering effect for sufficiently long, the United States might be drained of its entire stock of *(gold / Scotch whiskey)*.

---

pounds sterling; away from; gold.

---

5. So the gold standard keeps exchange rates steady; but demand-and-supply forces are still at work. Why don't some nations, trying to maintain that standard, run out of gold?

A nation must indeed "go off" the gold standard if it loses all or most of its gold by reason of a major rise in imports (such as that of question 4), or a sufficient drop in exports. However, there are some "equilibrating" forces that may operate to brake any such gold outflow.

The first major attempt to describe such an equilibrating mechanism was laid out by David Hume in the eighteenth century: the "gold-flow–price-level mechanism" (see text).

a. Suppose, as in question 4, the United States demand for imports increases. This American demand for foreign currencies pushes *(up / down)* their prices to the gold *(import / export)* point. According to Hume's gold-flow–price-level analysis, the resulting gold flow *(out of / into)* the United States *(increases / decreases)* the U.S. money supply, causing the price level to *(rise / fall)*.

b. In one or more foreign exporting countries, the *(same / reverse)* situation occurs. The gold which has left the United States flows into these countries, increasing their money stock and so causing their prices to be *(higher / lower)*. Since American prices have gone down while foreign prices have gone up, *(more / less)* American goods will be bought by foreigners, while Americans will tend to buy *(more / less)* foreign goods. That is, in America, exports will *(rise / fall)* and imports will *(rise / fall)*. So the rise in U.S. imports which began the process is offset.

In rough outline, for sufficiently large movements, Hume's analysis may have some validity. But today the link between a nation's total gold stock and its total money supply is not close at all. Moreover, Hume's analysis relies pretty heavily on the quantity theory of money (Chapter 15). Whether or not the price level responds to small or moderate changes in the total money supply is a debatable topic.

Hume's mechanism involves *price* changes. The chapter Appendix discusses another "equilibrator" (one which was first pointed out much more recently): *income* changes.

---

a. up; export; out of; decreases; fall. *b.* reverse; higher; more; less; rise; fall.

---

6. Although the old international gold standard is gone today, its influence persists—in two important respects especially. First, nations still consider their gold stocks as reserves for settling international balances. (But now they tend to regard gold as an "emergency" reserve; they do not part with gold unless events force them to do so. Here, the United States was one of the last to yield. Until 1971, she stood ready to give gold to any nation which had accumulated dollars and wanted them swapped for gold. Today—1976—she will no longer do so.)

Second, the desire for fixed or near-fixed rates persists. The gold standard is not the only possible mechanism to this end. You can hold the price of your currency steady—if you hold a sufficiently large inventory of foreign monies.

a. Canada, for example, relies heavily on exports to, and imports from, the United States. Suppose the Canadian authorities (to whom the exchange rate is consequently important) decide that for trading purposes it would be desirable to keep the price of the United States dollar at $(Can.)1.05. If the price of the U.S. dollar begins to drift below this figure, Canada will enter the foreign exchange market and support the price by *(selling / buying)* U.S. dollars. For this purpose, it will supply *(Canadian / American)* dollars. And if the U.S. dollar's price starts to move *above* $(Can.)1.05, Canada will *(buy / sell)* U.S. dollars.

b. Alternatively, Canada might choose a modified version of the same plan, keeping the price of the U.S. dollar within a "band" of (say) $(Can.)1.00 and $(Can.)1.10. Of course, she cannot keep the exchange rate indefinitely at a level not justified by supply and demand. If the price of the U.S. dollar keeps chronically trying to push *above* $(Can.)1.10, in due course Canada will *(accumulate too many / run out of)* U.S. dollars.

---

a. buying; Canadian; sell. *b.* run out of.

---

7. The great problem with fixed exchange rates, then, is that when maintained too long under changing world conditions, they grow outdated. Some nations then run dangerously low on their reserves of foreign currencies and gold; others pile up excess reserves. (But it is a most unusual nation that will concede that its reserves are "excessive.")

At the close of World War II, the international mood strongly favored fixed rates, to be altered only with changes in "fundamental conditions." This mood reflected a desire to regain, if possible, the stability which had characterized the old pre-World War I gold-standard days. Moreover, during the worldwide depression of the 1930s (after the gold standard had broken down), a "currency price war" had begun: some countries deliberately allowed their currencies to depreciate in price so as to gain a competitive advantage in world markets for their exporters. Thus the rules of the International Monetary Fund, created after World War II (see Chapter 36), reflected this desire for fixed rates. Thereafter, until the early 1970s, exchange-rate revisions were probably made too slowly. Some nations clung to overvalued rates, others to undervalued ones.

This disposition to stick to a fixed rate is understandable.

Such a rate removes uncertainty (see question 3). Moreover, any hint of a revision, whether upward or downward, will provoke strong opposition. Reduce the price of your currency, and there results *(upward / downward)* pressure on your domestic price level, since the domestic prices of all imported goods go *(up / down)*. Moreover, you suffer at least some loss of international prestige. In effect, you are admitting that you can't sell enough of your nation's merchandise for as high a price as you used to get. (In the early 1960s, it became increasingly apparent that the British pound was overvalued. Yet, for several years the British government clung to its $2.80 value, in the process losing foreign-currency reserves, borrowing abroad, and diverting the energies of government officials from critical domestic issues.)

On the other hand, if you *increase* the price of your currency, then prices of all your export goods, as foreigners see them, automatically go *(up / down)*. Any suggestion of such an increase will provoke howls of protest (perhaps justified, perhaps not) from exporting firms that such a price rise will destroy that tiny selling edge they have over their foreign competitors. (Japan appreciated the yen in 1972 because foreign pressure was so strong that she had to; but she did so by much less than some other nations thought appropriate in the light of her trade and reserve position.)

By the early 1970s, the consensus was that the price of maintaining fixed rates (the threat to reserves of gold and foreign exchange) had grown too high. All the major trading nations shifted to "floating rates." The West German mark and the Swiss franc thereupon rose notably; the U.S. dollar fell.

Thus far, the floating-rate system seems to have worked fairly well—although it has been described as a "dirty float." A "dirty float" is alternatively a "managed float"—i.e., not a totally free supply-and-demand one, but rather, a situation in which central banks still move in periodically, for what they consider to be good reasons, to check particular rises or falls in currency prices.

The fixed-rate system still has strong advocates. While usually conceding the need for an interim period of floating in turbulent conditions such as those of the 1970s, they insist that (*i*) in the longer term, fixed rates are necessary for stable, large-scale international trade; (*ii*) in conditions of recession or depression, floating rates degenerate into a "very dirty float" of competitive currency depreciation (see the second paragraph of this question); and (*iii*) such floating rates only invite currency speculation, hence needless ups-and-downs in the foreign-exchange markets. (Floating-rate proponents reply that fixed rates do not stop speculation, they just give speculators a periodic free ride. Thus when it becomes evident that a currency is undervalued, hence due for fixed-price revision, the speculators need only buy that currency, then sit back and await its new and higher price.)

A country which, for good reasons or bad, wants to maintain a fixed price for its currency in foreign-money terms, but is losing foreign-currency or gold reserves in the attempt thereat, may consider alternatives other than giving up and letting the price fall. It may impose new tariffs (see Chapter 35), or set even stronger restrictions on imports by establishing quota limits or even by banning the import of "nonessential goods." But such moves provoke strong resentment among other nations, and invite retaliation.

Alternatively, the country may follow what international bankers consider "the rules of the game": Raise interest rates and make fiscal policy more restrictive. This alternative is explored in Chapter 36 (see question 2, pp. 283–284).

_____

upward; up; up.

_____

8. Part of the international monetary problem is that of providing enough reserves so that every small shift in existing reserves does not set off a new monetary crisis. Most economists think that reserves cannot be based on gold alone: either gold must be supplemented, or else dispensed with entirely. (This topic also is further discussed in Chapter 36; see question 8, p. 287.) It is a curious use of scarce effort to expend it in digging gold out of the ground, only to bury that gold once again, deep in the vaults of some central bank. It is much easier to create "paper gold," through international agreement, in such total amount as seems appropriate. Such paper gold is now evolving; its technical name is

_____ .

_____

Special Drawing Rights.

_____

9. *a.* The terms "devaluation" and "depreciation" both indicate reductions in the value of a country's currency; yet they have different meanings. Devaluation means a reduction in a currency's value relative to (*other currencies* / *gold*). Depreciation means a reduction in its value relative to (*other currencies* / *gold*).

b. If the United States raises its official price of gold from (say) $100 to $200 per ounce, this change (*would* / *would not*) constitute a devaluation of the dollar. If all the other major countries make matching gold-price increases, this action (*would* / *would not*) be an all-around devaluation. However, if other countries do not follow the United States move, and if the price of the U.S. dollar on the foreign exchanges is therefore halved vis-à-vis the British pound, the West German mark, etc., then for the United States this would be an instance of (*devaluation only* / *depreciation only* / *both devaluation and depreciation*).

c. This exchange-rate shift would make foreign goods (*cheaper* / *dearer*) in dollar terms to Americans. To foreigners, in terms of their own currencies, American goods would appear (*cheaper* / *dearer*). That is, when a country's currency is depreciated, this move tends to (*increase* / *decrease*) the volume of its exports, and to (*increase* / *decrease*) the volume of its imports.

_____

a. gold; other currencies. *b.* would; would; both devaluation and depreciation. *c.* dearer; cheaper; increase; decrease.

_____

10. Taking the viewpoint of the United States for illustrative purposes, most international transactions fall into two categories: (1) export and export-like items whose effect is to bring foreign money to the United States; (2) imports and import-like items whose effect is to send American money abroad. If the total money volume in category (1) exceeds that in (2), then under a fixed-exchange-rate system, United States reserves tend to increase. Under a floating-rate system, the same excess of (1) over (2) tends to drive up the U.S. dollar price, expressed in any foreign money.

Assume a floating-rate system. As to each item following, indicate whether its effect would be to increase (I) or to decrease (D) the dollar's price in foreign-currency terms.
a. American demand for imports increases. . . . .(*I* / *D*)
b. Foreign demand for U.S. goods decreases. . . . .(*I* / *D*)
c. A recession in the United States results in falling GNP, employment, and imports. . . . .(*I* / *D*)
d. The rate of inflation in foreign countries is more rapid than that in the United States. . . . .(*I* / *D*)
e. Americans decide to invest less abroad—i.e., their demand for foreign IOUs decreases. . . . .(*I* / *D*)
f. Foreign firms increase their dividend payments, and some of the shareholders are Americans. . . . .(*I* / *D*)
g. Foreigners decide to hold fewer U.S. dollars. . . . .(*I* / *D*)

_____

a. D. *b.* D. *c.* I. *d.* I. *e.* I. *f.* I. *g.* D.

_____

11. A country's "balance of international payments" is the official record of all its transactions with foreign countries for some given time period, usually 1 year. It is customarily divided into three main sections. From text Table 33-1, write these down:

(1) _____

(2) _____

(3) _____

The "Capital account" sector records all purchases and sales of stocks, bonds, and other securities or IOUs. It includes all changes in bank accounts (both accounts within the country concerned but owned by foreigners, and accounts in other countries owned by residents of the country concerned).

The "Net reserve and gold assets" sector records only official shifts of reserves. The "Current" account records everything else—goods and services imported and exported, gifts, and a variety of miscellaneous items.

_____

(1) Current account; (2) Capital account; (3) Net reserve and gold asset movements.

12. The next few questions involve the recording of entries on the United States balance of payments (hereafter, BP). In all such transactions, one party gives some commodity, service, or security. The other party usually (not invariably) gives money in exchange. It makes no difference whether the money used was foreign or American; the BP treats all transactions as dollar transactions.

Every transaction involves both a credit and a debit of the same dollar amount. What the American resident *gives* is recorded as a credit; what the resident *receives* is a debit. Consider the following example: An American exporter sells goods to a French firm. Payment is made in francs (equivalent dollar value, $1,000). The American deposits these francs temporarily in a French bank. The BP entry is:

	Credit	Debit
Merchandise	$1,000	
Capital, Short-term		$1,000

The credit entry under Merchandise (in the BP's Current account section) records what the American gave in the transaction. The debit under Capital, Short-term, records the money received in exchange.

This Capital, Short-term (s/t), account records all changes in short-term IOUs, including currency and bank accounts. There is a debit entry whenever American holdings of short-term IOUs, foreign currency, or foreign bank accounts rise, and a credit whenever they fall. (So Capital, Short-term, is involved either as credit or as debit in the vast majority of transactions.)

Had the French customer not paid for the merchandise immediately upon delivery, the entry would be the same, for the American seller would not have shipped the goods without a promise to pay (a short-term IOU) from the customer.[1]

Show the needed BP entry if the American spends his French bank account on a vacation in Paris.

	Credit	Debit
_____	....	_____
_____	....	_____

Capital (s/t) credit, Travel & Transportation debit, $1,000.

13. On a separate sheet of paper, record the following transactions after the fashion indicated above. Use the account names provided in text Table 33-1. Use also the following memory aid if you find it helpful: Exports (what we give) are

[1]When the French customer does pay, say, 30 days later, no BP entry is necessary. Or we could say that payment entails both credit and debit entries under Capital, Short-term: a credit because the American has given up the short-term IOU, a debit because he has been given francs in exchange.

linked with credits; imports (what we receive) are linked with debits; hence:

In all instances, the BP is that of the United States.

a. An American manufacturer sells machine tools in England. The payment (equal to $1 million), in pounds sterling, is deposited in a British bank.

b. The manufacturer engages a British cargo steamer to carry the tools to the customer. Payment is made (equal to $10,000) from the British bank account.

c. An American importer buys Swiss watches worth $50,000. Payment is made in francs bought from an account owned by the Federal Reserve Bank of New York.

d. Visiting Russian scientists buy American vodka, value $50, to take home. They pay in dollars, provided them by their government.

e. A Frenchman buys picture postcards in New York, value $5, using dollars bought from a French bank.

The entries for these transactions indicate why "the BP always balances." This balance has nothing to do with the nation's good fortune, or bad one. The BP is simply an accountant's two-column statement, one column for Credits, one for Debits. For each and every transaction, the total Credit entry must equal the total Debit entry; thus the BP cannot possibly be "out of balance." The balance so recorded might (in extreme cases) reflect a state of near-bliss, or a serious impending crisis.

a. Merchandise credit, Capital (s/t) debit, $1 million.
b. Capital (s/t) credit, Travel & transportation debit, $10,000.
c. Capital (s/t) credit, Merchandise debit, $50,000.
d. Merchandise credit, Capital (s/t) debit, $50.
e. Merchandise credit, Capital (s/t) debit, $5.

14. When a security (a bond, any other form of IOU, or a stock) is bought or sold, it is entered as a particular kind of commodity for which an American gives or receives money. Record the following transactions as in question 13:

a. A West German firm sells 20-year bonds, value $500,000, in the United States. The dollar proceeds are temporarily deposited in an American bank.

b. These dollar proceeds are used to buy American merchandise.

a. Capital (s/t) credit, Capital (l/t) debit, $500,000.
b. Merchandise credit, Capital (s/t) debit, $500,000.

15. Interest paid on any IOU (e.g., a bond), or dividends paid, must be considered payment for a service—that service being the use of money capital. If an American firm pays a dividend to a British stockholder, this is an import of a service, hence a debit. Record the following transactions:

a. The West German firm of question 14 pays $50,000 interest on its bonds, buying dollars from a West German bank.

b. Later, this firm pays off its bond issue, using dollars similarly purchased. (It is now buying back, or importing, the IOUs which it sold in question 14.)

---

a. Investment Income credit, Capital (s/t) debit, $50,000.

b. Capital (l/t) credit, Capital (s/t) debit, $500,000.

---

16. When gold is involved in BP transactions, it is considered simply a commodity for which money is (usually) given or received in exchange, except that gold movements are recorded in the separate "Reserve and gold assets" section and not lumped in with other Merchandise items. Record the following:

a. The Bank of England, having accumulated a substantial dollar account in the Federal Reserve Bank of New York, uses part of this account to buy $5 million in gold from the United States government, or from the Fed.

b. The Russian government buys merchandise valued at $1 million from the United States. It pays in gold.

---

a. Reserve and gold assets credit, Capital (s/t) debit, $5 million. *b.* Merchandise credit, Reserve and gold assets debit, $1 million.

---

17. A gift or "unilateral grant" is by definition a one-sided transaction. But BP accountants make the transaction double-entry simply by using the vacant credit or debit line to record the fact that the transaction *is* a gift. If Americans send money abroad, that is a credit under Capital, Short-term; if they send merchandise abroad, it is a credit under Merchandise. In either case, the corresponding debit for a gift is an entry under Private remittances. Record these:

a. A private United States organization buys $1 million worth of surplus grain and ships it abroad as aid to a low-income country.

b. A foreigner sends $1,000 as a contribution toward a flood-relief program within the United States, having bought the dollars from his bank.

---

a. Merchandise credit, Private remittances debit, $1 million.

b. Private remittances credit, Capital (s/t) debit, $1,000.

---

18. *a.* Any reference to "the balance of trade" usually means the (*entire balance of payments / entire Current account / Merchandise account*).

b. The balance of trade is described as "favorable" if total (*exports exceed imports / imports exceed exports*). The word "favorable" is here (*correctly used / misleading*). A favorable balance of trade (*is / is not / may or may not be*) desirable. It is simply impossible to draw safe conclusions about the state of a country's welfare from the state of its balance-of-trade account (or even its entire Current account).

---

a. Merchandise account. *b.* exports exceed imports; misleading; may or may not be.

---

19. A less developed nation is typically one which borrows abroad insofar as it can do so. A mature, developed nation is typically one which lends to other countries. As a nation develops over a long time period, it may change from borrower to lender—and this shift will affect its BP position. The sequence outlined below (and in the text)—young debtor, mature debtor, young creditor, mature creditor—is an attempt to describe the likely BP changes involved.

a. The less developed nation is likely to try to build up its stock of capital goods through sales of its IOUs to more developed countries. On its BP, such security sales will be recorded as a (*credit / debit*). The import of capital equipment or other goods purchased with security-sale proceeds will appear on the Merchandise line as a (*credit / debit*). This country has (*a "favorable" / an "unfavorable"*) balance of trade. These facts make it a "young debtor" nation.

b. As time passes, this country ceases to borrow, or borrows in smaller quantities. It still pays interest and dividends on earlier years of bond and stock financing. But its exporting capacity has increased; it now shows a surplus of merchandise exports over imports, or an excess of (*credits over debits / debits over credits*). This (*"favorable" / "unfavorable"*) balance of trade is matched, or approximately so, by a surplus of debits on the BP Interest and Dividends account. The "mature debtor" stage has been reached.

c. In further time, this country may begin not only to repay its own earlier borrowings but to lend to other countries itself. This means a surplus of (*credits over debits / debits over credits*) in the BP Capital section. If this is matched, or approximately so, by a surplus of merchandise exports over imports, the "young creditor" stage has been reached.

d. Ultimately, the "mature creditor" stage may be attained. Such a country may still be lending capital abroad, but its inflow of interest and dividend payments is more than sufficient to offset this, so that on the BP Merchandise account, there is a surplus of (*credits over debits / debits over credits*)—i.e., the balance of trade is (*"favorable" / "unfavorable"*). This balance is supported by the (*debit / credit*) balance on the Interest and Dividends account.

---

a. credit; debit; "unfavorable." *b.* credits over debits; "favorable." *c.* debits over credits. *d.* debits over credits; "unfavorable"; credit.

QUIZ: Multiple Choice

1. *By the term "the gold points" is meant* (1) the exchange rates at which gold will begin to flow into or out of a country;

(2) the requirements which must be satisfied before a country is officially on the gold standard; (3) the exact relationship that is established between two currencies when both countries are on the gold standard; (4) the official buying and selling prices for gold set by a country on the gold standard; (5) the "mint parities" for the two countries.

2. *A "favorable balance of trade" means* (1) an excess of merchandise exports and other current account credits over merchandise imports and other current account debits; (2) an excess of foreign currency received by the home country over domestic currency received by foreigners; (3) an excess of merchandise exports over merchandise imports; (4) an excess of total credits over total debits in the balance of payments; (5) a situation in which the value of total imports exceeds the value of total exports.

3. *If we say that a country's currency has been devalued, we mean specifically with respect to that country that* (1) it has gone off the gold standard; (2) the domestic purchasing power of its currency unit has fallen; (3) its government has increased the price it will pay for gold; (4) it is experiencing an unfavorable balance of trade; (5) the prices of at least some foreign currencies, as expressed in that country's domestic currency, have fallen.

4. *To be fully on the gold standard, the government of a country must* (1) set a fixed price at which it is prepared to buy or sell gold in any quantity without restriction; (2) be prepared to buy or sell gold at any time without restriction, but at a price which it is free to vary from day to day as it chooses, provided the same price (or almost the same price) applies to both purchases and sales; (3) be prepared to buy gold in any quantity without restriction at a fixed price, but not necessarily to sell it; (4) be prepared to sell gold in any quantity without restriction, but not necessarily to buy it; (5) maintain a fixed gold content in its money unit, but not necessarily be prepared to buy or sell gold at any fixed price or without restriction.

5. *A Canadian province borrows money in New York via the sale of bonds, and temporarily deposits the U.S. dollar loan proceeds in a New York bank. The entry in the United States balance of payments for these events would be as follows:* (1) Credit entry under Capital, Long-term, debit entry under Capital, Short-term. (2) Credit entry under Invisibles, debit entry under Capital, Short-term. (3) Credit entry under Capital, Short-Term, debit entry under Income on Investments. (4) Credit entry under Capital, Short-term, debit entry under Capital, Long-term. (5) None of the above, since transactions of this type are not recorded on the balance of payments.

6. *The Canadian province of question 5 converts its U.S. dollars into Canadian dollars in the foreign exchange market. The effect of this conversion will be, if anything to* (1) depreciate the price of the U.S. dollar; (2) increase the total existing stock of U.S. dollars; (3) appreciate the prices of both U.S. and

Canadian dollars; (4) increase the United States' total foreign exchange reserves in the form of Canadian dollars; (5) decrease the total existing stock of Canadian dollars.

7. *Six months later, the Canadian province of question 5 makes its first interest payment to American bondholders, entering the foreign exchange market for the required U.S. funds. One alternative in question 6 could be correct as to the effect, if any, of this transaction. Which one?* (1). (2). (3). (4). (5).

8. *In a stable exchange-rate situation, if the price of the French franc is 25 United States cents, and the price of the United States dollar is 600 Italian lire, then the price of the French franc in Italian lire must be* (1) 90 lire; (2) 150 lire; (3) 200 lire; (4) 300 lire; (5) 600 lire.

9. *The exports of country A to country B increase substantially. Both A and B operate on the gold standard. According to David Hume's gold-flow–price-level mechanism,* (1) A's domestic price level will fall; B's domestic price level may or may not change; (2) A's price level may or may not change, but B's will fall; (3) A's price level will rise; B's will fall; (4) A's price level will fall; B's will rise; (5) none of the above will happen.

10. *If the exchange rate between Swiss francs and United States dollars changes from Sfr. 4 to the dollar to Sfr. 3 to the dollar, the franc's price has* (1) risen from 25 to 33 cents, and the dollar has appreciated relative to the franc; (2) fallen from 33 to 25 cents, and the dollar has depreciated relative to the franc; (3) risen from 25 to 33 cents, and the dollar has been devalued relative to the franc; (4) risen from 25 to 33 cents, and the dollar has depreciated relative to the franc; (5) fallen from 33 to 25 cents, and the dollar has appreciated relative to the franc.

11. *If American corporations make large dividend payments (in dollars) to foreigners,* (1) the effect on the price of the U.S. dollar, if any, will be to depreciate it; (2) the effect on the price of the U.S. dollar, if any, will be to appreciate it; (3) gold will tend to flow into the United States to compensate for the U.S. money going abroad; (4) imports into the United States will tend to increase to compensate for the U.S. money going abroad; (5) none of the above will be true.

12. *The five transactions listed below are all entries to be made on the U.S. balance of payments. For balance-of-payments purposes, four of the five are fundamentally similar. Which is the different one?* (1) The Federal Reserve Bank of New York receives gold from the Bank of England. (2) An American tourist on vacation spends francs in Paris. (3) A South American government sells long-term bonds in New York. (4) A British shipping firm is paid to carry an American export commodity abroad. (5) An American investor receives a dividend check from a West German steel company.

13. *If the exchange rate between Canadian and U.S. dollars is a floating one, and if the demand for Canadian dollars*

increases, then (1) the supply of Canadian dollars has decreased or will decrease; (2) the price of the Canadian dollar in U.S. currency will fall; (3) the supply of U.S. dollars has decreased; (4) the price of the U.S. dollar in Canadian currency will fall; (5) the U.S. dollar has been devalued.

14. *A substantial fall in the price of the dollar in foreign currencies (e.g., the price of the dollar in francs) could be expected to affect physical quantities of exports from the United States and imports into the United States as follows:* to (1) increase both exports and imports; (2) increase exports, decrease imports; (3) decrease both exports and imports; (4) decrease exports, increase imports; (5) have no perceptible effect on either imports or exports.

15. *If the United States and Italy are both on the gold standard, and the price of the Italian lira rises sufficiently,* (1) gold will begin to leave the United States when the gold export point is reached; (2) gold will begin to flow into the United States when the gold export point is reached; (3) gold will begin to leave the United States when the gold import point is reached; (4) gold will begin to flow into the United States when the gold import point is reached; (5) none of the above is correct, since the lira's price cannot rise with both countries on the gold standard.

16. *A mature-debtor nation is one whose balance of trade is* (1) unfavorable, the import surplus being paid for by borrowing; (2) unfavorable, thanks to the interest which is received from abroad; (3) favorable, the interest on past borrowing being paid out of the surplus of exports; (4) favorable, being made so by interest received from abroad; (5) not correctly identified by any of these descriptions.

17. *When countries A and B are both fully on the gold standard, the exchange rate linking their currencies is fixed, or almost so,* (1) in the sense that there is a mechanical relationship between the currencies of A and B, but not in a sense that is useful for exporters or importers; (2) because as a necessary part of being on the gold standard, country A must supply B's currency on demand at a fixed price, and vice versa; (3) because residents of A can always get B's currency at a fixed price through shipment and sale of gold to B, and vice versa; (4) because being fully on the gold standard requires both countries to use the same currency unit, so that there is really no foreign exchange problem; (5) in some circumstances, but not necessarily; the fact that A and B are both on the gold standard does not of itself imply any fixed exchange-rate relationship.

18. *If a country devalues its currency, and as a result it depreciates in value, the results will typically be as follows:* (1) Its imports will seem cheaper (from the viewpoint of its own citizens), and its exports will seem more expensive (from the viewpoint of foreigners). (2) Its imports will seem more expensive (from the viewpoint of its own citizens), and its exports will seem cheaper (from the viewpoint of foreigners). (3) Both its imports and its exports will seem cheaper (from the viewpoint of both its own citizens and foreigners). (4) Both its imports and its exports will seem more expensive (from the viewpoint of both its own citizens and foreigners). (5) None of the above, since there is no reason why the prices of either imports or exports should be affected.

QUIZ: Other

1. Below is a demand schedule for francs, at various dollars-and-cents prices. Convert it into a supply schedule for dollars, at various franc prices. [NOTE: Although this is not a simple problem, it is an interesting one. A "straight-line" demand schedule results in a supply schedule of quite unexpected shape. Convert in this way: If the price of 1 franc is $0.90, then 1.00 francs = 0.90 dollars, and so 1.00 dollars = 100/0.90 francs (i.e., the price of 1 dollar is about Fr. 1.1). The schedule below says that when the price of the franc is 90 cents, 100 francs will be demanded—i.e., 90 dollars will be supplied to buy them. In sum, when the dollar's price is Fr. 1.1., 90 dollars will be supplied. Work out other points on the supply schedule similarly.]

P of Francs (in $)	Q of Francs Demanded	P of Dollar (in Francs)	Q of Dollars Supplied
$1.00	0	_____	_____
0.90	100	_____	_____
0.80	200	_____	_____
0.70	300	_____	_____
0.60	400	_____	_____
0.50	500	_____	_____
0.40	600	_____	_____
0.30	700	_____	_____
0.20	800	_____	_____
0.10	900	_____	_____

2. The exchange rate between United States dollars and French francs is a floating one. What effect, if any, is each of the following events likely to have on *the price of the franc in dollars?*

Put U in the space if the effect should be to push the price of the franc (in dollars) up; D if down; N if there is no reason why the price of the franc should be affected.

a. French corporations have a large interest payment to make, in dollars, to American bondholders. ....( )
b. French corporations have a large interest payment to make, in francs, to American bondholders. ....( )
c. France emerges from a recession, and with this increase in incomes, the French people want to buy more American

merchandise. ....( )
d. American residents decide to buy French bonds. ...( )
e. The French government ships gold to the U.S. .....( )
f. French corporations sell bonds to Americans. They borrow in dollars and in New York because the interest rate is lower there; but the proceeds of the bond issue are to be spent on French labor and materials. ....( )
g. Foreign exchange speculators decide that the price of the dollar in francs is going to fall. ....( )
h. The taste of American gourmets for French wine is replaced by a taste for California wine. ....( )

i. The French government decides that American movies are immoral and refuses to admit them into France. ....( )
j. An American citizen sends a package of merchandise to her French relatives as a gift. ....( )
k. An American citizen sends a remittance of dollars to his French relatives as a gift. ....( )
l. A French bank, in possession of a dollar bank account, decides to convert these dollars into gold. ....( )
m. A French bank, in possession of a dollar bank account, decides to convert these dollars into francs. ....( )

APPENDIX: Unemployment Aspects of International Trade and Overvaluation

1. *a.* Part 2 of the text explored at length the change in GNP to be expected as the result of a change in domestic investment (*I*), or of a change in the propensity to consume. At that stage, no consideration was given to international trade—i.e., to the consequences of exports and imports.

Chapter 12 stated that if a rise in *I* spending occurs in the United States, and if there are unemployed resources, there will in consequence be a rise in employment and in real output—i.e., a rise in real GNP.

The same result is produced in the United States if foreigners decide to buy more American goods. With respect to effects on employment and GNP, we must include, along with the amounts of domestic *I* spending and *C* (consumption) spending, the amount of American *(exports / imports)*.

A rise in exports—i.e., a decision by foreigners to buy more American goods—*(will / will not)* have, in the United States, "multiplier effects" (see Chapter 12), just as a rise in *I* spending has multiplier effects.

b. Imports by Americans, on the other hand, constitute a "leakage" out of the flow of purchasing power not unlike personal saving. Chapter 11 noted that such saving does not flow directly back to producers in the same way as does consumption spending. (On this point, see especially Study Guide Fig. 11-7, p. 86, and the accompanying discussion.) Much the same is true of dollar expenditures on import goods. Those dollars should in due course find their way back into the American purchasing-power stream. But since for the moment they have passed into the hands of foreigners (in payment for foreign goods supplied to the United States), the route of return is somewhat more indirect.

For example, an American may decide to buy a Mercedes-Benz automobile in preference to a Cadillac. The dollars so spent pass into West German hands. They reappear within the United States spending stream only when a West German (or someone else who has, in the meantime, bought them) shows up, wanting to purchase American goods. Hence those dollars *do* reenter the spending stream—but not via the

exclusively domestic route such as the purchase of a Cadillac would have involved. In this indirect-route respect, import spending resembles domestic *(consumption spending / saving / investment spending).*

---

a. exports; will. *b.* saving.

---

2. *a.* If a country's GNP rises, ordinarily we would expect the total of its imports to *(rise also / remain unchanged / fall).* Imported materials used in production will *(rise / fall)* as output rises, and the rise in incomes will mean a *(rise / fall)* in imported consumer goods.

b. Chapter 11 introduced the "marginal propensity to consume"—that fraction of an extra dollar of income, or GNP, allocated to extra (domestic) *C* spending. We could speak similarly of a "marginal propensity to import"—meaning that fraction of an extra dollar of GNP typically allocated to *(imports / exports).*

---

a. rise also; rise; rise. *b.* imports.

---

3. *a.* For a long time, economists puzzled over possible "equilibrating effects" which might work to help keep a country on the gold standard, or simply help it to maintain a fixed exchange rate. Suppose a rise in imports leads to a gold outflow, or to loss of part of the country's foreign exchange reserves. The government of that country might take deliberate steps to check imports or encourage exports and so to restrain the gold or foreign exchange loss. But economists have always felt there might be some *automatic* equilibrators.

David Hume's gold-flow–price-level mechanism (review question 5, p. 258) was an attempt to describe just such a mechanism. But it is doubtful how much application this process has in a modern economy.

The income effects described in questions 1 and 2 above, it was then discovered, provided a much more plausible equilibrating effect. Suppose country A increases her imports from country B. As a result, A begins to lose gold or foreign exchange reserves (reserves meaning, in this case, her reserve supply of B's currency).

Because of the rise in exports to A, B's GNP *(rises / falls / does not change)*. As a result, B's imports from abroad *(rise / fall / do not change)*—including her imports from A.

This rise in B's imports will, to at least some degree, *(diminish / increase)* A's loss of gold or of foreign exchange.

b. Ordinarily, we can expect this rise in B's imports to be *(less than / equal to / greater than)* the original rise in B's exports. So, while these "income effects" provide an "automatic equilibrator," it is *(a full / only a partial)* equilibrator, and it may have to be supplemented by deliberate action (e.g., a change in monetary policy by the central bank).

---

a. rises; rise; diminish.   *b.* less than; only a partial.

---

4. *a.* The text discusses the case of an "overvalued currency"—a typical fixed-exchange-rate problem.

The countries involved are A and E. The exchange rate between their respective currencies is fixed. Costs and prices are gradually rising in both countries. But E is enjoying greater productivity increases. Because of this, E's prices and costs do not rise as fast as those of A.

As a result, people in A find that goods offered for sale by country E become *(more / less)* attractive in terms of price. To people in E, the *(same / reverse)* is true of goods which country A is selling. Thus the volume of country A's imports is likely to *(rise / fall)*, and the volume of her exports to *(rise / fall)*. Country A begins to experience a balance of payments problem.

b. If the rise in productivity and incomes in country E is particularly marked, business firms in A may well be persuaded to undertake or expand their foreign investment—i.e., to invest in new plant and equipment in country E. For this purpose, they will need E's currency; so they enter the foreign exchange market to buy it. In the short run at least, this will *(intensify / diminish)* A's balance-of-payments problem.

c. In sum, A is *(losing / gaining)* gold or foreign exchange reserves. *(A's / E's)* currency has become "overvalued" at the present fixed rate, in view of the change which has taken place between the two price levels.

This condition could be remedied if A *(appreciated / depreciated)* the price of her currency in the foreign exchange market. Alternatively, E could *(appreciate / depreciate)* her currency price. The stronger pressure is on the country losing reserves—that is, *(A / E)*. In the text's view, the needed *(depreciation / appreciation)* of A's currency will be, within A, strongly *(resisted / encouraged)*. And indeed, if A holds out long enough against this move, the winds may change. But if they do not change, then ultimately A has no recourse but to *(depreciate / appreciate)* the foreign value of her currency.

---

a. more; reverse; rise; fall.   *b.* intensify.   *c.* losing; A's; depreciated; appreciate; A; depreciation; resisted; depreciate.

QUIZ: Multiple Choice

1. *The "foreign-trade multiplier" is a responding factor which determines* (1) the amount by which exports increase as GNP rises; (2) the amount by which imports increase as GNP rises; (3) the amount by which GNP increases as exports increase; (4) the amount by which GNP rises as imports increase; (5) the amount of "leakage" to be expected from induced imports as GNP rises.

2. *The two items paired below have the same characteristics in terms of their multiplier consequences and their impact on the level of domestic GNP: A* (1) rise in imports and a rise in domestic investment; (2) rise in saving and a rise in exports; (3) fall in the propensity to save and a rise in exports; (4) rise in the propensity to consume and a rise in imports; (5) rise in imports and a rise in exports.

3. *The "gold-flow–price-level mechanism" was part of the traditional account of the gold standard's functioning. One of the following did not have any part to play in its account of how a gold inflow or outflow would tend to be self-correcting, namely, the* (1) gold outflow that would follow any large increase in imports; (2) reduction in quantity of imports to be expected following significant price rises abroad; (3) rise in money prices that might result from a large increase in exports; (4) increase in exports that might well follow upon a fall in the domestic price level; (5) rise in real and money incomes due to a rise in exports, and the consequent disposition to import more.

4. *A nation's exports rise by $5 billion. In terms of the effects on GNP and imports to be expected therefrom, a reasonable and normal set of consequences would be to find (in billions)* (1) GNP up by $12, imports up by $15; (2) GNP up by $12, imports up by $2; (3) GNP up by $12, imports down by $2; (4) GNP up by $4, imports up by $2; (5) GNP up by $2, imports up by $5.

5. *If GNP falls in the United States, and exchange rates are floating,* (1) imports will tend to decrease and the price of the U.S. dollar to increase; (2) imports will tend to decrease and the price of the U.S. dollar to decrease; (3) imports will tend to increase and the price of the U.S. dollar to increase; (4) imports will tend to increase and the price of the U.S. dollar to decrease; (5) none of these statements is true.

6. *American corporations have large investment projects to undertake in Europe (involving European labor, materials, and equipment). They finance these projects by floating bond or stock issues in the United States. The short-run or immediate effect, if any, upon the international position of the dollar will be this:* (1) The dollar will tend to weaken in price, or the

United States to lose gold or foreign exchange reserves. (2) The dollar will tend to strengthen in price, or the United States to gain gold or foreign exchange reserves. (3) The United States may gain gold or foreign exchange reserves, but there is no reason why the dollar's price should strengthen. (4) The dollar's price may well strengthen or rise, but there is no reason why the United States should gain gold or foreign exchange reserves. (5) Neither the dollar's price nor the United States gold or foreign exchange position is likely to be affected in any way.

7. *The projects described in question 6 have a significant effect in lifting Europe out of a recession. Should this occur, which alternative in question 6 would correctly describe the resulting effect, if any, upon the international position of the dollar?* (1). (2). (3). (4). (5).

8. *Substitute "European corporations" for "American corporations" in question 6. Everything else in question 6 is as before (including the reference to European labor, materials, and equipment). Which alternative is then correct?* (1). (2). (3). (4). (5).

34 INTERNATIONAL TRADE AND THE THEORY OF COMPARATIVE ADVANTAGE

IF THE UNITED STATES has no domestic sources of tin, obviously it must import the tin it needs. What is not so obvious is why the United States, or any other country, should import a commodity which it *could* produce.

The basic message of this chapter is that a nation *should* import some goods which it is capable of producing at home—if it wants to use its resources to the best advantage. Each country should *specialize* in production of those commodities it is best equipped to make, given its own resources, and given those available to other countries. It should export part of what it has produced, receiving in exchange other goods (imports) which it is less well equipped to make.

The "model" used in this chapter is intended to drive home this point in the simplest possible form. Much of the text chapter is actually taken up with qualifications to the simplified model, and with a review of some *wrong* ideas about international trade. One such incorrect idea holds that when a highly efficient country can outproduce another country in every line of activity, then profitable trade between them is impossible. Part of David Ricardo's great contribution to this subject was to show that even if a country is relatively inefficient in *all* lines of production, *this shows up in a lower living standard at home, and not in an impossible bargaining position in international trade.* The efficient and inefficient countries can still trade to mutual advantage, provided there are some differences in their *relative* costs of producing different goods. (Both the text and the review questions below develop this point at length.)

Before trying to understand why certain ideas about international trade are mistaken ideas, you must grasp the basic "comparative-advantage" idea: why, in real income terms, it pays each nation to specialize in production, to export, and to import.

The first group of questions below deals with a nation's situation *before* it engages in foreign trade. The idea is first to identify the country's before-trade real income position, then to show how foreign trade, when it begins, can improve real income.

The same simplifying assumptions are employed as in the text chapter. There are only two countries: "America" and "Europe." Only two commodities are involved: food (*F*) and clothing (*C*). All costs of producing *F* or *C* can be measured in man-hours of labor. For some reason or reasons, such as differences in climate

or in skills, the productivity of a man-hour of labor, both in *F* and in *C*, is different in America from what it is in Europe. (The specific productivity figures used are different from those employed in the text chapter.)

1. The quantities of *F* and of *C* yielded by a man-hour of labor in America and in Europe are as follows:

Yield of 1 Man-hour of Labor	Units of *F*	Units of *C*
In America	20	6
In Europe	10	8

Assuming "man-hours" to be the same in both countries, these figures indicate that, for some reason, America is more productive in *(F / both F and C / C / neither F nor C)*. Europe is more productive in *(F / both F and C / C / neither F nor C)*.

In an 8-hour day, a worker in America can produce either 160 units of *F* or *(10 / 48 / 64 / 80)* units of *C*. In Europe, in an 8-hour day, a worker can produce either 64 units of *C* or *(10 / 48 / 64 / 80 / 160)* units of *F*.

F; C; 48; 80.

2. *a.* This chapter assumes that all costs of producing either commodity in either country are solely labor costs, and that all revenue from sale of the commodity goes to that labor. (This simplifying assumption is dropped in the chapter Appendix.) Hence, if the market price of a unit of *F* in America is $1, the hourly wage earned by an American worker producing *F* will be *$(0.05 / 0.10 / 1.00 / 10.00 / 20.00)*.

If, instead, *F*'s price in America were to be $0.05 (5 cents), the corresponding hourly wage for an *F*-worker would be *$(0.05 / 0.10 / 1.00 / 10.00 / 20.00)*.

Similarly, if *C*'s price per unit in America is $2, the hourly wage of a *C*-worker would be *$(0.30 / 0.60 / 2.00 / 10.00 / 12.00)*.

b. If in Europe the price per unit of *F* is £1, the hourly wage of an *F*-worker there will be *£(1 / 4 / 6 / 8 / 10)*. If *C*'s price in Europe is £1, the corresponding hourly *C*-wage will be *£(1 / 4 / 6 / 8 / 10)*.

a. 20.00; 1.00; 12.00. *b.* 10; 8.

3. *a.* Suppose that, for some reason unspecified, the prices of *F* and *C* in America are both $1. A worker, free to choose either occupation, would earn more by going into *(F / C)* production. Specifically, in *F* production, earnings per hour would be $(1 / 6 / 8 / 10 / 20), and in C production, $(1 / 6 / 8 / 10 / 20).

Given freedom of labor to enter either occupation (and with no other preference between them), the prices noted above (both $1) (*could / could not*) characterize an "equilibrium" situation in America. If such prices *did* prevail—say the government tried to enforce them by law—then ultimately (*only F would be / only C would be / both F and C would continue to be*) produced.

b. In Europe, if the prices of both *F* and *C* were somehow £10, then (again assuming no barrier to movement between occupations) (*all workers would move into F / all workers would move into C / such prices would not affect F and C*) production.

a. F; 20; 6; could not; only *F* would be.
b. all workers would move into *F*.

4. *a.* Use question 1 data to record in the table below the number of minutes required to produce 1 unit of each commodity in each country. (It is easier to grasp the required "equilibrium" price relationship if the production facts are so set out.)

| | **Minutes of Labor Required to Produce:** | |
	1 Unit of *F*	1 Unit of *C*
In America		
In Europe		

b. The point of question 3 is that unless the prices of *F* and of *C* stand in the proper relation to one another, the entire resource supply (here, the entire labor force) will shift away from production of the "underpriced" commodity. If in America the price of *F* is $3, then, if both *F* and *C* are to continue to be produced, *C*'s price must be $(1 / 3 / 8 / 10 / 12). If *C*'s price in America is $2, then *F*'s price should be $(0.30 / 0.60 / 1.00 / 1.50 / 2.00). Prices of $2.40 for *F* and $9 for *C* (*would / would not*) constitute an equilibrium relationship.

Relative prices are what matter here. In America, the ratio between p_F and p_C must be (*1:1 / 3:10 / 5:10 / 10:3*) because that pair of figures matches the underlying ratio of production costs, measured in labor time needed to produce 1 unit of each commodity. (The *absolute* level of prices will be governed by such factors as the quantity of money circulating within the country.)

If prices of *F* and *C* somehow got stuck at $2.40 and $9 respectively, workers would move away from (*F / C*) production and into (*F / C*) production.

c. In Europe the same requirement holds, except that the relationship must match productive conditions therein. If the price of *F* in Europe is £4, then, for an equilibrium in which both commodities are produced, the price of *C* must be £(1 /

2 / 3 / 4 / 5 / 6). More generally, Europe's ratio p_F/p_C must be (*3:10 / 5:10 / 4:5 / 5:4*).

a. America, 3, 10; Europe, 6, 7½   *b.* 10; 0.60; would not; 3:10; *F*; *C*.   *c.* 5; 4:5.

The questions thus far have assumed that there is no international trade between America and Europe. Now, suddenly, the opportunity of such trading opens up. For simplicity, the costs of shipping goods from one region to the other are assumed to be so small that they can be considered zero. The prices of *F* and of *C* in America are respectively 60 cents and $2.

5. *a.* You are a shrewd, wealthy American entrepreneur. To be more specific, you have $9 in cash, and are the first to notice that *F*'s price in Europe is £4, and that *C*'s price is £5. Given such prices, how can you convert your $9 into $24? Describe the necessary operations in four steps.

Step 1: _____

Step 2: _____

Step 3: _____

Step 4: _____

b. If you were an entrepreneur in Europe with a capital of £15 and a similar desire to improve your financial and social standing, what would you do, and what would be the result?

Step 1: _____

Step 2: _____

Step 3: _____

Step 4: _____

a. 1: Buy 15 *F* for $9.   2: Sell the 15 *F* in Europe for £60. 3: Buy 12 *C* for £60.   4: Sell the 12 *C* in America for $24.
b. 1: Buy 3 *C* for £15.   2: Sell the 3 *C* in America for $6. 3: Buy 10 *F* for $6.   4: Sell the 10 *F* in Europe for £40.

6. *a.* As a result of this difference in price ratios between the two countries, the two commodities will accordingly begin to move internationally. Specifically (pick *two* alternatives), (*F moves from America to Europe / F moves from Europe to America / F moves in both directions / C moves from America to Europe / C moves from Europe to America / C moves in both directions*).

A quick rule of thumb (adapted from a text footnote) for determining which country will export which commodity in such circumstances is this: Write down the two before-trade price ratios as fractions, and take the smaller of the two, noting the country to which it belongs. (In question 5, the p_F/p_C fractions would be ³⁄₁₀ and ⁹⁄₁₀; America's ³⁄₁₀ is the smaller.) The *numerator* of that fraction indicates that country's export commodity. (The numerator is 3, and that 3 pertains to food price; so America will export food.) The *other* country will export the *other* commodity.

b. Had America's *F* and *C* prices been 30 cents and $1 respectively, rather than 60 cents and $2, the results described above *(would / would not)* change. Had Europe's *F* and *C* prices been £8 and £10 respectively, rather than £4 and £5, this *(would / would not)* change the results described.

---

a. *F* moves from America to Europe; *C* moves from Europe to America. *b.* would not; would not.

---

7. *a.* In America (and in Europe) the pre-trade domestic "equilibrium" has been disrupted. For example, in the United States, domestic supplies of *C* are supplemented by imports. Thus *C*'s price should *(rise / remain unchanged / fall)*. This in turn means that the ratio p_F/p_C will *(rise / remain unchanged / fall)*.

b. We know from questions 2 through 4 that if America's ratio p_F/p_C is anything other than 3:10 (or 0.3), workers will leave the "underpriced" occupation. In this case, workers will move from *(F / C)* to *(F / C)* production. Because of America's new export trade, more workers are needed in this commodity.

c. In Europe, which imports what America exports, there will *(be a / not be any)* change in domestic prices. There, the ratio p_F/p_C will *(rise / remain unchanged / fall)*. Workers will leave *(F / C)* production, moving instead to work in Europe's export commodity, namely *(F / C)*.

---

a. fall; rise. *b.* C; F. *c.* be a; fall; F; C.

---

8. *a.* The before-trade price ratios were 3:10 in America and 4:5 (or 8:10) in Europe. Clearly, such different ratios allow you to make a financial killing, when trade opens up, by going through the trading process of question 6. The profit you make would be an "arbitrage" one. (For the meaning of "arbitrage," see, if necessary, question 1, p. 167.)

These arbitrage profit opportunities will not last. They are in fact a symptom of disequilibrium. For, as question 7 indicated, when goods begin to move in volume between the two countries, prices are affected, Specifically (to repeat question 7), America's before-trade p_F/p_C of 3:10 will *(rise / fall)* and Europe's ratio of 4:5 (or 8:10) will *(rise / fall)*. That is, the two ratios move *(closer together / farther apart)*.

Suppose that America's ratio rises from 3:10 to 4:10, and Europe's falls from 8:10 to 7:10. There is *(no longer / still)* an arbitrage profit to be made; it persists so long as any difference at all persists between the two ratios. But as more and more people discover this opportunity, the trade volume *keeps increasing*. This increase in turn pushes the two ratios even *(closer together / farther apart)*. In the case here assumed, that of literally zero transport cost, the two ratios

must finally meet at a common figure, the same in both countries. A possible common figure would be 5:10. (It could be any figure between 3:10 and 8:10; but leave the matter of determination of the exact common ratio for question 12.)

b. Alas, when this common ratio is reached, your chances of getting rich quickly are ended; the arbitrage opportunity vanishes. Does this mean that international trade will stop? Not at all; it means only that the trade volume will *stop increasing*. Thereafter, a food producer gets the same return whether the output is sold in America or in Europe; the same is true of a clothing producer. An international equilibrium is established, comparable to the separate equilibria formerly prevailing in the two countries. The new equilbrium is one in which America produces only food, Europe only clothing.

If the trade volume were somehow greatly disrupted (say by serious and persisting shipping difficulties), the price ratios in the two countries would *(still remain at a common figure / draw apart again)*.

Introduce some transport cost, and the two price ratios will continue to differ somewhat—but by just enough to reflect that transport cost, not by enough to allow for any enduring arbitrage profit.

---

a. rise; fall; closer together; still; closer together.
b. draw apart again.

---

9. The result of this international exchange is that both countries enjoy an increase in real income. Specializing on *F* production, America will have available for consumption more of *F* than she did before, and more of *C* also. The same holds for Europe, which concentrates on *C* production.

This point is illustrated by comparing the labor costs of the two methods by which America may obtain clothing—producing that *C* at home, or producing and exporting *F*, and bringing back *C* in exchange.

America can produce 6 units of *C* per hour; each unit costs her 10 minutes of labor time (questions 1 and 4). Or she can produce 20 units of *F* per hour. Those 20 *F* units, exported to Europe—with the after-trade ratio p_F/p_C common to both countries still assumed to be 5:10—will yield as imports *(5 / 6 / 10 / 20 / 40)* C units. That is the result of 1 hour's labor effort; hence each *C* unit, obtained via such "indirect production," costs *(5 / 6 / 10 / 20 / 40)* minutes of labor time, as compared with the 10 minutes required in direct production.

(There is a geometric illustration of the real-income gain in the chapter Appendix.)

In this respect, international trade produces for America a result comparable to the development of a new technology greatly increasing labor productivity in the *C* industry.

This still assumes zero transport cost. The introduction of such cost would diminish this real-income gain; *very* high transport cost would destroy it completely.

10; 6.

10. Now change the productivity figures. *Double* America's yield per man-hour as to both commodities (leaving the figures for Europe unchanged). Thus, question 1's table becomes:

Yield of 1 Man-hour of Labor	Units of *F*	Units of *C*
In America	40	12
In Europe	10	8

The critical difference is that American labor is now assumed more productive than European labor as to *both* commodities. We do not ask what background factors would result in such differences. We simply accept the fact that there *are* "high-productivity" and "low-productivity" countries—in order to ask: Is trade that would be profitable to *both* participants possible in such circumstances?

In the table of question 4 (minutes of labor required for 1 unit of output), the "America" figures will now be (*doubled / unchanged / halved*). The ratio between these two figures will be (*doubled / unchanged / halved*).

In America's previous pre-trade situation (questions 1 through 4), her ratio p_F/p_C was 3:10. In the new situation—still pre-trade—that ratio will be (*higher / unchanged / lower*). (The two *absolute* prices may of course be different.)

Question 5 examined the trading opportunity arising out of the opening up of international trade. With the changed productivity figures introduced in this present question, this trading opportunity will (*no longer exist / be exactly as it was before*).

---

halved; unchanged; unchanged; be exactly as it was before.

---

11. The point, then, is that a "low-productivity" country should still be capable of dealing profitably with a "high-productivity" country; *both* should gain in real income from international trade. The cost of low productivity is a low per capita income within that country, not an inability to cope with international exchanges.

The essential factor upon which an opening up of trade (and profitable trade) *does* depend is a difference in the pre-trade price ratio as between the two countries.

Below are three sets of pre-trade price figures (each quite different from anything used earlier). In the right-hand column, indicate the proper conclusion by this code: (1) America would export *F*, Europe *C*. (2) America would export *C*, Europe *F*. (3) No opportunity for any trading gain here.

America		Europe		
P of *F* in \$	*P* of *C* in \$	*P* of *F* in £	*P* of *C* in £	Answer
1	2	3	4	
1	2	3	6	
1	2	3	8	

(To answer, use the question 5 technique—which between-country transfer of goods would earn you a profit?—or the rule of thumb suggested in question 6.)

b. All the foregoing may indicate why it was thought necessary to introduce such terms as *absolute* advantage (or disadvantage) and *comparative* advantage (or disadvantage).

America has an *absolute* advantage over Europe if her productive conditions are such that, domestically, she can produce the commodity in question at less real cost (which in this chapter means simply labor cost) than Europe can. (If America needs 1 hour to produce 1 unit of *F*, and Europe needs 1½ hours, then America has the absolute advantage with respect to *F*.)

Look back at the question 10 table. It indicates that America has the absolute advantage in (*F alone / both F and C / C alone*). Yet this circumstance does not prevent Europe from exporting good *C*, despite the absolute advantage of American producers. Thus it is said that Europe, regardless of her absolute disadvantage, still has a *comparative* advantage in production of good (*F / C*). (In terms of question 10 data, America is decidedly the high-productivity country. Yet, in comparative terms, her productivity shows up less prominently with respect to good *C*.)

In brief: No matter what absolute productive conditions may be, a country has a *comparative* advantage in production of (say) commodity *C*, if it can export *C* successfully, receiving some other good or goods (such as *F*) in exchange.

In a two-country, two-commodity example such as used herein, in order to determine the commodity as to which one country (Europe, say) has a comparative advantage, it is necessary to examine and compare the prices of both commodities (*in that one country alone / in both countries*).

---

a. 1; 3; 2. *b.* both *F* and *C*; *C*; in both countries.

---

12. At what exact level will the common, after-trade price ratio be established? This is essentially a supply-and-demand question. The trade process described earlier is just an exchange of one good for another. Indeed, for purposes of understanding how the common intermediate ratio is reached, it's easiest to think of this trade as simple barter. The exact quantities exchanged are settled by working out a barter rate which both countries find—in terms of the amounts exchanged thereby—satisfactory.

For convenience, we use here the same pair of pre-trade p_F/p_C ratios used earlier: America, 3:10, Europe 4:5 (or 8:10). In barter terms, the American ratio means that 10 of *F* is considered equal in value to 3 of *C*. Similarly, Europe's 4:5 ratio means that (*4 of F equals 5 of C / 5 of F equals 4 of C*).

When trade opens up, these two pre-trade ratios (recall questions 7 and 8) are pushed closer together. Consider any intermediate ratio, picked at random—say 1:2 (or 5:10). At that ratio—i.e., at such barter terms—there will be a particular quantity of *F* which America would wish to export, and corresponding quantity of C she would want to import. If the desired F-export quantity is 100 units daily, the quantity of C America wants in exchange (remember, the 1:2 ratio is expressed in p_F/p_C terms, as before) would be *(50 / 100 / 150 / 200 / 250)* units daily.

At that same 1:2 ratio, there are particular quantities of C and F which Europe would wish to export and import daily, respectively. But these quantities may not match the American ones. If so, then 1:2 is not an "equilibrium" common ratio.

The intermediate and common ratio finally established is one at which the two countries' wishes (in terms of F and C quantities exchanged) *do* match. The better the barter terms America is offered—the more the old 3:10 ratio moves upward—the *(more / less)* she will want to exchange. Europe, by contrast, will want to trade more extensively, the more that her pre-trade ratio of 4:5 moves *(up / down)*.

Somewhere between the two differing pre-trade price ratios, there should be a common price ratio that is mutually satisfactory.

---

5 of F equals 4 of C; 50; more; down.

---

13. The principal basis for mutually profitable international trade, then, is a difference in relative production costs and prices. (The country importing a commodity which at home it could not possibly produce at all is simply illustrating the extreme case of such differences-in-production-cost trade.)

It does not matter what factors account for these relative cost differences (e.g., climate, differences in labor education and skill, differences in capital equipment), just so long as these background factors emerge in the form of differences in relative prices.

Differences in "factor endowments" are usually cited as the principal source of such differences in relative production costs and prices (although this explanation is of the kind which may raise as many questions as it answers).

The text mentions briefly two other possible sources of mutually beneficial international trade. They are:

a. _____

b. _____

---

a. Decreasing cost. NOTE: In this case, we assume that the before-trade cost ratio between commodities F and C is the same in country A as in country E. But if A specializes in production of F, this may lower the per unit cost of producing F. Here, trade is still based on a difference in costs; but this difference emerges only *after* trade has begun.
b. Differences in tastes between the two countries.

QUIZ: Multiple Choice

1. *In comparative-advantage terms, the most correct explanation of why bananas are imported instead of being grown commercially in the United States is that* (1) bananas cannot be produced in the temperate zones; (2) it would take a great deal of effort to produce bananas in the United States; (3) bananas can be produced with less effort in other countries than they can in the United States; (4) United States resources are better employed in producing other commodities, and tropical-country resources are better employed in banana production than in other things; (5) the United States climate does not lend itself to banana production.

2. *David Ricardo's theory of comparative advantage, or comparative cost, is intended to show that trade between two countries will be mutually beneficial. An assumption made in this analysis, to which some objection might be raised on the ground that it influences and perhaps alters the conclusions reached, is the assumption that* (1) comparative advantage, not absolute advantage, is the important element in trade; (2) each country, in consequence of such trade, will specialize in the commodity it exports; (3) full employment is at all times maintained in both countries; (4) no tariffs exist in either of the two countries; (5) the before-trade ratio of prices within each country has no part to play in the determination of trade flows.

3. *A difference between a tariff on an imported good and a quota on such a good is* (1) that a quota can never be made to yield revenue for the government, whereas a tariff can; (2) that a tariff can never be made to yield revenue for the government, whereas a quota can; (3) that a quota can be used to shut off all, or virtually all, the inflow of the imported good, whereas a tariff cannot; (4) that a tariff can be used to shut off all, or virtually all, the inflow of the imported good, whereas a quota cannot; (5) not correctly stated by any of these descriptions.

4. *Before international trade begins, a country will have an equilibrium ratio of prices (determined by relative production costs) between any two commodities. If trade with another country begins, involving these commodities, this price ratio will ordinarily be altered* (1) only if a change in production costs results within the country; (2) in all cases (excepting only the one where the volume of international trade proves to be too small to affect it); (3) only in cases where the volume of international trade is small; (4) not at all, since it is an equilibrium relationship; (5) only in cases where the volume of international trade is exceedingly large.

5. *Arguments cited in favor of a protective tariff are that such a tariff (a) protects the domestic industry against foreign competition and (b) brings revenue for the government to offset the higher domestic price. As to these arguments, it may be said that* (1) actually the tariff reduces rather than increases the sales of the domestic industry; (2) if the industry in question enjoys an absolute advantage in production, it stands in no need of such a tariff; (3) the emphasis on government revenue may lead to a tariff per unit much higher than the domestic industry needs for protection; (4) an effective tariff may actually bring in no government revenue at all; (5) none of these statements is correct.

6. *The output of labor (assumed to be the only input involved) in production of wine and of cloth in two countries, Upper Utopia and Lower Utopia, is as follows:*

Production per hour	Upper Utopia	Lower Utopia
Yards of cloth	5	15
Quarts of wine	10	20

Comparing the two countries as to possible trade between them and as to production advantages, it would be correct to say that Upper Utopia has (1) an absolute advantage in cloth production; (2) an absolute advantage in wine production; (3) a comparative advantage in cloth production; (4) a comparative advantage in wine production; (5) a comparative advantage in neither commodity.

7. *Initially, there is no trade between the two countries of question 6; each lives in isolation. In Upper Utopia, the currency unit is the "up"; in Lower Utopia, it is the "down." The prices of cloth in Upper and Lower Utopia in their before-trade situations are respectively 20 ups and 60 downs. For an equilibrium in which each country continues to produce both commodities, the corresponding wine prices would have to be* (1) 5 ups, 20 downs; (2) 40 ups, 45 downs; (3) 10 ups, 45 downs; (4) 10 ups, 80 downs; (5) 40 ups, 80 downs.

8. *If trading opportunities were to be opened up, given the data of questions 6 and 7 (international transport cost assumed to be zero or negligible), then we should expect Lower Utopia to* (1) import wine; (2) export wine; (3) import both commodities; (4) export both commodities; (5) neither export nor import, since her productive situation is such that there is no prospect of profitable trade with Upper Utopia.

9. *Before the trading opportunity of question 8 emerged, each country had its own price ratio, reflecting domestic production costs. If trade develops between Upper and Lower Utopia, this ratio—specifically, the ratio of cloth price to wine price—will* (1) rise in Upper Utopia, fall in Lower Utopia; (2) fall in Upper Utopia, rise in Lower Utopia; (3) rise in both countries; (4) fall in both countries; (5) not change in either country, except perhaps during a short transitional period before equilibrium is reestablished.

10. *When international trade has become established, in the circumstances of questions 6 through 9, and a new equilibrium has been reached, the ratio of cloth price to wine price (transport cost still assumed zero) might reasonably be* (1) 1.2 in both countries; (2) 1.8 in Upper Utopia, 1.5 in Lower Utopia; (3) 1.6 in both countries; (4) 2.1 in Upper Utopia, 1.3 in Lower Utopia; (5) 2.3 in both countries.

11. *Given the price ratio or ratios set out in question 10, if we know that the total of cloth exports is 500 yards daily, then the daily wine exports must be* (1) 600 quarts, from Upper Utopia; (2) 600 quarts, from Lower Utopia; (3) 800 quarts, from Upper Utopia; (4) 800 quarts, from Lower Utopia; (5) 1,150 quarts, from Upper Utopia.

12. *The gain from trade is illustrated by the position of the wine-importing country (either Upper or Lower Utopia). Question 6 shows hourly output of wine if that wine is produced at home. If the country specializes in cloth production and gets its wine via imports, then—at the price ratio of question 10, transport cost still assumed zero—the number of quarts of wine resulting from 1 hour's labor is* (1) 16; (2) 20; (3) 24; (4) 28; (5) 32.

13. *Differences in comparative production costs are usually cited as the principal basis for international trade. Another (and different) possible source of such exchanges, mentioned in the text, is* (1) differences in climates; (2) fixed foreign exchange rates; (3) differences in transport costs; (4) differences in labor skills; (5) economies of mass production.

14. *Trade between countries of comparable size with different standards of living will be* (1) profitable to the country of lower living standards at the expense of the one of higher standards; (2) profitable to both as long as price ratios differ in the two countries, but of no profit to either once a common price ratio has been established; (3) profitable in some degree to both, even after a common price ratio has been established; (4) unprofitable to both because one country would be at an absolute disadvantage in all products; (5) profitable to the country of higher living standards at the expense of the one of lower living standards.

APPENDIX: Comparative Advantage Amplified and Qualified

This Appendix presents the same set of basic ideas found in the chapter. Only the manner of their presentation differs. The Appendix uses the production-possibility diagram first introduced in Chapter 2. The production-possibility line, or "frontier," represents *the limit of possible production,* given the resources and technology available. If international trade opens up, each country is still held to its frontier *with respect to its own production.* But *as to consumption,* it can—via exports and imports—move beyond the frontier to a higher real-income level.

One advantage of this approach, then, is the advantage a good graphical presentation always has (or at any rate, is supposed to have) over a presentation in words alone. A further advantage is that with the production-possibility diagram, there is no need to assume (as the chapter did, for convenience) that production costs are only labor costs. This awkward problem is now avoided. It makes no difference whether labor is the only resource, or whether (as is true in real life) capital and land are also involved. The critical fact is that when resource supplies are limited, there is a limit on production, and the production-possibility frontier illustrates that limit.

1. We begin, as in the chapter, with a country which does not engage in international trade; it lives in isolation.

In Fig. 34-1, the heavy solid line *AK* is this country's production-possibility line, or "frontier." (Disregard for the moment the other lines drawn on Fig. 34-1.)

The subject of production-possibility lines was dealt with at length in Chapter 2. (The frontiers there discussed were curved, whereas *AK* here is a straight line; but for immediate purposes, this difference is unimportant.)

As in the chapter preceding this Appendix, the symbol *F* represents food and *C* represents clothing. In brief review of Chapter 2, a production-possibility line is intended to depict *(the various possible F and C quantities which the country could produce with its available resources / the demand for F and the demand for C).*

the various possible *F* and *C* quantities which the country could produce with its available resources.

2. *a.* The *slope* of the production-possibility line or frontier is important here. The slope of line *AK* is $(-\frac{1}{2} / -1 / -2 / -4)$.

Slope simply records "what happens" in movement from one point to another along the line. A movement from *A* to *B* in Fig. 34-1 means that *C* production drops from 100 to $(0 / $

10 / 40 / 50). This is a reduction in *C* (a minus figure) of 60. But as part of the same *A*-to-*B* move, *F* production rises from 0 to (10 / 20 / 30 / 40 / 50)—an increase of 30. Slope is just the ratio between the two changes.

b. The slope of a production-possibility line reflects the swapping terms between the two goods imposed by the hard facts of production. (Slope here has nothing to do with tastes or preferences, only with what production possibilities will allow you to do.)

Line *AK* is straight: its slope has the fixed value of −2, no matter where on *AK* you may be. The message conveyed by this slope value is that *(no matter / depending on)* where you are on *AK*, if enough resources are withdrawn from *F* production to reduce *F* output by 1 unit, this will allow an increase in *C* production of $(\frac{1}{2} / 1 / 2 / 3 / 4 / 5)$ unit(s).

a. −2; 40; 30. *b.* no matter; 2.

3. Line *AK*'s slope reflects also the *prices* of *F* and *C* that must prevail. (REMEMBER: no international trade as yet.)

The same kinds of resources are used in *F* production as in *C* production. The owners of these resources (labor, etc.) are free to move them from one occupation to the other, and have no preferences or prejudices as between them. They will move if there is more income to be earned in the other occupation. The incomes they *do* earn in *F* or in *C* production are governed by the prices of the two goods.

a. Question 2 indicated that the resources capable of producing 2 units of *C* could (by changing occupation) instead produce 1 unit of *F*. Hence, if there is to be no incentive for resources to change occupation, the price of a unit of *F* must be *(one-half / the same as / twice / four times)* the price of a unit of *C*.

b. A pair of prices fitting this required ratio would be:
(1) $p_F = \$1$, $p_C = \$5$ (2) $p_F = \$2$, $p_C = \$4$
(3) $p_F = \$3$, $p_C = \$3$ (4) $p_F = \$4$, $p_C = \$2$
If the price ratio between *F* and *C* were to be anything other than the ratio 2:1 (for more on this, see, if necessary, the review questions for Chapter 34 preceding this Appendix), producers would leave the *(underpriced / overpriced)* occupation. If both commodities are to continue to be produced (remember again, there is as yet no international trade), then the ratio p_F/p_C must be 2:1.

a. twice. *b.* (4); underpriced.

4. In this case, consumers have no part to play in dictating the ratio p_F/p_C. (Had the production-possibility line been curved, things would have been different in this respect. But the essence of trade is more easily grasped by leaving this complication aside.)
a. The power of decision or choice left to consumers is this: *(They can still decide how much of F and of C to buy / They have no choice at all).* In Fig. 34-1 terms, this means that they

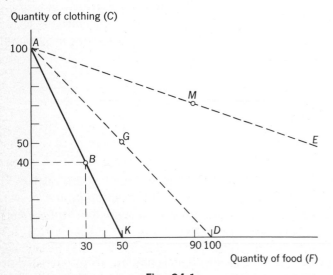

Quantity of clothing (C)

Quantity of food (F)

Fig. 34-1

can dictate the *(actual production point on / position of the entire)* line *AK*.

Suppose the point considered most desirable by consumers on line *AK* is *B*. That is, in the light of the constraint imposed by a limited resource supply, and faced with a p_F/p_C ratio of 2:1 which they cannot (except temporarily) change, the *F-C* combination they consider most desirable is 30 of *F* and 40 of *C*.

b. But suppose further that production somehow lands on a point *other than B*—say one midway between *A* and *B*. This means that more *(F / C)* is being produced, and less *(F / C)*, than consumers want. They respond to the supplies offered them by bidding up the price of *(F / C)* and bidding down the price of *(F / C)*.

This will change (temporarily) the p_F / p_C price ratio of 2:1. Hence some producers will shift from *(F production to C / C production to F)* production.

That is, consumer demands will push actual production toward point *B*—and in the process, carry the p_F/p_C ratio toward its level of 2:1.

a. They can still decide how much of *F* and of *C* to buy; actual production point on. *b.* *C; F; F; C; C* production to *F*.

Call the country discussed in questions thus far country X. The possibility of trade with another country, Y, is now opened up up for country X. The *before-trade* prices in these two countries are as follows:

	Food (F)	Clothing (C)
Country X	$2	$1
Country Y	fr. 10	fr. 30

At this point, we draw on material developed in review questions for the chapter preceding this Appendix. We begin with a situation in which the *F-C* price ratios differ in countries X and Y. Initially, there is no international trade. But trade opportunities between X and Y suddenly open up, and in consequence: (1) Goods begin to move between the two countries. (2) The pre-trade price ratio in each of X and Y will be affected by these movements of goods. (3) These two price ratios, hitherto different, will move toward one another. If we assume that costs of transporting goods between the two countries are zero, then the two price ratios will reach a single common figure, somewhere intermediate between their original, pre-trade levels. (4) Resources in each country will move out of the imported-good occupation, and into the export-good occupation.

5. To be more specific, in the light of the price data in the table above:
a. Country X will begin to export good *(F / C)*. The pre-trade

price ratio p_F / p_C in that country of 2:1 will *(fall / rise)*. Resources will move out of production of commodity *(F / C)* and into the other occupation.

b. Country Y will export commodity *(F / C)*. The pre-trade price ratio p_F/p_C in that country of 10:30 (or 1:3) will *(fall / rise)*. Resources will move out of production of commodity *(F / C)* and into the other occupation.

c. Look back at Fig. 34-1, which refers to country X. The shift of input resources will move production from B *(to between B and K / all the way to K / to between B and A / all the way to A)*. That is (given a straight-line production-possibility frontier), country X now specializes completely on the production of commodity *(F / C)*.

Similarly, country Y (if it too has a straight-line production-possibility frontier) will specialize completely in production upon commodity *(F / C)*.

a. *C;* fall; *F.* *b.* *F;* rise; *C.* *c.* all the way to *A; C; F.*

6. *a.* If, in country Y, p_F = fr. 10 and p_C = fr. 30, 3 units of *F* are there considered equal in value to 1 unit of *C*. For a citizen of country X who sells *C* there, and buys *F* to take back to his own country, it is as though there were barter terms of *(3 C for 1 F / 1 C for 1 F / 1 C for 3 F)* available.

b. Look back again at Fig. 34-1 (which refers, remember, to country X). Its production-possibility line is still *AK*, and the opening up of international trade has not changed that line. *Before* trade, point *B* marked both its production and consumption points. Now, with international trade, country X has moved to point *A* with respect to production. *With respect to consumption*, it can move *outside AK*—i.e., it can improve its real-income position.

Suppose country Y is willing to swap *any* quantity of *F* and *C* at terms of 3 *F* units for 1 *C* unit. (Almost certainly, country Y would *not* agree to such terms. They represent her before-trade price ratio, and they would mean that she gained no benefit from trade. But never mind about *that;* we'll reach that matter in a moment. Our immediate question is: What would country X do if she *did* have such an unrestricted exchange offer?)

In production, country X is at point *A*, producing 100 units of *C*. With country X operating at that point, a barter ratio of 3 *F* for 1 *C* would appear on Fig. 34-1 as the line *(AE / AD / AK)*.

Country X could then choose as her *consumption* equilibrium any point on that line—for example, point *(M / G / B)*. The choice of the exact point would be governed by *(the facts of production / consumer tastes)*, just as in question 4.

c. Continue to suppose that the barter terms of 1 *C* for 3 *F* are available, and that country X does choose point *M* as her consumption point. Country X's total *F* consumption per period would then be 90 units, and her total consumption of *C (40 / 50 / 70 / 100)* units. Since total *C* production is 100 units, this means the unconsumed part of C would be exported to Y—specifically, *(30 / 50 / 70 / 100)* units. If we compare this export total with the F imports of 90, we find it *(matches / does not match)* the ratio of 1 C for 3 F (on the basis of which line AE was drawn).

---

a. 1 C for 3 F. *b.* AE; M; consumer tastes. *c.* 70; 30; matches. (Be sure you have grasped the details of this question before moving on.)

---

7. *a.* The ratio of 1 C for 3 F is just one *possible* trading ratio. Another such would be 1 C for 1 F. This trading opportunity would appear on Fig. 34-1 as the line *(AK / AD / AE)*. If this *were* the opportunity facing the citizens of country X, they *(would / would not)* be disposed to export C. Country X would pick an equilibrium point for consumption just as in question 6—for example, a point such as *(M / G / B)*.

b. In sum, for every *possible* trading ratio which values 1 unit of C at more than ½ unit of F, country X will want to export C. And for each such ratio, there will be some specific C quantity that country X will want to supply, and some corresponding F quantity she will want to receive in exchange.

Note carefully one feature shared by all the possible after-trade exchange ratios. As lines AE and AD on Fig. 34-1 indicate, they allow country X to consume, by comparison with her pre-trade equilibrium of B, larger quantities of *(both C and F / C but not F / F but not C / neither commodity)*.

---

a. AD; would; G. *b.* both C and F.

---

8. *a.* Before trading opportunities arose, country X's ratio p_F / p_C was 2:1—i.e., 1 F unit cost twice as much as 1 C unit. Country X would thus want to export C for any ratio *(higher / lower)* than 2:1—for examples, 1:1 (line AD in Fig. 34-1), 1:2, or 1:3 (line AE). From country X's standpoint, the most attractive terms among these three examples would be *(1:1 / 1:2 / 1:3)*. For each such possible trading ratio, there will be particular quantities of C and of F which country X will want to export and import. The more attractive the exchange terms she can obtain, the larger will be the quantity of F she will likely want to import.

b. Country Y's position is the same except that the details are reversed. Her before-trade ratio p_F/p_C was 1:3 (i.e., an F unit cost only one-third of a C unit). She would want to export F and import C if offered any trading ratio *(higher / lower)* than 1:3. For each possible trading ratio, there will be particular F and C quantities she will want to export and import. If the trading ratio is particularly attractive—i.e., if it is markedly *(above / below)* 1:3—then the amount of C she will want to import will be in all likelihood be correspondingly increased.

---

a. lower; 1:3. *b.* higher; above.

---

9. As goods begin to move in volume internationally, each country's pre-trade price ratio p_F/p_C changes in conse-

quence. Country X's ratio falls below 2:1 (or 2/1, or just 2); country Y's ratio rises above 1:3 (or 1/3, or ⅓). If we retain the simplifying assumption of zero transport cost, these ratios will *(finally become equal / still remain unequal)*.

The matter of just where between 2 and 1/3 this common after-trade ratio will settle is (as question 12 for the chapter, p. 271, pointed out) just a supply-and-demand question. It is a matter of finding a ratio at which each country's desired export and import quantities just match that of the other country. For example, one of the following indicates a p_F/p_C ratio that would be mutually satisfactory:

(1) 1—if, at that ratio, X wants to import 50 food, Y wants to import 40 clothing.

(2) 1.5—if, at that ratio, X wants to import 30 food, Y wants to import 75 clothing.

(3) 1.1—if, at that ratio, X wants to import 40 food, Y wants to import 44 clothing.

(4) 0.5—if, at that ratio, X wants to import 30 food, Y wants to import 60 clothing.

---

finally become equal; (3). If, initially you find these p_F/p_C price-ratio figures difficult to handle, you are by no means the first to do so.

---

10. When the complication of "increasing costs" is introduced, production-possibility curves take on their more conventional shape, as in Fig. 34-2—or as they were depicted in the text's Chapter 2.

In Fig. 34-1, the production-possibility curve was a straight line. This was the "constant cost" case; the ratio p_F/p_C was fixed by the conditions of production. In the increasing-cost situation, this before-trade p_F/p_C ratio is *not* fixed; it varies according to the point on the "frontier line" at which production actually takes place. And *consumers* decide that operating point, just as they did in the constant-cost case (see question 4). However, so long as there is price competition, the price ratio p_F/p_C resulting must match the slope of the production-possibility line at that point. Otherwise, just as in Fig. 34-1's constant-cost case, producers find that there is an "overpriced" and an "underpriced" occupation, and they shift their production accordingly.

If, in Fig. 34-2, the pre-trade equilibrium of country X (at left) is indicated by E_0, the straight tangent line at that point should indicate the ratio p_F/p_C. (Strictly speaking, a minus

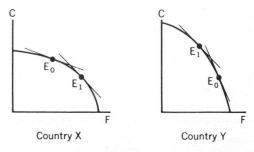

Country X   Country Y

Fig. 34-2

sign precedes that slope value, to indicate that "more of C must mean less of F," or vice versa. But, with the minus sign neglected—and in this question, we do neglect it—this slope value indicates the price ratio.)

Think of the tangency line at E_0 as though it were the actual production-possibility line for a tiny distance on either side of E_0. You can then employ the reasoning used with respect to Fig. 34-1 to understand why the pre-trade price ratio must equal the slope of this tangency line.

a. Let E_0 (in right-hand part) similarly indicate country Y's before-trade equilibrium. The tangency line here is steeper than that of country X—i.e., the ratio p_F/p_C is markedly higher in country *(X / Y)*. When trade opens up, country X would export *(F / C)* and import *(F / C)*.

b. The two points E_1 indicate a possible after-trade equilibrium, with respect to *production*. (Consumption equilibria are not shown, to avoid complicating the diagram.) The two slopes at the two points E_1 are equal, indicating a common after-trade price ratio. In the constant-cost case, each country gives up completely production of the good it imports. In the increasing-cost case as here illustrated, this *(is / is not)* the case. For example, country X *(continues / does not continue)* to produce some C. Nevertheless, her production has changed. She is producing *(more / less)* of F than she did before trade. Part of this additional F is exported, part she consumes at home. (REMEMBER: international trade allows the country to consume more of both commodities.)

---

a. Y; *F*; *C*. *b.* is not; continues; more.

QUIZ: Multiple Choice

1. *Country* H *both produces commodity* X *at home and imports it from country* K. *One of the following is* not *a possible explanation for this phenomenon, namely,* (1) with reduced output of X, H's producers of X can successfully compete with imports; (2) K's output of X is insufficiently large to be able to supply all H's needs; (3) H still has a comparative advantage in the production of X; (4) H and K have not yet reached their equilibrium price ratio or ratios and are still adjusting to foreign trade; (5) production is being carried on under conditions of increasing costs.

2. *If free international trade is opened up between two countries hitherto isolated from one another,* (1) the relative share of national income going to "scarce" factors in both countries may fall, but the absolute amount of real income going to such factors must rise because of the increase in total income; (2) the relative share of income going to all factors is likely to be increased; (3) the absolute amount of national income going to "scarce" factors in both countries may decrease, but the relative share going to such factors must increase; (4) it is possible for both the relative share and the absolute amount of income going to the "scarce" factors to be decreased; (5) none of the preceding will be true.

3. *In country* A, *before discovery of any international trade opportunity, the ratio* p_X/p_Y *is 2—i.e., 1 unit of commodity* X *is considered equal in value to 2 units of commodity* Y. *If country* A *were suddenly to be confronted with an international trading ratio* (p_X / p_Y) *of 1½, then it would wish to export* (1) some definite amount of X; (2) X, but would need to know X's absolute price before deciding *how much* of X to export; (3) some definite amount of Y; (4) Y, but would need to know Y's absolute price before deciding *how much* of Y to export; (5) either X or Y, depending on the absolute prices of X and Y.

4. *Country* A's *before-trade price ratio* p_X/p_Y *is 2, just as in question 3. The opportunity of trading with one other nation, country* B, *now opens up.* B's *before-trade price ratio* p_X/p_Y *is 3. Which alternative in question 3 would then be correct as to country* A's *export wishes?* (1). (2). (3). (4). (5).

5. *In question 4, the before-trade price ratios* p_X / p_Y *for countries* A *and* B *were 2 and 3 respectively. If free international trade opens up between* A *and* B, *with transport costs and other impediments to trade so low that they can be considered zero, then, after trade has become established,* (1) both the price ratios 2 and 3 will still persist; (2) there will still be two price ratios, one for each country, but their values will no longer be 2 and 3; (3) there will be only one common price ratio, whose value could possibly exceed 3 or be less than 2; (4) there will be only one common price ratio, whose value must be somewhere between the limits of 2 and 3; (5) none of the outcomes above is necessarily correct.

6. *The after-trade price ratio or price ratios described in question 5 will* (1) apply only to each country's comparative-advantage commodity; (2) apply only to the imported commodity, production costs still governing that of the exported commodity; (3) apply only for international trade purposes; (4) apply within both countries domestically, as well as in international trade; (5) not be correctly described by any of the above, necessarily.

7. *In the situation of questions 4 through 6, the resulting after-trade* p_X / p_Y *equilibrium price ratio could be as follows:* (1) 2.4, with A exporting 300 of X, B exporting 240 of Y; (2) 2.6, with A exporting 200 of X, B exporting 520 of Y; (3) 2.8, with A exporting 280 of Y, B exporting 100 of X; (4) 2.9, with A exporting 290 of X, B exporting 100 of Y; (5) 3.1, with A exporting 300 of X, B exporting 930 of Y.

8. *In Fig. 34-3, the production-possibility curves of three different countries are shown by the line DF. All three refer to the production of commodities X and Y (and the scales of measurement are the same in all). From these diagrams it is evident that* (1) A and B indicate increasing-cost situations, C a decreasing-cost one; (2) trade between A and B would be possible, but it is not likely that either A or B could trade profitably with C; (3) A and B indicate constant-cost situations, C an increasing-cost one; (4) all three indicate constant-

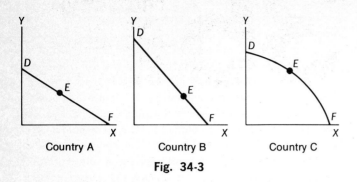

Fig. 34-3

cost situations; (5) C has greater freedom in choosing the quantities of X and Y it wants to produce than has A or B.

9. *If free international trade were to begin between countries A and B (Fig. 34-3), then we would expect country A to* (1) export Y and discontinue production of X; (2) export Y, but continue some production of X at home; (3) export X and discontinue production of Y; (4) export X, but continue some production of Y at home; (5) perhaps do any of the above—Fig. 34-3 does not furnish enough information to indicate what A would do in this situation.

10. *In Fig. 34-3, the E's represent each country's before-trade production and consumption point. If free international trade were to open up between countries A and B, we would expect these equilibrium points to change as follows:* (1) As to both production and consumption, each country would move toward point D or else point F, depending on whether its comparative advantage was in Y or in X. (2) As to consumption, each country would move toward D or else F, and as to production, E would remain unchanged. (3) As to production, each country would move to D or else to F, and as to consumption, to a point outside (northeast of) DF. (4) As to production, each country would move to D or else to F, and as to consumption, E would remain unchanged. (5) None of the above, since the changes resulting from trade would not be illustrated by diagrams such as this.

11. *If one country has a comparative advantage in producing X, then in terms of Fig. 34-3, when trade is opened up, its domestic production-possibility line will* (1) shift outward, toward the northeast; (2) rotate outward somewhat, pivoting on point F; (3) rotate outward somewhat, pivoting on point D; (4) shift inward somewhat; (5) remain unchanged.

12. *If country C (Fig. 34-3) enters into international trade with some other country or countries, it can be expected to* (1) import Y and discontinue home production of Y; (2) import Y, but continue some home production of Y; (3) import X and discontinue home production of X; (4) import X, but continue some home production of X; (5) continue some home production of the commodity imported, but the information given is insufficient to indicate if this will be X or Y.

QUIZ: Other

Below is a table (comparable to Table 34-2 in the text) showing production and consumption situations of two countries before trade. The exchange ratio of 4/5 in America means that 4 units of food are there considered equal in value to (and could be exchanged for) 5 units of clothing (hence that $p_F/p_C = 5/4$). Similarly, Europe's exchange ratio of 8/6 means that 8 units of food are considered equal in value to (and could be exchanged for) 6 units of clothing (hence that $p_F/p_C = 6/8$). Both countries produce under constant-cost conditions—i.e., their production-possibility curves are straight lines.

	Exchange Ratio, F for C	Food			Clothing		
		P	C	X(+) or M(−)	P	C	X(+) or M(−)
Before trade:							
America	4 / 5	200	200	0	250	250	0
Europe	8 / 6	80	80	0	180	180	0
World	None	280	280	0	430	430	0
After trade:							
America	_____	___	___	___	___	___	___
Europe	_____	___	___	220	___	___	___
World	11 / 10	___	___	___	___	___	___
Trade gains:							
America		___			___		
Europe		___			___		

After trade is opened up, the exchange ratio is 11/10, or 11 food exchange for 10 clothing. Europe exports 220 of food. From this scanty (but sufficient) information, complete all the remaining blanks, just as was done in the text. (You will probably find it necessary to figure out each country's production-possibility curve.) *P* signifies production; *C*, consumption; *X*, exports; *M*, imports.

35 PROTECTIVE TARIFFS, QUOTAS, AND FREE TRADE

THE COMPARATIVE-ADVANTAGE OUTLINE of trade, as presented in the preceding chapter, deliberately puts aside two sets of considerations that often are critical in actual economic decision making.

First, it disregards all financial aspects of international trade: capital movements, balance-of-payments deficits, overvalued currencies, foreign exchange shortages.

Second, it assumes that each country manages to operate continually at the full-employment level: it is always "on" its production-possibility frontier rather than inside it. There are no problems of widespread unemployment; there is no inflationary pressure.

Does its disregard of these hard problems mean that the comparative-advantage account of free trade is meaningless? Not at all. These matters *must* be pushed to one side in order to demonstrate the equally hard but often obscured fact of the gains from trade.

Three principal reasons (often working in combination) explain most of the actual or proposed restrictions on foreign trade: (1) The country fears unemployment, and regards imports as generators of unemployment, insofar as they are substitutes for domestically produced goods. (2) The country is short of foreign exchange reserves. (3) There are always particular groups which benefit from protection, and they bring (or try to bring) political pressure accordingly.

In a period of heavy unemployment, for example, it is hard to preach comparative advantage and free trade to legislators and businessmen. They may argue—and indeed may be correct in arguing—that a decrease in imports would raise domestic employment. So they may advocate an increase in protective tariffs.

Such an attempt to "export unemployment" may be canceled out when other countries retaliate with similar tariff increases aimed at us. However, it would be wrong to insist that import restrictions can never reduce unemployment, nor raise GNP. The proper objection is that such restrictions are clumsy and inappropriate methods. The use of fiscal and monetary policies, as discussed in Part 2 of the text, is far more effective. Moreover, these policies avoid the dubious ethics of trying to foist off your unemployment onto other nations; hence they do not incur the danger of retaliation.

There are other arguments, perhaps valid arguments, against free trade. Given reasonable assurance that unemployment can be handled by methods other than tariff or quota protection, most people in large, developed countries find it fairly easy to accept the free-trade principle. Those who live in a less developed country may be more hesitant. They look at the world's most prosperous nations; they hope that in due course their own country will enjoy equally high standards of production and income. And they wonder if some restriction on the import of particular goods may not be needed in order to widen productive and employment opportunities, and to foster their nation's industrial growth.

Less developed nations have made many misguided attempts to encourage the growth of local industry through protection. But as to what any such nation *should* do, the evidence is by no means all in yet.

1. *a.* The "mercantilist" approach to international trade argued that a nation should try to have (*exports / imports*) in excess of (*exports / imports*)—hence the phrase "favorable balance of trade." The surplus so obtained would be used to acquire (*merchandise / gold*). The mercantilist position was thus strongly disposed toward (*protectionism / free trade*). It was a convenient argument for many (*producer / consumer*) groups seeking protection against competition.

The underlying mercantilist philosophy was that a nation ought to apply the same principles of prudence appropriate for a family. It is prudent for a family to try to save part of its income. The nation, mercantilists said, is just the family on a larger scale. And they equated saving, at the national level, with the accumulation of gold.

The argument is not totally fallacious. Any nation will find it desirable to have reserves of gold (or foreign exchange) to cope with changing events which may produce balance-of-payments deficits. But even at the family level, the argument for "prudence" is wrong if interpreted as meaning that families must hoard their money. Saving which is not allowed to flow into investment spending (as Part 2 indicated) leads only to depression and to a fall in saving.

b. It would be quite (*possible / impossible*) for every nation to practice the mercantilist philosophy successfully, since it is (*possible / impossible*) for every nation to have a surplus of exports. A general attempt to practice this philosophy, by trying to expand exports and restrict imports, would lead to a major *(rise / fall)* in *(exports / imports / both exports and imports)*.

---

a. exports; imports; gold; protectionism; producer. *b.* impossible; impossible; fall; both exports and imports.

---

2. Often it is argued that a high tariff *(a)* brings revenue for the government, and *(b)* protects the domestic industry against competition. There is an inconsistency in using both of these arguments. Why?

_____

_____ .

The more revenue brought in, the less protection; and vice versa. A tariff sufficiently high to keep out all imports brings in zero revenue.

---

3. The "scientific tariff" is proposed as one which would be set at a level just sufficient to (pick one):
(1) Protect the domestic industry in time of recession.
(2) Cancel out the cost advantage enjoyed by foreign producers (e.g., "cheap foreign labor").
(3) Foster the growth of domestic industry whose development is considered in the national interest.

The text *(accepts / rejects with qualifications / rejects outright)* the scientific-tariff argument, on the grounds that (pick one):
(1) Such a tariff rarely succeeds in fostering industry growth.
(2) There are other and better means of coping with recession-induced unemployment.
(3) International cost differences form the basis for the greater part of international trade, and for the real income gains from such trade.

---

(2); rejects outright; (3).

---

4. *a.* In a country such as the United States, a pro-tariff argument sometimes put forward is that American producers cannot compete against "cheap foreign labor." The free-trade response to this argument is that (pick one):
(1) Such cheap labor is simply a particular illustration of the international cost differences on which mutually profitable trade is principally based.
(2) The cheap-labor argument is sometimes valid as to the imposition of a tariff, even though it has often been used to excess.
(3) Where cheap foreign labor does put the domestic industry at a disadvantage, the proper remedy is a subsidy or quota, not a tariff.

b. If the United States were to impose a tariff on imported industrial goods, it would reduce United States exports of (say) agricultural goods if (pick one):

(1) But only if, foreign nations retaliate with a counter-tariff against such agricultural goods.
(2) Foreign earnings of American dollars are reduced by this tariff to the point that other nations can no longer buy the agricultural goods, regardless of the imposition or nonimposition of a counter-tariff.

c. The "peril-point" provision in United States tariff legislation comes into play when import volume threatens the survival of domestic producers. The text's verdict as to a tariff so imposed is that (pick one):
(1) It is valid where considerations of national security are involved.
(2) On economic grounds, the industry ought to be exposed to that peril, even to the point of being killed off thereby.

d. If another country harms us by erecting a tariff against our goods, our own position *(will / will not)* normally be improved if we impose a retaliatory tariff.

e. If a country happens to be economically powerful, and also important in international trade, it may find that a moderate tariff improves its real-income position, due to a change in the

_____ .

---

a. (1). *b.* (2). *c.* (2). *d.* will not. *e.* terms of trade.

---

5. *a.* The text concedes that the "national-survival" argument for tariff protection for a particular industry *may* be valid—although it is one to be viewed with a beginning skepticism, since it has so often been used by special-interest groups. The text's suggestion is that where concern for national survival (particularly in wartime) does seem to warrant protection for some domestic industry, the best remedy is a *(quota / tariff / subsidy)*.

b. The text notes also that there *may* be a valid argument for imposition of tariffs in the case of the *(less developed / richer)* nations, because such tariffs *(may be one of the few sources of revenue for government that are administratively feasible / are almost the only effective means of protecting domestic employment in time of recession)*.

c. The "infant-industry" argument is one often invoked within the less developed nations. It is that the domestic industry needs protection when it is young and inexperienced, hence unable to stand up to the competition of mature foreign producers. The text's verdict on this argument is that (pick one):
(1) It has at least some validity in principle, although in practice many industries have proven perpetual infants, never able to survive without protection.
(2) It has no validity at all, since international trade is founded on natural cost advantages.

Tariff arguments such as the infant-industry one move us from the realm of static economic analysis to that of dynamic analysis. (Chapter 34, on comparative advantage, is a good example of static analysis. Such material puts its emphasis upon equilibrium, and the properties of equilibrium positions. Dynamic analysis deals with change—e.g., with growth—and with the process of change.) In general, the text's position is that the economic arguments for protection are probably stronger in the (static / *dynamic*) region of analysis.

---

a. subsidy. *b.* less developed; may be one of the few revenue sources administratively feasible. *c.* (1); dynamic.

---

6. *a.* Free trade is sometimes described as "a substitute for international factor mobility." That is, if country A is unusually short of some input or factor *X*, then A should import commodities which draw heavily upon *X* from country B, where *X* is more readily available and hence is cheaper. Therefore the import of commodities which "contain" the services of input *X* is a substitute for the (*export* / *import*) of *X* itself.

b. The "relatively scarce" input or factor of production in the United States is usually considered to be (*labor* / *capital*). (Note, however, that one study questions this conclusion— see footnote 4 in the text's Some Less Obvious Fallacies section.)

c. Given the assumption or conclusion of part *b*, it follows that the United States should specialize in the production (and export) of commodities requiring relatively (*large* / *small*) quantities of labor by comparison with capital and should import commodities requiring relatively (*large* / *small*) labor amounts.

d. As a result of such free trade, the total output available for consumption in the United States would be higher than in the absence of trade. If freer trade were to be adopted, the income position of certain labor groups—those suffering from import competition—would be harmed. The text suggests that with respect to labor as a whole, the adoption of such a freer trade policy (*would be bound to improve* / *most probably would improve*) labor's absolute real income. The income position of labor (taken as a whole) in absolute terms (*just possibly might* / *could not possibly*) decline, as a result of freer trade.

---

a. import. *b.* labor. *c.* small; large. *d.* most probably would improve; just possibly might.

QUIZ: Multiple Choice

1. *One argument for tariffs is that they should be imposed where the level of foreign wages is much below the level of domestic wages, to enable the domestic producer to compete. This argument* (1) is conceded by most economists to be correct, although sometimes exaggerated in order to justify some level of tariff protection; (2) is fallacious because there are almost no instances in which there is any real difference between the level of foreign and domestic wages; (3) ignores the fact that differences in relative costs constitute the princi-

pal basis for international trade; (4) may be correct with respect to money wages at home and abroad, but is not correct with respect to real wages; (5) is not correctly described by any of these.

2. *Country A imposes a new tariff on country B's products. Country B is considering a retaliatory tariff on A's goods. On economic grounds, B should (according to the text)* (1) reject the idea of a tariff increase, except perhaps as a bluff; (2) make the retaliatory tariff less than A's tariff; (3) make the retaliatory tariff more than A's tariff; (4) impose the retaliatory tariff only if B is in a situation of full employment; (5) appreciate the price of its currency relative to B's currency.

3. *The policy of the mercantilists with respect to foreign trade was that* (1) imports should exceed exports—i.e., the country should "get more than it gives"—in order to increase real income at home as much as possible; (2) exports should exceed imports in order to bring in gold; (3) since this trade represented commerce, it should be encouraged to the greatest possible degree—i.e., there should be free trade; (4) exports should be kept in balance with imports, and at the lowest possible level of both; (5) trade in agricultural products was more important than trade in industrial goods.

4. *The principal reason high-wage American labor does not require tariff protection from lower-paid foreign labor is because* (1) no American labor would be thrown out of work even if there were no tariffs; (2) the high per-man-hour productivity of American labor in many industries is an offset to the lower cost of foreign labor; (3) American consumers tend to buy American-made goods in preference to foreign-made goods; (4) a high-wage American industry can be presumed to have a comparative advantage over foreign competitors; (5) of none of these reasons.

5. *The argument by workers in a protected industry in the United States that free trade would worsen the income position of American labor is (according to the text)* (1) not valid even for workers in that industry after allowance is made for the improvement in real income afforded by cheaper imports; (2) not valid even for workers in that industry after allowance is made for the employment effect of increased exports; (3) valid for workers in that industry but probably not valid for American labor as a whole; (4) valid for workers in that industry and probably valid for American labor as a whole; (5) probably valid for workers in that industry but unquestionably invalid for American labor as a whole.

6. *From a purely economic point of view, the best level at which to set a tariff (under static assumptions) is* (1) the peril point; (2) the amount needed to bring the level of foreign costs up to the level of domestic costs; (3) zero; (4) a level sufficiently low so that it is not likely to invite retaliation by other countries; (5) the level at which revenues from the tariff will be at a maximum.

7. *If the principle of a scientific tariff were adopted with respect to all imports, the result would be as follows:* (1) A few commodity imports would be reduced, but the amount of most would remain unchanged. (2) There would be no basis in terms of cost savings for any international trade. (3) The flow of some imports would increase and that of others would decrease. (4) It is impossible to predict the result in terms of changes in import flows, but it would be the most reasonable compromise between the gains from free trade and the need for employment at home. (5) None of the preceding.

8. *One argument for tariff protection is that a tariff would improve the terms of trade in dealing with other nations. This argument, according to the text,* (1) is at bottom a refinement of the mercantilist argument that a nation's exports should exceed its imports; (2) may be valid if the tariff-imposing country is a relatively large one, and the tariff is a relatively small one; (3) is at bottom a refined version of the scientific-tariff argument, hence has no validity; (4) may be valid if the tariff-imposing country is unimportant in world trade for the commodity or commodities involved; (5) may be valid if it is applied to all the country's imports, without or almost without exception.

9. *It may be argued that a tariff should be imposed on a commodity if that commodity is considered essential to material well-being and if it is suspected that the foreign suppliers thereof might use their supply control for purposes of political blackmail—as in the case of oil. The text's verdict on this argument is that* (1) if the commodity is deemed really essential, the tariff is justified; (2) if the commodity is deemed really essential, a subsidy would be preferable to a tariff; (3) the best remedy for threats of political blackmail is to insist on all-around free trade; (4) although the imposition of a tariff might be used as a threat, political moves should be met by political countermoves (even to the threat of war), not by economic moves; (5) if the commodity is deemed really essential, its domestic production should be nationalized.

10. *If we reduce the flow of import goods by imposing heavy tariffs, our exports are likely to be affected as follows:* (1) They will be reduced if other countries retaliate by imposing tariffs against those exports (as is likely), but not otherwise. (2) There is little reason to expect that they will be affected at all, since retaliatory tariffs have usually proved ineffective. (3) They will be increased, since other countries will find it necessary to buy more from us to compensate for the higher cost of the goods they sell us. (4) They will be increased if the tariff raises the level of employment and national product at home, but not otherwise. (5) They are likely to be reduced in all or almost all circumstances.

11. *The argument for free trade relies essentially on the "comparative-advantage" analysis of Chapter 34—analysis which in turn relies on certain simplifying assumptions. The protectionist case is accordingly strengthened if it can point to any such assumption whose relaxation might perhaps alter the conclusions reached. One such comparative-advantage assumption is that* (1) the costs of transporting goods from one country to another are negligible; (2) trade is essentially a barter exchange, and there are no problems arising out of the establishment of foreign exchange rates; (3) comparative costs, not absolute costs, are what must be taken into consideration in understanding the nature of international trade; (4) production is "constant-cost" production—i.e., the production-possibility frontier is a straight line; (5) each country exports one good only, and imports one good only.

12. *The Latin American economist Raúl Prebisch believes that in the long run the terms of trade have been gradually shifting to the advantage of producers of industrial products and to the disadvantage of producers of agricultural products. Believing this trend will continue, he argues* (1) that "agricultural" nations should maintain or increase their tariffs on industrial products; (2) that "industrial" nations should maintain or increase their tariffs on agricultural products; (3) that "agricultural" nations should reduce or remove their tariffs on industrial products; (4) that "industrial" nations should reduce or remove their tariffs on agricultural products; (5) in none of the preceding ways.

13. *A valid counter to the argument that a tariff results in increased money wages in the protected industry is that* (1) workers in that industry will in all probability suffer a loss in real wages; (2) workers in other industries will suffer a loss in real wages; (3) the increase in money wages in the protected industry will cause unemployment; (4) tariffs cannot increase money wages in any industry; (5) any increase in real wages is likely to lead to inflation.

14. *The "peril-point" tariff argument is* (1) valid insofar as it does not increase the level of domestic prices; (2) an outright denial of the comparative-advantage principle; (3) generally invalid, but can (according to the text) be valid with respect to a few domestic industries which are growing in importance; (4) valid (according to the text) if the domestic unemployment level is unacceptably high; (5) one of the few recognized exceptions to the general application of the comparative-advantage principle.

EVERY DEVELOPED NATION must have a satisfactory monetary mechanism. The banking system's ability to create money and credit must be subject to some restraint, yet sufficiently flexible to expand as output increases over the years. The establishment of such a credit system does not come about automatically or easily. In the United States, it was not until the creation of the Federal Reserve System in 1913 that the earlier record of unstable banking and occasional "panics" was ended.

The needs of international trade for an effective money and credit system are essentially the same as those of domestic commerce. During the nineteenth century and up to World War I, the gold standard (see Chapter 33) was the ruling international money mechanism. Some students argue that the gold standard worked almost automatically; others insist that it worked only because Great Britain, as the world's banker, made it work. Moreover, it is not entirely clear to what extent the gold mechanism contributed to the relative stability of that period, and to what extent it worked, because the times were stable enough to permit it to work.

In any event, World War I ended this golden era. Britain returned to gold after the war, but in a weakened condition. Most economists think that Britain's domestic economy suffered dreadfully from her effort to keep the pound on gold at an overvalued rate. A crisis in 1931 ended the attempt. The period thereafter was one of international chaos. Restrictive trade policies became the rule as each nation struggled to protect its reserves of gold and foreign exchange. Mercantilist policies were adopted even if the mercantilist philosophy was not. Nations and corporations which had borrowed internationally were forced into default because they could not earn the foreign exchange needed to pay interest or principal on their borrowings. The characteristics of a domestic banking and credit crisis (including the damage to production and employment) were thus repeated on an international scale.

After World War II, two new international agencies were set up: the International Monetary Fund, and the World Bank. The operation of these agencies was intended to prevent any recurrence of the chaos of the 1930s. The World Bank has been reasonably successful. The difficulties of the 1930s have not been repeated.

But the IMF has been increasingly exposed to strains not envisaged at the time of its creation—so that, in 1975, it had to alter its operating rules. There is still disagreement (notably between the United States and France) as to the extent to which exchange rates should be stable or "floating." So the shape of the future international monetary system still remains unclear.

1. *a.* Experience before the Depression of the 1930s seems to indicate that loans made by the United States to foreign countries (*increased / decreased*) American employment and GNP, because the dollars so supplied led to (*an increase / a decrease*) in American (*exports / imports*).

b. During the Depression, many of these foreign borrowers defaulted on their loans. The problem here (in part) is that if a country is to pay principal or interest on a loan in dollars, it must earn dollars. And during the 1930s, the United States (*increased / decreased*) its tariffs, thus making it (*easier / harder*) for foreigners to earn the dollars needed. (Of course, the low level of American incomes and production in those years meant that it would have been more difficult to sell goods in the United States even without the tariff increase.)

c. In a depression, the incentive to "protect employment at home" by (*encouraging / discouraging*) imports is strong. But insofar as you succeed in reducing imports (say by higher tariffs), the foreign nation which formerly sold you those imports must suffer: you are "exporting your unemployment." This constitutes a "beggar-your-neighbor" policy.

The text's verdict is that a depression-level GNP should be remedied by (*tariff increases / tariff decreases / fiscal and monetary policies*). But even if the nature of this remedy is generally understood (in the 1930s, it was not), it may be difficult to put into practice if depression is virtually worldwide, as was true in the 1930s. If you adopt this policy while your neighbor countries do not, the increase in your GNP will (*increase / decrease*) your imports, and so may cause you to (*lose / gain*) gold or foreign exchange reserves.

---

a. increased; increase; exports. *b.* increased; harder. *c.* discouraging; fiscal and monetary policies; increase; lose.

---

2. The danger to your reserves of gold and foreign monies, outlined above, is most serious if you are trying to hold a fixed value for your own currency in the foreign exchange markets. Remember that this discussion still refers principally to the experience of the 1930s—a period when maintenance of fixed exchange rates was still considered very much a part of good international behavior. This emphasis upon fixed rates drew on past experience. It was in large part a heritage of the old gold standard. (For earlier discussion of the set of issues here involved, see questions 3 through 7, pp. 257–260.) The full gold standard, with all its requirements, had largely disintegrated after 1931. But its influence persisted.

By the 1930s, it was of course understood that if you stuck to a fixed exchange rate but were losing reserves in the process, there was no automatic mechanism that would go into action to check this reserve loss. Hence, as part of the good-behavior code, there had evolved the notion of "the rules of the game."

a. The first of these rules said that, if losing reserves, you should adjust the level of your domestic interest rates (particularly short-term rates) so as to attract foreign monies. That is, you should *(lower / raise)* interest rates. There are large amounts of "footloose" worldwide money capital; it is highly interest-rate-sensitive, and will move rapidly from one country to another—provided the nation which has raised its interest rates has good capital markets and is considered a stable country. This money capital, seeking your higher rates, shows up as a foreign demand for your domestic currency. You have been using foreign reserves to maintain the fixed international value of that currency. Now your need to do this is ended or diminished. The practice of adjusting interest rates in order to cope with reserve problems is widely used even today.

Up to a point, this policy works. If the reserve loss is minor, and if only a small *(increase / decrease)* in your interest rates is needed, the problem may be resolved with little impact on the domestic economy. However, if the interest-rate change must be pushed further, then clearly you are implementing *(an easier / a tighter)* monetary policy. This may be in keeping with your domestic needs—or it may not. Should your country happen to be in recession at the time, then you want *(an easy / a tight)* money policy. That is, in the matter of monetary policy, there arises the possibility of a clash between domestic needs and foreign needs.

b. Perhaps you may be able to reconcile this conflict by using the tighter monetary policy to improve your foreign-reserve position and, concurrently, using an easier *fiscal* policy to cope with your recession. But as you pull out of recession, the rise in GNP affects your imports: They probably will go *(up / down)*. This will *(add to / diminish)* the pressure on your exchange rate; it will *(improve / worsen)* your foreign-reserve position.

Moreover, there was a stronger interpretation of "the rules of the game"—one especially favored by some central banks and commercial banks with large international dealings. In this view, any nation experiencing a continuing loss of gold or foreign exchange was overspending its income and ought to use *both fiscal and monetary policies* to restrain or reduce its GNP. Reducing incomes would *(cut down on / increase)* import spending. It should free *(less / more)* of the nation's resources for export sales. Thus the foreign-balance position should be *(worsened / improved)*.

Under full-employment conditions, often it makes good sense to insist that a nation with persistent reserve-loss troubles is spending beyond its income. But in conditions of deep depression (like the 1930s), when it is obvious that the nation should try to develop *more* employment for its labor force, the notion that incomes should be *reduced* is abhorrent. In such situations, if you are trying to abide by "the rules of the game," you face a truly serious clash between domestic needs (to increase employment) and foreign needs (to maintain the value of your currency). The so-called good-behavior game rules then become stupid rules, by both domestic and international standards.

Hence, in the 1930s, some nations disposed of the problem of adhering to "the rules of the game" by dropping out of the game. That is, they allowed their currencies to depreciate in the foreign exchange markets. The text suggests that these countries recovered domestically *(more / less)* rapidly than those others which held to the vestiges of the gold standard by trying to maintain a stable price for their currencies.

---

a. raise; increase; a tighter; an easy. *b.* up; add to; worsen; cut down on; more; improved; more.

---

3. At the close of World War II, the Western nations created two new international agencies: the International Monetary Fund (IMF), and the World Bank. (The World Bank and other postwar developments, such as the European Common Market, are discussed in later questions for this chapter. The IMF was the agency principally concerned with the issues discussed in questions 1 and 2.)

The intended goal behind the IMF's formation was this: There were to be, so far as possible, stable exchange rates. But no nation would have to push itself deliberately into recession or depression just to maintain a steady international value for its currency—as strict application of "the rules of the game" mentioned in question 2 might sometimes have required it to do.

Each participating nation deposited with the IMF a supply of its own currency (and, in some cases, gold). These deposits established a "lending pool," from which any nation could borrow if temporarily losing reserves as a consequence of maintaining a fixed rate. It was of course understood that persisting reserve losses indicated some form of "fundamental disequilibrium" which could not be sustained by continual borrowing. A nation could depreciate its currency value by up to 10 per cent if it wished. Further depreciation required "consultation with the Fund"—in effect, international approval.

Today, with emphasis leaning strongly toward the need for "floating rates," it may seem odd that so much effort should have gone into establishment of a maintenance-of-fixed-rates system. But remember from question 7, p. 259, that there were—and are—valid arguments for steady rates as well as for floating ones.

In the course of time, it became evident that the IMF's "lending pool" of national currencies—dollars, pounds sterling, francs, etc.—was *(insufficient / excessive)* and in need of *(reduction / supplement)*. A new "international money"—although one to be used only in settlements between governments or central banks—was created. Its name was

_____ .

The prime movers behind this new money were those who felt that gold should be eliminated (or its status reduced, at least) as an international reserve. (For more on this, see question 8, p. 287.) Thus an alternative and more colloquial name

for these SDRs was "_____."

These SDRs are created just as commercial banks create money through their lending activity (Chapter 16). The total amount of their creation each year is settled by vote of IMF members. The extent to which any nation can draw SDRs is governed by its quota participation in the IMF.

For 25 years, the IMF operated successfully. Its rules were in general (although with exceptions) accepted. But in the mid-1960s, the strains of maintaining the system grew more apparent. Increasingly, nations took to changes in the international value of their domestic currencies with or without IMF approval. Finally, in 1975, the IMF conceded that in conditions of extreme economic turbulence, floating rates were (at least temporarily) necessary.

---

insufficient; supplement; Special Drawing Rights; paper gold.

---

4. Why all this turbulence, after a considerable period of relative stability? To answer, we must return again to the early post-World War II period.
a. At that time, the United States was not only the world's industrial giant; it was a nation whose productive capacity had emerged from the war unscathed. Consequently, there was a 10-year period of acute "dollar shortage." The dollar was the only currency that could buy much-needed United States goods. Had the period been a floating-rate one, the dollar's exchange-market value would have greatly *(depreciated / appreciated)*.

This dollar shortage was considerably relieved by the Marshall Plan, created by the United States to assist the war-ravaged nations in economic reconstruction. It was to the interest of the United States that these nations should once again become prosperous trading partners. Fear that they might turn communist also played its part. Nevertheless, by international standards, it was a notably generous act.

The war-damaged nations (especially those in Western Europe, and Japan) regained economic health with remarkable speed; the text describes their recovery as "a miracle." The Marshall Plan began this rehabilitation. Thereafter, in Europe, development of the Common Market (question 7, p. 287) was probably a major contributing factor. With recovery, the dependence of these nations on American goods was reduced. Indeed, with much-improved output capacity, their products became *(increasingly / less)* competitive with those American goods in world markets. The dollar shortage dwindled. In time, it became converted into a "dollar glut."

b. Many factors contributed to this turnaround in the dollar's standing. The text discusses them at some length; question 5 covers them briefly here. But some considerations require immediate mention.

Most of the big American corporations were attracted by the postwar opportunities for new markets abroad (mainly in Europe, but elsewhere in the world as well). They built new plants abroad; they bought up foreign corporations. Since foreign monies were needed for this activity (which means that U.S. dollars were being offered), the effect was to *(depress / increase)* the demand for foreign currencies—i.e., to *(depress / increase)* the supply of dollars offered.

Moreover, these corporations brought to their new foreign plants much American technology. This expertise improved foreign productivity—and with it, foreign ability to compete against American-produced goods.

Nevertheless, the dollar's shift from surplus to glut cannot possibly be explained solely in terms of a shift in relative productivities and competitive standings. What had happened, beginning in the early postwar years, was that the U.S. dollar had become the world's money. (Before the war, the pound sterling had played this role. Postwar Britain was so weakened that the burden—or most of it—had to be transferred. Tradition was strong, though, and the pound was still quite extensively used as a world money, even though its position was now decidedly second to the dollar.)

Recall the comments which began this Study Guide chapter: The international community needs a money stock to carry on its trading, just as the domestic economy needs one. Only central banks and governments dealt with the International Monetary Fund. Commercial banks, corporations, and other concerns involved in international trade and finance kept substantial deposits of dollars just in order to settle their accounts with one another.

The all-essential requirement in a money is confidence. So long as the dollar remained strong, it functioned well. But when evidence began to appear that changes in productivity and competitive positions had made it a little less strong than hitherto, some dollar holders began to *(reduce / increase)* their holdings. They started to switch to German marks, Swiss francs, Dutch guilders, and so on. In the money community, news spreads fast. There arose the danger of a kind of international "bank run," in which the dollar's value might have been driven fantastically (*above / below*) the value which a comparison between American and foreign price levels would have indicated.

This bank-run threat was averted because foreign central banks, aware of the major crisis it would have brought about, (*bought up / sold*) the dollars which nervous private holders wanted to unload—although their purchases left some of those central banks with large dollar holdings about which they were not entirely happy.

c. By the mid-1960s, it was common knowledge that the dollar's position was weak, if only because of the big dollar overhang in foreign central bank holdings. The British pound was weak for more fundamental reasons. Some currencies were overvalued, others undervalued. There had to be, at the very least, revisions in the fixed rates. Widespread speculation on prospective rate changes began. (For more on this, see again question 7, p. 259.) In the crises of the late 1960s and early 1970s, it became evident that much of this "speculation" was the activity of multinational corporations which handle many currencies, sometimes in huge amounts. To the treasurers of such companies, it was only the most elementary prudence, if any currency seemed in danger of falling in value, to shift (*into / out of*) that currency. By their actions, they (*intensified / diminished*) the prospect that the currency *would* fall in value.

Part of the problem was that no adequate substitute for the U.S. dollar as a world money existed. (Despite its tribulations, the dollar is still extensively used for this purpose. The status of the British pound continues to dwindle.) This year's strong currency may prove to be next year's weak one. Just as with money, the essential requirement for successful operation of a stable exchange-rate system is confidence. So, in the early 1970s, the nations abandoned their efforts to maintain that system. They switched to floating rates—although often "dirty floats"—i.e., those in which central banks (*still / refuse to*) intervene against what are considered to be unnecessary or undesirable rate fluctuations. In 1975, the IMF gave reluctant and qualified approval to the floating-rate system.

a. appreciated; increasingly. *b.* increase; increase; reduce; below; bought up. *c.* out of; intensified; still.

5. *a.* The text cites seven factors as having contributed to the gradual deterioration of the U.S. dollar's postwar international status and to the associated worsening of the United States' balance-of-payments position. Three of these factors have just been discussed in question 4: heavy investment abroad by American firms; the gradual postwar improvement in foreign productivity, especially in Western Europe and Japan; and a loss of confidence abroad in the secure value of the U.S. dollar.

The five-item list below includes the four remaining factors cited in the text. One item is alien—i.e., it is not so cited. Which one?

(1) A quadrupled price of foreign-produced petroleum.
(2) Too much domestic inflation, especially after the Vietnam war.
(3) Large deficits incurred by federal and state governments within the United States.
(4) Persisting remnants of foreign discrimination against the sale of American goods.
(5) Generosity on the part of the United States in the matter of economic and military aid.

b. Thereafter, the text lists a series of possible remedies which might improve the U.S. balance of payments, and hence the dollar's international position. The latter half of this list consists of "second-best" remedies—i.e., measures to which there should be resort only if conditions were to grow so much worse that the United States found itself in a desperate condition, one resembling the plight of Britain in the late 1970s.

The list below consists principally of "first-best" remedies—but includes (by the text's measure) two "second-best" resorts. Which two?

(1) Restrict foreign travel by American residents.
(2) Require other nations to assume a greater share of the burden of economic aid and defense programs.
(3) Improve domestic technical productivity.
(4) Press for further reductions in foreign discrimination against the sale of American goods.
(5) Improve the circumstances under which American firms make their sales abroad—i.e., strengthen their selling practices.
(6) Impose higher tariffs or other restrictions on the import of foreign goods into the United States.

a. (3). *b.* (1); (6).

6. *a.* We return now to topics discussed earlier in the text chapter—specifically, to the international agencies established after World War II. One such agency, the International Monetary Fund, has already been reviewed. Another is the International Bank for Reconstruction and Development—more concisely, the World Bank.

The World Bank's task, in brief, is to channel money from the richer nations to less developed ones. In slightly more detail, the Bank's function is, with respect to such poorer countries, to (*make short-term loans / make long-term loans / provide foreign exchange for balance-of-payments shortages*). It provides funds for a less developed nation (*even if that nation can / only if that nation cannot*) borrow privately at a reasonable interest rate.

b. The Bank can make loans (pick one):
(1) Only from its capital, subscribed by member nations.

(2) From its capital, or by floating bond issues with principal and interest payments guaranteed by member nations.

The text suggests that in its early years, the Bank was rather too (*liberal / conservative*) in its loan policies, but that when Robert McNamara became its president (in 1968), it (*expanded / curtailed*) the scope of its activity.

c. Still another agency, newly established in the postwar years, was the General Agreement on Tariffs and Trade (GATT). The task assigned this body (it now has a permanent office in Geneva) was to work toward less protectionist trade policies. This objective was to be accomplished by preliminary organization work leading up to periodic international conferences—e.g., the "Kennedy Round" of 1967—bringing nations together around the conference table. Through bargaining, haggling, and compromise, they are expected to reduce the barriers—of which tariffs are simply the most obvious instance—which impede the free flow of goods across national boundaries.

---

a. make long-term loans; only if that nation cannot.
b. (2); conservative; expanded.

---

7. *a.* The European Common Market (formally, the European Economic Community) began with the signing of the Treaty of Rome in 1957. Originally, the EEC had six members (strike out the two nonmember names): Belgium, Britain, France, Italy, Luxembourg, the Netherlands, Spain, and West Germany. Subsequently, three additional members were admitted (again strike out the two nonmember names): Britain, Denmark, Ireland, Norway, Sweden.

A principal objective in the EEC's formation was the creation of a mass-production free-trade market—i.e., a market big enough to encourage European firms to take full advantage of economies of scale.

b. Opinions differ as to the degree of political unity that was originally intended, or that will ultimately result, when the EEC structure is completed. But in economic terms, the EEC provides for (*low / zero*) tariffs among members. Tariffs applied by members against outsiders are to be (*low / uniform / the same as they were before EEC*). Among members, movement of labor is to be (*free / subject to moderate restriction only / still considerably restricted*). Movements of money capital among them are (*free / restricted*).

It is interesting to note that—harking back to the issue of stable versus floating exchange rates—there has been strong pressure within the EEC in favor of a single "Eurocurrency"—which in practice means a set of fixed or near-fixed exchange rates among EEC members. (France has been the principal advocate of this fixed-rate system.) It has been described as the "snake-in-the-tunnel" plan. The snake is the member country's actual exchange rate (vis-à-vis the rate of any other member). This snake-rate may wriggle up or down a little—but only within tight upper and lower limits imposed by the top and bottom of a narrow tunnel.

Thus far, the snake-in-the-tunnel plan has been only moderately successful. The EEC's weakest members, Italy and Britain, have been forced to depreciate their currencies—i.e., to push outside the lower limit of the tunnel.

---

a. Britain and Spain; Norway and Sweden.
b. zero; uniform; free; free.

---

8. Resort to floating exchange rates has substantially reduced the need for large national reserves. Yet *some* reserves must still be kept; there are still international settlements to be made. What should be the role of gold in such settlements, and in reserves?

Opponents of gold consider it a barbarous relic left over from the early days of money—a relic which has already disappeared from domestic monies, and which is overdue for removal from the international scene. Gold is inflexible in supply; its quantity cannot be increased so as to match smoothly the expanding needs of international commerce and finance.

This supply inflexibility could be overcome by periodic increases in the price of gold. Thus, doubling its price would make the same physical quantity of gold stand for (*half / twice*) as much money value. But this price-increase technique has at least two disadvantages: (1) It would be an open invitation for undesirable speculation in future gold-price movements. (2) Benefits would accrue unduly to the few major gold-producing nations, notably the Soviet Union and South Africa.

Moreover, gold's opponents points out, an international substitute for gold has been developed: Special Drawing Rights. These SDRs can be issued, and increased, as dictated by the needs of international trade.

In contrast, many advocates of gold insist that it has "inherent" or "intrinsic" value. Economists have grown skeptical of phrases like "inherent value"; in seeking to explain value, they have turned increasingly to the factors of supply and demand. The world's total gold supply vastly exceeds the quantity usable for jewelry, dentistry, and industrial applications. Gold is valuable only because people *think* (and for a long time have thought) it is valuable. Still, this belief is no worse than the belief (or convention) that a piece of paper money carrying the seal of some government or the name of a central bank is valuable. Indeed, by past experience, confidence in gold is more solidly based. There are many instances in history (European history especially) when people who held gold as their asset fared well (because gold is inflexible in supply), whereas those who held paper money fared badly, because a stupid or desperate government had grossly over-issued that paper money.

The crucial rule for success in any money medium—be it

gold, paper, or china beads—is, then: Neither underissue nor overissue. When the Spaniards brought back huge quantities of Inca gold from South America in the sixteenth century, the resulting inflation in European prices was the same as would have been produced by a vast increase in paper money.

A compromise view would run as follows: It is impossible to rely solely on gold for international settlements (for reasons such as those cited at the beginning of this question.) Nevertheless, the belief that "gold has value" is still widespread—even among some governments. (The strength of a government's advocacy of gold tends to be correlated with the amount of gold that government has stored in its vaults. France under de Gaulle was a particularly strong advocate.) This traditional confidence in gold may be misplaced. But confidence is always a vital element in money; there is no point in seeking to violate a traditional belief so long as that belief does no great harm. Of course, using gold does at least some damage by benefiting unduly those few nations which happen to have large quantities beneath their ground. Still, the international reserves can have *two* components: gold, and SDRs. Needed increases in this money stock should be created by increases in the *(total of SDRs / price of gold)*.

Gold's opponents are not happy with this compromise. They believe that gold's retention sustains the myth of its "inherent value." This makes SDRs the *("second-class" / "first-class")* international asset—in circumstances when the international trading world must rely increasingly on a regulated supply of such "paper gold," just as national economies have had to make increasing use of bank-deposit money, rather than stick exclusively to coins and paper bills.

---

twice; total of SDRs; "second-class."

QUIZ: Multiple Choice

1. *International trade and finance grew rapidly after the close of World War II. The resulting need for greater international liquidity (particularly during the 1950s, and up to the mid-1960s) was met principally by* (1) new gold production; (2) gold released by the Soviet Union; (3) the credit-creating facilities of the World Bank; (4) Special Drawing Rights; (5) gold released by the United States plus increased foreign holdings of dollars.

2. *Suppose that there is worldwide depression. All countries operate on the gold standard. If one country increases its GNP by expansionary domestic monetary and fiscal policy, that country can in consequence be expected to* (1) gain gold from other countries because of the rise in its exports; (2) gain gold from other countries because of the fall in imports; (3) lose gold to other countries because of the fall in exports; (4) lose gold to other countries because of the rise in imports; (5) neither gain nor lose gold necessarily, since changes in exports and imports would cancel one another out.

3. *The United States is conducting dollar aid and dollar loan programs for foreign countries. Imagine that substantial unemployment develops in the United States. With respect to the removal of unemployment, U.S. policy concerning the aid and loan programs should be to* (1) increase the scope of both (unless this can be construed as an "exporting of unemployment" policy), since an increase in either can reasonably be expected to increase GNP; (2) try to switch from aid programs, since their burden is painful in time of depression, to loan programs, which promise some future return; (3) maintain aid programs insofar as is economically possible despite their cost in employment, but reduce loans, since the outflow of dollars intensifies the depression at home; (4) reduce both programs on purely economic grounds—but make the final decision in terms of noneconomic considerations as well; (5) reduce, on both economic and noneconomic grounds, both programs as much as reasonably can be done.

4. *One factor which contributed significantly to the balance-of-payments deficits experienced by the United States during the 1950s and 1960s was* (1) the activity of U.S. corporations in expanding their plants and operations abroad; (2) a large excess of interest and dividends paid foreigners over similar investment income received; (3) a substantial excess of merchandise exports over merchandise imports; (4) the export of gold; (5) very heavy imports of miscellaneous "services" (other than travel).

5. *A country is at full employment and is experiencing an undesirable degree of price inflation. Its reserves of gold and foreign exchange are gradually being reduced as a result of balance-of-payments deficits. Particularly if this country wants to postpone any decision on changing the foreign price of its currency, the monetary policy indicated is* (1) a tighter policy concerning domestic prices, but an easier policy concerning foreign reserves; (2) a tighter policy as it concerns both domestic prices and foreign reserves; (3) an easier policy as it concerns both domestic prices and foreign reserves; (4) an easier policy concerning domestic prices, but a tighter policy concerning foreign reserves; (5) a tighter policy as it concerns domestic prices, but no special policy as to foreign reserves, since domestic interest rates have no part to play in this problem.

6. *Change the conditions of question 5 in one respect only: The country is experiencing heavy unemployment but not an undesirable degree of price inflation. Which alternative in question 5 then becomes correct?* (1). (2). (3). (4). (5).

7. *The principal task assigned to the International Monetary Fund at the time of its organization was to* (1) serve as a partial substitute for the old gold standard in maintaining stable exchange rates; (2) try to maintain a high level of employment within member countries, so as to avoid any danger of competitive depreciation policies in the foreign exchange markets; (3) make loans to private companies in any country where the funds could not otherwise be borrowed at any reasonable interest rate; (4) facilitate the development of free trade "regions" similar to the European Common Market; (5) coordinate the views of the larger and more developed nations concerning exchange-rate and trade problems.

8. *It could also be said that the principal task assigned to the International Monetary Fund was to* (1) act as the world's banker in matters of both short-term and long-term credit; (2) make direct long-term loans to less developed nations when necessary, so as to assist in their economic development; (3) control international credit sufficiently to enable member nations to maintain their price levels at reasonably noninflationary levels; (4) help bridge short-run disequilibrium in any member nation's balance of payments; (5) work toward the gradual reduction of tariffs and elimination of protectionist policies among nations.

9. *Which alternative in question 8 would be correct had that question referred to the World Bank, not to the International Monetary Fund?* (1). (2). (3). (4). (5).

10. *Which alternative in question 8 would be correct had that question referred to GATT (the General Agreement on Tariffs and Trade), not to the International Monetary Fund?* (1). (2). (3). (4). (5).

11. *A country's balance of trade is altered by an increase in volume of exports with no change in imports. From the standpoint of this country, this event would be regarded as* (1) desirable, since it means a favorable balance of trade; (2) undesirable, since it means that goods being sent abroad are of greater value than those received from abroad; (3) desirable if inflationary pressures are strong, since it will tend to lessen such pressures; (4) desirable if there is widespread unemployment, since it will tend to lessen the depression; (5) none of the above, since exports and imports are neutral in their effects on the domestic economy.

12. *A disturbance in its balance of payments may cause any nation to lose gold or foreign exchange reserves. This danger of loss is most acute whenever that nation* (1) increases its exports; (2) seeks to maintain a flexible exchange rate; (3) seeks to maintain a fixed exchange rate; (4) increases its borrowing from other nations; (5) experiences a drop in GNP—i.e., whenever any recession or depression occurs.

13. *The text speaks of action by a country which should increase its domestic employment, but at the possible expense of employment abroad. An example of such action by country A, to "export its joblessness" to country B, might be* (1) an appreciation of A's currency relative to B's; (2) a decrease in loans made to country B; (3) a depreciation of A's currency relative to B's; (4) a reduction in tariffs levied on imports from B; (5) an increase in the price of A exports—i.e., making buyers in B pay more for what they buy from A.

14. *A "dirty float" means* (1) an increase in protectionist policies by some device other than a tariff increase; (2) refusal by a nation to allow its currency to appreciate even though its reserves are large and increasing; (3) a beggar-my-neighbor policy; (4) introduction of a split exchange rate—a fixed rate for some transactions, a floating rate for others; (5) periodic intervention by a central bank to check excessive fluctuation in an otherwise-floating exchange rate.

15. *Sometimes it is argued that United States aid to less developed nations tends to worsen the payments deficit and weaken the dollar's position. Assuming such aid is not sufficiently large to have significant multiplier effects, this argument is valid if the aid takes the form* (1) only of U.S. dollars which are free to be spent on non-U.S. goods if the recipient wishes; (2) only of U.S. dollars which are to be used to purchase U.S. goods; (3) of U.S. merchandise other than surplus agricultural commodities; (4) of U.S. surplus agricultural commodities; (5) of any of the above, excepting alternative 4.

16. *The text chapter lists a series of possible remedies (both "first-best" and "second-best") for U.S. balance-of-payments deficits and consequent decline in the dollar's international value. One of the following five actions is not within that list. Which one?* (1) Insist that other nations assume more of the burden of foreign aid programs. (2) Hold down the rate of increase in the United States GNP. (3) Increase protectionist policies. (4) Adopt an easier (lower-interest-rate) monetary policy. (5) Impose tax penalties on certain foreign investments made by U.S. firms.

17. *A nation relies heavily upon a certain agricultural commodity for its export sales. Should this crop fail in a particular year, the nation could reasonably expect to ease the resulting shortage of foreign exchange by borrowing from* (1) the World Bank; (2) GATT (the General Agreement on Tariffs and Trade); (3) the Point Four reserve fund; (4) the International Monetary Fund; (5) none of these agencies.

18. *Suppose, among the countries of Western Europe, there is no significant flow of reserves. Exchange rates, and consequently reserves, are by and large "in balance." For some reason, one among these countries then experiences a substantial increase in domestic investment spending. The results to be expected for this country would be as follows:* (1) GNP up, import volume up, foreign reserves up. (2) GNP up, import volume down, foreign reserves up. (3) GNP down, import volume down, foreign reserves up. (4) GNP up, import volume down, foreign reserves down. (5) GNP up, import volume up, foreign reserves down.

6
CURRENT ECONOMIC PROBLEMS

THE THEORY OF GROWTH

DESPITE ITS SEEMING COMPLEXITY, the basic construction of this chapter is simple. It sets out the process of economic growth as an interplay between two elements: diminishing returns and technological progress.

Each new stage in this interplay affects the distribution of income between labor and capital. So what this chapter does is to outline how, *as a result of the interaction between diminishing returns and technological progress,* (1) the economy's output grows, and (2) income distribution as between labor and capital is affected.

The diminishing-returns law was introduced back in Chapter 2. It describes what happens when there are two productive inputs, one fixed in available supply, the other capable of being increased. As the quantity of the variable input increases, total output increases also. But "marginal-product" (extra output produced—Chapter 27) of this variable input diminishes. Finally, total output hits its maximum when nothing extra is being added by further units of the variable input—i.e., when its marginal-product has fallen to zero.

What matters most is that *input proportions change.* So diminishing-returns reasoning can be applied even when supplies of both inputs are increasing—but not at the same rate. The input with the slower rate of increase can be considered as "the fixed input," and the other as "the variable (and increasing) input."

At the moment, the most important aspect of all this is that *the payment made per unit to the variable input is closely associated with its marginal-product.* (If necessary, refer back to Chapter 27 to refresh your memory on this point.) So diminishing returns works against the well-being of this input. For example, *if* diminishing returns were to reach the point where the marginal-product of the variable input is zero, the competitive payment made to *every* unit of that input would be zero. (Ordinarily, diminishing returns will not proceed that far. For example, if labor is the variable input, its supply is bound to stop increasing when the "minimum-of-subsistence" wage is reached.)

Early discussions of economic growth were mainly conducted in terms of land (the fixed input) and labor (the variable input). With the emphasis on diminishing returns, it was inevitable that economists like Malthus should conclude that labor's future looked gloomy.

In more recent discussions, labor is considered the fixed input and capital the variable one (because the stock of capital is growing faster than population). Now the shoe is on the other foot: capital, it would seem, is the input to suffer from diminishing returns. But capital has another card to play: technological progress. So the diminishing-returns effect which continually works against the return to the owners of capital is more or less continually being offset (or more than offset) by technological advance.

1. In Fig. 37-1, p. 294, the solid line *OP* is the ordinary diminishing-returns diagram. (Disregard for the present the two broken lines *OQ* and *OR*.) *OP* shows how output of good X increases as more and more of variable input A is added to a *fixed* quantity of another input, B. The line is straight from *O* to *H*. This means that until the A quantity reaches *OD*, the marginal-product of A is *(increasing / constant / decreasing).* Thereafter, it is *(increasing / constant / decreasing).* This marginal-product is measured by the slope of the line; so marginal-product reaches zero when the line is *(flat / vertical)*—i.e., when A's quantity reaches *(OD / OE / OF / OG).*

constant; decreasing; flat; *OG.*

2. In very early attempts to construct economic theory (e.g., in Adam Smith's work), the discussion was often carried on as though production were exclusively a matter of labor cost (thus, the *labor* cost of hunting animals for food). So long as only one type of input is considered, there cannot be any conflict between two or more input classes over division of the output they cooperatively produce.

Soon, however, it became evident (and was noted in the works of Malthus and Ricardo) that land was likewise a productive input, and one scarce or limited in supply, whereas there was no comparable limit to the size of population that might ultimately appear. Hence "the law of diminishing returns" evolved—and with it, consideration of the clash between interests of the two input categories.

a. In the Malthus-Ricardo approach to diminishing returns— and in Study Guide Fig. 37-1 terms—*(land / labor / capital)* is the fixed input B, and *(land / labor / capital)* is variable input A. Malthus felt that a final "equilibrium" would be reached when labor had *(increased / decreased)* sufficiently to make the wage per worker just equal to the minimum-subsistence level.

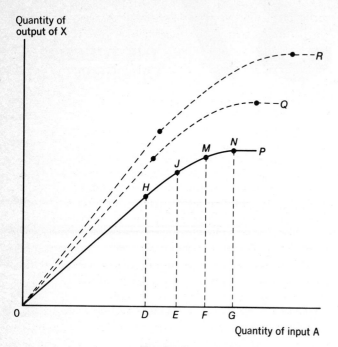

Quantity of
output of X

Quantity of input A

Fig. 37-1

b. This wage per worker would be labor's *(marginal- / total)* product. The remainder of total product, after these wages were paid, would go to landowners. In Fig. 37-1 terms, the Malthusian equilibrium would be reached with labor at a total *(of OG / necessarily less than OG, say OE or OF)*, and with total output *(NG / JE or MF)*.

---

a. land; labor; increased. *b.* marginal; necessarily less than *OG; JE* or *MF.*

---

3. *a.* As this "Malthusian equilibrium," in which labor earns only a subsistence wage, is approached, land becomes, in relative terms, more scarce. So its price (the rent per acre) must *(rise / fall).*

b. Offhand, one might think that as this painful situation (for labor) is approached, the relative share of landowners in total income must rise just as the price per unit of land rises. Strictly speaking, this is not necessarily so. The *absolute* amount of income going to landowners must rise; the *relative* share of landowners in total income *could* fall.

The total product and its division between the two input classes is as follows:

(1) Price of labor	×	(2) Number of units of labor	=	(3) Labor's total income
(4) Price of land	×	(5) Number of units of land	=	(6) Land's total income

$$(3) + (6) = \text{Total product}$$

As the labor supply increases, moving toward the Malthusian equilibrium, these six magnitudes behave as follows:

Item (1), the price of labor, *(rises / falls / remains constant).*
Item (2), number of labor units, *(rises / falls / remains constant).*
Item (3), labor's total earnings, may go either way. It may rise, remain constant, or fall (since its two components move in opposite directions).
Item (4), land's price, *(rises / falls / remains constant).*
Item (5), quantity of land, *(rises / falls / remains constant).*
Item (6), land's total earnings, *(rises / falls / remains constant).*

So item (3) could *possibly* rise sufficiently to outstrip, in relative terms, the rise in item (6). This is most likely when the "bite" of diminishing returns is not yet acute, so that increases in the labor quantity do not push down labor's marginal-product (the price of labor) by very much. But the more closely the point of zero marginal-product is approached (even though this point is never actually reached), the less likely this outcome becomes.

---

a. rise. *b.* (1) falls; (2) rises; (4) rises; (5) remains constant; (6) rises.

---

4. *a.* In Malthus-Ricardo analysis, the input ingredients of diminishing-returns analysis were land and labor. But in modern development theory, discussed later in the chapter, the fixed input is considered to be *(land / labor / capital)* and the variable input is *(land / labor / capital)*. A special name is given to increases in the variable input relative to the fixed one, namely:

---

b. As soon as we think of capital (that is, tools, machinery, and other equipment), it is natural to consider technological improvements in capital occurring over time. But if we assume such technological change to be absent and apply the analysis of question 3, the conclusion is that an increase in capital with labor or population fixed (or more generally, an increase in the proportion of capital to labor) would lead to *(an increase / a decrease)* in the return to each unit of capital—the profit rate or interest rate—and *(an increase / a decrease)* in the wage paid to labor.

c. More fully, if we designate the variable input capital as K, the fixed input labor as L, and quantity of output as Q, then (with no technological progress) the following results occur as K is increased relative to L:

(1) The capital-labor ratio, K/L, *(increases / decreases).*
(2) The capital-output ratio K/Q (see text), will *(increase / decrease)*, because when the law of diminishing returns is operating, any increase in the variable input—i.e.,*(in K / in Q / in L)*—yields an increase in output, Q, that is *(less than / exactly / more than)* proportionate to the K increase.
(3) As the K/L ratio increases, the interest or profit rate (price of K per unit) *(increases / decreases)*, and the wage rate (price of L) *(increases / decreases).*
(4) The fractional or percentage share of total output going to

K owners *(must increase / might increase / must decrease)*, just as in question 3.

---

a. labor; capital; deepening of capital. *b.* decrease; increase. *c.* (1) increases; (2) increase; in *K*; less than; (3) decreases; increases; (4) might increase.

---

5. The "classical" view was that the amount of money people save out of income is influenced by the rate of interest that is earned when such saved money is loaned out. Hence, by this view, the process described in question 4 would halt if and when (pick one):
a. The marginal-product of capital reached zero.
b. Wages reached the minimum-of-subsistence level.
c. The rate of interest fell so low that people chose to save no part of their income.

Thus, in this classical view, the drying up of saving ends the growth of *K*, because saving is the source by means of which increases in *K* are financed. Hence (disregarding the possibility of technological change), a long-run equilibrium might be reached in which net increases in the stock of capital are zero.

---

c.

---

6. In actual fact, the stock of capital in the United States has continued to grow, and it has grown more rapidly than population or the labor force. Since capital is increasing more rapidly than labor, it is appropriate to use a "model" in which labor *(L)* is fixed and capital *(K)* is increasing.

This *K* increase is seen as contending always with the law of diminishing returns, which steadily lowers *K*'s price and increases the price of the relatively scarce input *L*. *L* gains from the growth in *K*, just as landowners gained back in the Malthus-Ricardo model. However, the proportion of total output going to *L* may or may not increase (see question 4, last sentence), although *L*'s per-unit price will rise.

a. More important, *K*'s struggle against diminishing returns is helped by technical progress, which increases total output obtainable from any given combination of *K* and *L*, and raises *K*'s marginal-product. In terms of Study Guide Fig. 37-1 (where the variable input is now *K*), technical progress lifts the output curve from *OP* to *OQ*, and from *OQ* to *OR*. (The black dots on the *OQ* and *OR* lines mark the points at which curvature begins (the line begins to "bend over")—i.e., the point at which the influence of diminishing returns first begins to set in). Thus as *K* increases, say to the level of *OE*, the marginal-product of *K* will *(increase / decrease)*. The rate of interest or profit (per unit of capital) will thus *(fall / rise)* relative to labor's wage rate.

b. Combining the two effects (diminishing returns and technological progress), we see that the increase in the capital stock *(raises / lowers)* total output. Technical progress *(raises / lowers)* total output. The increase in the capital stock (disregarding technical progress) *(raises / lowers)* the demand

for labor. Hence we would expect labor's wage or price to *(increase / decrease)*. The exception to this is the case of technical progress which greatly *(increases / decreases)* the interest or profit rate and *(increases / decreases)* the demand for labor.

---

a. increase; rise. *b.* raises; raises; raises; increase; increases; decreases.

---

7. The facts of United States growth since 1900, as indicated in the text, are these:

a. The labor force has approximately *(remained constant / doubled / increased fourfold / increased sixfold)*. The stock of capital has approximately *(remained constant / doubled / increased fourfold / increased eightfold)*.

That is, the capital stock, in proportion to the labor force, has *(increased / decreased)* by a factor of *(2 / 4 / 6)*. There *(has / has not)* been a deepening of capital.

If *both* capital and labor had increased eightfold, we would expect output (disregarding technical progress) also to have increased by a factor of 8. But with labor only doubled, we would expect the output increase to be *(more / less)* than 8 times its value in 1900.

b. In fact, output has increased by a factor of about *(2 / 4 / 8)*. This means that the ratio of capital stock to annual output—the capital-output ratio—has *(increased / remained about constant / decreased)*. Things *(have / have not)* worked out as the simple law of diminishing returns would indicate, the reason evidently being

---

c. The actual capital-output ratio in the United States is at present about _____ .

d. Real wages *(have risen / have fallen / show no clear trend either up or down)*. The interest or profit rate—the "price of capital"—*(has risen / has fallen / shows no clear trend either up or down)*.

e. Output per man-hour, or *Q/L*, has *(risen / remained constant / fallen)*. The increase in the wage rate *(has exceeded / is approximately equal to / has fallen behind)* the *(increase / decrease)* in output per man-hour.

---

a. doubled; increased eightfold; increased; 4; has; less. *b.* 8; remained about constant; have not; technological progress. *c.* 3 years—i.e., value of the capital stock is reckoned as approximately equal to value of 3 years' output. *d.* have risen; shows no clear trend. *e.* risen; is approximately equal to; increase.

---

8. The terms "labor-saving" and "capital-saving" innovations lack precise, universally accepted meanings. The text suggests that an "X-saving" innovation is one which has the effect of reducing *(X's price / X's relative share in total product / amount of X employed per unit of output)*.

X's relative share in total product.

QUIZ: Multiple Choice

1. *Suppose agricultural output requires only two inputs, labor and land. The quantity of land available is fixed; the quantity of labor is variable. Then, as labor quantity is increased in order to increase output quantity, the law of diminishing returns will begin to operate, and* (1) the ratio of labor to land will increase; the ratio of land to output will fall; (2) both the labor-land ratio and the land-output ratio will fall; (3) both the labor-land ratio and the land-output ratio will increase; (4) the labor-land ratio will fall, and the land-output ratio will increase; (5) the labor-land ratio will increase, but the land-output ratio will not change.

2. *In the simple labor theory of value, demand for goods plays the following role: It* (1) interacts with supply to determine price, as in any other case; (2) dominates over supply in the determination of price, but does not influence quantities produced and consumed; (3) settles quantities produced and consumed, but has no influence on price; (4) has no influence either on quantities produced and consumed or on price; (5) dominates over supply both as to price and as to quantities produced and consumed.

3. *The most important single factor accounting for increased productivity and growth in the American economy thus far appears to have been* (1) a deepening of the capital stock; (2) technological change; (3) a widening of the capital stock; (4) the use of growth-encouraging monetary and fiscal policy; (5) the increase in skills of the labor force.

4. *Since 1900, the stock of capital in the United States has increased* (1) eightfold, and operation of the diminishing-returns law has significantly reduced the capital-output ratio; (2) tenfold, and operation of the diminishing-returns law has significantly increased the capital-output ratio, (3) only by an amount proportionate to the increase in the labor force, so that the diminishing-returns law has had no application; (4) threefold, and operation of the diminishing-returns law has significantly reduced the capital-output ratio; (5) eightfold, but the capital-output ratio has not increased significantly, despite the diminishing-returns law.

5. *In the United States, the share of wages and salaries in national product since 1900* (1) has significantly increased; (2) has remained about constant, or shown a very slight upward trend; (3) has significantly fallen, except for a period during and immediately after World War II; (4) rose fairly steadily until about 1930 and remained constant until 1945 (excluding World War II), but has fallen perceptibly since then; (5) is not correctly described by any of the above.

6. *If the amount of capital employed is increased, if the amount of labor and other inputs stays approximately fixed, and if the capital-output ratio remains constant, then* (1) the capital-labor ratio must have fallen; (2) the price of capital must have fallen; (3) the law of diminishing returns has been in operation; (4) technological improvements would explain this result; (5) total output must have fallen.

7. *In John Stuart Mill's "stationary state,"* (1) net capital formation (increases in the stock of capital) will still take place; (2) the rate of interest must be zero; (3) technical improvements may still increase the level of year-to-year output; (4) net personal saving will continue, although at a reduced rate; (5) none of the above descriptions is correct.

8. *According to the law of diminishing returns, if land is the fixed input and labor the variable input, then as the quantity of output is increased,* (1) the relative share of labor in total product must fall; (2) the price of land must fall; (3) the share of labor in total product or output must rise; (4) land's percentage share in total product or output must rise; (5) none of the above is necessarily correct.

9. *A deepening of capital must, in the absence of technological change,* (1) increase the capital-output ratio; (2) decrease the capital-output ratio; (3) increase output more than proportionately to the increase in capital; (4) increase output in proportion to the increase in capital; (5) increase the share of capital owners in the total of output.

10. *By "deepening of capital" is meant* (1) an increase in the stock of capital relative to the size of the labor force; (2) the introduction of new capital goods which embody technological change; (3) a change either in productivity or amount of capital which increases the share of capital-owners in total product; (4) an increase in the productivity of capital which reduces, or at least does not increase, the total of the capital stock; (5) none of the above.

11. *If capital is considered the variable input, then in the operation of the law of diminishing returns (without technological change), as output is increased,* (1) the share of capital owners in total output must increase; (2) the capital-output ratio must decrease; (3) the share of capital owners in total output must decrease; (4) the capital-output ratio must increase; (5) the capital-output ratio must, by definition, remain constant.

12. *Suppose technological change increases the output per man-hour of labor. If labor's hourly wage rises by exactly the same percentage as the rise in output per man-hour, then* (1) labor's share in total product must increase; (2) labor's real income will be unchanged; (3) there will be no increase in real total product, as distinct from the money value of total product; (4) labor's share in total product must decrease; (5) none of the above is correct.

APPENDIX: Modern Discussions of Development Theory

Because much of the material in this Appendix is at the frontier of economic knowledge, it is by no means as well organized or as well integrated as the topics outlined (for example) in Parts 2 and 3 of the text. Some of it may seem difficult—as, for example, the discussion of "Harrod-Domar growth models." These growth models are really fairly simple—but they do not seem simple at all until you have mastered the elements that go into their construction.

1. Economic growth analysis often begins by drawing on the Ricardo-Mill idea of "the stationary state." (For more on this idea, refer also to text Chapter 30 and Study Guide question 7, pp. 238–239; it is also mentioned briefly in the text Chapter 37 in reference to Mill's thought.) These classical economists thought that nations would grow until they reached a final "stationary-state" condition. Thereafter, there would be no further growth—not, at any rate, in the capital stock. When this final state is reached, the economy's stock of capital goods may be very large, but there is (*positive / zero / negative*) net investment—i.e., the capital stock (*is / is not*) being increased. There is just enough investment each year to balance that year's depreciation of the existing capital stock. The interest rate is (*positive / zero / negative*). No net investment is being undertaken because (1) all the capital-goods projects carrying a yield higher than the prevailing interest rate have already been undertaken, and (2) at that prevailing interest rate, the amount of saving out of income is (*positive / zero / negative*).

The points to note especially are these: (*a*) Capital growth stops because there is no saving to finance investment; (*b*) saving stops because the interest rate is insufficiently high to persuade people to save any part of income. So the classical belief that things ultimately gravitate toward a stationary state relies heavily on the view that the interest rate is important to people in deciding how much (if anything) they will save out of incomes.

zero; is not; positive; zero.

2. More recent views have been skeptical of this alleged tendency of things to drift toward a stationary state.

a. Joseph Schumpeter conceded that such a tendency might exist. But he argued that it is repeatedly offset by new

which create new profit possibilities. Innovators, seeking to exploit these opportunities, will bid (*down / up*) the interest rate and so will (*encourage / discourage*) saving out of income as financing for the new projects. Repeated innovations thus

keep pushing the economy into bursts of capital accumulation and growth.

b. Keynesian analysis calls into question the responsiveness of saving to the interest rate. In this view, people save against life's uncertainties, and they go on saving no matter how low the interest rate may be.

The interest rate is, instead, important in dictating *what people do* with income saved. People may save when interest rates are low—but they do not necessarily lend. Instead, they may display "liquidity preference" (see Chapter 18). In periods when profit opportunities look bleak, investment will be (*high / low*), and the reduced demand for investment money will make the interest rate (*high / low*). However, this (*high / low*) interest rate will *not* of itself reduce saving. So the disparity between saving and investment must be ironed out by a (*rise / fall*) in incomes and production, and by unemployment.

This is, of course, "short-run analysis" (as Schumpeter pointed out with respect to Keynes). These periods of unemployment may in time be overcome by further technological change, and consequently a surge of new investment. If we combine Schumpeter's views with those of Keynes, the conclusion is that capitalist economies are more likely to continue to grow rather than to drift toward a stationary-state equilibrium. Technological change will persistently create new investment opportunities, and the public's continued disposition to save will (except, just possibly, in certain low-interest-rate periods) provide financing for investment.

a. inventions (or innovations); up; encourage. *b.* low; low; low; fall.

3. Much of this Appendix deals with the concepts of "the natural rate of growth" and "the warranted rate of growth," used in Harrod-Domar growth models.

To understand the meaning of these models, and of the two "rates of growth" mentioned, begin with a review of the chapter's discussion of growth. It outlined how, as the capital stock *K* grows, output grows also. But if *K* grows more rapidly than the labor force *L*, the output increase will not be proportional to the increase in *K*. *K* will feel the impact of diminishing returns. However, *K*'s "marginal productivity" can be restored (and hence the return per unit of *K* can be increased) by technological innovation—the effect of which is likewise to increase total output.

Harrod-Domar analysis tries to explore more precisely the results arising out of increases in the capital stock and in the labor force, taking account of the two factors just mentioned, namely diminishing returns and technological change.

Because the diminishing-returns matter is handled a little

differently in these models, we postpone consideration of technological change. We begin by assuming that such change is absent.

Now as to diminishing returns, in the usual presentation (e.g., Study Guide Fig. 37-1, p. 294), the effect is described as occurring when you *vary* the proportions of the two inputs, say, K and L. Specifically, as you increase K relative to L, K's marginal-product gradually falls to zero.

Many economists think (on this, see text) that such outlines tend to exaggerate the extent to which variability of input proportions is possible in actual production. By and large, in this view, a given capital stock needs a given labor force to operate it. If there is insufficient capital for a given labor force, some of that labor will be unemployable. If there is insufficient labor for a given capital stock, some of that capital will be unusable. (Note that this is *not* a denial of the diminishing-returns effect. It says only that this effect will occur suddenly, not gradually.[1])

In Harrod-Domar models, it is assumed that the relationship (in production) between the total capital stock (K) and the total labor force (L) is pretty close to fixed. Hence it is no great distortion to think of this K/L ratio as actually fixed. If this ratio (dictated by technology) is not satisfied, the surplus K or the surplus L (whichever of the two happens to be in excess) will be unemployable.

We also have a given capital-output ratio, K/Q, where Q is total annual output (the same thing as GNP). This capital-output ratio is some figure such as $3\frac{1}{3}$. All that is meant here is that the value of the present total capital stock K is reckoned to be $3\frac{1}{3}$ times the value of annual output Q. Or to say the same thing differently, in order to double the size of K, the entire annual production (Q) for $3\frac{1}{3}$ years would have to go into investment production. (Investment *means* an addition to K.)

(Let's digress momentarily in order to clear away a small possible confusion. In growth analysis, the expression Q is conventional for "total annual output." As noted above, it is effectively the same thing elsewhere called GNP. For the balance of this question, to avoid duplication, only the term

Q, not GNP, is used. Remember, if it is a help for you: Q = GNP.)

Next, consider the fact that population ordinarily grows each year, so that the labor force, L, grows also. For example, say this growth rate is 3 per cent annually. (More generally, let this growth rate, expressed as a fraction, be designated g. Thus, in our example, $g = 3/100$.)

If the capital-labor relationship K/L is fixed by technology, this increase in L calls for a *matching* increase in K. *Will it occur?* That is the question underlying the "natural-growth" idea.

In brief, we want the annual increase in K to be 3/100 of K; by matching the increase in L, this increase will maintain the actual K/L ratio at its desired level. (More generally, we want the annual increase in K to be gK.) But this increase in K (whether the desired gK or some other figure) is what we more usually call investment, I. There must be just enough of Q channeled into investment (rather than into consumption) to provide the required addition to K.

This means that there must be just enough of Q *saved*, for I spending is financed out of S. (In this type of analysis, it is assumed there is no "Keynesian" problem whereby saving fails to flow smoothly into investment.)

So the problem is just this: How much must be saved out of Q (what fraction of Q must be saved) in order to produce the needed I (the K-addition desired so as to match the L-addition)?

Let s = the *fraction* of Q saved annually. Thus *total* annual saving will be sQ.

Now we can fit things together. By the assumption that all saving flows into investment, we have $sQ = I$. And the desired $I = gK$. Hence, if things are to go as desired, we must have $sQ = gK$. Or to put that equation in the text's form:

$$s = g \times \frac{K}{Q}$$

Note that K/Q is our old friend the capital-output ratio.

a. In our example, we used a g figure of 3/100 (i.e., annual increase in L of 3 per cent annually); and the capital-output ratio was assumed to be $3\frac{1}{3}$. So the percentage of income which must be saved, in order to produce the desired annual increase in K, must be *(3 / 4 / 5 / 6 / 7 / 8 / 9 / 10)* per cent.

Change L's annual growth rate from 3 to 4 per cent (with the same capital-output ratio). Then the required s-value would be approximately *(8.5 / 10.0 / 13.3 / 15.0 / 16.7)*. If the L growth rate were 5 per cent, then the required s-value would be approximately *(8.5 / 10.0 / 13.3 / 15.0 / 16.7)*.

b. If saving *does* take place at the percentage rate indicated, we have "balanced growth." Thus, in using the 3 per cent annual growth figure for L, if saving *is* 10 per cent of Q, then output will grow annually at *(3/10)* per cent. Allowing for population increase, output per capita and income per capita will increase *(by 3 per cent / by 10 per cent / not at all)*. The

[1]The essence of diminishing returns, expressed in terms of Study Guide Fig. 37-1 (p. 294) is that when you have too much of input A relative to input B, you cannot get further increases in output by adding more of A. But you are warned of this because the marginal-product of A *gradually* falls to zero. In the fixed-proportions case, there is no such warning. In Fig. 37-1 terms, when proportions are fixed, the output line OP no longer gradually "bends over." It is a straight line all the way from O to N. At point N, there is a kink. To the right of N, the output line is perfectly flat, just as in Fig. 37-1.

Suppose the available quantity of variable input A is only, say, OD. Then the A/B proportions are wrong; part of the given stock of input B is redundant, and that part cannot be employed in production. As the quantity of input A is increased beyond OD, more of B becomes employable. When the A quantity is OG, things are "just right" with respect to the specified fixed A/B proportions. Beyond OG, input A would become the redundant factor. Any such quantity of A in excess of OG would be unemployable for lack of available B with which it could work.

capital-labor proportion *K/L* will *(rise / remain constant / fall)*.

c. If saving falls short of what is required by population growth, the ratio *K/L* will *(rise / remain constant / fall)*, and there will be a tendency toward unemployment for lack of sufficient capital goods.

---

a. 10; 13.3; 16.7. *b.* 3; not at all; remain constant. *c.* fall.

---

4. *a.* In actual fact, as was pointed out earlier in the chapter, in the United States the ratio *K/L* has *(risen / fallen / remained constant)*. This suggests that the path followed has not been that of "balanced growth." But in the illustration of question 3, *technological change* was specifically excluded. When consideration is given this element, United States growth may still have been "balanced."

Technological innovation may take many forms. Typically, it appears in the form of new and different capital goods, which human labor is trained to operate. One way of handling technological change analytically is to think of it as a development increasing the productivity of labor.

By this approach, the increase in *L* (the labor *force*) does not fully indicate the increase in the "effective" labor supply—if *L* is increasing not only in numbers but in productive efficiency. The text uses the symbol *L** to measure the effective labor force. That is, if *L* grows, and this growth is accompanied by greater training and skill, *L** grows *(even faster / more slowly)*.

If the ratio *K/L* rises, as it has done in the United States, it is *(impossible / still possible)* for the ratio *K/L** to remain constant.

b. In the United States since 1900, the division of GNP between *K* owners and *L* owners has *(shifted in favor of K owners / shifted in favor of L owners / remained approximately constant)*. Further, the capital-output ratio *K/Q* (i.e., *K* / GNP) has *(increased significantly / decreased significantly / remained approximately constant)*. These two facts *(correspond / do not correspond)* to "balanced growth."

c. In the United States, the real wage per unit of *L* has *(risen / fallen / remained constant)*. In "balanced growth," the wage per unit of *L** *(rises / falls / remains constant)*. The actual rise in United States wage per unit of *L* *(can be / cannot be)* consistent with "balanced growth."

---

a. risen; even faster; still possible. *b.* remained approximately constant; remained approximately constant; correspond. *c.* risen; remains constant; can be.

"Balanced growth" analysis, in summary, notes that we must reckon with two basic and largely independent elements: growth in population (or the labor force), and the propensity of the population to save.

These two elements must harmonize in the sense that saving finances investment, and that investment takes the form of the new capital goods with which the increase in population must work. Growth is "balanced," and it occurs at "the natural rate," when these two basic elements are in reasonable harmony.

The elements are not in harmony when saving fails to provide the required amount of new capital goods. But they are not necessarily out of harmony when saving appears "too great," so that its tendency is to increase the *K/L* ratio. This is an incentive toward "labor-saving innovation"—i.e., technological change designed to *change* the fixed *K/L* ratio, to increase it to a higher "workable" level.

The economists who argue for relatively fixed factor proportions consequently do not regard the observed rise in *K/L* as a contradiction of their view. Typically, the fixed-proportions argument holds only that the *K/L* proportion is fixed or nearly fixed in any given state of technology (and with given equipment). The economists may argue that as *K* grows, this fixity can be a strong inducement toward technological development to *change* the proportion.

5. If the rate of saving is high in relation to the growth in the labor force, it is far from safe to assume that technological change will always save the day. Even if such output-increasing changes are directed toward an increase in the *K/L* ratio (i.e., toward "automation"), their effects typically appear rather slowly in actual production. The shorter-run consequences of a too-high flow of saving may be the Keynesian ones: a fall in incomes and employment, and a consequent fall in saving.

These considerations introduce Harrod's "warranted rate of growth." The warranted-rate case, like the natural-rate one, needs to be carefully spelled out. There are four beginning ingredients:

(1) In production, the ratio or proportion *K/L* is fixed. Because output is limited to what the available supplies of *K* and *L* can produce, the capital-output ratio, *K/GNP*, or *K/Q*, is also fixed.

(2) We start with more than enough *L* for the existing *K*. Part of the labor force is unemployed for lack of capital goods with which to work. An increase in *K* is needed if even part of this unemployment is to be removed. (For this question, it makes no difference whether total *L* is increasing annually, as in questions 3 and 4, or is fixed in amount.)

(3) Business firms are assured that there will be some extra *L* available to work with any extra *K* created. But they still must ask this question: *If* we build this extra *K*, will there be sufficient demand for the extra output thereby producible to have made that investment worth undertaking? In sum: Will there be a sufficient rise in GNP to justify building the extra *K*? So the underlying question is: What will be the rate of rise in GNP?

(4) The public wants to save *some fixed fraction* of GNP.

The problem resulting from this mixture of ingredients needs to be viewed in "Keynesian" terms. The public does the saving (*S*), and it has a firm plan as to the percentage of GNP (or *Q*) it will save. (As in question 3, hereafter we use only the term *Q*, not GNP.) A *different* group—business firms—does the investment (*I*) spending. Now the amount of *S* imposes an upper limit on the amount of *I* spending possible. But that is no guarantee that business firms will plan to spend on *I* *exactly as much as* the public plans to save.

Assuming the existing capital stock, *K*, to be fully employed, then the amount of *I* spending planned by businessmen will be governed by their expectations as to *Q*'s future level.

Suppose that business firms are pretty confident that *Q* will rise by 10 per cent—say from $100 to $110 billion. Since their present *K* is fully occupied, they will want to have built just enough extra *K* to meet that $10 billion increase in demand for output.

How do we translate that anticipated $10 billion *Q*-rise into a dollar total for extra *K*? The "rate of exchange" is provided by the (fixed) capital-output ratio, *K/Q*. If this ratio is 3, business will want to use saving of $30 billion (and not more), since that amount of investment (addition to *K*) is just capable of producing an extra $10 billion of *Q* annually. Thus the combination of business expectations and the *K/Q* ratio will settle the amount of *I* spending.

a. If business firms instead anticipate a *Q* rise from $100 to $120 billion, with the same *K/Q* ratio of 3, their desired *I* spending will be $(*zero / 20 / 40 / 60 / 80 / 100*) billion. If they expect *no* rise in *Q*, then their planned *I* spending will be $(*zero / 20 / 40 / 60 / 80 / 100*) billion.

If *W* is the expected rise in *Q* stated as a fraction, what is the general "rate of exchange" expression indicating the desired *I*-spending amount?

_____ .

b. At long last, we reach the "warranted rate of growth." It is that rate of annual growth in *Q*, expressed by the symbol *W* (a fraction of *Q*) that, once started, would just keep the economy progressing in a smooth, continuing rate of growth. Remember, the fraction of *Q* that people want to save is assumed to be fixed. That fixed fraction of *Q* saved would be *just* enough to equal the amount that business firms would want to invest, given their expectations as to future *Q*.

The essential requirement, then, is just *S* = *I*. And finding *W*, the warranted rate of growth, is just a matter of (i) putting *S* in place of *I* in the equation worked out in part *a* above, and then (ii) rearranging that equation so that *W* sits alone on the left-hand side thereof. Use a separate scrap of paper for the detail, then show the resulting equation below.

_____

c. In the equation above, *S* stands for *total* saving. The text equation uses the symbol s_a to indicate that fixed *fraction* of *Q* which the public insists on saving. Thus, $S = s_a Q$. Make this substitution in the equation above, and you get the text's equation, namely:

$$W = \frac{s_a}{K/Q}$$

If the fraction of *Q* that people wish to save is always 12 per cent, and the capital-output ratio is 4, the warranted rate of growth would be (*zero / 1 / 2 / 3 / 4 / 5*) per cent per annum. If *K/Q* is 5, and saving is always 10 per cent of income, the warranted rate would be (*zero / 1 / 2 / 3 / 4 / 5*) per cent growth per annum.

---

a. 60; zero; $I = W \times Q \times K / Q$ (or simply, $I = WK$).

b. $W = \dfrac{S}{Q \times K / Q}$.   *c.* 3; 2.

---

6. The "warranted rate of growth" idea is pretty clearly related to the "acceleration principle" view discussed in Chapter 14—i.e., investment spending is largely governed by the rate of growth in GNP (or *Q*). But in the warranted-rate outline, such spending is much more dependent upon businessmen's *expectations* as to the likely rate of GNP increase than it is in the acceleration-principle argument.

Notice that the "warranted rate of growth" is *not* envisaged as a growth rate that will necessarily remove all unemployment of *L*—even though the creation of new plant and equipment will of course create extra employment. (Unlike the "balanced growth" model of question 3, warranted-rate analysis pays relatively little attention to *L*'s size—i.e., is it fixed, or growing? There must be enough *L* on hand to operate the additional *K* created—that's about the extent to which warranted-rate analysis concerns itself with the *L* matter.)

The essential point to grasp about the warranted-rate argument is this: If the economy manages to get started along its warranted-rate growth track, it will (so the argument goes, anyhow) *continue* on that steady growth track (assuming the fixed capital-output and saving percentage figures persist) until and unless some disturbance bumps it off.

One possible source of disturbance is the limit on the labor force *L*. If *K* grows so rapidly as to overtake *L* (even though *L* may be rising), then, with unemployed *L* removed, *K* runs into the fixed *K/L* ratio, and investment meets a bottleneck. The amount of *I* spending will (*increase / decline*), saving will (*exceed / fall short of*) investment, and GNP will be thrown off its warranted-rate path. While in due course technology may change things by increasing the *K/L* ratio, the shorter-run adjustment may be the Keynesian one: a fall in incomes and in saving.

---

decline; exceed.

7. The Leontief input-output system (see text) is not concerned, as Harrod-Domar models are, with "aggregate growth." Indeed, although it also involves some interest in the matter of growth, the Leontief construction is "microeconomic" in the particular sense of dealing with the specific products which make up the GNP, and with the specific inputs needed for the manufacture of those products.

Suppose that GNP is made up solely of three types of goods: X, Y, and Z. This problem is posed: We need a 5 per cent increase in output of X, a 15 per cent increase in output of Y, and we can afford to reduce Z output by 10 per cent. What would these changes call for in the way of extra inputs needed?

This is the type of question the Leontief system is constructed to answer. As its base, it uses statistical material covering production in past years.

It is appropriate to illustrate the nature of the Leontief system through the example of a three-good GNP. But in real life, things are rather more complicated. Within any actual GNP, there are thousands upon thousands of different items. Even a computer-aided system cannot take full account of them all. The most appropriate simplification is to lump products together by industry—thus making *the industry* the microeconomic unit. Even a quite modest plan of division yields several hundred industries for a Leontief system to digest.

Typically, the output of any one industry goes in two directions. Part of that output may be a finished consumer good for households. But part (or all) may go *to other industries as inputs.* Fuel oil is an output used by families for home heating. It is also an input used by firms for their manufacturing needs.

A Leontief table is built to record this fact. Each industry gets a line (technically a *row*), showing where its output went. On the X-industry line, so much of X output went to the Y industry as a raw-material input, so much to the Z industry for similar use—and finally, so much of X to households for consumption purposes.

This arrangement of rows, one for each industry, means that each industry also gets a *column* (a vertical listing), showing the inputs it got from other industries—that is, the raw materials it needed to produce its own finished product. At the bottom of each column is a figure showing that particular industry's total *labor* input.

This is the information at the *surface* of a Leontief system. Suppose the table indicates that 6 labor units, L, were used per unit of X produced. This is only the *direct* requirement. X's *total L* requirements were greater, for X's production also called on inputs from Y and Z, and *they* used labor too. (Of necessity, a Leontief system must work in money terms, but these money figures are intended as equivalents of *real* input-output relationships.)

The Leontief system probes for *total* input-output needs: the *total L* per unit of X, *total* Y per unit of X, *total* Z/X

relation, and so on. Each such input-output figure (e.g., 10 L units per X unit) is assumed to be fixed; this is really the same "fixed factor proportions" assumption used in Harrod-Domar models.

If the Leontief system has developed these "input-output coefficients" correctly, it can then indicate the requirements for any given increase in output. Suppose (to use a simplified version of the illustrative problem with which this question began) the question is: What would be needed in order to obtain a 10 per cent increase in net final output of X—with no increase in net final outputs of Y and Z?

Insofar as Y and Z are needed as inputs in X production, more of these commodities will have to be turned out even though there is to be no increase in their final output. And the required increase in X output may have to be more than 10 per cent—if X is needed as an input in Y production or in Z production.

The Leontief system will accordingly report that such a 10 per cent increase in net final X output would require so many extra units of X, so many of Y, so many of Z, and so much extra L. We would expect the L requirement to be *(less than / the same as / greater than)* the extra L needed directly in the X industry. The rise in Y production will *(increase "final consumption" of Y / be fully absorbed as inputs for other industries).* The same is true of Z production. Of the increase in Y production, *(all will go directly to the X industry / some may go, for example, to the Z industry, hence only indirectly to the X industry).*

---

greater than; be fully absorbed as inputs; some may go to the Z industry.

QUIZ: Multiple Choice

1. A *"deepening of capital"* can be expected to reduce the rate of interest or profit unless (1) the capital-output ratio remains constant; (2) the capital-output ratio increases; (3) the capital-labor ratio increases; (4) the capital-labor ratio decreases; (5) output remains constant.

2. If saving and investment take place in the amounts indicated by the natural rate of growth, (1) the ratio of capital to labor in production will rise; (2) the ratio of capital to output will rise; (3) the rate of profit or interest will rise; (4) the share of labor-owners in GNP will rise relative to the share of capital-owners; (5) none of the above is correct.

3. According to the analysis of the "natural rate of growth," if the economy is actually growing at that rate, (1) the capital-output ratio will increase, but at a rate less than the natural rate of growth; (2) technological change will be taking place at a steady rate, and the rate of return on capital will be maintained at a steady level by this technological change; (3) there will be a widening of capital but no deepening of capital; (4)

there will be a deepening of capital but no widening of capital; (5) none of the above is correct.

4. *"Balanced growth," as the term is used in Harrod-Domar models, involves essentially a balance between* (1) saving and investment; (2) investment and the capital-output ratio; (3) total capital and total labor; (4) investment and the distribution of income between capital and labor; (5) saving and population growth.

5. *"Warranted" and "natural" rates of growth differ in this respect, namely that* (1) warranted-rate analysis assumes that capital can be deepened, natural-rate analysis that it cannot; (2) natural-rate analysis assumes unemployment of labor, and GNP is thrown off the natural-rate path when full employment is reached; (3) the natural rate indicates the fraction of income the public actually wishes to save; (4) the warranted rate is an unstable one, and any disturbance will throw GNP off the warranted-rate path; (5) not at all, since they are two words used by different economists to mean the same thing.

6. *A Leontief input-output system records, with respect to the total output of any one industry,* (1) only that part going to households, since to include the part going to other industries would be double counting; (2) only that part going to other industries, since its purpose is to record input-output relationships; (3) that part going to households and the part going to other industries as well, but the latter on a value-added basis to avoid double counting; (4) both the part going to households and the part going to other industries, in full; (5) none of the above, since for industries it records inputs, not outputs.

38 PROBLEMS OF ECONOMIC GROWTH AND DEVELOPMENT

1. All (or almost all) less developed countries have the following properties in common (pick as many as are correct):

a. A large population.

b. A low per capita income.

c. A considerable supply of underdeveloped natural resources.

d. Low life expectancy for most of the population.

e. A low ratio of capital equipment to population.

f. Land ownership heavily concentrated in the hands of a small number of landowners.

g. Total output in which agricultural goods bulk large.

---

b, d, e, g.

---

2. *a.* The United States has about *(1 / 6 / 13 / 20)* per cent of the world's population; it consumes about *(18 / 27 / 40 / 45)* per cent of total world income.

b. In the past 25 to 30 years, the difference in per capita incomes between advanced and less developed countries (according to the text) seems to have *(increased / decreased / remained about the same)*.

---

a. 6; 27. *b.* increased.

---

3. The characteristics of a nonsocialist "developed economy" are well understood. A country in this category has a large supply of capital goods per capita. Members of its population accept the principle of division of labor, and they are trained in skills adapted to that principle. Money is almost universally employed in place of barter, and money is used for the hiring of labor. There is an active "entrepreneur class," and the making of money is not frowned upon or treated with scorn. There are well-organized money and credit markets. There is general acceptance of the authority and trustworthiness of a central government which passes laws, imposes taxes, and enforces execution of private contracts. The laws are in general obeyed and the tax levies paid (which is not to say, of course, that there is no cheating at all on taxes). Ordinarily, it is not necessary to bribe government officials to have them carry out their ordinary jobs (which, again, is not to say that bribery and corruption are completely absent).

The developed economy accomplishes new things by reason of its entrepreneur class, its use of the money market mechanism, and its refusal to accept the dictates of tradition or of custom as to how things should be done. As a result, it produces high material living standards for its members and a greatly increased life expectancy. These benefits involve some costs: an uncertainty on the part of members as to where (if anywhere) they "belong" in society, and perhaps increased feelings of personal insecurity.

Since the characteristics described are common to all developed societies, it is agreed that they explain the higher material living standards and increased life expectancy. But the problem remains of *how* these characteristics were acquired. This is the central problem for planners in less developed societies. It is agreed that members of less developed societies want the benefits of development, and—presumably—they are willing to pay the costs. (The argument that such peoples are probably happiest as they are now, and best "left alone," has little application. Whether or not they are "happy" is an unanswerable question. But most certainly they will not and cannot be "left alone" in a world wherein methods of communication and transportation have increased so dramatically.)

"The theory of development" thus becomes an attempt to explain how the characteristics of developed societies emerged, or how they can be fostered.

a. Many of these explanations emphasize wholly, or in the main, one single factor—for example, geography. Here the view is usually that a cool, temperate climate is conducive to vigorous activity and hence to growth. The text *(accepts / accepts with qualifications / rejects)* the view that geography is a vital consideration.

b. Another explanation is race (white or nonwhite). (Often this is the geography explanation framed in a different way.) The test *(accepts / rejects)* the idea that race is the all-important consideration.

c. Still another factor emphasized is culture. The text *accepts with qualifications / rejects)* the view that *(accepts / some cultures have properties which impede growth.

Two questions are raised by the problem of cultures that seemingly oppose economic development: (1) *Can* established culture patterns be altered by planners for development? (2) Even if they can be broken, *ought* they to be?

There is a partial answer to the first of these questions. What appear on the surface to be well-established culture patterns sometimes break up quite easily, and without evidence of any great distress appearing among the people involved.

A more positive answer exists for the second question. No country can avoid the worldwide impact of economic development, so that proposals to "protect" an established culture are largely irrelevant.

---

a. rejects. *b.* rejects. *c.* accepts.

---

4. Max Weber, early in the twentieth century, put forward the view that cultural elements can be important in economic development (in opposition to the argument, attributed to Marx, that all determining forces in history are economic in origin). Weber stressed the significance of religion; specifically, he thought there was a close connection between the asceticism which Calvinism encouraged in its followers and capitalist development. The name given Weber's thesis is

_____ .

---

the "Protestant ethic."

---

5. In seeking to construct a "theory of development" as indicated in question 3, some economists speak of the "preconditions for growth" (see text)—a kind of foundation that must be laid before any lasting growth can be expected. These preconditions would include the development of a reasonably well-knit and cooperative society, the establishment of tolerable stability in that society, and acceptance of some degree of central authority.

a. Since "economic growth" means largely the creation of tools, machinery, and equipment—i.e., "capital formation"— there is a more specific prerequisite for the beginning of growth, pertaining to income and the disposition of that

income, namely, _____ .

b. Economists also single out "external economies" as being highly important in the development process. An external economy is something which reduces per unit cost for the individual producing firm or which facilitates production for that firm, yet which is quite outside the control of that firm— hence "external." (On external economies, see also the Appendix to Chapter 23). Examples would include developments in transportation facilities, health measures which improve the productivity of labor, and the development of a system of law which makes contracts enforcible and so encourages more widespread production.

The point about such external-economy projects is that the individual firm *(can / cannot)* undertake them. They *(must / can but need not necessarily)* be undertaken by government. Any individual firm which attempted such an external economy would find *(it worthless / that its benefits accrued also to other firms that did not bear any part of its cost).*

c. Paul Rosenstein-Rodan has given a particular name to these external-economy needs which cannot be left to private

entrepreneurs to develop. It is _____ .

---

a. ability (on the part of some fraction of population) to save part of income. *b.* cannot; must; that its benefits accrued to other firms. *c.* social overhead capital.

---

6. The text speaks of the four economic fundamentals in terms of which the problems of development must be reviewed and understood: population, natural resources, capital formation, technology.

a. As to *population*, the big question is (pick one):
(1) As economic development begins, will it bring about the population increase required for further development?
(2) Is it possible to improve health habits so as to control disease and so bring about a longer life span?
(3) Will development bring about a population increase such that real income per capita is no higher than before?

b. Concerning the second fundamental, *natural resources*, circle as many of the following as correctly indicate problems or difficulties in this area.
(1) Many less developed countries are resource-poor, so far as is known. How then are they to develop?
(2) Land reform is necessary for development in many countries, since land is not being used to the best advantage because individual holdings are too small.
(3) Land reform is necessary for development in many countries, since land is not being used to the best advantage because individual holdings are too large.

c. With respect to the third fundamental, *capital formation* (or the process of saving and investment), again circle as many statements as seem correct.
(1) Poor nations find it very difficult to save (to refrain from consumption) and so to free resources for investment activity.
(2) The social customs in some poor countries are such that rich people therein prefer to hoard their savings or use them in nonproductive ways, so that they are not used to finance investment projects which would raise the national product.
(3) The desire for development and the example of the developed countries have noticeably increased the amount of saving out of income in many poor countries.
(4) In many poor countries, investment expenditure tends to go heavily into housing, an investment form which does not have the highest priority in development.
(5) The amount of private lending for financing investment activity, by citizens in developed areas to those in less developed areas, is greater than it was in the nineteenth century, both absolutely and relatively.

d. With respect to the fourth fundamental, *technology*, again circle as many as seem correct.
(1) Less developed countries have the advantage that imitation of techniques already worked out is easier than the development of new and sometimes sophisticated techniques.
(2) Efforts by developed countries to export advanced "technological know-how" are frequently unsuccessful.

(3) Some advanced technologies are "capital-saving," and these are likely to be particularly well suited to adoption in less developed countries.

---

a. (3). *b.* (1), (2), (3). *c.* (1), (2), (4). *d.* (1), (2), (3).

---

7. *a.* Higher savings will be useless and productive investment will not take place in any country unless it has a class of vigorous, creative _____ .

b. Sometimes it is said that the recurring problem with which a developed country must cope is that of *(too much / too little)* saving and hence *(not enough / too much)* demand for goods. By contrast, the problem of the less developed country is that of *(too much / too little)* saving and hence *(not enough / too much)* demand for goods.

---

a. entrepreneurs. *b.* too much; not enough; too little; too much.

QUIZ: Multiple Choice

1. *One area of economic development in which the country's government must take the initiative and also participate, according to the text, is that of* (1) the maintenance of balanced growth; (2) heavy industry; (3) the transfer of resources needed in the shift from agricultural predominance to industrial predominance; (4) social overhead capital; (5) none of the above, there being no area in which such government involvement is always needed.

2. *The main reason population growth has spurted ahead so rapidly in many less developed countries in recent years is that* (1) birth rates have increased sharply with improvements in nutrition; (2) great strides have been made in keeping older people alive an extra 5 or 10 years; (3) infant mortality and mortality due to epidemics have been drastically lowered; (4) large-scale immigration has occurred in many countries since World War II; (5) birth rates have risen markedly as the natural result of widespread reductions in the customary age of marriage.

3. *The argument that a developing country should direct its efforts toward investment projects with a low capital-output ratio is* (1) valid only insofar as this ratio indicates the projects with the highest net productivity; (2) invalid, since the case of social overhead capital indicates that money productivity is not a proper consideration in development planning; (3) invalid because the process of development by its very nature demands an increase in the capital-output ratio; (4) valid only insofar as this ratio indicates the minimum cost of production for any given investment project; (5) not correctly described by any of the above.

4. *"Disguised unemployment" refers to a situation in which* (1) deficiencies in population statistics give a faulty picture of the labor force that is actually available; (2) workers who actually are effectively self-employed claim to be in need of work; (3) a country, having reached a certain stage in development, finds difficulty in recruiting workers for industrial jobs because of their reluctance to leave traditional occupations; (4) demand for finished consumer goods is insufficient; (5) for most (or all) of the year, the marginal productivity of labor in agriculture is actually very low.

5. *As a country develops economically and builds its own industry, one of the following usually does not occur, namely that* (1) it imports less and less from other developed and industrialized countries; (2) its total exports tend to rise; (3) it imports more and more from other industrialized, highly developed countries; (4) it imports more from less developed countries; (5) its total imports tend to rise.

6. *By "social overhead capital," as the term is used in the text, is meant* (1) the money investment required before any return is obtainable from a particular natural resource; (2) a particular form of "external economy"; (3) investment in those projects considered to have the highest net productivity; (4) projects which must be financed by the country itself, as distinct from those financed by external aid; (5) any capital investment the amount of which does not vary as the quantity of national output is increased.

7. *The idea of "social overhead capital," referred to in question 6, is particularly associated with the name of* (1) Jan Tinbergen; (2) Paul Rosenstein-Rodan; (3) Karl Marx; (4) W. W. Rostow; (5) Max Weber.

8. *A "precondition for growth" is the* (1) development of some excess of income over consumption; (2) creation of a surplus labor force for employment in manufacturing; (3) discovery and exploitation of some external economies; (4) cultural acceptance of free enterprise principles of economic behavior; (5) development of manufacturing to the point where it can begin to supplant agriculture.

9. *Four of the following five statements more or less repeat what the text says in discussing the problems of economic development. One is false—i.e., runs counter to what the text says. Which one?* (1) In some less developed countries, considerable investment takes place, but goes into items that are of low priority or even are undesirable from the standpoint of national economic development. (2) The development of adequate "social overhead capital" is usually essential if there is to be much economic development. (3) In history, political revolutions have often taken place *after* some economic progress has been achieved. (4) Most of the less developed countries are known to have substantial unexploited natural resources, if only the capital needed to bring them into effective use were available. (5) In poor countries, especially rural ones, often a large part of the manpower pool does almost nothing because there is nothing for it to do.

10. *Less developed countries have lower per capita incomes* than developed countries. The text suggests that the gap between the two income levels is (1) diminishing as to the "free enterprise" less developed countries, widening as to the socialist-oriented ones; (2) almost incapable of measurement, because of differences in cultures, tastes, and climates; (3) perceptibly diminishing, evidently as the result of foreign-aid programs; (4) diminishing with respect to those countries which have concentrated their investment upon social overhead capital; (5) probably growing wider.

11. "Land reform" is a topic often discussed with respect to economic progress within the less developed countries. Such land reform, insofar as it can contribute to higher real incomes therein, calls for (1) sometimes increasing, sometimes decreasing, the size of the plot operated by the individual owner, tenant, or cooperative; (2) the transfer of land from agricultural to industrial production; (3) decreasing the size of the plot operated by the individual owner, tenant, or cooperative; (4) the removal of land ownership from private to public ownership; (5) increasing the size of the plot operated by the individual owner, tenant, or cooperative.

12. Climate is a factor often mentioned with respect to the level of a nation's real income. The text's verdict on this factor is that (1) a temperate climate (neither excessively hot nor frigid) seems to be essential for a high level of per capita real income; (2) climate cannot be dismissed as one contributing factor, but in history the highest levels of civilization were sometimes reached outside the so-called "temperate" zone; (3) all things considered, climate usually turns out to be the critical element in economic development; (4) the earth's warmer regions, with allowance now made for modern developments such as air conditioning, actually have the greatest potential for future economic development; (5) climate has no real significance, nor will it have, in a careful analysis of past or future economic development.

QUIZ: Other

A less developed country is undertaking a large-scale development program and asks you to supply information on the following points. (Under each point, circle the number which you think furnishes the best answer.)

a. Change in population to be expected:
(1) Both the birth rate and the death rate are likely to remain high for some time.
(2) Both the birth rate and the death rate are likely to remain low for some time.
(3) Both the birth rate and the death rate are likely to fall substantially in the next few years.
(4) The death rate is likely to fall, and the birth rate to remain at its present high level for some time.

b. Capital-formation policy:
(1) In view of the post-World War II experience, primary reliance can be placed on borrowing and aid from abroad.
(2) The primary problem will be better allocation of existing saving rather than increasing total saving.
(3) Historical experience suggests that the percentage of national product put into personal saving and into capital formation will have to be increased and perhaps ultimately doubled.
(4) "Borrowing technology" will enable development at existing levels of saving.

c. Investment allocation:
(1) The government should make sure that it is undertaking adequate investment in social overhead capital.
(2) Private entrepreneurs can be relied upon to properly allocate available saving.
(3) Although inflation tends ultimately to discourage saving, it also tends to better allocate available saving.
(4) Modern technology makes heavy use of capital in production and hence should be avoided.

d. Change in foreign trade:
(1) Imports are likely to fall as domestic manufactures replace foreign manufactures.
(2) Imports are likely to rise because of the need for foreign capital goods—and possibly for food and fuel.
(3) Exports of primary products should be pushed, since this is where comparative advantage must lie.
(4) Exports should fall as the demand of developed countries for raw materials continues to decline.

39

ECONOMICS OF DISCRIMINATION: RACE AND SEX

1. The text examines two principal forms of discrimination by race. One arises when, as between two individuals of equal training and competence, one of them is discriminated against by reason of his race or the color of his skin. What is the other?

_____

_____

_____ .

Discrimination in educational-training opportunities, resulting in inequalities of training and competence.

2. _a._ According to the statistics, in the years immediately following World War II, the rate of unemployment was *(higher / lower)* among young blacks than among young whites. Today, the black unemployment rate is *(higher / lower)* than the white rate.

_b._ The text puts forward five possible explanations for this puzzling change. Cite at least four of these explanations.

_____

_____

_____

_____

_____

_____

_____

_____

_____

_____

_a._ lower; higher. _b._ (1) Unusually high black employment rate in World War II. (2) Migration of blacks into ghetto areas where employment is harder to find. (3) Young labor supply is now much greater, owing to lowering of average population age, and young-black employment is perhaps more affected by this development than young-white employment. (4) Blacks have not shared equally in rising trend toward college training, leaving more of them

for unskilled jobs (where unemployment rate is typically much higher). (5) Minimum-wage laws.

3. The United States has absorbed, with reasonable success, the greater part of many immigrant groups (particularly those from Europe) into the mainstream of its economic and social life. This has resulted in the "melting pot" thesis, which argues that discrimination against any particular group is in the United States a temporary phenomenon. In the view of the text, this thesis *(is / is not)* valid as applied to Negroes, American Indians, and many Spanish-speaking Americans. The problem of the integration of these groups *(should / cannot)* be left to the working of the "melting pot"—i.e., solely to private action.

is not; cannot.

4. _a._ In the 1950s, in the United States, the average of nonwhite family incomes was about one-half that of white families. By the mid-1970s, the fraction *(had fallen to almost two-fifths / was unchanged / had climbed to about three-fifths)*.

In the text's view, this change:
(1) Reflects a significant part of a trend toward greater equality between white and nonwhite.
(2) May have been, in part at least, a short-term swing, and may or may not be significant as part of the long-term trend.

_b._ Some people regard the control of price inflation as the most critical socioeconomic task facing the United States today. Others think it is even more important to provide greater opportunities to minority groups for the improvement of their position. Unfortunately, there may be some conflict between these two objectives; that is the significance of part _a_ of this question.

If the control of price inflation is treated as a matter of restraining aggregate money demand, then the objective of monetary and fiscal policy will be to *(encourage / restrain)* growth in GNP. As part of such an anti-inflationary policy, the rate of unemployment can be expected to *(increase / decrease)* somewhat. But black employment is frequently "marginal" employment: the black worker is last to be hired, first to be fired. Consequently, when GNP is restrained, black unemployment *(rises / falls)* sharply.

In contrast, when emphasis can be placed on *growth* in

307

GNP, as it was in the first half of the 1960s (after the doldrums of the 1950s), the position of minority groups *(improves / deteriorates)* significantly.

---

a. climbed to three-fifths; (2). *b.* restrain; increase; rises; improves.

---

5. The fact that job discrimination produces two different prices for labor of equal skill means, in supply-and-demand terms, that there are two separate markets for labor. The supply curve in one such market reflects the supply of privileged white labor; in the other, the labor supply of blacks and others discriminated against. The demand curve in each market is a "derived demand" (see Chapter 27), reflecting basically the marginal-product of labor.

The remedy for discrimination indicated in the text would be to *(unite / keep separate)* the two markets. The effect would be to *(increase / decrease)* total labor supply in the hitherto-white market. The consequence to be expected from any such supply increase is *(a decrease / an increase)* in the wage level in that market.

In the text's view, the resulting wage-rate change would probably be *(large / small)*. This conclusion assumes that the demand curve for labor is highly *(elastic / inelastic)* with respect to price (i.e., the wage level).

---

unite; increase; a decrease; small; elastic.

---

6. Almost all large-city ghetto areas in the United States have small supermarkets, liquor stores, and other retail establishments operated by white proprietors. Prices in such stores are typically somewhat higher than those charged in adjacent nonghetto areas. These prices, linked with white ownership, have sometimes been a source of resentment among residents—hence a demand for black proprietorship.

In the text's view, the evolution of "black capitalism" in this form *(probably will develop, and would be desirable / probably will develop, but would not be desirable / would be desirable, but probably will not develop / probably will not develop, and probably would not be desirable)*.

Behind this conclusion lie two principal considerations. First, a prospective black entrepreneur typically finds it *(more / less)* difficult to raise money capital than does his white counterpart. Second, the rate of return on capital investment among such ghetto enterprises is most likely to be *(above / about / below)* average, as compared with enterprises elsewhere.

In sum, this approach to "black separatism" might contribute something to Negro pride. But it seems *(likely / unlikely)* to improve the economic lot of the black community.

---

probably will not develop, and would not be desirable; more; below; unlikely.

---

7. White resentment of black progress is particularly evident when real-estate values are involved. The white family that sees black neighbors appear for the first time is beset by two fears. First, it thinks the character of the neighborhood may be destroyed (as though all blacks behaved as particular slum residents sometimes behave). Second, the white family is afraid real-estate values will fall when black families begin to "take over." The house is an important fixed asset for any family; for most families, it is the biggest investment made in a lifetime. Consequently, this property-value fear is understandable, whether or not it happens to be well-founded.

a. It is not unknown for unscrupulous real-estate operators to exploit this concern. They paint a grim picture of the future and persuade the white family to sell out "before it's too late." Then they resell (at a notably higher price) to a black family. This practice is known as (see text)

_____ .

According to the text, this fear of declining real-estate values *(has some foundation / is not, in general, well-founded)*. Middle-class black families often experience considerable difficulty in obtaining decent housing, because of tacit agreements to exclude them from particular neighborhoods. Consequently, when housing *is* available, they probably will offer a somewhat *(higher / lower)* price than a comparable white family would do.

b. Of course, it is difficult to generalize too freely concerning the effect upon real-estate values produced when black residents first enter a hitherto-white neighborhood. When black families seek to buy real estate, they *(add to the demand for / subtract from the supply of)* houses for sale. This tends to push the price of housing in that area *(up / down)*. But if white families begin an exodus from the region, this will *(add to the demand for / add to the supply of / subtract from the supply of)* housing for sale in the area involved. This action tends to push the price of real estate in that region *(up / down)*. Hence two effects are at work, and with respect to price, they work in *(opposite directions / the same direction)*.

---

a. "block busting"; is not well-founded; higher. *b.* add to demand for; up; add to supply of; down; opposite directions.

---

8. *a.* The text suggests that we should treat ghetto areas as we do the less developed countries. The program indicated by this approach would demand *(only governmental aid / only private aid, from business and the like / both governmental and private aid)*.

b. In the matter of governmental aid, several subsidy (or tax-credit) measures are suggested. Name the specific objectives of at least three of these subsidy proposals.

_____

_____

_a._ both governmental and private aid. _b._ To move industry to ghetto areas; to make cheaper capital and insurance available to black entrepreneurs; to provide more education in business skills; to provide better commuter-bus services.

QUIZ: Multiple Choice

1. _The young-black unemployment rate, which was lower than the young-white unemployment rate thirty years ago, is now higher. One explanation for this change (according to the text) may be_ (1) discrimination against young black workers; (2) the high proportion of blacks drafted for military service; (3) the heavy concentration of the black population in the Southern states; (4) more emphasis upon college training as a requirement for employment; (5) none of the preceding.

2. _In the United States, the profit earned from production and sale of slaves (according to the text)_ (1) fell significantly after the import of slaves from Africa was cut off in the early 1800s; (2) rose significantly after slave imports were cut off in the early 1800s, until the rate of return on investment was significantly higher than that obtained from field crops such as tobacco or cotton; (3) was significantly higher than the rate of return from investment in field crops, both before and after 1800; (4) was significantly below the rate of return obtained in other investments, both before and after 1800; (5) is not correctly described by any of the above.

3. _It is suggested that ghetto areas ought to be treated as less developed countries. One course of action suggested by the text as part of such a "development program" is that of_ (1) encouraging more small-scale, white-owned businesses in the ghetto area; (2) developing more and better bus lines leading out of the ghetto area; (3) supporting black separatism; (4) encouraging more small-scale, black-owned businesses in the ghetto area; (5) none of the above.

4. _Between the 1950s and the 1970s, average nonwhite family income rose somewhat relative to average white family income. This increase seems to have been, in considerable part, attributable to_ (1) the operation of the progressive income-tax system (since the figures refer to after-tax incomes); (2) a fall in the general unemployment level; (3) the imposition of anti-inflationary policies; (4) the migration of nonwhite families into large-city areas; (5) none of the above.

5. _With respect to discrimination by sex, which one among the following five statements is true, according to the text?_ (1) Women live a shorter time than men. (2) Over-all, women's earnings increase as they grow older, but not by as much as men's earnings increase. (3) Primitive societies show a fairly uniform pattern in the allocation of economic tasks between men and women. (4) Women are not capable of the same sustained acts of effort as men are. (5) If employers have found that men stay longer in employment than women do, it is rational for them to withhold from women some on-the-job training which they offer men.

6. _With respect to discrimination by sex, which one among the following five statements is true, according to the text?_ (1) Over the past 75 or 100 years, the percentage of women participating in the paid labor force has sharply increased. (2) There is a rough correspondence between differences in the earnings of men and women and their physical and psychological differences. (3) Discrimination against women in employment produces an economic gain for men which just matches the economic loss for women. (4) Overall, the average employed woman earns less than 50 per cent of what the average employed man earns. (5) In most societies, geographically and historically, women have been allowed to make a considerably smaller contribution to the total national product than men.

40

THE QUALITY OF LIFE: POVERTY AND INEQUALITY, ECOLOGY AND GROWTH, LOVE AND JUSTICE

THE GENERAL TOPIC of this chapter is social justice and social reform. Within that general topic, four specific issues are discussed:

1. Poverty and income inequality
2. The application of economic analysis to a wide range of matters not always regarded as falling within the scope of economics: time; human capital; law; and love
3. Pollution of the environment
4. The growth-versus-stability debate: zero population growth, and zero economic growth

1. The matter of poverty is not just a problem for the poor. It concerns the viability of our whole society.

Following World War II, there was an impressive rise in the output of material goods and services. This was largely accomplished by avoiding the serious recessions and depressions which for so long had plagued the more developed nations. In turn, this smoother year-to-year flow of output was largely the consequence of better understanding of the use of fiscal and monetary policies.

The resulting gains in real income were distributed widely—but not evenly. In extreme instances (notably among the American Indians and many blacks), there was almost no gain at all. More generally, the gains were somewhat uneven: some groups did better than others. Now a family's sense of material well-being depends substantially on the level of its own real income—but it depends also on its awareness of how well *other* families are doing. If those others seem to be gaining more, a sense of grievance may develop.

The worst-positioned groups (such as Indians and blacks) were usually outside the mainstream of economic activity; that is why they were nongainers. Unrest among them sometimes exploded into violence; they could see no other effective means by which to express their sense of grievance. Within the mainstream, the relative losers (or those who thought they were falling behind) had a different weapon available: the strike.

Thus all of us—even if only insofar as we want a smooth and well-ordered society, one within which at least a minimum sense of *community* exists—must be concerned about poverty and extreme inequalities in the distribution of income.

The study of poverty, as a subject for careful scientific inquiry, has barely begun. There is no simple explanation.

For example, the view that the poor are poor just because of their own shiftlessness has *some* validity in *some* situations. But why are they shiftless? As an overall explanation of poverty, the shiftlessness argument is thoroughly inadequate, however smugly reassuring it may be to those who happen not to be poor.

Some social scientists have insisted that the distribution of income is governed by law—not the laws of any government, but laws dictated by underlying social forces. Malthus' argument, for example (see Chapters 2 and 37), was that the mass of the population was ultimately doomed to a real-income level close to the survival minimum.

In broad outline, Karl Marx would have agreed with Malthus even though his background analysis was quite different. Marx regarded the immiserization of the workers as a consequence of the laws by which the capitalist system functioned. He believed that the dynamics of capitalism would ultimately lead to its overthrow by socialism.

Vilfredo Pareto (1848–1932), an Italian economist and sociologist who did much of his work at the University of Lausanne, examined the distribution of income in different countries at different periods. He was struck by the apparent constancy of the degree of income inequality (as, for example, the Lorenz-curve device of Chapter 5 would illustrate it). Pareto and his followers were thus inclined toward a belief in some underlying law which governed this inequality.

It is one thing to grope for an underlying law of income distribution; it is quite another to reach agreement with other seekers after truth as to the nature of this law. For example, the views of Pareto and of Marx on income distribution were probably quite different.

Figure 40-1 (similar in general construction to text Figure 40-1) illustrates this difference. The solid line *TT* illustrates a typical rise in *total* real income such as has occurred over the past 100 years in countries of the Western world. The broken line *AA* shows the growth in real income accruing to the less fortunate 50 per cent of the population, on the assumption that its share of total real income, at all times throughout the century, would be just 25 per cent of that total income. The dotted line *AZ* illustrates a share which does not increase at all. Had this been the share of the less favored 50 per cent of the population in 1880, the absolute real income of that 50 per cent would be exactly the same in 1980. In *relative* terms, this share would of course have decreased greatly.

Total real income

1880 1900 1920 1940 1960 1980

Fig. 40-1

Pareto's view as to the law of income distribution would be best illustrated by the line (AA / AZ).

If we assume for convenience a population of unchanged total size throughout the period, then Marx's view (allowing for possible dissent by some Marxian scholars) is probably best approximated by the line (AA / AZ).

AA; AZ.

---

2. If one believes that there are social forces which produce some law of income distribution, then it is only a short step to the further belief that attempts to change the distribution of income by means of legislation are attempts to violate natural laws; hence they are misguided, can do little good, and at worst can seriously reduce total real output. This happened in Malthus' case: his views were translated by those he had influenced into the argument that it does no good to try to alleviate the condition of the poor. Malthus' analysis was thus used in support of a harsh revision of the English Poor Laws in 1834.

Circle the numbers of those statements following which seem to repeat the text chapter's comments on this topic of governmental intervention.

(1) Laws such as those imposing a progressive personal income tax have changed income distribution—in the direction of greater income equality. These changes have not had the catastrophic effect on society which opponents predicted at the time the laws were passed.

(2) Statistics of income distribution are not sufficiently reliable or complete to permit firm conclusions, but it is probable that the share of income received by the lower 50 per cent of the population in the United States has increased somewhat over the past 100 years. In Fig. 40-1 terms, if the share of the

lower 50 per cent in 1880 was indicated by left-hand point A, its share in 1980 would be somewhat above right-hand point A.

(3) There are no immutable laws of income distribution. But it is exceedingly difficult to effect any significant change in the existing distribution, sometimes more difficult than proponents of change are willing to admit.

(4) Some proposals to improve the position of people at the bottom of the income scale, although seriously offered, can be shortsighted. If adopted, they probably would not better the real income position of the poor, and they would reduce total output.

(5) The proposal for a "negative income tax" falls within this category of shortsighted proposals.

(6) All proposals for the redistribution of income toward greater equality are likely to carry with them some "disincentive" effect. They are proposals that the real income pie be shared more equally, and their implementation would probably reduce somewhat the size of the total pie.

(7) If a redistribution-of-income proposal seems likely to result in a perceptible reduction in total real income, it should not be implemented.

(8) Proposals for income redistribution should be evaluated in tradeoff terms: Is the gain derived from greater equality of income (as measured by the emphasis society currently places on greater equality) worth the loss in terms of likely real output reduction?

---

(1), (2), (3), (4), (6), (8).

---

3. Figure 40-2 (similar in general construction to text Figure 40-2) illustrates the "disincentive" consequence attributable to income redistribution. Point A indicates the distribution of some given real income total (measured in money terms) between the two halves of the population. (These halves are equal in numbers, but unequal in terms of incomes received.) Total income of the upper-income half is OG. That of the lower-income half is AG. Because, together, they represent the incomes of the two halves, the sum of OG plus AG must equal that population's total income.

With the diagram's axes labeled as they are (i.e., with upper-half income recorded horizontally), if there is any inequality whatever in income distribution, then point A *must* lie below and to the right of the 45° line. With all incomes exactly equal (but only in that case), point A would land squarely on the 45° line.

a. Suppose that a dollar-for-dollar transfer of money (and real) incomes between the upper and lower income halves of the population is undertaken—specifically, a movement toward greater income equality. In terms of Fig. 40-2, it is a move of point A (*away from* / *toward*) the 45° line. Suppose further,

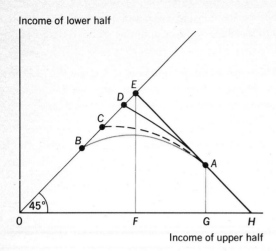

Fig. 40-2

and for the moment, that this transfer results in no "disincentive" consequences—i.e., the population's entire income total is *(not reduced at all / reduced)*.

The straight line *EH* also forms a 45° angle with the horizontal axis.[1] If there are no discentive consequences, then point *A* will move along this straight line toward point *E*. Because of *EH*'s 45° property, the increase in what was formerly *AG (will / will not)* be exactly matched by the reduction in what was formerly *OG*.

b. If greater-equality income redistribution were carried all the way to point *E* (still assuming no disincentive effect), there would *(still / no longer)* be "upper-income" and "lower-income" halves of the population. With no disincentive effect, the resulting total income, *EF* plus *OF*, would be *(greater than / the same as / less than)* the before-redistribution total income, namely *OG* plus *AG*.

c. Usually it is argued that any redistribution toward greater equality would have some disincentive consequences. Suppose redistribution is undertaken by means of heavier progressive income taxation. The extra tax proceeds so collected from higher-income people would be passed on to lower-income groups by transfer payments or by other such devices. Insofar as people try to avoid heavier taxation by working

[1]In a more advanced analysis, we would have to recognize that *EH* might not be a straight line. We put matters in terms of a transfer of *money* income between the two groups. But of course it is the resulting transfer of *real* income that matters: one group gains more purchasing power, the other group loses it. Of necessity, we measure real income in money terms; but it is still the transfer of *real* income we want to indicate by any move along *EH*. Suppose that money dollars are transferred from the upper-income half to the lower-income half. If the result is to change any of the money prices at which the items of real income are valued—and it probably will, if the tastes of the two groups are at all different—then things become more complicated. The dollar-for-dollar transfer can still be depicted as a movement along a straight 45° line, but the real income transfer will no longer be a straight line, even if there is no disincentive effect. This complication is best left completely to one side in an introductory survey.

shorter hours, or in other ways earning a little less income, the total of real GNP will *(fall / rise)*. The path of redistribution will no longer run from *A* toward *E*. Starting at *A*, it will gradually leave *EA*, and run more and more *(above / below)* *EA*, since the total of real income produced will be *(less / more)* than it was at point *A*.

The more sweeping the attempted redistribution—i.e., the farther the intended movement from *A* toward *E*—the *(less / more)* pronounced this disincentive effect is likely to be.

d. The three curved lines in Fig. 40-2, *DA*, *CA*, and *BA*, show three possible sets of disincentive consequences. Among them, the smallest disincentive effect is indicated by *(DA / CA / BA)*.

Notice that line *CA* is approximately flat in the region close to point *C*. This means that if redistribution toward complete equality were pressed hard enough, there would be a sufficient drop in *total* GNP that the real income of the lower half, in absolute terms, would *(increase only slightly / not increase at all / decrease)*. In *relative* terms—that is, relative to income received by the upper half—the share of the lower half would *(still increase / remain constant / decrease)*.

e. The most drastic disincentive effect is illustrated by line *BA*. If redistribution effects are such that total income follows this path, the lower half of the income distribution will at first (as the movement from *A* toward *B* commences) experience a moderate *(increase / decrease)* in real income. But thereafter the real income of this lower half of the population will *(increase / decline)*, in absolute terms.

If the likely redistribution path is as indicated by *DA*, society may well decide that some movement from *A* toward *D* is worth while: the sacrifice of total real income is justified by the resulting greater equality. But if the probable path of redistribution is indicated by *BA*, or even by *CA*, the cost in terms of total real income sacrificed is greater, and society must put a higher priority on income equality if either of these two paths is to be followed, even for a short distance away from *A*.

---

a. toward; not reduced at all; will. *b.* no longer; the same as. *c.* fall; below; less; more. *d.* DA; not increase at all; still increase. *e.* increase; decline.

---

4. Attempts to benefit lower-income groups by setting a ceiling or floor on particular prices can sometimes backfire. For example, some states have imposed a maximum on the legal interest rate to be charged on consumer loans, intending thereby to protect consumer borrowers. But if this maximum rate is set too low—taking into account the risk of default when such loans are made and the alternative opportunities existing for those with money to lend—the result may be that the supply of money available for low-income would-be borrowers *(dries up / increases)*. The loan business is then left to illegally operating loan sharks who exact rates (*even higher / lower*) than legitimate lenders would charge.

A similar problem may arise over rent ceilings. These may sometimes constitute an effective short-term remedy for rent gouging. Yet, if landlords are able to gouge because of a shortage of available housing, the only remedy that is ultimately satisfactory is an increase in housing supply. A legally imposed rent ceiling, if set too low, (*encourages / discourages*) construction of new housing. Those lucky enough to get housing at the legal price benefit. Yet the number who cannot find housing at all will (*increase / decrease*) as old housing becomes decrepit and new housing is not built.

dries up; even higher; discourages; increase.

5. The text cites five causes of income inequality. Name at least three, listing first the factor specified as responsible for the greatest disparities in income.

There are limits to the income which superior talent or energy can earn. A popular television personality may earn huge sums annually. But income is limited by the number of performances he or she is physically capable of giving. Moreover, earnings dwindle if popularity fades, or as old age begins to set in.

Property income is not subject to equivalent restraints. Ownership of stocks and bonds may demand comparatively little supervisory effort. If you have somehow made a good start in security ownership, you may reinvest your earnings and watch them grow. Moreover, unless checked by death or inheritance taxes, property and its income can be passed on to one's children, as talent and energy cannot.

Differences in property wealth. Differences in personal ability. Differences in education and opportunity. Class barriers to opportunity. Differences in age and health.

6. *a.* Circle the numbers of those among the following statements which repeat, at least approximately, the text's views on welfare programs—other than the "negative income tax" (discussed in part *b* of this question).

(1) The *disincentive* effect within many welfare programs means a loss of billions of dollars in potential national product.

(2) These programs are very costly; many are unnecessary and should be done away with as soon as reasonably possible.

(3) A welfare recipient who takes a minimum-wage job often

finds that with the consequent reduction or termination of welfare payments, he or she is worse off economically than when not working.

(4) Many, or most, programs are shot through with gross abuses. Most recipients could work, but avoid doing so because of the opportunity to remain on welfare.

(5) The cost of welfare programs has become a tremendous financial burden to many large metropolitan areas.

(6) Most of the programs are necessary, but they are costly, often inefficient, often degrading to the recipients.

b. The proposal for a "negative income tax" is a comparatively recent one. The text chapter's overall verdict upon it is (*favorable / unfavorable*).

Conservatives and liberals often join in support of this proposal. The difference is that the conservative frequently wants the negative income tax to *replace* most or all of the other welfare programs. The liberal often regards continuation of at least some of these other programs as still necessary; in this sense, the negative tax is wanted as a *supplement*.

One feature of the negative-tax proposal is important and gives it a resemblance to the ordinary tax system. Suppose you receive $3,000 annually from the government as a negative income tax. Through personal effort, you then manage to increase your own earnings by $3,000. The consequence will be that your negative-tax payment (*ceases entirely / remains at $3,000 / is reduced by some intermediate figure such as $1,500*). That is, your total receipts (negative tax plus earnings) (*go up / go down / are unchanged*). Hence, there (*is an / is not any*) incentive to increase total receipts built into the system. In this, it (*differs from / is the same as*) most other welfare programs.

a. (1); (3); (5); (6). *b.* favorable; is reduced by some intermediate figure; go up; is an; differs from.

7. Within its section "The New Microeconomics," the text chapter discusses such topics as time, investment in human capital, law and justice, and love. Most items within this varied list are usually considered as falling outside the purview of conventional economics. However, the argument is that you may encounter within any of these topics a principle which economic analysis has considered at length. The word "economics" derives from "economize," and it is the principle of *economy* that is involved. The crucial factor often applicable in matters of time, justice, or any other of the topics mentioned (it was discussed as early as Chapter 2 of the text) is this:

It is the extension of this basic principle that may be useful. Especially through Part 3 of the text, "the marginalist rule" was stressed (e.g., the equation of marginal revenue and marginal cost in profit maximization). In nontechnical language, that rule runs somewhat as follows: Whatever your objective, if you want to do the best you can in its attainment, *keep balancing the gain against its cost.* Pursue your objective, but if and when you observe that the (marginal) loss resulting from that pursuit begins to exceed the (marginal) gain, stop.

As an example, consider thalidomide. Its overhasty introduction as a tranquilizer produced sheer tragedy for many families: malformed children. Yet reaction to such a disaster in the form of overhasty regulation concerning the development of new drugs could produce equal (if perhaps less publicized) tragedy: People might suffer or die for lack of a drug that could have been made available.

Obviously, lack of complete information often makes the decision in such areas exceedingly difficult. The problem is further complicated by individual differences in value judgments. These considerations do not alter the fact that decisions must be made. They should be made by reference to the principle of trying to balance the gain against the loss.

Scarcity of the item (e.g., time, justice, love) in relation to the need or demand for that item.

---

8. *a.* In the matter of pollution (contamination of air or water, excessive noise, etc.), the text's conclusion is that the remedy must lie principally in *(voluntary cooperation by citizens in the cleanup / governmental action).* As to industrial pollution, the cost of the cleanup *(should be borne by the industry responsible / must ultimately be paid by the consumer in the form of a higher price for the industry's product).*

Again, question 7's cost-versus-gain rule applies. We want some areas of water sufficiently clean to be pleasant and safe for swimming. Do we want all water to be so cleansed? In proximity to some industrial regions, the costs of such a cleanup might be immense. There, settlement for a lower standard might be better: a sufficient reduction in pollution for the water not to be offensive to eye or to nose. We *(must / must not)* try to balance the gain against its cost. Again, the problem is complicated by the fact that different people value particular gains differently. Yet, again also, decisions must be made.

b. Unfortunately, in the early 1970s when the OPEC nations quadrupled the price of oil, a reevaluation of the benefits and costs in pollution control became necessary. Control standards were in general *(lowered / raised).* (Thus power-generating plants were allowed to use coal and oil with a higher sulphur content.)

We must understand the circumstances which enabled OPEC to exact its higher petroleum price. The huge rise in industrial output, spread over much of the world, greatly increased the demand for raw materials. Once again, then,

question 7's first principle reappears: scarcity in relation to demand.

There is no single remedy for the new scarcity pressures. There is much we can do, and in the past have not done, to economize on energy use. But, in the text's view, the problem must in considerable part be handled by *(price controls on / higher prices for)* raw materials.

---

a. governmental action; must ultimately be paid by the consumer; must. *b.* lowered; higher prices for.

QUIZ: Multiple Choice

1. *According to the text, the factor which has singly been most important in reducing economic inequality over the past 30 years has been* (1) the growth of universal suffrage (voting power); (2) the growth of the feminist (women's liberation) movement; (3) the provision of public education; (4) the attainment of high employment through effective fiscal and monetary policies; (5) death and inheritance taxation.

2. *The text emphasizes as important in reduction of economic inequality* another *of the five items listed in question 1—although this one has worked over a period much longer than 30 years. Which one?* (1). (2). (3). (4). (5).

3. *The benefit of higher education expenditure at the state level seems to have gone (the text suggests)* (1) mainly to the top 10 per cent in the income distribution; (2) mainly to the middle class; (3) mainly to the lower-income 50 per cent; (4) mainly to the poor; (5) to all income classes, quite uniformly.

4. *By the "inefficiency" of income redistribution is meant* (1) the reduction in total output caused by those unfavorably affected by redistribution, and by their decision to pay less in income tax by working less; (2) the administrative costs of redistribution; (3) the lesser skills of the gainers from redistribution; (4) the total amount of income transferred from upper-income to lower-income groups; (5) the resulting reduction in total taxes collected by the government.

5. *A poor family's employment earnings are supplemented by a "negative income tax"—in the amount, say, of $1,500. Under this tax proposal, if family employment earnings were to rise by $1,000, the income received from the "negative tax" would typically* (1) fall by $1,000; (2) fall by more than $1,000; (3) fall by some amount such as $500; (4) not fall at all; (5) rise by some amount such as $500.

6. *The text evaluates the negative income tax proposal as being* (1) undesirable because of its "disincentive" effect, even though in other respects it would be superior to existing welfare programs; (2) superior to existing welfare programs in its "incentive" effect, although some existing programs would probably have to be retained; (3) undesirable in that it would be inferior in most effects to existing welfare programs; (4) not much better and not much worse than existing programs, hence hardly worth introduction because of the costs of such introduction; (5) superior to existing welfare programs to such an extent that it would substitute for virtually all of them.

7. *Some social scientists have been convinced that the matter of income distribution is dictated by natural or social laws, beyond the power of any elected government to alter (except in the very short run). The text's verdict on this view is, in general, as follows:* (1) It is valid in that there is a reasonably close match between distribution of income and distribution of energy or talent, but in other respects the evidence fails to support it. (2) There is no supporting evidence, and it should be dismissed outright. (3) Elected governments *can* alter income distribution, and could easily have done much more than they have done were it not for pressure brought by special-interest groups. (4) It is almost completely valid, because the great bulk of the evidence supports it. (5) Elected governments *can* alter income distribution, although the redistribution process is much more complex and difficult than some reformers are prepared to admit.

8. *Individual A shops in supermarkets with careful regard for price charged per ounce of product. Individual B looks for convenience foods, with much less attention to their prices. The text's verdict on such behavior disparities is that* (1) because of resource scarcity and the pressure of increasing scarcity, A is behaving economically, whereas B is not; (2) because of the scarcity of time, both A and B may be acting rationally and economically, each in his or her own fashion, according to their different circumstances; (3) individual A, in emphasizing price, may completely overlook differences in product quality; (4) these choices simply reflect differences in tastes, and have nothing to do with scarcity or scarcities of any kind; (5) a compromise · between these disparities (less

emphasis on price for A, less on convenience for B) would improve the welfare of both of them.

9. *During some periods in United States history, income disparities appear to have widened; during other periods, to have narrowed. A period within which (the text suggests) the lower-income groups probably* lost *ground was that of* (1) World War II; (2) the Great Depression of the 1930s; (3) World War I; (4) the late 1960s; (5) the prosperity of the 1920s.

10. *Among the five time periods listed in question 9, there was one within which—again, the text suggests—the lower-income groups probably* gained *ground. Which one was it?* (1). (2). (3). (4). (5).

11. *Which one among the following five statements contradicts what the text chapter says concerning income and its redistribution?* (1) Attempts to redistribute income, if pressed too hard, may actually reduce the total of real incomes produced. (2) Most economists, even those within communist nations, expect that real wages in North America and Western Europe will rise by at least 30 per cent between today and the close of the twentieth century. (3) The provision of public education has been a powerful factor working toward reduced income inequality over the past century or more. (4) The overall effect of the welfare programs introduced during the past 25 or 30 years has been, ironically, to worsen the position of the lowest-income groups. (5) The greatest disparities in the distribution of income are due to differences in ownership of wealth.

12. *The problem of the pollution of air and of water by industry is an example of* (1) external diseconomies; (2) the working of the Invisible Hand; (3) the operation of the law of diminishing returns; (4) competitive disequilibrium; (5) none of the above.

41 FULL EMPLOYMENT AND PRICE STABILITY IN THE MIXED ECONOMY

THE CENTRAL MESSAGE of this chapter is a simple one: Economics has made enormous progress since 1930, but it still has far to go. One vital question concerning capitalism has been answered. Another question, perhaps of equal importance, remains unanswered.

1. It was (and is) a standard Marxist argument that capitalism's sheer productive power would be its ultimate ruin: it would be destroyed through inability to find adequate markets for its products. In the struggle to maintain their profits, capitalists would try to create a demand for military materiel by exercising their political power so as to push the nation to the edge of war, or even into war. And they would try to exploit the less developed nations by using them as a kind of dumping ground for excess production.

a. This thesis (discussed more fully in text Chapter 42) is, accordingly, one that forecasts a worsening series of crises arising out of a worsening deficiency of purchasing power. The Great Depression of the 1930s, with its gross (*shortage / excess*) of money demand, seemed to (*deny / confirm*) this thesis. World War II followed: military spending pushed all the nations involved into full employment. Again the thesis seemed (*denied / confirmed*).

The text's verdict is that this argument is (*invalid / valid*)— although it has just enough of truth to be persuasive. The total of capitalist purchasing power *can* fall short of its required full-employment level. Military spending *can* restore full employment.

The problem is that capitalism's market system cannot perform all the tasks sometimes expected of it. The credit-market mechanism is incapable of converting saving into investment at a continuous full-employment level. Thus a fall in investment spending can mean a fall in purchasing power below the full-employment level; and the multiplier process swells the resulting drop in GNP. Were the pricing system more "flexible," it might restore full employment by pulling supply prices down until a shrunken money-purchasing-power total was again sufficient to buy the full-employment output. But the pricing system lacks the requisite flexibility; it is not the sensitive, responsive instrument envisaged in pure (or perfect) competition theory. Finally, the money supply, dependent on the credit-creating power of commercial banks, is (in a sense) *too* flexible. Left to its own devices, this money supply will rise when GNP rises and fall when GNP falls, instead of remaining steady.

Until the early 1930s, economists had not grasped the significance of these conditions. The Great Depression forced them into a realization that their vision of the capitalist process was in some respects faulty, and that their grasp on some of the realities of that process was incomplete or nonexistent.

The outcome of this reconsideration was Keynesian economics. In its wake came the monetary and fiscal policies outlined in Part 2 of the text. These developments have vastly changed human affairs. Although the Great Depression was probably the worst of its kind, it was nevertheless one in a long series of such crises. Since World War II's close, these conditions have never been repeated—not even in the recession of the mid-1970s. If you have lived through both periods, you find it difficult to explain to anyone born too late for the Depression of the 1930s how immense the gap between the two eras really is.

Cold-war military spending has contributed to the difference. Yet it would be foolish to attribute everything to such spending. The change has come about mainly because of a somewhat improved grasp of capitalist mechanisms and, consequently, better handling of banking and governmental policies.

b. Accordingly, the text's verdict is that military spending is (*the only device / only one of many possible devices*) for influencing the GNP level. Governmental spending can be directed in many ways. An increase or a decrease in such spending, through its multiplier effects, influences consumer spending. Such consumer spending (*cannot otherwise be influenced / can also be influenced by tax changes*). Investment spending can perhaps be influenced via (*monetary policy alone / monetary policy and appropriate tax changes*).

---

a. shortage; confirm; confirmed; invalid. *b.* only one of many possible devices; can also be influenced by tax changes; monetary policy and tax changes.

---

2. The generation of economists emerging in the 1950s, having learned Keynesian theory, understood how an unrestrained free-market system could occasionally produce such disastrous results as those of the 1930s. They knew how fiscal and monetary policies could be used to increase purchasing power up to, or close to, a full-employment level.

Elsewhere, the new economists were more orthodox. They understood that the process of deliberate manufacture of purchasing power could be overdone. If pushed without proper

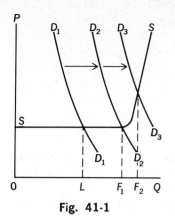 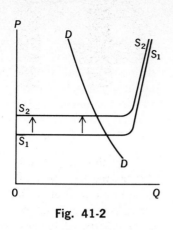

Fig. 41-1   **Fig. 41-2**

regard for full-employment limitations, it might yield a series of paper price increases. They knew also that prices might begin to rise *before* full employment was reached. However, there was reason to hope that "full employment" was a tolerably identifiable condition, and one that could at least be approached without significant upward price pressure. Most manufacturing plants reach their minimum-cost operating point at outputs quite close to capacity. Labor in any occupation is less likely to insist on higher wages if there is still substantial unemployment within that occupation.

Figure 41-1, at left above, illustrates in rough outline the prevailing 1950s view as to full-employment policy. It is an ordinary Chapter 4 or Chapter 20 supply-and-demand diagram. (Sometimes it is dangerously misleading to use this diagram, which pertains to a single commodity and hence to a tiny part of the whole economy, to illustrate overall price-level behavior. But it can be used as to the point here involved.) Demand curve D_1 represents a less-than-full-employment purchasing-power level. Fiscal and monetary policies can raise this to D_2, thereby increasing output from OL to OF_1, without significant increase in the price level. If such policies are pressed further—say to the D_3 level—there will be some additional output. But it will come at the cost of a sharp price rise. (So F_1 marks the beginning of the "full-employment zone." Full employment cannot be precisely defined. But it is not so vague a term as to be meaningless.)

The reasoning illustrated by Fig. 41-1 was (as already mentioned) pretty much the orthodox 1950s view. The movement from D_2 to D_3 is *(demand-pull / cost-push)* inflation. It is *(demand / supply)* that pushes prices up. Ever since the Spaniards brought vast quantities of gold to Europe in the sixteenth century, thereby setting off a considerable inflation, it has been well and widely understood that prices will rise if "there is too much money chasing too few goods."

---

demand-pull; demand.

---

3. *a.* In the 1960s, economists began to observe that price behavior was not always explainable in such demand-pull terms. Prices went up when there was no evidence of a

demand increase. In the late 1960s, when prices had begun to rise at a disturbing rate, fiscal and monetary policies were deliberately tightened in an effort to lower, or at least stabilize, prices. The reasoning behind these policies was that the inflation was *(demand-pull / cost-push)* in nature. The result of these policies was that unemployment *(rose / remained constant / fell)*. Prices *(fell / stabilized / continued to rise)*.

This, then, is—or appears to be, at any rate—cost-push inflation. In elementary supply-and-demand terms, the price rise must be attributed to a shift of the *(demand / supply)* curve, as illustrated by Fig. 41-2, the right-hand diagram in the adjoining column. Prices go up *(even when purchasing power is somewhat below / only when purchasing power is at)* the full-employment level.

b. In terms of economic theory, the problem is that "the Keynesian revolution" was an incomplete revolution.

A century ago, as the text chapter points out, economist Leon Walras worked out a model of the capitalist system in which unemployment and overproduction are both impossible—in a system where all prices and wages float so as to reach simultaneous-equation solutions for all the relative prices and wages that will clear all markets. The Keynesian breakthrough was to let the facts oust this beautiful but somewhat irrelevant theory. In reality, prices and wages did not behave in the manner required for the Walrasian model.

Unfortunately, this breakthrough was not sufficiently wide to allow *all* the critical facts to penetrate the theory. Keynes demonstrated that the system could get stuck at a level well below that of full employment. This unhappy situation had something to do with the failure of prices and wages to "float" in Walrasian fashion. But Keynes did not identify the *exact* property (or properties) of the real-life price-and-wage system that was (or were) responsible. He was too preoccupied with other facets of his new theory to be able to devote sufficient attention to this aspect of the problem. *Something* in the price-and-wage system was at fault. But the identification of that something was, for immediate purposes, less important than the fact that fiscal and monetary policies, properly devised, could be used as remedies for unemployment.

Thus the problem is that "micro" theory, which deals explicitly with prices, *(has / has not)* kept pace with "macro" (Keynesian) theory. In fact, micro theory was left almost completely untouched by the development of Keynesian analysis. (As to the deficiencies within micro theory, see the comments at beginning and end of question 2, pp. 205 and 207.) Just as the problem of widespread unemployment *(lies somewhere / does not lie anywhere)* within the functioning of the actual price system, so the current inflation problem (or much of it, at any rate) *(lies / does not lie)* within that less-than-perfect system. (The explanation that it is all just a matter of "monopolistic control over price" is such an oversimplified one that, even insofar as it has any analytic meaning at all, it is useless for purposes of anti-inflation policy.)

a. demand-pull; rose; continued to rise; supply; even when purchasing power is somewhat below.
b. has not; lies somewhere; lies.

4. *a.* One important factor in this "new inflation" is that most manufacturing corporations (as already noted) find that production costs reach their minimum at an operating level close to capacity. In recession, industry profits consequently suffer on *two* counts: (1) less business, and (2) higher per-unit output costs. Hence, in a recovery movement from recession to full employment, industry profits *(fall / rise)* sharply. Trade-unions, noting this *(decline / improvement)* in profits, become more militant in wage demands: there is *(more / less)* income to be shared, and labor wants its share. At a time when orders are pouring in and any production shutdown would mean the loss of profitable business, the industry may *(resist / yield to)* this demand as probably it would not have done under recession conditions. However, it *(pays / does not pay)* the higher wage bill out of its higher profits. It *(raises / lowers)* prices, pleading higher labor costs. Higher prices are more easily obtained under full-employment conditions; and insofar as the tradition is that "prices must be built on costs," the firms making up this industry will feel justified in their increase.

Question: Is this sequence of events demand-pull inflation—because these events arise only as the economy moves from recession to full employment? Or is it cost-push inflation—because the price increase follows the wage increase?

b. Trade-unions are often made the villain of the inflationary piece. They play their part. So do employers. Are a union's leaders wrong to ask for "more," when they know that at least part of their demands will be granted? Moreover, as the text points out, some price-level rises are almost certainly demand-pull in nature. The evidence is that the unionized industries then *(lag in / lead)* the upward price movement. They act as *(an incendiary / a restraining)* force. It is the nonunionized industries that *(lag in / lead)* the upward price movement.

When a union demands higher wages for its members on the ground that the industry is now earning higher profits, it is demanding that the former distribution of income between capital and labor be maintained. When the industry raises its price, it too is trying to protect an established pattern of income distribution. The profits that went up can go down; the industry thinks of the possibility that they *will* go down.

Management's first choice would be: no increase in wages or other costs, therefore no need for any cost-induced increase in price. Its second choice would be: if an increase in wages or other costs, then an increase in price. Labor's first choice would be: an increase in wages, no increase in prices. Its second choice would be: an increase in wages, even if it has to be followed by a price increase. Unfortunately, the two first choices clash. So the two sides settle on terms which represent the second choice for both. And prices go up.

The text quotes A. P. Lerner's observation that if all sellers, whether of labor or property services or finished goods, so determine their prices that, together, the demand is for more than 100 per cent of the available national product, the inevitable outcome is a rise in the price level. (But note that Lerner's argument is a little broader than that stated here. He is talking about overall "sellers' inflation"—which includes the sellers of raw materials as well as the sellers of labor service and of finished goods.)

a. rise; improvement; more; yield to; does not pay; raises.
b. lag in; a restraining; lead.

5 A strict "monetarist" would dissent vigorously from at least part of the analysis outlined above as to the nature and sources of present-day inflation. For this view, we must turn back to some Chapter 15 material—specifically, the Quantity Equation of Exchange, and the hypothesis derived therefrom, the Quantity Theory of Money.

The Quantity Equation is: $MV = PQ$ or $MV = $ GNP.

Here, M stands for the nation's money stock, and V for the "income velocity" of M's circulation—i.e., the number of times per year which each dollar within the M stock, on average, moves around the "income circuit." (For more on this, see, if necessary, Study Guide p. 113.) Recall that the Quantity Equation is not just an equation, but an *identity*. To emphasize this, Chapter 15 used the three-bar identity symbol $MV \equiv PQ$, not just the equality symbol $MV = PQ$. It is an identity because V, *by definition*, must always be the figure needed to make the two sides of the equation equal.

Within this equation (or identity), PQ is just an alternative expression for GNP. Any national product figure is a measure of the total volume of real goods and services produced, each item therein valued at its money price. The use of PQ as an alternative to GNP draws attention to these price (P) and physical quantity (Q) components. In such terms, the inflation question is: What makes P rise?

The monetarist's answer is that the critical element in the $MV = PQ$ expression is $(M / V / Q)$—i.e., the price level is governed by *(cost-push factors / the quantity of money / the exercise of fiscal policy)*.

The argument of the "nonmonetarist" (meaning here, any dissenter, even only a part-dissenter, from the monetarist view) is different. It is that the expression P (within $MV = PQ$) has a certain life of its own. That is, price changes often result from decisions or bargains made without reference to M, to V, or even to Q. They evolve from such decisions or bargains because the price-determining system is *(reasonably perfect / decidedly imperfect)* in the sense of being *(considerably removed from / quite close to)* the "ideal" Walrasian price mechanism mentioned in question 3.

The nonmonetarists do *not* dismiss the quantity of the money stock (M) as being unimportant in the inflationary process. They argue only for a different sequence of events. Price increases (especially within manufacturing industry) frequently arise out of the kind of bargaining process described in question 4. So prices (especially manufactured-good prices) go up.

This poses a difficult problem for the nation's central bank. Under constant-price conditions, the nation's money stock (M) presumably ought to be increased only at that annual rate of (say) 2 per cent or 3 per cent which matches the rate of increase in total real output. But prices, instead of being constant, are rising. So what do you do? Hold fast to your 2 or 3 per cent money-supply increase? This will probably generate substantial unemployment, since there is insufficient money purchasing power to buy the entire full-employment quantity of national product, as valued at its new and higher prices. Or give in, and increase M by an amount sufficient to allow for higher prices as well?

In principle, central banks in most Western nations are supposed to maintain some degree of independence from elected federal governments. In practice, a central bank which sticks so grimly to its independence as to ignore the needs and wishes of the elected government is headed for painful conflict.

The nonmonetarist argument is that central banks usually yield. They increase M, not by 2 per cent or 3 per cent, but by 10 per cent, by 15—or by whatever price circumstances dictate.

The monetarists' view of inflation is essentially a *(cost-push / demand-pull)* one. Increases in the money supply first reach the hands of buyers, and their extra demand pushes prices *(up / down)*. However, this transfers the new and extra money into the hands of suppliers. An increase in money demand means *(more / less)* pressure upon a limited supply of real resources. Hence the competitive money prices of inputs must rise. That is, costs go up.

Thus, to monetarists, the distinction between "cost-push" and "demand-pull" inflation is largely meaningless. Both are parts of an interacting process. To try to separate one from the other, within a general equilibrium system, is rather like asking: Which came first, the chicken or the egg?

M; the quantity of money; decidedly imperfect; considerably removed from; demand-pull; up; more.

---

6. The "Phillips-curve tradeoff" diagram (see text) implies an inverse relation between price rises and the degree of unemployment: the closer the approach to full employment, the larger the resulting price rise. One axis of the Phillips diagram measures percentage price rise; the other, percentage of the labor force unemployed. You consult a nation's statistics covering a series of years. Each year's figures (price rise and unemployment, both as percentages) yield one point to plot. If, joining the resulting set of points, you get approximately the northwest-southeast line of text Fig. 41-2, you have some confirmation of the hypothesis that price rises are a function of the approach to full employment.

The data from actual empirical studies frequently show *some* confirmation of the hypothesis—but not enough to verify it, still less to indicate the cost (in terms of higher prices) of any given reduction in unemployment.

A quite different diagram may illustrate the nature of this hypothesis: Study Guide Fig. 41-1. In that diagram, the rise in output and employment involved in moving from D_1 to D_2 sets off *(no / a substantial)* price-level increase. The move from D_2 to D_3 involves *(no / a substantial)* rise.

Now alter the shape of Fig. 41-1's SS curve. Smooth out the sharp bend: let SS begin to rise just beyond the D_1 intersection; let it rejoin the existing curve at or near the D_3 intersection. With this new SS curve, an increase in purchasing power from D_1 to D_2 yields *(no / some)* price increase. A further move from D_2 to D_3 produces *(no / another)* increase. This *(is / is not)* the kind of supply curve lying behind the Phillips hypothesis.

Whether the SS curve ought to appear as in Fig. 41-1, or redrawn as just described, is an open question. Of course, this is a crude illustration of a complex problem. (Indeed, many economists dislike the whole Phillips-curve approach as a major oversimplification.) Yet it illustrates a policy-making dilemma. What will a proposed expansion of purchasing power (say by use of fiscal or monetary policy) do to prices?

Note that the Phillips hypothesis, because it assumes that price-level rises are governed by the level of demand and of employment, is a *(demand-pull / cost-push)* hypothesis.

---

no; a substantial; some; another; is; demand-pull.

QUIZ: Multiple Choice

1. *Suppose relaxation of cold-war tensions made possible a major cutback in military spending. This reduction (the text indicates)* (1) could be, and would have to be, matched by an equal increase in private consumer spending, to maintain full employment; (2) would intensify the United States' international balance-of-payments deficit more than any full-employment problem; (3) would require an equal increase in governmental (nonmilitary) spending, to maintain full employment; (4) would require a reduction in tax rates but a tighter monetary policy; (5) is not correctly described by any of these statements.

2. *The use of contractionary fiscal and monetary policies as anti-inflationary weapons implies a belief regarding inflation that* (1) it is primarily demand-pull in nature; (2) it is primarily cost-push in nature; (3) substantial labor unemployment is the only remedy; (4) changes in the quantity of money govern the rate of price increase; (5) prices show little response to any change in buyer demand.

3. *The text mentions, early in this chapter, a view (Marxist in origin) as to capitalism's future. It is that capitalism must disintegrate because of* (1) inability to produce enough output to keep the proletariat from revolt; (2) inability to control the money supply, hence uncontrollable price inflation; (3) a falling rate of profit arising from inability to find sufficient markets for its products; (4) competition among capitalist nations in their imperialist ventures abroad; (5) cost-push inflation rather than demand-pull inflation.

4. *The text suggests that John Kenneth Galbraith's followers advocate, as the best remedy for inflation in the United States today,* (1) a reduction in structural unemployment; (2) giving priority to monetary policy over fiscal policy; (3) firm control over the money supply, then leaving matters to the free market; (4) a quasi-voluntary incomes policy; (5) permanent price and wage controls.

5. *The text discusses the experience of various Western nations with incomes policies, guidelines, and wage-price controls. Its overall verdict on such policies is that they have* (1) had almost no success; (2) had some short-run success, usually followed by a decline in effectiveness; (3) apparently been most successful, but credit really belongs to accompanying fiscal and monetary policies; (4) been much more successful than have restrictive fiscal and monetary policies; (5) been unequivocally successful, particularly so when accompanied by tight monetary policies.

6. *An "exogenous" factor which (according to the text) contributed to worldwide inflation during the mid-1970s was* (1) the aftermath of the Vietnam war; (2) bad weather and consequent poor harvests; (3) union pressure for major wage increases; (4) an increase in cold-war tensions and conflicts; (5) a series of excessive increases in world money supplies.

7. *By the "structural unemployment" mentioned near the close of this text chapter is meant the unemployment that* (1) would be removed by expansionary monetary or fiscal policy; (2) is created by the multiplier effect of any reduction in investment spending; (3) would not be removed simply by expansionary monetary or fiscal policy; (4) is created whenever the nation's growth rate drops below its appropriate level; (5) arises out of the fact that a mixed economy has no automatic mechanism to guarantee continuing full-employment operation.

8. *Cost-push (as distinct from demand-pull) inflation is indicated if* (1) expansionary fiscal policy sets off price rises without increasing employment; (2) a price increase is followed by a wage increase; (3) corporations yield too easily to labor demands in granting notably higher wages; (4) expansionary fiscal policy sets off price rises as well as increasing employment; (5) prices rise during a recession induced (at least in part) by a tighter monetary policy.

9. *Figure 41-3, alongside, is a Phillips-curve diagram. Lines A and B are alternative possible Phillips curves (drawn to the same scale). With respect to fiscal and monetary policies, and as between these two curves,* (1) line A would be

more desirable for expansionary policies, whereas line *B* would be near-ideal for anti-inflationary policies; (2) line *A* would make such policies (whether expansionary or contractionary) relatively easy to conduct, whereas *B* would make them difficult; (3) line *A* would be more desirable for anti-inflationary policies, whereas *B* would be near-ideal for expansionary policies; (4) line *A* shows the unemployment-and-price-change relation before use of such policies, and *B* the relation after their use; (5) there is no significant difference between *A* and *B* with respect to use of such policies.

10. *Figure 41-4, at right below, is again a Phillips-curve diagram. Alternative curves A and B are now in more extreme form, vertical and horizontal respectively. In such circumstances,* (1) line *A* suggests a situation in which inflation is entirely demand-pull, and *B* one that is entirely cost-push; (2) fiscal and monetary policies (whether anti-inflationary or expansionary) would be easy to administer in *A*, impossible in *B;* (3) line *A* suggests a situation in which inflation is entirely cost-push, and *B* one that is entirely demand-pull; (4) fiscal and monetary policies (whether anti-inflationary or expansionary) would be impossible in *A*, and easy to administrate in *B;* (5) there is no significant difference between *A* and *B* with respect to use of fiscal or monetary policies.

11. *Insofar as "cost-push inflation" is a real phenomenon, it can be explained in terms of* (1) the operation of the Quantity Theory of Money; (2) structural unemployment; (3) contractionary fiscal policies; (4) the fact that the available supply of real resources is limited; (5) imperfect price-and-wage markets, hence resort to such practices as union-management bargaining over wages.

12. *Insofar as an inflation is entirely cost-push in nature, then* (1) fiscal policy cannot be used to engineer any decrease in total employment; (2) the level of prices is actually governed by the Quantity Theory of Money; (3) monetary policy cannot be used to engineer any decrease in total employment; (4) a policy of wage and price controls would be totally ineffective against it; (5) macroeconomic fiscal and monetary policies would be totally ineffective against it.

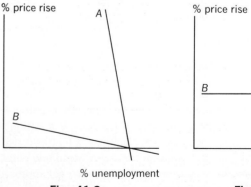

Fig. 41-3

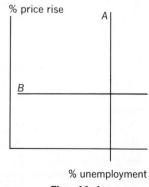

Fig. 41-4

42 WINDS OF CHANGE: EVOLUTION OF ECONOMIC DOCTRINES

1. The most prominent members of the early English "Classical School" of economists were:

> Adam Smith (1723–1790)
> Thomas Robert Malthus (1766–1834)
> David Ricardo (1772–1823)

Match these names with the following descriptions:

a. Sought, as a major part of his work, to discover "the laws of distribution"—i.e., the economic laws by means of which the national product was divided between three classes: laborers, landowners, and entrepreneurs (manufacturers and merchants): _____.

b. Enunciated the doctrine of laissez faire—i.e., government should not interfere with human activity, save in such restricted areas as the maintenance of law, police duties, and national defense: _____.

c. Best known today for his theory of population growth, but in fact dealt with a wide range of contemporary economic problems: _____.

d. Developed the hypothesis that, in the long run, land was the crucially scarce economic factor, so that economic growth would result in a continuing increase in the rental price per acre received by owners of land. (Note that although one of the three economists cited is particularly associated with this hypothesis, it is implicit also in the reasoning of another of the three.) _____.

e. Set out the doctrine of a self-regulating "natural order" of human affairs, and used the "Invisible Hand" concept to illustrate this doctrine: each individual, pursuing his own self-interest within a market system, is "led by an Invisible Hand to promote an end which was no part of his intention":

_____.

f. Relied heavily on the law of diminishing returns in his analysis. (NOTE: *Two* of the three economists did so.)

_____ and _____.

Adam Smith's *The Wealth of Nations* occupies a unique place in the esteem of economists, not so much because of its argument for laissez faire as because it was the first coherent account of the working of a market system. Much of what is found in Chapters 2 and 3 of the text derives from Adam Smith: the law of scarcity; the role of prices; the need for competition and the consequences of monopoly. Smith's argument is sometimes incomplete, sometimes confused, sometimes contradictory. Yet these are the inevitable shortcomings of a pioneer work of immense scope.

Two further points deserve mention as to the English classical economists. First, their work developed out of a lively and perceptive interest in contemporary issues. *The Wealth of Nations* is a frontal attack on the then-influential mercantilist philosophy of governmental interference in trade matters. Malthus and Ricardo dealt at length with issues arising out of the Napoleonic Wars, notably war-induced price inflation and tariff protection. When Napoleon's power play ended and normal shipping was resumed, the British food-growing aristocracy found itself exposed to new competition from American and other foreign grains. The English landowners contrived an increase in the grain tariff—the famous Corn Laws. Subsequently, and largely in consequence of the influential writings of the classical economists, the Corn Law rates were reduced—until finally, in 1846, the Corn Laws were abolished.

Second, there is just enough unanimity of viewpoint among the English classical economists to warrant grouping them together as a school—and no more. Malthus and Ricardo conducted a lengthy correspondence on innumerable issues. Almost always, they disagreed. (These disagreements did nothing to destroy a touchingly warm and enduring friendship which terminated only with Ricardo's death at the age of fifty-one.) For example, most of the classical economists accepted, at least in rough outline, Say's Law of full-employment purchasing power. Malthus did not—although he could not build an alternative theory. It was more than 100 years later that Keynes did construct such a theory.

It is this inner diversity of views, as well as its uniformity of views, that explains why the Classical School provided inspiration both for Marxists and "bourgeois" economists.

---

a. Ricardo. *b.* Smith. *c.* Malthus. *d.* Ricardo; Malthus. *e.* Smith. *f.* Malthus; Ricardo.

---

2. The English classical economists had, so to speak, roughed out the general shape of economic analysis. Thereafter, one group—the neoclassical economists, still predominantly English until the early twentieth century—undertook to correct, to refine, and to enlarge classical ideas. Another group—Marx and his followers—although drawing heavily on classical material, attempted a more fundamental revision.

The classical account, perhaps because it felt impelled to emphasize the basic scarcity of productive factors (Chapter 2), had stressed *supply* factors as the principal ingredient within commodity prices. Demand elements were not given much consideration. As the text puts it, it is almost as though all classical supply curves were *(horizontal / vertical)*, so that any shift in the demand curve *(would / could not)* change the level of price.

This classical supply-side account vacillated between a labor theory of value and a cost-of-production theory. (The latter asserts that the price of a commodity must be explained in terms of the quantities of labor, land, and capital required for its production.) Both labor and cost-of-production theories may seem plausible at first. But on closer inspection, they prove to be after-the-event explanations.

Marx handled this problem by accepting the labor theory of value, but adding to it his concept of *surplus* value (discussed in the Appendix). Prices, Marx said, are *not* equal to labor values in capitalist society; but they *would* be, in a properly functioning society. The labor theory of value, thus made over into "what ought to be" as much as "what is," became a banner in the crusade. Marxists sometimes called for acceptance of the labor theory somewhat as a fundamentalist Christian faith may demand unquestioning acceptance of the literal truth of everything in the Bible.

The Neoclassical School, in contrast, stuck (or tried to stick, at any rate) to "what is." They recognized labor cost, and costs of production generally, as *one* important element in price determination. But they added the element which earlier had

been neglected, namely: _____. The outcome— and here the work of Alfred Marshall (1842–1924) was most important—was the demand-curve and supply-curve approach of Chapters 4 and 20.

Demand and supply curves are graphs; therefore they have a mathematical background, whether that background is recognized or not. Economics was becoming more mathematical. The neoclassical introduction of "marginalist" concepts (marginal utility in Chapter 22, marginal cost and revenue in Chapters 23 through 25, marginal-product in Chapter 27) illustrates the point. If you have had training in calculus, you will know that "marginal" is a way of explaining the differential calculus.

It was as part of this more mathematical trend that the theory of general equilibrium (Chapter 32) was developed. The major figure here—the text quotes Joseph Schumpeter as saying he was "the greatest of the great economists"—was:

_____.

_____

horizontal; could not; demand; Leon Walras.

3. In the twentieth century, the major development in economics has been the development of Keynesian analysis, already discussed at length earlier in the text. Bitterly resented upon its introduction because it seemed to upset so many traditional beliefs, this analysis warns that in developed societies relying heavily on investment spending, the market system cannot be left to its own devices with assurance that a full-employment equilibrium will result. In brief, Keynesian analysis banished any belief in *(the law of scarcity / the law of supply and demand / Say's Law / the law of diminishing returns)*.

_____

Say's Law.

_____

4. The analytic method of classical and neoclassical economists was to try to develop some basic principles or truths (e.g., the law of diminishing returns), and then to use the process of deduction in order to reach particular conclusions (e.g., Malthus' prediction regarding population growth).

A minority opinion has held that economists are too complacent about their conclusions, and insufficiently disposed to check them against "the facts." Thus they have revised their thinking only when forced by some crisis to do so. (It took not only an extraordinary mind to produce Keynes' *General Theory;* it took also the experience of the Great Depression.)

a. Both the German Historical School and the American Institutionalist School were in considerable degree reactions against the classical analytic method. They were expressions of the view that economics was filled with *(too much theory, not enough facts / too many facts, not enough theory)*.

b. A somewhat similar view, holding that much of economic theory is out of touch with the important current trends, is expressed contemporarily by John Kenneth Galbraith (although Galbraith's criticism is not much directed against analytic method). Circle as many of the following statements as seem to repeat the text's conclusions on Galbraith.
(1) His theory is basically Marxist both in its origins and its conclusions.
(2) His work is more a criticism of existing theory than an outline of an identifiable and testable alternative theory.
(3) His argument presents a serious challenge to Keynesian economics.
(4) His reasoning is in large part a synthesis of other men's ideas; his role has been to merge these ideas, and to present them in unusually persuasive fashion.

_____

a. too much theory, not enough facts.   *b.* (2), (4).

_____

5. *a.* Karl Marx's principal work was his three-volume *Das Kapital.* In the text's evaluation, referring particularly to opinion among rebels and dissenters, *Das Kapital* is *(no longer so often / still)* considered Marx's major contribution to reform.

b. Marx's forecasts in this work (already briefly noted on p. 316) included the following: The real wage of laborers would *(rise / fall);* the "reserve army of the unemployed" would *(increase / decrease)* in number; the rate of capitalist profit would *(rise / fall);* business cycles would *(grow / diminish)* in intensity; the capitalist system would collapse by reason of *(an excess / a deficiency)* of purchasing power.

Thus far, these forecasts *(have / have not)* been vindicated.

c. The text suggests that interest in Marx is today turning toward other aspects of his thought. Two ideas in particular are mentioned, namely:

(1) _____

(2) _____

---

a. no longer so often. *b.* fall; increase; fall; grow; a deficiency; have not. *c.* (1) Alienation. (2) The economic interpretation of history (the view that behavior is shaped by material interests, or in more Marxian terms, by the conditions of production).

QUIZ: Multiple Choice

1. *The concept of a "natural order" is associated in economics particularly with the name of* (1) John Maynard Keynes; (2) Leon Walras; (3) Adam Smith; (4) Karl Marx; (5) Alfred Marshall.

2. *Which of the five economists cited in question 1 was the author of the statement, "People of the same trade seldom meet together, even for merriment and diversion, but the conversation ends in a conspiracy against the public or in some contrivance to raise prices"?* (1). (2). (3). (4). (5).

3. *An important part of David Ricardo's argument was that* (1) the income or payment received by each productive factor or input would be governed by that factor's marginal productivity; (2) economists relied to excess on the deductive process, and neglected the requirement of verifying their conclusions empirically; (3) supply and cost factors alone could not explain price or value, since demand was a factor of equal importance; (4) the rate of business profit was bound to fall; (5) land's rental price would gradually increase, and labor's price would gradually fall.

4. *Which alternative in question 3 would be correct, had that question referred to Karl Marx (and to capitalist society) rather than to David Ricardo?* (1). (2). (3). (4). (5).

5. *The contemporary economist whose name is most prominently associated with the principle of laissez faire earlier advocated by Adam Smith is* (1) Milton Friedman; (2) Thom-

as Kuhn; (3) Robert Solow; (4) John G. Gurley; (5) John Kenneth Galbraith.

6. *The law of diminishing returns played a prominent part in* (1) Leon Walras' theory of general equilibrium; (2) the mercantilist theory of tariff protection; (3) Adam Smith's principle of "the Invisible Hand"; (4) David Ricardo's theory of income distribution; (5) Karl Marx's theory of the business cycle.

7. *Neoclassical theory (according to the text) contributed to the development of economic analysis in that it* (1) developed a mathematical theory of general equilibrium and in the process brought marginalist concepts into use; (2) developed the theory of econometric measurement of economic variables; (3) in large part reversed the classical emphasis on deduction, insisting that economists verify empirically the hypotheses on which they relied; (4) set out a non-Marxist account of how the economy might reach an equilibrium which was substantially below the level of full resource employment; (5) gave the first clear account of the significance of the law of scarcity as applied to both demand and supply sides of the market.

8. *The "economic interpretation of history" doctrine set out by Marx and Engels says that* (1) the distribution of income by class is governed by the iron law of marginal productivity; (2) the driving force behind entrepreneurial behavior is the maximization of money profit; (3) each class has its own economic interest, and beliefs and behavior are dictated by such economic interest; (4) an authoritarian leader, thrown up by world revolution, is an imperative before any change in the conditions of production can be accomplished; (5) the inescapable scarcity of land must lead to the progressive immiserization of the growing body of laborers who must work on that land.

9. *Karl Marx, according to the text, received much of his inspiration from one English writer, namely* (1) Jeremy Bentham; (2) David Hume; (3) John Locke; (4) David Ricardo; (5) Adam Smith.

10. *According to the text's evaluation, today's reformers and radicals regard Marx, and his major work* Das Kapital, *as follows:* (1) Das Kapital is no longer read, and none of Marx's other ideas has perceptible influence. (2) The doctrine of the declining real wage in *Das Kapital* is the major inspiration for contemporary thought. (3) Marx's influence is still powerful, but interest has shifted away from *Das Kapital* to his earlier writings. (4) The theory of surplus value within *Das Kapital* is still the most powerful concept within Marxian thought. (5) Interest has shifted to Marx's later writings, since he had already begun to reject some of the ideas in *Das Kapital* in his closing years.

APPENDIX: Rudiments of Marxian Economics

1. A considerable part of this Appendix deals with Marx's concept of *surplus value.* Perhaps it is a pity that what began as a kind of ethical principle should be reduced to the tedious

level of algebra. But Marx intended surplus value to be a scientific principle as well as an ethical one; it is legitimate to subject it to such examination.

The detail of the material below follows the text example. There are only two commodities, coal and corn. Coal is not a consumer good. It is merely something required in order to produce corn, and completely used up in corn production. The entire goal of economic activity is the production of corn, the only consumer good.

The requirements for producing coal and corn (the production functions for these commodities) are as follows:

▶ Coal: 4 hours of direct labor alone suffice to produce 1 unit of coal. No other input is needed.

▶ Corn: 4 hours of direct labor are needed for 1 unit of corn. Also, for each such unit of corn, 1 unit of coal is needed.

a. Hence with respect to corn, adding the indirect labor requirement (that needed to produce 1 unit of coal) to the direct labor requirement, it takes *(4 / 8)* hours of labor for each unit of corn.

b. In the Marxian system, the measure of all values is socially necessary labor. The unit of value is 1 hour of such labor time. We shall use the British-pound symbol £ (because it resembles an L) to indicate anything measured or valued in such labor units. (The text does not do this.)

We begin with a situation in which there is no capitalism, no exploitation, no surplus value. Each laborer receives the full value of his production. Hence:

▶ A laborer working a 12-hour day, whether he works in coal or in corn, receives a wage of £12 daily.

▶ The price of coal per unit, because it takes 4 labor hours to produce, is £4.

▶ The price of corn per unit, because in total it takes 8 labor hours to produce, is £8.

Check to be sure that the total of purchasing power in wages is just sufficient to buy the total output of finished goods—meaning here, the total output of corn. Suppose there are 10 men, 5 working in coal, 5 in corn. The working day is 12 hours. Total daily earnings would be £*(12 / 40 / 60 / 80 / 120)*. Total daily output of corn would be *(1 / 4 / 5 / 10 / 15 / 20 / 30)* units. Value of this corn would be £*(40 / 60 / 100 / 120 / 150 / 200)*. So total consumer purchasing power is *(less than / equal to / greater than)*· total value of output produced.

One further detail: Marx used the term "variable capital" (*v*) to refer to direct labor cost, and the term "constant capital" (*c*) with respect to indirect labor cost. (By "constant capital," he was doubtless thinking of machines and tools, and thinking of them as the result of past labor expenditure. But the example of coal illustrates this "stored-up labor" idea equally well, and it is simpler.)

Thus the two prices, with coal as product 1 and corn as product 2, are as follows:

▶ (1) Price of coal = £$(c_1 + v_1)$ = (0 + 4) labor hours

▶ (2) Price of corn = £$(c_2 + v_2)$ = (4 + 4) labor hours

---

a. 8. *b.* 120; 15; 120; equal to.

---

2. Now the Serpent enters this rural Eden, in the form of capitalism. We now recognize that *time* is a factor in production, in a somewhat different sense from labor hours. It may take only 8 hours of labor to produce a unit of corn; but that does not mean that corn is ready for harvest 8 hours after it is planted. The workers who produce corn must wait for it to ripen. However, they cannot wait for the corn needed to feed their families. So there emerges a capitalist class that will supply corn immediately (from stocks accumulated from past harvests). Laborers are paid a money wage, which they spend to buy corn. Capitalists now set the price of corn. And they set it at a price which exceeds wage costs (direct and indirect).

In effect, the capitalists are lending corn to the workers to tide them over the period from planting to harvest. Presumably, they are entitled to *some* interest on their loan. They collect this interest by increasing appropriately (or inappropriately) the price they charge for corn.

a. The important thing is that the price now charged for corn is no longer explainable solely in terms of the labor hours required to produce corn. Price now *(falls short of / exceeds)* this labor cost. This *(excess / deficiency)* is Marx's surplus value. (Surplus value enters likewise into the price of coal; this we shall reach in a moment.)

The symbol *s* is used for the amount of surplus value. This surplus value is measured in terms of labor hours, since in the Marxian labor-theory world, *everything* is so measured— even though these particular hours of toil exist only in the capitalists' imagination. So the prices of coal and of corn (commodities 1 and 2 respectively) are now:

(1) Coal price = £$(c_1 + v_1 + s_1)$
(2) Corn price = £$(c_2 + v_2 + s_2)$

Marx said that labor is the thing that is exploited, and that the surplus value would be proportionate to the direct labor (variable capital) needed for each commodity. Why to direct labor only and not to indirect labor (constant capital) as well? Because indirect labor was exploited at that earlier stage of production when it was direct labor. Coal workers are exploited in that surplus value is built into the price of coal. When the coal reaches corn workers as an input needed for corn production, the surplus-value-inflated price of coal is used as the cost of this input. Corn workers are likewise exploited in that more surplus value is added into the price of corn.

In the text example, surplus value is assumed to be just *twice* the amount of direct labor. That is:

(1) Surplus value exacted in coal = $s_1 = 2v_1$
(2) Surplus value exacted in corn = $s_2 = 2v_2$

b. It is at some stage such as this that one wonders if Marx did not grow a little weary (or uneasy) as to the algebra required to set out his surplus-value principle. On this point, he left no message; your task is still to compute prices, with surplus value included, according to his instructions.

With all assumptions as before, compute the prices (in labor value) of coal and of corn. (Repeated for convenience, coal's indirect labor or constant capital requirement is 0; its direct labor or variable capital requirement is 4 labor hours per unit. The corresponding figures for corn are 4 and 4. But remember: In corn production, coal is now valued at its surplus-value-included price.)

	c	+	v	+	s	=	price
(1) Coal:	_____	+	_____	+	_____	=	_____
(2) Corn:	_____	+	_____	+	_____	=	_____

c. Because the labor hour is the value measure, a worker who works a 12-hour day is paid £(6 / 12 / 24). This will enable him to buy (½ / 1 / 1½ / 2 / 3) unit(s) of corn daily. In the days before surplus value (if there were such days), the same wage would have bought (½ / 1 / 1½ / 2 / 3) unit(s) of corn.

---

a. exceeds; excess. *b.* $0 + 4 + 8 = 12$; $12 + 4 + 8 = 24$. *c.* 12; ½; 1½.

---

3. *a.* If the rate of surplus value were to be reduced, the real wage of each worker would *(increase / decrease)*. The actual surplus-value rate is set at such a level that the resulting real wage of labor is just high enough for labor to survive and maintain itself. It is easiest to explain this as Malthus did: If real wages rise above the minimum-of-subsistence level, population will thereupon rise until wages are pulled down again. But, as the text points out, Marx did not draw on Malthusian theory. He simply said that capitalists would set wages at their minimum level because the existence of a "reserve army of the unemployed" would enable them to do so.

For example, if workers need 1 full unit of corn daily for survival, the rate of surplus value of 2 used above *(must be lowered / can be increased)*. If workers can survive on ¼ unit daily, this rate *(must be lowered / can be increased)*.

b. This surplus value would, outside of Marxian economics, be called "profit." If surplus value is so translated, it suggests an inconsistency in the analysis just set out. The surplus-value amount recorded at the end of question 2 was 8 for both coal and corn. If we think of direct and indirect capital $(c + v)$ as the amount of money tied up in production, then the rate of profit (the rate of return on capital)—compare the *s* amount with the $(c + v)$ total—is higher in *(coal / corn)*.

As the text points out, if you adjust the surplus-value figures by industry so as to get equal rates of profit, you then have unequal rates of surplus-value exploitation of direct

labor. Had Marx lived longer, he might have been able to sort this problem out.

---

a. increase; must be lowered; can be increased. *b.* coal.

---

4. Setting aside the unequal-rate-of-return problem, it is clear that the workers' total income is grossly *(excessive / insufficient)* to buy the total output of corn produced. This purchasing-power deficiency would vanish were the capitalists willing to buy the remaining output (and they have sufficient income, after paying wages, to do so). But, according to Marx, the capitalist instinct is to produce, to save, and to accumulate—not to consume. If we accept this view, it is easy to see why the system faces a crisis of purchasing power. If capitalists refuse to give workers the needed buying power, and if they refuse to buy the remainder of the consumer-good output because they want to save and to invest, then who is there to buy it? It may be possible to postpone the crisis through exploitation of the less developed nations. But this is only a temporary solution; the system's ultimate collapse is inevitable.

Perhaps the matter can be summed up as follows. Marx thought that the distribution of income was grossly unfair— and remember he was looking at the nineteenth-century consequences, sometimes dreadful, of the Industrial Revolution. He saw, correctly, that the major factor in inequality of income distribution is property ownership. He saw also that a system which relies heavily on the processes of saving and investment may from time to time suffer from deficiencies of purchasing power. Again he was correct—see, for example, question 1, p. 316.

Evidently Marx thought that he could take the labor theory of value and, by adding to it his surplus-value concept, make the resulting theory a vehicle for scientific expression of *all* the problems just cited.

With the benefit of hindsight, it seems likely that on the labor-theory matter, Marx was mistaken. Possibly some later Marxist may be able to sort things out and make surplus value as powerful a scientific device as was intended. But for now, surplus value seems a hopeless tangle, and more of a liability than an asset to Marxian analysis.

It is a tribute to Marx's intellectual power that so many contemporary critics of capitalism, affronted by its income distribution or by some of its other properties, still turn to Marx for inspiration despite the defects of his analysis.

---

insufficient.

---

5. Chapter 27 of the text outlined the "marginal-productivity" theory of income distribution. The originator of this theory, John B. Clark, cannot decently be labeled as a mere apologist for capitalism: he was an economist, trying to sort things out sufficiently that one could make at least rough statements as to how total output gets itself distributed among the various groups which contribute to production of that output. And yet the message which Clark's analysis seemed to convey—assuming it to refer to actual distribution within a real world—was this: Each input, whether capital or labor or anything else, is paid according to its productivity (more specifically, its *marginal* productivity). So (it would appear) there is a certain justice in the world after all, albeit perhaps a firm or harsh justice: as you produce, so shall you consume. (For more on this, see question 13, Study Guide p. 219.)

Like so much of economic theory (Marxian theory included), this marginal-productivity theory was a matter of deduction: begin with certain assumptions, and from them reach particular conclusions. Applied to the distribution of income between capital and labor, this theory assumes that (1) there *is* an identifiable input called "capital," and (2) there exists the particular kind of substitutability between capital and labor needed to make marginal-products identifiable.

The truth of these assumptions is by no means fully established, and they have been attacked by Joan Robinson, a competent economist and a defender of much of Marxist theory (although not of the labor theory of value).

There must be *some* theory of income distribution, however imperfect (which is perhaps why marginal-productivity theory survives). The text Appendix cites one equation which it is suggested evolves out of the argument of Joan Robinson and others, namely:

$$\pi = g/\sigma_s$$

where π is the rate of profit on capital, g is a specified annual rate of growth in the labor force, and σ_s is the fraction of profit income saved (all saving being done out of profit), in a balanced-growth situation.

If you are interested in such esoteric problems and wish to develop the meaning of this equation more fully, note that it has the same background as that of question 3, p. 297 (Appendix to Chapter 37). The two situations are similar in that (*i*) the capital-labor (K/L) proportions are assumed fixed (no substitution between them), (*ii*) the labor force grows at a specified rate, and (*iii*) for "balanced growth," capital must grow at the same rate.

The problem in the earlier question was: In order for capital (K) to grow at the required rate, how much investment (I) and saving (S) must there be each year? The answer was that for any specified rate of labor-force growth g, the required figure for I and S is governed by the capital-output ratio, K/Q. The equation cited in that earlier question was: $s = g \times K/Q$, s being the fraction saved out of annual real output, Q.

Two substitutions can be made in this equation: (*i*) If s is the *fraction* of income saved, then *total* saving $S = sQ$. (*ii*) Using p to stand for total annual profit, then by the definition of σ_s above, $\sigma_s p = S$. With these two substitutions, the equation above converts into:

$$\sigma_s p = gK \text{ or } g/\sigma_s = p/K$$

And p/K is the ratio of profit earned to total capital; it is the text's π, the rate of profit.

6. The text Appendix suggests that the Marxist method of interpreting surplus value can be extended into a newer approach: input-output analysis. The results indicated (and they are not part of what is usually considered "Marxian economics") are these: (1) If capitalists save no part of their profit income, but instead spend all of it on consumption, then there will be no crisis of purchasing power. Nor will there be any growth of output. The system will remain in stationary full-employment equilibrium. (2) At the other extreme, if capitalists save *all* their income—but put *all* this saving into investment—there will be "balanced growth." Output will grow at a steady percentage rate. So long as labor is willing to spend all its income to buy the increasing output of consumer goods, and capitalists continue to put all their income into new investment, there will be no purchasing-power crisis. Full employment will prevail throughout this balanced-growth period.

QUIZ: Multiple Choice

1. *In Marxian terminology, "constant capital" signifies* (1) equipment or materials which represent the fruit of past labor; (2) the value of total output in a capitalist society; (3) the money cost that would be incurred even if production were zero; (4) the value of total output in a socialist society; (5) the markup of price over the actual value of labor incurred in production.

2. *In a socialist regime, according to Marx, the price per unit of each commodity would (or should) equal* (1) the value of direct labor required for that commodity's production; (2) variable capital per unit plus constant capital per unit; (3) the value of one hour of socially necessary labor; (4) the costs of that commodity's production, including all necessary services of land, labor, and capital, but excluding profit; (5) none of the above.

3. *Marx's argument was that the output which requires labor effort is given a price which exceeds the money wage paid that labor. The verdict of neoclassical economic theory on this argument is that it* (1) may have some validity as to labor-intensive production, but not as to capital-intensive production; (2) is entirely false; (3) is correct, since inputs other than labor contribute to production; (4) may have some validity as to capital-intensive production, but not as to labor-intensive production; (5) is meaningless, since demand is a more powerful factor in price determination than is labor cost.

4. *Marx's approach to the economic problem of values was that* (1) the emphasis of the classical economists upon values was a distraction, the important thing being the exploitation of labor; (2) the important thing is relative values, the valuation of one commodity as against another; (3) surplus value has to be measured altogether differently from labor value; (4) there has to be an absolute measure of value, that measure being labor value; (5) in capitalist societies, prices bear no consistent relationship to values whatsoever.

43 ALTERNATIVE ECONOMIC SYSTEMS

1. The term "socialism" has been applied to a variety of political and economic movements. It is generally agreed that the characteristic common to most of these movements is a belief that the privilege of unlimited ownership of private property is not an inalienable right. In particular, socialists challenge the right of private ownership of productive resources in the form of land and capital goods.

While the origins of socialist thought can be traced back to the Greeks and beyond, the socialist movement developed its real momentum in the eighteenth and nineteenth centuries. The Industrial Revolution profoundly altered European economic and social conditions. It brought immense wealth to some members of the new entrepreneur class. It brought degradation and misery to many workers employed in the new industries. To people of conscience, it seemed that in the new economy, the dice were stacked against anyone unlucky enough to be forced to try and earn his or her living from labor alone. Members of this "proletariat" class would inevitably be exploited by a small group of employers exercising power acquired through ownership of productive inputs other than labor.

However unanimous socialists may have been on the indignities of the new industrial society, they were far from agreement on the proper method of reform. The anarchists believed in total abolition of the state; later, anarchism came to be associated with the view that capitalism (and the state) can be overthrown only by violent means. The "utopian" socialists hoped to reform society by establishing as seeds within that society small communal groups whose behavior would be governed by "high-minded" rules.

Karl Marx regarded these utopian projects as fatuous diversions of reform effort. He insisted on a socialism that would be "practical" in the essential sense of being based on a *scientific* analysis of human society. In 1848, to express these views, he and Friedrich Engels published a famous document, namely _____ .

Marxism's intellectual foundation is "dialectical materialism," an adaptation of Hegel's "dialectical idealism." This Marxian system describes human history in terms of movement and change. Each stage of development within that history contains some inner contradiction which is the seed of its own destruction. Change is the process by which one contradiction is removed, only to produce another. The fundamental assumption in Marxism, as stated in the *Communist*

Manifesto, is that "the history of all hitherto-existing society is the history of class struggles." In this history, the ruling class exploits one or more other classes. Feudalism was one stage in human history, in which the ruling class consisted of land-owning nobility. The inner contradiction within this system led to its overthrow by capitalism. According to Marx, the bourgeois ruling class of capitalists would in due course be overthrown by the proletarian laboring class. Marx thought this would be the final stage of the class struggle, since the overthrow of capitalism would result in a classless society.

To enlarge his argument that capitalism carries within it an inner contradiction leading to its own destruction, Marx developed his theory of surplus value, already discussed in the Appendix to Chapter 42.

The sheer power and scope of Marxian analysis overwhelmed much of utopian socialism. But it did not stop the division of views among socialist thinkers. The subsequent division became, roughly, that between Marxist Communists who considered world revolution a necessity for reform and Marxist socialists advocating gradual evolution through parliamentary means. The British "Fabian movement" (see text) constituted a particular branch of the *(revolutionist / gradualist)* movement.

---

the *Communist Manifesto;* gradualist.

---

2. While fascism has intellectual roots quite different from those of socialism, it became in the nineteenth century a reaction against revolutionary socialism. Fascism laid emphasis on the protection of law and order and the sanctity of private property. Socialist thinkers were typically "internationalist" in outlook; fascism appealed to sentiments of national pride. Fascist thinkers were contemptuous of parliamentary democracy, which they considered to be either irresolute and irresponsible or else a thinly veiled device for the exercise of mob rule. An authoritarian national leader was considered essential to political salvation.

When Communist leaders assumed political control in Russia, they resorted to authoritarian measures for execution of their plans. Thus, despite the ideological hostility between the two movements, communism acquired one of the very characteristics of fascism most despised by Western thinkers with a regard for individual rights. The division between "evolutionary" socialism and communism was greatly widened.

Put F in the space below if the description fits the fascist system of economic or political organization. Put S if it is characteristic of European "evolutionary" socialism. Put B if both; N if neither.

a. Strong emphasis placed on obedience to authority....( )
b. Extensive centralized planning of investment, foreign trade, and domestic output. ....( )
c. Strong emphasis on the recognition of democratic rights and on avoidance of change by force. ....( )
d. Highly nationalistic in sentiment and opposed to "internationalism." ....( )
e. Strong emphasis on avoiding major inequalities in distribution of income. ....( )
f. Recognition of individual initiative as a major force in maintaining a satisfactory rate of growth. .... ( )
g. Considerable government ownership of certain basic or key industries, such as transportation..................( )
h. The nation is considered an entity different from the total of its citizens, and the duty of the citizens is to further the ends of the nation. ....( )
i. The money pricing system is typically not used or used very little for the distribution of consumer goods among the population. ....( )

a. F. *b.* B. *c.* S. *d.* F. *e.* S. *f.* N. *g.* S.
h. F. *i.* N.

3. Circle as many of the following as correctly indicate characteristics of the Soviet Union:

a. The state owns all land.
b. The state owns almost all capital equipment.
c. Consumer goods are given money prices, and workers choose among these consumer goods according to these prices; the wages of workers are paid in money.
d. Central planners once were plagued with the problem of a widespread piling up of consumer goods which could not be sold; now this problem is much less acute.
e. Workers have, in general, no choice as to the geographic area in which they may work.
f. Workers have very little choice as to the occupation they would like to enter.
g. In Stalin's day, no attempt was made to respect civil liberties in the Western sense; today, these civil liberties are by and large respected.
h. There are no important differences in wages or salaries— i.e., no significant departures from equality of income distribution.
i. Such inequalities of income distribution as do exist tend to reflect political influence rather than special competence or skill in some occupation.
j. In the decision on WHAT goods to produce, top priority is given to investment projects and defense production, consumer goods being produced to the extent possible after these requirements have been satisfied.

k. Industrial workers are now given a fair degree of freedom to bargain collectively with plant managers on wages and other terms of employment.
l. Industrial plants operate by being given a quota of output which they are expected to meet or exceed.
m. The quota system of output has now been discarded. Plant managers now operate on an incentive system which closely resembles profit maximization.
n. Plant workers and plant managers now have some share in the ownership of the plants they operate.
o. Advertising is now being used to further the sale of some consumer goods.
p. Political control of economic planning has moved gradually but steadily away from centralization and toward decentralization.
q. Proposals to use the interest rate as a device for giving priorities among different investment projects are increasing and may possibly be used to some extent.
r. The state levies a tax on the sale of goods at each production stage, so that consumer-good prices considerably exceed wages paid to produce those goods.
s. Marxist concepts with respect to value are still employed with respect to relative prices set on consumer goods and on investment goods.

a, b, c, j, l, o, q, r,

4. Westerners who think that "criticism of the system" is discouraged (and dangerous) in the Soviet Union are correct as to *political* criticism. However, complaints over shoddy consumer goods or poor production techniques, via gripe letters to the newspapers, are *encouraged.* Such criticism evidently performs a corrective function. Russian production is still governed, in part, by authoritarian direction from above, rather than by consumer demand. Consumers still must resort to this clumsy letter-to-the-editor device to get things changed. In Western societies, the equivalent corrective device is one of

_____ .

a system of markets, prices, and profit incentives.

5. Circle as many of the following as correctly describe comparisons between the United States, the Soviet Union, and other economies (according to the text).

a. The Soviet Union's rate of growth in GNP since World War II has exceeded that of all Western countries.
b. As the Soviet Union's output grows and in consequence turns more toward services, it is estimated that her rate of growth will increase, since services do not involve the same heavy investment in capital equipment.
c. GNP in the Soviet Union is somewhere between one-half and three-quarters of the United States GNP, according to the presently available statistics.

d. The Soviet Union has been able to imitate technologies already developed elsewhere. This fact has made it somewhat easier for her to maintain a high GNP growth rate.

e. The long-term rate of growth in GNP in the United States is fractionally above 5 per cent annually.

f. The Soviet Union devotes a larger fraction of her GNP to military expenditure than the United States does.

g. Experience with GNP figures since World War II furnishes no clear answer to the question of whether collectivist societies or decentralized societies are better adapted to rapid rates of growth.

c, d, f, g.

QUIZ: Multiple Choice

1. *British socialism and Russian communism differ in this respect:* (1) Since World War II, the emphasis on public ownership of industry has been somewhat moderated in communism but not in socialism. (2) Significant inequalities of income are accepted as necessary in socialist thinking but not in communist. (3) Socialism accepts and encourages the trade-union movement; communism does not. (4) Significant inequalities of income are accepted as necessary in communist thinking but not in socialist. (5) None of the above.

2. *Which of the following labels is more properly regarded as fascist rather than socialist?* (1) Guild socialism. (2) Marxian socialism. (3) National socialism. (4) Christian socialism. (5) Fabian socialism.

3. *In the Soviet Union (according to the text), the problem of* WHAT *to produce is settled as follows: The decision is made* (1) first on total consumer-good production, then defense, the residual in total output being capital goods; (2) principally through a pricing system, except for defense and defense-related production; (3) according to a system of national priorities, among which any of consumer goods, capital goods, or defense may rank highest at any particular time; (4) by the central authority, but there is no clear evidence as to the priority system; (5) on defense and capital-good production first, consumer goods being the residual in total output.

4. *"Fabian socialism" refers to* (1) the major body of socialist thought existing before publication of Marx and Engels' *Communist Manifesto;* (2) British thought stressing the inevitability of gradual socialism; (3) socialist theory developed by the Trotsky wing of the communist movement; (4) socialist thinking which denies the view that industry should be government-owned; (5) none of the above.

5. *A characteristic of French "indicative planning" is that* (1) with respect to investment plans, it applies only to industries owned or operated by the state; (2) participation by private industry in the plan is voluntary or quasi-voluntary; (3) the work of planning and coordination is carried out by private industry, not by the state; (4) it is principally concerned with the economic aspects of relations with other Common Market members, not with domestic growth; (5) while members within each industry develop their plans for expansion and have them approved by the state, no attempt is made at an over-all "comprehensive" plan.

6. *"Anarchism," as that term has most generally been interpreted, means a belief that* (1) there need be, and should be, no government of any kind; (2) socialism is best developed through the establishment of small "seed" groups which carry out in practice the principles of socialism; (3) capitalism is a tolerable economic and political system, provided the conditions of "pure" or "perfect" competition are reasonably satisfied; (4) the status and wishes of the individual must be considered secondary to the status and needs of the state; (5) trade unions have proven to be a major barrier in moving toward attainment of a socialist state.

7. *Which alternative in question 6 would be correct, had that question referred to a central belief with respect to fascism, rather than to anarchism?* (1). (2). (3). (4). (5).

8. *The Soviet government acquires much of the revenues needed for its operation through* (1) levying of an income tax, although not a progressive income tax; (2) levying of a turnover tax applied on goods at each stage of production; (3) payments made by each industrial plant in proportion to cost of plant construction, much as a Western company might pay interest on a bond issue; (4) levying of taxes on privately owned property; (5) levying of a progressive income tax.

9. *Yugoslav socialism differs from Russian socialism in that, in Yugoslavia* (1) there has been much less dependence on market pricing as a device for resolving the basic problem of WHAT goods to produce; (2) state revenues are largely obtained through imposition of a progressive personal income tax, not unlike those of Western capitalist societies; (3) nominally at least, workers have much greater control over the factory in which they work, in such senses as that they may elect (or hire) their own managers; (4) no plant has any freedom as to the nature of the product which it may produce; (5) any person may still own land, without restriction as to the total quantity of land so owned.

10. *According to the text, the best available estimates suggest that total and per capita real GNPs in the United States and in Soviet Russia compare about as follows: The U.S.S.R.'s total GNP (as compared with that of the United States)* (1) is somewhat over one-half, but her per capita GNP is less, perhaps about one-half; (2) is approximately equal, and her per capita GNP is slightly higher; (3) is about one-third, and her per capita GNP is even less, perhaps about one-quarter; (4) has by now risen slightly above that of the United States, although her per capita GNP is still only about five-sixths; (5) simply cannot be compared with that of the United States, because commodities consumed in the two countries are so different as to make comparisons meaningless.

ANSWERS TO QUIZ QUESTIONS: Multiple Choice

Chapter 2
1. 4. **2.** 4. **3.** 4. **4.** 2. **5.** 2.

Chapter 3
1. 1. **2.** 5. **3.** 2. **4.** 3. **5.** 5.

Chapter 4
1. 4. **2.** 4. **3.** 1. **4.** 1. **5.** 2.
Appendix
1. 4. **2.** 3.

Chapter 5
1. 1. **2.** 3. **3.** 4. **4.** 4. **5.** 2.

Chapter 6
1. 2. **2.** 1. **3.** 5. **4.** 5. **5.** 2.
Appendix
1. 3. **2.** 3. **3.** 2. **4.** 2. **5.** 1.

Chapter 7
1. 3. **2.** 4. **3.** 3. **4.** 3. **5.** 2.

Chapter 8
1. 3. **2.** 2. **3.** 2. **4.** 4. **5.** 5.

Chapter 9
1. 5. **2.** 3. **3.** 2. **4.** 2. **5.** 1.

Chapter 10
1. 3. **2.** 4. **3.** 5. **4.** 4. **5.** 3.
Appendix
1. 4. **2.** 3.

Chapter 11
1. 4. **2.** 5. **3.** 1. **4.** 2. **5.** 1.

Chapter 12
1. 2. **2.** 4. **3.** 5. **4.** 5. **5.** 1.

Chapter 13
1. 4. **2.** 2. **3.** 5. **4.** 5. **5.** 3.

Chapter 14
1. 4. **2.** 2. **3.** 4. **4.** 1. **5.** 2.

Chapter 15
1. 1. **2.** 1. **3.** 4. **4.** 1. **5.** 5.

Chapter 16
1. 1. **2.** 2. **3.** 3. **4.** 2. **5.** 5.

Chapter 17
1. 5. **2.** 4. **3.** 2. **4.** 3. **5.** 1.

Chapter 18
1. 5. **2.** 1. **3.** 4. **4.** 2. **5.** 3.
Appendix
1. 3. **2.** 4.

Chapter 19
1. 3. **2.** 2. **3.** 4. **4.** 1. **5.** 3.
Appendix
1. 3. **2.** 2.

Chapter 20
1. 5. **2.** 4. **3.** 2. **4.** 3. **5.** 2.
Appendix
1. 2. **2.** 3. **3.** 1. **4.** 1. **5.** 3.

Chapter 21
1. 4. **2.** 1. **3.** 4. **4.** 4. **5.** 3.
Appendix
1. 4. **2.** 5. **3.** 4. **4.** 4.

Chapter 22
1. 4. **2.** 1. **3.** 2. **4.** 4. **5.** 1.
Appendix
1. 5. **2.** 4.

Chapter 23
1. 4. **2.** 2. **3.** 4. **4.** 4. **5.** 5.

Chapter 24
1. 3. **2.** 5. **3.** 1. **4.** 1. **5.** 4.

Chapter 25
1. 1. **2.** 3. **3.** 1. **4.** 3. **5.** 3.
Appendix
1. 3. **2.** 4.

Chapter 26
1. 2. **2.** 4. **3.** 1. **4.** 3. **5.** 4.

Chapter 27
1. 3. **2.** 4. **3.** 4. **4.** 3. **5.** 4.
Appendix
1. 3. **2.** 4. **3.** 4. **4.** 2. **5.** 1.

Chapter 28
1. 3. **2.** 1. **3.** 1. **4.** 2. **5.** 4.

Chapter 29
1. 2. **2.** 1. **3.** 5. **4.** 3. **5.** 5.

Chapter 30
1. 4. **2.** 3. **3.** 2. **4.** 1. **5.** 3.

Appendix
1. 1. **2.** 3.

Chapter 31
1. 3. **2.** 4. **3.** 5. **4.** 2. **5.** 4.

Chapter 32
1. 2. **2.** 5. **3.** 2.
Appendix
1. 2. **2.** 1.

Chapter 33
1. 1. **2.** 3. **3.** 3. **4.** 1. **5.** 4.
Appendix
1. 3. **2.** 3. **3.** 5.

Chapter 34
1. 4. **2.** 3. **3.** 5. **4.** 2. **5.** 4.
Appendix
1. 3. **2.** 4. **3.** 3. **4.** 1. **5.** 4.

Chapter 35
1. 3. **2.** 1. **3.** 2. **4.** 2. **5.** 3.

Chapter 36
1. 5. **2.** 4. **3.** 1. **4.** 1. **5.** 2.

Chapter 37
1. 1. **2.** 3. **3.** 2. **4.** 5. **5.** 2.
Appendix
1. 1. **2.** 5.

Chapter 38
1. 4. **2.** 3. **3.** 1. **4.** 5. **5.** 1.

Chapter 39
1. 4. **2.** 5. **3.** 2.

Chapter 40
1. 4. **2.** 3. **3.** 2. **4.** 1. **5.** 3.

Chapter 41
1. 5. **2.** 1. **3.** 3. **4.** 5. **5.** 2.

Chapter 42
1. 3. **2.** 3. **3.** 5. **4.** 4. **5.** 1.
Appendix
1. 1. **2.** 2.

Chapter 43
1. 3. **2.** 3. **3.** 5. **4.** 2. **5.** 2.

ANSWERS TO QUIZ QUESTIONS: Other

Chapter 6 Appendix

1.

Income Statement—1976		
Sales		$80
Less manufacturing cost of goods sold:		
Manufacturing cost:		
Depreciation	$ 5	
Other mfg. cost	37	
	42	
Add beginning inventory	20	
	62	
Deduct closing inventory	24	38
Gross profit		42
Deduct selling and admin. costs, interest, taxes .		22
Net profit		20
Dividends paid		15
Addition to retained earnings		$ 5

Balance Sheet—December 31, 1976

Assets			Liabilities and Net Worth		
Current:			Current liabilities:		
Cash	$ 4		Accounts payable	$ 2	
Inventory	24		Long-term liabilities:		
Fixed:			Bonds	30	$32
Bldgs. and					
equipment .	$94		Net worth:		
Less dep'n.			Capital stock	40	
allowance ..	27	67	Earned surplus	23	63
		$95			$95

2. *a,b,c.* Expenditures for purchase of capital equipment are not recorded on an Income Statement. The Income Statement *does* record the depreciation on such equipment, each year that it is used—until, at the end of the equipment's life, the total of such year-after-year recorded depreciation equals the original expenditure amount (minus any scrap value the equipment may have). See Review questions 3–5, pp. 43–44.

Any expenses incurred each year for maintenance and routine repair of equipment are recorded on the Income Statement, in addition to the depreciation expense entry.

d. The "Retained Earnings" total (sometimes called "Earned Surplus"), as recorded within the Net Worth section of a Balance Sheet, does not stand for cash. This Retained Earnings figure is simply whatever figure is needed to make the two sides of the Balance Sheet balance. Whatever cash the company may have is recorded as Cash on Hand, on the Asset side of the Balance Sheet. See Review question 2b, p. 43.

Chapter 10

1. GNP: Consumption, $30,000; Gross investment, $600; Total GNP, $30,600. NNP: Consumption, $30,000; Net investment, $100; Total NNP, $30,100. National income: Rent, $3,000; Interest, $1,000; Wages & salaries, $12,000; Proprietors' income, $12,100; Total National income, $28,100. Difference between NNP and National income totals is Indirect business taxes, $2,000. **2.** *a.* It decreased. *b.* $338. *c.* $250.

Chapter 11

1. No. All families have the same MPC. Decrease in *C* spending would just match increase in *C* spending. **2.** Yes, if each family's MPC were to decline as its income increased.

Chapter 12

1. *a.* $44, $56, $80. *c.* $100. **2.** *a.* (3). *b.* (2). NOTE: You may find this question difficult at first. But when you grasp it, you will understand much of the content of this chapter.

You *cannot* add the cited *C* figure of $80 to the *I* figure of $10, and so declare equilibrium GNP to be $90. The *C* figure of $80 is valid *only if GNP is $100*.

At any GNP less than $100, *C* spending will be *less than $80*. Specifically, at GNP of $90—because the MPC is 0.8—*C* spending would be only $72. So there will not be enough spending to sustain an equilibrium GNP of $90. If you are still puzzled—and you will not be the first—try a Fig. 11-7 circular-flow diagram. On such a diagram, write in a GNP of $100 at top, with *C* spending of $80 and *S* of $20. Now add *I* spending of $10 (at bottom left). Is GNP in equilibrium at this figure of $100? No. Will it rise or fall? It will fall, at first to $90. Will it be in equilibrium at $90? No, because at GNP of $90, *C* spending will fall below $80.

Part *b* is much easier. If you work it out, it may help you with part *a*. We want the total *I* figure that must be added to a *C* spending figure of $80 in order to bring GNP up to $100. (If GNP is $100, then the *C* spending figure of $80 will be valid.) Obviously, the needed *I* figure is $20. That is, the needed *I increase* is $10.

Now we have a quick way of figuring what equilibrium GNP would be, in the circumstances of part *a*—i.e., with total *I* spending of $10. Start with total *I* of $20, and consequently with equilibrium GNP of $100. Now let *I* fall from $20 to $10. If the MPC is 0.8, then the multiplier is 5 (see review question 9 for this chapter). The resulting drop in GNP will consequently be $50. So with I spending at $10, equilibrium GNP will be $50.

Chapter 13
1. *a.* 450. *b.* 0.4. *c.* 400. *d.* 25 / 11.

Chapter 16
1. *a.* No; coin-and-bill money is down; bank money is up. *b.* Yes; bank money is up by $800; no change in coin-and-bill money. *c.* No. *d.* The single bank *can* create money (as we have here defined "the money supply"). *e.* Money supply would again be up by $800, just as in part *b;* but it would be an increase in coin-and-bill money, not in bank money.

Chapter 22 Appendix
1. *d.* **2.** *b.*

Chapter 24
1. *a.* 16. *b.* $2.40 profit. *c.* 20¢ profit. *d.* 11, loss $3.10. *e.* Yes; loss is less than Fixed Cost. **2.** *a.* (3). *b.*

(5)—price is the same thing as average or per-unit revenue. *c.* (2). *d.* (5). *e.* (1). *f.* (2). *g.* (3).

Chapter 25
1. *a.* AR. *b.* $7. *c.* $6. *d.* 5 *e.* $6.75. *f.* $20. *g.* $33.75. *h.* $13.75. *i.* 6. *j.* $5. *k.* $5. *l.* $4.20. *m.* $6.50. *n.* $13.80.

Chapter 27
1. No; 3. **2.** Yes; 1.

Chapter 27 Appendix
1. 4.50; 6.00; 36; 12; 4 of X, 3 of Y; 54.

Chapter 33
1. (fr. 1.00, 0), (fr. 1.11, 90), (fr. 1.25, 160), (fr. 1.43, 210), (fr. 1.67, 240), (fr. 2.00, 250), (fr. 2.50, 240), (fr. 3.33, 210), (fr. 5.00, 160), (fr. 10.00, 90).

Chapter 38
a. (4). *b.* (3). *c.* (1). *d.* (2).